FOR THE LOVE OF

Literature

Children & Books in the
Elementary Years

FOR THE LOVE OF *Literature*

Children & Books in the Elementary Years

JOHN F. SAVAGE
Boston College

Boston   Burr Ridge, IL   Dubuque, IA   Madison, WI   New York   San Francisco   St. Louis
Bangkok   Bogotá   Caracas   Lisbon   London   Madrid
Mexico City   Milan   New Delhi   Seoul   Singapore   Sydney   Taipei   Toronto

McGraw-Hill Higher Education

*A Division of The **McGraw-Hill** Companies*

FOR THE LOVE OF LITERATURE: CHILDREN & BOOKS IN THE ELEMENTARY YEARS

This book is printed on acid-free paper.

1 2 3 4 5 6 7 8 9 0 DOC/DOC 0 9 8 7 6 5 4 3 2 1 0

ISBN 0–07–290534–4

Editorial director: *Jane E. Vaicunas*
Sponsoring editor: *Beth Kaufman*
Developmental editor: *Cara Harvey*
Senior marketing manager: *Daniel M. Loch*
Project manager: *Marilyn M. Sulzer*
Production supervisor: *Sandy Ludovissy*
Designer: *K. Wayne Harms*
Senior photo research coordinator: *Lori Hancock*
Supplement coordinator: *Stacy A. Patch*
Compositor: *GAC—Indianapolis*
Typeface: *10/12 ACaslon Regular*
Printer: *R.R. Donnelley & Sons Company/Crawfordsville, IN*

Cover/interior designer: *Jamie O'Neal*
Cover image: *Christian Pierre/Super Stock*

The credits section for this book begins on page 567 and is considered an extension of the copyright page.

Library of Congress Cataloging-in-Publication Data

Savage, John F., 1938–
    For the love of literature: children & books in the elementary
years / John F. Savage. — 1st ed.
        p.   cm.
    Includes index.
    ISBN 0–07–290534–4
    1. Children's literature—Study and teaching (Elementary)
2. Children's literature—History and criticism. 3. Children's
literature—Bibliography. 4. Children—Books and reading.
I. Title.
LB1575.S28   2000
372.64'044—dc21   99–18073
                                                              CIP

www.mhhe.com

THIS BOOK IS DEDICATED TO
STACEY, JAY AND DONNA
WHO, OVER THE YEARS, HAVE DEMONSTRATED THEIR LOVE OF LITERATURE AND TO
MARY JANE
WHO CONTINUES TO SHOW HER LOVE IN SO MANY WAYS.

ABOUT THE AUTHOR

John F. Savage began his career as a classroom teacher, and he still spends as much time as he can in classrooms with teachers and children. He earned a doctorate from Boston University and has worked with the Xerox Education Division. At the present time, he is a professor in the School of Education at Boston College, where he has directed the Reading/Literacy Program for over 30 years.

Dr. Savage has written four professional books on reading and language arts, including *Teaching Reading and Writing: Combining Skills, Strategies, and Literature* (McGraw-Hill, 1997). He has also authored a children's trade book on dyslexia, scores of professional articles, and other material that ranges from newspaper columns to basal stories.

A popular speaker, John Savage has conducted workshops and worked with teachers all over the United States, in Canada, Europe, Asia, and Australia, where he was a Senior Fulbright Scholar. He lives on Cape Cod where he loves the sea, the sand dunes, and reading children's books on lazy summer afternoons.

John Savage shares his love of literature by reading *Caps for Sale* by Espher Slobodkina in a classroom of special needs students.

CONTENTS

Preface

CHAPTER 1   *Children's Literature in Children's Lives*

CHAPTER 2   *Children's Literature with Diverse Perspectives*

CHAPTER 3   *Sensitive Subjects in Children's Literature*

CHAPTER 4   *Picture Books*

CHAPTER 5   *Fantasy*

CHAPTER 6   *Traditional Folk Literature*

CHAPTER 7   *Contemporary Realistic Fiction*

CHAPTER 8   *Historical Fiction*

CHAPTER 9   *Informational Books*

CHAPTER 10   *Biography and Autobiography*

CHAPTER 11   *Poetry*

CHAPTER 12   *Media, Technology, and Children's Literature*

CHAPTER 13   *Children's Literature in the Curriculum*

APPENDIX A   *Award-Winning Children's Literature*

APPENDIX B   *Sources of Information About Good Books*

APPENDIX C   *Sources of Information About Children's Authors*

APPENDIX D   *Publishers and Their Addresses*

Credits

Name Index

Subject Index

CONTENTS

Preface XV

CHAPTER 1 CHILDREN'S LITERATURE IN CHILDREN'S LIVES 1

Introduction 1

Literature for Children 2

A Brief History of Children's Literature 4

Children's Literature Helps Children Grow 10
Personal/Social Development 10
Cognitive Development 11
Language Development 13

What Makes a Good Book? 14

Literary Elements in Children's Books 19
Plot 19
Setting 20
Character 20
Theme 21
Other Literary Elements 21

Children's Literature and Learning to Read 22

Censorship 25

❧ Special Perspectives
Children's Literature in Children's Lives: A Young Person's Perspective by Julia Lowd 12
Tell Me a Story by Kim Keller 15
Children's Literature in Children's Lives: A Parent's Perspective by Monique Lowd 23

❧ List of Ten
Books that Sell Well 8
Children's Books Awards 17

❧ Author Profile
Dr. Seuss 3
Judy Blume 6

Conclusion 28

Questions and Activities for Action and Discussion 28
Children's & Young Adult Books Cited in This Chapter 28
References 31

CHAPTER 2 CHILDREN'S LITERATURE WITH DIVERSE PERSPECTIVES 33

Introduction 33

Why Multicultural Children's Literature? 35

African-American Children's Literature 39

Latino Children's Literature 42

Asian-American Children's Literature 47

Native American Children's Literature 48

Children's Literature that is Really Multicultural 50

The International Dimension of Multicultural Literature 51

Multicultural Literature at Home and in School 51

❧ Special Perspectives
The Indian in the Cupboard and the Politics of Children's Books by Marilyn Cochran-Smith 52

❧ List of Ten
Multicultural Alphabet Books 38
Young Black Heroines 41

❧ Author Profile
Mildred D. Taylor 40
Gary Soto 46
Virginia Driving Hawk Sneve 49

ⱥ**Awards**

Coretta Scott King Award Winners   43

The Americas Award and the Pura Belpre
Award   45

Conclusion   57

Questions and Activities for Action and Discussion   58

*Children's & Young Adult Books Cited in this
Chapter*   59

References   61

**CHAPTER 3   SENSITIVE SUBJECTS IN
CHILDREN'S LITERATURE**   63

Introduction   63

Books About Sensitive Issues   64

Death   65

Divorce   67

Different Family Structures   68

Foster Families   70

Abuse   71

Homelessness   72

People with Special Needs   73

Books on Other Sensitive Subjects   73

Using Books on Sensitive Subjects at Home
and in School   74

ⱥ**Special Perspectives**

Children's Literature as a Tool for Social and
Emotional Development by Maureen E.
Kenny   75

ⱥ**Author Profile**

Eve Bunting   64

Betsy Byars   70

Conclusion   78

Questions and Activities for Action and Discussion   79

Children's & Young Adult Books Cited in this Chapter   79

References   82

CHAPTER 4   PICTURE BOOKS   83

Introduction   83

Picture Books in the Lives of Young Children   86

Language Development and Imagination   86

Early Experiences with Art   86

Introducing Children to Reading   86

Formats for Picture Books   87

Art in Picture Books   88

Literary Elements in Picture Books   90

Plot   90

Characters   90

Setting   90

Theme   91

Types of Picture Books   92

Wordless Books   92

Alphabet Books   94

Counting Books   95

Concept Books   97

Picture Story Books   97

Traditional Folk and Fairy Tales   99

Historical Stories   100

Realistic Stories   101

Fantasy   101

Informational Books   102

Biography   102

Poetry   102

Picture Books in School and at Home   102

ⱥ**Special Perspectives**

Postmodern Picture Books by Amy Seldin   103

ⱥ**List of Ten**

People Who Write Books Without Words   93

Alphabet Books   94

Counting Books   96

Some Wonderful Picture Books   100

ⱥ**Author Profile**

Faith Ringgold   85

Allen Say   91

Maurice Sendak   97

Conclusion   106

Questions and Activities for Action and Discussion   107

*Children's & Young Adult Books Cited in this
Chapter*   107

References   111

CHAPTER 5 FANTASY 113

Introduction 113

Fantasy in Life and in Literature 114

Literary Qualities of Fantasy 115

Flights of Fancy 117
  Animal Fantasy 117
  Toys and Other Inanimate Objects 118
  Fantastic Characters 119
  Fantasy Families 120
  Kings and Queens 122
  Happenings 122
  Historical Fantasy 123
  High Fantasy 123

Science Fiction 125

Fantasy in School and at Home 126

✎Special Perspectives
  Making it Real by Audrey A. Friedman 127
✎List of Ten
  Ghost Stories 121
✎Author Profile
  Roald Dahl 119
  C. S. Lewis 124

Conclusion 130
Questions and Activities for Action and Discussion 130
Children's & Young Adult Books Cited in This Chapter 131
References 133

CHAPTER 6 TRADITIONAL FOLK LITERATURE 135

Introduction 135

The Appeal of Folk Literature 138
  Plot 139
  Setting 140
  Character 140
  Theme 141

Types of Folk Literature 142
  Folktales 143
  "Literary" Folktales 147
  Fairy Tales 147
  Myths 150
  Fables 151
  Legends 152
  Tall Tales 153
  Epics 154
  Ballads and Folk Songs 154

Folk Literature at Home and in School 155

✎Special Perspectives 136
  Who Owns the Fairy Tale? By Bonnie Rudner 136
✎List of Ten
  A Multicultural Sampler of Collections of Traditional Folktales 148
  A Multicultural Sampler of Cinderella Stories 149
✎Author Profile
  Robert D. San Souci 140
  Gerald McDermott 145
  Verna Aardema 153

Conclusion 156
Questions and Activities for Action and Discussion 157
Children's & Young Adult Books Cited in This Chapter 157
References 161

CHAPTER 7 CONTEMPORARY REALISTIC FICTION 163

Introduction 163

The Appeal of Realistic Fiction 166

Literary Qualities in Realistic Fiction 169

Topics in Realistic Fiction 170
  Home Life 170
  School Life 171
  Growing Up 172
  Mysteries 175

Sports   175
Animal Stories   176
Humor   176
History   177
Multicultural Stories   177

Series Books   179

Realistic Fiction at School and at Home   181

❧Special Perspectives
Making Connections with Realistic Fiction by
Pamela O'Day   166

❧List of Ten
Ten Realistic Fiction Titles that Have Won
the Newbery Medal   174

❧Author Profile
Angela Johnson   165
Gary Paulsen   173
Laurence Yep   178

Conclusion   182
Questions and Activities for Action and Discussion   183
Children's & Young Adult Books Cited in This
Chapter   183
References   186

CHAPTER 8 HISTORICAL FICTION   187

Introduction   187

Why Historical Fiction?   189

Historical Fiction as Literature   192

History Through Fiction   195
World History   195
Multicultural Dimensions of Historical Fiction   198

Historical Fiction in the Classroom and at
Home   200

❧Special Perspectives
Historical Fiction Brings the Past Alive by
Ann Carmola   201

❧List of Ten
Scott O'Dell Award for Historical Fiction   188
Brief Historical Fiction Books   193

❧Author Profile
Scott O'Dell   190
Karen Cushman   194
Patricia and Frederick McKissack   198

Conclusion   203
Questions and Activities for Action and Discussion   203
Children's & Young Adult Books Cited in This
Chapter   204
References   206

CHAPTER 9 INFORMATIONAL
BOOKS   209

Introduction   209

Fact and Fiction   210

What Makes Good Nonfiction Literature
for Children?   211
Accuracy   211
Content   213
Style   213
Organization   214
Format   214
Vocabulary   214
Interest   214

Concept Books   215

Types of Informational Books   216
General Interest and Information   218
Informational Trade Books About School Subjects   218
Science   219
Mathematics   221
Social Studies   222
The Arts   224

Nonfiction Literature in School and at
Home   225

❧Special Perspectives
Fiction Forbidden: When Nonfiction Takes
Over the School by Kathleen Tower   226

❧List of Ten
Concept Books for Young Children   216
Informational Trade Books About Science   220

Informational Trade Books About Social
   Studies   223

꙳Author Profile
   Gail Gibbons   212
   Seymour Simon   219

꙳Award-Winning Nonfiction Books   226

Conclusion   229
Questions and Activities for Action and Discussion   229
Children's & Young Adult Books Cited in This
   Chapter   230
References   233

**CHAPTER 10   BIOGRAPHY AND
AUTOBIOGRAPHY**   235

Introduction   235

Examining Biographies   236

Biographies Abound   239
   Multicultural Dimensions   241

Biographies in Different Forms   242

Autobiographies   244

Biographies and Autobiographies in School
   and at Home   246

꙳Special Perspectives
   "It's Just Plain Real!": Introducing Young
   Children to Biography and Autobiography
   by Christine Duthie   247

꙳List of Ten
   Autobiographies of Children's Authors   245

꙳Author Profile
   Jean Fritz   237
   David A. Adler   241
   Russell Freedman   243

Conclusion   248
Questions and Activities for Action and Discussion   248
Children's & Young Adult Books Cited in This
   Chapter   249
References   252

CHAPTER 11   POETRY   253

Introduction   253

Elements in Poetry   255
   Language   255
   Rhythm   255
   Rhyme   255
   Imagery   256
   Content   256
   Humor   257

Types of Poetry   258
   Rhymes and Chants   259
   Narrative Poetry   261
   Ballads   263
   Lyric Poetry   265
   Free Verse   265
   Structured Poetry   267
   Limericks   267
   Haiku   267
   Cinquain   268
   Concrete Poems   268

Poetry: Multicultural Focus   269

Poetry at Home and in School   271

꙳Special Perspectives
   Diamonds in the Rough: How Do You
   Teach Someone to Love Poetry? by
   Elizabeth Gonsalves   271

꙳List of Ten
   A Sampler of Mother Goose   260
   A Sampler of Poetry Books   263
   Books of Poetry By and About African
   Americans   269

꙳Author Profile
   Shel Silverstein   257
   Jack Prelutsky   262
   Eloise Greenfield   266

Conclusion   276
Questions and Activities for Action and Discussion   276
Children's & Young Adult Books Cited in This
   Chapter   277
References   279

CHAPTER 12 MEDIA, TECHNOLOGY, AND CHILDREN'S LITERATURE   281

Introduction   281

Literature and Media   283
    Audiotapes   284
    Movies and Videotapes   285

Computer Technology   286
    Books on CD-ROM   286
    Databases of Children's Literature   290
    Children's Literature on the Internet   290

Technology and Children's Literature in School and at Home   293

•Special Perspectives
    Integrating Literature and Technology in the Classroom by Robin Fitzgerald and Mary Carr   294

•List of Ten
    Children's Books Available on CD-ROM   288
    Internet Sites Related to Children's Literature   291

•Author Profile
    Jan Brett   282

Conclusion   297
Questions and Activities for Action and Discussion   298
Children's & Young Adult Books Cited in This Chapter   298
CD-ROMs Cited in This Chapter   299
References   299

CHAPTER 13   CHILDREN'S LITERATURE IN THE CURRICULUM   301

Introduction   301

Encountering Literature in the Classroom   302
    Reading Aloud   303
    Basal Readers   304
    Core Books   305
    Anchor Books   305
    Classroom Libraries   305

How Children's Literature is Used in the Classroom   307

    Shared Reading   307
    Guided Reading   309
    Literature Circles and Readers' Workshops   311
    Transactional Literature Discussions   312
    Grand Conversations   313
    Skills and Strategy Development   313
    Thematic Teaching   314
    Content Themes   316
    Literature Themes   317
    Literature Logs or Reader Response Journals   318

Parents as Part of a Literature-Based Program   320

•Special Perspectives
    The Impact of Literature in the Classroom by Pamela G. Amster   315

•List of Ten
    Favorite Books to Read Aloud in School   303
    Characteristics of Literature-Based Classroom Programs   309

•Author Profile
    Jane Yolen   306
    Cynthia Rylant   319

Conclusion   321
Questions and Activities for Action and Discussion   322
Children's & Young Adult Books Cited in This Chapter   322
References   324

APPENDIX A AWARD-WINNING CHILDREN'S LITERATURE   327

APPENDIX B SOURCES OF INFORMATION ABOUT GOOD BOOKS   359

APPENDIX C SOURCES OF INFORMATION ABOUT CHILDREN'S AUTHORS   363

APPENDIX D PUBLISHERS AND THEIR ADDRESSES   367

Credits   375
Name Index   377
Subject Index   406

"Every night my Dad used to read to me before bedtime. That became my favorite time of the day. I loved it!"

"Remember the character Madeline? I loved her as a kid!"

"Every year, I read *Alexander and the Terrible, Horrible, No Good, Very Bad Day* to my children. They love that book."

"The other day, I watched a teacher do a lesson on the *sh* sound with Nancy Shaw's *Sheep on a Ship*. The kids loved learning phonics that way."

Love is a word constantly connected with children's literature. Long after children have forgotten which state grows the most winter wheat or what the structure of an igneous rock is, they remember laughing at the antics of *Curious George* or crying when the dogs are buried in *Where the Red Fern Grows*. Literature quickly becomes part of children's lives and remains with them forever.

Children's literature is currently enjoying unprecedented popularity in American education at all levels. In the elementary grades, trade books are being widely used as the centerpieces of language arts instruction, and literature is used as a vehicle for instruction across the curriculum. Even conventional basal programs have become "literature-based," featuring unexpurgated selections written by the most widely recognized and well-respected authors in the field. Text series designed to teach reading incorporate children's trade books.

At the college level, courses in children's literature are typically oversubscribed, not only with teacher education students, but also with students from all areas of study across campus. College students, it seems, are rediscovering the joys of their interactions with Amelia Bedelia, Henry Huggins, Anastasia Krupnik, and other story characters from their past.

Outside academic settings, society is even more tuned in to literature for children. Sales of juvenile paperback books for 1995 topped half a billion dollars, up almost 30 percent from the previous year. Over 4,000 books for children were published in the United States in 1997. Children's book reviews are carried regularly in newspapers and magazines. The internet is full of Web sites related to children's books. Interest and awareness in children's literature has never been higher, and it's growing by leaps and bounds.

But why another children's literature text? How is this book different from other books about children's literature? Most of these texts are compendiums of information that people ought to know about the stories and poems that children read. Information about the field of children's literature is important. Without such information, one can neither comprehend nor appreciate the field. Indeed, this book is replete with such information. But experiencing children's literature involves more than knowing about it. Children's literature is more than information; it is something that touches children's lives. It's one thing to know the characters, plot, and setting of *Bridge to Terabithia:* it's something else entirely to be moved by this touching story. And, as the title of this book suggests, its emphasis is on the affective dimensions of literature, and it is geared toward children's aesthetic responses to the stories and poems that they read.

For the Love of Literature also deals with issues in the field of children's literature today—how to use multicultural literature to impact the curriculum; what to do when a school committee bans a favorite book from the classroom; how to teach from trade books without "basalizing" them; how to use technology in school and at home to help children interact with literature.

In a nutshell, the book is designed to accomplish three major goals: to help the reader (1) discover the joys of literature for children, (2) acquire a general knowledge of the field, and (3) develop an awareness of ways to share children's literature both inside and outside the classroom.

The importance of the first goal—to foster a love of literature—can hardly be overstated. Educators frequently talk about "reluctant readers." But humans are rarely reluctant to spend time with what they love. We're not reluctant to be with the people we love, to eat the food we love, or to go to the places we love. Literature provides a powerful incentive for readers who are "reluctant" as well as for those who read enthusiastically and well.

A Word About Content and Organization

For the Love of Literature: Children & Books in the Elementary Years contains thirteen chapters, eight of which cover genres and forms of children's literature and five of which explore the use of literature for children inside and outside the classroom.

The opening chapter is an introduction to and overview of the field of children's literature. In light of the importance of recognizing diversity in the twenty-first-century classroom, the second chapter examines the general topic of multicultural literature, and this topic is further explored in more detail in most of the chapters that follow. Chapter 3 considers sensitive subjects in children's literature and books that address some of the harsh realities and difficult issues that children face in their lives.

The next eight chapters survey the genres of literature that children encounter in their home and school lives. Chapter 4 focuses on picture books, since this is the form through which young children typically encounter literature for the first time. Chapter 5 is about fantasy, an essential element in the lives of children and an important area in the field of children's literature. The sixth chapter is about traditional folk literature, since much literature has its origins in the oral tradition. The next two chapters—7 and 8—cover genres that have great appeal to children as they gain independence in reading, realistic fiction and historical fiction. Chapter 9 examines nonfiction, or informational trade books, as a genre of children's literature, and Chapter 10 addresses biographies and autobiographies. Chapter 11 explores poetry for children.

The final two chapters examine topics that are of concern to teachers (and often parents) in their use of children's books in the classroom. Chapter 12 examines how technology is impacting the field of children's literature both in school and at home. Because literature is so central to language arts instruction in school today, the final chapter places literature in the school curriculum and considers ways to use stories and poems for teaching children how to read and write.

Each chapter has three special features: author profiles, essays about literature, and lists of children's books:

Author Profiles are brief biographical sketches of popular authors and/or illustrators of children's books. These profiles are included because knowledge about and appreciation of children's literature are enhanced tremendously by an awareness of the people who create this literature. The first chapter, for example, profiles Theodor Geisel (Dr. Seuss) and Judy Blume, two authors who have done so much to make children's literature part of children's lives. It's rare to find a student in high school or in college who has not read a book by Seuss or Blume.

Special Perspectives on Children's Literature are essays that present opinions about, insights into, information about, and/or application of some aspect of children's literature pertinent to each chapter. The essays are authored by scholars and practitioners who offer unique perspectives on the chapter topics and who are currently involved in the field of literature for children. The writers of these essays include college professors, classroom teachers, book editors, and even a middle school student.

Lists of Ten are lists of children's books in various categories. They have been deliberately and judiciously limited to ten items. (Lists of award-winning books are longer.) More extensive lists of children's books on many topics (books for preschool children, alphabet and counting books, books for twenty-first-century girls, books offering positive Asian-American images, and so on) are published frequently in books, in reference sources, on the Internet, and in databases (like the one that accompanies this book). So many new children's books are becoming available so rapidly that lists are typically outdated even as they appear.

For the Love of Literature: Children & Books in the Elementary Years is designed to be user-friendly—chapter organizers at the beginning of each chapter summarize the chapters' offerings; headings and graphic devices are used to clarify content throughout, the lists of books are concise and carefully selected, and chapter summaries and post-chapter discussion questions/activities enhance college students' learning and or teachers' professional development.

APPENDICES

Four appendices are included. Appendix A contains descriptions of major awards in children's literature, including lists of titles and authors who have won some of these awards. Appendix B presents the names of books and magazines that teachers and parents can use in selecting books for children. Appendix C lists sources of information about children's authors, including print and nonprint sources. Appendix D has a list of publishers and their addresses.

ACKNOWLEDGMENTS

For the past thirty years, I have been fortunate to have been associated with colleagues and students who have constantly enhanced my intellectual, academic, personal, and professional lives. Thanks are due to the thousands of students who have enriched my knowledge and love of literature with their enthusiastic, "Have you seen this new kid's book, Dr. Savage?" More specifically, an enormous debt of gratitude is due to my graduate assistant Pamela O'Day who consistently provided indispensable help. The staff of our Educational Resource Center, especially its Director, Monique Lowd, and its librarian, Cindy Jones, were tremendously helpful and supportive. My undergraduate research assistants—Sandra Luciano, Amy Rebert, Shannon Murray and Alicia Nardi—helped dig up information that was not always easy to find. By lending their own expertise, insights, and effort, a gifted group of graduate students helped me understand and write about the different topics covered by this book: Patricia Marino, Francesca Lyons, Caterina Da Silva, Laura Rey, Nicole Malik, Liz McDonough, and others. I especially appreciate the work of the friends and colleagues who contributed their own special perspectives to the various chapters.

Thanks are due to the reviewers whose suggestions and critical comments improved the final product enormously: Linda DeGroff, University of Georgia; Margot Papworth, Cazenovia College; Angela Ferree, Western Illinois University; Walter Prentice, University of Wisconsin, Superior; Terrell Young, Washington State University; Amy Meekins, Salisbury State University; Jack Haynes, Florida Southern College; Terrance Flaherty, Minnesota State University, Mankato; Paul Dale Hauser, Kirkwood Community College; Donna Camp, University of Central Florida; Linda Leonard Lamme, University of Florida; Monica Gordon Pershey, Cleveland State University; Dee Storey, Saginaw Valley State University.

To the editors at McGraw Hill—Beth Kaufman, who was instrumental in getting me started and who stood by me throughout, Cara Harvey, whose help and support have been constant, and Marilyn Sulzer, my project manager, who guided me through the production process—I give my thanks and gratitude. Their interest and efforts kept me going when my get-up-and-go occasionally got up and went.

FOR THE LOVE OF *Literature*

Children & Books in the Elementary Years

CHAPTER 1

CHILDREN'S LITERATURE IN CHILDREN'S LIVES

T he field of children's literature is an enormous and exciting field. Thousands of books published every year are read to and by children for purposes of entertainment, information, and enjoyment. Literature is more than something that children learn about in school; it is something that becomes part of their lives.

THIS CHAPTER

- explores the values that literature has in enriching children's intellectual and emotional lives;
- traces the history of children's literature from its beginnings to the present time;
- identifies elements that contribute to quality in children's literature; and
- considers the impact of censorship in the selection and use of children's books.

Not long ago, I was driving with my daughter, an attorney who was practicing law in New York City. We were engaged in a friendly but very animated argument, the substance of which I can no longer remember. I was (at least in my opinion) gaining the upper hand in the argument and I made a particularly cogent and convincing point. My daughter looked at me, smiled, and retorted, "Oh, Dad! I say the same thing to you that Madeline said to the tigers in the zoo!"

Those who remember Ludwig Bemelmans's wonderful little *Madeline* will recall that

> To the tigers in the zoo,
> Madeline said, "Pooh Pooh."

When I reflect on that incident, I continue to be struck by how much children's literature remains part of my daughter's life. Here was a thirty-something attorney practicing law in the rough-and-tumble world of New York City who still remembered the lines of a book that she heard and read at the age of two or three. Madeline had remained part of my daughter's life all the way into adulthood.

LITERATURE FOR CHILDREN

Children's literature is a body of prose and poetry written to be read by and to young children. The content of children's literature reflects children's emotions and experiences, and it engages them in real and imagined encounters that expand their worlds. "Literature brings literacy and the learner together forging a pervasive and enduring connection that begins in infancy and continues throughout life" (Doiron 1995, 35).

Literature for children covers many ages, from simple concept and board books for the very young to novels and informational books for adolescents and young adults (although young adult literature is often considered a separate field of study). It covers many genres, including traditional folk literature, fantasy, historical and realistic fiction, biography and autobiography, informational books, and, of course, poetry.

While written primarily for a young audience, some well-known works of children's literature were not designed originally for children. Jonathan Swift wrote *Gulliver's Travels* (1726) as a critique of humanity addressed to a mature imagination, but it quickly became a glamorous children's adventure story. Daniel Defoe did not write *Robinson Crusoe* (1719) with a young audience in mind, but the story immediately appealed to young readers. And even many of the rhymes of *Mother Goose Tales*, a staple of children's literature from their very earliest years, were originally written and recited as political parodies of royalty and other authority figures who could not be outwardly mocked or criticized at the time.

Nor is the appeal of children's literature limited to young children alone. Beyond offering the pleasure of sharing simple books with youngsters, some children's books have inherent appeal to adult tastes. Robert Munsch's *Love You Forever*, a book about the love between a mother and her child, rarely fails to generate emotional response and praise from an adult audience. Shel Silverstein's *The Giving Tree*, while it has been criticized on the basis of its perceived gender bias, is frequently given as a gift by adults to symbolize genuine love and admiration. And Dr. Seuss has written books with direct appeal to adult audiences such as *You're Only Old Once!* "a book for obsolete children" that spoofs a trip to a health clinic, and *Oh, the Places You'll Go*, which is as appropriate for college graduates as it is for children in the elementary grades.

Within the recent past, there has been an explosion of interest in children's literature. As many as 5,000 new children's titles are published in the United States every year. Annual sales of juvenile books top $2.5 billion and these figures are projected to increase each year. Children's books are reviewed regularly by major newspapers. Journals and magazines devoted exclusively to children's literature are getting more and more attention, and new publications are appearing all the time. Schools have placed children's literature at the heart of the curriculum. More and more families are recognizing the importance of books as part of home life. In short, children's literature has come into its own and is claiming an increasingly prominent place on the American literary landscape.

Children's literature is more than a field of study, however; it is part of children's lives. It's not unusual for every student in a college class to have read books by Dr. Seuss and Judy Blume. These and other authors have touched the lives of generations of children, and their work has become part of American culture.

Literature never leaves the minds and hearts of those fortunate enough to grow up with books. Throughout their lives, children recall their encounters with literature in the early and elementary school years—the security of being tucked in with Margaret Wise

Author Profile: DR. SEUSS

Theodor Seuss Geisel was born and raised in Springfield, Massachusetts. After graduating from Dartmouth College, he attended Oxford University, presumably to earn a doctorate. Although his educational accomplishments fell short of his (and his father's) expectations, he arrived home with the self-awarded title "Doctor," which he placed in front of his middle name, making him Dr. Seuss.

As a young man, Geisel worked for a New York advertising agency writing snappy copy for radio and newspaper ads and, in Los Angeles, wrote documentary films that won Academy Awards. All the while, he was trying to get his first children's book published. After it had been rejected by over twenty publishers, *And to Think That I Saw It on Mulberry Street* was finally published in 1937. Other children's books quickly followed including *The 500 Hats of Bartholomew Cubbins* (1938), *Horton Hatches the Egg* (1940), and *McElligot's Pool* (1947), all with lively language, zany illustrations, and often subtle messages.

In 1957, Dr. Seuss became a household name with the publication of *The Cat in the Hat*, which he wrote in response to a publishing executive's challenge that a children's book could not be interesting and have a limited vocabulary. The book was an instant success and it raised the author's fame to a new level. *The Cat in the Hat* was quickly followed by other easy-to-read works like *Green Eggs and Ham* (1960) and *One Fish, Two Fish, Red Fish, Blue Fish* (1968).

Dr. Seuss's work is noted for its humor and imagination. His books don't preach, yet many are not without lessons and common sense morals. *Yertle the Turtle* (1979) illustrates the stupidity of uncontrolled ambition; *The Lorax* (1971) speaks to the problem of pollution; *The Butter Battle Book* (1984) has an important message about war. Dr. Seuss shows a range of insight and style unparalleled in the field. His *Dr. Seuss's A B C Book* (1974) is enormously popular with preschoolers, while his *Oh, the Places You'll Go* (1990) has been required reading in MBA programs at prestigious business schools (as a motivational piece and as a model of clear writing.)

Dr. Seuss's final book was published posthumously. Years before his death in 1991, Theodor Geisel casually mentioned to his editor that he was working on a book about a teacher. After he died, his secretary sent manuscript notes and rough sketches from this book to his editor, who contacted the talented children's poet Jack Prelutsky and the skilled illustrator Lane Smith (of *The Stinky Cheeseman* fame) to finish the work that Seuss had started. The result of this collaboration was *Hooray for Diffendoofer Day!* published in 1998.

Theodore Geisel died in 1991. Dr. Seuss, however, will live forever—or at least as long as the Grinch steals Christmas every year and as long as that pesky cat in the hat intrudes on children's lives and on their imaginations.

Here are some other books by Dr. Suess that can be found on bookshelves in classrooms and children's bedrooms:

If I Ran the Zoo (1950)

Horton Hears a Who! (1954)

The Cat in the Hat Comes Back (1958)

If I Ran the Circus (1984)

I Am Not Going to Get up Today (1987)

Brown's *Goodnight, Moon;* the fun of clapping to the rhythm of "To Market to Market to Buy a Fat Pig," and other Mother Goose rhymes; the thrill of marching with Madeline in two straight lines; the fear about what could happen to Hansel and Gretel; the fun of responding to the finger rhymes and the chanting rhymes in John Foster's *First Verses;* the enjoyment of sharing *We're Making Breakfast for Mother* by Shirley Neitzel; the delight of laughing at the silliness of Amelia Bedelia; the satisfaction of learning what time it is with Dan Harper's *Telling Time with Big Mama Cat;* the fascination of learning about huge sea creatures from the simple text and detailed illustrations in Nichola Davies's *Big Blue Whale;* the shedding of tears at the death of Jesse in Katherine Paterson's *Bridge to Terabithia;* the resentment at the unfair treatment of the Logans in Mildred D. Taylor's *Roll of Thunder, Hear My Cry;* the apprehension shared with Marty in his attempts to rescue the dog from an abusive master in Phyllis Reynolds Naylor's award winning *Shiloh* and in her two sequels, *Shiloh Season* and *Saving Shiloh.*

There is a joy to children's literature that never quits. Helping children experience this joy is one of the greatest gifts that teachers and parents can give.

A Brief History of Children's Literature

Just as no study of humans would be complete without attention to their history, no study of children's literature would be complete without looking at its history. Beginning in the oral tradition, children's literature has progressed to an art form that touches the lives of millions of children and adults today.

Children's literature traces its beginnings to preliterate times, when ancient bards and storytellers passed tales and legends from generation to generation in the oral tradition in caves and clearings, castles and cottages, and wherever people gathered. These ancient stories were not just for children; they were a means of information, inspiration, and entertainment of everybody in the society. Some of these stories remain part of the canon of children's literature today.

William Caxton, who established England's first printing press, published books of etiquette, fables, and legends. Hornbooks—with pages mounted on wooden paddles covered by a protective film similar in consistency to an animal horn—contained psalms, prayers, lessons, and other didactic reading material designed for young readers. Chapbooks—works printed crudely on cheap sheets of paper folded into quarters and sold by street vendors—contained some popular stories about Robin Hood and King Arthur, along with plenty of advice on how to behave. All of these materials did not, however, constitute a body of work that could be considered literature for children.

Because children at that time were considered "miniature adults," books were didactic in nature. The content of books for young readers consisted mainly of religious instruction, rules of behavior, ethical messages, and moral platitudes. "When books for children first appeared, they were either prosaically instructive or gloomily minatory. They were used as vessels for instilling precepts of good behavior, piety, respect for parents, and other worthy goals that did little for enjoyment on the part of young readers. Some of this lingered for a very long time in children's books" (Sutherland 1997, 21).

With the Puritan influence, books had such horribly didactic titles as *Spiritual Milk for Boston Babies in Either England, Drawn from the Breasts of Both Testaments for their Souls' Nourishment* and *A Token for Children of New England, or Some Examples of Children in Whom the Fear of God Was Remarkably Budding Before They Died*. Some authors wrote adventure stories for adults that were embraced by younger readers, but few books were designed exclusively for children's reading pleasure.

In 1744, the Englishman John Newbery changed the face of children's publishing when he began to create books with attractive formats, quality illustrations, and sturdy bindings that were designed primarily for children to enjoy. Newbery opened the door to material written for children's entertainment and amusement with books like *A Pretty Little Pocketbook*. He also published *Mother Goose Tales*, which Charles Perrault had collected and published in France several years earlier, along with other books designed for children's pleasure. The oldest (and arguably most prestigious) award given for children's books published in the United States, the Newbery Medal, appropriately bears his name.

In the following century, children's literature began to bloom. Hans Christian Andersen's wonderful stories like "The Ugly Duckling" and "The Little Mermaid" were translated from Danish into English. Jacob and Wilhelm Grimm collected two volumes of German folktales that included such stories as "Snow White" and "Rumpelstiltskin." Childhood came to be recognized as a joyful and carefree period of life, and books celebrating it began to be published. Charles Dodgson (writing under the pseudonym Lewis Carroll) wrote the enormously popular fantasy *Alice's Adventures in Wonderland*, the first book that was intended purely for children's enjoyment without any pretense of instruction. Edward Lear's books of nonsense poetry delighted both young and old readers. Robert Louis Stevenson wrote his famous adventure stories *Treasure Island* and *Kidnapped* and later his *Child's Garden of Verse* with young readers in mind. From France came Jules Verne's science fiction stories. From India (via England) came Rudyard Kipling's animal stories. A body of literature for children was beginning to grow.

In North America, books for a young audience were becoming popular as well. Kate Douglas Wiggin wrote *Rebecca of Sunnybrook Farm*. Louisa May Alcott wrote *Little Women*. Samuel Clemens (writing as Mark Twain) created Tom Sawyer and Huckleberry Finn. Washington Irving wrote *The Legend of Sleepy Hollow*, which was popular with older children. By the end of the century, the pious and moralistic books of earlier times had been replaced by writing designed to amuse and entertain a young audience.

In the 1800s, when color printing was introduced, artists began to achieve greater recognition and enjoy greater influence in books produced for children. Caxton's publications had rough illustrations and John Comenius's *Orbis Sensualium Pictus*, published in 1658, has been called "the first picture book" because it had text and woodcut illustrations on each page. By the middle of the nineteenth century, the rough illustrations that characterized earlier books had moved to works of art that captured the word and some of the stories. Illustrators like Randolph Caldecott and Kate Greenaway were reflecting the vitality and joy of childhood in their artwork.

As the world entered the twentieth century, people began to take children's literature more seriously. Beatrix Potter wrote *The Tale of Peter Rabbit* and other wonderful stories about woodland creatures, and she illustrated these stories meticulously. On both sides of the Atlantic appeared quality stories for young readers, such as Frank Baum's *The Wonderful Wizard of Oz*, Kenneth Graham's *The Wind in the Willows*, L. M. Montgomery's *Anne of Green Gables*, and Frances Hodgson Burnett's *The Secret Garden*. The entrepreneurial Edward Stratmeyer established "stables" of anonymous writers who produced hundreds of series books about the Hardy Boys, the Rover Boys, the Bobbsey Twins, and Tom Swift.

In the 1930s, the American picture book came of age. Publishing companies recruited studio artists to work on children's books, and the results were marked by striking illustrations and vigorous text, such as *Millions of Cats,* which Wanda Gag wrote and illustrated. Author/illustrators such as Robert McCloskey, Margaret Wise Brown, Robert Lawson, and Theodor (Dr. Seuss) Geisel produced books that became classics. The Caldecott Medal was established for distinguished illustration in picture books.

A. A. Milne created Winnie-the-Pooh and his friends in the Hundred Acre Wood. Laura Ingalls Wilder wrote her *Little House* stories. Pamela Travers wrote about Mary Poppins. Collections of poems expressly written for children were produced by well-known contemporary poets. Children's book genres expanded to include nonfiction as well.

In the 1940s and 1950s, children's literature expanded dramatically. Illustrators such as Maurice Sendak, Eric Carle, and Barbara Cooney made their indelible mark on children's publishing. Writers like Beverly Cleary, E. B. White, and C. S. Lewis produced books that became classics. American publishing companies issued collections of folktales from around the world. Poets like David McCord and John Ciardi kept poetry alive in the children's world. More and more children's libraries were established, and writing for children came to be recognized and admired.

Through the 1960s and 1970s, topics addressed in children's literature opened up considerably. In 1964, Louise Fitzhugh presented young readers with *Harriet the Spy*, a character who broke the mold of the idealized Goody Two Shoes image of previous generations of children's book characters. Judy Blume became wildly popular with young readers by addressing topics that were considered untouchable in earlier decades. Other authors wrote about death, divorce, abuse, addiction, and other sensitive subjects, bringing a new realism into the world of childrens' literature. New authors emerged—Patricia MacLachlan, Lois Lowry, Betsy Byars, Jerry Spinelli, Katherine Paterson, and others—each addressing topics important to a young audience and writing critically acclaimed and widely read stories.

Author Profile: JUDY BLUME

Judy Blume is one of the most popular and one of the most controversial writers in the field of children's literature. She's popular because her stories deal with issues that young readers can relate to and understand; she's controversial because of the straightforward way in which she handles topics that touch the raw nerves of some adults.

Blume was born in a New Jersey town much like the ones she often writes about in her books. While at New York University, she married and, after graduation, she settled down to raise a family. When her children started school, she began writing. Her first book, *The One in the Middle Is the Green Kangaroo*, was first published as a magazine story. After that, her career as a writer took off.

A series of enormously successful books followed in the 1970s—*Are You There, God? It's Me, Margaret* (1972), *Then Again, Maybe I Won't* (1973), *Deenie* (1974), *Blubber* (1976), and *Tales of a Fourth Grade Nothing* (1976). Her books became wildly popular with a young reading audience. Ten of the top 100 all-time best-selling paperbacks were written by Judy Blume.

Blume's writing has a wide audience, from books for young children like *Freckle Juice*, which is full of humor, to an adult novel *Wifey* (1989), which contains some fairly explicit sexual content. Because she deals with relationships between the sexes in a frank and open manner, Blume has been a constant target of censors. Partly in response to criticism, she wrote *Letters to Judy: What Kids Wish They Could Tell You* (1987) containing letters she received in response to her books.

Judy Blume continues to live in the New York City area, where she recently finished her most recent adult novel, *Summer Sisters* (1998).

Here are some of Judy Blume's other popular titles, along with her more recent books:

> *Iggy's House* (1976)
>
> *Otherwise Known as Sheila the Great* (1976)
>
> *Superfudge* (1981)
>
> *Tiger Eyes* (1982)
>
> *Fudge-A-Mania* (1990)
>
> *Here's to You, Rachel Robinson* (1993)

Until the 1960s, children's literature was generally an all-white world. People of color, when they were included in children's books, usually appeared in stereotypical or cameo roles. In 1962, Ezra Jack Keats won the Caldecott Medal for *The Snowy Day*, a book that featured a young African-American child as its central character. Children's books by and about African Americans, Latino/as, Native Americans, and Asian Americans became more widely available. In 1977, Mildred D. Taylor won the Newbery Medal for *Roll of Thunder, Hear My Cry*, the story of an African-American family living in the segregated South in the 1930s. Virginia Driving Hawk Sneve, John Steptoe, Virginia Hamilton, Gary Soto, Lawrence Yep, Allan Say, and other talented authors wrote stories about people other than white Americans. The traditional folktales and fairy tales of different cultures became popular. Children's literature took on a distinct multiethnic, multicultural dimension. Today, children acquire cultural values and seek entertainment in media other than books. But stories are still used to give children a sense of who they are within a larger social context. And stories expose children to the traditions of others in our multicultural world.

In the modern era, the number of books published for children has skyrocketed, and books for young children have taken on new and different forms; for example, now there are board books and pop-ups. New authors like Karen Cushman and Faith Ringgold continue to demonstrate their talent in connecting with children. Illustrators like Chris Van Allsburg, Jerry Pinkney, David Wiesner, and Lane Smith have made an indelible mark on the field with their attractive and stunning illustrations. The work of writers like Jack Prelutsky and Shel Silverstein keep children involved in poetry. Authors like Gail Gibbons and Seymour Simon will continue to fascinate children with informational books about the world around them.

The modern history of children's literature is still in progress. We will all be witnesses to the introduction of new folktales and legends. Our history will be presented in children's books through different perspectives. Authors will continue to expand children's book topics, addressing contemporary controversial issues in realistic fiction and other genres. New artistic techniques will enhance the art of picture books. As knowledge expands, informational books for children will keep pace with the expansion. New biographies will appear and the lives of yet-unchronicled individuals will be written for children. Poets will continue to produce work that will make children laugh and sigh. This is a history of which we will all be a part!

Children's literature will continue to have a living history, continually evolving and changing to serve the needs of the succeeding generations of children who love it.

LIST OF TEN

BOOKS THAT SELL WELL

Book sales figures provide an indication of popularity, and, while quantity certainly doesn't equal quality, something might be said about the books that have remained the most widely circulated over the years. *Publishers Weekly*, the well-recognized trade journal of the book publishing industry, lists the all-time best-selling children's books from the original date of publication through the end of 1995. The top ten *hardcover* titles and their circulations follow:

The Poky Little Puppy by Jeanette Sebring Lowrey
(Golden, 1942)   14,000,000

The Tale of Peter Rabbit by Beatrix Potter
(Frederick Warne, 1902)   9,331,266

Tootle by Gertrude Crampton
(Golden, 1945)   8,055,500

Saggy Baggy Elephant by Kathryn and Bryon Jackson
(Golden, 1947)   7,089,000

Scuffy the Tugboat by Gertrude Crampton
(Golden, 1955)   7,065,000

Pat the Bunny by Dorothy Kunhardt
  (Golden, 1940)   *6,146,543*

Green Eggs and Ham by Dr. Seuss
  (Random House, 1960)   *6,065,197*

The Cat in the Hat by Dr. Seuss
  (Random House, 1957)   *5,643,731*

The Littlest Angel by Charles Tazewell
  (Children's Press/Ideals, 1946) *5,434,709*

One Fish, Two Fish, Red Fish, Blue Fish by Dr. Seuss
  (Random House, 1960)   *4,822,331*

Dr. Seuss is very well represented, with fourteen of the 100 best-selling hardcover titles. Other authors who have several books on the list are Shel Silverstein, Beatrix Potter, Richard Scarry, and A. A. Milne. A number of *Where's Waldo?* books, along with several titles from the Hardy Boys and Nancy Drew series also appear on the list. Other old favorites on the list include Margaret Wise Brown's *Goodnight, Moon*, Watty Piper's *The Little Engine That Could*, E. B. White's *Charlotte's Web*, Eric Carle's *The Very Hungry Caterpillar*, Maurice Sendak's *Where the Wild Things Are*, Robert McCloskey's *Make Way for Ducklings*, and Laura Numeroff's *If You Give a Mouse a Cookie*. Disney's books are on the list, of course, as are those about Barney and Big Bird.

Interesting to note in the hardback list is the number of titles published by Golden Books. In the 1930s and 1940s, executives at Golden Books determined that their policy would be to place children's literature into the hands of as many children as possible, so they produced books in inexpensive formats. For many families, children's literature was synonymous with Golden Books.

Publishers Weekly also lists the all-time best-selling paperback children's books from the original date of publication through the end of 1995. The *paperback* titles that have proven most popular over the years and their circulations follow:

Charlotte's Web by E. B. White
  (HarperCollins, 1974)   *7,894,103*

The Outsiders by S. E. Hinton
  (Dell, 1968)   *7,798,000*

Tales of a Fourth Grade Nothing by Judy Blume
  (Dell, 1976)   *6,371,000*

Shane by Jack Schaefer
  (Bantam, 1983)   *6,161,000*

Are You There, God? It's Me, Margaret by Judy Blume
  (Dell, 1972)   *6,015,000*

Where the Red Fern Grows by Wilson Rawls
  (Dell, 1974)   *5,625,000*

A Wrinkle in Time by Madeleine L'Engle
  (Dell, 1973)   *5,617,000*

List of Ten continued

Island of the Blue Dolphins by Scott O'Dell
   (Dell, 1971)   *5,513,000*

Little House on the Prairie by Laura Ingalls Wilder
   (HarperCollins, 1971)   *5,291,059*

Little House in the Big Woods by Laura Ingalls Wilder
   (HarperCollins, 1971)   *5,227,120*

Of the other books in the top 100 best-selling paperback titles, the Berenstain Bears dominate, representing about one-fifth of the titles listed. Popular authors of paperbacks are Judy Blume, Laura Ingalls Wilder, S. E. Hinton, and Roald Dahl, all of whom have multiple copies on the best-selling paperback list. Familiar old favorites on the list are E. B. White's *Stuart Little*, Marjorie Willliams's *The Velveteen Rabbit*, Patricia MacLachlan's *Sarah, Plain and Tall*, Mildred Taylor's *Roll of Thunder, Hear My Cry*, Katherine Paterson's *Bridge to Terabithia*, George Selden's *The Cricket in Times Square*, Don Freeman's *Corduroy*, William Armstrong's *Sounder*, and John R. Gardiner's *Stone Fox*.

This list originally appeared in *Publishers Weekly*, February 5, 1996. Reprinted with permission of *Publishers Weekly*.

CHILDREN'S LITERATURE HELPS CHILDREN GROW

As children grow from infancy through adolescence and young adulthood, they pass through a number of developmental stages. Their cognitive competencies grow. Their language expands. Their personalities develop. Children's literature contributes to this human development every step along the way.

Personal/Social Development

Children's literature contributes mightily to the personal and social development of young people. Just as it stimulates cognitive and language growth, it contributes to children's emotional growth. It enables them to observe others with empathy and provides a means by which children deal with their own fears and emotions.

The themes of children's stories relate to the experiences of growing up—overcoming fears, developing trust, learning the importance of truthfulness, assuming responsibility, getting along with others, coping with challenges, and finding one's own place in the world. By reading about how others handle moral dilemmas, children learn to make decisions about their own behavior in such situations.

Bibliotherapy involves the dynamic interaction between a book and a reader. It relates to the therapeutic dimensions of children's responses to literature. Through the characters they meet in books, children get to walk vicariously in another person's shoes. Ideally, by understanding the feelings of others, children can deal more effectively with some of their own emotions. Even when children's literature is not used for helping children deal with such serious issues as death or family breakups, books can be used to help young children deal with everyday emotions. Consider how the following emotions might be explored through literature:

- **anger:** Judith Viorst's *Alexander and the Terrible, Horrible, No Good, Very Bad Day,* in which Alexander faces setbacks at home, in school, and everywhere he goes;
- **fears:** Dick Gackenbach's *Harry and the Terrible Whatzit,* in which Harry conquers his fears of the imagined Whatzit in his basement;
- **jealousy:** Ezra Jack Keats's *Peter's Chair,* in which Peter is worried about the arrival of a new baby;
- **concern about physical stature:** Susan Meddaugh's *Too Short Fred,* in which good things happen to Fred because he is short; and
- **concern over conflicts:** Crosby Bonsall's books *Mine's the Best* and *It's Mine!— A Greedy Book,* in which children find ways to resolve their conflicts.

Developmental psychologist Peggy J. Miller says that "children's stories do not just evoke emotions but provide an arena in which children can act upon and transform their emotional experience" (Miller, 1997, 282). As children grow socially and emotionally, they find support in the books they read.

Cognitive Development

Children's literature opens the doors of knowledge to young people. From basic concept books like Tana Hoban's *Colors Everywhere* for very young children to Jim Murphy's *Gone-a-Whaling: The Lure of the Sea and the Hunt for the Great Whale* for upper elementary grade students, books help children learn about the world around them, provide information that expands their world, and help them develop their cognitive abilities.

Cognition involves a complex set of mental functions, all of which might be engaged through experiences with trade books. For example, consider how the following mental functions, all of which are essential to reading success, are engaged through literature:

- **recall:** children repeat the repetitive language of simple books such as Eileen Christelow's *Five Little Monkeys Jumping on the Bed,* just as they recall the events in trade books that they read as they get older.
- **prediction:** children anticipate what happens next in Tana Hoban's concept book *Look! Look! Look!* by peeking through a hole in the page, and they predict what will happen next in stories like Patricia MacLachlan's *Sarah, Plain and Tall;*
- **comparing and contrasting:** children find similarities and differences in the illustrations of simple books like Peter Spier's *Fast-Slow, High-Low: A Book of Opposites,* and they compare Esther Forbes's straightforward *Johnny Tremain* and James and Christopher Collier's more ambiguous *My Brother Sam is Dead* which offer contrasting accounts of the American Revolution.
- **critical thinking:** children talk about what they might do if they were a character in a picture story book, just as they decide if they might act like Jonas did leaving his perfect society in Lois Lowry's *The Giver.*

Children's literature nurtures and expands the imagination, which is a vital component of cognition. Children stretch their minds as they travel with new friends through new worlds. Some well-known scientists have attributed their scientific imaginations to the fiction they enjoyed as children (Raymo 1992; Tunnell 1994). Television has made everything explicit for today's children who still need experiences with books to develop their power to visualize and imagine.

Special Perspectives on Children's Literature

CHILDREN'S LITERATURE IN CHILDREN'S LIVES: A YOUNG PERSON'S PERSPECTIVE
by Julia Lowd

Saturday. No soccer game.
No trumpet lesson with Miss Nye.
A perfect chance.
I packed some food.
I kissed my mom and dad good-bye.

I climbed the stairs to my room.
I closed the door.
I turned away while reaching toward the globe, then looked.
My finger rested on Bombay.

I scanned my bookcases.
I pulled out Travels in India, *Kipling's* Tales, Flora and Fauna of Southern Asia,
Hindu Ways, Himalayan Trails, *and* Northern Indian Cooking *by J. K. McGreft.*
Then I settled myself on my bed.
And I left.

Ever since I found this poem—"Bound for Discovery" by Paul Fleischman—on a bookmark, it has been one of my favorites. It perfectly describes what I think about reading. Whenever I read, I go on a different adventure.

Curled up in bed the lamp casts a yellow shadow upon the words. I am living in
another time. Horses pull carriages through the dirt streets. Ladies in their
Sunday best walk sedately with their parasols. Happy children run about looking
at the storefronts. . . .

When I was a young child I loved it when people read to me, but I got annoyed when they wouldn't read to me at every moment, so I learned to read on my own. My parents had no problem finding books for me to read. Every time my mom came home with a pile of books, it seemed like Christmas to me. It still does. I also have a good sized collection of my own books. I don't think that merely reading a book is enough. I believe you have to absorb it, think about it, reread it. I have read a few of my books at least fifty times. Literally.

Whenever I am feeling sad, I go to my bookcase and pull out a book to cheer me up. My friends often complain that they get bored on lazy afternoons, but that's not my experience. Books have always provided plenty of excitement. I have read everything from Roald Dahl to C. S. Lewis, but if someone were to ask me to identify my favorite book, I'd have to say *The Polar Express* by Chris Van Allsburg.

Ever since I first read *The Polar Express*, I have been enthralled. The deep, vibrant illustrations combine with the thrilling words to send shivers up my spine. This special book has instilled in me a desire to write something exciting and mysterious, yet comforting.

The heat holds everything in its wake. The wind has lost its breath, the fog has fallen. Everything is stopped except me. I lie in the hammock, yet I am really not there. I am in an Arabian desert watching the caravans. Everything is foreign. I am alone. Suddenly a sand storm comes streaking out of the horizon. . .

Now, as I grow older and spend more and more time writing, there is nothing that I treasure more than a cold winter night in my warm bed with a captivating book.

Julia Lowd is a twelve-year-old student at the Bigelow Middle School in Newton, Massachusetts.

Good literature piques children's curiosity and develops their interests. It leads children to constantly consider the question, "What if . . . ?"

Language Development

Children begin to acquire language the day they are born and their language develops more dramatically during their first three years than at any other time in their lives. As children examine the print and pictures in board books, listen to simple stories about personified objects and well-loved animals (stuffed and otherwise), and meet storybook characters like Madeline and Amelia Bedelia, they are presented with opportunities for stimulating this amazing language growth.

Wide reading has been shown to be the major avenue of vocabulary growth. In their early encounters with concept books and other books like Richard Scarry's *The Best Word Book Ever* and *My First Word Book*, children acquire the meanings of new words and learn new meanings for the words they already know. And when they hear that Peter Rabbit was "naughty" and that the lion walked away from the rock "confused, perplexed, puzzled, and bewildered" in William Steig's *Sylvester and the Magic Pebble*, these words creep into their daily lexicon.

The word play in books like Nancy Shaw's *Sheep on a Ship* (and her other "sheep books" like *Sheep in a Jeep* and *Sheep out to Eat*) and Wendy Cheyette Lewison's *Buzz Said the Bee* help children develop phonemic awareness, an understanding that spoken language consists of combinations of individual speech sounds, a crucial factor in learning how to read.

Literature provides opportunities for children to experience the best that language has to offer throughout their preschool experiences and during their school years. Since authors of good children's stories write "up" to children (rather than down to them), children encounter in such stories a high level of language. Finally, as children hear, repeat, and embellish narrative structures in retelling and talking about stories, they use language in a way that will serve them well throughout their lives.

Schools have come to recognize the role of literature in stimulating children's language development. Literature has been placed at the heart of the language arts curriculum. Even contemporary basal readers, which used to be the bailiwick of good old Dick and Jane, are saturated with high-quality literature written by widely respected authors. Skilled teachers learn to use these programs without "basalizing" the stories; that is, without killing children's interest in literature by inappropriately overusing the literature for skill development.

Children's literature supports children's growth and development in every possible way. In the words of the respected literary educators, Ralph Peterson and Maryann Eeds, "Writers make stories for people to live in as carpenters make houses. While living within the story world, readers have access to insights, experiences, and perceptions they would otherwise not have available. A story illuminates what it is to be human as it describes the joys, triumphs, and sorrows of specific characters. By being aesthetically ordered, the literary form makes accessible the most fundamental experiences of life: love, aloneness, belonging, alienation, hopelessness, hope. Feeling becomes thinkable through story form" (Peterson and Eeds 1990, 15).

Children's literature clearly contributes to the growth and development of youngsters in many ways, but the bottom line is enjoyment. The enchantment of books enhances the lives of children in a way that remains with them from cradle to grave.

WHAT MAKES A GOOD BOOK?

What makes a good book for children? The answer to this question, like beauty, often rests in the eye of the beholder. Yet parents and teachers daily face decisions about books to read with their children and students.

Certain children's books retain their appeal and remain on everybody's lists of favorites. Children have enjoyed *Mother Goose Tales* and traditional fairy tales like "Snow White" and "Cinderella" for centuries. *Alice's Adventures in Wonderland* and *The Tale of Peter Rabbit* have retained their appeal for generations. Young children consistently enjoy *The Very Hungry Caterpillar* and other books by Eric Carle, and they continue to love anything that Dr. Seuss has ever written. As they grow into reading on their own, they delight in books like Janet and Allan Ahlberg's *The Jolly Postman*, Arnold Lobel's *Frog and Toad Are Friends*, and Holly Keller's *I Am Angela*, stories that they learn to read independently. Reading *Mother Goose Tales* leads to enjoyment of poetry by Jack Prelutsky and Eloise Greenfield. Children learn to sample legends such as those about Paul Bunyan and folk tales like *Why Mosquitoes Buzz in People's Ears* by Verna Aardema. They grow to enjoy the company of Ramona Quimby and Henry Huggins. Their tastes expand as they sample historical fiction and fantasy. They enjoy the perennial favorites that they meet in their classroom programs, like John R. Gardiner's *Stone Fox* and Natalie Babbitt's *Tuck Everlasting*. They vicariously live the lives of the characters in the stories that Judy Blume has written for them. They discover books like Lois Lowry's *Number the Stars* and Katherine Paterson's *Bridge to Terabithia*. And they move into adolescence with authors like Jerry Spinelli *(Wringer)*, S. E. Hinton *(The Outsiders)*, and Louis Sachar *(Digging)*. Selecting books for children is indeed a subjective enterprise. If we look at these and other "hardy perennials" from the field of children's literature, we can begin to discover what makes "good" literature for children.

Young children enjoy books that have pictures that grab and hold their attention, action that moves quickly, language that delights, characters who are charming and courageous, and the assurance that all will be well at the end of the story. Books need to give older readers a story that speaks directly to their minds and hearts, characters to whom they can relate (positively or negatively), and messages that allow them to derive satisfaction from the reading experience even when things don't work out perfectly well at the end.

Temple et al. (1998) identify the following qualities that make for outstanding children's literature:

- expanding awareness by broadening children's understanding;
- providing a good read without being overly didactic or moralizing;
- dealing with significant truths about human experience; and
- having integrity and showing originality

Literature for children is full of action. It avoids racial, ethnic, and other stereotyping and presents material that children can "get into."

Special Perspectives on Children's Literature

TELL ME A STORY
by Kim Keller

When asked what I look for in children's books, I remember the response of a publisher I will always admire. She would say that if she knew what she was looking for, she could commission someone to write it for her.

It's true; as children's book editors, we don't know what we want, but we do know what we like when we read it. I could fill pages with examples of manuscripts that do not work because they're too didactic, too personal, too long, too short, too adult, too serious, too badly rhymed or written. But I often find that manuscripts that don't work are simply lacking story—that's all, a satisfying story. When I read novels for adults, that's what I desire most too—a good story. Children deserve the same. Of course, characterization and writing style are crucial as well, but without a problem to be solved or a goal to be achieved, what is even the most fascinating of characters going to do?

The Carrot Seed, for example, by Ruth Krauss with illustrations by Crockett Johnson (Harper, 1945) is entirely about story. A boy plants a seed and we follow him as he nurtures it day after day, despite the disparaging comments by his skeptical family. Over time and with considerable patience, a carrot grows. It's not quick or easy, but it happens. And oh how satisfying to see him cart away that great big carrot! I now realize as an adult reader that the boy's name is not even mentioned. His name is not important— it's the story that counts.

Owen, by Kevin Henkes (Greenwillow, 1993), has humor and character—remember Mrs. Tweezers?—and a perfect interdependence of words and pictures, but it is the story that keeps us reading it over and over again. Although Owen is growing up, he still has a security blanket. Henkes allows readers to witness the ways Owen's very careful parents try to break him of his blanket habit and all the ways the boy remains attached to it. When Owen's mother cleverly thinks of cutting his blanket into pocket-sized swatches to carry inconspicuously wherever he goes, we're thrilled that there is resolution to Owen's blanket problem. So is Owen.

Of course, there are many books for children that don't have a story at all—particularly concept books—but they aren't my favorites. Yet even nonfiction books—especially biographies—are best when they tell the *story* of a person's life rather than merely listing events and dates in a dry, albeit thorough, academic manner.

Perhaps this seems too simple a criterion for judging good literature for children. I'm not suggesting that *composing* a good story is simple, and it's certainly not easy. In fact, I think that finding the succinct words to write a children's book is a skill worthy of much more praise than it now receives. But even the best-chosen words don't make a great tale.

When I think about what makes a good children's book, I think about expressions often heard by parents: "Tell me a story, Mama" or "*Then* what happened, Papa?" Children are pleading for stories.

Then, when a young child has heard a good story, what's the first word out of her mouth?

"Again!"

Kim Keller is the Assistant Managing Editor in the Children's Book Department of Houghton Mifflin Company and a former bookseller.

Later in this chapter, we'll explore in more detail the literary elements that are often used as measures of quality in children's literature. For now, consider the elements that pertain exclusively to picture books. Artwork needs to be attractive and appealing, and should draw the child into the story just as the words do. The criteria for the annual Caldecott award for the best picture book include "excellence of execution in the artistic technique employed; excellence of pictorial interpretation of story, theme, or concept; of appropriateness of style of illustration to the story theme, or concept; of delineation of plot, theme, characters, setting, mood, or information through the pictures" (Association for Library Service to Children 1997, 6).

Different genres of children's literature demand their own qualities of excellence. Fantasy needs drama and action; poetry needs rhythm and well-chosen language; historical fiction demands authenticity in setting and character; realistic fiction demands honesty; nonfiction requires accuracy, clarity, and organization of information. And all genres demand that the writing elicit a positive affective response from the children who read it.

Even when objective criteria are applied, judging the quality of a children's book can be a subjective enterprise. A book that appeals to one child (or adult) may not appeal to another. The appeal of the book may be in the context in which it is shared rather than inherent in the work itself. Opinions differ. Even the Newbery and Caldecott award committees allow for some subjective interpretation. They define *distinguished* as "marked by eminence and distinction; marked by excellence in quality; marked by conspicuous excellence or eminence; and individually distinct" (Association for Library Service to Children 1997, 5), a definition that leaves a great deal of room for interpretation.

Children's tastes in reading matter differ according to their developmental stages and their ability to handle text of increasing levels of difficulty and complexity. Many children are inclined to read mostly one type of literature, such as historical fiction or science fiction. Adults are apt to share with children the types of books they themselves prefer, which can influence children's taste. Children often go through phases, from reading nothing but realistic fiction to reading nothing but fantasy. When children discover an author like Betsy Byars, they may read everything by her that they can get their hands on.

In promoting children's love of literature, finding "just the right book" for a child at a given point in time is a subjective challenging matter. It's hard to go wrong with the classic literature that has been enjoyed by generation after generation. Books that appealed to parents and teachers when they were children are likely to be presented to new readers in a way that will ensure their continued popularity.

LIST OF TEN

CHILDREN'S BOOK AWARDS

One way to keep abreast of the release of good children's books is to monitor the awards that are given every year for distinguished contributions to the field of children's literature. The Council for Children's Books has identified over 125 awards given annually for writing, illustration, and overall quality in literature for children (Hiebert and Raphael 1998). Here are ten widely recognized awards:

List of Ten continued

The Newbery Medal was initiated in 1922 and named after the great British children's publisher John Newbery, this award is given by the American Library Association for the most distinguished contribution to literature for children authored by a citizen or resident of the United States. Other books worthy of attention are designated "Honor Books."

The Caldecott Medal is an award, named in honor of the nineteenth-century British illustrator Randolph Caldecott, that is given to the most distinguished picture book for children in the United States, a book that provides the reader with a visual experience. The award is given for illustration rather than text. As in the case of the Newbery Award, other books that merit attention are designated "Honor Books."

The Coretta Scott King Award is an annual award that is given to an African-American writer and African-American illustrator whose books make an inspirational and educational contribution to literature for children and young adults. (Books that have won The Coretta Scott King Award recognition are listed on pages 43–44.)

Children's Choice is a children's book award that is voted on by children rather than by librarians or other adult experts. It is jointly sponsored by the International Reading Association and the Children's Book Council. Award-winning books are announced in the October issue of *The Reading Teacher*.

***The Boston Globe–Horn Book* Award** is an award that recognizes outstanding works in the areas of fiction/poetry, nonfiction, and illustration.

The Hans Christian Anderson Award is named in honor of the great Danish storyteller; this award is given to an author and an illustrator who make a significant international contribution to the field of children's literature.

The Laura Ingalls Wilder Award is named in honor of the author of the famous *Little House* series; this award goes to authors whose cumulative work has represented a significant contribution to children's literature.

The Mildred L. Batcheler Award is an annual award that is given to a children's book originally published outside of the United States in a language other than English.

The Obis Pictus Award is given annually by the National Council of Teachers of English, and recognizes achievement in nonfiction books (see p. 226).

The Ezra Jack Keats Award is named in honor of the popular Caldecott Medal–winning author and is given to a promising writer who has written six or fewer children's books and whose work reflects the qualities of Keats's stories.

Many other local, national, and international awards are given for distinguished work in the field of children's literature, and these awards, along with books that have won the awards, are listed in Appendix A.

While awards acknowledge quality and reflect some of the finest writing and illustration for children's enjoyment, they are not always the best determinants of popularity among children. Some of the books honored have not proven to be tremendously popular with children, and some of the most enduring books have been overlooked by the awards committees. Nevertheless, these awards do generate annual attention for works of quality in the field of children's literature and alert parents and teachers to books that are, at the very least, worth examining.

LITERARY ELEMENTS IN CHILDREN'S BOOKS

What makes a piece of children's literature especially notable is often found in its literary elements. These elements include plot, setting, character, and theme. Style, tone, mood, and language also contribute to the overall appeal of a book.

Plot

Plot is the structure or action of a story. It consists of the events and the order of events in stories. Children are drawn into stories by the action, excitement, and suspense that are embedded in the plot.

The plot of most children's stories has four basic parts: a beginning, rising action, climax, and falling action or resolution. The beginning sets the scene, introduces the characters, and gets the story going. As the action rises, the plot progresses. The story peaks at the climax, which comes from one or more of the following:

- a conflict between the protagonist and other people, as in Robb White's young adult novel *Deathwatch*, in which young Ben is hunted like an animal in the desert by the ruthless Madec;

- a conflict between the protagonist and nature, as in Jean Craighead George's *Julie of the Wolves*, in which the Eskimo girl Miyax struggles against the forces of nature as she makes her way across the Alaskan wilderness;

- a conflict between the protagonist and society or social values, as in Mary Hoffman's *Amazing Grace*, which is about a girl who learns that she cannot take the lead role in the school production of "Peter Pan" because she is black and female but who also learns that she can do anything she wants when she puts her mind to it; and

- a conflict between the protagonist and him- or herself, as in Paula Fox's *One-Eyed Cat*, in which Ned struggles with guilt and remorse for disobeying his father and shooting a stray cat.

Some stories have more than a single element of conflict. In most stories, the plot concludes with a successful resolution and a speedy tying up of loose details.

Some plots may have an anticlimax or use flashbacks. Others may follow an episodic series of events in a "bed-to-bed" sequence from the time the protagonist gets up in the morning until he or she goes to bed at night; for example, Judith Viorst's *Alexander and the Terrible, Horrible, No Good, Very Bad Day* opens with, "I went to sleep with gum in my mouth and now there's gum in my hair," and ends with, "When I went to bed Nick took back the pillow he said I could keep." The appeal of other children's books—such as Robert McCloskey's *A Time of Wonder*, for example, or Byrd Baylor's *If You Are a Hunter of Fossils*—comes from their evocative, lyrical, almost poetic language. But most children's stories follow a direct, well-defined plot sequence with a great deal of action.

Plot, however, is more than a simple linear series of events. It's a plan that dynamically develops the relationship between events and characters throughout the story. Plot is the element that holds the story together. Tension undergirds plot in Patricia MacLachlan's *Sarah, Plain and Tall*, the tension readers experience over whether Sarah will stay or leave. Suspense undergirds William Steig's *Sylvester and the Magic Pebble* as the reader continues to wonder, "Will Sylvester ever be found again?" A good plot makes the reader want to continue reading.

Plot reinforces children's sense of story which continues into adulthood. The narratives of everyday life—what happened in school, what happened on a trip to the zoo, what happened at the birthday party—are comprised of events that children relate in story form. Narrative remains an important dimension of communication throughout our lives. The success of the salesperson introducing a new product, the attorney presenting a case, and the teacher instructing a group of children is often determined by the effectiveness of the stories each tells. Early exposure to children's literature provides a solid foundation for this sense of narrative throughout life.

Setting

The background against which the story action takes place—when and where the action happens—is the setting. The location can be as specific as the subway tunnel in New York City, as generic as a nameless suburban middle school, or as vague as a cottage deep in the woods. The time can be the ancient past, the here and now, or the unseen future. Whether general or specific, setting constitutes "the story stage."

Some stories draw their credibility and authenticity from the setting. Authors may carefully craft the setting so that, whether it is a medieval village in historical fiction or a space station in science fiction, the setting is believable to the reader.

Character

Peter Rabbit, Madeline, Anastasia Krupnik, Henry Huggins, Cassie Logan, Pippi Longstocking, and Gilly Hopkins are the characters we remember and love from long-ago encounters with literature. Authors of children's stories create dynamic characters to whom young children can relate. The way an author develops character can make or break a children's story.

Authors create characters by describing their appearance; by describing or showing what they think, say, feel and do; and by relating what others in the story say and think about them. For young children, the main character may be an animal or personified object. Older children generally prefer characters their own age or older.

Traditional folk literature is full of "flat" characters, stock characters such as the evil witch or the handsome prince. Most children's literature, however, is full of well-rounded, fully developed, authentic, human characters, the kind of people with whom children form a special relationship while they read. The characters become believable through what they say and do. They talk, behave, and think in ways that are consistent with their age, background, and role in the story.

Theme

Theme is the major idea or essential meaning of the entire literary work, the interconnecting thread that brings all the other literary elements together. The theme is the central core of the story. It's not just the topic of a book, not just "what the story is about." Rather, theme is the large idea that undergirds the entire work.

Children's literature is full of timeless themes that are woven into the fabric of stories—the triumph of good over evil, overcoming obstacles, valuing friendships, conquering fears, finding oneself. Themes are not (or should not be) so heavy-handed that they overpower the story. The theme emerges and evolves. It is not didactic. Most children's literature is written for enjoyment, not for moral development, although some authors believe that literature still should be used primarily for morally didactic purposes and as platforms from which to preach (Bennett 1996; Kilpatrick, Wolfe, and Wolfe 1994). In good literature, however, theme does not become so dominant that it overrides the plot, character, or other literary elements.

The criteria for the Newbery Medal awarded to the most distinguished children's book published in the United States each year include these literary elements: "interpretation of theme or concept," "development of plot," "delineation of characters," "delineation of setting," and "appropriateness of style (and) excellence of presentation for a child audience" (Association for Library Service to Children 1997, 4). Plot, setting, character, and theme will continue to be treated in the chapters that follow on different genres of children's literature.

Other Literary Elements

Beyond the major elements of plot, setting, character, and theme, other literary devices are used to create stories to amuse and enlighten.

Mood is the emotional atmosphere that an author creates with words or that an illustrator creates with artwork. In *Sounder*, for example, William Armstrong creates a mood of hostility and sadness with his language; in *Sam, Bangs and Moonshine*, Evaline Ness creates a somber, foreboding mood through the use of dark colors in her pictures. Mood draws the reader into the text and can shape the reader's personal reaction or response.

Tone is so closely related to mood that the terms are sometimes used interchangeably. Tone reflects an author's attitude toward a topic. "A story can be told as a personal experience shared with a friend (à la Judy Blume) or as an outrageous joke that an adult tells to a child (à la Roald Dahl)" (Savage 1998, 57). Whether removed or intimate, tone creates a context in which the reader might respond to the story.

Style, the way an author uses language to tell a story, is another literary element. Style is not easy to define. Authors use style as a way of developing characters or describing settings; compare the aristocratic style of Father Rabbit's speech in Robert Lawson's *Rabbit Hill* with the vernacular adolescent style of Jill in Judy Blume's *Blubber*. Style is the author's distinctive way of writing—use of words, figures of speech, sentences, and other language constructions to make the characters, setting, and action come alive. Karen Hess wrote her Newbery Medal winner *Out of the Dust* in the form of free verse, for example.

Point of view, the position that authors take in the worlds that they create, is a dimension of the author's style. Most stories are told through the eyes of a third person or omniscient narrator who knows all the events in the story, including what the characters are saying, thinking, and feeling. Jon Scieszka told *The True Story of the Three Little Pigs* through the eyes of the wolf (who portrays himself as an innocent victim of circumstances). Jane Yolen and Bruce Coville, both accomplished children's authors, collaborated on the young adult novel *Armageddon Summer* and told the story in alternating voices with Yolen writing in the girl's voice and Coville writing in the boy's.

Irony, outcomes contrary to what was or might have been expected in the text, is occasionally found in children's books. Ellen Raskin's *Nothing Ever Happens on My Block* is the story of a boy sitting on a curb and complaining of boredom, as all kinds of exciting events are taking place in his neighborhood behind him.

Symbolism, the use of qualities, objects, people, animals, and even places to represent or symbolize abstract ideas, can sometimes be found in children's books. The silver bell that represents the spirit of Christmas in Chris Van Allsburg's *The Polar Express*, for example, or the metal toy man who had been buried in the garden for ages and who comes to breathe new life into the garden of the old woman in William Joyce's *The Leaf Man* are symbols that represent ideas. More characteristic of stories written for adults, symbolism is a subtle part of writing for children.

The quality of children's literature is often determined by these literary devices. Fast-moving plots, believable characters, authentic settings, relevant themes, the use of stylistic devices, and (in the case of picture books) appealing artwork all contribute to making books that are meaningful, important, appealing, and engaging to young readers. Despite the fact that some of these qualities can be judged objectively to some extent, the overall appeal of a book to a child is a subjective matter. And while experts will continue to analyze these features and teachers will continue to make children consciously aware of them in the books they encounter, a child's intuitive response to a book is what determines whether a book is a good choice to generate a love of literature.

CHILDREN'S LITERATURE AND LEARNING TO READ

Traditionally, children's literature was seen as a supplement to and enrichment of the school's reading curriculum. This is no longer the case. Literature has become an integral part of reading and writing instruction in today's classrooms. From emerging literacy stages in the preschool years to developing strategies for fluency and independence in the upper grades, children's literature is an important part of helping children learn to read.

Children's literature has long been recognized as an important element in preparing children for formal reading instruction. The link between exposure to literature and reading success has been clearly established. Children who are read to in the preschool years, whose toys include books, and who come from homes where books are talked about have a tremendous head start when they enter school for the first time. Children whose in-school instruction is literature-based also show gains in reading ability, while maintaining a positive attitude toward reading as an out-of-school activity.

Given the close connections between reading and writing, exposure to children's literature has a positive effect on children's writing as well. Through literature, children encounter figures of speech, dialogue, descriptive writing, and different models of elaborated structure that children's authors use. These elements often can be observed as well in the writing of children who read widely and well.

Bushner (1997) examined how reading and writing are reflected in quality children's books. She found that reading is portrayed in books for children as a bedtime activity with a parent reading to a child, as a family activity with family members reading together, as a school experience (usually an unpleasant one), as an activity modeled by a teacher or peer, and as an activity involving older children with younger ones, among other portrayals. She discovered that children's books usually portray reading in a very traditional context—that is, one "reads" only when pronouncing all the words correctly like an adult; the teacher is the dominant force in teaching reading; and reading aloud is the most frequently portrayed reading activity.

Special Perspectives on Children's Literature

CHILDREN'S LITERATURE IN CHILDREN'S LIVES: A PARENT'S PERSPECTIVE
by Monique Lowd

When my daughter was born, I received only one book as a present: *The Story of Babar* by Jean de Brunhoff—a wonderful book, but for a newborn? So I went shopping and brought home books, lots of books. That was the beginning of a wonderful journey, a journey that's continuing still.

I brought home *Goodnight, Moon* and *The Real Mother Goose*, and I started reading to my child. I read and I read. We moved quickly to *The Very Hungry Caterpillar*, *Curious George*, Richard Scarry's *Best Word Book Ever*, and *Madeline*—very special Madeline! Then we moved to Robert McCloskey, a good move since we spend our family vacations in Maine. Some experts tell us that a book must have a story, a plot to give meaning and sustain interest. Perhaps so, but what to make of *A Time of Wonder*? Robert McCloskey's marvelous evocative piece that takes place on the coast of Maine doesn't have much of a plot but it does have luminous illustrations and a wonderful poetic text. Feel the fog lifting in the following words:

> *Now the fog turns yellow.*
> *The bees begin to buzz,*
> *and a hummingbird hums by.*
> *Then all the birds begin to sing,*
> *and suddenly the fog has lifted!*

My daughter and I both loved it!

Winter becomes a very special time with Karen Gundersheimer's *Happy Winter* (unfortunately now out of print) and Ezra Jack Keats's *Snowy Day*. Christmas brings special treats—*The Polar Express* by Chris Van Allsburg, Peter Spier's *Christmas!*, *The Story of Holly and Ivy* by Rumer Godden, and *The Year of the Perfect Christmas Tree: An Appalachian Story* by Gloria Houston. These last two books were illustrated by another wonderful illustrator from Maine, Barbara Cooney. Over and over we read these books, and of course, on Christmas Eve night, there is always Clement C. Moore's poem "The Night Before Christmas" beautifully illustrated by Anita Lobel.

Dr. Seuss, that wacky storyteller, was instrumental in teaching my daughter to read. Never mind the debates about phonics and whole language; the faster you learn to read, the quicker you'll discover the Grinch. Then there were the books that generated gales of laughter. The funniest one to both of us was *The Pea Patch Jig* by Thatcher Hurd about a mischievous little mouse on Farmer Clem's farm where tomatoes go "splat" and zucchinis go "thwack!" And *Much Bigger Than Martin* by Steven Kellogg and *Tell Me, Grandma, Tell Me, Grandpa* by Shirlee P. Newman, and George and Martha, and Fudge, and so, so many more! Chris Van Allsburg provided mysticism, magic, and mystery as much for me as for my daughter. We still have dreams about flying sailboats!

As we progressed to chapter books, we spent hours dreaming about *Hans Brinker and the Silver Skates*, a difficult book to read on one's own, but with a little adapting here and there, a tragic story still relevant today. However, Roald Dahl was the hit of those early chapter books. The misanthropic adults were disturbing to me but a joy to the listener. And those revolting rhymes: How could you not laugh, yet how could you explain the idea of Snow White as a "slut" to a nine year old?

The days of reading aloud waned, as my daughter progressed and started discovering series books, starting with the *Baby-Sitter's Club* series by Ann Martin. My librarian friends assured me that this was a necessary phase and that my daughter was not going to be bound to romances in perpetuity. They were right, of course. She moved right into *The Chronicles of Narnia* and soon afterwards Brian Jacques's *Redwall* books. Fantasies reigned supreme. Then followed the realistic fiction of L. M. Montgomery *(Anne of Green Gables)* and Maud Hart Lovelace (the *Betsy Tacy* books). These stories, with their strong female protagonists, provided hours of entertainment and dreamy contemplation.

During a recent summer vacation, Maine Public Radio opened our eyes and hearts to *The Homecoming* by Cynthia Voigt. Every Monday night we spent half an hour glued to the radio to listen to the journey of Dicey Tillerman and her brothers and sisters down the East Coast to their grandmother's house in Maryland. Later, we read other books about the Tillerman family and compared notes. And we continue to read books together, laughing and crying at *Letters to Rifka* and *Walk Two Moons*.

I hope that what started for my daughter as a baby will last a lifetime. Her love of books was engendered not by threats—"Don't come out of your room until you finish the chapter" or "Twenty more minutes of reading and you can watch TV." Rather, it evolved gently and naturally as reading became part of our daily activities. Teachers along the way enhanced the pleasure by creatively interweaving books into the curriculum.

Just think of what's ahead—Dickens, Tolstoy, and eventually Proust! Who has time for television when there are so many marvelous books?

Monique Lowd is Head Librarian of the Educational Resource Center in the School of Education at Boston College and the mother of Julia (who wrote the first of the Special Perspectives on Children's Literature *in this chapter).*

Some children's books portray illiteracy and stress the importance—and the joy—of learning how to read. Eve Bunting's *The Wednesday Surprise* is about a little girl who tutors her illiterate grandmother as a birthday surprise for her father. Muriel Stanek's *My Mom Can't Read* is a touching story of a mother who gives classic excuses to avoid reading to her first grade daughter but who seeks help when her problem is revealed. A similar story is Vashanti Rahasman's *Read for Me, Mama* about an illiterate mother who finally admits her problem and shares the experience of learning to read with her son. The sheer joy of reading is portrayed in David McPhail's *Edward and the Pirates*, a delightful fantasy about young Edward who reads a story to pirates who step out of the pages of a book and tell Edward that they are unable to read the story about themselves. In *Thank You, Mr. Falker*, a book based on the author's own childhood experience, Patricia Polacco describes the problems of a young girl struggling with learning how to read and the teacher who finally helps her succeed. For older readers, Jerry Spinelli has written four lively and humorous accounts of young people who find amazing possibilities in the public library in *The Library Card*.

Society tends to see reading and writing as functional skills. We read newspaper accounts of the mother who nearly poisoned her child because she was unable to read the warning on the label or of the airplane mechanic who installed an engine part incorrectly because he couldn't read the directions. While failure to read can have these disastrous effects, the essence of reading extends beyond the ability to decipher a want ad or the directions on the back of a frozen pizza box. The essence of reading is summed up by a character in Patricia Polacco's picture book, *Pink and Say*.

Pink and Say is about two young Civil War soldiers, Pinkus Aylee (Pink) who is black and Sheldon Curtis (Say) who is white, separated from their units. Pink, who has been taught to read by his former slave master and who promises to teach his illiterate friend to read, speaks to the power of literacy: "To be born a slave is a heap o' trouble, Say. But after Aylee taught me to read, even though he owned my person, I knew that nobody, ever, could really own me." Pink thus summarizes the potential importance of literature in all of our lives.

CENSORSHIP

Censorship impacts the selection of children's books for libraries and schools by attempting to remove or limit access to materials and ideas on the grounds that they contain immoral or otherwise objectionable characteristics.

There is a difference between self-selection and censorship. For a variety of reasons, teachers may choose not to use particular books in their classrooms. These choices are based on a teacher's personal and professional judgment. Censorship, however, is an external force that prohibits teachers from making choices about books.

Schools and libraries are the battlefields on which wars over the restriction of children's books are waged. In a school context, censorship occurs at a macro level and at a micro level.

At the macro level, groups bring pressure on school boards and other policy-making bodies to eliminate particular titles from school libraries or from use in the curriculum. These pressure groups typically mount well-organized campaigns in order to challenge reading materials that they perceive as objectionable, and they often succeed at imposing on others their ideas regarding the use of books for instructional and recreational purposes.

At the micro level, individual teachers face objections from parents for using particular books in the classroom as core books, read-aloud titles, free reading selections, summer reading recommendations, and for other purposes. A parent or group of parents may object to the entire content of a book such as the portrayal of a same-sex relationship in *Daddy's Roommate* by Michael Willhoite. Or the objection may be to a single passage, word, or illustration such as to the use of the words *hell* and *damn* by the protagonist of *The Great Gilly Hopkins* by Katherine Paterson or to Maurice Sendak's drawing of Mickey in *In the Night Kitchen* in which the boy is nude (even though the cartoonish nature of the artwork makes the illustration inoffensive to most).

Censors have attempted to remove—and sometimes have succeeded in removing—from the shelves of libraries and classrooms some classic works of children's literature, including Mark Twain's *The Adventures of Huckleberry Finn* for what is perceived as a racist portrayal of Jim the slave and for Huck's "outrageously objectionable" behavior. While this book is generally regarded as one of America's greatest novels and has been translated into many languages, the book has been banned somewhere in the United States every year since it was published (Foerstel 1994). The censors seem to overlook the context of the times in which the book was written and fail to recognize the book's literary qualities.

Among the hundreds of children's books that are repeatedly challenged are some of the most widely read books by young readers, including the following:

- *Bridge to Terabithia* by Katherine Paterson, because of "offensive language";
- *A Light in the Attic* by Shel Silverstein, because some of the poems "show disrespect";
- *Halloween ABC* by Eve Merriam, because it has to do with ghosts, spirits, and "otherworldly" things (books about Halloween are frequently challenged because they deal with "the occult");
- *The Witches* by Roald Dahl, because it deals with witchcraft; and
- *A Wrinkle in Time* by Madeleine L'Engle because "it sends mixed messages to children around good and evil" (Pistolis 1996).

Popular traditional stories like "Goldilocks and the Three Bears" (in which there is a bad role model), "Little Red Riding Hood" (Trina Hyman's illustrations have a bottle of wine in the basket), and "Cinderella" (the original version contains violence; stepsisters chop off their toes to fit into the glass slipper) have also drawn objections.

Judy Blume has long been a lightning rod for the censors. *Are You There, God? It's Me, Margaret,* which deals with a girl's concerns about the physical changes that accompany puberty, *Blubber,* which deals with the unfair and obnoxious behavior of middle-school children, and *Then Again, Maybe I Won't,* which deals with a boy's spying on the girl next door, are repeatedly challenged, yet they remain in demand among young readers. Blume has drawn so much ire and fire over the years that some of her other delightfully unobjectionable books like *Freckle Juice* and *The One in the Middle Is the Green Kangaroo* have been tainted by their association with her more controversial work, and children have been deprived of reading them. In her book *Letters to Judy: What Kids Wish They Could Tell You,* Blume includes some of the correspondence she received from young readers wishing to share with her their reactions and responses to her books.

Censors usually act out of sincere concern for the welfare of children, and few would deny the right of parents to regulate their own children's access to books. However, censors impose their own particular point of view on everyone and dictate what everyone else can and cannot read, and censorship thus can have chilling effects. Teachers shy away from using quality books for fear of stirring up controversy, and librarians remove books from shelves to avoid being hassled. Many educators see censorship as a violation of personal rights and intellectual freedom and as an affront to the professional autonomy and integrity of teachers and librarians.

When choosing books that others may find objectionable, teachers need to be ready to support their choices. They must be able to articulate sound reasons for selecting a work, have a clear idea of what they hope to accomplish by using the book, and identify expectations for student learning from the work, which aspects of it will be discussed and emphasized, and the reasons. Censorship can best be confronted with sound curriculum decisions.

What can schools and libraries do in the face of a wave of censorship that seems to be increasing all the time? An important initial step is to formulate a written policy governing the selection and use of books for children. A written policy can bring cool logic to an otherwise heated and often passionate debate. A policy can be a means of avoiding angry confrontations and can provide a strategy for responding to protests.

A policy should contain guidelines for selecting children's books; for example, a policy might require that selected books be positively reviewed in recognized journals, address some clearly identified curriculum need, or portray some clearly stated values. A policy should justify the use of a book on the basis of its literary merit or instructional importance. The policy should be drawn up by everyone with a stake in children's education, especially those who oppose censorship. Once formulated, the policy should be promulgated and followed. Teachers have the right to expect the support of administrators for using books that meet established guidelines. They also should expect administrative support in their efforts to instill in students a love of literature.

Help is available for educators battling censorship. The National Council of Teachers of English (NCTE) has produced a CD-ROM, *Rationale for Challenged Books,* that can be used as ammunition. The program contains plot summaries, explanations of the strengths of books that are most often challenged, counterarguments, and teaching ideas and suggestions related to the books. NCTE and the American Library Association offer materials to help schools and communities formulate policies regarding the choice and use of books.

CONCLUSION

Love is a powerful word. To help children come to love literature is one of the greatest gifts from parents and teachers to children.

In dealing with children, parents and teachers have obligations and opportunities. One opportunity parents have is to introduce their children to the world of children's books. By exposing children to books in their earliest years and by continuing to read and discuss books throughout childhood, parents plant a seed and nourish a love that continues long after their children have discovered the joy and satisfaction of reading on their own.

Teachers have the important obligation to develop children's ability to read. But they also have the equally (if not more) important job of developing in children the *inclination* to read. It has been said that a reader is not someone who *can* read; it's someone who *does* read. Teachers play a central role in developing children's preference for reading during leisure time.

To help children develop the love of reading along with the ability to read is indeed a great gift to give!

Questions and Activities for Action and Discussion

1. What was your favorite book as a child? Describe the reasons you loved this book so much, including reasons related to the book and to the context in which you enjoyed it. If you were going to share a book with a child today, which book would it be? Explain the reasons for your choice.

2. Select a children's book and analyze its literary qualities (plot, setting, characters, theme, etc.).

3. Review the work of a children's author who has written several books—Eric Carle, Patricia McKissack, Virginia Hamilton, Paul Goble, Laurence Yep, Gary Soto, and so on. Describe the quality of this author's work.

4. Describe how different types of books can be used to promote children's cognitive, language, and personal/social development at different ages.

5. Research the topic of censorship. Find a book that has been challenged or banned in your community. Explain why the book should (or should not) be used.

CHILDREN'S & YOUNG ADULT BOOKS CITED IN THIS CHAPTER

Aardema, Verna. 1975. *Why Mosquitoes Buzz in People's Ears.* Illustrated by Leo and Diane Dillon. New York: Dial.

Ahlberg, Janet, and Allan Ahlberg. 1986. *The Jolly Postman.* Boston: Little Brown.

Alcott, Louisa May. 1993. *Little Women.* New York: Henry Holt. (Other editions available.)

Armstrong, William. 1969. *Sounder.* New York: Harper and Row.

Babbitt, Natalie. 1995. *Tuck Everlasting.* New York: Farrar, Straus and Giroux.

Baum, Frank. 1983. *The Wonderful Wizard of Oz*. New York: Puffin. (Other editions available.)

Baylor, Byrd. 1980. *If You Are a Hunter of Fossils*. Illustrated by Peter Parnall. New York: Scribner's.

Bemelmans, Ludwig. 1939. *Madeline*. New York: Viking.

Blume, Judy. 1971. *Freckle Juice*. New York: Dell.

_____ 1971. *Then Again, Maybe I Won't*. New York: Bradbury.

_____ 1972. *Are You There, God? It's Me, Margaret*. New York: Dell.

_____ 1974. *Blubber*. New York: Bradbury.

_____ 1981. *The One in the Middle Is the Green Kangaroo*. Illustrated by Amy Aitken. New York: Bradbury.

_____ 1987. *Letters to Judy: What Kids Wish They Could Tell You*. New York: Pocket Books.

Bonsall, Crosby. 1964. *It's Mine!—A Greedy Book*. New York: Harper and Row.

_____ 1973. *Mine's the Best*. New York: Harper and Row.

Brown, Margaret Wise. 1947. *Goodnight, Moon*. Illustrated by Clement Hurd. New York: Harper & Row.

Bunting, Eve. 1989. *The Wednesday Suprise*. New York: Clarion.

Burnett, Frances Hodgson. 1912. *The Secret Garden*. New York: Harper and Row.

Carle, Eric. 1971. *The Very Hungry Caterpillar*. New York: Crowell.

Carroll, Lewis. 1994. *Alice's Adventures in Wonderland*. Illustrated by Dianne Good. New York: Random House. (Other editions available.)

Christelow, Eileen. 1989. *Five Little Monkeys Jumping on the Bed*. New York: Clarion.

Collier, James, and Christopher Collier. 1984. *My Brother Sam Is Dead*. New York: Four Winds Press.

Dahl, Roald. 1983. *The Witches*. New York: Farrar, Straus and Giroux.

Davies, Nichola. 1997. *Big Blue Whale*. Illustrated by Nick Maland. Cambridge: Candlewick.

Fitzhugh, Louise. 1964. *Harriet the Spy*. New York: Harper and Row.

Forbes, Esther. 1945. *Johnny Tremain*. Boston: Houghton Mifflin.

Foster, John. 1996. *First Verses*. Illustrated by Carol Thompson. New York: Oxford University Press.

Fox, Paula. 1984. *One-Eyed Cat*. New York: Bradbury.

Gackenbach, Dick. 1977. *Harry and the Terrible Whatzit*. New York: Clarion.

Gag, Wanda. 1928. *Millions of Cats*. New York: Putnam.

Gardiner, John R. 1980. *Stone Fox*. New York: Harper and Row.

Geisel, Theodor (Dr. Seuss). 1986. *You're Only Old Once!* New York: Random House.

_____ 1990. *Oh, The Places You'll Go*. New York: Random House.

George, Jean Craighead. 1972. *Julie of the Wolves*. New York: Harper and Row.

Graham, Kenneth. 1987. *The Wind in the Willows*. New York: Scholastic. (Other editions available.)

Harper, Dan. 1998. *Telling Time with Big Mama Cat*. Illustrated by Barry Moser and Cara Moser. San Diego: Harcourt Brace.

Hess, Karen. 1997. *Out of the Dust*. New York: Scholastic.

Hinton, S. E. 1967. *The Outsiders*. New York: Viking.

Hoban, Tana. 1988. *Look! Look! Look!*. New York: Greenwillow.

_____ 1995. *Colors Everywhere*. New York: Greenwillow.

Hoffman, Mary. 1991. *Amazing Grace*. Illustrated by Carolyn Binch. New York: Scholastic.

Hyman, Trina. 1983. *Little Red Riding Hood*. New York: Holiday House.

Irving, Washington. 1994. *The Legend of Sleepy Hollow*. New York: Random House. (Other editions available.)

Joyce, William. 1996. *The Leaf Man*. New York: Scholastic.

Keats, Ezra Jack. 1962. *The Snowy Day*. New York: Penguin.

_____ 1967. *Peter's Chair*. New York: Harper and Row.

Keller, Holly. 1997. *I Am Angela*. New York: Greenwillow.

Lawson, Robert. 1944. *Rabbit Hill*. New York: Viking.

L'Engle, Madeleine. 1962. *A Wrinkle in Time*. New York: Farrar, Straus and Giroux.

Lewison, Wendy Cheyette. 1992. *Buzz Said the Bee*. Illustrated by Hans Wilhelm. New York: Scholastic.

Lobel, Arnold. 1962. *Frog and Toad Are Friends*. New York: Harper and Row.

Lowry, Lois. 1989. *Number the Stars*. Boston: Houghton Mifflin.

_____ 1994. *The Giver*. Boston: Houghton Mifflin.

MacLachlan, Patricia. 1985. *Sarah, Plain and Tall*. New York: Harper and Row.

McCloskey, Robert. 1957. *A Time of Wonder*. New York: Viking.

McPhail, David. 1997. *Edward and the Pirates*. Boston: Little Brown.

Meddaugh, Susan. 1978. *Too Short Fred*. Boston: Houghton Mifflin.

Merriam, Eve. 1987. *Halloween ABC*. Illustrated by Lane Smith. New York: Macmillan.

Montgomery, L. M. 1982. *Anne of Green Gables*. New York: Bantam. (Other editions available.)

Munsch, Robert. 1986. *Love You Forever*. Toronto: Firefly Books.

Murphy, Jim. 1998. *Gone-a-Whaling: The Lure of the Sea and the Hunt for the Great Whale*. New York: Clarion.

Naylor, Phyllis Reynolds. 1991. *Shiloh*. New York: Dell.

_____ 1996. *Shiloh Season*. New York: Atheneum.

_____ 1997. *Saving Shiloh*. New York: Atheneum.

Neitzel, Shirley. 1997. *We're Making Breakfast for Mother*. Illustrated by Nancy Winslow Parker. New York: Greenwillow.

Ness, Evaline. 1966. *Sam, Bangs and Moonshine*. New York: Henry Holt.

Paterson, Katherine. 1977. *Bridge to Terabithia*. New York: Harper and Row.

_____ 1978. *The Great Gilly Hopkins*. New York: Harper and Row.

Polacco, Patricia. 1994. *Pink and Say*. New York: Philomel.

_____ 1996. *Thank You, Mr. Falker*. New York: Philomel.

Potter, Beatrix. 1903. *The Tale of Peter Rabbit*. New York: Dover. (Other editions available.)

Rahasman, Vashanti. 1997. *Read for Me, Mama*. Illustrated by Lori McElrath-Eslick. Honesdale, Penn.: Boyds Mills.

Raskin, Ellen. 1966. *Nothing Ever Happens on My Block.* New York: Antheneum.

Sachar, Louis. 1998. *Digging.* New York: Farrar, Straus and Giroux.

Scarry, Richard. 1963. *The Best Word Book Ever.* New York: Western.

_____ 1986. *My First Word Book.* New York: Random House.

Scieszka, Jon. 1989. *The True Story of the Three Little Pigs.* Illustrated by Lane Smith. New York: Viking.

Sendak, Maurice. 1970. *In the Night Kitchen.* New York: Harper and Row.

Shaw, Nancy. 1986. *Sheep in a Jeep.* Illustrated by Margot Apple. Boston: Houghton Mifflin.

_____ 1989. *Sheep on a Ship.* Illustrated by Margot Apple. Boston: Houghton Mifflin.

_____ 1992. *Sheep out to Eat.* Illustrated by Margot Apple. Boston: Houghton Mifflin.

Silverstein, Shel. 1964. *The Giving Tree.* New York: Harper and Row.

_____ 1981. *A Light in the Attic.* New York: Harper and Row.

Spier, Peter. 1972. *Fast-Slow, High-Low: A Book of Opposites.* New York: Doubleday.

Spinelli, Jerry. 1997. *The Library Card.* New York: Scholastic.

_____ 1997. *Wringer.* Boston: Little Brown.

Stanek, Muriel. 1986. *My Mom Can't Read.* Illustrated by Jacqueline Rogers. Niles, Ill.: Albert Whitman.

Steig, William. 1969. *Sylvester and the Magic Pebble.* New York: Simon and Schuster.

Stevenson, Robert Louis. 1972. *Treasure Island.* New York: Scholastic. (Other editions available.)

_____ 1993. *A Child's Garden of Verse.* Illustrated by Thea Kliros. New York: Dover. (Other editions available.)

_____ 1995. *Kidnapped.* New York: Dutton. (Other editions available.)

Taylor, Mildred D. 1976. *Roll of Thunder, Hear My Cry.* New York: Dial.

Travers, Pamela. 1934. *Mary Poppins.* New York: Harcourt Brace.

Twain, Mark. 1982. *The Adventures of Huckleberry Finn.* New York: Scholastic. (Many editions available).

Van Allsburg, Chris. 1985. *The Polar Express.* Boston: Houghton Mifflin.

Viorst, Judith. 1972. *Alexander and the Terrible, Horrible, No Good, Very Bad Day.* Illustrated by Ray Cruz. New York: Macmillan.

White, Robb. 1972. *Deathwatch.* New York: Doubleday.

Wiggin, Kate Douglas. 1986. *Rebecca of Sunnybrook Farm.* New York: Dell. (Other editions available.)

Willhoite, Michael. 1991. *Daddy's Roommate.* Boston: Alyson.

Yolen, Jane, and Bruce Coville. 1998. *Armageddon Summer.* San Diego: Harcourt Brace.

REFERENCES

Association for Library Service to Children. 1997. *The Newbery and Caldecott Awards: A Guide to the Medal and Honor Books.* Chicago: American Library Association.

Bennett, W. 1996. *The Children's Book of Virtues.* New York: Simon and Schuster.

Bushner, D. E. 1997. A Look at How Children's Authors Depict Books or Reading in Literature for Children. *Primer: The Journal of the Massachusetts Reading Association* 26:4–19.

Doiron, R. 1995. An Aesthetic View of Children's Nonfiction. *English Quarterly* 28:35–41.

Foerstel, H. N. 1994. *Banned in the U.S.A.: A Reference Guide to Book Censorship in Schools and Public Libraries.* Westport, Conn.: Greenwood Press.

Hiebert, E. H., and T. E. Raphael. 1998. *Early Literacy Instruction.* Fort Worth: Harcourt Brace.

Kilpatrick W., G. Wolfe, and S. Wolfe. 1994. *Books That Build Character: A Guide to Teaching Your Child Moral Values Through Stories.* New York: Simon and Schuster.

Miller, P. J. 1997. Peter Rabbit and Mr. McGregor Reconciled, Charlotte Lives: Preschoolers Re-Create the Classics. *The Horn Book* 74: 282–288.

Peterson, R., and M. Eeds. 1990. *Grand Conversations: Literature Groups in Action.* New York: Scholastic.

Pistolis, D. R., ed. 1996. *Hit List: Frequently Challenged Books for Children.* Chicago: American Library Association.

Raymo, C. 1992. Dr. Seuss and Dr. Einstein: Children's Books and Scientific Imagination. *The Horn Book* 68: 560–567.

Savage, J. F. 1998. *Teaching Reading and Writing: Combining Skills, Strategies and Literature.* Boston: McGraw Hill.

Sutherland, Z. 1997. The Newbery Award: Changing with the Times. In *The Newbery and Caldecott Awards: A Guide to the Medal and Honor Books.* Chicago: American Library Association.

Temple, C., M. Martinez, J. Yokota, and A. Naylor. 1998. *Children's Books in Children's Hands: An Introduction to Their Literature.* Boston: Allyn and Bacon.

Tunnell, M. O. 1994. The Double-Edged Sword: Fantasy and Censorship. *Language Arts* 81:606–612

CHAPTER **2**

CHILDREN'S LITERATURE WITH DIVERSE PERSPECTIVES

 n today's society, multiculturalism has become an educational imperative. That we live in a diverse society is undeniable. How we deal with that diversity will determine the quality of our lives and the lives of our children. Knowledge and appreciation of the characteristics and values of other cultures are essential to children's education, and multicultural children's literature provides a natural vehicle for promoting cross-cultural understandings.

THIS CHAPTER

- addresses the values of multicultural literature for all children;

- identifies literature in different genres related to African-American, Latino/a, Asian-American, and Native American cultures; and

- describes the use of multicultural literature at home and in school.

In 1965, as the Civil Rights Movement was picking up steam, Nancy Larrick wrote an article entitled "The All-White World of Children's Books" for the widely respected magazine *Saturday Review*. In the article, Larrick expressed her concern about "millions of nonwhite children learning to read and to understand the American way of life in books which either omit them entirely or scarcely mention them" (63) and about the impact of this phenomenon on white children as well. The author noted that only a tiny fraction of books available at the time had characters and content related to African Americans and also noted the frequency with which people of color were shown in stereotypical or menial roles.

Times have changed since Larrick's article. As education moves into the twenty-first century, schools are becoming increasingly aware of the importance of diversity in their curriculum and programs. Diversity in the student population has become a hallmark of North American education. In many schools today, children from non-Anglo backgrounds constitute the solid majority of students, and demographic projections suggest that students of color will constitute half the population of public schools in the near future (Lara 1994). Multicultural children's literature has become an important component in the effort to address the needs of this diverse population.

What is multicultural children's literature? *The Literacy Dictionary* defines it as "writing that reflects the customs, beliefs, and experiences of people of differing nationalities and races" and as "materials designed to reflect the interests, vocabulary, and experiences of students from various cultural or ethnic backgrounds" (Harris and Hodges 1995, 158).

Bishop (1997, pp. 2–3) calls it literature "that represents all the diversity to be found in this society" and "literature by or related to people of color". Diamond and Moore (1995, p. 43) define it as "literature that focuses on specific cultures by highlighting and celebrating their cultural and historical perspectives, traditions, and heritage, language and dialects, and experiences and lifestyles . . . [including] literature of diverse cultures outside the United States, from which the people of color in this nation claim their ancestral heritage". Norton's (1995, 560) definition is "literature about racial or ethnic minority groups that are culturally and socially different from the white Anglo-Saxon majority in the United States, whose largely middle-class values and customs are most represented in American literature".

Some definitions of *multicultural literature* include literature related to religious groups (such as Jewish or Amish religions), regional literature (as in stories from Appalachia), nonethnic underrepresented groups (such as gays or lesbians), and other groups in society (the aging or disabled, for example). And sometimes the umbrella spreads to include literature related to mainstream groups who maintain a sense of cultural identity within a broader social context such as Irish Americans or Italian Americans.

While the debate continues about exactly what constitutes multicultural literature (Cai 1998), in most contexts the term refers to stories and poems that relate to groups that have been traditionally marginalized or disenfranchised in American society—African Americans, Native Americans, Latinos, and Asian Pacific Americans. This is literature that authentically reflects non-Western cultures, with characters and content other than those of mainstream society.

A distinction is sometimes made between *multiethnic* and *multicultural* literature. Ethnicity relates to race; culture relates to the beliefs, customs, art, values, and other qualities that people acquire as members of a social group. So a black person living in Boston, Massachusetts, one living in Kingston, Jamaica, and one living in Nairobi, Kenya, may all share the same ethnicity, but they hardly share the same culture. Within the context of children's literature, the terms *multiethnic* and *multicultural* are often used interchangeably. *Multicultural* is the term that will generally be used throughout this chapter.

While the term *minorities* is often used in connection with multicultural literature, the chapter generally eschews the use of this term. *Minority* often has a pejorative connotation. Reflecting on what the world might be like for African Americans in the twenty-first century, comedian and author Bill Cosby wrote, "The word *minority* has connotations of weakness, lesser value, self-doubt, tentativeness, and powerlessness" (Cosby 1990, 61). Besides, in a school in which 40 percent of the students are African American, 30 percent are Latino, 20 percent are Asian American and 5 percent are Native American, these students hardly constitute a "minority" of the school population.

WHY MULTICULTURAL CHILDREN'S LITERATURE?

In our multicultural mosaic of the twenty-first century, children will bring different backgrounds, language, perspectives, and skills to their educational experience. Schools need to be increasingly aware of these dimensions of diversity and the importance of helping children develop knowledge and appreciation of other people. From the earliest stages of education, books affect the way children view their worlds. That's why multicultural literature plays such an important part in children's classroom lives.

Bishop (1997) identifies five functions that literature about people of color can serve: "(1) it can provide knowledge or information, (2) it can change the way students look at their world by offering varying perspectives, (3) it can promote or develop an appreciation for diversity, (4) it can give rise to critical inquiry, and (5) like all literature, it can provide enjoyment and illuminate human experience, both its unity and its variety" (4–5).

Teachers who integrate literature from many different cultures into their classrooms send a message that diversity is valued in the learning environment. Children come to see similarities among people of different cultures and recognize the universality of some human experiences.

Multicultural children's literature has values for all children. For children from non-Anglo backgrounds, multicultural literature holds up to young readers images of themselves. A curriculum that includes a rich diet of multicultural literature answers the question, "Where are the books about us?" Seeing one's own ethnic group and cultural values reflected on the pages of books improves children's self-images and shows them that their culture is valued. When children see people like themselves and familiar experiences authentically reflected in what they read, their identities are affirmed and they experience pride in their cultural heritage. Children react more positively when they relate to the events and characters in a story. Readers prefer stories about people like themselves—characters with whom they can identify, settings in which they are comfortable, actions and ideas with which they are familiar. In sum, multicultural literature can be a means of empowerment for children from diverse cultures.

Multicultural literature also has direct academic payoffs. The reading and writing of children from diverse backgrounds improves with the use of multicultural literature. Summarizing research in this area, Diamond and Moore (1995) conclude, "When students encounter literature that includes characters, settings, and themes that resonate with other prior experiences, they will attain higher levels of reading and writing performance" (8). Improved achievement is not limited to reading and writing. Multicultural literature provides a means of drawing on children's cultural capital to enhance and promote learning in all areas of the curriculum.

While multicultural literature has special value for members of particular ethnic groups, its value is for *all* children. Multicultural literature gives pupils opportunities to view their own culture from different perspectives. "Literature written by and for people from marginalized groups can provide to students from more privileged backgrounds a sense of lived experience of people who suffer from the effects of poverty and discrimination. Literature offers all students an opportunity to talk about the meaning of difference, to imagine how the world could be different, and to consider how to challenge practices that diminish the lives of our fellow citizens" (Dudley-Marling 1997, 125).

Misconceptions are perpetuated when ethnic and cultural realities are distorted or ignored in the curriculum. The converse is also true, and multicultural literature can be a way to fight racism. When children read how the black characters in Mildred D. Taylor's *Mississippi Bridge* are treated by their white neighbors, they feel the effects of prejudice. Yamate (1997) addresses this topic directly: "If children are not given the opportunity to read multicultural books, we run the risk of condemning future generations of Americans to the perpetuation of the stereotypes, misperceptions, and misunderstandings that fuel the racial tensions and disharmony that have plagued our past" (126). In the hands of skilled and sensitive teachers, multicultural literature can be a powerful tool used to chip away at stereotypical images that children have of people different from themselves.

By providing a diverse focus, multicultural literature injects a whole new dimension into the way we look at education. Our educational system has traditionally been very Eurocentered. "Consider that educators regularly designate books 'multicultural' if they represent other cultures, whereas books reflecting a Eurocentric perspective are viewed as normative" (Wollman-Bonilla 1998, 287–288).

In reaction to the eurocentricity of the traditional school curriculum, Banks (1997) has developed a model for transforming the curriculum to include multiethnic studies. His model, which looks at what children study from diverse perspectives rather than primarily or exclusively from a mainstream point of view, includes four approaches or stages for transforming the curriculum:

1. *the contributions approach* focuses on heroes, holidays and discrete cultural events;
2. *the additive approach* makes content, concepts and issues related to diverse ethnic groups part of the curriculum but still studies them from a mainstream perspective;
3. *the transformation approach* changes the structure of the curriculum so that students view issues and themes from different ethnic and cultural perspectives; and
4. *the social action approach* engages students in identifying social issues and taking action to resolve social problems.

Using Banks's model, Rasinski and Padak (1990) and Bieger (1996) suggest the use of multiethnic literature at various stages during the transformation of the curriculum to a multiethnic focus. At the contributions stage, children would read a book like Andrea Davis Pinkney's *Seven Candles for Kwanzaa* as the holidays approach or read the biographies of Martin Luther King Jr. and other famous African Americans in celebration of Black History Month in February. At the additive level, students would read and discuss books like Mildred D. Taylor's *Roll of Thunder, Hear My Cry*, a story about racial prejudice in the rural South, or Byrd Baylor's *Amigo*, the story of an impoverished Latino child in the Southwest who adopts a prairie dog as a pet. At the transformation level, students may read James and Christopher Collier's *War Comes to Willy Freeman*, the story of a young black girl who witnesses the death of her father in battle with the British and then finds that the Redcoats have captured her mother, for their studies of the American Revolution or Barbara Brenner's *Wagon Wheels*, the story of an African-American pioneer family, for their studies of the westward expansion. At the highest social action level, students would decide what to do about racial prejudice and sanctioned bigotry after reading books like Taylor's *Song of the Trees* or Yoshiko Uchida's *Journey to Topaz*, the story of the internment of Japanese Americans during World War II.

Multicultural literature provides a powerful vehicle to enhance children's learning and broaden their viewpoints. Banks (1997) maintains that "only by looking at events from many different perspectives can we fully understand the complex dimensions of American culture and society" (19). Children's trade books provide age-appropriate means for young people to examine school subjects from different perspectives.

Banks's model is intended as a blueprint to transform the school curriculum rather than as a means of integrating multicultural literature into the school program. Nevertheless, it provides a useful framework for using multicultural trade books in the classroom, even at the contributions or additive stages. Multicultural materials often are seen as superficial because "they fail to consider institutional racism and other oppressive social structures" (Oakes and Lipton 1999, 24). Using multicultural trade books at the *transformation* or *social action* levels begins to counteract racism at its foundation.

The use of multicultural literature is not without its risks. It's unrealistic to think that a single piece of literature can speak to the actual experiences of all pupils from a specific ethnic group. There is no such thing as *an* African or *an* Asian culture. There are, for example, as many as fifty distinct ethnic groups of Asian Pacific Americans living in North America today, yet they are often viewed as one large population. To complicate matters, a child's cultural identity may be more related to the region or social class of the family in the child's original homeland than to his or her ethnicity. Also, it's naive to think that a particular trade book will represent fully the heritage and experiences of an entire cultural group. Culture is a dynamic and complex phenomenon, it can be influenced by a person's class, age, gender, or other status within the culture, and it cannot be distilled into a single book.

Children who are members of nonmainstream groups may reject a teacher's attempt to use multicultural literature. Educators' attempts to use multicultural literature to acknowledge and celebrate a particular child's unique and diverse cultural background may conflict with the child's (and perhaps his or her parents') struggle to "fit in" and become part of the mainstream. In implementing multicultural literature in his third grade classroom, Dudley-Marling (1997) found that "I tried to use particular texts to represent the ethnic and religious identities of my students without regard to how they themselves would have chosen to represent those identities" (131).

Not all children in an ethnic group respond to multiethnic literature in the same way. Cultural conflicts between American-born children of Asian descent versus recently arrived immigrants can influence the choice and use of children's literature related to Asian-American cultures. In researching the responses of children to Jean Fritz's *Homesick: My Own Story*, an autobiographical account of growing up as the child of missionaries in China, Leung discovered that "Chinese-American students experience their ethnic culture in different ways, and these cultural experiences influence their literary response" (Leung 1998, 39). African-American children can be embarrassed when vernacular speech patterns of Ebonics are used to add authenticity to stories. The child recently arrived from Eastern Europe may be angered by Barbara Cohen's *Molly's Pilgrim*, a story with implicit and explicit parallels between the experiences of today's immigrants seeking freedom from religious persecution and the experiences of those who arrived on the Mayflower.

Authenticity is sometimes an issue in multicultural literature; that is, can a person outside the culture write accurate and realistic portrayals of the experiences and values of that culture? Bishop (1992) classifies books according to their approaches to the culture and the people they portray as *culturally specific*, *generic*, or *neutral*. "A culturally specific book illuminates the experience of growing up within a particular non-white cultural group" (44). Some picture story books, such as Elizabeth Fitzgerald Howard's *Aunt Flossie's Hats (and Crab Cakes Later)* and Camille Yarborough's *Cornrows,* depict the strong intergenerational relationships characteristic of African-American culture. *Nim and the War Effort* by Milly Lee describes Nim's efforts to win a paper drive contest, even when her efforts place her in conflict with the traditional cultural values of her grandfather. Stories such as these portray for young readers characters and actions from an "insider's" perspective. Stories such as Laurence Yep's *Dragonwings,* which paints a picture of life in a Chinatown after the turn of the century, and *Jazmin's Notebook* by Nikki Grimes, the personal reflection of a young African-American girl facing the joys and challenges of growing up in Harlem during the 1960s, do the same thing for older readers. One gets the sense of cultural specificity on the first page of Irene Small's *Irene and the Big Fine Nickel* in which the author exuberantly describes Harlem as a place where "you never questioned being black because there were millions of people who looked just like you."

In comparison to *culturally specific* books, *culturally generic* books, according to Bishop, feature children who are members of non-Anglo groups but don't contain details that define cultural characteristics. Books such as *Peter's Chair* by Ezra Jack Keats feature an African-American family, even though the story is about the universal theme of an older sibling's concern when a new baby is being brought into the family.

A third type of book Bishop calls *culturally neutral.* These books may feature illustrations of people from different ethnic backgrounds, but the book's subject has nothing to do with ethnic diversity.

Knowing these classifications of multicultural literature is useful in introducing books with a multicultural focus to children. Parents and teachers can choose and use books according to the ways they represent diverse cultures.

LIST OF TEN

MULTICULTURAL ALPHABET BOOKS

A plethora of alphabet books gives young children a taste of cultures other than their own. A sample of these books follows:

Gathering the Sun: An Alphabet in Spanish and English by Alma Flor Ada (translated by Rosa Zubizarreta and illustrated by Simon Silva)
A bilingual book that honors Latino farm laborers (Lothrup, 1997)

The Calypso Alphabet by John Agard (illustrated by Jennifer Bent)
Introduces words that have to do with the Caribbean culture (Holt, 1989)

Caribbean Alphabet by Frane Lessac
Matches letters of the alphabet to objects related to life in the Caribbean (Morrow, 1994)

A Is for Aloha by Stephanie Feeney
Alphabet book focusing on Hawaiian-American life (University of Hawaii Press, 1985)

A Is for Asia by Cynthia Chin-La (illustrated by Yumi Heo)
Focuses on objects and ideas related to Asian cultures (Orchard, 1997)

Jambo Means Hello: Swahili Alphabet Book by Muriel Feelings (illustrated by
Tom Feelings)
Features letters related to African experiences (Dial, 1976)

Ashanti to Zulu: African Traditions by Margot Musgrove
*Facts and illustrations about twenty-six African tribes, one for each letter of the alphabet
(Dial, 1976)*

Many Nations: An Alphabet Book of Native Americans by Joseph Bruchac (illustrated
by Robert F. Goetzel)
Alphabet book that reflects the diversity of Native American peoples (Troll, 1997)

A to Zen by Ruth Wells
*Introduces Japanese words from A to Z and is designed to be read back to front and right
to left (Simon and Schuster, 1992)*

Navajo ABC: A Diné Alphabet Book by Luci Tapahonso and Eleanor Schick
*Illustrations of Navajo words and samples of the Navajo alphabet (Simon and
Schuster, 1995)*

AFRICAN-AMERICAN[1] CHILDREN'S LITERATURE RELATED TO AFRICAN AMERICANS

For many years, children's literature that included African Americans perpetuated racist
attitudes and negative stereotypes. Blacks were largely ignored or they were depicted in an
unattractive stereotypical fashion, as "happy-go-lucky, childlike creatures who wanted nothing more from life than something good to eat and a chance to sing and dance. What is
remarkable is how long-lasting this image proved" (Bryson 1994, 152). Today, however, there
is a wealth of material in all genres that respects, celebrates, and appreciates people of color.

An interesting contrast between past and present is the case of *The Story of Little
Black Sambo*. Helen Bannerman, the wife of a British colonial officer in India, wrote this
story in 1899 for the amusement of her children. The story, with its crudely drawn characters and simplistic story line, remained a popular part of the canon of children's literature
for decades. Eventually, however, the book was recognized as offensive to many people and
viewed as the epitome of racism, so it was removed from schools and libraries across this
country. *Little Black Sambo* was so thoroughly expunged that whole generations of young
adults today have not even heard of the book.

Almost a century after *The Story of Little Black Sambo* was originally published, the
talented African-American writer Julius Lester teamed up with the award-winning
African-American illustrator Jerry Pinkney to produce a latter-day version of the story, *Sam
and the Tigers*. Both men had remembered the original story with genuine fondness from

1. In this section, the term *African American* is used in a generic sense. Some children's stories and poems about people of color
come directly from one of several African cultures; some are rooted in one of the various Caribbean cultures. Much of the
English-language literature by and about people of color is related to African-American people and traditions, however, and so
this term is used throughout.

their youth, and so they reconceptualized and retold the tale with a style, humor, and visual images that combine to make a delightful fantasy that can be enjoyed by children from all ethnic groups, despite the historical baggage that the story carries. (Fred Marcello also adapted Bannerman's famous, or infamous, story by changing the setting to India, where Bannerman lived when she wrote it, and the characters' names to Babaji, Mamaji, and Papaji, and by redoing the illustrations to create *The Story of Little Babaji*.)

Children's books that reflect African-American culture span all the genres: traditional folk literature, fiction and fantasy, biography and informational books, and poetry. These books will be identified in subsequent chapters on particular genres. In poetry as in prose, such literature is characterized by high literary quality and artistic excellence that reflects many dimensions of the African-American experience, and promotes the love of literature in all children, whatever their cultural background.

Author Profile: MILDRED D. TAYLOR

Mildred D. Taylor is author of some of the most powerful multicultural literature ever written for children. Her stories about the Logan family have informed and inspired children of all ethnic groups.

Taylor was born in Jackson, Mississippi, in 1943. Not long after she was born, her family, in part to avoid the segregation that was law in southern states at the time, moved to Toledo, Ohio, where Taylor grew up. She majored in Education at the University of Toledo and, after graduation, joined the Peace Corps. She worked in Ethiopia for two years and, when she returned home, she attended the University of Colorado School of Journalism, where she honed her writing skills and earned a Master's degree.

The Taylor family was a family of storytellers. Taylor was fascinated by the detailed stories that her father and her uncles told at family gatherings about growing up in the South. She realized that the stories she heard from her family did not match the stories she read in books, and so she decided to write some of them. In 1975 her first book, *Song of the Trees*, was published. The book introduced the Logans, an African-American family living in Mississippi during the 1930s who had to fight to maintain ownership of their land.

The following year, *Roll of Thunder, Hear My Cry* was published and it won the Newbery Medal for 1977. The story told about more struggles of the Logan family—the indomitable Cassie, her parents, and her three brothers, Stacey, Christopher-John, and Little Man—as they strove to overcome racial prejudice and social injustice that African Americans endured in the segregated South of the 1930s.

Taylor continued to write books about the Logan family: *Let the Circle Be Unbroken* (1981), *The Friendship* (1987), *The Gold Cadillac* (1987), *The Road to Memphis* (1990), *Mississippi Bridge* (1990), and *The Well* (1995). All of her books feature strong, engaging characters who encounter prejudice and injustice in a racially segregated environment.

Mildred Taylor resides in Colorado, where she continues her career as a writer.

Certain books authentically reflect the values and qualities that are essential to African-American history and culture. Sharon Bell Mathis's *The Hundred Penny Box*, about a boy's warm relationship with his great-great aunt, is a story that exemplifies cross-generational love. So is Angela Johnson's *Toning the Sweep*, a young adult novel about the love and care given by three generations of African-American women. In the picture storybook *Old Cotton Blues* by Linda England, an old blues musician gives a young boy a harmonica, and the two make special music, and *Ma Dear's Aprons* by Patricia McKissack is a warm and sensitive story about an African-American boy who knows what day of the week it is by the apron his mother is wearing for work.

LIST OF TEN

YOUNG BLACK HEROINES

Kathleen Odean (1998) has suggested a list of books that feature young black females as the central characters. These protagonists, either African or African American, are brave, intelligent, risk-taking, strong, and vibrant. A sample of ten titles from this list follows:

Off to School by Gwendolyn Battle-Lavert (illustrated by Gershom Griffith)
> *This story tells about the perserverance of Wezielee who wants to go to school (Holiday House, 1995)*

Just Us Women by Jeannette Caines (illustrated by Pat Cummings)
> *A story of independence in which a girl and her aunt take a car trip together (HarperCollins, 1982)*

Darkness and the Butterfly by Ann Grifalconi
> *Set in Africa, this story tells how Osa learns to conquer her fear of darkness (Little Brown, 1987)*

Masai and I by Virginia Kroll (illustrated by Nancy Carpenter)
> *An American girl imagines what a Masai girl is doing at the same time (Simon and Schuster, 1992)*

Nanta's Lion: A Search-and-Find Adventure by Sue MacDonald
> *A fascinating presentation of a brave girl who sets out to find a lion (Morrow, 1995)*

I Want to Be by Thylias Moss (illustrated by Jerry Pinkney)
> *A celebration of a girl's dream of what she wants to be (Dial, 1993)*

Molly the Brave and Me by Jane O'Connor (illustrated by Sheila Hamanaka)
> *A cheerful story about an interracial friendship in the second grade (Random House, 1990)*

JoJo's Flying Side Kick by Brian Pinkney
> *A story about a girl who achieves her goals in martial arts (Simon and Schuster, 1995)*

Jenny Reen and the Jack Muh Latern by Irene Small (illustrated by Keinyo White)
> *A story about a girl who tricks a scary monster (Simon and Schuster, 1996)*

Cherries and Cherry Pits by Vera B. Williams
> *A wonderfully illustrated book about a girl and the stories she tells (Greenwillow, 1986)*

In African-American children's literature, the genres of historical fiction, realistic fiction, and information often merge. *The Watsons Go to Birmingham-1963* by Christopher Paul Curtis, for example, is a work of fiction, yet children can gain from it an historical sense and much information about the Civil Rights Movement.

Some children's books related to the African-American experience contain African-American Vernacular English (AAVE) or Ebonics. For example, the grandmother in Valerie Flournoy's warm and touching book *The Patchwork Quilt* says, "Stuff? This ain't stuff. These little pieces gonna make me a quilt." A rich Jamaican dialect is reflected in Regina Hanson's *Face at the Window:* "Lureen said, 'Why you look? Any time Miss Nella show her face at her window, something terrible gonna' happen.' 'Yes,' said Trevor. 'My mama say if you see Miss Nella's face in de window, you is in big trouble.'"

Authors use language like this to give more fullness to characters and authenticity to stories. Such language in stories that portrays the most obvious features of sound, lexicon, and grammar of a dialect is called *eye dialect.*

Language is a collection of dialects, and people are often characterized by the way they speak. Ebonics is a form of language with its own sound system, internal syntactic structure, and unique lexicon (van Keulen, Weddington, and DeBose 1998). It is another dialect of our language. AAVE is different from standard English, but it is not a deficient form of language. Standard written language does not have the dialect features that mark people's speech, and therefore when eye dialect is used, it throws some people—black and white alike—for a loop. Nevertheless, eye dialect is an attempt to reasonably represent colloquial speech patterns in order to add an element of authenticity and enjoyment to a story. More important by far than a story's use of eye dialect, however, is the quality and appeal of the story.

The rich montage of children's literature can "inform children of all cultures about the African-American experience of joy, struggle, perserverance, and hope" (Diamond and Moore 1995, 47). With attractive artwork, exciting plots, memorable characters, and interesting settings, literature about African Americans furthers the love of literature in children from all cultures.

LATINO[2] CHILDREN'S LITERATURE

Children's literature related to Latino cultures is an essential part of children's experiences with books. As with other marginalized groups, the traditional portrayal of Spanish-speaking people in children's books was stereotypical and generally negative. But more striking was the dearth of books about Latinos. While books by and about African Americans have increased in the past several years, books about Latinos and their contemporary lives lag far behind. Only a tiny percentage of children's books published each year are by or about Latinos. While the number of Latino children in schools continues to climb, their presence in children's trade books has not kept pace. "A recent issue of *The New York Times Book Review* that included a look at 'fifty years of children's books' did not mention one

---

2. As in the case of *African American, Latino* is a generic, all-encompassing term in this case for Americans of Latin American heritage. While Latinos share the Spanish language, they come from different cultures in the Caribbean, Central America, and South America. Puerto Rican history and traditions differ from Mexican history and traditions, which differ from the history and traditions of other cultures in the Caribbean. Since a bond of recognition often exists among Spanish-speaking people, the term Latino is used; however, cultural differences are recognized.

CORETTA SCOTT KING AWARD WINNERS

Since 1970, the American Library Association has given awards to commemorate the work of Dr. Martin Luther King Jr. and Coretta Scott King in promoting peace and world brotherhood. The awards are given to the African-American author and, since 1974, the African American illustrator whose works have made outstanding inspirational and educational contributions to literature for children and young people. Award winners over the years follow:

1970 Lillie Patterson for **Martin Luther King, Jr.: Man of Peace** (Garrard)

1971 Charlemae Rollins for **Black Troubador: Langston Hughes** (Rand)

1972 Elton C. Fax for **17 Black Artists** (Dodd)

1973 Jackie Robinson (with Alfred Duckett) for **I Never Had It Made** (Putnam)

1974 Sharon Bell Mathis for **Ray Charles** (Crowell)

George Ford, illustrator, for **Ray Charles** (Crowell)

1975 Dorothy Robinson for **The Legend of Africana** (Johnson)

Herbert Temple, illustrator, for **The Legend of Africana** (Johnson)

1976 Pearl Bailey for **Duey's Tale** (Harcourt)

1977 James Haskins for **The Story of Stevie Wonder** (Lothrop)

1978 Eloise Greenfield for **Africa Dream** (Crowell)

Carole Bayard, illustrator, for **Africa Dream** (Crowell)

1979 Ossie Davis for **Escape to Freedom** (Viking)

Tom Feelings, illustrator, for **Something on My Mind** by Nikki Grimes

1980 Walter Dean Myers for **The Young Landlords** (Viking)

Carole Bayard, illustrator, for **Cornrows** by Camille Yarborough

1981 Sidney Poitier for **This Life** (Knopf)

Ashley Bryan, illustrator, for **Beat the Story Drum, Pum-Pum** (Atheneum)

1982 Mildred D. Taylor for **Let the Circle Be Unbroken** (Dial)

John Steptoe, illustrator, for **Mother Crocodile: An Uncle Amadou Tale from Senegal** adapted by Rosa Guy (Delacorte)

1983 Virginia Hamilton for **Sweet Whispers, Brother Rush** (Philomel)

Peter Mugabane, illustrator, for **Black Child** (Knopf)

1984 Lucille Clifton for **Everett Anderson's Goodbye** (Holt)

Pat Cummings, illustrator, for **My Mama Needs Me** by Mildred Pitts Walter

1985 Walter Dean Myers for **Motown and Didi** (Viking)

1986 Virginia Hamilton for **If People Could Fly: American Black Folktales** (Knopf)

Jerry Pinkney, illustrator, for **Patchwork Quilt** by Valerie Flournoy (Dial)

1987 Mildred Pitts Walter for **Justin and the Best Biscuits in the World** (Lothrop)

Jerry Pinkney, illustrator, for **Half Moon and One Whole Star** by Crescent Dragonwings (Macmillan)

1988 Mildred D. Taylor for **The Friendship** (Dial)

John Steptoe, illustrator, for **Mufaro's Beautiful Daughter** (Lothrop)

1989 Walter Dean Myers for **Fallen Angels** (Scholastic)

Jerry Pinkney, illustrator, for **Mirandy and Brother Wind** by Patricia McKissack

1990 Patricia and Frederick McKissack for **A Long Hard Journey** (Walker)

Jan Spivey Gilchrist, illustrator, for **Nathaniel Talking** by Eloise Greenfield (Black Butterfly Press)

1991 Mildred D. Taylor for **Road to Memphis** (Dial)

Leo and Diane Dillon, illustrators, for **Aïda**, retold by Leontyne Price (Harcourt)

1992 Walter Dean Myers for **Now It's Your Time! The African-American Struggle for Freedom** (HarperCollins)

Faith Ringgold, illustrator, for **Tar Beach**

1993 Patricia McKissack for **The Dark Thirty: Southern Tales of the Supernatural** (Knopf)

Kathleen Atkins Smith, illustrator, for **Origins of Life on Earth: An African Creation Myth** by David A. Anderson (Sight Productions)

1994 Angela Johnson for **Toning the Sweep** (Orchard)

Tom Feelings, illustrator, for **Soul Looks Back in Wonder** (Dial)

1995 Patricia and Frederick McKissack for **Christmas in the Big House, Christmas in the Quarters** (Scholastic)

James E. Ransome, illustrator, for **The Creation** by James Weldon Johnson

1996 Virginia Hamilton for **Her Stories** (Blue Sky Press)

Tom Feelings, illustrator, for **The Middle Passage: White Ships, Black Cargo** (Dial)

1997 Walter Dean Myers for **Slam!** (Scholastic)

Jerry Pinkney, illustrator, for **Minty: A Story of Young Harriet Tubman** by Alan Schroeder (Dial)

1998 Sharon M. Draper for **Forged by Fire** (Atheneum)

Javaka Steptoe, illustrator, for **In Daddy's Arms I Am Tall: African Americans Celebrating Fathers** (Lee and Low)

1999 Angela Johnson for **Heaven** (Simon & Schuster)

Michele Wood, illustrator for **i see the rhythm** (Children's Book Press)

book about or by a Latino, did not include one Latino reviewer, nor was an ad bought for a book written or illustrated by a Latino" (Mora 1998, 282). Even of books that are about Spanish-speaking people, most depict those of Mexican or Puerto Rican heritage, not those who belong to other Latino cultures in our society. Nevertheless, those books that do exist can be effectively used in the classroom.

For Latino students, sharing literature that reflects their history, values, experience, and language fosters pride and stimulates interest. For non-Latino students, the literature creates awareness and broadens children's reading backgrounds with stories and poems that appeal.

THE AMERICAS AWARD AND THE PURA BELPRE AWARD

Two major awards are given annually for Latino children's books. The Americas Award, initiated in 1993, honors books that present engaging and authentic representations of Latin American and Latino life experiences. It is sponsored by the Consortium of Latin American Studies Programs. Named in honor of the New York Public Library's first Latina librarian, the Pura Belpre Award was initiated in 1996 and is given biannually to authors and illustrators of Latino heritage. It is sponsored by the American Library Association. Winners of the two awards follow:

THE AMERICAS AWARD

1993 **Vejigante Masquerader** by Lulu Delacre (Scholastic)

1994 **The Mermaid's Twin Sister** by Lynn Joseph (Clarion)

1995 **Tonight by Sea** by Francis Temple (Orchard)

1996 Picture Book: **In My Family/En Mi Familia** by Carman Lomas Garza (Children's)
     Fiction: **Parrot in the Oven**: **Mi Vida** by Victor Martinez (HarperCollins)

1997 Picture Book: **The Face at the Window** by Regina Hanson (Clarion)
     Fiction: **The Circuit**: **Stories from the Life of a Migrant Child** by Francisco Jimenez (University of New Mexico Press)

THE PURA BELPRE AWARD

1996 Author: Judith Ortiz Coffer, **An Island Like You: Stories from the Barrio** (Orchard)
     Illustrator: Susan Guevara for **Chato's Kitchen** by Gary Soto (Putnam)

1998 Author: Victor Martinez, **Parrot in the Oven** (HarperCollins)
     Illustrator: Stephanie Garcia for **Snapshots from the Wedding** by Gary Soto (Putnam)

1999 **Barrio: Jose's Neighborhood** by George Ancona (Harcourt Brace, 1998)

The importance of using Latino literature cannot be overstated. When students see their own culture and experiences reflected in books like Gary Soto's picture book *Too Many Tamales* about a Christmas celebration in a Latino household and his *Local News*, with stories about growing up in a Mexican-American neighborhood in California, even the most reluctant readers are apt to become enthusiastic. For many Latino children, exposure to these books consists of their first encounter with characters who resemble themselves and with experiences to which they can relate, thus validating their own linguistic and cultural experiences. Barry (1998) emphasizes the power of literature in helping children make the connection between home and school. For Latino pupils, this is especially important.

Children's literature related to Latino cultures crosses different genres. A rich tradition of folk literature comes from the stories of native cultures colonized by the Spanish when they arrived in this hemisphere. Historical fiction often focuses on the role of the early Spanish explorers and the Spanish pioneers in the West, and realistic fiction frequently reflects the experiences of Latino youth growing up in a largely Anglo society. Nonfiction books present information about Spanish-speaking peoples and their cultures, and poetry celebrates the rich tradition of the cultures.

Much children's literature related to Latino cultures is bilingual with parallel Spanish and English text, such as *Medio Pollito/Half-Chicken* by Alma Flor Ada, a pourquoi tale from Cuba, and *Tortillas Para Mamá and Other Spanish Nursery Rhymes*, a collection of poems by Margot Griego. These books allow teachers to share fine literature in two languages and help both Spanish-speaking and English-speaking children to see the connections between their respective languages. Some popular children's titles have been translated into Spanish: *Jorge el Curioso* (*Curious George*) and *Donde Viven los Monstruos* (*Where the Wild Things Are*).

Other books embed individual Spanish words, expressions, and whole sentences within the story so that the meaning of the language in context is clear to the reader. In Arthur Dorros's *Abuela*, a simple story in which Rosalba and her grandmother take an imaginary aerial journey, the dialogue includes passages such as, " 'El parque es lindo,' says Abuela. I know what this means. I think the park is beautiful too." Many of Gary Soto's books, such as *Snapshots from the Wedding*, a book that depicts a festive family wedding including the exciting preparations, dancing to a mariachi band at the reception, and the delicious food enjoyed by the guests, integrate Spanish expressions throughout. In fact, the humor of Soto's *The Old Man and His Door* centers on the similarity between two Spanish words, *puerco* (pig) and *puerta* (door) and on the confusion of a guest who brings la puerta instead of el puerco as the main dish for a barbecue.

Author Profile: GARY SOTO

Gary Soto is one of the most popular and versatile authors in the field of children's and young adult literature today. Both in his life and in his writing, he maintains a strong commitment to his Latino roots.

Gary Soto was born in Fresno, California, to Mexican-American parents. His grandparents had emigrated from Mexico and found work as farm laborers. He earned a degree in English from California State University at Fresno and a Master of Fine Arts in Creative Writing at the University of California at Irvine.

Soto's versatility as a writer is remarkable. He has written nine poetry collections for adults, and his award-winning poems regularly appear in literary magazines. But his appeal to young readers comes from his picture books and young adult novels. He sees his role as a writer "to make readers out of nonreaders," and his work continues to accomplish this goal.

Soto's writing is rooted in his experiences as a Mexican American, and his stories capture the flavor of life in the barrio. His first book for young readers was *Living up the Street* (1985), narrative recollections about his youth. Other books of short stories about life in his Fresno neighborhood followed—*Baseball in April and Other Stories* (1990), *A Summer Life* (1990), and *Local News* (1993).

Soto's picture books integrate the English-language text with Spanish words and expressions that reflect the content. *Too Many Tamales* (1993, illustrated by Ed Martinez), *Chato's Kitchen* (1995, illustrated by Susan Guevara), *The Old Man and His Door* (1996, illustrated by Joe Cepeda), and *Snapshots from the Wedding* (1997, illustrated by Stephanie Garcia) all authentically reflect the author's cultural traditions and share experiences to which Latino children can relate.

Gary Soto lives with his family in Berkeley, California, where he continues to write and teach at the University of California at Berkeley. Here are some of his other books that children can enjoy:

Neighborhood Odes (1992)

Taking Sides (1992)

The Cat's Meow (1995)

Off and Running (1996)

Boys at Work (1996)

As children from Latino cultures continue to constitute a substantial proportion of our school population, teachers will continue to use books by Spanish-speaking authors and books about Latino cultures as an important dimension of multicultural literature, and the number of these books available can be expected to increase. Stories and poems related to Latino cultures will continue to be used to enrich the curriculum and promote the love of literature for all children.

ASIAN-AMERICAN[3] CHILDREN'S LITERATURE

Asian Pacific Americans represent the fastest growing groups of ethnic "minorities" in the United States today. Traditionally, as portrayed in children's literature, Asian Americans fared no better than other marginalized groups. Children's books "presented stereotypes suggesting that all Asian Americans look alike, choose to live in 'quaint' communities in the midst of large cities, and cling to 'outworn, alien' customs" (Norton 1995, 564). Children's literature perpetuated the image of Asian Americans as "foreigners." More recently, an increasing number of books recognizing diversity among Asian Americans have begun to appear, presenting Asian Americans and their ways of life in more realistic and positive fashions.

As in the case of the literature of other cultural groups, children's literature related to Asian Americans crosses different genres. Unfortunately, many stories that are characterized as "folk literature" perpetuate stereotypes of Asian Americans. Margaret Mahy's version of *The Seven Chinese Brothers*, for example, suggests that all Chinese people look exactly alike, and *Tikki Tikki Tembo* (retold by Arline Mosel) suggests that Asian names are somehow amusingly bizarre. While many more authentic traditional folktales and fairy tales related to Asian cultures are available, stereotypes often persist. Some traditional folk

---

3. *Asian American* is a very general term. Asian Pacific Americans represent up to 50 different ethnic groups. The expression is used generally to include literature related to the cultures of China, Japan, Cambodia, Vietnam, and other countries in Southeast Asia and the Pacific Islands.

literature reflects the universality of fairy tales. Ed Young's Caldecott Medal winner *Lon Po Po* recounts the Chinese version of Little Red Riding Hood, and Ai-Ling Louie's *Yeh Shen* is subtitled *A Cinderella Story from China*. Shirley Climo's *The Korean Cinderella* casts this universally popular story in a Korean context.

Stories about Asian Americans often tell about the life of immigrants in a new land. Laurence Yep's popular story *Dragonwings* tells about a boy who follows his dreams in coming to America, accurately reflecting life in the Chinese-American community at the turn of the century. Allen Say's Caldecott Medal–winner *Grandfather's Journey* is about the immigration of the author's grandfather from Japan to the United States. In *Chinatown* by William Low, a boy and his grandmother enjoy the colorful sights and sounds of China-town as they participate in Chinese New Year. Books such as these provide authentic im-ages of the Asian-American experience.

Themes in stories about Asian Americans often involve conflicts created by the tug between old values and new lifestyles. Lensey Namioka's *Yang the Youngest and His Terrible Ear* is a funny story about a nine-year-old boy who, to his family's consternation, prefers baseball to music. Laurence Yep's *Ribbons* is a sensitive contemporary story about a young girl's struggle to pursue her interest in ballet in the face of problems. Michele Surat's *Angel Child, Dragon Child* is about the difficulties of a young Vietnamese girl in adjusting to life without her mother in a new country. Linda Crew's *Children of the River* offers to older readers the same theme about a Cambodian teenager.

Many stories about Asian Americans have strong autobiographical elements. Beth Bao Lord's *In the Year of the Boar and Jackie Robinson* is based on the author's experience as a young girl moving from a small village in China to Brooklyn, New York. In *Year of Impossi-ble Good-Byes*, Sook Nyul Choi recalls the difficulties of life in North Korea under enemy oc-cupation and the courage involved in the family's escape. In *The Land I Lost: Adventures of a Boy in Vietnam*, Huynh Quang Nhuong takes the reader back to his home village.

Traditionally, books related to Asian-American cultures have been set in Asian coun-tries or have presented Asian Pacific Americans living in North America as being exotic and removed from the mainstream of society. Talented writers like Allen Say, William Low, and Laurence Yep are changing that image by producing fine literature that depicts Asian Americans more realistically as members of contemporary society. Literature related to Asian Americans continues to constitute part of the rich montage of material that educates, entertains, and inspires children inside and outside the classroom.

NATIVE AMERICAN[4] CHILDREN'S LITERATURE

As in the case of other ethnic groups, Native Americans were for years stereotyped in the mass media as well as in literature for children. The derogatory image of the bloodthirsty warrior bedecked in feathers and smeared with war paint dehumanized Native American peoples and diminished their cultures. The popular cowboy movie image of the "American Indian" as a wild and primitive creature attacking wagon trains and waging war on noble settlers was often perpetuated in books written for children. Laura Ingalls Wilder's popu-

---

4. *Native American* is a very broad expression. As anyone familiar with the history of North America knows, many different tribes populated this continent prior to the arrival of Europeans, each with its own distinct language, tradition, and literature.

Author Profile: VIRGINIA DRIVING HAWK SNEVE

A noted Native American author of books for children, Virginia Driving Hawk Sneve adds sensitivity and authenticty to material that she writes for young readers.

Born and raised on the Rosebud Sioux Reservation in South Dakota, Sneve attended the Bureau of Indian Affairs School on the Reservation and graduated from St. Mary's High School for Indian Girls. She continued her education at South Dakota State University, where she earned both Bachelor's and Master's degrees. After graduation, she taught English, music, drama, and speech and worked as a guidance counselor at the high school and elementary school levels.

When her daughter began reading the *Little House* books, some of which were set in South Dakota where she grew up, Sneve became interested in writing for children. She produced a number of novels with Native American protagonists—*Jimmy Yellow Hawk* (1972), *High Elk's Treasure* (1972), *Betrayed* (1974), and *The Twelve Moons* (1977).

Sneve sees her writing as an extension of her work as an educator. She wants readers to have a positive and accurate picture of her Native American heritage, unlike the image of brave boy warriors and noble princesses who saved settlers from savage Indians that she encountered in her own reading as a child. Her writing reflects an honest attempt to dispel stereotypes and to show that Native Americans have a proud past, a viable present, and a hopeful future. In 1989, she collected poems of Native American young people into a well-known volume, *Dancing Teepees*.

In the 1990s, Sneve turned her talented hand to writing nonfiction books for children. She authored the *The First Americans*, a series that accurately describes the history, customs, and present lifestyles of different groups of Native Americans. The books in the series include *The Seminoles* (1994), *The Hopi* (1995), *The Cherokees* (1996), and *The Apaches* (1997).

Today, Virginia Driving Hawk Sneve continues to write fiction and nonfiction that help children come to love literature as they come to understand better Native American culture.

lar *Little House* series, for example, depicted Native Americans as untrustworthy and dangerous.

More recently, much has changed as contemporary authors have created stories that reflect Native Americans in a more realistic and positive light. *Morning on the Lake,* a picture book by Jan Bourdeau Connelly depicts a modern day Ojibway boy learning about the ways of nature from his grandfather. *Sacred Fire* by Nancy Wood captures in prose and verse the traditional wisdom of the Pueblo Indians of the Southwest. Traditions of the past are preserved in books like Joseph Bruchac's *Between Earth and Sky: Legends of Native American Sacred Places*, which contains stories about the three directions: Above (sky), Below (earth), and Within (ourselves). Virginia Driving Hawk Sneve has written an informational series called *The First Americans* that portrays different groups of Native Americans as they lived in the past and as they live now.

As in the case of other socially marginalized groups, there is a dearth of children's literature related to Native Americans, especially stories that reflect Native Americans in contemporary settings, although some is beginning to appear. Two very well-known children's authors have written books about young people seeking to reconnect with their ancient heritage in a modern age: Jean Craighead George's *The Talking Earth* is about a Seminole girl who searches for her heritage in the Florida swamps, and Gary Paulsen's *Dogsong* is about a contemporary Eskimo boy who rediscovers his heritage in the Arctic wilderness. As mainstream society comes to recognize the rich tradition of Native American cultures, more and more children's books that are free of language, appearance, and behavior stereotype will find their way into homes, libraries, and classrooms to enhance the literary experience of children.

Children's Literature that Is *Really* Multicultural

"Children come in all the colors of the rainbow." So begins *All the Colors of the Earth* by Sheila Hamanaka. Children's literature that is classified as "multicultural" often only offers the perspective of a single culture that has been traditionally outside the mainstream of society. Many children's stories are, however, truly *multi*cultural, in that they depict the experiences of people from two or more ethnic groups or cultures interacting. Some of these books follow:

- *Black Is Brown Is TAN* by Arnold Adoff

  a story with lyrical text about children growing up in an interracial family

- *Smoky Night* by Eve Bunting

  an account of a city riot in which Mrs. Kim, Mr. Raminez, Mr. Jackson, and others are residents of a diverse urban neighborhood

- *Jamaica and Brianna* by Juanita Havill

  about two friends—one Asian American and one African American—who discover the bumps and smooth spots in friendship

- *Pink and Say* by Patricia Polacco

  about a white soldier and a black soldier who develop mutual respect and friendship

- *How My Parents Learned to Eat* by Ina Freedman

  the account of an American sailor who marries a Japanese woman

- *Dumpling Soup* by Jama Kim Rattigan

  a story about a family whose members are Japanese, Korean, Hawaiian, and Caucasian

- *Run Away Home* by Patricia McKissack

  about an African-American family who befriends a runaway Apache boy in Alabama during the 1800s

Books such as these portray people from diverse backgrounds living and working together, which is one of the aims of using multicultural literature at home and in school.

THE INTERNATIONAL DIMENSION OF MULTICULTURAL LITERATURE

While more children's books are published in the United States than in any other country in the world, many books published in other countries find their way to classroom and library shelves in North America. These books constitute another dimension of multicultural literature in children's lives and reflect some of the best works of literature available for children.

Multicultural understanding crosses national boundaries. Through international children's literature, children come to know and appreciate stories from other countries and establish a framework for international understanding. This body of literature helps children learn about people in other lands and presents a rich and accessible view of life in other countries.

Often, because they are published outside North America, international children's literature reflects times, places, and situations with which children may not be familiar. "It is not unreasonable to assume that an author from a particular country, writing for the children of that country, would write differently than if writing for American children" (Lo and Leahy 1997, 217). *Hiroshima No Pika* by Toshi Maruki, for example, was written for a Japanese audience whose perspective on survival after an atomic attack is very different from the perspective on this side of the world. However, "When students compare their own experiences and customs against those of another, a clearer perspective of their own place in the world can emerge" (Lo and Leahy 1997, 221).

While international children's literature can help broaden horizons, some of its aspects can create certain barriers in reading comprehension. Young readers in the United States and Canada have the background to understand and enjoy the humor of Mary Jane Auch's *I Was a Third Grade Science Project*, the story of a school science experiment gone awry, but they may not have the schemata to appreciate of the humor of Garry Crew's *The Watertower*, the story of two friends who decide to go swimming in the water tower of their village in the Australian outback.

Through international literature, children can gain perspectives into cultures different than their own. By reading Beverley Naidoo's *Chain of Fire*, the story of the destruction of villages in South Africa, or her *No Turning Back*, a novel about a runaway boy during apartheid, children can gain insights into that place and time. And by reading *Why Goats Smell So Bad and Other Stories from Benin*, translated and retold by Raouf Mama, they can enjoy the trickster tales, the pourquoi tales, and other traditional stories from the Fon people of Benin. International children's literature links children across national boundaries and helps them discover the similarities and differences among them.

Each year, the Batchelder Award is given to books originally published in a foreign language and translated for publication in the United States (see Appendix A). Other awards are given to books published in Great Britain, Canada, Australia, and New Zealand. Teachers and parents can find annotated references to notable international books in *Children's Books from Other Countries*, edited by Carl M. Tomlinson (Scarecrow, 1998).

MULTICULTURAL LITERATURE AT HOME AND IN SCHOOL

With a rich diet of children's literature in the home, it is likely that children will encounter books related to diverse cultures. For children who are African American, Native American,

Asian American, or Latino or who are from multiracial homes, early encounters with literature that represents their own cultures is important. When very young children look at books, it's important that they see characters who look like them looking back at them. Multicultural trade books can be powerful vehicles in the lives of so-called "minority" children.

Experiencing the diversity of multicultural literature is important for children's reading experiences in the home. The strikingly brilliant artwork in the picture books of illustrators such as Faith Ringgold or Gerald McDermott are a treat to the eyes of children (and adults) of all ethnic backgrounds. Children delight in stories about the trickery of Anansi the spider or Iktomi the coyote just as much as they delight in the antics of Peter Rabbit or Curious George. Multicultural realistic books such as *Anna in Charge* by Yoriko Tsutsui, a contemporary picture book about two sisters, gives young readers the sense that children from other cultures share many of their same values and experiences. In sum, a rich variety of multicultural literature belongs in the home just as it belongs in the classroom.

Within the school setting, multicultural literature needs to be an integral part of the curriculum, not something that is used only on occasion as when teachers read biographies of African Americans by Patricia and Frederick McKissack during Black History Month or share stories by Laurence Yep as Chinese New Year approaches. Yamate (1997) identifies the goals of multicultural literature in the classroom as "(1) the validation of minority experiences not commonly represented in literature, media and the arts . . . (2) preparing students for life in a world characterized by diversity . . . (and) (3) cultivating and instilling in students a greater appreciation of all people as valued and important individuals" (122).

Children need to encounter different ethnic images in their initial encounters with trade books. In prekindergarten and other early childhood settings, multicultural titles should constitute a major part of the children's literature collection, so that children will be exposed to diversity in the stories they experience early on in school. Picture storybooks like Margaree King Mitchell's *Uncle Jed's Barbershop*, a wonderful story about an African-American man who achieves his dream, and Taro Yashimo's *Crow Boy*, a haunting story of a boy rejected by his classmates, are important for children as they begin to interact with literature. In early childhood settings, read-alouds, book sharing, story time, creative dramatics, show-and-tell or sharing, and other language activities should include poems and stories representing a variety of different cultural groups.

Special Perspectives on Children's Literature

THE INDIAN IN THE CUPBOARD AND THE POLITICS OF CHILDREN'S BOOKS
by Marilyn Cochran-Smith

James Finn Garner's *Politically Correct Bedtime Stories* is riotously funny. Cinderella's ball is thrown because the prince wants to "celebrate his exploitation of the dispossessed and marginalized peasantry," while the seven dwarfs debate whether to let Snow White stay with them because she might "disrupt [their] strong bond of brotherhood." Smith's parody makes it clear that the whole modern enterprise—altering language and excising certain images of gender, culture, and oppression in something as harmless as the stories read to children—is ludicrous, carried to ridiculous extremes by radical feminists, Marxists, or worse.

Does it really matter that in Richard Scarry's *Postman Pig and His Busy Neighbors* all the cute little bunnies and kitties who are teachers and nurses and beauticians are girl creatures, while all the cute little squirrels and puppies who are truck drivers and lawyers and doctors are boy creatures? Does it matter that upper elementary grade teachers who want to include in what they read aloud to their classes books they refer to as "relationship novels" with male main characters have a hard time finding more than a handful while the relationship novels with female characters are plentiful? Does it matter that the Indians in Laura Ingalls Wilder's *Little House* books are portrayed (particularly in Ma's eyes and in her words) as slinking, greasy, foul-smelling, bloody savages? Does it matter that young African-American and Korean and Puerto Rican men and women preparing to be teachers consistently report that they can remember no books from their childhoods in which the characters looked like them?

During more than twenty-five years as a teacher and teacher educator, I have come to believe strongly that these things do matter. And what makes them matter, even at the beginning of the twenty-first century, is not the copyright date of a particular book (after all, Wilder's books were written between 1930 and 1950, and *Postman Pig* first appeared in 1978), but whether a book is widely available now on library shelves and bookstore carousels and whether teachers regularly choose (or are required) to read or "teach" a book to groups of schoolchildren.

The books we read to and with children are not neutral or value-free. Far from it, they contain explicit and implicit messages about the way the world works or should work. In the fictive worlds they offer to readers, particularly in their portrayals of major as well as trivial characters, children's books convey subtle and not so subtle messages about preferred values, attitudes, and beliefs as well as sometimes powerful images of culture, gender, race, and ethnicity. This view of literature—not as something to be critiqued only on aesthetic or literary grounds but as something that also provides statements about a complex array of important social and political questions— is sometimes referred to as "the politics of children's literature." As Joel Taxel suggests, "Discussions about the sociocultural and political dimensions of literature have become part of a broader critique of society that, among many things, seeks to explain how and why ideologies such as racism and sexism are so ingrained in consciousness as to become part of our common-sense understanding of how the world works."

The evolution of a course on literature for children, which I have taught in various iterations once or twice a year for the past twenty years, has given me some insights into these issues. A few years ago I began to use Lynne Reid Banks's *The Indian in the Cupboard* as one of the six to eight novels my students read in common for the course. Published in 1980 when *The New York Times* called it "the best novel of the year," the book continues to be highly acclaimed and widely used as a whole class text in upper elementary or middle schools, and its popularity has increased since it was recently made into a major motion picture. A fantasy about Omri, a British boy who receives as a present a collector's cupboard, the book revolves around a plastic Indian figure who comes to life (but remains three inches high) when the boy casually places him inside the cupboard and closes the door. A toy cowboy and soldier eventually come to life too and interact with the Indian and the boy. The book is charming in many ways, well written and pivoting on premises that are extremely appealing to children—being bigger than adults, having toys come to life, and keeping a powerful secret.

But in addition to positive reviews about the popularity of the book and the high quality of its writing, the book has also been criticized as racist, perpetuating stereotypes about Native Americans at the same time that it charms and appeals. The first year I used the book, my students were all prospective teachers who were just completing a year of student teaching in urban schools where the population was primarily African American, Asian, and Puerto Rican. I asked them to read the novel, jotting down their responses and then read the critical literature I had assigned. In an excoriating critique of images of Native Americans in children's books, Dorothy MacCann argues that the vast majority of children's books with Native American characters or themes are written from a non-Native perspective, with few exceptions portraying Native American cultures as futile and obsolete. About *The Indian in the Cupboard* (and its sequel) specifically MacCann writes,

> The cultural content is rooted in the image of the Indian as presented in
> Hollywood westerns and dime novels. . . . At every turn of plot, Little Bear
> is either violent or childishly petulant until he finally tramples upon his
> ceremonial headdress as a sign of remorse. The historical culpability of the
> cowboy and others who invaded [American Indian] territory is ignored.
> Native Americans are seen as the primary perpetrators of havoc, even as
> they defend their own borders (145).

In a collection of articles about children's books written primarily by Native Americans, the review of *Indian in the Cupboard* is also wholly negative. Beverly Slapin and Doris Seale conclude,

> My heart aches for the Native child unfortunate enough to stumble across,
> and read, these books. How could she, reading this, fail to be damaged?
> How could a white child fail to believe that he is far superior to the
> bloodthirsty, sub-human monsters portrayed here? (122)

Most of my students reported that they were completely engrossed in the unfolding story, and some were shocked by the negative critiques and even embarrassed that they hadn't noticed the racist overtones (and undertones) until after they finished the book. Many were uncertain about what to think, and the student discussion that followed was intense and animated:

"The book is full of stereotypes. If a book has stereotypes, does that mean you just shouldn't use it in your classroom?"

"There are stereotypes about Indians, but there are also stereotypes about cowboys and soldiers—doesn't this make the book sort of balanced?"

"The very idea of an American Indian adult as the possession (and a miniature possession at that) of a white English child is totally offensive and off-putting—does it really matter what else the book does or doesn't do?"

"Since the boy's faulty assumptions about Indians are for the most part pointed out and corrected as the story goes along, doesn't it actually sort of "teach" some correct facts?"

"In the final analysis, isn't what really matters how engaging the story is and what the quality of the writing is?"

"How can we evaluate the realism of the portrayal of characters in a story that is obviously fantasy rather than history or biography?"

" Since none of us had any Native American children in the classes we student taught this year, does this make the issue of potentially hurting a Native child reader irrelevant?"

At some point in this intense discussion, I inserted, "What if it were *The* Jew *in the Cupboard* or *The* Black *in the Cupboard?* Would that be all right?" This was a turning point. At first there was dead silence. The looks on the faces of many students indicated that it would decidedly *not* be all right to have a children's book with those titles or story lines. Why, then, was it all right for elementary and middle school teachers each year to teach to the whole class a children's book with an Indian in the cupboard? Several African-American and Latino students said this opened their eyes to children's books in a new way by making them think differently about "self" and "other." Everybody seemed to have new questions. Nobody seemed as sure about the answers.

So what do we do with books like this one? What do we do once we have learned to pay attention to the politics of children's books? It does not follow from this perspective, as Garner would have us believe, that we rush to establish the "language police" of the literary world, making sure that every children's book is scrutinized and stripped until harmless or that every children's book has a miniature United Nations delegation standing on the corner. It also does not follow that we either censor or lionize books on the basis of somebody's standard of what is "politically correct."

But it does follow that we, as educators, recognize that children's literature—like all other literature—is not neutral and value free. We need to pay particularly careful attention to the images of race, gender, and culture implicit in the books we share with children, and we need to make choices based on thoughtful consideration of these issues. More than five thousand new children's books are published every year. As educators, we have the opportunity to share only the tiniest portion of these with our students. It is our responsibility—particularly given a school population that is increasingly diverse in race, culture, ethnicity, and language background—to choose wisely and to choose proactively for a more just society.

Marilyn Cochran-Smith is professor of Education and Chair of the Department of Teacher Education at Boston College.

SOURCES CITED:

Garner, J. F. 1994. *Politically Correct Bedtime Stories: Modern Tales for Our Life and Times.* New York: Macmillan Publishing Company.

MacCann, D. 1993. Native Americans in books for the young. In *Teaching Multicultural Literature in Grades K–8,.* ed. V. Harris. Norwood, Mass.: Christopher-Gordon Publishers, Inc.

Slapin, B., and D. Seale. 1992. Review of *Indian in the Cupboard.* In *Through Indian Eyes,* B. Slapin and D. Seale. Philadelphia, Penn.: New Society Publishers.

Taxel, J. 1993. The Politics of Children's Literature: Reflections on Multiculturalism and Christopher Columbus. In *Teaching Multicultural Literature in Grades K–8,* ed. V. Harris. Norwood, Mass: Christopher-Gordon Publishers, Inc.

As a dimension of multicultural literature, international books belong in the classroom too. "International and U.S. books work well together. Selecting a good mix of U.S. and international books for units of instruction, read-alouds, or independent reading is a daily reminder to students that similarities outweigh differences between cultures" (Tomlinson 1998, 8).

Zarrillo (1994) recommends literature units involving multicultural materials. These units consist of an integrated set of instructional activities for large and small groups in the following categories:

- **author studies**, using the work of people like Paul Goble and Virginia Hamilton;
- **genre studies**, with a focus on pourquoi stories and historical fiction;
- **thematic topics**, including the theme of growing up and the theme of family and friends; and
- **cross-curricular subjects**, such as studying about China and famous people.

These units include listening activities, journal and story writing, filmstrips and videos, independent reading, storytelling, listening to and writing poetry, artwork, small group lessons on reading skills and strategies, and a full range of other language arts activities that are a normal part of a literature-based language arts program.

Within the classroom, multicultural literature is not only used to expose students to other cultures but also to engage children in discussing issues. For example, *Angel Child, Dragon Child* by Michele Surat is a story about a Vietnamese girl who must adjust to a new life in America. The book explores interracial tensions in school and offers opportunities for students to talk about ways for children of different ethnic groups to understand one another. The question, "What would you do if . . . ?" gives children a chance to examine their own attitudes and actions regarding cultural groups different from their own. When used well, multicultural literature gives children more than a chance to examine a way of life from the outside; it also creates opportunities to examine how we interact with people different from ourselves.

Multicultural literature offers possibilities for the same range of instructional activities that any children's literature does. Beginning with traditional folk literature, children can compare common folktales from different cultures, dramatize some of these folk stories, and use the content and themes for storytelling (since these stories have their roots in the oral tradition of the cultures from which they come). Works such as Mildred D. Taylor's *Song of the Trees* or Yoshiko Uchida's *The Bracelet* are ideal for generating readers' workshop discussions because they are such powerful stories on important topics. Poetry such as found in Eloise Greenfield's *Honey I Love and Other Poems* and the rhythmical language of Camille Yarborough's *Cornrows* lend themselves to choral reading. Historical fiction like Laurence Yep's *Dragon's Gate* and Scott O'Dell's *Carlota* extend literature across the curriculum and help move students away from an eurocentric view of the history of this country. (European immigrants indeed traveled west in settling the United States, but Latinos traveled north, Chinese immigrants traveled east, and many Native Americans were forced to travel south.) Reading the biographies of famous people from different cultures creates awareness of the contributions that all ethnic groups have made to our modern world. In sum, multicultural literature provides a vehicle for a full range of listening, speaking, reading, and writing activities, while it enhances and enriches the classroom curriculum.

Finally, teachers committed to using children's literature as a vehicle for instruction need to educate themselves about the cultures represented in the literature their students are reading. Teachers with the best of intentions often encounter land mines as they try to make multicultural literature part of their classroom programs. The support and information provided by parents of children from diverse cultures can enhance a teacher's perspective and improve the use of multicultural literature in the classroom, while creating another link between home and school.

CONCLUSION

The twenty-first century reflects a pluralistic society. Whatever metaphor we use—the traditional "melting pot" in which all differences are melded into a single social entity; the "salad bowl" in which all the ingredients maintain their own unique features while adding to the overall taste and texture of the salad; the "mosaic" in which the colored tiles unite and balance to create a beautiful image; the "quilt" in which elements of different shapes, sizes, and colors join together to produce a whole; the "rainbow" in which different colors retain their own hues but together produce something truly beautiful—our survival depends on our living together with understanding, respect, and appreciation. Multicultural literature reflects the rich diversity of the global village in which we live.

Multicultural literature is about more than diversity, however; it's also about inclusion. It is not meant to be a separate part of the language arts program to be alternately studied and put aside at various times during the year. Also, books representing different cultures are not just for children from the represented cultures. And multicultural literature should not be used as an external sign of political correctness. Instead, multicultural literature reflects a "bringing together" that will help children understand and appreciate the contribution of people of all backgrounds to our resulting way of life.

Multicultural poems, stories, and informational books that teachers use in classrooms must first represent quality literature. That picture books represent artistic quality is vital. That stories include multiracial and multiethnic characters is essential. That settings be authentic is important. That stories have compelling, interesting plots is critical. But most important by far is that multicultural literature lead children toward understanding and appreciation of the diverse world in which they live, while promoting a love of literature.

Questions and Activities for Action and Discussion

1. There are many views about what constitutes multicultural literature. The one adopted in this chapter is that multicultural literature consists of books by and about marginalized ethnic and cultural groups in our society. Another view broadens the definition to include as many cultural groups as possible. A third broadens the definition even further to encompass all literature. Prepare a position statement about what you believe multicultural literature is and be ready to defend it.

2. Review an African-American, a Latino, an Asian-American, and a Native American picture book. What do all four books have in common? Which of their features are unique? What conclusions can you draw about books written from an "outsider" versus an "insider" perspective?

3. Select several books by a well-known author of multicultural literature. In what ways do the author's works reflect his or her knowledge and understanding of the culture that he or she has written about?

4. Respond to a new immigrant parent who tells you, "Please don't use multicultural literature with my child. We have recently arrived in this country and are trying to fit in. We want our children to accept American values, so please use only literature that will generate understanding for and appreciation of these values."

5. Explore the children's literature of some of the mainstream cultural groups not addressed in this chapter—Jewish Americans, Irish Americans, and Italian Americans, for example. Contrast this body of literature with the multicultural literature described in this chapter.

CHILDREN'S & YOUNG ADULT BOOKS
CITED IN THIS CHAPTER

Ada, Alma Flor. 1995. *Medio Pollito/Half-Chicken*. Illustrated by Kim Howard. New York: Doubleday.

Adoff, Arnold. 1973. *Black Is Brown Is TAN*. Illustrated by Emily McCully. New York: Harper and Row.

Auch, Mary Jane. 1998. *I Was a Third Grade Science Project*. Illustrated by Herm Auch. New York: Holiday House.

Bannerman, Helen. 1899. *The Story of Little Black Sambo*. London: Chatto &.Windus.

_____ 1996. *The Story of Little Babaji*. Illustrated by Fred Marcello. New York: HarperCollins.

Baylor, Byrd. 1989. *Amigo*. Illustrated by Garth Williams. New York: Simon and Schuster.

Brenner, Barbara. 1978. *Wagon Wheels*. New York: HarperCollins.

Bruchac, Joseph. 1996. *Between Earth and Sky: Legends of Native American Sacred Places*. Illustrated by Thomas Locker. San Diego: Harcourt Brace.

Bunting, Eve. 1994. *Smoky Night*. Illustrated by David Diaz. New York: Harcourt Brace.

Choi, Sook Nyul. 1991. *Year of Impossible Good-Byes*. Boston: Houghton Mifflin.

Climo, Shirley. 1983. *The Korean Cinderella*. New York: HarperCollins.

Cohen, Barbara. 1990. *Molly's Pilgrim*. New York: Dell.

Collier, James, and Christopher Collier. 1983. *War Comes to Willy Freeman*. New York: Dell.

Connelly, Jan Bourdeau. 1998. *Morning on the Lake*. Buffalo, N.Y.: Kids Can Press.

Crew, Garry. 1996. *The Watertower*. Illustrated by Steven Wollman. Brooklyn, N.Y.: Crocodile Books.

Crew, Linda. 1989. *Children of the River*. New York: Dell.

Curtis, Christopher Paul. 1995. *The Watsons Go to Birmingham–1963*. New York: Delacorte.

Dorros, Arthur. 1991. *Abuela*. Illustrated by Elisa Klevin. New York: Dutton.

England, Linda. 1998. *Old Cotton Blues*. Illustrated by Theresa Flavin. New York: Simon and Schuster.

Flournoy, Valerie. 1985. *The Patchwork Quilt*. Illustrated by Jerry Pinkney. New York: Dial.

Freedman, Ina. 1987. *How My Parents Learned to Eat*. Boston: Houghton Mifflin.

Freedman, Russell. 1987. *Indian Chiefs*. New York: Holiday House.

Fritz, Jean. 1982. *Homesick: My Own Story*. Illustrated by Margot Tomes. New York: Putnam.

George, Jean Craighead. 1983. *The Talking Earth*. New York: Harper and Row.

Greenfield, Eloise. 1978. *Honey I Love and Other Poems*. Illustrated by Diane and Leo Dillon. New York: HarperCollins.

Griego, Margot. 1981. *Tortillas Para Mamá and Other Spanish Nursery Rhymes*. Illustrated by Barbara Cooney. New York: Holt.

Grimes, Nikki. 1998. *Jazmin's Notebook*. New York: Dial.

Hamanaka, Sheila. 1994. *All the Colors of the Earth*. New York: Morrow.

Hanson, Regina. 1997. *Face at the Window*. Illustrated by Linda Saport. New York: Clarion.

Havill, Juanita. 1993. *Jamaica and Brianna*. Boston: Houghton Mifflin.

Howard, Elizabeth Fitzgerald. 1991. *Aunt Flossie's Hats (and Crab Cakes Later)*. Illustrated by James E. Ransome. New York: Clarion.

Johnson, Angela. 1993. *Toning the Sweep*. New York: Scholastic.

Keats, Ezra Jack. 1967. *Peter's Chair*. New York: Harper and Row.

Lee, Milly. 1997. *Nim and the War Effort*. Illustrated by Yansook Choi. New York: Farrar, Straus and Giroux.

Lester, Julius. 1996. *Sam and the Tigers*. Illustrated by Jerry Pinkney. New York: Dial.

Lord, Beth Bao. 1984. *In the Year of the Boar and Jackie Robinson*. New York: Harper and Row.

Louie, Ai-Ling. 1982. *Yeh Shen, A Cinderella Story from China*. New York: Philomel.

Low, William. 1997. *Chinatown*. New York: Henry Holt.

Mahy, Margaret. 1990. *The Seven Chinese Brothers*. Illustrated by Jean and Moo-Sien Tsang. New York: Scholastic.

Mama, Raouf. 1998. *Why Goats Smell So Bad and Other Stories from Benin*. Illustrated by Imna Arroyo. North Haven, Conn.: Linnet.

Maruki, Toshi. 1982. *Hiroshima No Pika*. New York: Lothrup.

Mathis, Sharon Bell. 1975. *The Hundred Penny Box*. Illustrated by Leo and Diane Dillon. New York: Viking.

McKissack, Patricia. 1997. *Ma Dear's Aprons*. Illustrated by Floyd Cooper. New York: Atheneum.

_____ 1997. *Run Away Home*. New York: Scholastic.

Mitchell, Margaree King. 1993. *Uncle Jed's Barbershop*. Illustrated by James Ransome. New York: Simon and Schuster.

Mosel, Arline. 1968. *Tikki Tikki Tembo*. New York: Henry Holt.

Naidoo, Beverley. 1990. *Chain of Fire*. Illustrated by Eric Velasquez. New York: HarperCollins.

_____ 1997. *No Turning Back: A Novel of South Africa.* New York: HarperCollins

Namioka, Lensey. 1992. *Yang the Youngest and His Terrible Ear*. Illustrated by Kees de Kiefe. Boston: Little Brown.

Nhuong, Huynh Quang. 1982. *The Land I Lost: Adventures of a Boy in Vietnam*. New York: Harper and Row.

O'Dell, Scott. 1981. *Carlota*. Boston: Houghton Mifflin.

Paulsen, Gary. 1984. *Dogsong*. New York: Bradbury.

Pinkney, Andrea Davis. 1993. *Seven Candles for Kwanzaa*. Illustrated by Brian Pinkney. New York: Dial.

Polacco, Patricia. 1994. *Pink and Say*. New York: Philomel.

Rattigan, Jama Kim. 1990. *Dumpling Soup*. Boston: Little Brown.

Say, Allen. 1993. *Grandfather's Journey*. Boston: Houghton Mifflin.

Small, Irene. 1991. *Irene and the Big Fine Nickel*. Illustrated by Tyrone Geter. Boston: Little Brown.

Sneve, Virginia Driving Hawk. 1989. *Dancing Teepees: Poems of American Indian Youth*. New York: Holiday House.

_____ 1994–1997. *The First Americans*.

Snyder, Dianne. 1988. *The Boy of the Three-Year Nap*. Illustrated by Allen Say. Boston: Houghton Mifflin.

Soto, Gary. 1993. *Local News*. Orlando, Fla.: Harcourt Brace.

_____ 1993. *Too Many Tamales*. Illustrated by Ed Martinez. New York: Putnam.

_____ 1996. *The Old Man and His Door*. Illustrated by Joe Cepeda. New York: Putnam.

_____ 1997. *Snapshots from the Wedding*. Illustrated by Stephanie Garcia. New York: Putnam.

Surat, Michele. 1983. *Angel Child, Dragon Child*. Illustrated by Vo-Dinh Mai. Austin, Tex.: Raintree.

Taylor, Mildred D. 1976. *Roll of Thunder, Hear My Cry*. New York: Dial.

_____ 1984. *Song of the Trees*. New York: Bantam.

_____ 1990. *Mississippi Bridge*. New York: Dial.

Tsutsui, Yoriko. 1991. *Anna in Charge*. Illustrated by Akiki Hayashi. New York: Puffin.

Uchida, Yoshiko. 1971. *Journey to Topaz*. Illustrated by Donald Carrick. New York: Scribner.

_____ 1993. *The Bracelet*. Illustrated by Joanna Yardley. New York: Philomel.

Wood, Nancy. 1998. *Sacred Fire*. Illustrated by Frank Howell. New York: Doubleday.

Yarborough, Camille. 1979. *Cornrows*. New York: Coward-McCann.

Yashimo, Taro. 1976. *Crow Boy*. New York: Puffin.

Yep, Laurence. 1975. *Dragonwings*. New York: Harper and Row.

_____ 1993. *Dragon's Gate*. New York: HarperCollins.

_____ 1996. *Ribbons*. New York: Putnam.

Young, Ed. 1989. *Lon Po Po: A Red-Riding Hood Story from China*. New York: Philomel.

REFERENCES

Banks, J. A. 1997. *Teaching Strategies for Ethnic Studies* (6th ed.). Boston: Allyn and Bacon.

Barry, A. 1998. Hispanic Representation in Literature for Children and Young Adults. *Journal of Adolescent and Adult Literacy* 41:630–637.

Bieger, E. M. 1996. Promoting Multicultural Education Through a Literature-Based Approach. *The Reading Teacher* 49:308–311.

Bishop, R. S. 1992. Multicultural Literature for Children: Making Informed Choices. In *Teaching Multicultural Literature in Grades K–8*, ed. V. J. Harris, Norwood, Mass.: Christopher-Gordon Publishers.

_____ 1997. Selecting Literature for a Multicultural Curriculum. In *Using Multiethnic Literature in the K–12 Classroom*, ed. V. J. Harris. Norwood, Mass.: Christopher-Gordon Publishers.

Bryson, B. 1994. *Made in America: An Informal History of the English Language in the United States.* New York: Avon.

Cai, M. 1998. Multiple Definitions of Multicultural Literature: Is the Debate Really Just "Ivory Tower" Bickering? *The New Advocate* 11:311–324.

Cosby, B. 1990. 45 Years from Today. *Ebony* 46:61.

Diamond, B. J., and M. A. Moore. 1995. *Multicultural Literacy: Mirroring the Reality of the Classroom.* New York: Longman.

Dudley-Marling, C. 1997. "I'm Not from Pakistan": Multicultural Literature and the Problem of Representation. *The New Advocate* 10:123–134.

Harris, T. L., and R. E. Hodges, ed. 1995. *The Literacy Dictionary: The Vocabulary of Reading and Writing.* Newark, Del.: International Reading Association.

Lara, J. 1994. Demographic Overview: Changes in Student Enrollment in American Schools. In *Kids Come in All Languages: Reading Instruction for ESL Students.* eds. K. Spangenbert-Urbschat and R. Prichard. Newark, Del.: International Reading Association.

Larrick, N. 1965. The All-White World of Children's Books. *Saturday Review* 46:63–65, 84–85.

Leung, C. B. 1998. Bicultural Perspectives and Reader Response: Four Young Readers Respond to Jean Fritz's *Homesick.* Unpublished manuscript. Fargo, N.D.: North Dakota State University.

Lo, D. E, and A. Leahy. 1997. Exploring Multiculturalism Through Children's Literature: The Batchelder Award Winners. *The New Advocate* 10:215–224.

Mora, P. 1998. Confessions of a Latina Author. *The New Advocate* 11:279–290.

Norton, D. E. 1995. *Through the Eyes of a Child: An Introduction to Children's Literature.* Columbus, Ohio: Merrill.

Oakes, J., and M. Lipton. 1999. *Teaching to Change the World.* Boston: McGraw-Hill.

Odean, K. 1998. Young Black Heroines. *Book Links* 7:36–39.

Rasinski, T. V., and N. D. Padak. 1990. Multicultural Learning Through Children's Literature. *Language Arts* 67:576–580.

Tomlinson, C. M. 1998. International Children's Literature. *Book Links* 8:8–13.

van Keulen, J., G. T. Weddington, and C. E. DeBose. 1998. *Speech, Language, Learning and the African American Child.* Boston: Allyn and Bacon.

Wollman-Bonilla, J. E. 1998. Outrageous Viewpoints: Teachers' Criteria for Rejecting Works of Children's Literature. *Language Arts* 75: 287–295.

Yamate, S. S. 1997. Asian Pacific American Children's Literature: Expanding Perceptions About Who Americans Are. In *Using Multiethnic Literature in the K–12 Classroom,* ed. V. J. Harris. Norwood, Mass.: Christopher-Gordon Publishers.

Zarrillo, J. 1995. *Multicultural Literature, Multicultural Teaching: Units for the Elementary Grades.* Fort Worth, Texas: Harcourt Brace.

FIRST he ate some lettuces
and some French beans ;
and then he ate some radishes ;

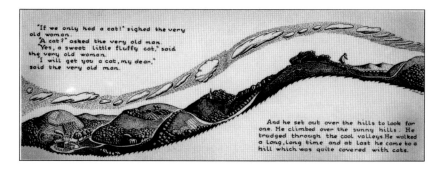

Early illustrators added the indispensable element of art to children's picture books. Randolph Caldecott's illustrations, such as those in *The Diverting History of John Gilpin* (1878), added action and expression heretofore missing in literature for children (top). Beatrix Potter's drawings of the rabbits and other animal characters in books like *The Tale of Peter Rabbit* (1903) were done with meticulous detail (middle). Wanda Gag used a two-page sweep integrating words and dramatic black ink illustration in *Hundreds of Cats* (1928), which has been called the first American picture story book (bottom).

And Black Mumbo made him a beautiful little Red Coat, and a

The simplistic characterizations and crude illustrations in Helen Bannerman's original *The Story of Little Black Sambo* were so offensive to so many people that the book was virtually expunged from the canon of American children's literature (top). However, writer Julius Lester and artist Jerry Pinkney, both African Americans, revised (and revived) the story with a new style of language and illustration in *Sam and the Tigers (bottom)*.

One winter morning Peter woke up and looked out the window. Snow had fallen during the night. It covered everything as far as he could see.

Prior to the 1960s, people of color were virtually invisible in the pages of literature for children. In 1963, Ezra Jack Keats won the Caldecott Medal for *The Snowy Day,* a book which featured an African American child as the main character (top). Illustrations by Floyd Cooper complement text by Patricia C. McKissack to reflect African American history and traditions in *Ma Dear's Aprons* (bottom).

Here's a boy named Danny bearing a pillow with rings.
If he looked down, he would see that his left shoe is untied.
If he looked up, he would see his mother snapping his picture,
Little gentleman with combed hair.

There are bridesmaids, one taller than the next,
And the groomsmen, straight as soldiers.
There is Father Jaime,
And a yawning altar boy with a dirty tennis shoe peeking
From under his robe.

Once again he exchanged stories and laughed with his old friends.

In Gary Soto's *Snapshots from the Wedding*, illustrator Stephanie Garcia used three dimensional figures sculpted out of clay, along with acrylic paints, wood, fabric and other "found objects" to create unique and creative "snapshots" for the book (top). The muted tones that Allen Say used in the watercolor illustrations in his 1994 Caldecott Medal winner *Grandfather's Journey* reflect the author's background and his topic for this book (bottom).

CHAPTER 3

Sensitive Subjects in Children's Literature

 oday's children's literature addresses some of the harsh realities that many children face in their lives. In stories for young readers, authors deal with topics such as death, divorce, homelessness, disabilities, and abuse. Books about these sensitive subjects often contain strong material about painful life experiences.

This Chapter

- identifies children's books that deal with some of the difficult issues children face in their lives and

- suggests ways of using these books at home and in school.

Throughout the ages, children's literature has reflected society's view of children. As the ancients shared their myths and legends around the campfires, children were undoubtedly part of the audience, but the stories were told for all, not just the young. The Greek slave Aesop wrote simple, childlike fables with animal characters, but these too were designed for the edification of adults. Children were seen as miniature adults, and writing for them was designed to teach them lessons.

Even Charles Perrault's collection of French fairy tales was intended for the amusement of the ladies of the court of Louis XIV, not for their children. The Brothers Grimm gathered and published German folk and fairy tales as a scholarly effort, not to amuse youngsters.

Literature written expressly for children began to emerge in response to the ideas of the seventeenth-century British educational philosopher John Locke. Locke promoted the concept of *childhood* as a stage in life with particular interests and needs, and he urged a milder approach to child raising than had heretofore been followed. Children were seen as children, not as miniature adults. Locke believed that children should be provided with easy books to read as soon as they were able. John Newbery, influenced by Locke's thinking, began to publish books designed specifically for children's enjoyment, and a body of children's literature was born. When school books designed to teach reading appeared, such as the

McGuffey Eclectic Readers they featured stories with child characters engaged in age-appropriate activities, but the stories still maintained a heavy dose of lessons on moral principles, along with prayers, psalms, and other religious material.

The early years of the twentieth century brought a new day in children's literature. Lots of books were produced for children's enjoyment without pretense of didactic intent, but books still maintained an air of innocence. In schools, Dick and Jane ruled reading instruction. They lived in a "typical" suburban neighborhood as members of a nuclear family with Mother, Father, Baby Sally, Spot the dog, and Puff the cat. Father went to work while Mother stayed home. Dick assumed the leadership role while Jane supported him. All was right with the world. In children's trade books, this idealized image was maintained by authors like Robert McCloskey in *Lentil* and by Beverly Cleary in *Ramona the Pest* and *Henry Huggins*.

In the 1960s, changes in society were reflected in children's literature. The Civil Rights Movement, the Vietnam War, the 1969 Democratic National Convention, and other movements and events jarred the national conscience. Society was forced to confront the realities of racism, sexism, divorce, drug abuse, and violence. Authors chose to acknowledge in their writing the fact that children were touched by many of these circumstances. The age of New Realism was ushered into children's literature.

Books About Sensitive Issues

Much contemporary realistic fiction relates to topics that reflect the harsh realities that children encounter directly and indirectly in their everyday lives—the loss of a friend or family member through death; the trauma of divorce and the effects of living in single-parent or "merged" families after the marriage of one or both parents; the experience of being abandoned by a parent and/or placed in a foster home; homelessness; living with a cognitive or physical disability; experiencing or witnessing physical or sexual abuse. These stories, many of which are troubling to adults, often strike strong chords in the minds and hearts of young readers and require tactful handling in the classroom. For many young children, subjects like death, divorce, and disability need to be approached in very sensitive ways.

Author Profile: Eve Bunting

Eve Bunting is a popular and prolific author who has written over 150 books for children and young adults. Her books address an incredible range of sensitive subjects. She has a unique talent to present tender and complex topics in simple terms.

Anne Evelyn Bunting was born in Northern Ireland and lived there for thirty years before coming to the United States with her husband and three children in 1952. She had no aspirations to be an author until she took a writing course at a local community college when her prodigious writing career took off. Her Irish background was evidenced in her writing from the beginning. Her first book, *The Two Giants* (1972), was about the legendary Irish folk hero Finn McCool. Other books that reflect her Irish heritage followed—*St. Patrick's Day in the Morning* (1980), about a boy who climbs to the top of the village hill to prove he is old enough to march in a parade; *Clancy's Coat* (1984), about two grouchy old villagers who become friends again; *Spying on Miss Muller* (1995), a young adult novel set in a boarding school in Belfast; and *Market Day* (1996), about a young girl who accompanies her father to an Irish country fair.

Bunting has a unique ability to tackle sensitive subjects in a touching manner and in terms that young children understand. She has written about homelessness in *Fly Away Home* (1991) and in *December* (1997), the effects of war in *The Wall* (1990), the travails of boat people in *How Many Days to America? A Thanksgiving Story* (1988), adult illiteracy in *Wednesday's Surprise* (1989), the heartbreak of people in nursing homes in *Sunshine Home* (1994), the internment of Japanese Americans during World War II in *So Far from the Sea* (1998), urban riots in *Smoky Night* (1994), sibling rivalry in *Twinnies* (1997), and urban youth gangs in *Your Move* (1998). She has also written about joyful and amusing topics in *The Valentine Bears* (1983), *Coffin on a Crime* (1992), *A Turkey for Thanksgiving* (1995), and other books, and she has written science fiction, informational books, and books about the environment.

While she has written over a hundred picture books, Bunting does not illustrate her own work. Her books have been illustrated by artists who are well known in their own right, including Jan Brett (who nearly caused Bunting to stop writing when deciding that she would only work on her own original books), David Wiesner (who later won a Caldecott award for *Tuesday*), and Susan Meddaugh (the creator of Martha the talking dog). Of late, Bunting has worked extensively with David Diaz, whose distinctive mixed media illustrations for *Smoky Night* (1994) won the 1995 Caldecott Medal for its distinguished artwork. Diaz has also illustrated some of Bunting's other works, including *Going Home* (1996) and *December* (1997).

Eve Bunting now lives in California, where she continues to write for children about a rich range of topics. Here are some of her other recent books:

A Day's Work (1994)

The Blue and the Gray (1996)

SOS Titanic (1996)

Train to Somewhere (1996)

Moonstick (1997)

Death

Many children find death mysterious and frightening. The devastation of losing someone they love, fear about what happens after death, and the ceremonies that surround burial of the dead all create uneasiness in the mind of the young child. Books about death and dying provide vehicles for discussing this topic and for helping children come to grips with the fear and sadness that often surround it.

Death can have a traumatic impact on the life of a young child. Children often first encounter death with the loss of a pet, and stories about how children handle this grief are presented in books such as the following:

- *The Tenth Good Thing About Barney* by Judith Viorst, an engaging picture book in which a father helps his son deal with the loss of his cat Barney by listing all the good things about Barney;
- *Mustard* by Charlotte Graeber, in which family members support one another after the death of a beloved cat who had been the family pet for over a decade;
- *I'll Always Love You* by Hans Wilhelm, in which a boy is reassured after the death of his dog Elfie by knowing that he often told Elfie, "I'll always love you."

Books like these help children understand that it's okay to be sad at the loss of a pet, and they suggest strategies for dealing with that sadness. The death of a beloved pet is the subject of books for older children by Wilson Rawls: *Where the Red Fern Grows* and *Summer of the Monkeys*.

Young children have a hard time understanding or accepting the death of someone in the family. A number of books have been written for children about the death of a family member:

- *Saying Good-Bye to Grandma* by Jane Rush Thomas, about a seven-year-old boy who attends his grandmother's funeral and encounters many of the traditions and rituals surrounding death;
- *Snowdrops for Cousin Ruth* by Susan Katz, about the devastating effects that death has on a family when one of the children is killed by an automobile and about the family's recovery from their grief;
- *Losing Uncle Tim* by MaryKate Jordan, a sensitive story about a boy who loses an especially close uncle to AIDS;
- *Missing May* by Cynthia Rylant, the 1992 Newbery Medal winner about the grief of a girl at the loss of a beloved great-aunt and about her realization that love is never truly lost
- *Out of the Dust* by Karen Hesse, the poetic 1998 Newbery Medal winner about a fourteen year old who runs away from home (but later returns) after her mother dies in a fire.

Often, death comes earlier to people in poorer communities. The grief and sadness associated with death is presented with different multicultural perspectives in books such as:

- *Everett Anderson's Good-Bye* by Lucille Clifton, the poetic story of a young African-American boy who struggles through stages of pain and grief over his father's death;
- *A Pillow for My Mom* by Charissa Sgouros, a sad story about a girl who makes a pillow for her sick mother, and receives the pillow back when her mother dies
- *Annie and the Old One* by Miska Miles, in which a young Navajo girl tries to forestall the death of her beloved grandmother, only to have the old woman explain death in terms of the cycle of nature;

- *First Snow* by Helen Coutant, a warm and touching story about a Vietnamese-American girl who faces her grandmother's death but learns about death from another cultural and religious perspective.

A unique Latino perspective on the topic of death is presented in books like George Ancona's *Pablo Remembers: The Fiesta of the Day of the Dead* and Kathryn Lasky's *Days of the Dead*. These books describe the Latino tradition of celebrating Días de los Muertos, a commemoration of family members who have died. Stemming from ancient traditions, the Day of the Dead is a time of family get-togethers to reflect on the lives of loved ones. Since this celebration occurs each year on the last day of October and the first day of November, some teachers use these books as a supplement to (or as an alternative to) literature about Halloween.

Children are also affected by the loss of friends. Some books for younger children about the death of a friend are:

- *A Taste of Blackberries* by Doris Smith, a story about the shock and grief of a young boy who witnesses the death of a friend when he is fatally stung by a bumblebee (to which he is allergic);

- *Empty Window* by Eve Bunting, a sensitive treatment of grief that surrounds the death of a friend;

- *Remember the Good Times* by Richard Peck, which deals with the reaction and response of two friends when their third friend commits suicide.

An enormously popular book among children in the upper elementary grades is *Bridge to Terabithia* by Katherine Paterson, the story of a girl and a boy (Leslie and Jess) who create their own secret kingdom called Terabithia. When Leslie drowns on the way home from their secret hideaway, Jess is left with an enormous sense of loss. This book about the death of a friend has remained one of the most widely read children's books on the market, despite the objections of many adults to its subject matter and to some of the language.

Books about death and dying provide children with information about this topic and the emotions that surround it, while allowing them to engage in a quality literary experience.

Divorce

Divorce is a common fact of family life in our society. By the time they reach the middle grades, most children have experienced divorce in their own families or are familiar with it in the families of friends. Despite the frequency with which it occurs, the separation of parents can be a tremendously traumatic experience for children. Books about divorce provide a means of helping children come to grips with this highly emotional event in their own lives and to understand the impact that divorce has on the lives of their friends and classmates.

In many books about divorce, children express their raw feelings about the breakup of their parents' marriage. Children often feel torn between two parents who have separated, and they may even feel a degree of responsibility for the breakup. Books that help them deal with these difficult emotions follow:

- *Priscilla Twice* by Judith Caseley, in which a young girl feels divided between her mother and her father, and the emotional tug that she experiences when the two separate;

- *As the Crow Flies* by Elizabeth Winthrop, the story of a second grade boy who lives in Arizona with his mother and who discovers that distance does not diminish a special father-son relationship when his dad visits him from Delaware;
- *My Mother's House, My Father's House* by C. B. Christiansen, which describes the life of a girl who splits her time by living with her mother from Monday through Thursday and with her father at alternate times in the week.

Stories such as these reflect the range of relationships that occur between former spouses (from friendliness to hostility) and the range of children's emotions in response.

A book that is very popular with upper elementary grade children is Beverly Cleary's *Dear Mr. Henshaw*, winner of the 1984 Newbery Medal. After his parents split, sixth grader Leigh Botts writes to his favorite author, Mr. Henshaw. His letters reveal much about himself, including his feelings about the divorce of his parents. (Cleary has also written *Strider*, a sequel told in the form of Leigh's diary two years later.)

While divorce is rarely funny, children's authors can sometimes inject humor into their books on the topic:

- *The Harmony Arms* by Ron Koertge is about a boy who visits Los Angeles from Mississippi with his divorced father and encounters some terribly amusing characters and situations;
- *Mitzi's Honeymoon with Nana Potts* by Barbara Williams is a story in which Mitzi engages in some very amusing entanglements when she stays with her new stepfather's mother during her own mother's honeymoon.

In virtually all instances, divorce leads to living situations that differ from those that children are used to, and this can be anxiety-producing for children (and often for their parents also). Different family structures are described in children's literature as well.

Different Family Structures

In traditional children's literature, even in the genre of realistic fiction, children and parents usually live together as "one big happy family," forming a nuclear unit of mother, father, brothers, sisters, occasionally grandparents, and sometimes pets. But not all children live like that and didn't, even in "the good old days." Today's books reflect a variety of family structures. Children live in single-parent households, merged families when one or both divorced parents remarry, and families headed by two adults of the same gender. Each of these family structures is included in literature for children.

Books that describe single parent family situations do so candidly, describing the emotional and financial stress that these families often experience:

- *A Chair for My Mother* by Vera Williams, a touching story about a child, her mother, and her grandmother, in which Rosa buys a chair for her perpetually tired waitress-mother;
- *Good-Bye and Keep Cold* by Jenny Davis, about a Kentucky family who first must deal with the sudden accidental death of their father and then deal with life in a single-parent household.

When parents divorce and one or both parents remarry, children may begin new lives as members of merged families with children from different marriages:

- *What Hearts* by Bruce Brooks, in which a boy's intelligence and sensitivity help him deal with the instability of his new world when his mother divorces and re-marries;

- *Bummer Summer* by Ann M. Martin, about Kammy who must adjust to a new family when, after several years, her widowed dad marries the mother of two young children;

- *The Animal, The Vegetable, and John D. Jones* by Betsy Byars, the story of "a merged family in the making" in which two sisters plan to spend their vacation with their divorced father, only to discover that he has brought along his new girlfriend and her son.

Adopting children is not uncommon in today's families, and stories about adopted children range from picture books to longer works of realistic fiction:

- *How I Was Adopted* by Joanna Cole, a picture book that honestly and realistically addresses the delicate topic of adoption of young children;

- *The Day We Met You* by Phoebe Koeler, an easy-to-read book about how parents prepare for the arrival of a new adopted baby;

- *The Adopted One* by Sara Burnett Stein, a rather objective story about Joshua, an adopted boy who fits into his new family and some of the concerns that he has.

Families in the United States and Canada often adopt children from Asia, Eastern Europe, or South America, and this topic has become part of literature for children. *Allison*, by Allen Say, is a beautiful and sensitive picture story book about an Asian child who begins to notice that she resembles her doll more than she resembles her Anglo parents and about how her parents help her cope with that discovery. Two other picture books about adopting a child from another country are *Over the Moon: An Adoption Tale* by Karen Katz and *An Mei's Strange and Wondrous Journey* by Stephan Molnar-Fenton. In Angela Johnson's *Heaven*, a first person narrative for upper grade readers, a teenage girl's life is shattered when she learns that her parents are not her birth parents.

With more gay households and greater acceptance of gay lifestyles, books on families that involve same-gender partners have become part of children's literature. Some people object to children's books that portray same-gender relationships. Homosexuality offends their moral and social values, and they find the subject inappropriate in reading material for children. On the other hand, others see same-gender relationships as a lifestyle that is openly followed and discussed in today's society. Books on this topic typically generate discussion in living rooms, teachers' rooms, and school board meeting rooms and are the targets of different forms of censorship. Whether or not an adult chooses to share these books with children in a home or school setting, books about same-gender relationships are part of literature for children today:

- *Daddy's Roommate* by Michael Willhoite, the story of a boy who spends weekends with his divorced father and male roommate who live in an openly gay relationship;

- *Heather Has Two Mommies* by Lesléa Newman, about three-year-old Heather, the daughter of a lesbian couple; when she joins a playgroup, she learns as other children describe their different family structures;
- *My Two Uncles* by Judith Vigna, a straightforward account of the gay relationship of two men and the open resentment that one of the men's father shows about the relationship.

These books describe gay lifestyles in a matter-of-fact fashion, without any value judgment. They typically attract controversy when used in schools and libraries.

Foster Families

When families disintegrate, children may be placed in foster care. Foster homes are the setting in the following books:

- *Mama One, Mama Two* by Patricia MacLachlan, a picture book about a loving relationship between a foster child and his foster mother;
- *The Pinballs* by Betsy Byars, the story of spunky and difficult twelve-year-old Carlie who has bounced from foster home to foster home, but who finally learns compassion and maturity in her relationship with other foster children who, like her, "have been bounced around like pinballs."

Some books for children deal with the heartbreaking subject of abandonment:

- *Journey* by Patricia MacLachlan, a poignant story in which a mother leaves her son and daughter with their grandparents, and both generations have to cope;
- *The Great Gilly Hopkins* by Katherine Paterson, the enormously popular story of a feisty adolescent who lives in foster homes and maintains dreams and expectations about her "flower child" mother, only to have these hopes dashed.

Stories that portray the efforts of siblings to avoid being separated and placed in different foster home include:

- *Homecoming* by Cynthia Voight, the story of Dicey Tillerman who gathers her siblings around her when their mother abandons them in a Connecticut parking lot, and leads them on a journey to the grandmother's house in Maryland;
- *Mama, Let's Dance* by Patricia Hermes, a touching story of three children who try to keep their mother's desertion a secret because they don't want to be separated from one another.

Author Profile: BETSY BYARS

Betsy Byars is an author who writes with humor, sensitivity, and a deep understanding of children. A prolific writer who has authored over fifty books, Byars has a special talent for writing about children who feel marginalized.

Born in North Carolina, Betsy Byars received her education in her home state, graduating from Queens College as an English major. She began writing magazine articles, and reading to her own family spurred her interest in writing children's books. Her first novel, *Clementine*, was rejected by nine publishers before being published in 1962.

Eight years and five books later, Byars wrote *Summer of the Swans*, for which she won the 1971 Newbery Medal. The novel is a moving story about Sara, an awkward adolescent girl who is charged with caring for her mentally disabled brother. Her brother becomes lost but, with the help of a friend, Sara is able to find him and find confidence and a sense of self-worth as well.

Byars has a unique ability to tackle sensitive subjects with humor and compassion. In *Night Swimmers* (1980), she explores the emotions of Retta, the oldest child in a motherless family who has to care for her younger siblings while her father works. In *Pinballs* (1977), she writes about children who form a bond and learn to care about each other while living in a foster home. In *The Animal, the Vegetable, and John D. Jones* (1982), she writes about children who have to share their divorced father with his new girlfriend on their annual vacation. In *Cracker Jackson* (1985), she deals with child abuse. In these and other books, the author avoids sentimentality and shows respect and admiration for children's strength and resiliency. Her writing combines humor and compassion beautifully.

Not all of Byars's books deal with sensitive subjects. She has written humorous books like *The Two Thousand Pound Goldfish* (1982), *The Not-Just-Anybody Family* (1986), and *McMummy* (1995), in which the characters find a mummy-shaped pod on a plant in an eccentric scientist's greenhouse. She has also created three series: the *Bingo Brown* books, very funny stories about a boy's first love; the *Herculeah Jones Mystery Series* about a girl detective and her male friend; and *The Golly Sisters*, easy-to-read books about two sisters who travel through the Old West. Byars's books have been adapted for television, and her work has been translated into nine languages.

Betsy Byars lives in South Carolina, where she enjoys flying her private airplane and continuing to write. Here are some of her recent books:

Coast to Coast (1992)

The Joy Boys (1996)

My Brother, Ant (1996)

Ant Plays Bear (1997)

Death's Door (1997)

Abuse

Child abuse is an issue that children's authors deal with in a very sensitive fashion. Stories for young children about physical or sexual abuse explore the fear and shame associated with the secretive nature of abuse. Such stories often show children where help is available and how to get it. Some of these books follow:

- *What Jamie Saw* by Carolyn Coman, a simply written and sensitive story about a boy, his mother, and his baby sister who try to recover from an abusive home relationship from which they escape;
- *Chilly Stomach* by Jeanette Caines, a simply written story about a child's reaction to an overly friendly uncle;
- *Cracker Jackson* by Betsy Byars, about an eleven-year-old boy who tries to save a former baby-sitter from an abusive relationship with her husband;
- *I Hadn't Meant to Tell You This* by Jacqueline Woodson, in which two friends share the secret of one of them being abused by her father.

Young adult titles that make realistic reading on the topic of abuse for older children include the following:

- *Weeping Willow* by Ruth White, in which a teenager deals with her stepfather's abuse and tries to protect her younger sister;
- *The Watcher* by James Howe, about a thirteen-year-old girl who longs for a happier life in the face of a father who physically and emotionally abuses her and a mother who drowns her daughter's cries with opera music;
- *When She Was Good* by Norma Fox Mazer, an account of the effects of abuse of a young girl by an older sister, but one which ends on a positive note.

Homelessness

For obvious reasons, it's difficult to precisely measure the size of our national homeless population, but estimates place the number around 7,000,000 people, many of them children of elementary-school age. Homelessness is not just an "urban" problem; books about this sensitive subject belong in classrooms in affluent suburbs just as they belong in schools where homeless shelters are part of the neighborhood.

As early as 1958, Natalie Savage Carlson addressed the issue of homelessness in *The Family Under the Bridge*, a charming story about a homeless old man in Paris and three youngsters who become his "grandchildren." More recently, homelessness has been addressed in a more stark and realistic fashion in picture books for younger readers:

- *Mr. Bow Tie* by Karen Barbour is about two children who befriend a homeless man and help reunite him with his family;
- *Fly Away Home* by Eve Bunting is about a boy and his father who live at an airport because "the airport is better than the streets."
- *December* by Eve Bunting is about a mother and son who share their cardboard shelter on a city street with an old woman on Christmas eve, after which their fortunes change.

Most books about homelessness are aimed at older readers, and they feature protagonists who are in their early teen years:

- *The Midwife's Apprentice* by Karen Cushman is about a homeless waif who finds her place in the world of medieval England;

- *The Beggar's Ride* by Theresa Nelson is the story of a 12-year-old girl who is befriended by the homeless people in Atlantic City after she runs away from home;
- *Monkey Island* by Paula Fox is about a boy who lives with his mother in a hotel room until she leaves, and then he joins the homeless population in New York City, where he is befriended by two homeless men who help him survive;
- *The Planet of Junior Brown* by Virginia Hamilton is about three characters who find each other in New York and survive through their mutual support.

When Jerry Spinelli won the 1991 Newbery Medal for *Maniac Magee*, the story of an engaging homeless boy who makes friends easily and becomes something of a legend to the kids in a Pennsylvania town, many teachers and critics feared the book was "glorifying" homelessness Nevertheless, it remains popular with young readers, not only because of the topic but because of the characters and plot. Solid counterarguments are found in the non-fiction book *No Place to Be: The Voices of Homeless Children* by Judith Breck, which contains interviews with children living in New York shelters.

People with Special Needs

Society is far more open today than it was in the past about children with physical and mental disabilities. As federal law and educational practice have brought children with special needs more into the mainstream of school life, books have brought children with disabilities into the mainstream of children's literature.

Books that focus on characters who have physical or cognitive disabilities include the following:

- *Knots on a Counting Rope* by Bill Martin, Jr. and John Archembault, a picture storybook about a Native American boy who is blind, told in a very interesting narrative style;
- *Summer of the Swans* by Betsy Byars, a Newbery Medal winner about a young adolescent responsible for caring for her mentally retarded brother Charlie;
- *The Alfred Summer* by Jan Slepian, about friendships formed by a 14-year-old boy with cerebral palsy, told with humor, insight, and compassion;
- *Crazy Lady!* by Jane Leslie Conly, a wonderful story about a boy who becomes friendly with a mentally handicapped neighbor and his mother;
- *Ian's Walk: A Story about Autism* by Laurie Lears, a sensitive picture story book about a child whose autism makes his brain "not work like other people's."

Realistic fiction in which major characters have physical or cognitive impairments are not merely books about exceptional children. They are also compelling stories that happen to involve children with handicaps. In writing these stories, authors project positive images and break down stereotypes, creating fresh and interesting characters with complex personalities and human emotions that all children share.

Books on Other Sensitive Subjects

The topics addressed in this chapter—death, divorce, alternative family structures, foster families, physical and sexual abuse, homelessness, disabilities—are certainly not the only sensitive issues that are addressed in realistic fiction for today's children. Environmental issues, the impact of nuclear disaster, aging and illness, sibling rivalry, violence, crises of conscience, mental illness, and drug and alcohol addiction are just some of the many other topics addressed in books for children.

Authors will undoubtedly break new ground in writing stories about some of the harsh realities of some children's lives. Poverty is an element in Vera Williams's *A Chair for My Mother* and Karen Hesse's *Out of the Dust*. Eve Bunting's picture book *Your Move* is about a boy who takes his six-year-old brother on a gang-initiation assignment, and her *Smoky Night* deals with urban violence. The young adult novel *Raven in a Dove House* by Andrea Davis Pinkney deals with the decision that a twelve-year-old girl faces when she is asked to hide a handgun belonging to a cousin whom she loves. In *Nine Candles*, Maria Testa tells the story of Raymond, a seven year old who every Sunday visits his mother in prison. Sensitive teachers will find ways to discuss these sensitive issues as children encounter them in their reading.

The field of children's literature is always expanding. Books mentioned in this chapter represent only a few of the sensitive issues that are contained in books for young readers. See the end-of-chapter references for more such books.

Using Books on Sensitive Subjects at Home and in School

Books on sensitive subjects include the finest examples of quality literature. Betsy Byars's *Summer of the Swans*, Jerry Spinelli's *Maniac Magee*, Beverly Cleary's *Dear Mr. Henshaw*, and Cynthia Rylant's *Missing May* did not win their Newbery Medals because they were about a handicapped child, a homeless boy, a divorce, and the death of a beloved relative, respectively; these books won this prestigious award because they represent distinguished contributions to the field of children's literature.

Books on sensitive subjects feature some of the strongest, most engaging, and most well-developed characters that children will encounter in what they read. Plots are exciting and move quickly. Themes extend beyond the sensitive subjects to include maturity, self-discovery, the importance of others in one's life, and the like. Most of these books offer hope for children who face problems. Such stories help children deal with issues in their own lives and help them understand some of the issues that their friends and classmates face. Since parents typically understand their children more intimately than teachers do, they are in the position to use books on these topics to help their children with their needs and concerns. Some books have direct application to sensitive events that arise in the family. Allen Say's *Allison* is a story about an Asian child who has been adopted by Anglo parents. Charlotte Graeber's *Mustard* suggests itself when a beloved family pet dies.

Books on sensitive subjects can be vehicles for parent-child discussions about strong emotions. Sharing Doris Smith's *A Taste of Blackberries*, for example, creates opportunities to talk about fear, sadness, guilt, love, and other feelings within the context of a good story. As children read upper-level books like Betsy Byars's *The Pinballs* or Patricia MacLachlan's *Journey*, parents can discuss some controversial issues; consider, for example, the language of Gilly Hopkins or the attitude of Vernon in Jane Leslie Conly's *Crazy Lady!*. Such books can generate some animated and productive family discussion.

Special Perspectives on Children's Literature

CHILDREN'S LITERATURE AS A TOOL FOR SOCIAL AND EMOTIONAL DEVELOPMENT
by Maureen E. Kenny

As a counseling psychologist who has worked with children in schools and clinical settings, I have found children's literature to be a useful adjunct to therapy and often an important tool in the counseling process. Through reading stories, children can learn that the problems they face and the feelings they hold are not unique. Others must know about these experiences—parental divorce, death, abuse, adoption, foster care, disability—and feelings—sadness, despair, anxiety, fear—or they would not be able to write about them.

When selected carefully, children's literature can also provide good examples for problem solving and coping with life's challenges. Persistence in the face of difficulty, ways of responding to teasing and peer rejection, and how to deal with a "perfect" sibling when one never seems to be able to do things right are just a few examples of the kinds of lessons that can be learned. The process of reading about children similar to the child client can be helpful in developing feelings of trust and confidence in the early stages of therapy. Children who are not yet ready to talk about their own feelings and difficulties may feel more comfortable discussing the feelings of a fictional character, thus able to examine how they are like the character later in the counseling process.

The therapeutic potential of children's literature is not limited to troubled children or children who have experienced unusual stress. In work with classroom groups, I have tried to use excerpts from prose and poetry to help children gain knowledge about normal developmental transitions as a means of making sense of their own experiences. This fits with my commitment to prevention and my desire to enhance children's resources for coping with typical daily hassles as well as life's major stressors. Entering a new grade, changing schools, making new friends, failing a test, asking for help, and feeling different are everyday transitions and experiences that can often be discussed more easily with the use of a poem or a story as a stimulus. Efforts to promote empathy, along with cultural and social understandings, can also be enhanced by reading about children from other races, cultures, and times. Children can reflect on the similarities and differences between their own lives and those of the characters they encounter. Ethnic identity and pride can also be enhanced when ethnic minority children examine literature from their own cultures (Holman 1996).

The use of children's literature to enhance social and emotional development is not limited to mental health professionals. Just as parents, teachers, and other caring adults teach children about their lives, emotions, values, and coping skills through their daily interactions, they can extend these lessons with the use of literature. Counselors often view the reading of carefully selected literature within the home and family as a way of promoting positive development. This process can also benefit children indirectly through its impact on adults. As parents and teachers read about fictional characters and discuss them with children, the adults can gain awareness of and sensitivity to how children think and feel about sensitive topics. For the young child who cuddles with a parent while reading about a tender topic, feelings of mutual trust and understanding may increase. Sharing literature relevant to current concerns can also enhance the meaningfulness of reading for some children as they discover that reading is a way to learn more about themselves and their own lives.

What should parents and teachers know if they want to use children's literature in therapeutic ways? Through this essay, I have emphasized the importance of carefully selecting stories and poems to be shared. Selected literature should offer positive coping strategies. Books that offer more than one possible solution are useful for discussing the advantages and disadvantages of each choice. Poems and books that fail to provide correct information, that fail to offer hope, or that provide false hope should be avoided (Holman 1996; Pardek 1994). Children's literature achieves its therapeutic potential through a process of guided dialogue and reflection. Creative writing, art, discussion, and role playing can be used to facilitate reflection (Pardek 1994).

Following the model of community-based and service learning, the reading of literature can be coupled with community experience (e.g., service), classroom discussion, and reflection. The reflection and discussion processes require skill and sensitivity on the part of teachers and parents. Although the therapeutic potential of literature is achieved when children can relate personally with the characters and can apply what they have read to their own lives, children should not be pushed to do this too soon. Since the goal is to deepen children's understanding, adults need to recognize children's current level of emotional/social understanding and help them move to the next level. Pushing children too hard on tasks for which they may not be developmentally ready may be perceived by children as a "put down" and negatively affect self-esteem (Gladding and Gladding 1991).

Through response to literature, teachers sometimes become aware of children who are overwhelmed by the stress in their lives. Teachers may then seek consultation from a school counselor in determining such children's need for therapeutic intervention. If need is determined, these children may be appropriately referred (with parental permission) to a school counselor or other mental health professional. Within these guidelines, it is my experience that reading and discussing children's literature has great potential for enhancing the social and emotional development of young people.

A licensed psychologist and certified school psychologist in the Commonwealth of Massachusetts, Dr. Maureen Kenny is currently associate professor in the counseling psychology program and Chair of the Department of Counseling, Developmental and Educational Psychology in the School of Education at Boston College.

REFERENCES

Gladding, S. T., and C. Gladding. 1991. The ABCs of Bibliotherapy for School Counselors. *The School Counselor* 39:7–12.

Holman, W. D. 1996. The Power of Poetry: Validating Ethnic Identity Through a Bibliotherapeutic Intervention with a Puerto Rican Adolescent. *Child and Adolescent Social Work Journal* 13: 371–383.

Pardek, J. T. 1994. Using Literature to Help Adolescents Cope with Problems. *Adolescence* 29:421–427.

Books on sensitive subjects need not be reserved for family situations or circumstances that suggest a crisis, however. Books about sensitive subjects can offer the same potential for enjoyment of literature as can any other book. Books like Vera Williams's *A Chair for My Mother* and Miska Miles's *Annie and the Old One* make marvelous material for lap reading under any circumstances.

In the classroom, books about sensitive subjects take their place in a literature-based program along with books used for instruction and enjoyment. Picture books like Eve Bunting's *Fly Away Home* and Elizabeth Winthrop's *As the Crow Flies* can be part of the classroom collection in the lower grades and used in directed lessons to help build children's reading competencies. These books become part of show and tell, classroom discussion, creative dramatics, and other oral language activities.

Books about sensitive subjects can be used in classroom reading lessons, just as any quality piece of children's literature can. These books can be particularly effective in generating critical discussions about anger, sadness, grief, pity, acceptance, friendship, companionship, and other emotions that children experience. As part of readers workshop, books like *Bridge to Terabithia,* for example, can produce discussion that comes from the heart. Books on sensitive subjects can be used as part of the classroom literature-based reading activities that are suggested in Chapter 13. They can also be part of core literature selections and included on recommended summer reading lists.

In some very popular children's books, sensitive issues are merely incidental. In Jean Craighead George's *Julie of the Wolves*, for example, the young protagonist Miyax heads into the Alaskan wilderness because she is attempting to escape an abusive relationship in an arranged marriage. And in Lois Lowry's *The Giver*, children take daily medication to suppress their awakening emotional and sexual development. While these issues are not central to the story, they can be discussed when children raise them while reading the book.

As read-aloud selections, books on sensitive subjects need to be selected with care and sensitivity. Teachers need to judge whether a book on abuse or abandonment will be especially upsetting or embarrassing to a particular child asked to read it aloud. When a book strikes a personal chord with a child, teachers may need the support of counselors or other mental health professionals to help the child deal with the issues raised. Not all books on sensitive subjects strike such deep personal responses of course. But books like Wilson Rawls's *Summer of the Monkeys* that are quite sad may bring tears to the eyes of children, and some children may be embarrassed to cry in front of peers.

Because books on sensitive subjects typically generate genuine emotional responses in children, these books provide authentic stimuli for reader response journals. Children can express their connections to characters and their responses to events in a personal manner in such journals. Sensitive-subject books can also be the starting point for a full range of classroom writing activities. Children can compose different endings to stories, create sequels, or suggest different solutions to problems posed in books. After they have read or heard Katherine Paterson's *Bridge to Terabithia*, for example, and written standard book reports or entries in response journals, children might also write the following:

- a sequel about what happens to Jess;
- an obituary for Leslie;
- a newspaper account of the accident;
- a description of their own real or imagined Terabithia;
- a letter to a friend; and
- a script or dialogue based on a scene from the story.

In short, opportunities for oral language and reading-writing activities abound in books on sensitive subjects. Such books are another avenue for developing children's love of literature.

CONCLUSION

While childhood may be seen as a time of carefree enjoyment and joyous experiences, reality for many children falls well short of that ideal. A growing body of children's literature recognizes some of the issues that children face and builds stories around these sensitive subjects. But such books are not written solely for children who deal with difficult issues in their daily lives any more than multicultural titles are designed solely for "minority" youngsters. Such books can be used to help all children develop insights about the world in which they live and the many different people who inhabit it.

Books on sensitive subjects are not always the easiest books to use in the classroom. These stories can raise raw issues that adults will find bothersome and that some children will find painful. However, whether we like the fact or not, these stories reflect the realities of contemporary society. And, despite the challenges that such books may pose, quality literature about sensitive subjects can be used for educating, inspiring, and entertaining all children. In so doing, such books contribute to children's love of literature.

Questions and Activities for Action and Discussion

1. Some people think that many of the sensitive topics addressed in today's children's books—child abuse, homelessness, same-gender relationships, and the like—ought not to be presented in picture books for young children. Others say that these books reflect the realities of today's world and that all children should be made aware of these issues. What do you think? Take a stand in this debate and give arguments to support your position.

2. Revisit the topic of bibliotherapy, the process of helping children deal with personal problems through reading. Describe how a book about death or divorce might be used with a child who has just experienced either in his or her own family. Identify cautions that should be exercised in using books on sensitive issues for therapeutic purposes.

3. Select three or four books written at different reading levels about one of the tender topics addressed in this chapter. Make lists comparing and contrasting how the authors approach the topic for different reading levels.

4. Examine a book that describes family structures that differ from the traditional nuclear family—foster families, same-gender parents, single parent families. List ways in which the author describes the settings and the places of the characters therein. What other ways might the author approach the topic? From your own experience, how realistically does the author portray the family situation?

5. Imagine that a child brings a book on a sensitive issue to class and asks you to share the book with the group. You are aware that the book would be embarrassing, offensive, or hurtful to one of your students. Describe how you would handle the situation.

CHILDREN'S & YOUNG ADULT BOOKS CITED IN THIS CHAPTER

Ancona, George. 1993. *Pablo Remembers: The Fiesta of the Day of the Dead*. New York: Lothrup, Lee and Shepard.

Barbour, Karen. 1991. *Mr. Bow Tie*. San Diego: Harcourt Brace.

Breck, Judith. 1991. *No Place to Be: The Voices of Homeless Children*. Boston: Houghton Mifflin.

Brooks, Bruce. 1992. *What Hearts*. New York: HarperCollins.

Bunting, Eve. 1980. *Empty Window*. Illustrated by Judy Clifford. New York: Frederick Warne.

_____ 1991. *Fly Away Home*. Illustrated by Ronald Himler. New York: Clarion.

_____ 1994. *Smoky Night*. Illustrated by David Diaz. San Diego: Harcourt Brace.

_____ 1997. *December*. Illustrated by David Diaz. San Diego: Harcourt Brace.

_____ 1998. *Your Move*. Illustrated by James Ransome. San Diego: Harcourt Brace.

Byars, Betsy. 1970. *Summer of the Swans*. New York: Viking.

_____ 1977. *The Pinballs*. New York: Harper and Row.

_____ 1983. *The Animal, the Vegetable, and John D. Jones*. New York: Delacorte.

_____ 1985. *Cracker Jackson*. New York: Penguin.

Caines, Jeanette. 1986. *Chilly Stomach*. New York: Harper and Row.

Carlson, Natalie Savage. 1958. *The Family Under the Bridge*. Illustrated by Garth Williams. New York: Scholastic.

Caseley, Judith. 1995. *Priscilla Twice*. New York: Greenwillow.

Christiansen, C. B. 1989. *My Mother's House, My Father's House*. Illustrated by Irene Trivas. New York: Atheneum.

Cleary, Beverly. 1950. *Henry Huggins*. New York: Morrow.

_____ 1968. *Ramona the Pest*. New York: Morrow.

_____ 1983. *Dear Mr. Henshaw*. Illustrated by Paul O. Zelinsky. New York: Morrow.

_____ 1991. *Strider*. Illustrated by Paul O. Zelinsky. New York: Morrow.

Clifton, Lucille. 1983. *Everett Anderson's Good-Bye*. New York: Henry Holt.

Cole, Joanna. 1995. *How I Was Adopted*. New York: Morrow.

Coman, Carolyn. 1995. *What Jamie Saw*. Arden, N.C.: Front Street.

Conly, Jane Leslie. 1993. *Crazy Lady!* New York: HarperCollins..

Coutant, Helen. 1974. *First Snow*. New York: Knopf.

Cushman, Karen. 1995. *The Midwife's Apprentice*. New York: Clarion.

Davis, Jenny. 1987. *Good-Bye and Keep Cold*. New York: Orchard.

Fox, Paula. 1991. *Monkey Island*. New York: Orchard.

George, Jean Craighead. 1972. *Julie of the Wolves*. New York: Harper and Row.

Graeber, Charlotte. 1982. *Mustard*. Illustrated by Donna Diamond. New York: Macmillan.

Hamilton, Virginia. 1971. *The Planet of Junior Brown*. New York: Macmillan.

Hermes, Patricia. 1991. *Mama, Let's Dance*. Boston: Little Brown.

Hesse, Karen. 1997. *Out of the Dust*. New York: Scholastic.

Howe, James. 1997. *The Watcher*. New York: Antheneum.

Johnson, Angela. 1998. *Heaven*. New York: Simon and Schuster.

Jordan, MaryKate. 1989. *Losing Uncle Tim*. Illustrated by Judith Friedman. Niles, Ill.: Whitman.

Katz, Karen. 1997. *Over the Moon: An Adoption Tale*. New York: Henry Holt.

Katz, Susan. 1998. *Snowdrops for Cousin Ruth*. New York: Simon and Schuster.

Koeler, Phoebe. 1990. *The Day We Met You*. New York: Bradbury.

Koertge, Ron. 1992. *The Harmony Arms*. Boston: Little Brown.

Lasky, Kathryn. 1996. *Days of the Dead*. Photos by Christopher G. Knight. New York: Hyperion.

Lears, Laurie. 1998. *Ian's Walk: A Story About Autism*. Illustrated by Karen Ritz. Morton Grove, Ill.: Whitman.

Lowry, Lois. 1993. *The Giver*. Boston: Houghton Mifflin.

MacLachlan, Patricia. 1982. *Mama One, Mama Two*. Illustrated by Ruth Bernsten. New York: HarperCollins.

_____ 1991. *Journey*. New York: Delacorte.

Martin, Ann M. 1983. *Bummer Summer*. New York: Holiday House.

Martin, Bill, Jr., and John Archembault. 1987. *Knots on a Counting Rope*. New York: Henry Holt.

Mazer, Norma Fox. 1997. *When She Was Good*. New York: Scholastic.

McCloskey, Robert. 1978. *Lentil*. New York: Puffin.

Miles, Miska. 1971. *Annie and the Old One*. Illustrated by Peter Parnell. Boston: Little, Brown.

Molnar-Fenton, Stephan. 1998. *An Mei's Strange and Wondrous Journey*. Illustrated by V. Flesher. New York: DK Ink.

Nelson, Theresa. 1992. *The Beggar's Ride*. New York: Orchard.

Newman, Lesléa. 1990. *Heather Has Two Mommies*. Illustrated by Diana Souza. Los Angeles: Alyson Publications.

Paterson, Katherine. 1977. *Bridge to Terabithia*. New York: Harper and Row.

_____ 1978. *The Great Gilly Hopkins*. New York: Harper and Row.

Peck, Richard. 1985. *Remember the Good Times*. New York: Delacorte.

Pinkney, Andrea Davis. 1998. *Raven in a Dove's House*. San Diego: Harcourt Brace.

Rawls, Wilson. 1961. *Where the Red Fern Grows*. New York: Doubleday.

_____ 1989. *Summer of the Monkeys*. New York: Doubleday.

Rylant, Cynthia. 1992. *Missing May*. New York: Orchard.

Say, Allen. 1997. *Allison*. Boston: Houghton Mifflin.

Sgouros, Charissa. 1998. *A Pillow for My Mom*. Illustrated by Christine Ross. Boston: Houghton Mifflin.

Slepian, Jan. 1980. *The Alfred Summer*. New York: Macmillan.

Smith, Doris. 1973. *A Taste of Blackberries*. New York: Crowell.

Spinelli, Jerry. 1990. *Maniac Magee*. Boston: Little, Brown.

Stein, Sara Burnett. 1984. *The Adopted One*. Photos by Erika Stone. New York: Walker.

Testa, Maria. 1996. *Nine Candles*. Illustrated by Manda Schaffer. Minneapolis: Carolrhoda.

Thomas, Jane Rush. 1988. *Saying Good-Bye to Grandma*. Boston: Houghton Mifflin.

Vigna, Judith. 1995. *My Two Uncles*. Morton Grove, Ill.: Whitman.

Viorst, Judith. 1971. *The Tenth Good Thing About Barney*. New York: Atheneum.

Voight, Cynthia. 1981. *Homecoming*. New York: Simon and Schuster.

White, Ruth. 1992. *Weeping Willow*. New York: Farrar, Straus and Giroux.

Wilhelm, Hans. 1985. *I'll Always Love You*. New York: Crown.

Willhoite, Michael. 1990. *Daddy's Roommate*. Los Angeles: Alyson Publications.

Williams, Barbara. 1983. *Mitzi's Honeymoon with Nana Potts*. New York: Dell.

Williams, Vera. 1982. *A Chair for My Mother*. New York: Greenwillow.

Winthrop, Elizabeth. 1998. *As the Crow Flies*. Illustrated by Joan Sandin. Boston: Houghton Mifflin.

Woodson, Jacqueline. 1994. *I Hadn't Meant To Tell You This*. New York: Delacorte.

REFERENCES

Friedberg, J. B., J. B. Mullins, and A. W. Sukiennik. 1992. *Portraying Persons with Disabilities: An Annotated Bibliography of Nonfiction for Children and Teenagers.* New Providence, N.J.: Bowker.

Rasinski, T. V. and C. S. Gillespie. 1992. Sensitive Issues: An Annotated Guide to Children's Literature, K–6. Phoenix: Oryx Press.

Rudman, M. K., K. D. Gagne, and J. E. Bernstein, eds. 1994. *Books to Help Children Deal with Separation and Loss: An Annotated Bibliography* (4th ed.). New Providence, N.J.: Bowker.

CHAPTER 4

PICTURE BOOKS

Picture books are books in which illustrations are an integral part of the work. Picture books can entertain, inform, inspire, amuse, and otherwise contribute to children's cognitive and affective development. They are typically the first form of children's books that children encounter and children often remember them for a lifetime.

THIS CHAPTER

- examines the artistic and literary qualities of picture books;
- describes the various types of picture books available to young (and older) readers; and

- identifies the genres of children's literature found in picture book format.

Picture books are the first form of books that children typically encounter. When bedtime includes reading *Goodnight Moon* by Margaret Wise Brown, when parents follow up watching the annual Christmas television special by reading *How the Grinch Stole Christmas* by Dr. Seuss, when parent and child snuggle up together to share Beatrix Potter's stories about Flopsy, Mopsy, Cottontail, and Peter Rabbit or to laugh about the antics in David Shannon's *No, David!* then children are getting their first delicious taste of literature.

In picture books, pictures and text go together as partners in a happy marriage. "Picture books present the reader with a succession of images, some in the presence of written text, some alone, which taken together provide an aesthetic experience which is more than the sum of the parts" (Kiefer 1988, 261).

Illustrations complement or add to the text by providing information not present in the words or by helping create the mood or tone of the story. Picture books involve "the interdependence of art and text, which together merge to present a story, theme or idea as an organic whole" (Flowers 1998, 67). Text and illustration work together so readers must attend to both elements. While picture books come in different forms and deal with different topics, all have "collective unity of story-line, theme or concept, developed through a series of pictures of which the book is comprised" (Association for Library Service to Children 1997, 5).

Technically, picture books are not a genre of children's literature. "Genre" refers to a category used to classify a type of literary work; for example, poetry, folktale, or historical fiction. Picture books cross genres. Some picture books are traditional folk literature, some present realistic stories from children's worlds, some are fantasies, and some are nonfiction presentations of informational material. Picture books constitute a category of artistic endeavor, and they are considered a major form of literature for children.

Included in the category of picture books are

wordless books, books that tell a story without the benefit of text;

alphabet books, which contain letters of the alphabet and pictures corresponding to each letter;

counting books, which aim to develop number concepts by pairing numerical characters with pictures of the equivalent number of objects;

picture story books, in which words and pictures are used to tell a story; and

informational books, which combine pictures with expository text to help children develop concepts.

In short, picture books include all types of books in which illustrations are an essential component. Not included are *illustrated books*, books that contain occasional illustrations to help children visualize what they read but whose text is sufficient to convey the story without the pictures.

Pictures have long been used to tell stories or record information. The prehistoric sketches on the walls of caves and on the sides of rocks recorded the activities of prehistoric people. Our alphabetic writing system evolved from Egyptian hieroglyphics, which began as picture writing.

Prior to the development of mechanical printing, art that accompanied stories was hand-produced. William Caxton, who brought the printing press to England, produced an illustrated edition of *Aesop's Fables* in 1484, and many of the chapbooks sold by street vendors in the seventeenth and eighteeenth centuries had crude illustrations. Since the major purpose of books for children at the time was to promote certain virtues and values, illustrations were not considered essential.

The publication of picture books flourished during the latter half of the nineteenth century, partly because improvements in printing allowed for more colorful and attractive illustrations, and partly because a middle class had emerged with enough leisure time for reading and enough money to buy books for their children. With the introduction of color printing, illustrations improved enormously. The names of illustrators Randolph Caldecott and Kate Greenaway, which have been attached to the coveted awards given annually to the most distinguished picture book published in the United States and in Great Britain respectively, became well-known in the children's books industry.

In the early twentieth century, author/illustrators like Beatrix Potter made pictures an integral part of their books. Artists like Wanda Gag turned their hands to illustrating books for children and the results were striking illustrations and vigorous text. In the 1930s and 1940s, the popularity of picture books exploded. Author/illustrators like Robert Lawson and Robert McCloskey produced books that sold in the millions. Golden Books put inexpensive editions of picture books into the hands of millions of young readers. Authors like Maurice

Sendak and Ezra Jack Keats broke convention by combining words and pictures to entertain and inform children. The work of contemporary authors and illustrators like Chris Van Allsburg and Lane Smith continue to make the creation of picture books a fine art.

As it developed and evolved, the American picture book remained largely an all-white enterprise through the 1960s. People of color, when they appeared at all, made cameo appearances or were stereotyped. In 1962, Ezra Jack Keats introduced Peter, an African-American child and the main character in *The Snowy Day*. While some people raised questions about the way Peter and his mother were depicted, the book won the Caldecott Medal, and Keats continued to write books like *Whistle for Willie* and *Peter's Chair* in the same vein. In 1969, *Stevie*, by John Steptoe, became the first major picture book by an African-American artist. Subsequent contributions by other minority artists—Faith Ringgold, Jerry Pinkney, Stephanie Garcia, Allen Say, and many, many others—have made the body of contemporary picture books multiethnic.

Author Profile: FAITH RINGGOLD

Faith Ringgold was born in New York City and grew up in Harlem during the Great Depression. As a child, Ringgold was often sick, and so she spent much of her time indoors. While her siblings and friends attended school and played outdoors, she spent her time drawing and sewing as well as visiting museums and attending musical performances in the city. The roots of her work are found in these experiences.

Ringgold graduated from City College of New York as an art teacher. She began to use quilts in her art and began to incorporate stories into her quilts. *Tar Beach* (1991), which began as a quilt story, tells the story of Cassie, a young girl who spends her summers on the roof of her apartment building in New York and imagines that she flies over Manhattan. This book, which won numerous awards and accolades (including designation as a Caldecott Honor Book), firmly established Ringgold's reputation as an author/illustrator of children's books.

Ringgold's quilt stories reflect the traditions of African Americans. *Aunt Harriet's Underground Railroad in the Sky* (1992) continues the theme of flying as Cassie and her brother find a train while they are flying, and they learn from the train's conductor (Harriet Tubman) about the Underground Railroad. *Dinner at Aunt Connie's House* (1993) is about two girls who find portraits of African-American women while visiting their aunt's house, and the paintings speak to them about the women's historical significance.

Faith Ringgold is a wonderful artist and an elegant writer. The pages of her books are filled with brilliant illustrations and beautiful language. She has continued to weave words and art into new picture books like *The Invisible Princess* (1999) and *If a Bus Could Talk: The Story of Rosa Parks* (1999).

Improvements in materials and techniques, experiments with different types of media, advances in printing technology, the development of computer-generated art, and the willingness of authors to "push the envelope" in exploring new content and format have all added levels of artistic sophistication to make contemporary picture books an art form and a popular form of children's literature that will carry into the twenty-first century.

Picture Books in the Lives of Young Children

Picture books have many functions in children's lives, not the least of which is to provide an initial encounter with literature. The characters in Mother Goose, Cinderella, Peter Rabbit, and The Little Engine that Could enter children's lives through the world of picture books. Children develop concepts and acquire information as they play with board books, examine concept books, encounter alphabet books, share counting books, and enjoy a variety of different types of picture story books. Children delight in the language and actions of Corduroy and Winnie-the-Pooh, laugh at the antics of the Cat in the Hat and of Ferdinand the Bull, and join in the refrain "hundreds of cats and thousands of cats and millions and billions and trillions of cats." Children's love of literature begins with picture books.

Language Development and Imagination

Early encounters with picture books stimulate children's language development. As they hear the words and look at the pictures, children are exposed to the best that language has to offer. Picture books introduce children to new words, enriching their rapidly expanding vocabularies. These books teach children to explore verbal concepts by engaging them in discussion about the characters and events. Rhyming language helps them develop their phonemic awareness.

Picture books not only promote children's language development; they also stimulate children's imaginations. Stories fill children's minds with wonderful images. At a very young age, children move easily from the world of their own bedroom to the bedroom to which Max returns from the kingdom of the Wild Things or across the world to listen to what the moon would say in *And If the Moon Could Talk* by Kate Banks.

Early Experiences with Art

Picture books provide children with early experiences with art. Pictures foster children's visual literacy and their awareness of the power of art. Sometimes this awareness develops through simple conversations about what children like and don't like about the pictures they see in books.

Introducing Children to Reading

Picture books provide a pleasant introduction to learning how to read. Reading aloud to children is perhaps the single most important way to help them acquire the background that will lead to their eventual success in learning to read on their own (Lesiak 1997). Even when direct instruction is incidental or nonexistent in the very early years, sharing books gives children a sense of story, helps them gain language and linguistic concepts that will support later reading success, gives them practical experiences with handling books, and generally introduces them to the pleasures of reading. It also helps young children develop an awareness of the metalinguistic aspects of reading—left-to-right and top-to-bottom directionality in reading, letter and word recognition, and the way to handle a book. Through picture books children enter the literacy community at a very early age.

As children acquire the ability to read independently, picture books continue to play a major role in their literacy development. Children gain confidence by recognizing the words of their favorite books, and they learn to read on their own by practicing with easy-to-read picture books. As they grow with picture books, their pleasure and satisfaction in reading continues.

With the combination of art and text, picture books provide stimulation for the eyes and the ears. Illustrations feed the child's imagination; words feed the child's language abilities. Together they introduce children to a world that they will never leave.

Because picture books are designed primarily for younger children (although they can be used with older children as well), they are generally intended to be read aloud. In listening to picture books read aloud, children discover and delight in the rhythm of language. Because picture books contain relatively few words, their writers have chosen their words very carefully and picture books thus feature an economical use of language, telling complete and often complex stories in a limited space. Children's author Karla Kuskin speaks about the magic of words in picture books: "Like poetry, a picture book has to be written in two ways. It must work when read aloud and also when read silently to oneself. Every syllable counts. Most importantly, the well-chosen words need to be simple but never simplistic, clear and strong enough to interest a child and hold her attention" (Kuskin 1998, 160).

Formats for Picture Books

While most picture books are published in standard hardback or paperback formats, some are published as board books, three-dimensional books, interactive books, or big books.

Board books are constructed of heavy laminated cardboard or light plastic pages that are bound together between two covers or are connected edge-to-edge to fold out as an accordion. These books are usually made to withstand the rigorous toy-treatment of the most vigorous child. Some of these books are made of vinyl or cloth, so that they can be read virtually anyplace. The content of these books ranges from simple illustrations and label words to simple stories that reflect young children's authentic interests and experiences such as Cynthia Rylant's *Everyday Children* and her other board books on everyday experiences, and Rosemary Wells's *Max's Bath* and other Max books. Board books have come to be regarded as real books rather than as mere playthings.

Three-dimensional books include pop-up books, die-cut books, and books with movable parts or three-dimensional illustrations. Eric Carle's well-loved *The Very Hungry Caterpillar* eats holes through the pages as he voraciously devours the food in the pictures. Holes cut through the pages of Simms Taback's *There Was an Old Lady Who Swallowed a Fly* allow children to look through the pages to glimpse the menagerie that the old woman swallows, and Tana Hoban's *Look! Look! Look!* uses openings in pages to reveal parts of the illustrations on successive pages so that children can guess what's coming. Lois Ehlert's three-dimensional book *Hands* is actually shaped like a hand. Children are fascinated with the animals that pop off the pages in *The Wide-Mouthed Frog: A Pop Up Book* by Keith Faulkner, a colorful book about animals in the food chain, and in *Dinosaur Stomp! A Monster Pop-Up Book* by Paul Strickland, featuring three-dimensional pop-up dinosaurs and colorful action words. Children can manipulate the flaps and tabs of Paul Zelinsky's *The Wheels on the Bus*. Tiny computer chips embedded in pages provide light and sound in Eric Carle's *The Very Quiet Cricket*. To the extent that children become involved in three-dimensional books, these books become interactive entities.

Interactive books stimulate children's participation. Of course, any book that uses heavily patterned language or rhyme will stimulate children to add words or rhymes on their own, but some interactive books are structured to induce children to participate. A good example is Dorothy Kunhardt's classic *Pat the Bunny*, the pages of which contain tactile surfaces (sandpaper for Daddy's unshaven face, for example) that extend reading beyond sight and sound. Janet and Allan Ahlberg's *Each Peach Pear Plum* is a delightful book in which children play "I Spy" with characters from nursery stories.

Big books are oversized versions of regular picture books with enlarged illustrations and print. Chart-sized versions of the Dick and Jane readers had been used in classrooms for some time, before the idea of using big books as teaching tools in American schools was imported from New Zealand in the 1980s. In big books, text and illustrations are large enough to be seen by a group of children so that they can join in shared reading lessons and other classroom activities that are part of reading instruction. Many excellent picture story books have been published in big book format. While big books are designed primarily for teaching reading in schools, publishers have also developed a home market for enlarged editions of picture books.

Board books, three-dimensional books, interactive books, and big books all constitute unique opportunities for early interaction with language and art. As children turn flaps to find objects, clap and repeat words, touch the three-dimensional objects on a page, and otherwise interact with these books, they practice language and engage in behaviors that bring them into the community of readers and lovers of literature.

ART IN PICTURE BOOKS

Illustrating books for children is a unique art form that involves special talent and technique. Pictures do more than just show what's happening in a book. Art reinforces text by showing what the characters are doing, as in Kevin O'Malley's illustrations in *Colliding with Chris* by Dan Harder, a story about a boy who can ride a bike but doesn't know how to use the brakes. Art establishes setting and reinforces or conveys mood in books like *Good-Bye Charles Lindbergh* written by Louise Borden and illustrated by Thomas B. Allen. Art helps define and develop characters—Dav Pilkey's illustrations for Angela Johnson's *Julius* leave no doubt in the reader's mind about how delighted Maya is with the pig her granddaddy sends her or about what her parents think of the whole situation. Art provides a different angle on the story, as in the illustrations of Pulitzer Prize–winning cartoonist Jules Feiffer in his amusing *I Lost My Bear*. It provides interesting, often subtle visual asides that foster children's joy in discovery; when looking carefully at the cork tree in Robert Lawson's illustrations for *The Story of Ferdinand* by Munro Leaf, one can see clusters of corks hanging like bunches of grapes from the branches. The use of space, the arrangement of print, the level of detail in pictures and drawings, colors, texture, and perspective all contribute to the overall quality and value of a picture book.

In books for young children, color is very important. Color suggests a mood or adds background to the story. In the Navajo legend *Arrow to the Sun*, Gerald McDermott used golds, yellows, and desert browns to suggest the Southwest; in *Anansi the Spider*, McDermott used bold greens and reds to reflect West African folk culture. The dark tones that Evaline Ness used in her Caldecott Medal winner *Sam, Bangs and Moonshine* underscore the drama and impending tragedy of the story.

While color is an important part of illustration in picture books for children, some of the finest examples of picture books have been illustrated in black and white. Wanda Gag's early classic *Millions of Cats* and Shel Silverstein's black-line sketches in *The Giving Tree* are good examples.

Artists and illustrators who create picture books often demonstrate unique and distinctive styles. The trained eye can often spot at a hundred paces a book by Eric Carle, Jerry Pinkney, Chris Van Allsburg, Jan Brett, Lane Smith, and other skilled illustrators.

Artists use a variety of media in creating artwork in picture books—pen and ink, pencil, lithographs, oil paintings, crayons and felt-tip pens, water colors, wood- or linoleum cuts, acrylic, gouache, tempera, fabrics, and various combinations of mixed media. In some picture books, the artist's media are specifically described in an afternote. Susan Campbell Bartoletti's traditional Polish tale *Dancing with Dziadziu*, for example, has the following note on Annika Nelson's illustrations: "The illustrations in this book are hand-colored linoleum cuts printed on Daniel Smith archival printmaking paper." Readers are informed that Greg Sked's illustrations in *The Turning Year* by Bill Martin Jr. were done in designer gouache on canvas. Jules Feiffer used watercolor and ink for the full-color illustrations in *I Lost My Bear*. Eric Carle paints on tissue paper and then cuts and pastes the paper to create the images in his books.

The artist's talents and imagination are often brought to bear in unusual ways. Illustrations may consist of collages made with twigs, string, or cloth. Aminah Brenda Lynn Robinson used cloth, thread, buttons, raw cotton, wood scraps, clay, and sand to enhance her illustrations in Evelyn Coleman's *To Be a Drum*. David Diaz used acrylic paintings set against a collage of mixed media for the Caldecott winner *Smoky Night* by Eve Bunting. Stephanie Garcia sculptured figures out of clay for *Snapshots from the Wedding* by Gary Soto. Benny Andrews brilliantly used fabric collages to create artwork in keeping with the theme of Libby Hathorn's *Sky Sash So Blue*, about a young slave girl who offers her older sister a special blue sash to use as part of her wedding dress.

Picture books reflect a variety of artistic styles and art forms, including the following:

- the representational style, typified in the painstaking accuracy (although she does dress them in human clothing) of Beatrix Potter's drawings of Peter Rabbit and other animals;

- the expressionistic style, with the slightly distorted shapes and unusual colors that Ludwig Bemelmans uses in *Madeline* and that Vera Williams uses in *A Chair for My Mother*;

- the cartoon style used by Theodor (Dr. Seuss) Geisel reflecting the energy and vitality of American illustrators at the time;

- the simple folk style that Barbara Cooney uses in Donald Hall's *Ox-Cart Man* reflecting the simplicity of the era that the book depicts;

- the surrealistic style with colors and shapes and forms representing the nightmarish action of Chris Van Allsburg's *Jumanji*.

The style that artists use often sets the tone and mood of the books they are illustrating. As part of their artistic style, some author/illustrators include pictures around the edge of the page to contribute to the story and/or the information contained in text. In *Comet's Nine Lives*, set on Nantucket Island, Jan Brett's marginal illustrations not only highlight the nautical setting but also foreshadow what will happen in the next part of the story. Brett uses marginal illustrations brilliantly in other books as well.

Photographs are also used to illustrate children's picture books. While sometimes used in picture story books, photographs are usually reserved for informational books. A photograph might offer a panoramic view of a rain forest or a close-up of a tiny bug on the leaf of a plant.

Design is another artistic element that is an important dimension of picture books. Design includes the style, size, and color of type and the arrangement of type and illustrations on the pages of the book. Page breaks need to be designed so that the reader is left with "What's next?" anticipation at the end of a page.

Good art is good art by any standard, whether it is hanging in a frame on a museum wall to be analyzed by critics or placed between the covers of a picture book to be enjoyed by children.

LITERARY ELEMENTS IN PICTURE BOOKS

Picture books contain the major literary elements found in other forms of children's literature: characterization, setting, plot, and theme.

Plot

Given the short attention span of the young child, the plots of picture books are usually short and uncomplicated (although there are elements of irony and levels of meaning that mature readers can appreciate in many picture books). Some plots follow a normal narrative structure, moving from the beginning with a rising action to the climax and finally the resolution. Other stories, such as Ezra Jack Keat's *The Snowy Day* and Judith Viorst's *Alexander and the Terrible, Horrible, No Good, Very Bad Day*, follow a "bed-to-bed" plot structure, beginning when the main character gets up in the morning and ending when the character goes to bed at night.

Informational picture books obviously don't follow the narrative structure of fiction. Nonfiction picture books present information with well-structured expository text organized by main idea/detail, cause-effect relationships, comparison/contrast, or sequence. Whatever text structure is used, information is presented in an organized manner that helps children understand and that is supported by drawings and pictures that extend and clarify the facts and concepts presented in text.

Characters

Picture books typically contain characters with whom children can identify—the mischievous Peter Rabbit (who gets caught in Mr. McGregor's garden), the nervous Ira (who sleeps over at his friend's house with his favorite teddy bear), the daring Max (who tames the Wild Things). Authors of picture books create full and rich characters in the same way that authors of longer novels do—through a character's speech, thoughts, and actions; through other characters' attitudes toward the character; and through direct description. Skilled artists use illustration to show the emotions and other qualities of the characters. Pictures of characters' faces help us see what they are like and how they react to a story's events.

Setting

As in all children's literature, setting—the time and place of a story—is important in children's picture books. Illustrations combine with text to create settings. Scenes depict details of time and location—from city streets and country roads to the insides of children's houses and the inside of their minds. Illustrations indicate the time of the story by showing characters' appearance, how they dress, and what their houses and towns look like. In pictures,

children can see the castles and forests, the cities and meadows, and all the other places that
that form backdrops for stories.

Author Profile: ALLEN SAY

Allen Say is a talented and popular author/illustrator who captures the nuances of
Japanese culture along with the emotions and experiences common to all people.

Say's interest and talent in art was fostered and developed from a young age. He
was born and spent his early years in Yokohama, Japan, during the Second World War.
At the age of twelve, Say moved to Tokyo, where he apprenticed himself to the famous
Japanese cartoonist Noro Shimpei, a man who became his mentor. His later book, *The
Ink-Keeper's Apprentice* (1994), is an autobiographical account of his life at that time.
When he was sixteen years old, Say's father took him to California, where he continued
to study and practice his art.

Say became involved in children's literature by illustrating the books written by
well-known authors, works like Eve Bunting's *Magic and the Night River* (1978), Ina
Friedman's *How My Parents Learned to Eat* (1985), and Diane Snyder's *The Boy of the
Three-Year Nap* (1988), which earned Say distinction when named as a Caldecott Honor
Book.

In 1982, Say wrote and illustrated his first children's book, *The Bicycle Man,* a
post–World War II story about two American soldiers and their friendly encounter with
a group of Japanese schoolchildren. He continued to write and illustrate his own books,
such as *A River Dream* (1988), which focused on his favorite hobby of fly fishing; *Tree
of Cranes* (1988), about a boy who learns about Christmas when his mother decorates a
pine tree with Japanese paper cranes; and *El Chino* (1990), a biography of Billy Wong, a
Chinese American who became a famous matador in Spain.

In 1994, Say won the Caldecott Medal for *Grandfather's Journey,* a simple and
poignant account of an old man's journey to North America, his return to his village in
Japan to marry his childhood sweetheart, his subsequent emigration to America, and his
ultimate return to his homeland. While Say wrote the book about his grandfather, it is
a reflection of Say's own experiences of living in two countries, Japan and the United
States.

After winning the Caldecott Medal, Say continued to write and illustrate books
such as *Emma's Rug* (1993), the story of a young artist who finds that her creativity
comes from within, and *Allison* (1997), the story of an Asian child who has been
adopted by an Anglo couple.

Allen Say continues to write children's books in his California home where he
lives with his wife and daughter.

Theme

Picture books contain messages that have meaning for young readers, but these messages
are implied rather than driven home in a didactic fashion. Vera Williams's *A Chair for My
Mother*, in which a child saves her money to purchase a chair for her hard-working mother,

speaks to the themes of love and sacrifice. Evaline Ness's *Sam, Bangs and Moonshine* is a clear lesson about the dangers of confusing fantasy and reality. Through the humor and nonsense of *Yertle the Turtle*, Dr. Seuss conveys a message about selfishness. As in any good piece of literature, the underlying ideas that govern the story are woven into the story itself.

Even in wordless books, children first experience the literary qualities that they will continue to encounter as they explore children's literature independently and as adult readers.

FACTORS FOR CONSIDERATION

FIVE FACTORS IN EVALUATING PICTURE BOOKS

In reviewing picture books, here are five factors to look for:

1. Are illustrations attractive and interesting enough to grab and hold the reader's attention?
2. Is text integrated and balanced with artwork to achieve unity?
3. Do the illustrations use visual elements like line, color, and texture to convey ideas and enhance the content of the text?
4. Do illustrations add to the reader's understanding of characters and settings in stories?
5. How does the book relate to other works by the same author and/or other books on the same topic?

TYPES OF PICTURE BOOKS

The broad category of picture books includes wordless books, alphabet books, counting books, and concept books. The largest category of picture books is picture story books, most of which are meant to be read to children but some of which are designed to be read by children on their own.

While there are differences among different types of picture books, many categories of these books overlap and a single book can fall into more than one category. Tana Hoban's *26 Letters and 99 Cents*, for example, is both an alphabet and a counting book.

Wordless Books

Wordless books are picture books in which stories are told with little or no print at all. Illustrations alone develop a cohesive narrative. Wordless books provide fail-safe reading material for all children—even the very young—because there are no words to get "right" or "wrong."

While they don't contain text, quality wordless books do include literary elements that mark good children's literature. Illustrations not only convey the story or plot, but also develop character, portray setting, and convey theme. Martha Alexander's *Bobo's Dream*, for example, is the story of a boy and his dog's trip to the park. The characters of the boy, the dog, and the "supporting cast" are made very apparent; the setting is clear; the plot moves from beginning to climax through resolution as any good narrative does; the themes of loyalty and overcoming one's fear with confidence are clear. Yet not one printed word appears in the text.

The skill with which illustrators tell stories without words is remarkable. Artists like Jan Omerod in books like *Sunshine* and *Moonlight* convey mood and tone through their illustrations alone. Such stories can be delightful (as is Tomie de Paola's *Pancakes for Breakfast*) and heartbreaking (as is Tom Feeling's *The Middle Passage*).

Wordless books are appropriate across grade levels. Although some wordless books are too sophisticated for young children to fully appreciate, interpret, and understand, many present simple stories that reflect young children's experiences and stimulate language development and imaginations. Young children can laugh at the animals in Tomie de Paola's *Pancakes for Breakfast* and make up stories about the scenes in David Wiesner's *Tuesday*. Older children (and adults) can relate to these stories on multiple levels.

Informational wordless books present content in fascinating and effective ways. John Goodall's *The Story of an English Village*, for example, shows the changes that occurred in an English village between the fourteenth and twentieth centuries, and Eric Rothman's *Time Flies* follows a bird flying out of the mouth of a dinosaur skeleton back in time to when dinosaurs roamed the earth.

LIST OF TEN

PEOPLE WHO WRITE BOOKS WITHOUT WORDS

What follows is a list of well-known authors and illustrators of wordless books:

Mitsumasa Anno, whose brilliantly designed wordless books such as *Anno's Journey* are among the most fascinating and the most popular available

Alexandra Day, who wrote the hilarious and popular accounts of Carl the caring rottweiler in such books as *Good Dog, Carl* and *Carl's Christmas*

Tomie de Paola, whose *Pancakes for Breakfast* is a widely enjoyed wordless book

John S. Goodall, whose wordless books such as *The Story of an English Castle* delight and inform young and old alike

Pat Hutchins, who authored the fascinating *Changes, Changes*, a wordless book that is frequently identified as a classic in the field

Fernando Krahn, whose clever illustrations contribute to lively action in a number of wordless books

Mercer Mayer, whose wordless books about a boy, a dog, and a frog are well known and whose other wordless books make millions of children and adults laugh

Jan Omerod, whose brilliant wordless books focus on family relationships and everyday life experiences

Peter Spier, who consistently entertains and informs with his books

David Wiesner, the brilliant artist who authored the enormously engaging Caldecott Medal–winning *Tuesday*

Some of these authors—such as Mitsumasa Anno and Jan Omerod—specialize in wordless books. Others—such as Pat Hutchins, and Tomie de Paola—are authors of award-winning picture storybooks as well.

This list is adapted from one that originally appeared in Savage, John F. 1998. *Teaching Reading and Writing: Combining Skills, Strategies and Literature* (2nd ed.). Boston: McGraw-Hill, Co.

Alphabet Books

Alphabet books help make children familiar with the name, form, and sometimes the sound of the individual orthographic symbols that constitute our writing system. From simple to sophisticated, these books are a popular type of picture book that informs and entertains young and old alike.

Most people are familiar with the ordinary "A is for Apple, B is for Ball" type of alphabet book. While this simple type of alphabet book can be used to introduce young children to letter names and sounds, most alphabet books are vehicles for writers to express their ideas and for artists to display their work. Quality alphabet books go well beyond the mere presentation of sound-symbol relationships and do the following:

- **tell a story:** *Chicka Chicka Boom Boom* by Bill Martin Jr. and John Archambault, an enormously popular alphabet book in which letters climb a tree, told in a jazzy style that children love;

- **feature exquisite artwork:** Jonathan Hunt's *Illuminations*, a lavishly illustrated account of various aspects of life during the Middle Ages;

- **present information:** Jerry Palotta's popular *The Icky Bug Alphabet Book*, full of scientific information, and Ann Whitford Paul's *Eight Hands Round: A Patchwork Alphabet* which presents a history lesson by illustrating various types of patchwork quilts;

- **focus on multiculturalism:** Margaret Musgrove's *Ashanti to Zulu: African Traditions* which gives facts and illustrations about twenty-six African tribes, associating them with the twenty-six letters of the alphabet;

- **use imaginative language:** Cathi Hepworth's ***Ant**ics! An Alphabet **Ant**hology*, a sophisticated work in which the word *ant* is embedded in each entry (F is **fant**astic).

LIST OF TEN

ALPHABET BOOKS

Hundreds of alphabet books are published each year. Here is a sample of ten of the more notable (and often unusual) alphabet books available for classrooms and homes:

Anno's Alphabet by Mitsumasa Anno
  a wonderfully illustrated book full of intriguing visual illusions (Crowell, 1975)

The Z Was Zapped by Chris Van Allsburg
  explains each ingenious illustration on the reverse side of the page (Houghton Mifflin, 1987)

The A to Z Beastly Jamboree by Robert Bender
  *in which an alphabet of creatures performs silly actions and a chain of marginal
  illustrations links all the animals and reinforces the sequence of letters (Dutton, 1996)*

The Handmade Alphabet by Laura Rankin
  a striking presentation of sign language through finger-spelled letters (Dell, 1991)

Hullaboo ABC by Beverly Cleary, illustrated by Ted Rand
  colorful watercolors illustrating letters for objects on a farm (Morrow, 1998)

Alphabet Soup: A Feast of Letters by Scott Gustafson
a book in which animals bring to a potluck meal food for each letter of the alphabet (Greenwich Workshop Press, 1994)

Down in the Garden: An Alphabet Book by Anne Geddes
connects letters with pictures in the author's unique photographic style, which consists of images of children's faces superimposed on flowers and plants in a garden setting (CEDCO, 1996)

Animalia by Graeme Base
a book of stunning (sometimes bizarre) illustrations of animals, with alliterative descriptors (Abrahams, 1986)

The Extinct Alphabet Book by Jerry Palotta
gives information about creatures that no longer exist (Charlesbridge, 1994)

The Accidental Zucchini by Max Grover
represents each letter with an unusual alliterative combination, such as "octopus overalls" and "umbrella underwear" (Harbrace, 1993)

Additional alphabet books with a multicultural focus are listed on pages 38–39.

A delightfully playful alphabet book is Reeve Lindbergh's *The Awful Aardvarks Go to School*. When the awful aardvarks visited the school, they wreaked havoc in an alliterative manner: They did such things as "bullied the bunny, gobbled green gum, and hassled the hamster." Tracey Campbell Pearson's illustrations add to the delight of the book. Another alphabet book with letters woven into the story is Michael J. Rosen's *Avalanche*, in which the *A*valanche starts when *B*obby throws a ball that hits a *C*an of cat food and so on through the alphabet. Clever wordplay and silly humor is characteristic of Richard Wilbur's *The Disappearing Alphabet*, which explores what happens when letters are dropped from words; David Diaz's illustrations add to the delight of the book.

While some alphabet books can be used to introduce letter symbols to young children, most are better appreciated by a more mature reading audience as a vehicle for demonstrating artistic talent or presenting information. Whatever their purpose, alphabet books represent a category of picture books that continues to retain popularity in the field of children's literature.

Counting Books

Counting books integrate numerals and illustrations to help develop number concepts and numerical awareness and to entertain. Generally, these books are designed to help children learn to establish one-to-one relationships between objects and numbers and to count, usually up to ten. Counting books take different approaches to developing number awareness:

- books like Eric Carle's *1, 2, 3 to the Zoo* focus on one-to-one relationships between numbers and objects;
- books like Peter Sis's brilliant and colorful *Going Up!* teach the concept of ordinal numbers;

- books like Muriel Feeling's *Moja Means One: A Swahili Counting Book* focus on multicultural as well as numerical dimensions of learning; and
- books like Lloyd Moss's *Zin! Zin! Zin, a Violin* present number-object relationships with elegant verse.

LIST OF TEN

COUNTING BOOKS

Here is a sample of ten especially unique and interesting counting books available to teachers and parents:

Anno's Counting Book by Mitsumasa Anno
includes, in addition to spectacular illustrations containing subtle features, the concept of zero (Putnam, 1977);

Amazing and Incredible Counting Stories by Max Grover
a collection of hypothetical newspaper headlines on subjects ranging from missing skyscrapers to radio refrigerators (Scholastic, 1995)

One, Two, One Pair by Bruce McMillan
shows how objects can come in pairs—feet, socks, and even humans (Scholastic, 1991)

The M&M's Brand Chocolate Candies Counting Book by Barbara Barbieri McGrath
a mouthwatering presentation of numbers, colors, shapes, and simple math using pictures of M&M candies (Charlesbridge, 1994)

Pigs from 1 to 10 by Arthur Geisert
a book in which children are encouraged to find and count the pigs in the illustrations (Houghton Mifflin 1992)

Ten, Nine, Eight by Molly Bang
features a father and child who observe objects in a room at bedtime and count back until the drowsy child is ready to go to sleep (Scholastic, 1992)

One Sun Rises: An African Wildlife Counting Book by Wendy Hartmann
counts numbers from one to ten by showing African wildlife, and then from ten to one by showing nocturnal animals (Dutton, 1994)

Fiesta! by Ginger Furglesong Guy
a bilingual counting book with numbers one to ten (uno a diez) representing what children need at a party (Greenwillow, 1996)

The Crayon Counting Book by Pam Muniz Ryan, illustrated by Frank Massola
numbers and colors combined with clever rhymes to present the concept of counting by twos (Charlesbridge, 1996)

How Many Feet in the Bed? by Diane Hamm
a counting book in a family setting (Simon and Schuster, 1991)

In addition to developing number concepts, counting books often explore concepts of color, shape, and size. Many counting books contain excellent artwork, creative language, and useful information that extends beyond helping children learn to count to ten. The concept of numbers is also built into some picture story books. In Eric Carle's *The Very Hungry Caterpillar*, the voracious bug eats one apple, two pears, three plums, and so on, and in David Kirk's *Miss Spider's Tea Party*, the hostess invites two timid beetles, three fireflies, and other insects all the way up to nine spotted moths.

Concept Books

Concept books are a type of informational picture book. These books focus on a single concept such as color, shape, opposites, trains, trucks, airports and other ideas that attract children's interests or are part of their world. Concept books are written to present information and explain ideas in a manner appropriate to very young children. As a type of children's literature, concept books are described more fully in Chapter 9.

While wordless books, alphabet books, counting books, and concept books are essential components of children's early encounters with books, when people think "picture book," they usually think of books that tell a story or present information through a combination of words and pictures. Picture story books constitute by far the largest category of picture books.

PICTURE STORY BOOKS

Picture story books combine words and artwork to tell a story. In a picture story book, words and illustrations work together. In Maurice Sendak's classic picture story book *Where the Wild Things Are*, readers know what mischief Max was punished for by looking at the pictures rather than by reading the text. Pat Hutchins's popular *Rosie's Walk* is another good example of how words and pictures work together in picture story books. Rosie the hen strolls around the barnyard, followed by a fox who encounters all kinds of mishaps. Even though the story is really about the fox, the hapless animal is never mentioned in text and is shown only in Hutchins's illustrations.

Author Profile: MAURICE SENDAK

One of the most remarkable author/illustrators in the history of American children's literature is Maurice Sendak. Sendak has attracted a greater combination of criticism and acclaim than any other creator of American picture books.

Sendak was born in Brooklyn, New York, in 1928. From an early age, he loved to read and draw. His sisters would take "real books" out of the library for their little brother when he had tired of children's books. While still in high school he began his work as an illustrator, working on the comic strip "Mutt and Jeff." After high school, he continued his education as an artist at the Art Students' League and, at nineteen years of age, coauthored his first published book, *Atomics for the Millions* (1947).

Early in his career, Sendak illustrated books written by other authors such as Ruth Krauss's *A Hole Is to Dig* (1952) and Beatrice de Regnier's *What Can You Do with a Shoe?* (1955). His own early work includes *Chicken Soup with Rice* (1962) and *Alligators All Around: An Alphabet Book* (1962), books that are still very popular today.

Sendak's most famous work is *Where the Wild Things Are* (1963), a benchmark in American children's publishing. The book generated both criticism and praise. Many adults feared that the book was "too frightening" for children; others praised it for the way it handled children's fantasy and dealt with children's emotions. The book won the 1964 Caldecott Medal and garnered other awards.

Sendak continued to write and illustrate children's books that continued to prove popular with children—*Hector Protector* (1965), *Really Rosie* (1986), and *Pierre: A Cautionary Tale* (1991). Much of his work was converted to videos and stage productions.

Some critics continue to find aspects of Sendak's work disturbing—the nudity of the boy in *In the Night Kitchen* (1970), the portrayal of the babies' experiences in *Outside over There* (1981), the deplorable conditions of the children in *We Are All in the Digs with Jack and Guy* (1993), a book in which Sendak intertwined two very old and obscure nursery rhymes.

Despite some people's concerns, Sendak's work continues to be popular because he connects with children. He recognizes that everyday fear and anxieties are part of children's lives. In his stories, children overcome their fears and end up safe and sound in the end. His books are full of symbolism from his own childhood.

Sendak's writing extends beyond picture books for children. He wrote the lyrics for an animated film version of the book *Really Rosie*, and he has written lyrics for an opera based on *Where the Wild Things Are* (for which he has also designed the sets and costumes).

Throughout his distinguished career, Maurice Sendak has earned recognition as an author, illustrator, and creative genius. He continues to maintain an office in New York City and a home in Connecticut.

Some picture story books are more appropriate for use with very young children. In a book like Bruce Degen's *Jamberry*, for example, the words and pictures explode off the page in joyful celebration. Laura Jaffe Numeroff's *If You Give a Mouse a Cookie* and her subsequent *If You Give a Moose a Muffin* and *If You Give a Pig a Pancake* appeal to our senses of humor and the absurd.

Other picture story books explore topics of interest to children in the preschool and early elementary years. For the very young, Peter Sis's *Fire Truck* is about a boy who wakes up to find, to his delight, that he has become a fire engine. For elementary school children, Bernard Waber's *Ira Sleeps Over* is a favorite book about a boy who is apprehensive about bringing along his teddy bear to sleep at his friend's house, only to discover that his friend sleeps with a stuffed animal too.

Some picture books appeal to children and to older readers. David Macaulay's *Black and White*, a book that contains four stories (or possibly only one story; it's up to the reader to decide) can be as intriguing to adults as it is to upper grade pupils. Chris Van Allsburg's haunting Christmas story *The Polar Express* is enjoyed by young children, but adults typically appreciate the book's symbolism and sentiments even more than children do. A few picture books by children's authors appeal primarily to an adult reading audience; for example, Dr. Seuss's *You're Only Old Once!* billed as "A Book for Obsolete Children," recounts a physical examination at the Golden Age Clinic. While young children can laugh at the language and illustrations, older folks can enjoy the book at a much more personal level.

For the most part, picture story books are intended to be read aloud to children. The stories may involve predictable language with structured and repeated text that is often rhymed, or they may be written in a more descriptive and narrative style. But, no matter what style of writing the author uses, picture story books are designed to be taken in through the ear and the eye, to be savored as an auditory and visual experience. "We take pleasure in the images and the ideas that the illustrations evoke and pleasure in the words themselves" (Austin 1998, 120).

Predictable picture story books are those that use repeated words or language patterns. Many traditional stories use repeated language patterns as a storytelling technique; for example, in *The Little Red Hen* "Not I, said the fox" is repeated, and in *The Gingerbread Man* "Run, run, run as fast as you can" is repeated. Bill Martin Jr. used the technique effectively in his well-known *Brown Bear, Brown Bear, What Do You See?* So did Pat Hutchins in *Goodnight, Owl!* The repeated words and sentence patterns quickly become familiar to children, and so they are soon able to repeat the lines of the story and move into reading the story independently.

Not all easy-to-read stories are written in a patterned, predictable style. Dr. Seuss's *The Cat in the Hat* is considered an easy reading book; in fact, the author wrote it in response to a publisher's request to produce an interesting story with a limited vocabulary as an antidote to the vapid stories that children had to deal with in their typical school reading books. Many (but not all) of Seuss's subsequent works, like *Green Eggs and Ham* and *One Fish, Two Fish, Red Fish, Blue Fish* were written in the same vein. Rhyming text combined with wonderful illustrations in books like *Snow Dance* by Leslie Evans and *Mouse Mess* by Linnea Riley provide interesting introductions to reading.

Some easy-to-read stories are labeled as such and are designed to be read by children on their own as they enter the beginning reading stage. These books provide material that children use to build fluency and confidence as independent readers. Books like Arnold Lobel's *Frog and Toad* stories (such as *Frog and Toad Are Friends*), Cynthia Rylant's *Henry and Mudge* books (such as *Henry and Mudge: The First Book of Their Adventures*), and *Emma's Magic Winter* by Jean Little are often the first books that children learn to read on their own. These books typically contain more text, but the writing consists of a controlled vocabulary and language style that children are able to read and understand.

While they sometimes focus on a single story or series of events, easy-to-read picture books are often broken into short "bite-sized" chapters that get children ready for reading longer chapters as their reading ability progresses and their interests expand. Picture story books like Jean Van Leeuwen's *Tales of Oliver Pig* and Susan Meddaugh's *Too Short Fred* provide chapters of three to eight pages connected by a theme or a story line.

Picture story books cover the gamut of genres in the field: traditional folk and fairy tales, realistic stories and fantasies, biographies and information books.

Traditional Folk and Fairy Tales

Fairy tales, folk tales, myths, and legends are popular material for picture books. Versions of old favorite fairy tales such as "Cinderella," "Hansel and Gretel," "Jack and the Beanstalk," and "Little Red Riding Hood" have been illustrated by the likes of Jan Brett, Paul Galdone, Marcia Brown, and Trina Shart Hyman. The 1998 Caldecott Medal for excellence in illustration was awarded to Paul O. Zelinsky for his illustration of the traditional fairy tale *Rapunzel*, and Lane Smith won Caldecott recognition for his illustration of Jon Scieszka's off-the-wall variation of fairy tales in *The Stinky Cheese Man and Other Fairly*

Stupid Tales. Traditional literature also includes the many beautifully illustrated editions of *Mother Goose Tales,* such as *The Glorious Mother Goose,* selected by Cooper Edens, with illustrations by famous illustrators of the past.

Folktales and fairy tales from many cultures are available in picture story book form; examples are Verna Aardema's very popular West African folktale *Why Mosquitoes Buzz in People's Ears* and John Steptoe's *Mufaro's Beautiful Daughters.* Children meet other folk characters from different cultures such as:

- the American legendary woodsman Paul Bunyan in Steven Kellog's *Paul Bunyan;*
- the Italian legendary character Strega Nona in Tomie de Paola's *Strega Nona;*
- the African folk trickster Anansi the Spider in Gail E. Haley's *A Story, a Story;*
- the Irish legendary hero Fin McCool in Tomie de Paola's *Fin M'Coul: The Giant of Knockmany Hill;* and
- the Russian witch Baba Yaga, of whom a kinder and gentler version is portrayed by Patricia Polacco in *Babuska Baba Yaga.*

Picture story books provide parents and teachers with a full range of traditional literature that they can offer to their children. The topic of traditional literature will be treated in more detail in Chapter 6.

Historical Stories

Stories rooted in the past are sometimes presented in picture story book form. Some of these stories are historically accurate such as Alice and Martin Provensen's *The Glorious Flight Across the Channel with Louis Bleriot,* an account of the first human flight across the English Channel in 1909. Some of these stories are fictional such as Emily Arnold McCully's *Mirette on the High Wire,* the story of a young girl's efforts to restore the courage of a high-wire daredevil. Whether factual or fanciful, the language and illustrations in these stories bring to life for young children long ago times and places.

Historical fiction picture books can leave a vivid impression of important events from history. Historical fiction is the subject of Chapter 8.

LIST OF TEN

SOME WONDERFUL PICTURE BOOKS

If you could own only ten picture books, which ones would they be? Over 1,000 children's picture books are published in the United States each year, and many more are published across the globe. To select only ten seems an impossible task. Here are ten extraordinary picture books that might be chosen by many bibliophiles for their "essential collections":

Where the Wild Things Are by Maurice Sendak
broke the mold of American picture story book writing (Harper and Row, 1963)

Make Way for Ducklings by Robert McCloskey
written decades ago, a gentle story of a mallard family's search for a home in the Boston Public Gardens (Viking, 1941)

Owl Moon by Jane Yolen, illustrated by John Schoenher
 lyrical text and striking illustrations about a girl and her father who go owling in the winter woods (Putnam, 1987)

Miss Rumphius by Barbara Cooney
 story about a woman who spreads beauty in the world by planting flowers (Viking, 1982)

Polar Express by Chris Van Allsburg
 with text and illustrations that suggest the magic of Christmas Eve, on its way to becoming a classic (Houghton Mifflin, 1985)

The Talking Eggs by Robert D. San Souci, illustrated by Jerry Pinkney
 Creole folktale from the American South with a special style of language and illustration that captures a special mood (Dial, 1989)

Tuesday by David Wiesner
 brilliant and imaginative illustrations in a wordless book about what would happen if pigs or frogs could fly (Clarion, 1991)

Drummer Hoff by Barbara Emberley, illustrated by Ed Emberley
 rhyming and repeated text and brilliant illustrations, a treat to both ear and eye (Simon and Schuster, 1967)

Hooray for Diffendoofer Day! by Dr. Seuss, with help from Jack Prelutsky and Lane Smith
 exuberant account of a school, a refreshing reflection on standards-based education from Dr. Seuss's sketches and notes (Knopf, 1998)

My Very First Mother Goose by Iona Opie, illustrated by Rosemary Wells
 one of the best of many good collections available (Candlewick, 1996)

This list of ten could be expanded a hundredfold or more by lovers of children's literature.

Realistic Stories

Some picture books tell what really happened or really could happen. Books like *Window Music* by Anastasia Suen allow children to share scenes from the window of a passing train. *Sam and the Zamboni Man* by James Stevenson is about a boy who visits his grandfather, the driver of a Zamboni at an ice rink. Many of the books on sensitive topics identified in Chapter 2 are picture books. Dealing with such topics within the confined space of a picture book takes incredible skill and sensitivity.

Fantasy

Some of the most popular picture story books in the marketplace are fantasy books. Such books give animals human qualities, make toys and other inanimate objects come alive, and involve magic or other supernatural forces. Through picture story books in this genre, children meet such marvelous human characters as the friendly safety officer whose dog steals his thunder during presentations in Peggy Rathman's *Officer Buckle and Gloria* and such fabulous nonhuman characters as Miss Spider in *Miss Spider's Wedding* and David Kirk's other Miss Spider books such as *Miss Spider's New Car*. Fantasy feeds the imaginations of children and will be treated in more detail in the next chapter.

Informational Books

While technically not story books, many outstanding informational picture books are published every year. Some informational picture books present information through strong narrative elements. For example, *A Tree Is Growing* by Arthur Dorros traces the growth of a tree throughout the seasons of a year, explaining how each part of the tree contributes to its growth, and *Bald Eagle* by Gordon Morrison is a well-researched and stunningly illustrated book about our national bird. Other picture books that are informational books will be included in Chapter 9.

Biography

Another form of nonfiction picture books is the biography. Illustrated accounts of the lives of famous people from different eras and different fields—such as Diane Stanley's biography of the great Russian Emperor *Peter the Great* and Kathleen Krull's biography of the great Olympic athlete Wilma Rudolph in *Wilma Unlimited*—bring characters alive in the minds of young readers. Chapter 10 deals with biography and autobiography in more detail.

Poetry

Illustrations and poetry usually complement each other in picture books. The clever and colorful illustrations that accompany Karla Kuskin's humorous and charming poems in *The Sky Is Always the Sky* and the more gentle illustrations that accompany Nancy White Carlstrom's nature poems in *Midnight Dance of the Snowshoe Hare: Poems About Alaska* work to enhance enjoyment of the poems.

In sum, quality picture books represent a very special form of artistic endeavor. Writers and illustrators integrate words and pictures to entertain and inform young readers through the ear and eye. Picture books are the very first literature that children encounter, and they remain favorites long into adulthood.

PICTURE BOOKS IN SCHOOL AND AT HOME

For parents, grandparents, and other adult caregivers, there are few experiences as enjoyable as sharing a picture book with a child. "Lap reading" describes the activity of reading with a child, sharing a well-loved book, and responding to a child's repeated request, "Read it again." Lap reading creates a connection between older and younger reader that few other activities can.

Books advising parents on the effective use of literature in the home (Trelease 1995; Butler 1998) suggest ways to share books, recommend books to share at particular ages, and give other information that helps parents start their children on the road to academic success and a love of reading.

It's never too early to introduce books to children. All types of picture books have a place in the home reading experiences of the young child. Board books become playthings before the child learns to talk. Simple concept books allow children to point to and name objects as they acquire language. Mother Goose becomes a staple in their daily diet of reading and recitation. Alphabet books familiarize them with letter symbols (although most alphabet books are not written for the specific purpose of teaching children letter names and sounds). Counting books familiarize children with numbers. Wordless books encourage children to make up their own stories to go along with the pictures.

Picture story books are the mainstay of children's early encounters with literature. Favorite storybook characters like Corduroy and Madeline become as familiar as members of the family. As adults share picture books with them, children learn to count the ducks in *Make Way for Ducklings* and to name the colors of the fruits and vegetables that *The Very Hungry Caterpillar* eats. The verbal exchange that occurs in response to books is invaluable in language and cognitive development and develops an awareness of and appreciation for literature. Here is where children develop language and a sense of story that will stay with them throughout their lives. Children ask that favorite stories be read over and over and over (often to a tired parent's consternation) until they can recite the stories word for word by themselves (or recognize that the reader has skipped a part).

The key to sharing picture books in the home is the child's involvement and response. Some books—like *Each Peach Pear Plum* and *Brown Bear, Brown Bear What Do You See?*—invite child participation. But with any book, clapping to accompany the rhythm of the language, talking about the pictures, laughing at the humor, describing the characters, completing the rhyming elements, reading along with the reader, and retelling the story are part and parcel of the reading experience.

Sharing books at home does not stop when children learn to read independently. Reading mysteries, fantasies, and historical fiction together continues to cement the bond between parent and child established by picture books.

Picture books are no less important in the classroom than they are in the home. And just as there are references to help parents choose and use picture books at home, there is a wealth of professional references available to suggest to teachers how to effectively use picture books in the classroom (Beaty 1994; Bromley 1996; Savage 1998).

In nursery and kindergarten programs, book nooks and classroom libraries that children have a chance to visit all day should be part of the learning environment. Concept books are used to stimulate language, sharpen perception, and enhance learning. Collections of picture books on curriculum topics like dinosaurs or the moon add to children's expanding knowledge. Alphabet books focus attention on letters and the sounds these letters represent. Counting books illustrate number-symbol relationships.

In early childhood settings, teachers and other caregivers share picture books several times each day, and children share the books with which they are familiar. Children have opportunities to talk about books, dramatize stories, dictate their own versions of familiar stories, and draw new illustrations. Books are part of show and tell, big books are used for shared reading lessons, and books are sent home to establish a link with parents. Children's literature dominates a good early childhood educational program.

In primary grade classrooms, picture books remain important, both as vehicles for instruction and as sources of enjoyment. At this level, children develop the skills and strategies that will lead to independence in reading and writing. Classroom libraries offer these children many opportunities to browse through books that they enjoy and are learning to read. Picture books are integral to the instructional process, as children learn new words and apply comprehension strategies to their reading. Oral and written language activities center around picture story books and children's responses to books. Picture books are used for guided reading, lessons are built around predictable books, and teachers use informational picture books across the curriculum. Easy-to-read picture story books provide material with which children can practice their developing reading competency, and they provide stepping stones to growing reading independence.

The use of picture books in the classroom extends beyond the early stages of literacy development. Many picture books hold fascination for children well beyond the primary grades. While some picture books are "baby books" in the estimations of some youngsters, others—such as Patricia Polacco's *Pink and Say*—contain language and content appropriate for the upper grades. Books like *The True Story of the Three Little Pigs* are used for developing students' understanding of and ability to use point of view, and wordless books are used in story writing activities. Picture books can remain part of children's literacy development into the later years of elementary school, as teachers design creative ways to make them part of children's learning experiences.

Special Perspectives on Children's Literature

POSTMODERN PICTURE BOOKS
by Amy Seldin

…We live in a post-modern,
post-literate age;
an age of doubt;
an age of uncertainty;
AN AGE OF PLAYFULNESS—
to be playful is to be open;
to be playful is to be spontaneous;
to be playful is to expect the unexpected…
(Nikola-Lisa 1994, 37)

Postmodernism is a movement within contemporary literature, art, philosophy, and the social and natural sciences that questions and critiques traditional forms and their functions. Since World War II, postmodernist eclectic, aggressive works have deliberately experimented with traditional ideas and structure in literature, art, and architecture.

Postmodern literature and art may include ambiguous text and images. Postmodern artists and writers actively display a lack of faith in traditional art forms, and thus use nontraditional art forms as means of gaining knowledge about life. Because a consistent portion of the text and images in postmodern books is ambiguous, this type of picture book is a wonderful form of literature for helping children develop skill in negotiating meaning and in critical thinking.

How are postmodern picture books different from traditional picture books? Authors and illustrators of postmodern picture books follow few conventions. Traditional picture book authors typically subscribe to usual conventions: consistent use of layout, materials, space, and size and shape of text throughout the book. Creators of postmodern picture books consistently break these conventions by using different combinations of different textures and collage, black and white spaces, images, and print that may or may not comment on the surrounding text. Often, the art is highly detailed and defined, and the colors used are rich and dark. Text is often discontinuous, chaotic, and ambiguous. All of these details contribute to postmodern picture books that are colorful, eclectic, energetic, inviting, and enjoyable to read.

How do readers negotiate meaning from a postmodern picture book? These books are typically entertaining, humorous, witty, and challenging to read. They are crafted in such a way that they leave multiple gaps that readers must fill with critical information. Usually, some information is omitted or misplaced, and readers must read the entire story with a critical eye to continually update it for overall comprehension. Readers must juxtapose the unusual, unconventional, ambiguous details with what they already know about the world and traditional picture books, and then decide how to make sense of the juxtaposition. Readers must maintain attention to details such as space, color, texture, art media, print, and then decide how, when, and why they all fit together.

Postmodern picture books have enjoyed both popularity and critical recognition in the field of children's literature. Jon Scieszka and Lane Smith's *The Stinky Cheese Man and Other Fairly Stupid Tales* (Viking, 1992), a humorous parody of traditional fairy tales, was a Caldecott Honor book. The author and illustrator make dramatic use of various print sizes, colors, and page arrangements. The dialogue of the narrators—Jack (from Jack and Jill) and the familiar Little Red Hen—is interwoven throughout the book, but the narrators never tell their own stories. Distinctive features of the book are upside-down illustrations and print. The princess in the book is not a gorgeous, Disneylike, Barbie-proportioned princess but rather a skinny witch with a crooked mouth, two eyes on one side of her head, and very curly dark hair. These details challenge the assumption that all princesses are stunning creatures and calls for interpretation and discussion. Similar postmodern features can be found in Scieszka's and Lane's earlier popular creation, *The True Story of the Three Little Pigs* (Viking, 1989).

Another strong example of a postmodern picture book is David Macaulay's Caldecott Medal–winning *Black and White* (Houghton Mifflin, 1990). In this book, Macaulay plays with form by using both sides of the opened book pages as one plane to hold four quadrants of varying background colors. At first, there appear to be four distinct stories taking place in the four quadrants of each two-page spread. As one continues reading, however, possibilities for connections among all four corner stories emerge. Some of the same postmodern features can be found in Macaulay's *BAAA* (Houghton Mifflin, 1985) and *Shortcut* (Houghton Mifflin, 1986).

Using postmodern picture books encourages students to think critically and to exercise their own negotiating skills and devices. Teachers and parents need to create opportunities for children to critically assess the authority of texts and social mores. Many conventional approaches to teaching and using literature in classrooms are more concerned with initiating students into an existing mainstream school culture rather than educating students to question or change it.

Teachers and students together need to examine and make deliberate attempts to influence how and what knowledge and identities are produced within the social classroom structure. Group negotiation of stories draws attention to ways in which knowledge, power, and experience are produced under specific conditions of learning. Parents and teachers can use the content of postmodern picture books and student-initiated discussion to generate critical thinking. We can create a place for students to critique postmodern books (which, in turn, critique society) and create a social context within which this critique can occur.

Using postmodern picture books creates opportunities to make sense of, to construct, to defend, and to critique stories and allows children to create their own forum for negotiating text. By using these materials and processes, teachers and parents help students to develop as critical and active citizens of the world.

As a teacher, Amy Seldin has used postmodern picture books with young children and has found that children are able to fill in gaps, can interpret what happens in text, can collectively track characters all the way through the book, and can observe, negotiate, and make connections between stories.

REFERENCES

Bodmer, G. 1989. The Postmodern Alphabet: Extending the Limits of Contemporary Alphabet Books, from Seuss to Gorey. *Children's Literature Quarterly* 14:115–117.

Giroux, H. 1992. Textual Authority and the Role of Teachers as Public Intellectuals. In *Social Issues in the English Classroom,* eds. C. Hubert and S. Totten. Urbana, Ill.: National Council of Teachers of English.

Nikola-Lisa, W. 1994. Play, Panache, Pastiche: Postmodern Impulses in Contemporary Picture Books. *Children's Literature Association Quarterly* 19:35–40.

Palye N. 1992. Post-Modernist Impulses and the Contemporary Picture Book: Are There Any Stories to These Messages? *Journal of Youth Services in Libraries.* Winter.

CONCLUSION

Picture books combine language and art. Karla Kuskin, a noted children's author, describes the picture book as "a complicated form of collaborative art. When it is very well done, it is an artistic achievement worthy of examination and honor. Even failures, especially near misses, deserve the kind of attention and understanding given to serious creative endeavors" (Kuskin 1998, 159–160).

The appeal of good picture books never diminishes. The bedtime story *Goodnight, Moon* by Margaret Wise Brown, published in 1939, remains popular with today's cyber-generation. Over 1,000 new picture book titles are published each year, and a few of them have the endearing qualities of old favorites. The elegant simplicity of *Nocturne*, a book combining Jane Yolen's poetic language and Anne Hunter's wonderful illustrations to help children appreciate the nighttime sky, is one such newer story that may be shared with children at bedtime for generations to come.

Picture books start children on the road to a love of literature. Even before a child is able to talk, books are sources of engagement and enjoyment, and they remain so into the adult years.

Questions and Activities for Action and Discussion

1. Identify a favorite picture book that you remember from your own childhood. In what ways did the artwork contribute to making this book a favorite?
2. Select several books by a well-known contemporary children's book illustrator—such as Chris Van Allsburg, Allen Say, Lane Smith, Faith Ringgold, or Jan Brett. Note the illustrator's use of line, color, and other artistic elements to create his or her unique style. Describe the appeal of the artist's style.
3. Review a concept book, an alphabet book, and a counting book. Make a list of ways you would use each for instructional purposes with a prekindergarten child.
4. Research and report on the use of wordless books as vehicles for enjoyment and instruction. Include specific examples of how these books can be used for reading and writing instruction in the classroom.
5. Compare two informational picture books, one that uses photographs as the only graphic element and one that uses drawings. What does each graphic element contribute? Describe which you prefer and be ready to defend your position.

CHILDREN'S & YOUNG ADULT BOOKS CITED IN THIS CHAPTER

Aardema, Verna. 1975. *Why Mosquitoes Buzz in People's Ears*. Illustrated by Leo and Dianne Dillon. New York: Dial.

Ahlberg, Janet, and Allan Ahlberg. 1979. *Each Peach Pear Plum*. New York: Viking.

Alexander, Martha. 1970. *Bobo's Dream*. New York: Dial.

Banks, Kate. 1998. *And If the Moon Could Talk*. Illustrated by Georg Hollennleben. New York: Farrar, Straus and Giroux.

Bartoletti, Susan Campbell. 1997. *Dancing with Dziadziu*. Illustrated by Annika Nelson. San Diego: Harcourt Brace.

Bemelmans, Ludwig. 1939. *Madeline*. New York: Viking.

Borden, Louise. 1998. *Good-Bye Charles Lindbergh: Based on a True Story*. Illustrated by Thomas B. Allen. New York: Simon and Schuster.

Brett, Jan. 1996. *Comet's Nine Lives*. New York: Putnam.

Brown, Margaret Wise. 1947. *Goodnight Moon*. Illustrated by Clement Hurd. New York: Harper.

Bunting, Eve. 1994. *Smoky Night*. Illustrated by David Diaz. New York: Harbrace.

———1998. *Going Home*. Illustrated by David Diaz. New York: HarperCollins.

Carle, Eric. 1960. *1, 2, 3 to the Zoo*. New York: Putnam.

———1969. *The Very Hungry Caterpillar*. New York: Philomel.

———1990. *The Very Quiet Cricket*. New York: Philomel.

Carlstrom, Nancy White. 1998. *Midnight Dance of the Snowshoe Hare: Poems About Alaska*. Illustrated by Ken Kuroi. New York: Philomel.

Coleman, Evelyn. 1998. *To Be a Drum*. Illustrated by Aminah Brenda Lynn Robinson. New York: Whitman.

Degen, Bruce. 1983. *Jamberry*. New York: Harper and Row.

de Paola, Tomie. 1975. *Strega Nona*. New York: Simon and Schuster.

———1978. *Pancakes for Breakfast*. New York: Harcourt Brace.

———1981. *Fin M'Coul: The Giant of Knockmany Hill*. New York: Holiday House.

Dorros, Arthur. 1997. *A Tree Is Growing*. Illustrated by S. D. Schindler. New York: Scholastic.

Edens, Cooper. 1988. *The Glorious Mother Goose*. New York: Atheneum.

Ehlert, Lois. 1997. *Hands*. San Diego: Harcourt Brace.

Evans, Leslie. 1997. *Snow Dance*. Illustrated by Cynthia Jabar. Boston: Houghton Mifflin.

Faulkner, Keith. 1996. *The Wide-Mouthed Frog: A Pop-Up Book*. Illustrated by Jonathan Cambert. New York: Dial.

Feelings, Muriel. 1971. *Moja Means One: A Swahili Counting Book*. New York: Dial.

Feelings, Tom. 1995. *The Middle Passage*. New York: Dial.

Feiffer, Jules. 1998. *I Lost My Bear*. New York: Morrow.

Gag, Wanda. 1928. *Millions of Cats*. New York: Putnam.

Geisel, Theodor (Dr. Seuss). 1957. *How the Grinch Stole Christmas*. New York: Random House.

———1957. *The Cat in the Hat*. New York: Random House.

———1960. *Green Eggs and Ham*. New York: Random House.

———1966. *One Fish, Two Fish, Red Fish, Blue Fish*. New York: Random House.

———1979. *Yertle the Turtle*. New York: Random House.

———1986. *You're Only Old Once*. New York: Random House.

Goodall, John. 1986. *The Story of an English Village*. New York: Macmillan.

Haley, Gail E. 1970. *A Story, a Story*. New York: Antheneum.

Hall, Donald. 1979. *Ox-Cart Man*. Illustrated by Barbara Cooney. New York: Viking.

Harder, Dan. 1997. *Colliding with Chris*. Illustrated by Kevin O'Malley. New York: Hyperion.

Hathorn, Libby. 1998. *Sky Sash So Blue*. Illustrated by Benny Andrews. New York: Simon and Schuster.

Hepworth, Cathi. 1992. ***Ant**ics! An Alphabet **Ant**hology*. New York: Putnam.

Hoban, Tana. 1987. *26 Letters and 99 Cents*. New York: Greenwillow.

———1988. *Look! Look! Look!* New York: Greenwillow.

Hunt, Jonathan. 1989. *Illuminations*. New York: Bradbury.

Hutchins, Pat. 1968. *Rosie's Walk*. New York: Macmillan.

———1972. *Goodnight, Owl!* New York: Macmillan.

Johnson, Angela. 1993. *Julius*. Illustrated by Dav Pilkey. New York: Scholastic.

Keats, Ezra Jack. 1962. *The Snowy Day*. New York: Viking.

———1964. *Whistle for Willy*. New York: HarperCollins.

———1967. *Peter's Chair*. New York: HarperCollins.

Kellogg, Steven. 1984. *Paul Bunyan*. New York: Morrow.

Kirk, David. 1994. *Miss Spider's Tea Party*. New York: Scholastic.

———1995. *Miss Spider's Wedding*. New York: Scholastic.

———1997. *Miss Spider's New Car*. New York: Scholastic.

Krull, Kathleen. 1996. *Wilma Unlimited: How Wilma Rudolph Became the World's Fastest Woman*. Illustrated by David Diaz. San Diego: Harcourt Brace.

Kunhardt, Dorothy. 1942. *Pat the Bunny*. New York: Western.

Kuskin, Karla. 1998. *The Sky Is Always the Sky*. Illustrated by Isabelle Derraux. New York: HarperCollins.

Leaf, Munro. 1936. *The Story of Ferdinand*. Illustrated by Robert Lawson. New York: Viking.

Lindbergh, Reeve. 1997. *The Awful Aardvarks Go to School*. Illustrated by Tracey Campbell Pearson. New York: Viking.

Little, Jean. 1998. *Emma's Magic Winter*. Illustrated by Jennifer Plecas. New York: HarperCollins.

Lobel, Arnold. 1970. *Frog and Toad Are Friends*. New York: Harper and Row.

Macaulay, David. 1990. *Black and White*. Boston: Houghton Mifflin.

Martin, Jr., Bill. 1994. *Brown Bear, Brown Bear, What Do You See?* Illustrated by Eric Carle. New York: Holt.

———1998. *The Turning Year*. Illustrated by Greg Sked. San Diego: Harcourt Brace.

Martin, Jr., Bill and John Archambault. 1989. *Chicka Chicka Boom Boom*. New York: Simon and Schuster.

McCloskey, Robert. 1940. *Lentil*. New York: Penguin.

———1941. *Make Way for Ducklings*. New York: Puffin.

McCully, Emily Arnold. 1992. *Mirette on the High Wire*. New York: Putnam.

McDermott, Gerald. 1972. *Anansi the Spider: A Tale from the Ashanti*. New York: Holt.

———1974. *Arrow to the Sun*. New York: Viking.

Meddaugh, Susan. 1978. *Too Short Fred*. Boston: Houghton Mifflin.

Morrison, Gordon. 1998. *Bald Eagle*. Boston: Houghton Mifflin.

Moss, Lloyd. 1995. *Zin! Zin! Zin, a Violin*. Illustrated by Marjorie Prueman. New York: Simon and Schuster.

Musgrove, Margaret. 1976. *Ashanti to Zulu: African Traditions*. Illustrated by Leo and Diane Dillon. New York: Dial.

Ness, Evaline. 1966. *Sam, Bangs and Moonshine*. New York: Henry Holt.

Numeroff, Laura Jaffe. 1985. *If You Give a Mouse a Cookie*. New York: Harper and Row.

———1991. *If You Give a Moose a Muffin*. New York: HarperCollins.

———1998. *If You Give a Pig a Pancake*. New York HarperCollins.

Omerod, Jan. 1981. *Sunshine*. New York: Lothrup.

———1982. *Moonlight*. New York: Lothrup.

Palotta, Jerry (1986) *The Icky Bug Alphabet Book*. Illustrated by Ralph Masiello. Watertown, Mass.: Charlesbridge.

Paul, Ann Whitford. 1991. *Eight Hands Round: A Patchwork Alphabet*. New York: HarperCollins.

Polacco, Patricia. 1993. *Babuska Baba Yaga*. New York: Philomel.

———1994. *Pink and Say*. New York: Putnam.

Provensen, Alice, and Martin Provensen. 1983. *The Glorious Flight Across the Channel with Louis Bleriot*. New York: Puffin.

Rathman, Peggy. 1995. *Officer Buckle and Gloria*. New York: Putnam.

Riley, Linnea. 1998. *Mouse Mess*. New York: Scholastic.

Rosen, Michael J. 1998. *Avalanche*. Illustrated by David Butler. Cambridge, Mass.: Candlewick.

Rothman, Eric. 1994. *Time Flies*. New York: Crown.

Rylant, Cynthia. 1987. *Henry and Mudge: The First Book of Their Adventures*. New York: Simon and Schuster.

———1993. *Everyday Children*. New York: Bradbury.

Sandin, Joan. 1981. *The Long Way to a New Land*. New York: Harper and Row.

Scieszka, Jon. 1989. *The True Story of the Three Little Pigs*. Illustrated by Lane Smith. New York: Viking.

———1992. *The Stinky Cheese Man and Other Fairly Stupid Tales*. Illustrated by Lane Smith. New York: Viking.

Sendak, Maurice. 1963. *Where the Wild Things Are*. New York: Harper and Row.

Shannon, David. 1998. *No, David!* New York: Scholastic.

Silverstein, Shel. 1964. *The Giving Tree*. New York: Harper and Row.

Sis, Peter. 1989. *Going Up!* New York: Greenwillow.

———1998. *Fire Truck*. New York: Greenwillow.

Soto, Gary. 1996. *Snapshots from the Wedding*. Illustrated by Stephanie Garcia. New York: Putnam.

Stanley, Diane. 1996. *Peter the Great*. New York: Morrow.

Steptoe, John. 1969. *Stevie*. New York: HarperCollins.

———1987. *Mufaro's Beautiful Daughters*. New York: Lothrup, Lee and Shepard.

Stevenson, James. 1998. *Sam and the Zamboni Man*. Illustrated by Harvey Stevenson. New York: Greenwillow.

Strickland, Paul. 1996. *Dinosaur Stomp! A Monster Pop-Up Book*. New York: Dutton.

Suen, Anastasia. 1998. *Window Music*. Illustrated by Wade Zahares. New York: Viking.

Taback, Simms. 1997. *There Was an Old Lady Who Swallowed a Fly*. New York: Penguin.

Van Allsburg, Chris. 1981. *Jumanji*. Boston: Houghton Mifflin.

———1985. *The Polar Express*. Boston: Houghton Mifflin.

Van Leeuwen, Jean. 1979. *Tales of Oliver Pig*. Illustrated by Arnold Lobel. New York: Dial.

Viorst, Judith. 1971. *Alexander and the Terrible, Horrible, No Good, Very Bad Day*. New York: Macmillan.

Waber, Bernard. 1972. *Ira Sleeps Over*. Boston: Houghton Mifflin.

Wells, Rosemary. 1985. *Max's Bath*. New York: Dial.

Wiesner, David. 1991. *Tuesday*. New York: Clarion.

Wilbur, Richard. 1998. *The Disappearing Alphabet*. New York: Harcourt Brace.

Williams, Vera. 1987. *A Chair for My Mother*. New York: Harcourt Brace.

Yolen, Jane. 1997. *Nocturne*. Illustrated by Anne Hunter. New York: Harcourt Brace.

Zelinsky, Paul. 1990. *The Wheels on the Bus*. New York: Dutton.

———1997. *Rapunzel*. New York: Dutton.

REFERENCES

Association for Library Service to Children. 1997. *The Newbery and Caldecott Awards: A Guide to the Medal and Honor Books*. Chicago: American Library Association.

Austin, P. 1998. Math Books as Literature: Which Ones Measure Up? *The New Advocate* 11:119–132.

Beaty, J. J. 1994. *Picture Book Storytelling*. Fort Worth: Harcourt Brace.

Bromley, K. D. 1996. *Webbing with Literature* (2d ed.). Boston: Allyn and Bacon.

Butler, D. 1998. *Babies Need Books: Sharing the Joy of Books with Children from Birth to Six*. Portsmouth, N.H.: Heinemann.

Flowers, A. A. 1998. Nineteenth Century Origins of the Modern Picture Book. *Teaching and Learning Literature*: 67–72.

Kiefer, B. 1988. Picture Books as Contexts for Literacy, Aesthetic, and Real World Understandings. *Language Arts* 65: 260–270.

Kuskin, K. 1998. To Get a Little More of the Picture: Reviewing Picture Books. *The Horn Book* 74: 159–165.

Lesiak, J. L. 1997. Research Based Answers to Questions about Emergent Literacy in Kindergarten. *Psychology in Schools* 34:143–159.

Savage, J. F. 1998. *Teaching Reading and Writing: Combining Skills, Strategies, and Literature*. Boston: McGraw Hill.

Trelease, J. 1995. *The Read-Aloud Handbook* (4th ed.). New York: Penguin.

CHAPTER 5

FANTASY

s a genre of children's literature, fantasy involves stories that are highly improbable yet quite believable. Fantasy transports children into the world of make-believe and extends their imaginations in exotic settings with incredible characters engaged in improbable adventures. In this chapter, science fiction is also considered part of modern fantasy.

THIS CHAPTER

- examines the role that fantasy plays in children's lives and in their encounters with literature;

- presents categories of fantasy frequently found in literature for children; and

- suggests ways for using fantasy as part of children's diet of reading material.

Fantasy plays an important part in the lives of children. Young children typically have regular conversations with their pets and stuffed animals, soar on wings above their neighborhoods, go to the ball with Cinderella, sail the seas with Captain Hook, and walk the decks with Captain Crunch. The child's mind is a fertile garden of imagination.

Adults engage in flights of fancy from time to time as well. Who among us has not imagined winning a million dollars in the lottery, scoring the winning touchdown in the Super Bowl, winning a beauty pageant, or writing a best-selling book? It is our dreams, however unrealistic, that often keep us going.

In the world of children's literature, fantasy involves stories of the impossible that readers can still believe. A fantasy is "a highly imaginative story about characters, places, and events that, while sometimes believable, do not exist" (Harris and Hodges 1995, 82). While characters and events remain beyond the realm of possibility, they capture the imagination and bring readers into worlds with limitless possibilities.

As a genre, fantasy traces its roots to the folktales, legends, and myths of ancient peoples. The witch in *Hansel and Gretel*, the giant in *Jack and the Beanstalk,* and the fairy godmother of *Cinderella* are all fantasy creatures who are part of traditional stories. The fox in Aesop's fables talks and teaches us about "sour grapes." The difference between traditional literature and fantasy is that traditional tales spring from the oral tradition of stories passed from generation to generation by word of mouth in a society, while fantasies are original stories that come from the imaginations of known authors. The former is born of the oral tradition and the latter, of the literary tradition.

Fantasy tales composed and told in a traditional style such as those written by Hans Christian Andersen and Rudyard Kipling are known as *literary fantasies.* Other fantasy stories that challenge conventions, such as those written by Roald Dahl and E. B. White, are *modern fantasies.*

FANTASY IN LIFE AND IN LITERATURE

The noted child psychoanalyst Bruno Bettelheim (1978) speaks to the important role that fantasy plays in the lives of children. According to Bettelheim, children have a real need for fantasy, and this need should be satisfied from the early years. The world of make-believe is important to the child. Fantasy not only provides a healthy relief from some of the realities of daily living, but also gives children a sense of hope and encouragement. Children vent some of their frustrations through their vicarious experiences with fantasy characters. Fantasy satisfies the child's need for justice because, in this genre, justice prevails as evil characters get what they deserve.

Fantasy opens a world of wonder to children of all ages. Reality is suspended as children enter strange new worlds that involve demons and dragons, witches and goblins, space travelers and aliens. These tales of enchantment open limitless possibilities and develop the minds of young readers.

Fantasy stimulates children's imaginations. While other literary genres such as historical fiction and traditional folk literature require children to extend their imaginations to "get into" the story, fantasy requires that they extend their imaginative powers a bit further to deal with the characters and events of fantasy. "Fantasy deliberately challenges our perceptions of reality and forces us to explore new, uncharted realms of thought. Not all readers are willing to accept the challenge. But for those who do, the rewards can be manifold" (Russell 1991, 106).

Fantasy can help children develop their powers of creative thinking. It leads children to see the world in new ways and to ask the question "What if . . .?" Fantasy is part of what educates the imagination, and imagination is a prime source of creative invention. "Many scientists have credited scientific advancement to the creative seeds sown by fairy stories, fantasy, and science fiction novels" (Tunnell 1994, 610). Examining the role that fantasy plays in developing children's scientific imaginations, Raymo (1992) notes that fantasy helps open children's minds to new possibilities and thus improves their thinking.

For some children, fantasy provides an escape from reality, an escape that can be cathartic. Children leave their everyday worlds behind as they soar into imaginative realms in which they can vicariously experience adventures in a land of magic. Seeing magic in other worlds can sometimes help children discover the magic in their own lives.

One of the paradoxes of fantasy is that it must be believable. While readers must suspend reality when they enter the world of fantasy literature, they still must be able to believe in what they are reading. Authors of fantasy provide detailed descriptions of scenes and characters in their stories, and characters act in a way consistent with the environments in which they find themselves. Readers become totally absorbed in fantasy, and time ceases to exist when they fall down a rabbit hole as Alice did in her journey to Wonderland or crawl through a door at the back of a wardrobe as the children did in their journey to Narnia.

How do authors make their fantasy believable to readers? Shapiro (1996, quoted in Temple et al. 1998) identifies six devices that writers use: (1) Authors ground their stories in the real world before taking the reader into a secondary world. (2) The narrator or one of the characters assures the reader that events are normal or real. (3) Scenes, characters, and actions are described in vivid detail. (4) The language is consistent with the context of the story. (5) Sometimes, something from the fantastic world is brought back to the real world. (6) Story plots are marked by logic and consistency. In sum, authors draw readers into stories by describing worlds well and by relating events in an internally consistent way.

Early fantasies were not intended for children. Jonathan Swift's *Gulliver's Travels* (1726), for example, was written as a political satire, but the characters that Swift created captured the fancy of young readers. But in later centuries, fantasy has been created specifically for children. For example, Lewis Carroll's *Alice's Adventures in Wonderland* (1865), which chronicled the fantasy adventures of a young girl, was written solely for the purpose of entertaining children. Authors like Beatrix Potter with *The Tale of Peter Rabbit*, A. A. Milne with *Winnie-the-Pooh*, and Pamela Travers with *Mary Poppins* continued the British tradition of writing wonderful fantasy stories for children. American authors like Frank Baum with *The Wonderful Wizard of Oz*, Victor Appleton with his *Tom Swift* stories, and Robert Lawson with *Rabbit Hill* added to the growing body of fantasy literature for children. Today, the content and themes of fantasy continue to appeal to a twenty-first–century audience of children.

Literary Qualities of Fantasy

Writers of children's fantasy lead young readers to accept what is far-fetched and exaggerated, yet they maintain an internal consistency. Settings, although sometimes unusual, are described in such detail that children can reconstruct them in their minds. Characters are well developed and behave in believable ways. Plots are well structured and keep children involved. Themes are appropriate and woven into the natural fabric of the story.

Settings transcend the world of reality. The time can be past, present, or future. The place can be as ordinary as a cabin by the side of a lake or a spaceship hurtling through the galaxy. While some stories take place entirely in a fantasy world, other stories travel back and forth between the real world and the world of make-believe. Whenever and wherever the story takes place, the setting is consistent with the action.

Characters are equally credible. They may be fantastic creatures like the Cauldron Warrior in Lloyd Alexander's *The Book of Three* or they can appear to be ordinary like Jonas's parents in Lois Lowry's *The Giver*. They can be humorous characters like Harry Potter, the surviving son of wizards, who discovers his magical powers in *Harry Potter and the Sorcerer's Stone* by J. K. Rowling. Even when characters have magic powers—the Rats in NIMH, Peter Rabbit, the little engine that could, the unusual creatures of Narnia—they are believable.

The plot is also believable. Actions are logical. Magic is an essential element of the plot, whether that magic is as simple as a spider spinning messages with her web in *Charlotte's Web*, as ordinary as Raymond's being called by his mother in Jules Feiffer's *Meanwhile . . .*, or as dramatic as the power of Aslan the Golden Lion in *The Lion, the Witch, and the Wardrobe*. Plots are well crafted.

Even in fantasy there are lessons to be learned. The themes reflect the same universal ideas present in other forms of children's literature—the value of friendship, loyalty, the overcoming of fear, respect for others, coming of age. Themes can teach important lessons and be the basis of decision making. Themes are typically woven into the story and developed metaphorically through the characters and their actions. While the tone of fantasy is often serious, stories can also be light, airy, and humorous.

Considerable differences exist in terms of literary qualities among different types of fantasy. The protagonists in an animal fantasy like Don Freeman's *Corduroy* behave very differently than do characters in a heroic fantasy like Tolkien's *The Lord of the Rings* trilogy. Plots in high fantasy typically follow the "hero cycle" in which the hero is called to an adventure and enters another world. The hero endures trials, often with the help of a mentor or protective figure. The hero matures and returns home, having conquered evil and discovered his or her true destiny. This type of fantasy involves a quest in which the hero seeks justice and self-fulfillment in serious adventure.

While "unreal" in many ways, fantasy tells truths. It captures emotions and reflects the realities of the human condition. It reflects our aspirations, our dreams, and our fears. It is, in essence, a bridge between the world in which we live and the world that our imaginations are capable of creating.

FACTORS FOR CONSIDERATION

FIVE FACTORS IN EVALUATING FANTASY

In reviewing children's fantasy, here are five factors to look for:

1. What devices does the author use to encourage readers to suspend their belief?
2. Do characters and settings grab the attention and interest of the reader?
3. Is the story logical and consistent within the framework that the author establishes?
4. Does the author draw the reader in and make the reader grow comfortable in the fantasy world that the author creates?
5. Even though the work is fantasy, are there connections to the real world or lessons to be learned from the work?

Flights of Fancy

Through the genre of fantasy, literature takes children on flights of fancy to places beyond their ordinary worlds. They travel back to the past to meet wicked witches and dangerous dragons. They fly into the future to encounter space aliens. Their toys talk. Their bicycles fly. Their pets behave like humans. And all of this remains credible to the young (and older) mind.

Animals, toys and other inanimate objects, unusual characters who live alone or as members of a fantastic family, ghosts and goblins, kings and queens, and wild and crazy events all take center stage in fantasy for children. High fantasy brings the genre to another level, engaging heroes in serious conflicts between good and evil. Science fiction also comes under the umbrella of fantasy literature.

Animal Fantasy

A type of fantasy that has long enjoyed popularity with young children is animal fantasy. Animals come to life and think, feel, talk, and behave like human beings. This technique, known as *anthropomorphism*, is used to make a connection with young (and sometimes old) readers. The animals become humans in animal form, thus teaching lessons about human behavior without being oppressively didactic.

Some of the best known and most loved children's stories of all time are animal fantasies such as Beatrix Potter's classic *The Tale of Peter Rabbit*—along with her other animal stories such as *The Tale of the Flopsy Bunnies* and *The Tale of Squirrel Nutkin*. It has been suggested that Potter's stories were an attempt to break away from the strict upbringing that she endured in a straitlaced Victorian society (Lurie 1990). Whether or not her writing stemmed from rebellion, it has remained a favorite with children for a century. Another classic in this genre is E. B. White's *Charlotte's Web*, in which the life of Wilbur the pig is saved by the enduring friendship of Charlotte the spider.

In addition to old favorite fantasy characters like Michael Bond's *A Bear Called Paddington*, H. A. and Margaret Rey's *Curious George*, and William Steig's mouse dentist *Dr. De Soto* and the unfortunate donkey *Sylvester*, children meet new animal characters such as:

- Poppleton the pig in Cynthia Rylant's *Poppleton Everyday*, which contains three short stories about this lovable character;
- Leon the pig in Christine Davenier's *Leon and Albertine,* in which Leon falls in love with Albertine the chicken and gets advice from all the barnyard animals about how to win her heart;
- the two cool cats in *Chato's Kitchen* by Gary Soto; and
- Miss Spider in David Kirk's *Miss Spider's Tea Party*, in which wary bugs avoid the hospitable spider's invitation to tea, and in Kirk's other Miss Spider books.

Animal fantasies for older children feature more intricate and complex narratives that engage children in thoughtful reading. Stories in this vein that older readers enjoy include the following:

- Kenneth Grahame's classic *The Wind in the Willows*, one of the original animal fantasies, involving woodland animals who form a bond and deal intelligently with the human dimensions of life;
- Robert C. O'Brien's *Mrs. Frisby and the Rats of NIMH*, an intriguing and absorbing story about a group of incredibly intelligent rats who escape from a lab and create their own society; and
- Brian Jacques's *Redwall,* the first in a series of animal fantasies about a troupe of mice who inhabit Redwall Abbey and who fight to protect their home against the onslaught of a succession of enemy animal invaders.

Through fantasy, authors create worlds in which animals retain enough animal traits to separate them from humans yet think and act in human ways. People, when they appear in these stories, typically play minor and incidental roles, like Mr. McGregor in *The Tale of Peter Rabbit*. In some animal fantasies, the relationship between animal and human is closer, usually when children are involved. In Beverly Cleary's fantasies *The Mouse and the Motorcycle* and *Runaway Ralph*, for example, a young boy interacts with a mouse who rides his toy motorcycle while the family is staying in a motel.

The remarkable characters from animal fantasies are often more real, more appealing, and more memorable than the humans in these stories. They are the type of characters that children come to love.

Toys and Other Inanimate Objects

Young children talk to their teddy bears and other stuffed animals all the time, so authors of children's fantasy build stories around this fertile dimension of children's imaginations. Pinocchio, the nineteenth-century wooden puppet who came to life, is well known to children (in part because of Walt Disney's portrayal of this fantasy character). A. A. Milne's *Winnie-the-Pooh* seems so real it's hard to envision that he and his friends in the Hundred Acre Wood are stuffed animals (with the exception of Christopher Robin, of course). In toy fantasies, toys are magically transformed into animated beings who talk, think, live, breathe, and love like humans do.

Other stuffed animals that have come alive in the pages of well-loved children's fantasies include the following:

- *Corduroy* by Don Freeman, the department store teddy bear who longs to be loved and is finally purchased by a little girl and
- *The Velveteen Rabbit* by Margery Williams, the favorite toy that is brokenhearted when placed in the rubbish heap but who later becomes real.

Through anthropomorphism, inanimate objects also do wonderful things. Machines in stories like Hardie Gramatky's *Little Toot*, Virginia Lee Burton's *Katy and the Big Snow*, and Watty Piper's *The Little Engine That Could* are classic stories that children encounter (and believe) early in their lives.

For older readers, Lynne Reid Banks's *The Indian in the Cupboard* and her sequel *The Secret of the Indian* are based on the concept that toys magically come alive and engage in different types of human activities. While both of Banks's books have been criticized because they stereotype the language and behavior of Native Americans (see pp. 52–56), they have captured the imaginations of children and remain popular.

Fantastic Characters

All fantasy includes unusual or peculiar characters, but some stories focus on larger-than-life eccentric human beings. Astrid Lindgren's *Pippi Longstocking*, for example, is a protagonist who enjoys outrageous and far-fetched adventures. Less outrageous than Pippi is Peggy Parish's literal-minded but delightful *Amelia Bedelia*, the maid who follows directions to a ridiculous degree. It's interesting to note that these characters are so well-known that books about them always include their names in the titles: *Pippi in the South Seas* or *Good Work, Amelia Bedelia*. This phenomenon is repeated in other genres with the likes of Anastasia Krupnik or Ramona Quimby, but Anastasia and Ramona live in a world closer to children's realities.

Some of the most popular and famous fantasy characters ever have been created by Roald Dahl. Characters like Willy Wonka in *Charlie and the Chocolate Factory*, James and his companions in *James and the Giant Peach*, and the giant in *The BFG* leave an indelible impression on the minds of those who meet them. The characters and actions that Dahl created are not free of controversy, however. James's parents are eaten by a wild rhinoceros and his aunts (however miserable their behavior) are crushed by a giant peach, and some adults consider such material inappropriate for young minds. Children, however, seem not to be bothered.

Fantasy literature is filled with fascinating characters—the Queen of Hearts and the Mad Hatter in *Alice's Adventures in Wonderland*, Peter and his siblings in *The Tale of Peter Rabbit*, Wilbur and Charlotte in *Charlotte's Web*—who live and breathe in children's imaginations.

Author Profile: ROALD DAHL

One of the most prolific and popular authors of children's fantasy was Roald (pronounced RU-ald) Dahl. Born in Wales of Norwegian parents who had immigrated to England, Roald attended British boarding schools, where he had a generally miserable educational experience.

Dahl did not set out to become an author for children. When he finished high school in 1934, he went to work for an oil company, traveled widely in Africa, and became a pilot in the Royal Air Force during the first years of World War II. Injuries sustained in a plane crash grounded him, however, and he became a military official in the British Embassy in Washington. There he discovered his talent as a writer.

Dahl was invited by *The Saturday Evening Post* to write an article about his early war experiences. The article was so well done that the magazine invited him to write several others. His first novel, *The Gremlins*, was published in 1943, and he continued to write collections of short stories through the 1940s and 1950s.

He married American actress Patricia Neal, and the couple had children. Dahl decided to put on paper stories that he had been telling his children. The result was *James and the Giant Peach*, published in 1961. For nearly three decades, other highly successful children's books followed: *Charlie and the Chocolate Factory* (1964), which was made into the popular movie "Willie Wonka and the Chocolate Factory," *Fantastic Mr. Fox* (1970), *Charlie and the Great Glass Elevator* (1972), *Danny, Champion of the World* (1975), *The BFG* (1982), *The Witches* (1983), and *Matilda* (1988).

All of these stories featured memorable characters (some realistic, some outlandish) engaged in often outrageous adventures to the delight of a young reading audience. While his books sold millions of copies, Dahl's work did not escape the wrath of censors because of violence (the parents of James are eaten by a wild rhinoceros, for example, and his aunts are crushed by the giant peach), racism (for his portrayal of the Oompa-Loompas in the chocolate factory, a description that Dahl revised in later editions of the book), and the occult (for his treatment of witches, for example). He was also criticized for the behavior of some of his characters and for some of his language. However, while his books have been challenged by adults, they have remained at the top of the all-time favorite list for children.

Dahl's writing was not limited to children's books. He wrote several books of short stories (many with sexual overtones and undertones) and a number of screenplays and scripts for Hollywood, including the script for James Bond's "You Only Live Twice" and the screenplay for another popular work of fantasy, Ian Fleming's *Chitty Chitty Bang Bang*. Dahl also wrote some poetry, including *Revolting Rhymes* (1983), humorous tongue-in-cheek rhymed versions of famous fairy tales like *Snow White* and *Cinderella*. He wrote two autobiographies as well: *Boy: Tales of Childhood* (1984) and *Going Solo* (1986).

Roald Dahl died in 1990. He left behind a legacy of characters, settings, and stories that will keep him in the minds and hearts of children for generations to come. Here are some of his other works for children:

George's Marvelous Medicine (1981)

The Twits (1991)

The Minpins (1991)

The Vicar of Wibbleswicke (1991)

Fantasy Families

Children love to be in on a secret, especially when adults are kept in the dark. That's why series involving characters who are unseen by adults have maintained such popularity over the years. Examples are:

- Mary Norton's *The Borrowers,* about a family of miniature people who live in the walls of a house and create their own world with ordinary objects that the full-size residents discard or that the little people "borrow" and adapt for their own use;
- Roald Dahl's *The Minpins*, about a family of little creatures who live in hollow trees in a secret forest; and
- Sylvia Waugh's *The Mennyms*, about a family of life-size rag dolls who "pretend to live and live to pretend" that they are human, hide behind bulky clothes and under umbrellas, and live a full and happy life (not without normal family conflicts and problems) behind the doors of their big old Victorian house at 5 Brocklehurst Court.

LIST OF TEN

GHOST STORIES

Children always love a good ghost story. Fantasy often involves the supernatural, and tales that involve the supernatural often involve ghosts. Here are ten ghost books that children will enjoy and that are written at different reading levels:

The Boggart by Susan Cooper
in which an ancient spirit inhabits an unsuspecting family's computer (Macmillan, 1993)

A Time for Andrew: A Ghost Story by Mary Downing Hahn
a ghost story involving a boy who travels eighty years into the past to meet his great-great-uncle (Clarion, 1994)

The Dark-Thirty: Southern Tales of the Supernatural by Patricia C. McKissack
a collection of ghost stories rooted in the African-American heritage, told during the "Dark-Thirty," the half hour before sunset (Knopf, 1992)

Rollo and Tweedy and the Ghost at Dougal Castle by Laura Jen Allen
an easy-to-read story about finding a ghost that is haunting an old Scottish castle (HarperCollins, 1992)

Even More Short and Shivery by Robert D. San Souci
a collection of ghost stories from around the world told by a master storyteller (Delacorte, 1997)

The Man Who Tricked a Ghost by Laurence Yep
a Chinese folktale about a man who shows his bravery when he meets and outwits a ghost (Troll, 1993)

Chills in the Night: Tales That Will Haunt You by Jackie Vivels
seven ghost stories that explore the emotions of those who participate in Brian's school games (DK Pub. Inc, 1997)

The Doll in the Garden: A Ghost Story by Mary Downing Hahn
a story of two girls who take a ghostly trip back in time when they find an old doll buried in the garden (Clarion, 1989)

The Ghost Comes Calling by Betty Ren Wright
in which a boy tries to clear the name of a ghost who is haunting his vacation cabin on the lake (Scholastic, 1994)

Ghost Abbey by Robert Westall
in which Maggie discovers that ghosts are haunting a dilapidated English abbey (Scholastic, 1989)

Ghost stories sometimes generate controversy, since they deal with supernatural topics that some critics think ought not to be part of the reading diet of young children.

A fantasy family that many elementary school-aged children are familiar with is the Tuck family. Natalie Babbitt's *Tuck Everlasting* is widely used in literature-based language arts programs and is enjoyed by children whether they encounter it in school or at home. Having discovered a water source that prevents people from ever getting old, the family drinks from the magic spring and so will live forever. However, they bear the burden of hiding their secret from other human beings. This engaging story explores moral dilemmas that frequently lead to lively classroom discussion.

Kings and Queens

Royalty remains a popular topic of fantasy written for children. Kids like to "rule" things (as Max ruled the Wild Things in Maurice Sendak's fantasy *Where the Wild Things Are*), and so it's hardly surprising to see kings and queens and their entourages reflected in fantasies written for children. Some of these stories are outrageous and funny. Others are symbolic and touching.

Some children's fantasies that include royal characters follow:

- Antoine de Saint Exupéry's *The Little Prince*, a lovely story full of symbolism and written at multiple levels of meaning;
- Dr. Seuss's *The 500 Hats of Bartholomew Cubbins*, a hilarious parody about a vain king who could not get young Bartholomew to remove his hat in his presence; and
- Jane Yolen's *The Emperor and the Kite*, in which a young princess rescues her father from his enemies.

Stories like Hans Christian Andersen's literary fantasy *The Princess and the Pea* and *The Emperor's New Clothes* feature the foibles and vanities of royalty. Such books have long been popular with young readers.

"Wild and Crazy" Happenings

Fantasy sometimes feeds on the preposterous. Some of the "crazy" ideas that children have find their way into fantasy stories like the following:

- *Cloudy with a Chance of Meatballs* by Judi Barrett, about a town called Chewandswallow where food falls from the sky until the residents have to dispose of a mountain of garbage (which suggests some problem-solving activities);
- *Tar Beach* by Faith Ringgold, the brilliantly illustrated picture book of a girl who soars over Manhattan island (what child has not envisioned him- or herself soaring like a bird above the neighborhood?);
- *Bored—Nothing to Do!* by Peter Spier, in which two brothers construct their own airplane with the odds and ends they find around their house and yard;
- *The Phantom Tollbooth* by Norman Juster, about Milo's journey through an enchanted world featuring phenomenal attractions and told with ingenious language;

- *The Chocolate Touch* by Patrick S. Catling, a modern fantasy based on the Midas legend in which everything the main character touches turns to chocolate.

Stories like these, as preposterous as they may seem to adults, delight children and make their encounters with print enjoyable.

Historical Fantasy

Historical fantasy takes children back in time to experience authentic historical settings and involves supernatural or fantastic forces. "Quite a few historical novels have been successfully disguised as fantasy. These are the 'time slip' novels, in which a contemporary child slips back to some former time, assumes the identity of some person of the past, and remains there for the major part of the book, leading its way around the alien culture" (Rahn 1991, 22). Here are some examples:

- *John Midas in the Dreamtime* by Patrick S. Catling, a story of a young American boy who travels back in time to live among the early Australian Aborigines;
- *A Girl Called Boy* by Brenda Hurmence, in which an African-American girl goes back in time to the mid-1800s and experiences slavery; and
- *The Root Cellar* by Janet Lunn, the story of an orphan girl who has a time-warp experience that takes her back to Canada in the 1860s.

In some time-slip novels, children encounter a variety of supernatural characters:

- **dragons,** in books like Patricia Wrede's *Calling on Dragons* and *Talking to Dragons*, two fantasies involving characters from the enchanted forest who battle evil wizards;
- **witches,** in books like Bill Brittain's *The Devil's Donkey*, in which a boy is changed by a witch into a donkey, and Roald Dahl's *The Witches*, in which a boy and his grandmother foil a plot to turn all the children of the world into mice; and
- **legendary characters from the past,** such as Merlin in T. A. Barron's *The Lost Years of Merlin* (the first book in a Merlin trilogy), in which the Arthurian wizard finds his power and identity, and Maid Marian in Theresa Tomlinson's *The Forestwife*, a fantasy that emerges from the Robin Hood legends.

Like historical fiction, these stories take young readers into the past to help them gain a sense of antiquity. Unlike historical fiction, however, historical fantasies incorporate elements of magic or the supernatural.

High Fantasy

Sometimes called *heroic fantasy*, high fantasy is a more serious type of writing that appeals to older readers. High fantasy involves sophisticated stories with a serious tone that usually involve the struggle between the forces of good and evil, the quest for justice, or the quest for "the boon." Entire worlds may be at stake.

High fantasy rekindles myths, ancient stories, gothic fantasies featuring fear of the unknown, and epic fantasies in which heroic characters engage in high deeds for the purpose of seeking higher rewards. Sometimes, traditional folk literature and fantasy interact, as in Jane Yolen's *Merlin and the Dragons*, in which young King Arthur hears about his mentor-magician's childhood.

The central character in high fantasy is the hero, a strong, virtuous, compassionate, and courageous individual who consistently seeks the good. Heroes may possess unusual, noble characteristics and also represent "everyperson." They often possess magical qualities that enable them to engage in fantastic actions. High fantasy always involves universal values—compassion, courage, selflessness, striving for the "greater good."

High fantasy books that have been popular with young readers for a long time include the following:

- C. S. Lewis's *The Lion, the Witch, and the Wardrobe*, the most popular of the Narnia Chronicles, which sends children into the world of animal characters and into battle between the forces of good and evil;
- J. R. R. Tolkien's *The Hobbit*, in which the Hobbit does battle with the evil creatures of Middle Earth; and
- Lloyd Alexander's *The Book of Three*, the first book in the Prydan Chronicles, a quest series in which a young assistant pig keeper gallantly protects his beloved land from the forces of evil.

The Lion, the Witch, and the Wardrobe, other titles in the Chronicles of Narnia, and *The Hobbit* have acquired a devoted following of young readers who never seem to lose their taste for literature that lets them join a noble quest to conquer evil forces in a fantasy world. Newer works of fantasy—Garth Nix's *Slade's Children*, in which four young fugitives attempt to overthrow the cruel rule of the bloodthirsty Overlords, for example, and Eva Ibbotson's *The Secret of Platform 13*, about a fantasy world under an abandoned railroad platform in London and behind a door that opens for nine days every nine years—will also be enjoyed as children encounter them.

Many works of high fantasy—C. S. Lewis's Chronicles of Narnia, for example, or Lloyd Alexander's Prydain Chronicles—are written as series. While each of the books is a self-contained story, readers who "begin at the beginning" with the first book better understand the works that follow.

Author Profile: C. S. LEWIS

Clive Staples Lewis was born in Northern Ireland in 1898. As a child, he read widely and wrote stories about talking animals, foreshadowing the inhabitants of the kingdoms he would create in his later writing.

Best known for his famous Chronicles of Narnia, C. S. Lewis saw himself as more of a scholar than a children's author. In fact, his children's works were often scoffed at by his more staid academic colleagues at Cambridge University where Lewis taught philosophy and Medieval and Renaissance literature. It was not until he was fifty-two years old that *The Lion, the Witch, and the Wardrobe*, the first of his seven Chronicles of Narnia, was published, in 1950. In that book, children playing in a wardrobe find a door that opens onto a magic land called Narnia. Entering this magic world, they join the White Lion Aslan in a struggle to free Narnia from the spell cast by the evil White Witch.

Other books in this series of high fantasy followed, one a year until the seven books were completed:

Prince Caspian, the Return to Narnia (1951)

The Voyage of the Dawn Trader (1952)

The Silver Chair (1953)

The Horse and His Boy (1954)

The Magician's Nephew (1955)

The Last Battle (1956)

Lewis's fantasies are highly symbolic, reflecting the author's strong religious beliefs and his spiritual journey from atheism to devout Christianity. He communicated his ideas in myth, satire, and fantasy, imbuing them with reason and logic.

Although he is most noted for his writing for children, Lewis also wrote for adults, including *The Screwtape Letters* (1941) and *'Til We Have Faces: A Myth Retold* (1956). His other writing includes theology and literary criticism.

C. S. Lewis died in 1963. He left behind a legacy of high fantasy that continues to shine in the galaxy of literature for children.

SCIENCE FICTION

Science fiction is an imaginative form of literature based on hypothesized scientific advances and imagined technology. Some people make a distinction between *science fantasy* and *science fiction;* the former deals with a world that never was and never could be, while the latter speculates on events that one day may be possible. However, this distinction is neither clearly defined nor universally accepted, so science fiction is included here as part of fantasy.

Science fiction provides a different view of reality. It deals with fantastic events, but the characters and actions are scientifically plausible and technologically possible. It may involve extensions of technology already familiar to readers. Technology replaces magic in these fantasies, but the stories are marked by the same sound literary qualities as other forms of fantasy.

Science fiction had its beginnings in the 1800s with books like Mary Shelley's *Frankenstein* and Jules Verne's classic works *20,000 Leagues Under the Sea* and *Journey to the Center of the Earth*. These nineteenth-century works still fascinate twenty-first-century readers, in part because their themes are timeless and in part because we've seen many of Verne's "fantastic futuristic events and devices" come to actuality in our times.

Science fiction that is popular with children involves space travel and time travel, genetic engineering and social engineering, robots and real human beings. More contemporary works of science fiction that many children have enjoyed include the following:

- Madeleine L'Engle's Newbery Medal winner *A Wrinkle in Time*, about children who travel to the planet Comozotz in search of their scientist father who has been captured by an evil space creature;
- Annette Curtis Klause's *Alien Secrets*, a space adventure/mystery set on a space freighter carrying a twelve year old trying to join her parents on a distant planet;
- Jean Marzollo's and Claudio Marzollo's *Jed's Junior Space Patrol*, an easy-to-read space adventure involving robots (including a robot teddy bear) and space creatures who save planet X-5;
- Robert Silverberg's *Letters from Atlantis*, about a scientist who transforms his mind and travels to the lost continent of Atlantis to report what life was like there 180 centuries ago; and
- Philip Pullman's *The Golden Compass*, in which the heroine must find a way to prevent kidnapped children from being used for scientific experimentation.

Science fiction extends beyond the gimmicks and gadgets of unrealized technology and the fantastic events that occur on some distant planet in the far reaches of outer space. Lois Lowry's compelling Newbery Medal winner *The Giver*, a book that seems destined to become a classic, is the story of a boy who escapes from a utopian futuristic world where all is perfect (and perfectly controlled) but is devoid of memory and emotion. This compelling and complex novel poses deep questions about the effect of future scientific advances on basic human values. A similar utopian theme is explored in Nancy Farmer's *The Ear, the Eye, and the Arm*, about a technologically managed futuristic society set in Zambia whose equanimity is disturbed by the emergence of the vlei people who live in the former city dump.

The continuing popularity of the "Star Trek" television series and the movie *2001: A Space Odyssey*, the revival of the *Star Wars* trilogy, and the regular release of new blockbuster sci-fi movies make it easy to understand the continuing popularity of science fiction in children's literature.

FANTASY IN SCHOOL AND AT HOME

Children often learn to love literature through fantasy. Many lucky children have experienced fantasy stories at home as part of their emerging reading experiences in the preschool years. At bedtime, they have heard "warm and cuddly" fantasy stories like *Corduroy* and *Winnie-the-Pooh*. Classics like *Where the Wild Things Are* and *The Little Engine That Could* have been part of their shared home reading experiences.

Home is the place where parents can talk about the elements of fantasy that worry some of the critics. Parents can explain, for example, that, although Max travels to the scary kingdom of the Wild Things, he returns to a warm meal in the security of his own bedroom. Fantasy make takes young children to distant places, but it also brings them back to the security of their own lives.

Elements of fantasy can remain the subject of parent-child interactions as children get older. Fantasy is full of supernatural happenings, and anything that smacks of the supernatural continues to be the object of criticism and censorship by some groups. The fact that Miss Nelson comes into the classroom dressed as Viola Swamp (a witch) in Harry Allard's very popular and notably inoffensive *Miss Nelson Is Missing* has drawn criticism for including "witchcraft," and classics like *The Wonderful Wizard of Oz* have been targeted for the same reason. Such issues can be the subject of fruitful discussion when fantasy is shared in the home.

In school, fantasy takes its place alongside other types of children's literature in a classroom program. Classic fantasy picture books such as Munro Leaf's *The Story of Ferdinand* ought to be part of the reading experiences of young children. Fantasy children's books make ideal material for reading aloud to children in the lower grades. The sheer fun of hearing about Deborah Howe's and James Howe's *Bunnicula* (the rabbit-turned-Dracula) or about the adventures of the Big Friendly Giant as he tromps around, whizpopping all over the place, makes young children laugh.

Fantasies like Beverly Cleary's *The Mouse on the Motorcycle* can be enjoyed by children independently as free reading material or can be used in the classroom as vehicles for directed reading-writing-thinking lessons and for other activities described in Chapter 13. Fantasy can be part of a theme in reader's workshop. Popular titles like *The Giver* or *Tuck Everlasting* can be used as core books for directed reading activities. Fantasy stories can be the focus of critical-thinking, creative-thinking, and problem-solving discussions. In sum, fantasies can be included in the full spectrum of reading activities that characterize literature-based instruction in any classroom.

Special Perspectives on Children's Literature

MAKING IT REAL
by Audrey A. Friedman

Real isn't how you are made. . . .
It's a thing that happens to you.
(from *The Velveteen Rabbit* by Margery Williams)

The other evening I watched the movie "Close Encounters of the Third Kind." As a childlike ET with an ethereal and engaging smile escorted a mesmerized Richard Dreyfuss on an adventure certainly out of space and time, I marveled enviously at the genius of Stephen Spielberg in making this fantasy so real to his audience. Vivid natural settings, intense light shows, and eerie repetitions of hypnotic music invited us to suspend disbelief and venture into a world of fantasy where travel and imagination are timeless and boundless, a world where dreams are so real that we can see them, touch them, smell them, hear them, and even taste them, a world where in the comfort of our living rooms we can experience a personal, close encounter of the third kind.

Fantasy is among the most sophisticated, engaging, and challenging children's literature. Experts note that modern fantasy helps children expand their curiosity, become more astute observers of the world around them, learn to be sensitive to differences, and open their minds to unusual possibilities. Margery Williams's *The Velveteen Rabbit*, E. B. White's *Charlotte's Web*, Madeleine L'Engle's *A Wrinkle in Time*, Roald Dahl's

James and the Giant Peach, and David Wiesner's picture fantasy *Tuesday* entice the reader into imaginary worlds featuring a raggedy rabbit, a sagacious arachnid, a tentacled beast, a gargantuan grasshopper, and acrobatic amphibians. These writers and artists transport readers into a place and time where the impossible is possible. Like Spielberg, they make the unimaginable real!

Despite the genius of Williams, White, L'Engle, Dahl, Wiesner, Spielberg, and others, not all readers delightfully embark on a mother ship, ready to roam the galaxies. For some people, reading fantasy is a sometimes difficult and often frustrating misadventure. Sometimes, a teacher must help children "make it real." How do we help students understand elaborate description, decipher profound metaphors, identify with complex characters, discern subtle nuances of text—all which enable them to suspend disbelief and become fantasy adventurers? **How do we help our students make it real?** In the *Velveteen Rabbit*, Williams provides the answer: The Skin Horse tells the rabbit that only when the boy loves him for a long time will he become real. The boy rubs and kisses the rabbit, takes him for wheelbarrow rides and picnics, builds fairy huts for him, and finally utters the magic words "He's real!" When the boy sees, touches, hears, and smells the rabbit, he makes the rabbit real. We need to help readers see, touch, hear, smell, and even taste the setting, the time, the event, and the fantasy; we need to help students make the words real.

How do we help students visualize the warm and wonderfully soft healing haunches and tentacles of Aunt Beast? Preservice English teachers eyed me incredulously as I passed out large sheets of newsprint, scented markers, crayons, colored pencils, and sketching pens and instructed them to draw Aunt Beast. In forty-five minutes, I learned about my students' ability to read, comprehend, organize, lead, listen, share, collaborate, and suspend disbelief. I watched as they made Aunt Beast real for themselves. Collaborative drawings captured the rhythmic and flowing tentacles, the most delicate fur imaginable, and the soothing music that flowed from the "Beast." Some students remarked that they had always disliked high fantasy; it was too hard, too confusing, too abstract. But they commented that drawing Aunt Beast was fun; it made science fiction easier to understand, made the text accessible, made the words real.

Did Charlotte really write, "some pig" and "terrific!" in her wondrous web? Was Wilbur right? Did Charlotte really have hairy legs? Twenty fourth graders set out on a mission to learn the truth, and in the web-strewn hedges around the school yard, they found the answer. Children witnessed the handiwork of many Charlottes. Arachnid's fabric glistened patterns, letters, and even words. More astute observers saw snowflakes, and some who ventured close enough even saw hairy legs! Charlotte's wisdom and words were real indeed.

Imagine bags of magic, an enormous peach, a grasshopper larger than a boy! How preposterous! The giggles and delight as second graders designed and decorated bags of magic and intoned accompanying chants paled only in comparison with their screeches as they studied preserved specimens of "Texas-sized" grasshoppers, earthworms, centipedes, and garden spiders (the very large variety) and living, breathing, flying lady bugs. Like naturalists, the children counted legs, spots, and segments, opened wings, noted nubs, rings, and large eyes, talked about the variety of colors, how the creatures moved, what they ate, and where they lived, and occasionally complained about the wretched smell of formaldehyde. They compared what they saw to what they read and concurred that Roald Dahl had done his homework. James's friends were larger than life perhaps but definitely real.

Giant bullfrogs on flying lily pads are another story. Or are they? Wiesner's vivid greens, rich violets, hot yellows, and deep indigos convince the reader to accompany acrobatic amphibians on a visual sojourn. This time, students created text, engendering personal, fantastic tales in which the frog-characters had names, personalities, likes, dislikes, and, most of all, attitude. As fantasy writers, they made the visual text real.

Modern fantasy weaves intricate plots, magical settings, contagious characters, and universal themes into tapestries that delight and challenge the reader. Fantasy literature invites all children to embark on strange, mysterious, and unusual adventures. All that readers need to bring to the task are natural curiosity and a desire to dream. Madeleine L'Engle has remarked that we should never underestimate the capacity of a child for a wide and glorious imagination. All children are capable of exploring the mysterious, strange, and powerful worlds that fantasy literature offers. All children can become fantasy adventurers if we can excite their senses to see, hear, smell, touch, and even taste the words—if we can help them "make it real!"

Audrey A. Friedman is a member of the faculty of the School of Education at Boston College, where she teaches courses in literacy and teacher research.

Teachers often find curriculum connections with fantasy, such as between ecology and *Cloudy with a Chance of Meatballs*, contemporary space travel and *A Wrinkle in Time*, or social issues and *The Giver*. Even without these specific curriculum connections, however, fiction has its own value as part of children's encounters with literature. A major purpose of using fantasy in the classroom is to help children enjoy books as they become critical readers.

High fantasy offers especially fertile ground for studying literary elements in stories. Plots are clear. Characters are well defined. Settings are vividly described. Themes are apparent. As children compare Tolkien's Middle Earth and Lewis's Narnia, for example, they can develop an understanding of settings.

Science fiction offers specific classroom applications. Children can compare the science they read in science fiction with the science they study in class. They can learn to separate fact from fiction by reading about invented futuristic worlds.

Modern fantasy and science fiction offer as many springboards to writing as do other forms of children's literature. Children can create their own fantasy stories about their pets and favorite toys or imagined experiences. They can invent their own worlds and write stories about their adventures in these worlds. They can write follow-ups to the stories they read; for example, what happens to Jonas when he escapes into the real world at the end of

The Giver? (In fact, sequels have been written to a number of children's fantasies; for example, Jane Leslie Conly wrote *Rasco and the Rats of NIMH* as a sequel to her father's *Mrs. Frisby and the Rats of NIMH*).

Opportunities for classroom reading and writing activities related to fantasy are limited only by the imagination of the teacher and the time available in a usually full school schedule.

CONCLUSION

Fantasy has been called "fundamentally the most important kind of story" to share with children (Tunnell 1994, 606). It is an essential quality in children's lives as well as an important characteristic in their reading materials.

Fantasy characters endure. Characters that we met as children—Mr. Toad of Toad Hall in *The Wind in the Willows*, the Scarecrow and the Tin Woodsman in *The Wonderful Wizard of Oz*, the Mad Hatter and the Queen of Hearts in *Alice's Adventures in Wonderland*—stay with us for life. Some fantasy characters have become franchises. The images of Peter Rabbit and Winnie-the-Pooh continue to appear on T-shirts, tableware, coloring books, CD-ROMs, and other merchandise.

While fantasy may demand more of readers than do other genres of children's literature, it also rewards the reader in significant ways. Most important, fantasy leads children deeper into the love of literature.

Questions and Activities for Action and Discussion

1. List the advantages and disadvantages of using fantasy as part of a literature-based reading program in the classroom. Give examples of the type of activities and questions you would use with *Cloudy with a Chance of Meatballs* in the lower grades and *Tuck Everlasting* in the upper grades, for example. Or focus specifically on science fiction and describe how you might use this genre as part of a literature-based reading program. How, for example, might you relate science fiction to subjects that children are studying?

2. E. B. White's *Charlotte's Web* is an enormously popular book. How do you account for its popularity? On a sheet of paper make two columns, one headed "Could Happen" and one headed "Couldn't Happen." Use these categories to explain how the author made the story believable to his readers.

3. Anthropomorphism—the assigning of human qualities to animals or inanimate objects—is a technique that fantasy writers for young children often use. Examine a picture book by an author like William Steig or Bernard Waber and list how the author/illustrator made objects and animals act and think like human beings. Explain why this technique is so popular with children.

4. Fantasy often involves ghosts, goblins, witches, and otherworldly creatures. Critics often argue that supernatural topics have no place in the lives of children. Prepare a position statement challenging or supporting this point of view.

5. High fantasy involves its own unique qualities and characteristics. Report on how these qualities are manifest in works like C. S. Lewis's *The Lion, the Witch, and the Wardrobe* or Lloyd Alexander's *Book of Three*. How do these qualities differ from the fantasy elements of television programs like "The X-Files"?

CHILDREN'S & YOUNG ADULT BOOKS CITED IN THIS CHAPTER

Alexander, Lloyd. 1964. *The Book of Three*. New York: Dell.

Allard, Harry. 1977. *Miss Nelson Is Missing*. Boston: Houghton Mifflin.

Andersen, Hans Christian. 1973. *The Princess and the Pea*. Illustrated by Paul Galdone. New York: Seabury. (Other editions available.)

_____ 1982. *The Emperor's New Clothes*. New York: Harper & Row. (Other editions available.)

Babbitt, Natalie. 1975. *Tuck Everlasting*. New York: Farrar, Straus and Giroux.

Banks, Lynne Reid. 1985. *The Indian in the Cupboard*. New York: Doubleday.

_____ 1990. *The Secret of the Indian*. New York: Avon.

Barrett, Judi. 1978. *Cloudy with a Chance of Meatballs*. New York: Macmillan.

Barron, T. A. 1996. *The Lost Years of Merlin*. New York: Philomel.

Baum, Frank. 1900. *The Wonderful Wizard of Oz*. New York: World. (Other editions available.)

Bond, Michael. 1960. *A Bear Called Paddington*. Illustrated by Peggy Fortnum. Boston: Houghton Mifflin.

Brittain, Bill. 1981. *The Devil's Donkey*. Illustrated by Andrew Glass. New York: Harper & Row.

Burton, Virginia Lee. 1943. *Katy and the Big Snow*. Boston: Houghton Mifflin.

Carroll, Lewis. 1963. *Alice's Adventures in Wonderland*. New York: Macmillan. (Other editions available.)

Catling, Patrick S. 1979. *The Chocolate Touch*. Illustrated by Margot Apple. New York: Morrow.

_____ 1986. *John Midas in the Dreamtime*. Illustrated by Jean Loener. New York: Morrow.

Cleary, Beverly. 1965. *The Mouse and the Motorcycle*. Illustrated by Louis Darling. New York: Morrow.

_____ 1970. *Runaway Ralph*. Illustrated by Louis Darling. New York: Morrow.

Conly, Jane Leslie. 1986. *Rasco and the Rats of NIMH*. Illustrated by Leonard Lubin. New York: Harper & Row.

Dahl, Roald. 1961. *James and the Giant Peach*. Illustrated by Nancy Ekbolm Burket. New York: Knopf.

_____ 1972. *Charlie and the Chocolate Factory*. Illustrated by Joseph Schindelman. New York: Knopf.

_____ 1982. *The BFG*. Illustrated by Quentin Blake. New York: Putnam.

_____ 1983. *The Witches*. Illustrated by Quentin Blake. New York: Farrar, Straus and Giroux.

_____ 1991. *The Minpins*. Illustrated by Patrick Benson. New York: Viking.

Davenier, Christine. 1997. *Leon and Albertine*. New York: Orchard.

de Saint-Exupéry, Antoine. 1943. *The Little Prince*. New York: Harcourt.

Farmer, Nancy. 1994. *The Ear, the Eye, and the Arm*. New York: Orchard.

Feiffer, Jules. 1997. *Meanwhile . . .* New York: HarperCollins.

Fletcher, Susan. 1993. *Dragon Kyn*. New York: Antheneum.

Freeman, Don. 1968. *Corduroy*. New York: Viking.

Geisel, Theodore (Dr. Seuss). 1937. *The 500 Hats of Bartholomew Cubbins*. New York: Vanguard.

Grahame, Kenneth. 1940. *The Wind in the Willows*. Illustrated by E. H. Shepard. New York: Scribners.

Gramatky, Hardie. 1939. *Little Toot*. New York: Putnam.

Howe, Deborah, and James Howe. 1983. *Bunnicula*. Illustrated by Leslie Morrill. New York: Atheneum.

Hurmence, Brenda. 1982. *A Girl Called Boy*. Boston: Houghton Mifflin.

Ibbotson, Eva. 1998. *The Secret of Platform 13*. New York: Dutton.

Jacques, Brian. 1968. *Redwall*. New York: Philomel.

Juster, Norman. 1961. *The Phantom Tollbooth*. Illustrated by Jules Feiffer. New York: Random House.

Kirk, David. 1994. *Miss Spider's Tea Party*. New York: Scholastic.

Klause, Annette Curtis. 1993. *Alien Secrets*. New York: Delacorte.

Lawson, Robert. 1944. *Rabbit Hill*. New York: Viking.

Leaf, Munro. 1936. *The Story of Ferdinand*. Illustrated by Robert Lawson. New York: Viking.

L'Engle, Madeleine. 1962. *A Wrinkle in Time*. New York: Farrar, Straus and Giroux.

Lewis, C. S. 1961. *The Lion, the Witch, and the Wardrobe*. New York: Macmillan.

Lindgren, Astrid. 1959. *Pippi in the South Seas*. Illustrated by Lois S. Glanzma. New York: Viking.

Lowry, Lois. 1994. *The Giver*. Boston: Houghton Mifflin.

Lunn, Janet. 1983. *The Root Cellar*. New York: Scribners.

Marzollo, Jean, and Claudio Marzollo. 1982. *Jed's Junior Space Patrol*. Illustrated by David Rose. New York: Dial.

Milne, A. A. 1981. *Winnie-the-Pooh*. New York: Dell. (Other editions available.)

Nix, Garth. 1997. *Slade's Children*. Illustrated by Leo Dillon and Dianne Dillon. New York: HarperCollins.

Norton, Mary. 1953. *The Borrowers*. New York: Harcourt. (Several more books in this series.)

O'Brien, Robert C. 1971. *Mrs. Frisby and the Rats of NIMH.* New York: Macmillan.

Parish, Peggy. 1980. *Good Work, Amelia Bedelia.* Illustrated by Lynn Sweat. New York: Avon.

Peterson, John. 1967. *The Littles.* New York: Scholastic. (Several more books in this series.)

Piper, Watty. 1929. *The Little Engine That Could.* New York: Putnam.

Potter, Beatrix. 1903. *The Tale of Peter Rabbit.* New York: Dover (Other editions available.)

_____ 1903. *The Tale of Squirrel Nutkin.* New York: Dover. (Other editions available.)

_____ 1903. *The Tale of the Flopsy Bunnies.* New York: Dover.

Pullman, Phillip. 1996. *The Golden Compass.* New York: Knopf.

Rey, H. A., and Margaret Rey. 1941. *Curious George.* Boston: Houghton Mifflin.

Ringgold, Faith. 1991. *Tar Beach.* New York: Crown.

Rowling, J. K. 1998. *Harry Potter and the Sorcerer's Stone.* New York: Scholastic.

Rylant, Cynthia. 1998. *Poppleton Everyday.* Illustrated by Mark Teague. New York: Scholastic.

Sendak, Maurice. 1963. *Where the Wild Things Are.* New York: Harper & Row.

Silverberg, Robert. 1990. *Letters from Atlantis.* New York: Atheneum.

Soto, Gary. 1995. *Chato's Kitchen.* Illustrated by Guzan Guevara. New York: Putnam.

Spier, Peter. 1978. *Bored—Nothing to Do!* New York: Doubleday.

Steig, William. 1982. *Dr. DeSoto.* New York: Farrar, Straus and Giroux.

Tolkien, J. R. R. 1938. *The Hobbit.* Boston: Houghton Mifflin.

Tomlinson, Theresa. 1995. *The Forestwife.* New York: Orchard.

Waugh, Sylvia. 1990. *The Mennyms.* New York: Avon. (Several more books in this series.)

White, E. B. 1952. *Charlotte's Web.* New York: Harper & Row.

Wrede, Patricia. 1993. *Calling on Dragons.* San Diego: Harcourt Brace.

_____ 1993. *Talking to Dragons.* San Diego: Harcourt Brace.

Williams, Margery. 1969. *The Velveteen Rabbit.* Illustrated by William Nicholson. New York: Doubleday.

Yolen, Jane. 1995. *Merlin and the Dragons.* Illustrated by Li Ming. New York: Dutton.

_____ 1993. *The Emperor and the Kite.* Illustrated by Ed Young. New York: Putnam.

REFERENCES

Bettleheim, B. 1978. *The Uses of Enchantment.* New York: Knopf.

Harris, T. L., and R. E. Hodges, eds. 1995. *The Literacy Dictionary: The Vocabulary of Reading and Writing.* Newark, Del.: International Reading Association.

Lurie, A. 1990. *Don't Tell the Grown-Ups: Subversive Children's Literature.* Boston: Little Brown.

Rahn, S. 1991. An Evolving Past: The Story of Historical Fiction and Nonfiction for Children. *The Lion and the Unicorn* 15:1–26.

Raymo, C. 1992. Dr. Seuss and Dr. Einstein: Children's Books and Scientific Imagination. *The Horn Book* 68:560–567.

Russell, D. L. 1991. *Literature for Children: A Short Introduction.* New York: Longmen.

Temple, C., M. Martinez, J. Yokota, and A. Naylor. 1998. *Children's Books in Children's Hands: An Introduction to Their Literature.* Boston: Allyn and Bacon.

Tunnell, M. O. 1994. The Double-Edged Sword: Fantasy and Censorship. *Language Arts* 71:606–612

CHAPTER 6

TRADITIONAL FOLK LITERATURE

uch children's literature springs from the folk tradition of bards and storytellers inspiring and entertaining their audiences, orally transmitting the values of their cultures to the next generation through story. From this oral tradition come the folktales and fairy tales, myths and legends, tall tales and fables that children continue to love today.

THIS CHAPTER

- examines the background and characteristics of folk literature;

- describes various forms of traditional literature that today's children enjoy; and

- suggests ways in which this literature can be used at home and in school to promote children's love of literature.

From ancient times, people have gathered in grand halls and in humble dwellings, in caves and clearings, in temples and at campsites to hear storytellers recount tales for those gathered around them. In some ancient societies, these bards and storytellers had priestlike powers, and they enjoyed prestige second only to that of the chief or king. They told about the heroic adventures of ancient ancestors, about how the world came to be, and about the gods who created it. Their stories conveyed the values that needed to be passed from elders to the young. The accumulation of these stories is traditional folk literature.

Folk literature had its origin in the oral tradition in preliterate societies, and it developed independently of the written word. Traditional stories, poems, and songs were passed by spoken word from generation to generation for centuries before they were ever written down.

Castle tales—stories about Beowulf and King Arthur, for example—centered on the great deeds and chivalrous actions of nobility. *Cottage* tales were shared by the common folk who relied on their imaginations and the power of magic to transcend their daily grind of poverty and servitude; examples are, "Hansel and Gretel" and "Jack and the Beanstalk."

In the seventeenth and eighteenth centuries, people began to write down these stories that had been passed along by word of mouth. Charles Perrault, a courtier in the court of Louis XIV, gathered a collection of French fairy tales to amuse the members of the court, a collection that included such classic stories as "Cinderella" and "Puss in Boots." But perhaps the best-known gatherers of traditional European folk literature were the Brothers Grimm.

Jacob and Wilhelm Grimm were scholars whose primary interest was language, not literature. Grimm's Law is a linguistic principle that accounts for sound shifts that occurred in the evolution of Germanic languages (including English) into their modern forms. But the Grimms have become far more famous for their contributions to folk literature than to language study.

In their efforts to study authentic spoken language, the Grimms collected stories from many people, most of them peasants. The stories, including "Hansel and Gretel" and "Snow White," were meticulously transcribed and published in two collections of *Nursery and Household Tales*, in 1812 and 1815 respectively.

An interest in folklore continued to spread throughout Europe. A Norwegian collection of folktales published in 1851 contained such stories as "The Three Billygoats Gruff" and "Henny Penny." An English compilation about fifty years later included "The Three Bears" and "The Three Little Pigs."

As these books were published, they became exceedingly popular with young and old alike. While they reflected the oral tradition and were repeatedly passed along by word of mouth, they were preserved in written form from the 1700s and 1800s on.

Special Perspectives on Children's Literature

WHO OWNS THE FAIRY TALE?
by Bonnie Rudner

In his edited collection of feminist fairy tales *Don't Bet on the Prince*, Jack Zipes tells a story, "A Fairy Tale for our time." In this tale, a little girl named Steffie awakens, having had a horrible nightmare:

> The fairy tale had been kidnapped,
> and if she did not find it by nightfall,
> there would be silence, eternal silence,
> like the dreadful dark that surrounded her room.

Steffie knows that her dream is true and she sets out on a quest to rescue the fairy tale.

Zipe's use of the word *kidnapped* in the story is very interesting and revealing. The word *kidnap* means to snatch something from its rightful place. If we assume that the fairy tale has been kidnapped, we are faced with a number of questions:

- Who has kidnapped the fairy tale?
- What is/was its rightful place?
- Who owned the fairy tale to begin with?
- Have fairy tales been corrupted by Disney? The religious right? Feminists? Freudians? The fabulists?
- Should we, like Steffie, be trying to rescue the fairy tale?

In the original fairy tale, when little Snow White, seeking refuge in the forest, awakens from her nap, she is confronted by the owners of the cottage, "seven dwarfs who dug and delved in the mountains for ore." They are friendly, and she agrees to cook and clean for them in return for shelter and protection. The dwarfs are also indistinguishable from one another. In Disney's 1937 movie *Snow White and the Seven Dwarfs*, the dwarfs are seven distinct characters, each with his own name.

Disney's Little Mermaid is no longer, like Andersen's, a victim of her own desires who willingly bargains with the sea witch. In Disney's version, Ariel is tricked by a malevolent Ursula, who is merely using the mermaid to avenge herself against King Triton. The entire conflict is worked out as a confrontation between good and evil. And, of course, true love wins out in the end. Children who read Andersen's version, having fallen in love with Disney's Ariel, often feel very disappointed.

Walt Disney was not the first artist to adapt the narrative of the fairy tale for his own purposes. Charles Perrault deliberately eliminated Little Red Riding Hood's rescue by the hunter in his collection because he wanted to demonstrate to his audience that once a girl succumbs to a wolf's temptation, she will be forever ruined:

> Little Girls, this seems to say,
> Never stop along the way.
> Never trust a stranger friend;
> No one knows how it will end. . . .

In the feminist version of "Little Red Riding Hood," "The Company of Wolves," Angela Carter explores another option for little girls. Her character deliberately chooses to stray from the path in order to encounter the wolf. The wolf says, "All the better to eat you with, my dear. The girl bursts out laughing; she knew she was nobody's meat."

In the "Merseyside Snow White," a Marxist version of the tale, the heroine does not marry her prince. Instead, she leads her people in a rebellion against the queen, and they decide to keep the diamonds they have been mining for the greedy monarch.

Are these and other altered versions of fairy tales to be considered "kidnapped"? The answer for teachers and parents who use fairy tales is a pragmatic one. Many of the new versions of the tales have become part of the fairy tale canon. Who owns the fairy tale? No one and everyone. These great narratives have evolved throughout the course of human history, and we can expect them to continue to be changed, enhanced, and corrupted. Tanith Lee, in her story of an evil Cinderella, knows that an old story can also be a new story:

> Possibly you have been told this story?
> No? Oh, but I am certain that you have
> heard it in another form.

As teachers and parents, we can and should present many versions of these stories. In this way, children can begin to appreciate how rich and creative a source of materials the fairy tales are.

Bonnie Rudner, a member of the faculty of the English Department at Boston College, specializes in children's folklore and fantasy.

REFERENCES:

1. Brothers Grimm. 1972. "Little Snow-White." *The Complete Grimm's Fairy Tales.* New York: Pantheon.
2. Carter, Angela. 1979. "The Company of Wolves." *The Bloody Chamber and Other Stories.* New York: Penguin.
3. Lee, Tanith. 1983. "When the Clock Stikes." *Red as Blood or Tales from the Sisters Grimmer.* New York: DAW.
4. Perrault, Charles. 1969. "Little Red Riding Hood." *Perrault's Fairy Tales.* Mineola, NY: Dover.
5. Zipes, Jack. 1986. "A Fairy Tale for Our Times." *Don't Bet on the Prince.* London: Methuen.

THE APPEAL OF FOLK LITERATURE

The appeal of folk literature is timeless. Twenty-first-century children delight in stories recounted in Aliki's *The Gods and Goddesses of Olympus* in the same way their counterparts did in ancient Greece, although the characters in these stories were more integral to the lives of ancient Greek youngsters. The appeal of folk literature may be found in its essential literary elements—plot, setting, character, and theme—which are simple. They had to be. Stories were shared orally among a largely uneducated, unsophisticated audience whose attention had to be held during the telling. Plots don't have many extraneous details. Characters remain uncomplicated. Settings are general. Themes are simple. Also, the language is direct and easy to understand and remember; otherwise, it would not have survived retellings across generations.

Plot

Folk literature has clear structure with well-defined, economical plots. Plots are simple, ordered, and well designed, and they move quickly since the storyteller had to immediately capture and maintain the interest and attention of an audience. Traditional story structure progresses directly from a beginning, through elements that build toward a classic climax, to a speedy resolution. Conclusions quickly follow the climax, leaving no loose ends or unattended details. "The quest begins, the tasks are initiated and performed, the flight gets under way, and obstacles of every kind appear, with the hero or heroine reduced to despair or helplessness or plunged into more and more perilous action. This is the heart of the story—action that mounts steadily until it reaches a climax, when the problem or conflict will be resolved one way or the other" (Sutherland 1997, 177).

Repetition is a basic element in the plot of folk literature. Events often occur in sets of three. Language is often repeated as well:

> *Who's that tromp, tromp, tromping over my bridge?*

Repeated language often rhymes:

> *Little pig, little pig, let me come in.*
> *Not by the hair of my chinny chin chin.*
> *Fee, fi, fo, fum, I smell the blood of an Englishman.*

In the oral tradition, this linguistic style lends itself to repeated and dramatic retelling.

In folk literature plots, good invariably triumphs over evil. Snow White awakens and marries the prince. Hansel and Gretel are reunited with their loving father. Red Riding Hood is saved by the woodsman. This reliable, uncomplicated, and uncompromising outcome has enormous appeal for children.

Campbell (1968) describes a type of plot often characteristic of folk literature as the *hero cycle*. In the hero cycle, the protagonist is called from home to an adventure. He or she quickly faces a challenge and meets it with cleverness or courage. Helpers may assist the hero in entering the place where the object of the quest is found. In this "Land of Adventures" the hero often faces death and rebirth. A hero may meet an authority figure who confirms his or her worthiness or a father figure who poses a challenge. The hero successfully captures or wins the "boon," the object of the quest, and then returns home.

The hero cycle can be found in folk literature that ranges from such simple stories as "Jack and the Beanstalk" to the great Greek epic *Odysseus*. The cycle is not limited to folk literature alone; it can be found in fantasies such as C. S. Lewis's The Chronicles of Narnia.

In most folk literature, contrasts are clear. A David and Goliath type of conflict may be found in both plot and characters—the young Hansel and Gretel versus the old witch, tiny Jack versus the huge giant, the kind and gentle children of Lir versus their cruel and evil stepmother. This type of conflict, in which justice always triumphs, adds to the appeal of folk literature for children.

Setting

Setting consists of the time and place in which a story occurs. In folk literature, time and place are quickly established. Action happens "Once upon a time," which, because of its implied distance in time, allows for anything to happen—animals can talk, giants can roam the land, and magic can occur. In folk literature, time speeds by: four hundred years pass with a single phrase.

Place is equally simple and briefly sketched: a dark forest, an opulent palace, a grassy meadow. Often, settings reflect the cultures from which the stories come: Imagine the dark German woods through which Hansel and Gretel traveled, the glittering ball that Cinderella attended at the palace of the French "Sun King," the vast expanses of mother Russia in the Baba Yaga tales, or the great American wilderness that Paul Bunyan tamed.

Character

Folk literature typically uses stock characters—the evil stepmother, the kindly king, the poor beggar. The characters are *flat;* that is, they are one-dimensional, completely good or entirely evil. They may possess combinations of qualities like kindness, strength, or cruelty, but they are not well developed.

Physical descriptions of characters are rarely provided. With the exception of a hero being identified as "fair haired," people in traditional folk stories are characterized mostly in terms of their inner qualities. Most of this characterization is conveyed through their actions.

Author Profile: ROBERT D. SAN SOUCI

Robert D. San Souci is a talented and versatile teller of tales. The settings of his stories range from the United States to Armenia and from early American history to the Middle Ages.

San Souci was born and raised in the San Francisco area. Before he could read or write, he delighted in listening to stories, which he embellished as he repeated them for family and friends. He received a bachelor's degree from St. Mary's College and did graduate work at the University of California at Hayward. He supported himself by writing magazine articles and newspaper stories and by working in bookstores and for publishing companies.

In 1978, San Souci published his first children's book, which was a work of folk literature and a Blackfoot Indian Tale, *The Legend of Scarface.* In this story a man is alienated by others because of a birthmark on his face. The book received critical acclaim and garnered several awards. Other works of folk literature for children followed: *Song of Senda* (1981), an Eskimo myth; *The Talking Eggs* (1988), a Creole folktale from the American South; *The Little Seven-Colored Horse* (1991), a Spanish-American folk story;

The House in the Sky (1996), a Bahamian folktale; *The Hired Hand* (1997), an African-American story set in Virginia in the 1700s; and *A Weave of Words* (1998), an Armenian folk tale of adventure and love.

San Souci has retold Arthurian legends in *Young Guinevere* (1996), *Young Lancelot* (1996), and *Young Arthur* (1997). He has also retold the Medieval legend of *Nicholas Pike* (1997), a merman and the woman who falls in love with him. And he has produced several *Short and Shivery* volumes of ghost stories.

San Souci has a unique ability to bring old stories to life for young readers. He doesn't illustrate his own stories but he works closely with his illustrators, who include his brother Daniel, David Shannon, and the award-winning Brian Pinkney.

Robert D. San Souci lives in California where he has several "works in progress" for children, adolescents, and adults. Here are some of his other works:

Sukey and the Mermaid (1992)

Sootface: An Ojibwa Cinderella Story (1994)

The Faithful Friend (1995)

The Samurai's Daughter (1997)

The Legend of Fa Mulen (1998)

Theme

The themes found in traditional folk literature are the basic, unchangeable needs and concerns of human beings, such as justice, wisdom, and love. Virtue is rewarded; evil punished. The weak prevail over the strong, the wise over the foolish. Faithfulness and truth are requited; cruelty and treachery are reviled. These themes typically reflect what is valued in a culture: courage, strength, wisdom, mercy, persistence.

The universal appeal of folk literature is evident in the parallel stories found in many different cultures. People in different parts of the world share emotions and respond in similar fashion to human conditions. While a particular tale will be told in a cultural context, its narrative patterns and themes will resonate with people unconnected in space and time. It's not surprising, then, to see similar stories develop in different cultures. The European Cinderella has her Chinese counterpart in *Yeh-Shen*, her Algonquin counterpart in *The Rough-Faced Girl*, and her Irish male equivalent in *The Irish Cinderlad*, tales retold by Ai-Ling Louie, Rafe Martin, and Shirley Climo respectively. Stories found in many different cultures from different parts of the world are sometimes called *migratory tales*.

Some experts believe that the appeal of folk literature is that it meets basic psychological needs. Stories reflect a child's need for love, nurturing, and affirmation. Folktales and fairy tales provide safe vehicles for dealing with deep emotions or unconscious drives. The noted child psychoanalyst Bruno Bettelheim (1975) interpreted fairy tales—along with nursery rhymes and other forms of children's literature—as the vehicle through which children deal with their unconscious fears and insecurities. Hansel and Gretel represent the fear of abandonment and separation from family; the three little kittens who lost their mittens embody children's fear of losing something valuable. Children are relieved when the brother and sister are reunited with their loving father and reassured when the kittens are ultimately rewarded with their pie.

Not everybody, however, subscribes to this psychoanalytic spin. While traditional folk literature may indeed fulfill basic human needs, these needs are social as well as psychological. These stories fulfill a need for entertainment, and many believe they should be enjoyed rather than analyzed. Traditional folk literature is often full of violence and sexism, and this is a concern to some critics. These elements, like the fantasy and magic found in these stories, need to be viewed within the context of the source of the original tales.

The original, authentic versions of most fairy tales are generally more violent than their modern versions. Blackbirds peck out the eyes of Cinderella's mean sisters. At Snow White's wedding, the evil queen is forced to dance in red-hot iron shoes until she falls over dead. Current versions typically smooth the rough edges found in earlier versions, and punishments in contemporary tales are far less severe. Comparing different endings of familiar stories can provide an interesting exercise in critical thinking for children.

Many folk stories are sexist—Snow White is carried away by the Prince and kings capriciously give their daughters in marriage as rewards for deeds well done.

Such sexism, just like the magic and fantasy of folk literature, must be viewed within the social and historical context of the original tellings of these tales. While we live in times that are more enlightened in many ways, these aspects of folk literature give teachers, librarians, and parents interesting points of discussion as they share folk literature with their children. Moreover, some contemporary retellings of traditional folk tales feature women and girls in proactive roles; examples are *Cinder Edna* by Ellen Jackson and *Princess Smartypants* by Babette Cole. James Finn Gardner's tongue-in-cheek *Politically Correct Bedtime Stories* offers more "enlightened and liberated" versions.

Each culture has its own folk tradition—consider the Baba Yaga tales from Russia, the legendary Irish hero Fin McCool, the British legend of King Arthur and the Knights of the Round Table which is derived from old tales of earlier Celtic heroes, and the Scandinavian tales of the mighty supernatural powers Thor and Woden. From Africa, Latin America, Asia, and the Middle East, folk stories perpetuate local legendary figures, account for creation and other natural events, and celebrate human accomplishments.

In comparison to many other countries, the United States is a young nation. Nevertheless, it has developed its own collection of folk literature, featuring characters like Paul Bunyan and John Henry who reflect the values and experiences of a people challenged with expansion into vast territories. American Indians had a rich heritage of folk literature that had developed independently of such traditions in other parts of the world long before Europeans first set foot on the shores of North America. African Americans have developed a special and unique folk tradition based on their experiences in the Americas. Folk literature from different American groups adds to the rich montage of traditional literature for children to enjoy.

TYPES OF FOLK LITERATURE

Traditional folk literature includes folktales and fairy tales, myths and legends, fables, epics, and tall tales. Also included are ballads and folk songs passed from generation to generation in the oral tradition.

FACTORS FOR CONSIDERATION

EVALUATING TRADITIONAL FOLK LITERATURE

In reviewing traditional folk literature for children, here are five factors to look for:

1. Does the story appeal to children's imaginations and their sense of right and wrong?
2. To what extent does the work help children understand aspects of the values of the culture from which the story came?
3. Does the literature suggest possibilities for extending children's imaginations and creative thinking?
4. Do illustrations make the story more interesting and understandable for children?
5. Is this the type of story the child will want to hear again and again, or the type of story that he will want to retell to others?

Folktales

Folktales are narratives that have been retold within a culture for generations. Different versions of the same story may emerge as storytellers put their own twists and embellishments on their tales.

Single, illustrated retellings of folktales are among the best known and most loved picture books that young children encounter:

- *The Mitten*, the popular Ukrainian folktale about an animal who makes a winter home in a child's lost mitten, has been retold and illustrated in picture books by Jan Brett and by other illustrators as well;
- *Strega Nona*, a folktale from the Italian tradition about a character with a cooking pot that can produce unlimited amounts of pasta, has been retold and illustrated by Tomie De Paola; and
- *Stone Soup*, the French story about the clever traveler who shows an old lady how to make soup from a stone, has been retold and illustrated by Marcia Brown. (A Jewish version of the same folktale is *Bone Button Borscht* by Aubrey Davis.)

Just as ancient storytellers often added their own embellishments to their retellings, modern authors and illustrators sometimes take literary license by adding their own unique touches to a story.

Classic folktales from different cultures have also been adapted in picture book form for young children:

- *The Children of Lir*, the oft-told Irish story of four beautiful children turned into swans by a jealous stepmother, retold by Sheila MacGill-Callahan;

- *East of the Sun and West of the Moon*, the classic Norwegian folktale about a prince who is saved by the perseverance of the woman who loves him, retold by Kathleen and Michael Hague; and

- *The Seven Chinese Brothers*, about seven brothers who use their unique talents to bring about the downfall of the evil Emperor, retold by Margaret Mahy.

Folk literature from all cultures shares certain characteristics. In *cumulative tales*, such as "The Gingerbread Man" and *One Fine Day*, the Armenian folktale for which Nonny Hogrogian won a Caldecott Medal, in which a fox approaches a series of characters in an attempt to have his severed tail reattached, the same action and language are repeated over and over.

In traditional folk stories from many cultures, animals think, act, and talk like humans. Such stories like "Puss in Boots" and "Henny Penny," are called *talking beast tales*.

Another type of folk literature is the *pourquoi tales*. *Pourquoi* is the French word for *why*. Early people mystified by the world around them, told pourquoi tales to explain natural phenomena. Modern pourquoi tales include the retelling of a well-known African story in *Why Mosquitoes Buzz in People's Ears* by Verna Aardema, the Navajo account of *How the Stars Fell into the Sky* by Jerrie Oughton, and *Musicians of the Sun*, Gerald McDermott's account of how the Lord of the Night frees the musicians who are held captive by the Sun. Pourquoi tales have long been popular with children. (More examples of pourquoi tales are presented in the section on myths.)

Another type of folk literature particularly popular with young children is the *trickster tale*. In these stories, the main character outsmarts everyone else and achieves goals through wit, cunning, and trickery. The character may be a mischief-maker or helpful. Often, tricksters are small and weak characters who prevail over stronger and more powerful forces. In some stories, they set out to trick others only to be tricked themselves. (Most youngsters are familiar with this scenario as replayed through the "Roadrunner" cartoons.)

Like all folk literature, trickster tales come from the oral tradition. They "contain reference to a society's values: what the people value; what they laugh at; what they scorn, fear, or desire; and how they see themselves" (Young and Ferguson 1995, 491).

Trickster tales emanate from many cultural traditions:

- from the African-American tradition come tales of Brer Rabbit, as recounted in Julius Lester's *The Tales of Uncle Remus: The Adventures of Brer Rabbit* and other stories that have delighted children for a long time;

- from the West African tradition come tales of Anansi the spider recounted in such books as *Anansi and the Talking Melon* by Eric A. Kimmel. (When West Africans were taken as slaves to the Caribbean, they brought their Anansi stories with them, often adapting the stories to the climate and the environment of the people's new land.);

- from the tradition of the Plains Indians come stories about the Coyote, portrayed by Gerald McDermott in *Coyote: A Trickster Tale from the American Southwest* and by Paul Goble in *Iktomi and the Berries* about Iktomi, a man who sometimes disguised himself as a coyote. (Different American Indian groups had their own trickster characters such as Raven, who appears in Gerald McDermott's *Raven: A Trickster Tale from the Pacific Northwest*.);

- from the American South come tales of the trickster Lapin, the clever and cunning Cajun rabbit, recounted in books like *Why Lapin's Ears Are So Long and Other Tales from the Louisiana Bayou* by Sharon Arms Doucet; and

- from Ireland come stories about leprechauns, fairy creatures also known as "little people" or "wee folk" who live in the otherworld under the earth and who protect hidden pots of gold, portrayed by Linda Shute in *Clever Tom and the Leprechaun* and Teresa Bateman in *Leprechaun's Gold.*

Trickster tales can be found in the literature of Asian countries, in which the trickster takes the form of a human or a clever animal who achieves his or her ends through wit and guile. Indeed, the trickster has long been part of the traditional stories of people the world over.

Trickster tales are fun. They're entertaining. But they also provide an effective springboard into multicultural literature. Young and Ferguson (1995) suggest many different ways to use trickster tales with children, including readers theater, drama, puppetry, storytelling, art, and bookmaking. They also provide a rich bibliography of trickster tales from around the world.

Author Profile: GERALD MCDERMOTT

You'd hardly know it by looking at his work, but author/illustrator Gerald McDermott didn't start his career working on children's books. He was a filmmaker, creator of animated films like *Anansi the Spider* (1972) and *The Stonecutter* (1975).

McDermott began attending art classes in Detroit at the age of four. At nine, he participated in a radio show, where he acted out folktales and legends for a live audience. After graduating from high school (where he had spent more time working on out-of-school cinematographic projects and television than on school work), he attended Pratt Institute in New York.

It was for a school project at Pratt that the young artist created his first animated film, *The Stonecutter*, based on a Japanese folktale. He then moved to Europe, where he began making his films into children's books. Much of his work has focused on the folk literature of Native Americans. His *Arrow to the Sun: A Pueblo Indian Tale* (1974) won him a Caldecott Medal. Other Native American stories that he retold and brilliantly illustrated include *Coyote: A Trickster Tale from the American Southwest* (1994) and *Raven: A Trickster Tale from the Pacific Northwest* (1993).

McDermott also writes mythical stories from other cultures. *The Voyage of Osiris* (1997) tells how the Egyptians saw the miracle of new growth after the flooding of the Nile, and *Zomo the Rabbit* is a trickster tale from Africa. He has written two Irish tales, *Daniel O'Rorke* (1988) and *Tim O'Toole and the Wee Folks* (1990). *Musicians of the Sun* (1997) is a hero tale in which the Lord of the Night sends Wind to free four musicians, whom the Sun is holding prisoner, so that they can bring joy to the world.

Gerald McDermott uses his brilliantly colorful art style and understanding of the cultures of origin of his stories to bring traditional folk literature to children.

African-American, Native American, Asian-American, and Latino writers have made many contributions in retelling children's folktales from diverse cultures. African-American folktales reflect the African tradition. Tony Fairman's *Bury My Bones but Keep My Words: African Tales for Retelling* is a collection of traditional folktales selected from several different African cultures. John Steptoe's *Mufaro's Beautiful Daughters* and Verna Aardema's *Bringing the Rain to the Kapiti Plain: A Nandi Tale* are among scores of African folktales that are popular with children from all ethnic groups. The trickster Anansi remains a popular fixture in folk literature for children, and so does his wife Aso whose clever schemes are used to trick the Sun God in Verna Aardema's *Anansi Does the Impossible: An Ashanti Tale*.

Another body of folk literature developed in communities of slaves on early plantations. The distinctive style of storytelling that characterized traditional oral tales about Brer Rabbit and other characters is preserved in such books as *Flossie and the Fox* by Patricia McKissack, *The Talking Eggs: A Folktale from the American South*, Robert D. San Souci's retelling of the Creole folktale, and *The Hired Hand: An African American Folktale*, a story also by Robert D. San Souci set in the 1700 in Virginia.

Folktales from Latino cultures include the following:

- *The Lady of Guadeloupe* by Tomie De Paola, a Mexican tale with religious content;
- *The Rooster Who Went to His Uncle's Wedding*, a cumulative tale from Cuba retold by Alma Flor Ada; and
- *Night of the Stars*, an Argentinean pourquoi tale about how the stars came to the sky, by Douglas Gutierrez and Maria Fernandez Oliver.

Multiple Latino folktales are presented in collections such as John Bierhorst's *The Monkey's Haircut and Other Stories Told by the Maya*, which recounts the folktales of the ancient Maya, and Nicholasa Mohr's *The Song of el Coqui and Other Tales of Puerto Rico*, which contains folk stories from three groups: the indigenous Tainos, the African people who were brought to the island as slaves, and the Spanish who invaded the island.

Many picture books, such as the following, retell folktales from Asian countries:

- *The Crystal Heart: A Vietnamese Legend*, a touching tale retold by Aaron Shepard;
- *The Boy of the Three-Year Nap*, a traditional trickster tale retold by Diane Snyder;
- *The Crane Wife* by Odds Bidken, the sad story of a humble sailmaker and a beautiful woman;
- *Liang and the Magic Paintbrush* by Demi, based on an ancient Chinese legend about the traditional universal theme of good triumphing over evil; and
- *Nine-in-One, Grr! Grr!* by Blia Xiong, a folktale from the Hmong people of Laos.

The rich store of traditional folk literature from Native American cultures includes myths and legends, creation tales and trickster tales, and other stories that reflect traditions that developed long before Europeans set foot on North American soil. Many of these traditional stories have been retold by contemporary children's authors:

- Tomie De Paola, whose *The Legend of Bluebonnet* is a Comanche tale about the importance of living in harmony with nature;
- Paul Goble, whose Buffalo Woman recounts the important relationship the Plains Indians maintained with the buffalo;

- Douglas Wood, whose *Rabbit and the Moon* is an adaptation of a Cree pourquoi tale about how the crane got its long legs; and
- Michael J. Caduto and Joseph Bruchac, whose collection *Keepers of the Earth* contains stories from many different Native American nations.

Helping children come to enjoy this rich tradition of multicultural folk literature is another way of helping them understand and appreciate the peoples from which the stories come.

"Literary" Folktales.   Traditional literature has its roots in the oral tradition and so the original authors are unknown. The work of some authors who have since written in the folk style, however, has achieved a level of popularity that matches that of famous folk and fairy tales. Such *literary folktales* do not come from the cultural tradition of an ancient people and are written by known authors. However, they are crafted in the form of traditional literature, featuring strong conflict, little character development, fast-moving plots, and the triumph of good over evil (or of common sense over foolishness). Among the best known literary folktale author is the Danish writer Hans Christian Andersen.

Andersen's "The Ugly Duckling," "The Emperor's New Clothes," and "The Little Mermaid" earned international recognition and have appeal that remains strong today. Andersen's stories are available in collected works such as *Fairytales* illustrated by Arthur Rackham and in individual picture books:

- *The Ugly Duckling*, retold by Lillian Moore and illustrated by Daniel San Souci;
- *The Emperor's New Clothes*, illustrated by Virginia L. Burton; and
- *The Little Mermaid*, illustrated by Charles Santore.

Many other editions of these popular stories by Hans Christian Andersen are available to delight young children and enrich their lives. Contemporary authors have written variations of Andersen's stories. Jane Yolen makes frogs the central characters in *King Long Shanks* (a takeoff on "The Emperor's New Clothes"), and Jon Scieszka's ugly duckling grows up to be a really ugly duck in *The Stinky Cheese Man and Other Fairly Stupid Tales*.

Another author of literary folktales is Rudyard Kipling. After serving as a British soldier in colonial India, Kipling wrote his own stories in the traditional folk style for children. Kipling's *The Elephant Child, How the Rhinoceros Got Its Skin, How the Camel Got Its Hump*, and other "Just So" pourquoi stories have remained popular with children and continue to inspire creative writing in the classroom.

Fairy Tales

Fairy tales, stories that have imaginative characters and magical events, are an integral and popular form of traditional folk literature. Sometimes called *wonder tales*, these stories typically feature enchanted creatures with supernatural powers. First told primarily by and for adults, fairy tales have become, for the most part, the exclusive property of young children. For lack of a better term, *fairy tale* has also been applied to other types of nursery stories like "Goldilocks and the Three Bears," stories that have nothing to do with fairies or supernatural beings.

LIST OF TEN

A MULTICULTURAL SAMPLER OF COLLECTIONS OF TRADITIONAL FOLKTALES

Many folktales from different cultures are available in picture books and story books for children. Here's a "United Nations Selection" of folk literature collections that can be used as read-alouds or as independent reading in school or at home:

The People Could Fly: American Black Folktales by Virginia Hamilton, illustrated by Leo and Diane Dillon
a classic collection of African-American Folk Literature (Knopf, 1985)

The Rainbow People by Laurence Yep, illustrated by David Wiesner
twenty Chinese folktales retold by a famous author and illustrated by a talented artist (Harper & Row, 1989)

Cut from the Same Cloth: African American Women of Myth, Legend, and Tall Tale by Robert D. San Souci, illustrated by Brian Pinkney
a collection of folk literature with female characters (Putnam, 1993)

BoRabbit Smart for True: Folktales from the Gullah by Patricia Jaquith, illustrated by Ed Young
four tales that originated from the islands off the Georgia coast (Philomel, 1981)

Folktales from India: A Selection of Oral Tales from Twenty-Two Languages by A. K. Ramanujan
a rich collection of stories from many different cultures in India (Pantheon, 1991)

The Girl Who Dreamed Only Geese and Other Tales of the Far North by Howard Norman, illustrated by Leo and Diane Dillon
a collection of ten Inuit folktales from northern Canada (Harcourt Brace, 1997)

The Golden Carp and Other Tales from Vietnam by Lynette Dyer Vuong, illustrated by Manabu Saito
six folktales from Vietnam (Lothrop, Lee and Shepard, 1993)

Korea's Favorite Tales and Lyrics by Peter Hyun, illustrated by Dong-il Park
a collection of Korean folk stories and poems (Tuttle, 1998)

Tales for the Telling by Edna O'Brien, illustrated by Michael Foreman
twelve Irish folk and fairy stories from the Emerald Isle (Pavilion, 1986)

A Bag of Moonshine by Alan Garner, illustrated by Patrick James Lynch
a collection of twenty-two stories from various parts of the British Isles (HarperCollins, 1986)

Collections of folktales that trace their origins to other parts of the globe—Italy, Russia, Norway, and other countries—are available to support and enrich the multicultural dimension of curriculum through traditional literature.

Magic is a central feature of fairy tales. Trolls, witches (both good and evil), fairy god-parents, and other magical characters feature prominently in these stories. Fairy tales have wonder and romance, and the characters—at least the good ones—live happily ever after. As with other forms of traditional folk literature, fairy tales have no known authors and have been passed on (and often embellished and altered) by repeated retellings from generation to generation.

For hundreds of years, traditional fairy tales like "Cinderella," "The Three Little Pigs," and "Little Red Riding Hood" have been the most frequently told stories to young children. Among the authors and illustrators who provide today's illustrated versions of these stories are

- Paul Galdone, who has illustrated such classics as *Puss in Boots*, *The Little Red Hen*, and *Rumpelstiltskin;*
- Glen Rounds, who has illustrated *The Three Little Pigs and the Big Bad Wolf* and *The Three Billygoats Gruff;* and
- Paul Zelinsky, who has illustrated (among other fairy tales) *Rumpelstiltskin* and whose classic oil paintings for *Rapunzel* won the 1998 Caldecott Medal.

As is the case with traditional folk tales, classic stories are often retold in different ways. Hayward (1998) details the multiple retellings of "The Gingerbread Boy," including Paul Galdone's classic retelling, Eric A. Kimmel's more recent retelling, Jim Aylesworth's *The Gingerbread Man,* which invites children's participation in a read-aloud experience, Barbara Baumgartner's simple version geared to beginning readers, and Richard Egielski's *The Gingerbread Boy* who leads a chase through New York City. Hayward also finds connections in *The Gingerbread Rabbit* by Randall Jarrell.

Altered versions of fairy tales abound, including the following parodies:

- Jon Scieszka's *The True Story of the Three Little Pigs* (written under the pseudonym A. Wolf), in which the wolf is portrayed as the innocent victim of a plot;
- Diane Stanley's engaging and entertaining *Rumpelstiltskin's Daughter*, in which the miller's daughter marries Rumpelstiltskin; and
- Michael Emberley's *Ruby*, the story of Red Riding Hood in an urban setting with animal characters.

These spoofs often provide an entertaining change of pace for children and adults alike.

Myths

A myth is "a traditional tale common to members of a tribe, race, or nation, usually involving the supernatural and serving to explain some natural phenomenon" (Hornstein 1956, 309). Myths combine science and religion. They typically involve gods and goddesses,

LIST OF TEN

A MULTICULTURAL SAMPLER OF CINDERELLA STORIES

Cinderella stories are found in many cultures. Some of these stories date from ancient times, while others have been created more recently. Here are ten of these stories:

Mufaro's Beautiful Daughters: An African Tale by John Steptoe
> *in which one of Mufaro's two daughters is chosen to marry the King because of her kindness (Lothrup, 1987)*

The Rough-Faced Girl by Rafe Martin, illustrated by David Shannon
> *an Algonquin story about a girl whose face is scarred from sitting by the fire and who, rather than her stepsisters, recognizes and marries the Invisible Being (Putnam, 1992)*

Ye-Shen: A Cinderella Story from China by Ai-Ling Louie, illustrated by Ed Young
> *about a girl, forced by her cruel stepmother to do the housework, who finds magic bestowed on her by a magical fish (Philomel, 1982)*

The Egyptian Cinderella by Shirley Climo, illustrated by Ruth Heller
> *a tale dating to the days of the pharoh about a girl who finds happiness (Crowell, 1989)*

Princess Furball by Charlotte Huck, illustrated by Anita Lobel
> *a Grimm brothers' story in which the heroine wins the prince because of her own independence and clever resourcefulness rather than her beauty (Greenwillow, 1989)*

The Korean Cinderella by Shirley Climo, illustrated by Ruth Heller
> *the story of Pear Blossom, who is chosen by the magistrate to be his wife (HarperCollins, 1993)*

The Golden Sandal: A Middle Eastern Cinderella Story by Rebecca Hickox, illustrated by Will Hilderbrand
> *about Maha, who despite the machinations of her evil stepmother, marries the man of her dreams (Holiday House, 1998)*

The Irish Cinderlad by Shirley Climo, illustrated by Loretta Krupinski
> *about Becan who, rejected by his stepmother and stepsisters, rescues and marries a princess (HarperCollins, 1996)*

The Way Meat Loves Salt: A Cinderella Tale from the Jewish Tradition by Nina Jaffe, illustrated by Louise August
> *from Eastern Europe, about a rejected daughter who finds happiness and acceptance when she wins the hand of the rabbi's son (Holt, 1998)*

Smoky Mountain Rose: An Appalachian Cinderella by Ann Schroeder, illustrated by Brad Sneed
> *a Cinderella story set in the Smoky Mountains and retold in Appalachian language— "One night, while Rose was fryin' a mess o' fish, the trapper, he starts lookin' dejected-like" (Dial, 1997)*

This list by no means exhausts the various versions of Cinderella stories that children can enjoy as part of their reading experiences.

powerful forces in the universe. In Greek myth, Zeus ruled the sky and Poseidon the sea. Each culture has its own mythological characters to account for the mysteries of the world.

Traditional myths often explain what was unfathomable to early people—the origin of the world, the creation of humans, the order of the universe, the rising and setting of the sun, the turning of the seasons. These myths were known as *pourquoi tales* and are available to today's children in the following books:

- *The Orphan Boy* by Tololwa Mollel, a Masai story that explains the positioning of the planet Venus;

- *How the Sea Began: A Tiano Myth* by George Crespo, about the origin of the ocean; and

- *Dragonfly's Tail* by Kristina Rodanas, a Zuni myth that warns of the drastic results if people take the earth's bounty for granted.

How the world came to be has fascinated humankind from the beginning, and every culture has its own myth about the creation of the world. Many of these stories have been gathered by Virginia Hamilton in *In the Beginning: Creation Stories from Around the World*.

With the development of science and the spread of writing, the term myth came to mean "the unreliable lore of unsophisticated people" (Temple, Martinez, Yokota, and Naylor 1998, 138). Yet myths persist as an enchanting part of children's literature, amusing and entertaining and pushing children to think about the world in different ways.

Fables

Fables are short allegorical narratives presenting a moral or a lesson to be learned. Most fables have a compressed didactic style and contain a clearly stated moral. Although a prominent part of children's literature, fables were not, in antiquity, written for the young. They were composed and recounted by adults, often with satirical intent.

Most of our classical fables are attributed to the ancient Greek slave Aesop who supposedly lived over 600 years before the birth of Christ. So little is known about Aesop himself that some people insist that he was only an invention of later generations, not unlike Mother Goose. Others maintain that Aesop was a real person and provide historical facts about his life. Whatever the truth, classical Greeks attributed almost all the fables they knew to Aesop.

A typical Aesop fable is a brief anecdote that describes a single incident designed to teach some rule of wise conduct. The characters are typically animals who behave like humans; in fact, they have been called "humans in disguise." They are each assigned a stereotypical quality: The ass is stupid, the fox cunning, the lamb meek and mild. The moral is typically drawn from common human experiences and is easy to understand. The behavior of the animal concretizes abstract principles. The tortoise who defeats the rabbit teaches us that slow and steady wins the race; the crow who loses his cheese when he tries to sing speaks to the danger of vanity; the city mouse and country mouse remind us that striving for comfort and elegance may come with a price.

There are numerous editions of Aesop's fables, illustrated in various styles:

- *The Caldecott Aesop*, a facsimile of the 1883 edition by Alfred Caldecott, with original illustrations by Randolph Caldecott;

- *Twelve Tales from Aesop*, retold and illustrated by Eric Carle; and
- *Aesop's Fables*, illustrated by Safaya Salter.

Children can also enjoy fables in picture books such as the following:

- *Town Mouse, Country Mouse*, retold and illustrated by Jan Brett;
- *Milly and Tilly: The Story of a Town Mouse and a Country Mouse*, a British adaptation by Kate Summers;
- *The Hare and the Tortoise*, retold and illustrated by Carol Jones; and
- *The Boy Who Cried Wolf*, adapted by Ellen Schechter.

As with other forms of folk literature, Aesop's fables have not escaped tongue-in-cheek treatment by Jon Scieszka and Lane Smith whose *Squids Will Be Squids* modernizes and pokes fund at the tales.

Other fables that children can enjoy are Arnold Lobel's *Fables*, a collection that won the Caldecott Medal, and Dennis Nolan's retelling of the classic *Androcles and the Lion*, the story of a runaway slave who befriends a lion.

Fables can be appreciated at many different levels—the story itself can be enjoyed, the art with which the fable is told may be appreciated, and the way a fable reflects a truth may be admired. However, as for the didactic dimension of fables, "the lessons are frequently too sophisticated and are therefore lost on the audience. . . . Most adult and child readers prefer that didacticism be saved for school texts, how-to-books, and Sunday sermons" (Russell 1991, 29). In other words, children enjoy fables as stories but frequently may miss the message.

Legends

While all folk literature has a legendary quality, *legend* is a general term applied to tales handed down first in oral and then in written form that are popularly believed to be true even though their accuracy has not been verified. Whereas forms of folk literature such as epics and fairy tales tend to be purely imaginary, legends tend to have some roots in history. Whether King Arthur or Robin Hood really lived is a question that historians continue to debate. It is likely however, that, at the very least, such characters are either composites or greatly enhanced versions of actual figures.

Many legends have flourished about English King Arthur and his Knights of the Round Table, and several books for children and young adults recount the life and adventures of this legendary British monarch. Jane Yolen tells about Arthur's childhood in *The Dragon's Boy*, and Michael Morpurgo retells events from Arthur's life in *Arthur, High King of Britain*. The many adventures of Arthur's fascinating magic mentor Merlin are recreated for young adult readers by T. A. Barron in *The Lost Years of Merlin* and *The Seven Songs of Merlin*. Robert D. San Souci has written about Arthurian figures in *Young Arthur* and *Young Guinevere*. No less popular are the legends of Robin Hood, told by Ann McGovern in *Robin Hood of Sherwood Forest*.

In addition to chronicling Arthurian legends, Michael Morpurgo has retold the legend of the Irish pirate-queen in *The Ghost of Grania O'Malley*. The story of this fascinating and powerful woman who commanded a fleet of pirate ships that prowled the seas off the west coast of Ireland in the 1500s and who challenged Queen Elizabeth face-to-face is also retold in the picture book *The Pirate Queen* by Emily Arnold McCully. While Grania O'Malley actually lived, her deeds are recounted in legendary proportions.

Each culture has its own heroes—real and imagined—whose lives and deeds entertained and inspired people to perpetuate legends about them. Myths and legends from around the globe have been gathered by Geraldine McCaughrean in *The Bronze Cauldron* and in *The Silver Treasure: Myths and Legends of the World*. Collections such as these contain hours of reading material that foster the love of literature in children.

Tall Tales

Similar to legends but more lighthearted are tall tales, exaggerated accounts of the deeds of legendary local heroes. Most American children are familiar with the deeds of Paul Bunyan, the prodigiously powerful lumberjack who could fell whole forests with a few swings of his mighty ax and who ate flapjacks the size of skating rinks. Steven Kellogg has brought Paul Bunyan alive, along with other American legendary folk heroes like Pecos Bill and Johnny Appleseed, in a series of tall tales for children. Julius Lester and Jerry Pinkney have done the same for *John Henry*, the legendary African American with the mighty hammer. Anne Issacs has added some gender balance with *Swamp Angel*, an original tale about a female character who saves the people of Tennessee from Thundering Tarnation, a bear so big that his hide covers the state of Montana.

Tall tales are marked by outlandish exaggeration and humor. Their larger-than-life characters tickle children's fancy.

Author Profile: VERNA AARDEMA

It seems that Verna Aardema, storyteller extraordinaire, was destined from a young age to be a famous writer for children. Born the third of nine children in the little town of New Era, Michigan, Aardema learned to read as a very young child and discovered early in her life that she loved to write and tell stories. As a child, she became known as a bookworm. Her special place for reading and writing was a swamp behind her house where she would also go to tell tales to the neighborhood children.

Aardema attended college in Michigan, where she won several awards for her writing. After college, she taught and she wrote for a local newspaper. In 1973, she retired to become a full time storyteller and writer, and she developed a special talent for retelling the ancestral folk tales of Africa.

Aardema's name burst onto the children's literature stage when her retold West African tale *Why Mosquitoes Buzz in People's Ears*, illustrated by Leo and Diane Dillon, won the 1976 Caldecott Medal as the most distinguished picture book published in the United States the previous year. Her *Borreguita and the Coyote* (1980) is also an award winner.

Aardema has continued to retell folk literature from Africa in books such as *Bringing Rain to the Kapiti Plain: A Nandi Tale* (1981) and *What's So Funny, Ketu? A*

Nuer Tale (1982). She has also retold trickster tales like *Anansi Finds a Fool* (1992) and *Rabbit Makes a Monkey out of Lion* (1989).

Aardema researches her topics thoroughly. She often visits with African students studying in the United States, and they share with her legends from their native lands. Her stories capture the spirit of their cultures of origin, and her language preserves the folk nature of the tales she retells. As with so much traditional literature, many of her stories contain lessons for children.

Verna Aardema lives with her husband in Florida, where she continues to write and spends time telling stories in schools, colleges, and libraries.

Here are other African folktales that Verna Aardema has retold:

The Lonely Lioness and the Ostrich Chicks (1996)

Jackal's Flying Lesson: A Khoskhoi Tale (1995)

The Crocodile and the Ostrich: A Tale from the Akambba of Kenya (1993)

Traveling to Tondo: A Tale of the Nkundo of Zaire (1991)

Epics

Epics are lengthy accounts of the adventures of legendary superheroes. Rooted in mythology, these great tales embody the ideals of a culture through the great feats of their protagonists.

Epics—such as the Greek *Odyssey*, the British *Beowulf*, the French *Song of Roland*, and the Spanish *El Cid*—are not typically part of children's reading fare in the elementary grades. They are usually reserved for study in high school and beyond. However, Rosemary Sutcliff has adapted some of these stories for elementary readers in books like *Dragon Slayer*, an adaptation of *Beowulf*, and *Black Ships Before Troy: The Story of the Iliad*, which retells the famous Greek epic.

All epics have heroes, and *hero tales* are enjoyed by children and young adults. Rosemary Sutcliff's *The Hound of Ulster* describes the deeds of the Irish warrior-hero Cuchulain, and David Wisniewski tells about Sundiata, the African hero-king, in *Sundaita: Lion King of Mali*.

Ballads and Folk Songs

Music has always played an important role in human gatherings. Out of musical traditions come folk songs and ballads that entertain, inform, and inspire.

Like all folk literature, ballads and songs were transmitted orally, and most were modified in the process. Generally, the authorship is unknown. Subject matter is vivid and concrete, with little attention given to character analysis or setting. Lines and stanzas are repeated. People often chanted such songs to help them do rhythmical work such as hauling nets, sawing wood, and pounding spikes.

Ballads and songs, like other forms of folk literature, reflect the values and the experiences of the people who sang them. The popular American ballad "I've Been Working on the Railroad," for example, recounts the labors of those who built the tracks that connected the two coasts of a new nation. *Follow the Drinking Gourd*, adapted in story form by Bernardine Connelly, is based on the old ballad about the Underground Railroad that led so many slaves to freedom prior to the Civil War.

Traditional music that has been made into picture books—such as Nadine Wescott's *Skip to My Lou*, Pete Seeger's adaptation of the South African folksong *Abiyoyo*, Woody Guthrie's folksong *This Land Is Your Land*, and some of John Langstaff's songs—offer opportunities to integrate music and children's literature into the classroom program.

FOLK LITERATURE AT HOME AND IN SCHOOL

Traditional folk literature has a prominent place in the reading diet of children at home and in school. The fairy tales that are part of this genre are as much a part of children's early encounters with books as is Mother Goose. Before they come to school, children—if they are fortunate—will be familiar with Snow White and Cinderella, will have clapped to the rhythm of "The Gingerbread Man," and will have imitated the gruff voice of the troll as the three billy goats tromp across his bridge.

All forms of folk literature can be shared and discussed in the home environment. Folktales such as *The Legend of Bluebonnet* or fables such as "The Town Mouse and the Country Mouse" provide a wealth of wonderful material for lap reading. Young children enjoy a fast-moving adventure, whether the story is about the antics of Wile E. Coyote in Saturday morning cartoons or found in the pages of *The Tale of Rabbit and Coyote* by Tony Johnson which weave tales about the traditional tricksters into a Mexican context. Tall tales and myths make wonderful bedtime stories. In short, opportunities abound for using the multiple resources of folk stories at home during the preschool years and well beyond.

When they come to school, children encounter folk literature in more structured and sequenced learning experiences. Traditional folk literature evolved from the oral tradition, so it lends itself especially well to oral language activities in the classroom. Retelling favorite tales gives students opportunities for developing oral language proficiency. Folk stories like Esphyr Slobodkina's beloved *Caps for Sale* or Nonny Hogrogian's cumulative tale *One Fine Day* lend themselves to creative dramatics that children thoroughly enjoy. Children can discuss the themes of folk stories such as the theme that beauty is only skin deep in Rafe Martin's *The Rough-Faced Girl*, some of the lessons embedded in Aesop's fables, or issues like sexism and violence in traditional folk stories.

Folk literature can be an integral part of reading instruction. Simple versions of stories like Janet Stevens's presentation of the Grimm brothers' *The Brementown Musicians*, for example, can be read by children in instructional settings or independently. For vocabulary development, word walls can be made from new words encountered in the folk stories that children read. Children can be challenged to find words to describe characters like Manyara and Nyasha, the two sisters in *Mufaro's Beautiful Daughters*. Children can make story maps based on the clearly defined plots of folktales and arrange sentence strips to indicate the sequence of events in these stories. Comparing the traditional versions of stories like "Little Red Riding Hood" and "Rumpelstiltskin" with multicultural versions like Ed Young's *Lon Po Po* or Diane Stanley's extended version *Rumpelstiltskin's Daughter* develops critical thinking. This type of instructional activity can be part of a classroom program where love of literature is the central focus. And, of course, traditional folk literature provides a rich source of material for reading aloud at any grade level.

The various types of folk literature suggest a cornucopia of opportunities for writing activities. Pourquoi tales can inspire children to write their own accounts of how the mountains came to be or what makes snow. The stories of Paul Bunyan and John Henry provide models for children to write about the adventures of their own legendary characters. Writing in many modes—journal responses, alternative versions, sequels to traditional stories, letters, poems—can be integrated into the classroom.

Traditional folk literature will extend across the curriculum when children examine the types of communities from which folk literature comes, such as the Pueblo Indians in Gerald McDermott's *Arrow to the Sun* or the Nandi community in Verna Aardema's *Bringing the Rain to the Kapiti Plain*. Making a world map to trace the roots of folk stories develops a sense of geography as it deepens global understanding. Comparing the explanations of natural phenomena given in pourquoi tales to scientific explanations based on current knowledge extends folk literature into science. Children can create for the stories they write original artwork in response to the often striking illustrations they find in fairy tales and folktales that they share in the classroom. And in the area of music, folk songs past and present make interesting and enjoyable musical experiences for children.

Traditional folk literature is an essential ingredient in a multicultural curriculum. Traditional stories that come to us from preliterate times all over the populated world have survived and retained their popularity for centuries. As children discover the rich folk traditions of Africa and of African Americans, as they enjoy the stories that come from Asia, as they meet the characters in Native American folklore, and as they engage in the wealth of imaginative material characteristic of Latino literature, children come to understand and appreciate the contributions that so many people have made to our literary heritage.

CONCLUSION

Traditional folk literature is an important part of the literary heritage for children of all ages. Folk stories run the gamut of literature for children, from simple picture books for young children to more sophisticated novels for young adults. Folklore is also an area of study for serious scholars.

Folk literature bridges the gap from past to present. Ancient stories link us to our ancestors and connect us to the pasts of many cultures. At the same time, many of the themes and characters of folk literature we can relate to today. We often see our own personalities (real or imagined) in the foolish fox, the brave warrior, or the beautiful princess. Cinderella hits the lottery. The wicked witch gets her comeuppance. Everyone likes the idea of living happily ever after. At the core of folk literature is its universality.

Folk literature enables very young children to share the joy and magic of Ye-Shen's good fortune and to escape the frightening giant by clambering down the beanstalk after Jack. It allows older children to attend a meeting of the Knights of the Round Table and to work alongside Paul Bunyan in the North Woods. Today, as technologically oriented as we are, we still love traditional folk literature, just as people loved these stories long ago, and just as those who follow us will continue to love the stories. Traditional folk literature is part of who we are and what we are.

Questions and Activities for Action and Discussion

1. Compare different versions of popular fairy tales—renditions of "The Gingerbread Man" by different authors, versions of "Cinderella" from different cultural perspectives, "adapted" versions of stories by authors like Jon Scieszka. Make a chart or graphic organizer comparing and contrasting different versions.

2. Select a folk tale and analyze it for its literary elements of plot, setting, character, and theme. Prepare the story for retelling to a group of peers or young children.

3. Using the library or your school's Educational Resource Center, gather several examples of pourquoi tales or trickster tales. Explain why these stories may have been so important to earlier people and why they remain so popular with children today.

4. Compare an older version of a classic legend, an epic, or one of Aesop's fables with a contemporary version of the same story. List similarities and differences between the traditional and the modern versions.

5. After reading Bonnie Rudner's essay (see. pp. 136–138), watch the movie version of a popular fairy tale and read one of the variant versions of the same story. Prepare a presentation for a group of parents in which you explain why you would (or wouldn't) use each with their children.

CHILDREN'S & YOUNG ADULT BOOKS CITED IN THIS CHAPTER

Aardema, Verna. 1975. *Why Mosquitoes Buzz in People's Ears*. Illustrated by Leo and Diane Dillon. New York: Dial.

_____ 1981. *Bringing the Rain to the Kapiti Plain: A Nandi Tale*. Illustrated by Beatriz Vidal. New York: Dial.

_____ 1997. *Anansi Does the Impossible: An Ashanti Tale*. Illustrated by Lisa Desimini. New York: Simon and Schuster.

Ada, Alma Flor. 1993. *The Rooster Who Went to His Uncle's Wedding*. Illustrated by Kathleen Kuchera. New York: Putnam.

Aesop. 1992. *Aesop's Fables*. Illustrated by Safaya Salter. San Diego: Harcourt Brace.

Aliki. 1994. *The Gods and Goddesses of Olympus*. New York: HarperCollins.

Andersen, Hans Christian. 1932. *Fairytales*. Illustrated by Arthur Rackham. New York: Weathervane Books.

_____ 1979. *The Emperor's New Clothes*. Illustrated by Virginia L. Burton. Boston: Houghton Mifflin.

_____ 1988. *The Ugly Duckling*. Retold by Lillian Moore and illustrated by Daniel San Souci. New York: Scholastic.

_____ 1993. *The Little Mermaid, the Original Story*. Illustrated by Charles Santore. New York: Random House.

Aylesworth, Jim. 1998. *The Gingerbread Man*. Illustrated by Barbara McClintock. New York: Scholastic.

Barron, T. A. 1996. *The Lost Years of Merlin*. New York: Philomel.

_____ 1997. *The Seven Songs of Merlin*. New York: Philomel.

Bateman, Teresa. 1998. *Leprechaun's Gold*. Illustrated by Rosanne Litzinger. New York: Holiday House.

Baumgartner, Barbara. 1998. *The Gingerbread Man*. Illustrated by Norman Messenger. New York: DK Ink.

Bidken, Odds. 1998. *The Crane Wife*. Illustrated by Gennady Spirin. San Diego: Harcourt Brace.

Bierhorst, John. 1986. *The Monkey's Haircut and Other Stories Told by the Maya*. Illustrated by Robert Andrew Parker. New York: Morrow.

Brett, Jan. 1989. *The Mitten*. New York: G. P. Putnam.

_____ 1994. *Town Mouse, Country Mouse*. New York: G. P. Putnam.

Brown, Marcia. 1975. *Stone Soup*. New York: Macmillan.

Caduto, Michael J., and Joseph Bruchac. 1988. *Keepers of the Earth: Native American Stories and Environmental Activities for Children*. Golden, Colo.: Fulcrum.

Caldecott, Alfred. 1978. *The Caldecott Aesop: Twenty Fables Illustrated by Randolph Caldecott*. Garden City, N.Y.: Doubleday.

Carle, Eric. 1980. *Twelve Tales from Aesop*. New York: Philomel.

Climo, Shirley. 1996. *The Irish Cinderlad*. Illustrated by Loretta Krupinski. New York: HarperCollins.

Cole, Babette. 1986. *Princess Smartypants*. London: Hamish Hamilton.

Connelly, Bernardine. 1997. *Follow the Drinking Gourd*. Illustrated by Yvonne Buchanan. New York: Simon and Schuster.

Crespo, George. 1993. *How the Sea Began: A Tiano Myth*. Boston: Houghton Mifflin.

Davis, Aubrey. 1997. *Bone Button Borscht*. Illustrated by Dusan Patricic. Toronto: Kids Can Press.

Demi. 1980. *Liang and the Magic Paintbrush*. New York: Henry Holt.

De Paola, Tomie. 1975. *Strega Nona*. Englewood Cliffs, N.J.: Prentice Hall.

_____ 1980. *The Lady of Guadeloupe*. New York: Holiday House.

_____ 1996. *The Legend of Bluebonnet*. New York: Putnam.

Doucet, Sharon Arms. 1997. *Why Lapin's Ears Are So Long and Other Tales from the Louisiana Bayou*. Illustrated by David Catrow. New York: Orchard.

Egielski, Richard. 1997. *The Gingerbread Boy*. New York: HarperCollins.

Emberley, Michael. 1992. *Ruby*. Boston: Little Brown.

Fairman, Tony. 1993. *Bury My Bones but Keep My Words: African Tales for Retelling*. Illustrated by Meshack Asare. New York: Holt.

Galdone, Paul. 1975. *The Gingerbread Boy*. New York: Clarion.

_____ 1983. *Puss in Boots*. Boston: Houghton Mifflin.

_____ 1985. *The Little Red Hen*. Boston: Houghton Mifflin.

_____ 1985. *Rumpelstiltskin*. Boston: Houghton Mifflin.

Gardner, James Finn. 1994. *Politically Correct Bedtime Stories: Modern Tales for Our Life and Times*. New York: Macmillan.

Goble, Paul. 1984. *Buffalo Woman*. New York: Simon and Schuster.

_____ 1989. *Iktomi and the Berries*. New York: Orchard Books.

Guthrie, Woody. 1998. *This Land Is Your Land*. Illustrated by Cathy Jacobson. Boston: Little Brown.

Gutierrez, Douglas, and Maria Fernandez Oliver. 1988. *Night of the Stars*. Translated by Carmen Diana Dearden. New York: Kane/Miller Books.

Hague, Kathleen, and Michael Hague. 1980. *East of the Sun and West of the Moon*. Illustrated by Michael Hague. San Diego: Harcourt Brace.

Haley, Gail. 1970. *A Story, a Story: An African Tale*. New York: Atheneum.

Hamilton, Virginia. 1988. *In the Beginning: Creation Stories from Around the World*. Illustrated by Barry Moser. San Diego: Harcourt Brace.

Hogrogian, Nonny. 1971. *One Fine Day*. New York: Macmillan.

Issacs, Anne. 1994. *Swamp Angel*. New York: Dutton.

Jackson, Ellen. 1994. *Cinder Edna*. Illustrated by Kevin O'Malley. New York: HarperCollins.

Jarrell, Randall. 1996. *The Gingerbread Rabbit*. Illustrated by Garth Williams. New York: HarperCollins.

Johnson, Tony. 1994. *The Tale of Rabbit and Coyote*. Illustrated by Tomie De Paola. New York: Putnam.

Jones, Carol. 1996. *The Hare and the Tortoise*. Boston: Houghton Mifflin.

Kellogg, Steven. 1984. *Paul Bunyan*. New York: Morrow.

_____ 1986. *Pecos Bill*. New York: Morrow.

_____ 1988. *Johnny Appleseed*. New York: Morrow.

Kimmel, Eric A. 1993. *The Gingerbread Boy*. Illustrated by Megan Lloyd. New York: Holiday House.

_____ 1995. *Anansi and the Talking Melon*. Illustrated by Janet Stevens. New York: Holiday House.

Kipling, Rudyard. 1988. *The Elephant Child*. Illustrated by Lorinda B. Cauley. San Diego: Harcourt Brace.

_____ 1991. *How the Rhinoceros Got Its Skin*. Illustrated by Tim Raglin. New York: Simon and Schuster.

_____ 1991. *How the Camel Got Its Hump*. Illustrated by Tim Raglin. New York: Simon and Schuster.

Lester, Julius. 1987. *The Tales of Uncle Remus: The Adventures of Brer Rabbit*. Illustrated by Jerry Pinkney. New York: Dial.

_____ 1994. *John Henry*. Illustrated by Jerry Pinkney. New York: Dial.

Lobel, Arnold. 1980. *Fables*. New York: HarperCollins.

Louie, Ai-Ling. 1982. *Yeh-Shen: A Cinderella Story from China*. Illustrated by Ed Young. New York: Philomel Books.

MacGill-Callahan, Sheila. 1993. *The Children of Lir*. Illustrated by Gennady Spirin. New York: Dial.

Mahy, Margaret. 1992. *The Seven Chinese Brothers*. Illustrated by Jean Teng and Mouslen Tseng. New York: Scholastic.

Martin, Rafe. 1992. *The Rough-Faced Girl*. Illustrated by David Shannon. New York: G. P. Putnam's Sons.

McCaughrean, Geraldine. 1996. *The Silver Treasure: Myths and Legends of the World*. Illustrated by Bee Willey. New York: Simon and Schuster.

_____ 1997. *The Bronze Cauldron*. Illustrated by Bee Willey. New York: Simon and Schuster.

McCully, Emily Arnold. 1995. *The Pirate Queen*. New York: Putnam.

McDermott, Gerald. 1986. *Arrow to the Sun: Pueblo Indian Tale*. New York: Puffin.

_____ 1993. *Raven: A Trickster Tale from the Pacific Northwest*. San Diego: Harcourt Brace.

_____ 1994. *Coyote: A Trickster Tale from the American Southwest*. San Diego: Harcourt Brace.

_____ 1997. *Musicians of the Sun*. New York: Simon and Schuster.

McGovern, Ann. 1970. *Robin Hood of Sherwood Forest*. Illustrated by Tracy Sugarman. New York: Scholastic.

McKissack, Patricia. 1986. *Flossie and the Fox*. Illustrated by Rachel Isadora. New York: Dial.

Mohr, Nicholasa. 1995. *The Song of el Coqui and Other Tales of Puerto Rico*. Illustrated by Antonio Mertorel. New York: Viking.

Mollel, Tololwa. 1991. *The Orphan Boy*. Illustrated by Paul Morin. Boston: Houghton Mifflin.

Morpurgo, Michael. 1995. *Arthur, High King of Britain*. San Diego: Harcourt Brace.

_____ 1996. *The Ghost of Grania O'Malley*. London: Heinemann.

Nolan, Dennis. 1997. *Androcles and the Lion*. San Diego: Harcourt Brace.

Oughton, Jerrie. 1996. *How the Stars Fell into the Sky*. Illustrated by Lisa Desimini. Boston: Houghton Mifflin.

Rodanas, Kristina. 1995. *Dragonfly's Tail*. Boston: Houghton Mifflin.

Rounds, Glen. 1992. *The Three Little Pigs and the Big Bad Wolf*. New York: Holiday House.

_____ 1993. *The Three Billygoats Gruff*. New York: Holiday House.

San Souci, Robert D. 1989. *The Talking Eggs: A Folktale from the American South*. Illustrated by Jerry Pinkney. New York: Dial.

_____ 1993. *Young Guinevere*. Illustrated by Jamichael Hunterly. New York: Doubleday.

_____ 1997. *Young Arthur*. Illustrated by Jamichael Hunterly. New York: Doubleday.

_____ 1997. *The Hired Hand: An African American Folktale*. Illustrated by Jerry Pinkney. New York: Dial.

Schechter, Ellen. 1994. *The Boy Who Cried Wolf*. New York: Bantam.

Scieszka, John. 1989. *The True Story of the Three Little Pigs*. Illustrated by Lane Smith. New York: Viking.

_____ 1992. *The Stinky Cheese Man and Other Fairly Stupid Tales*. Illustrated by Lane Smith. New York: Viking.

Scieszka, John, and Lane Smith. 1998. *Squids Will Be Squids: Fresh Morals, Beastly Fables*. New York: Penguin.

Seeger, Pete. 1994. *Abiyoyo*. Illustrated by Michael Hays. New York: Simon and Schuster.

Shepard, Aaron. 1998. *The Crystal Heart: A Vietnamese Legend*. Illustrated by Joseph David. New York: Atheneum.

Shute, Linda. 1988. *Clever Tom and the Leprechaun*. New York: Lothrup, Lee and Shepard.

Slobodkina, Esphyr. 1947. *Caps for Sale*. New York: Harper and Row.

Snyder, Diane. 1988. *The Boy of the Three-Year Nap*. Illustrated by Allen Say. Boston: Houghton Mifflin.

Stanley, Diane. 1997. *Rumpelstiltskin's Daughter*. New York: Morrow.

Steptoe, John. 1987. *Mufaro's Beautiful Daughters*. New York: Lothrup, Lee and Shepard.

Stevens, Janet. (1992). *The Brementown Musicians*. New York: Holiday House.

Summers, Kate. 1996. *Milly and Tilly: The Story of a Town Mouse and a Country Mouse*. Illustrated by Maggie Kneen. New York: Dutton.

Sutcliff, Rosemary. 1964. *The Hound of Ulster*. New York: Dutton.

_____ 1976. *Dragon Slayer*. New York: Puffin.

_____ 1993. *Black Ships Before Troy: The Story of the Iliad*. Illustrated by Alan Lee. New York: Delacorte.

Wescott, Nadine Bernard. 1990. *Skip to My Lou*. Boston: Little Brown.

Wisniewski, David. 1992. *Sundiata: Lion King of Mali*. Boston: Houghton Mifflin.

Wood, Douglas. 1998. *Rabbit and the Moon*. Illustrated by Leslie Baker. New York: Simon and Schuster.

Xiong, Blia. 1989. *Nine-In-One, Grr! Grr!* Illustrated by Cathy Spagnoli. San Francisco: Children's Books.

Yolen, Jane. 1990. *The Dragon's Boy*. New York: HarperCollins.

_____ 1998. *King Long Shanks*. Illustrated by Victoria Chess. San Diego: Harcourt Brace.

Young, Ed. 1996. *Lon Po Po*. New York: Putnam.

Zelinsky, Paul O. 1986. *Rumpelstiltskin*. New York: Dutton.

_____ 1997. *Rapunzel*. New York: Dutton.

REFERENCES

Bettelheim, B. 1975. *The Uses of Enchantment*. New York: Vintage Books.

Campbell, J. 1968. *The Hero with a Thousand Faces*. Princeton, N.J.: Bollingen.

Hayward, C. 1998. "Run, Run as Fast as You Can": Stories of Gingerbread Men and Other Runaways. *Booklinks* 8:20–24.

Hornstein, L. H., ed. 1956. *The Reader's Companion to World Literature*. New York: Dryden.

Sutherland, Z. 1997. *Children and Books* (9th ed.). New York: Longman.

Russell, D. L. 1991. *Children's Literature: A Short Introduction*. New York: Longman.

Temple, C., M. Martinez, J. Yokota, and A. Naylor. 1998. *Children's Books in Children's Hands: An Introduction to Their Literature*. Boston: Allyn and Bacon.

Young, T. A. and P. M. Ferguson. 1995. From Anansi to Zumo: Trickster Tales in the Classroom. *The Reading Teacher* 48: 490–503.

Paul Zelinski won the 1996 Caldecott medal for his elegant illustration of the fairy tale *Rapunzel* by using oil paints to create portrait-like illustrations (top). As part of her brilliant style, Jan Brett uses borders around pages to create a "story within a story" and to foreshadow what is about to happen, in books like *The Mitten* (middle). The fact that Faith Ringgold began her career as a quilt maker accounts for her style of illustration in books like *Tar Beach*, with pictures in colorful acrylics that reflect the author's dreams and experience growing up as an African American female in Harlem (bottom).

They looked in Louisburg Square, but
there was no water to swim in.

That's nothing to tell of,
That won't do, of course . . .
Just a broken-down wagon
That's drawn by a horse.

That *can't* be my story. That's only a *start*.
I'll say that a ZEBRA was pulling that cart!
And that is a story that no one can beat,
When I say that I saw it on Mulberry Street.

Robert McCloskey used sepia paints to portray the realistic details in his American picture book classic, *Make Way For Ducklings,* which won the 1942 Caldecott Medal (top). Dr. Seuss used a colorful cartoon style that reflected the energy of the illustrators of the 1930s in *To Think That I Saw It On Mulberry Street* and other books (bottom).

Two timid beetles — Ike and May —
Crept from the woodwork that same day.
But when Miss Spider begged, "Please stay?"
They shrieked, "Oh no!" and dashed away.

On Saturday
he ate through
one piece of
chocolate cake, one ice-cream cone, one pickle, one slice of Swiss cheese, one slice of salami,   one lollipop, one piece of cherry pie, one sausage, one cupcake, and one slice of watermelon.

That night he had a stomachache!

The Spider Queen laughed at them, but
the doodle bug leader stopped her short.
"Tiny of body but brave of heart, we will
finish what we start!" he said proudly.

   This angered the spider.

   The Long-Lost Toy smiled. He'd never
liked the Spider Queen.

David Kirk paints pictures in vivid colors to portray Miss Spider, two timid beetles, and other multi-legged creatures in *Miss Spider's Tea Party* and his other Miss Spider books (top). Eric Carle's use of color is no less brilliant, but his technique is different; he uses painted tissue paper in collage style in producing books like the enormously popular *The Very Hungry Caterpillar* and other work (middle). In *The Leaf Men*, William Joyce creates a mood of fantasy that reflects the nature of the story (bottom).

I knew that I could have any gift I could imagine. But the thing I wanted most for Christmas was not inside Santa's giant bag. What I wanted more than anything was one silver bell from Santa's sleigh. When I asked, Santa smiled. Then he gave me a hug and told an elf to cut a bell from the reindeer's harness. The elf tossed it up to Santa. He stood, holding the bell high above him, and called out, "The first gift of Christmas!"

Illustrators often help create the mood of a story with their artwork. Chris Van Allsberg captures the magic and mystery of Christmas Eve in his evocative pastel illustrations in *The Polar Express* (top). The pale blues and facial expressions that Don Wood used in Audrey Wood's *The Napping House* reflects a quiet mood conducive to dozing off (bottom).

Authors of wordless books tell stories with pictures alone. The expressions on the faces of each family member after they have been tossed out of a fancy restaurant because of the antics of the boy's frog in Mercer Mayer's *Frog Goes To Dinner* speaks volumes about their reactions (top). David Wiesner's illustrations in his Caldecott Medal winning *Tuesday* raises children's imaginations to another level (bottom).

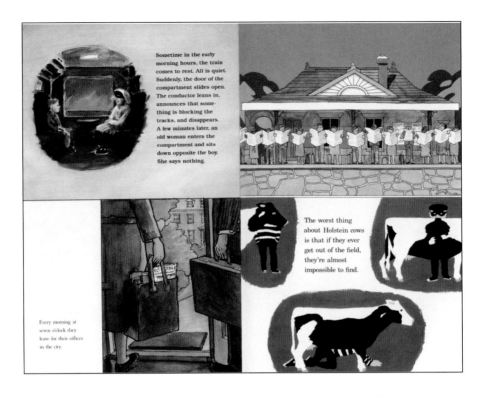

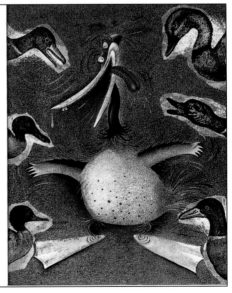

Well, as it turned out, he was just a really ugly duckling. And he grew up to be just a really ugly duck. The End.

Illustrations in postmodern picture books are often untypical of what one finds in more conventional titles. Readers are left to decide if the series of illustrations in David Macaulay's *Black and White* are four different stories or four parts of a single story (top). Lane Smiths's zany illustrations such as the ugly duckling "who grew up to be a really ugly duck" complement the text created by his writing partner John Scieszka in such books as *The Stinky Cheeseman and other Fairly Stupid Fairy Tales* (bottom).

In October of 1288, when the walls and towers of the castle were finished, the exterior of the entire structure was whitewashed with lime, giving it the appearance of having been carved from a single enormous piece of stone and greatly enhancing its already powerful image.

The following spring saw only a handful of laborers returning to Aberwyvern.

There was very little left to do, and the day-to-day maintenance of castle and town wall could now be managed by the craftsmen who had settled permanently in the town. At this point Lady Catherine considered the castle ready for occupation and, on April 29, arrived with her ladies in waiting, children, and servants to join Lord Kevin in their Welsh home.

Then one day the boy came to the tree
and the tree said, "Come, Boy, come and climb
up my trunk and swing from my branches
and eat apples and play in my shade
and be happy."
"I am too big to climb and play," said the boy.
"I want to buy things and have fun.
I want some money.
Can you give me some money?"
"I'm sorry," said the tree, "but I have no money.
I have only leaves and apples.
Take my apples, Boy, and sell them
in the city. Then you will have money
and you will be happy."

Some picture books are effectively illustrated in black and white. David Macaulay's drawings of the planning and construction of a castle in *Castles* are incredibly detailed and informative (top). By contrast, Shel Silverstein's black-and-white line drawings in *The Giving Tree* are less detailed, but they effectively enhance the text (bottom).

River Drinker
took a big drink.

Now the iguana was not at the meeting. For he had not heard the summons.
The antelope was sent to fetch him.
All the animals laughed when they saw the iguana coming, badamin, badamin, with the sticks still stuck in his ears!

King Lion pulled out the sticks, purup, purup. Then he asked, "iguana, what evil have you been plotting against the python?"
"None! none at all!" cried the iguana. "Python is my friend!"
"Then why wouldn't you say good morning to me?" demanded the snake.

It goes forth at night
to prowl around the fires.
It even likes to mingle
with the dancers.
Then it is both prowler and dancer.

Traditional folktales have been illustrated in interesting ways. In *Anansi the Spider: A Tale from the Ashanti*, Gerald McDermott used geometric, African-style illustrations in bold colors (top). In *Why Mosquitoes Buzz in People's Ears*, the pourquoi tale retold by Verna Aardema, illustrators Leo and Diane Dillon use soft colors and symbolic drawings of the animals in the story; the book won the 1976 Caldecott Medal (middle). By contrast, translator and illustrator Marcia Brown used dark images in a collage to create a mood and tone in her 1983 Caldecott Medal winner *Shadow,* a folktale from India (bottom).

CHAPTER 7

CONTEMPORARY REALISTIC FICTION

antasy and fairy tales are at one end of the literary spectrum, and realistic fiction is at the other end. Contemporary realistic fiction addresses situations that children face in their daily lives. It paints pictures of home and school, family and friends, the places where children live and the places to which their imaginations might take them.

THIS CHAPTER:

- examines the qualities and appeal of this genre of children's literature;

- describes topics that authors of realistic fiction address in their novels; and

- considers the use of realistic fiction inside and outside the classroom.

Contemporary realistic fiction deals with the realities of children's lives, the joys, sorrows, and challenges that children encounter in their everyday experiences. The genre "consists of stories that attempt to portray people and events as they are in real life. It mirrors children's experiences. It often explores the problems and conflicts that children face as they grow up, and it sometimes gives them insights and outlets in dealing with these issues and concerns" (Savage 1998, 45).

Realistic fiction presents an account of what it is like to pass into adolescence and to grow toward the independence of adulthood. It deals with circumstances that really exist and situations that could really occur. While some of the plots may be outside a child's everyday existence, realistic fiction always remains within the realm of possibility.

Russell (1991) defines the genre in this way: "Realistic fiction consists of those stories set in the world as we know it, governed by the laws of the natural world as we understand them, and intended to provide a believable verisimilitude to life as we experience it. . . . The appeal of realistic fiction resides in its ability to recreate artistically a vision of the human condition and to enable the readers either to identify or empathize with the characters and their predicaments" (111).

In approaching realistic fiction, it's important to distinguish between what is *possible* and what is *probable*. For most children, it is highly unlikely that they will ever find themselves marooned on the shores of a lake in the Canadian wilderness as a result of a plane crash (as Brian did in Gary Paulsen's *Hatchet*) or locked overnight in New York's Metropolitan Museum of Art (as Claudia and her brother Jamie were in E. L. Konisgberg's *From the Mixed-up Files of Mrs. Basil E. Frankweiler*). While improbable, these stories are within the realm of possibility. Authors tell stories in such a way that the readers believe the story could really happen, however exaggerated or unusual the circumstances. Authors of realistic fiction remain faithful to the essential rules of nature and stay within the bounds of what really might occur.

The link between the genres of realistic and historical fiction occasionally blurs. It may be difficult to judge a story written in the 1950s by contemporary standards. A book like Theodore Taylor's *The Cay*, for example, is set during World War II, but its plot and theme remain as contemporary and appealing today as they were when the story was originally written. On the one hand, the world has changed greatly since Judy Blume wrote *Tales of a Fourth Grade Nothing* in the early 1970s; on the other hand, the contemporary issues that are portrayed in that book are as relevant today as they were over thirty years ago.

As a genre, realistic fiction traces its origins to moralistic tales of the 1600s that were told for purely didactic purposes. The year 1719 brought Daniel Defoe's *Robinson Crusoe*, the survival tale of a man marooned on a desert island, written for the reading pleasure of adults but in time became enormously popular with children as well. In the late 1800s, two great authors working on different sides of the Atlantic brought realistic fiction to a new level. Robert Louis Stevenson wrote *Treasure Island* (1876) and *Kidnapped* (1886), while the American Samuel Clemens (under the pseudonym Mark Twain) wrote *The Adventures of Tom Sawyer* (1876) and *The Adventures of Huckleberry Finn* (1884), books that have remained classics across generations. Other books from the early days of realistic fiction that have become classics are *Little Women* by Louisa May Alcott (1868), *Rebecca of Sunnybrook Farm* by Kate Douglas Wiggins (1903), and *The Secret Garden* by Frances Hodgson Burnett (1909).

In the 1930s, 1940s, and 1950s, realistic fiction became extremely popular with young readers. As Dick and Jane dominated reading instruction in schools, realistic fiction presented an idealized and conventional image of the world in which children lived. Girls wore dresses; well-scrubbed boys ran errands for neighbors; all seemed right with the world. Confronting personal problems or social issues in books for children was taboo.

In the 1960s and later, a new realism entered the genre, and realistic fiction began to become more "real." Harriet, the main character in Louise Fitzhugh's *Harriet the Spy*, didn't wear dresses and didn't get along very well with her parents. Judy Blume's *Are You There, God? It's Me, Margaret* was straightforward in addressing a girl's emotional reaction to the physical changes that puberty brings. Novels began to include some of the harsh realities that were part of the lives of some children—death, family breakups, homelessness, addiction, alienation, physical and mental handicaps, abuse, and racism. (See Chapter 3.) Some authors won top awards for dealing with these issues. Jerry Spinelli won the 1991 Newbery Medal for *Maniac Magee*, a story about a homeless boy. Cynthia Rylant won the same award for *Missing May*, a story about the death of a loved one. Children, it seemed, could not get enough of this new reality in their reading, and books reflecting new realism became enormously popular.

Author Profile: ANGELA JOHNSON

Angela Johnson is an author who has created powerful realistic fiction. Drawing on her own family experiences, she creates stories with loving family themes.

Johnson was born in Alabama and raised in Ohio, where she attended Kent State University. As a teenager in the 1970s, she wrote very personal and often angry beat poetry. After college, Johnson began to write stories for young audiences. Her first book, *Tell Me a Story, Mama* (1989) reflected all the times she had begged her father to tell her stories that she had already heard countless times.

The works that followed all reflected the author's experiences as a member of a close-knit African-American family: *Do Like Kyla* (1990), *When I Am Old Like You* (1990), *One of Three* (1991), and *The Leaving Morning* (1992). All are related to the stories passed on to her from her parents and grandparents.

In 1993, Johnson's first novel, *Toning the Sweep*, was published. A touching and powerful story about the warm and loving relationships among daughter, mother, and grandmother, the book won the Coretta Scott King Medal. This very powerful story was followed by a lighthearted and delightfully amusing picture book *Julius* (1993), about a pig who comes to live with an unsuspecting family. She won her second Coretta Scott King medal in 1999 for *Heaven*, a first-person narrative of an adolescent's struggle when she learns that her parents are not her birth parents.

Angela Johnson still lives in Ohio, where she continues to write books for children and young adults. Here are some of her more recent books:

Shoes Like Ms. Alice's (1995)

Humming Whispers (1995)

The Aunt in Our House (1996)

Daddy Calls Me Mom (1997)

The Rolling Store (1997)

Realistic fiction also began to reflect the multicultural makeup of society. People of color became the main characters in books, and stories were set in other than middle class suburban settings. Characters like Virginia Hamilton's *Zeeley* and Nicholasa Mohr's *Felita*, African-American and Latina characters respectively, appeared as protagonists in realistic fiction. Issues of racism and prejudice were addressed in books like Alma Flor Ada's *My Name Is Maria Isabela* and the many books of Mildred D. Taylor.

As realistic fiction has evolved, it has not been without its share of concern for and criticism of some of the hard issues it currently addresses. While critics always find reasons to attack many types of children's books, contemporary realistic fiction is the genre that seems to elicit the loudest protests. Some stories touch raw nerves, and critics consider current books too stark in treating the harsh realities that are part of the lives of some children. The debate continues in school board rooms, in faculty lounges, and in living rooms. And as contemporary realistic fiction continues to reflect the changing world in which children live, it's unlikely that the debate will abate very soon.

THE APPEAL OF REALISTIC FICTION

Contemporary realistic fiction consists of stories to which children can relate. In these novels, children interact with familiar characters—the class bully, the pesky sibling, the loyal friend, the overbearing adult.

Realistic fiction offers children stories that they care about. While fantasy takes them to the outer reaches of their imaginations and historical fiction takes them into the past, realistic fiction gives them the here and now. Even when settings are beyond the reader's direct experiences and story situations are highly improbable in terms of the child's own life, the reader can relate to the characters and the qualities that these characters show in meeting life's challenges.

Special Perspectives on Children's Literature

MAKING CONNECTIONS WITH REALISTIC FICTION
by Pamela O'Day

Children's literature opens new worlds to young and old alike. Books create limitless opportunities for children to make connections with interesting people doing exciting things in fascinating places. As a child, I remember being immersed in stories and sharing adventures with the Bobbsey Twins and making friends with *Rebecca of Sunnybrook Farm* and Jo in *Little Women*. As a teacher, I helped children connect with the characters in books, share experiences that were similar to their own, and find new and creative solutions to their problems in the world of books.

An important part of enjoying and interacting with literature involves making a personal connection to the text. Realistic fiction provides opportunities for children to make this connection, a connection that will "hook" a reader into the story. This genre provides opportunities for children to talk about their feelings, to laugh and cry with the characters they encounter, to rejoice in their victories and suffer in their defeats, and to brainstorm suggestions for solutions to problems that occur in their lives.

We usually think of realistic fiction as an upper grade enterprise. We think of fifth and sixth graders relating to the dilemmas that Judy Blume describes or the challenges that Gary Paulsen's characters face. A wealth of wonderful realistic fiction exists for upper elementary school and middle school children.

The primary grades, however, also have ample opportunities to connect with realistic fiction. Children sit spellbound while listening to a story that could happen to them. They eagerly and enthusiastically offer ideas about the problems faced by characters in the stories while making their own important personal connections. Through these connections, literature becomes real.

In the primary grades, children connect to the characters in the stories they experience. Primary grade children can understand Rosa's feelings in *A Chair for My Mother* by Vera Williams. Even though they may have never experienced the tragedy of a fire personally, they know about the issue through school and community fire prevention programs. They can relate to the young girl's concern about her mother and about how hard her mother works. They share in the excitement when Rosa and her family purchase the chair for their home and appreciate the sentiments that the purchase represents. They extend their connections through a variety of cross-curricular activities.

A book that consistently captures children's attention is *Ira Sleeps Over* by Bernard Waber. Young children relate to the conflicting feelings of excitement and apprehension about staying over at a friend's house for the first time. They understand the difficult decision that Ira faces: whether or not to bring his teddy bear to Reggie's house. Many can relate to the frustration of having an older sibling who knows all, just like Ira's sister. Through their connection to the characters, children talk about difficult decisions in their own lives and suggest possible solutions.

Another book to which children consistently connect is *Don't Forget to Write* by Martina Selway. In this book, Rosie is going to visit her Granddad and Aunt Mabel on their farm. She is apprehensive about going away by herself. Rosie's mother reassures her and reminds her, "Don't forget to write." The letter that Rosie begins evolves into a journal that highlights her experiences and the changes in her attitude that occur throughout her visit. Children eagerly await to see what new experience each day brings and they share Rosie's feelings of disappointment when it's time to go home.

Realistic fiction provides young children with opportunities to discuss difficult issues. *Smoky Night* by Eve Bunting highlights the experiences and feelings of a boy and his mother on a night of urban rioting. This powerful book is supported by vivid illustrations by David Diaz. It can be a catalyst for discussions about difficult issues surrounding the topic.

Older pupils connect with Anastasia Krupnik and Encyclopedia Brown, and younger pupils connect with *Nate the Great*, the main character in Marjorie Weinman Sharmat's mystery series. Children look for clues to solve the mysteries and think of alternative endings for stories.

Realistic fiction provides many more opportunities for children to connect with literature. The genre stimulates discussion and encourages children to think of alternative solutions to problems. It gives children a chance to make personal connections with story characters through mutually shared experiences, ideas, and emotions. As teachers plan activities to expand and enrich the literature experience, children become personally involved in literature at a young age. Realistic fiction provides children's bond to books.

Pamela O'Day is a former first grade teacher who is currently pursuing graduate studies.

Through contemporary realistic fiction, children gain insights into the lives of others. In Cynthia Voight's *The Homecoming*, for example, as readers travel with the Tillerman kids from Connecticut where they have been abandoned by their mother in the parking lot of a shopping center to their grandmother's house in Maryland, they develop empathy with the family. Katherine Paterson's *Jacob Have I Loved* helps children get a grip on some of the issues and emotions surrounding sibling rivalry. Realistic fiction gives children insights into the problems of others and, while extending the limits of their experience, insights into themselves.

Contemporary realistic fiction often addresses the sensitive issues discussed in Chapter 3. When readers meet story characters who experience divorce, abuse, and other problems similar to their own, they may gain insight and understanding into some of the issues they face in their own classrooms, neighborhoods, or homes. *Bibliotherapy* is the term that psychologists use to describe the process of helping children cope with their personal problems through reading. Bibliotherapy is the interaction between a reader and literature that helps the reader satisfy emotional needs, find solutions to problems, or learn to cope with fear, guilt, anger, and other emotions. Common sense suggests that bibliotherapy be used judiciously because we can't always assume that the realism of the fiction mirrors the reality of a child's situation. Bibliotherapy requires skillful guidance by a professional who understands children and the nature of their problems and careful discussion about the problems that characters face and the ways issues are resolved.

Realistic fiction can sometimes be used to broaden children's knowledge of the world beyond their immediate environments. Consider these books, for example:

- James Heneghan's *Torn Away*, a story about an angry and hostile thirteen-year-old Irish lad named Delcan Doyle who is sent from Belfast to live with his uncle in Canada after his whole family had been killed in the Northern Ireland conflict, can help children come to understand more about the "Troubles" in that part of the world.
- Frances Temple's *Tonight, by Sea* introduces readers to Paulie who may help them understand some of the problems people face in Haiti and the dangers that they are ready to risk in seeking freedom in the United States.
- Beverley Naidoo's *Chain of Fire* brings readers into contact with the oppression of blacks under apartheid in South Africa.

The fact that a novel is "realistic" doesn't mean that it can't stretch the reader's imagination, since elements in realistic fiction are sometimes possible but not probable. While children may never have directly experienced some of the situations that characters in realistic fiction find themselves in, a well-told story can draw a reader into a situation. Realistic fiction can even personalize the images children see on the evening news.

One of the striking features of realistic fiction is its tendency to remain pertinent and contemporary, even as time passes. Girls who once read Judy Blume's *Are You There, God? It's Me, Margaret* while they were dealing with their own issues of puberty are now mothers witnessing their daughters' experience of the book. Even books like Beverly Cleary's *Ribsy*, which may be considered "corny" and hardly contemporary by today's standards, remain popular with young readers.

Beyond the personal and social needs met by realistic fiction, there is another outcome derived when children read it—they love it! Realistic fiction provides children with stories in which they can become involved, characters that they can admire or dislike, events that make them laugh or cry.

LITERARY QUALITIES IN REALISTIC FICTION

Contemporary realistic fiction has the same literary qualities or characteristics as other genres of children's literature—well-developed characters, well-described settings that seem real to young readers, well-constructed plots that center on realistic conflicts, and well-chosen themes that evolve from the story.

Plots revolve around events that have happened or that could possibly happen in the lives of young readers. Conflict is essential, as it is in any story. Realistic fiction features conflicts with self, with adults and peers, with social values, and with others. More than one conflict often exists in a contemporary realistic plot.

Typically, characters in realistic fiction are about the same age as (or slightly older than) the readers. They are developed in a convincing, credible fashion.

Setting is most often contemporary. Settings may be improbable but they're not impossible. They range from urban neighborhoods to suburban schools and malls to mountain meadows and wilderness areas. They are usually described so that children can easily envision and understand them.

Themes in realistic fiction frequently consist of the normal day-to-day challenges of growing up. In most stories, good is rewarded and evil punished. Themes often revolve around lessons to be learned, but the lessons evolve naturally in the story and are not hammered home in a pedantic fashion. Authors like Bennett (1995) and Kilpatrick et al. (1994) promote children's literature as a vehicle for teaching moral values. While there may indeed be a lesson to be learned in realistic fiction, the lesson is a by-product of the story rather than the reason the story was written.

Obviously, an author does not need to limit a work of realistic fiction to a single theme. Cynthia Voight's *Dicey's Song*, for example, is a compelling novel that involves the loss of a parent, family responsibilities, problems associated with poverty and learning disabilities, friendship, and an adolescent's search for independence, all woven into a warm and beautiful story.

FACTORS FOR CONSIDERATION

EVALUATING REALISTIC FICTION

Here are five factors to look for in evaluating realistic fiction:

1. Do young readers quickly connect with the ideas or themes of the story?
2. Can readers identify with the characters and settings portrayed?
3. Does the story deal with contemporary social and personal concerns critical to children's lives?

Factors for Consideration continued

4. If sensitive issues are part of a story, are the issues handled realistically, with care, and with an eye to children's own needs and relationships?

5. Will children be likely to pick up the book on their own and to talk about the book with friends and classmates?

TOPICS IN REALISTIC FICTION

Much contemporary realistic fiction consists of young adult novels for children in the upper elementary grades and middle school. These stories feature adolescent and preadolescent protagonists and deal with problems typically faced at this stage of development. Some contemporary realistic fiction, however, is presented in picture books and features situations in which younger children may sometimes find themselves:

- Charlotte Zolotow's *William's Doll* is about a young boy who wants to own a doll and his family's concerns about this desire;
- Bernard Waber's *Ira Sleeps Over* is an enormously popular picture book about a boy's reluctance to take his favorite teddy bear on a sleep-over at his friend's house;
- Eve Bunting's *Smoky Night* tells how the people of Los Angeles came together after a riot; and
- Vera Williams's *A Chair For My Mother* is the touching story of a child's concern for her very tired working mother.

For children in the upper elementary and middle school grades, realistic fiction deals with conflicts with adults, with siblings, with friends, and within themselves. It includes mystery stories, sports stories, stories about animals, and humorous stories. Contemporary realistic fiction is, in short, the staple of children's reading as they move toward independent stages of reading levels and more independent stages of their young lives.

Home Life

Children's relationships with parents and siblings in family settings are popular in the field of contemporary realistic fiction. Stories about living as part of a family often mirror life's challenges as they entertain.

In the 1930s and 1940s, Beverly Cleary created the families of *Ramona Quimby* and *Henry Huggins*, nuclear families that were happy, secure, well adjusted, and mostly Anglo, families in the "Leave It to Beaver" mode. Less saccharine and sentimental than their nineteenth-century precursors, Cleary and similar authors injected warmth and humor to accounts of growing up, but they chose to overlook some of the harsh realities of contemporary families.

As times changed, authors like Lois Lowry in *Anastasia Krupnik* and Judy Blume in *Tales of a Fourth Grade Nothing* and *Superfudge* combined humor with more realism about the ups and downs of modern family life. The joys and vicissitudes of family relationships are presented with charm and humor in easy-to-read level books like the following:

- Judy Blume's *The One in the Middle Is the Green Kangaroo*, the story of a second grader who feels like peanut butter squished in the middle in a sandwich between an older brother and a younger sister; and
- Betsy Byars's *My Brother, Ant*, the story of a likable boy and his younger brother Ant(hony).

Stories of home life are not always presented through rose-colored glasses, however. Realistic fiction also explores some of the more serious complexities of family relationships. For example, the issue of sibling rivalry and envy between sisters is treated in two powerful stories, *Jacob Have I Loved* by Katherine Paterson and *A Summer to Die* by Lois Lowry. Works of realistic fiction that deal with serious issues in family relations include the following:

- Betsy Byars's *Summer of the Swans*, the story of a girl who is responsible for caring for her special needs brother;
- Virginia Hamilton's *M. C. Higgins, the Great*, which describes an African-American family whose family pride helps them survive hardships; and
- Maude Casey's *Over the Water*, about an alienated adolescent who comes of age with the help of her extended Irish family.

Growing up is rarely easy because it involves coping with many family problems. Stories about the pressures, responsibilities, and satisfactions of relating to family members is a theme that rarely fails to strike a familiar chord in young readers.

Realistic fiction also explores alternative types of families such as the following:

- single-parent families, as in Beverly Cleary's *Dear Mr. Henshaw* in which a boy reacts to his parents' divorce;
- families in which both parents work, as in Lois Lowry's *Anastasia on Her Own* in which the irascible Ms. Krupnick must cope with housekeeping responsibilities when her parents are professionally engaged;
- children living with grandparents, as in Cynthia Voight's *Dicey's Song*, about children who travel to their grandmother's house after their mother abandons them;
- merged or reconstructed families, as in Betsy Byars's *The Animal, the Vegetable, and John D. Jones*, about two sisters who go on a vacation with their divorced father only to discover that his girlfriend and her son have been invited too; and
- temporary family arrangements, as in Betsy Byars's *The Pinballs*, the story of children living in foster care.

In any classroom, one is likely to find children living in a number of different family situations. Realistic fiction has moved beyond the stable family structure consisting of a happy and well-adjusted mom and dad with two-and-a-half kids to include the variety of family structures that exist today.

School Life

School plays a major part in the lives of children, so it's not surprising to see much contemporary realistic fiction on a variety of school-related problems. These books typically focus more on the social than on the academic aspects of school life—fitting in, making friends, adjusting to life in schools. Some books that have proven popular with young readers follow:

- Vicki Grove's *Reaching Dustin*, in which sixth grader Carley Cameron discovers the many problems that her troublesome classmate Dustin Groat faces;
- Barthe deClements's *Nothing's Fair in Fifth Grade*, the story of a girl who has problems entering a new school;
- Gail Gauthier's *A Year with Butch and Spike*, a funny story about some quirky kids and their school lives;
- Ralph Fletcher's *Flying Solo*, about a class that handles itself when the substitute for Mr. Fabiano doesn't show up; and
- Lorri Hewett's *Lives of Our Own*, about a girl who moves to a small Georgia town and discovers racism and resentment in her new school.

Many school stories focus on the topics of acceptance by peers and developing friendships. The search for such acceptance typically spills over into out-of-school settings. Some books that involve getting along in the community beyond the school follow:

- Vera Williams's *Scooter*, about a girl whose mother literally pushes her into the neighborhood;
- Zilpha Keatley Snyder's *Libby on Wednesday*, in which Libby reaches out to school friends by allowing them to use her tree house; and
- Deborah Savage's *Under a Different Sky*, a young adult novel about two teenagers who become friends despite the differences in their social backgrounds.

Getting along with others in today's diverse society may involve overcoming prejudice. Vaunda Micheaux Nelson's *Mayfield Crossing* is about white children who are unwilling to accept African Americans in their school. Carol Fenner's *Yolanda's Genius* is about a girl who overcomes discrimination by promoting the musical talents of her brother. Books like these help children understand some of the insidious dangers of racism and add an important multicultural dimension to their reading.

Growing Up

Passing from childhood to adolescence is a concern for elementary and middle school students, and much realistic fiction deals with this topic. Preadolescent children are concerned about physical, social, and emotional growth, topics explored by the following stories:

- Gary Paulsen's *The Haymeadow*, in which fourteen-year-old John Barron spends the summer alone in the mountains tending his father's herd of sheep;
- Barbara Park's *The Kid in the Red Jacket*, in which fifth grader Howard finds himself removed from his familiar environment and living in a new city; and
- Bill and Vera Cleaver's *Where the Lilies Bloom*, in which young Mary Call makes independent decisions following the death of her father.

Author Profile: Gary Paulsen

Gary Paulsen has written over fifty books for young readers. He writes with a tone and in a style that young people appreciate and enjoy.

Paulsen had a difficult family life, and he had to develop a fierce sense of independence and find comfort in books. As a young man, he worked at several jobs (including for a magazine) before his first book, *Special War*, was published in 1966.

Much of Paulsen's work is intensely personal. In his early life in Minnesota, his family was largely dysfunctional; many of the characters in his books have dysfunctional backgrounds as well. He is a committed outdoorsman; many of his novels are set in the wilderness. He has faced challenges in his life; his protagonists face strong conflicts in virtually all his work. He often writes in the first person; his first successful young adult novel, *Winterkill* (1976), was so true to life that it resulted in a lawsuit (which the author won).

Paulsen's experience with nature is a thread that runs through all his work. The very popular *Hatchet* (1987) is a tale of a boy's survival after a plane crash in the Canadian wilderness. *Voyage of the Frog* (1993) is about survival at sea. In *The Island* (1988), fourteen-year-old Wil Newton is forced to leave the comforts of life in a city when his father is transferred to an isolated wilderness island. *The Haymeadow* (1992) is about a boy who spends the summer alone tending his father's herd of sheep in the mountains. Paulsen is an Iditarod dogsled racer, and his experiences in this race have resulted in three books: *Dogsong* (1985), *Winterdance* (1994), and *Woodsong* (1990). The theme of teenagers facing and meeting life's challenges runs through his work.

Paulsen has also written an award-winning book of historical fiction, *Nightjohn* (1993), about the effects of slavery and the power of literacy. He has also written nonfiction books about outdoor sports (*Father Water, Mother Woods: Essays about Fishing and Hunting in the North Woods*, 1994) and about sailing (*Sailing: From Jibs to Jibing*, 1983).

Gary Paulsen splits his time between his homes in Minnesota and New Mexico. Here are some more of his books:

> *Sarny, a Life Remembered* (1977)
>
> *The Schernoff Discoveries* (1977)
>
> *Brian's Winter* (1996), a sequel to the popular Hatchet
>
> *Tucket's Ride* (1997)

Independence is often achieved through facing and overcoming one's fears. In realistic fiction, this theme is frequently developed in *survival stories*, stories in which a character confronts obstacles in nature and in the self. Survival stories popular with young readers include the following:

• *My Side of the Mountain* by Jean Craighead George, about a boy who spends a year alone living off the land in the Catskill Mountains of New York State;

- *Julie of the Wolves* by Jean Craighead George, about a girl who survives in the Alaskan tundra with the help of a wolfpack;
- *Slake's Limbo* by Felice Holman, about a boy who survives in the tunnels of the New York City subway system;
- *Call It Courage* by Armstrong Sperry, about the son of a tribal chief who must prove his courage by making a solo ocean journey;
- *Island of the Blue Dolphins* by Scott O'Dell, about a girl who survives on an island off the coast of California;
- *Hatchet* by Gary Paulsen, about a boy stranded by a plane crash in the Canadian wilderness;
- *Deep Dream of the Rainforest* by Malcolm Bosse, a survival story set in the rain forests of Borneo;
- *The Cay* by Theodore Taylor, about a young white boy and an elderly Jamaican black man who depend on one another after they are shipwrecked on a deserted Caribbean island; and
- *Weirdo's War* by Michael Coleman, about two boys trapped in an underground cavern.

Many other survival stories are available to entertain children. These provide both male and female protagonists, settings that range from the wilds of Alaska to the exotic South Seas to the grubby subway tunnels of New York City, characters of different ethnicities, and heaps of excitement.

LIST OF TEN

TEN REALISTIC FICTION TITLES THAT HAVE WON THE NEWBERY MEDAL

The Newbery Medal is awarded by the American Library Association each year to the most distinguished contribution to children's literature. In the past, this most prestigious award has been given to biography, poetry, fantasy, science fiction, and historical fiction. Here are ten works of realistic fiction that have won this prestigious award in the last quarter of the twentieth century:

Julie of the Wolves by Jean Craighead George
　　(Harper, 1973)

M.C. Higgins, the Great by Virginia Hamilton
　　(Macmillan, 1975)

Roll of Thunder, Hear My Cry by Mildred Taylor
　　(Dial, 1977)

Bridge to Terabithia by Katherine Paterson
　　(Crowell, 1978)

Dicey's Song by Cynthia Voight
(Atheneum, 1983)

Dear Mr. Henshaw by Beverly Cleary
(Morrow, 1984)

Maniac Magee by Jerry Spinelli
(Little Brown, 1991)

Shiloh by Phyllis Reynolds Naylor
(Atheneum, 1992)

Missing May by Cynthia Rylant
(Orchard, 1993)

Walk Two Moons by Sharon Creech
(HarperCollins, 1995)

Mysteries

The long-standing popularity of series like the Hardy Boys and The Bobbsey Twins is an indication that children love mystery stories. Current series about children who solve mysteries range from easy-to-read books like David Adler's *Cam Jensen* mysteries and Donald Sobol's *Encyclopedia Brown* stories to more difficult reading like Betsy Byars's *The Herculeah Jones* series about a female sleuth and her friend. Once introduced to these junior detectives, children typically want to read all the books in a series.

More complex and sophisticated mystery stories that are part of children's literature include the following:

- Eve Bunting's *Coffin on a Case*, the story of a twelve-year-old boy who becomes adept at solving mysteries when he takes over his father's detective business;
- Ellen Raskin's clever *The Westing Game*, which requires children to carefully follow a complicated series of clues to solve a mystery;
- Jean Ferris's *Love Among the Walnuts*, about Alexander Hunting-Ackerman who foils relatives' attempts to kill his eccentric family; and
- E. L. Konigsberg's *From the Mixed-up Files of Mrs. Basil E. Frankweiler*, an intriguing mystery that unravels in a museum setting.

Both Raskin and Konigsberg have won Newbery Medals for their excellence in writing and their ability to weave mystery stories that engage young minds.

Sports

Athletics are an important part of the lives of real children, and so stories involving sports are a popular part of contemporary realistic fiction. Here is a sampling of books about sports, in which the characters face more than the challenges of the games themselves:

- *Fighting Tackle* by Matt Christopher (who has written many realistic sports stories), about a boy whose involvement in football is complicated by his brother's special needs;
- *Grandmas at Bat* by Emily Arnold McCulley, an easy reading book about two grandmothers who take over as coaches of a little league team;
- *Skinnybones* by Barbara Park, a funny story about a Little League baseball player who talks his way into a situation he later wishes he hadn't;
- *Jo Jo's Flying Sidekick* by Brian Pinkney, about a girl who passes a difficult test in her tae kwon do class and overcomes some of her other problems at the same time; and
- *My Underrated Year* by Randy Powell, a book for older readers about the keen athletic competition that develops between a boy and a girl.

While these stories typically include a great deal of play-by-play action football, baseball, basketball, track, soccer, hockey, wrestling, and other sports, they also deal with issues and dilemmas outside the athletic arena that force the protagonists to learn valuable lessons about growing up.

Animal Stories

From the days of Anna Sewell's *Black Beauty* (1877), stories in which animals play a central role are popular in realistic fiction. Classic stories such as Marjorie Kinnan Rawlings's *The Yearling* and Fred Gipson's *Old Yeller* still retain a readership among today's young audience. Animal stories that have won the attention and the hearts of children include Wilson Rawls's *Where the Red Fern Grows*, a tear-jerking story about a boy who becomes the proud owner of two redbone hounds with whom he loves to hunt, and Phyllis Reynolds Naylor's 1992 Newbery Medal winner *Shiloh*, the story of a West Virginia mountain boy's courageous efforts and sacrifices to save a lovable dog from his abusive master, and her two sequels, *Shiloh Season* and *Saving Shiloh*.

Unlike writers of animal fantasy, authors of realistic fiction about animals avoid anthropomorphism, or making animals think, talk, and behave like humans. A fascinating realistic story about animals is Sheila Burnford's *Incredible Journey*, a story about a Labrador retriever, a bull terrier, and a Siamese cat who cross the northern Canadian wilderness in search of their family. While these three house pets often demonstrate an uncanny intelligence and ability to communicate while they survive in the wild, they never lose their animal identity and cross over into being human.

Humor

Children like stories that make them laugh—humor is more often found in realistic fiction than in any other form of children's literature. Children typically giggle at the antics of the Herdmans in Barbara Robinson's *The Best Christmas Pageant Ever* and smile at the improbable predicaments of Billy and his friends in Thomas Rockwell's *How to Eat Fried Worms*.

Among the many books that provide genuine amusement for children are the following:

- Judy Blume's *Freckle Juice* in which Andrew drinks an awful concoction in order to develop freckles;
- Paula Danzinger's *Make Like a Tree and Leave* (one of many books by this author who can tickle children's funnybones), which deals with some of the absurd ideas that children have about adults;
- Bonnie Pryor's *Toenails, Tonsils, and Tornadoes*, which chronicles the trials and tribulations of Martin Snodgrass and the adjustments he must make in his life when his great-aunt Henrietta shows up at his home; and
- Sheila Greenwald's *Rosy Cole: She Walks in Beauty*, a tongue-in-cheek story about a girl who wants to be a model.

In some realistic fiction, plots center around the absurdity and incongruity of the situations in which the characters find themselves. In other books, humor is an incidental part of the story itself, not its central focus. Whether direct or incidental, humor is a feature that helps make realistic fiction appealing to many children.

History

Many books of realistic fiction are set in the past. Books like Patricia MacLachlan's *Sarah, Plain and Tall* and Paula Fox's *Slave Dancer* present life as it was lived a long time ago. These books will be described in the next chapter as another genre of children's literature, *historical fiction*.

Multicultural Stories

More and more contemporary realistic fiction has people of various cultural and ethnic backgrounds as its main characters. These books focus on the same topics and themes as all realistic fiction—facing the challenges of growing up by dealing with self and others at home, in school, in the neighborhood, and beyond. Books ranging from picture story books to young adult novels reflect the experiences of different nonmainstream cultures in American society:

- Sharon Bell Mathis's *The Hundred Penny Box* deals with cross-generational conflicts in an African-American household;
- Nancy Van Lann's *Mama Rocks, Papa Sings* is a realistic, fact-based, fast-paced picture story book about an extended Haitian family;
- Rob Thomas's *Slave Day* is about a student who objects to the high school's annual "slave day" fund raising activity,

Gary Soto has written a number of contemporary realistic fiction books about growing up in a Mexican-American culture:

- *Taking Sides*, about a young Latino's search for his cultural identity when he moves from the city to a middle-class suburban neighborhood;
- *Baseball in April*, short stories about Soto's experiences as a young man; and
- *The Skirt*, a warm and touching story about a girl who leaves a very special skirt on the bus after school.

Contemporary realistic fiction about Asian Americans sometimes focuses on events set in the original homeland and sometimes deals with young people's attempts to adjust to lives in a new country while continuing to honor the values and traditions of their culture. Among stories set in Asia are the following:

- Eleanor Coerr's *Sadako and the Thousand Paper Cranes*, a moving account of a child stricken with leukemia following the bombing of Hiroshima;
- Pearl Buck's *The Big Wave*, a compelling story set in Japan about human tragedy and human friendship that follow a tidal wave off the coast of Japan; and
- Yukio Tsuchiya's *Faithful Elephants*, a touching and historically accurate (some people consider it historical fiction) about the fate of elephants in a Japanese zoo after the bombing of Japan during World War II.

Stories set in the United States include the following:

- Laurence Yep's *Dragonwings* and *Thief of Hearts,* rooted in the culture of San Francisco's Chinatown;
- Linda Crew's *Children of the River*, a young adult novel about a Cambodian teenager's struggle with the values and lifestyles of conflicting cultures; and
- Michele Surat's *Angel Child, Dragon Child*, a picture story book about the difficulties faced by a young Vietnamese girl when entering a new school in the United States.

Author Profile: LAURENCE YEP

Laurence Yep is a widely acclaimed writer of realistic fiction for children and young adults. His work has enabled countless young (and older) readers to gain insight into and appreciation of the culture and tradition of Chinese Americans.

Yep was born in San Francisco. He began to write stories when he was in high school there as a means of clarifying and examining his cultural identity. The theme of cultural identity runs through much of his later work as well. By the age of eighteen, when he was a freshman at Marquette University, Yep became a published author. He transferred to the University of California at Santa Cruz and later completed a doctorate in English at the State University of New York at Buffalo.

As a writer, Yep first worked in science fiction. His first book was *Sweetwater* (1973). He soon turned his hand to realistic fiction for which he has won widespread acclaim and popularity.

Dragonwings, published in 1975, was named a Newbery Honor Book. In this novel, based on a true story, Yep recounts the tale of Young Moon Shadow who leaves China in the early 1900s to join his father and share his dream of flying. Based on his research on Chinese-American history, Yep created in *Dragonwings* a compelling story with memorable characters. Other works in the same vein followed: *Child of the Owl* (1977), *Sea Glass* (1979), and *The Star Fisher* (1991).

Much of Yep's writing deals with the conflict between respecting and preserving the ancient traditions of a Chinese heritage and dealing with life in a modern American environment. *Child of the Owl* (1977), for example, is about a girl raised outside Chinatown who must examine her ethnic heritage when she goes to stay with her grandmother in Chinatown. *Ribbons* (1996) is about a young Chinese-American girl who wants to continue her ballerina lessons but is unable to because her grandmother comes to stay with the family, creating an economic burden.

Yep has demonstrated his writing talents in other genres as well. *Dragon's Gate* (1993) is a historical novel about the work of Chinese laborers in building the Transcontinental railroad, and *Dragon Lost at Sea* is a series of fantasies based on Chinese myths. He has gathered traditional Chinese folk stories in *The Rainbow People* (1989), and he retold a Mongolian folktale in *The Khan's Daughter* (1997). *Kind Hearts and Gentle Monsters* (1982) is a teenage romance novel. Yep has also written plays that have been staged in theaters on both coasts of the United States.

Laurence Yep lives in California, not far from where he grew up, and continues to write for children and adults. Here are some of his other books:

Later, Gator (1995)

Hiroshima (1995)

The Thief of Hearts (1995)

Contemporary realistic fiction about Native Americans is not as readily available as are titles about other cultural groups. Picture books like Barbara Jossee's *Mama, Do You Love Me?* is a warm story about an Indian family living in the Arctic region. Miska Miles's *Annie and the Old One* is a book for young readers about a Navajo family living on a reservation and facing the death of the family matriarch.

Teachers owe it to children to share these stories to reflect the diversity that characterizes today's society. For children of any ethnic background, reading stories like these contributes to an understanding of others and to a love of literature.

SERIES BOOKS

One can hardly consider the topic of realistic fiction without addressing series books, books that are part of numbered series such as R. L. Stine's *Goosebumps*, Ann M. Martin's *The Baby-Sitter's Club*, and Francine Paschal's *Sweet Valley High*. While some experts regard these books "not as a work of literature but as a commodity" (Jenkins 1977, 194), series books are enormously popular with pupils from the upper elementary grades through high school. They outsell regular single author works in bookstores by as much as four to one, and they consistently rank at or near the top of sales figures for young adult fiction.

The pioneer of the series book was an ingenious entrepreneur named Edward Stratemeyer who, shortly after the beginning of the twentieth century, began a "fiction factory" at which anonymous hack writers would complete preconstructed plots under fictious names.

"Hundreds of series books about the Rover Boys, the Hardy Boys, Tom Swift, the Bobbsey Twins, and others were products of Stratemeyer's fertile imagination" (Temple et al. 1998, 269). His daughter, Harriet Stratemeyer Adams began writing the *Nancy Drew* series under the pen name Carolyn Keene, and she is said to have written 300 titles in this series. For generations, these series books remained among the most popular book choices of young readers.

Today, although the number and quality of excellent children's books far exceeds that available in Stratemeyer's times, contemporary series books remain enormously popular. They offer preadolescents and adolescents familiarity in reading material. Written for mass markets, they feature a level of language that's easy to read, predictable plots that are easy to follow, and familiar characters and settings. Young readers may use them to practice their reading skills, and these books offer a recreational alternative to television and video games. Because they are so widely read by young readers, popular series books provide a means of socialization in a literary community. For many children, contemporary series books promote reading fluency and provide reading pleasure.

On the down side, series books are, in a word, trite. Characters and plot structures differ very little from title to title. Characters live in homogeneous suburban settings. The books do little to expand children's literary horizons or to improve their literary tastes. Another problem involves the images that they project, particularly the images of girls in friendship/romance series.

In a study of young adult fiction series, Motes (1998) examined how female identity and roles were portrayed. She found that girls are "helpless dolls and deficient scholars" with three goals in life: boys, cheerleading, and popularity. She found that girls living in the pages of series fiction are obsessed with their physical appearance, because beauty is linked to success with males and/or positions of prestige; that girls constantly maintain a competitive hostile relationship with one another; and that attracting the right boyfriend is the ultimate success in a girl's life. Calling the books "breeding grounds for bulimia," Motes writes, "These authors teach readers that in order to be happy, successful, and sane, females must have boyfriends. And not just any boyfriend, but the right kind, even if it means placing kindness and responsibility in the shadow of his prestige. Females are trained to feign incompetence or actually believe in their incompetence and then be desperately grateful to a man for his chivalrous rescue. Finally, females are enticed into honoring romance before their own intellectual development" (Motes 1998, 49).

Despite the drawbacks of such books, skyrocketing sales figures are indicative of these books' popularity with young readers. As a result, it makes little sense to ignore these books. Perhaps the best course of action is to help children develop a critical consciousness about series books. Greenlee and her colleagues (1996) found that children are capable of comparing series and nonseries books that they have read. When a child selects a series book for a book report, the focus might be on how that book compares with another, more conventional children's literature title. Read-aloud selections of quality literature can be discussed vis-à-vis series books that students are reading independently. Critical questions about plot, setting, character, and theme can also raise children's critical consciousness about these books.

As Monique Lowd wrote in her essay in the opening chapter of this book (pp. 23–25), most children pass through the phase of series books. They are comparable in function to the "junk novel" that adult readers often enjoy on vacation. However, if children read nothing but series books, problems may arise. Readers may perceive these as realistic fiction when actually they seriously distort reality. Series books must be recognized as part of children's reading, but the goal should be for children to become aware of some of the critical elements of series books and to expand their reading horizons.

REALISTIC FICTION AT SCHOOL AND AT HOME

Given the popularity of contemporary realistic fiction with young readers, this genre is a natural for inclusion in a classroom reading and writing instructional program. Apart from having an enormous appeal, many of these books are quality literature and can form the core of reading material in the classroom. Given the popularity of books like John Reynolds Gardiner's *Stone Fox* and Katherine Paterson's *Bridge to Terabithia*, teachers can find numerous occasions to use realistic fiction to help students develop a full vocabulary and the comprehension strategies that are part of reading instruction. Contemporary realistic fiction can be used as an integral part of core literature and as free-time reading material in the classroom.

One of the marks of a skilled and mature reader is the ability to relate events in books to one's own life. Realistic fiction deals with events that happen or could happen in the lives of real children. Teachers can use discussion questions and reader response journals to get children to focus on how events in a story relate to their own lives and to think about which characters they relate to most closely. Such events and characters can be incorporated into children's own stories about their experiences.

"Is it real?" is a question that teachers ask children about books they read from kindergarten onward. Distinguishing fact from fiction and opinion is a skill practiced in basic reading throughout the grades. Realistic fiction always stays within the bounds of reality and the range of possibility, but students can construct "Degrees of Probability" charts to gauge how likely a story's event would be in their own lives.

Most works of realistic fiction follow a clearly delineated plot structure—a beginning that introduces the problem; a series of events that build up to a climax; a climax that involves a confrontation; and a resolution that brings the story to a satisfying conclusion. A few novels have an anticlimax that heightens the interest of the reader. As children read realistic fiction in directed activities or for independent projects, they can complete plot diagrams about the stories.

Realistic fiction lends itself particularly well to literature circles. Children reading different survival stories, for example, can compare the characters, settings, conflicts, and other features of these novels. In author groups, children can read books by Betsy Byars, Jerry Spinelli, Gary Paulsen, and other authors who have written several works of contemporary realistic fiction. The beauty of using theme groups and author groups in the classroom is that books on a range of reading levels can be used to meet the different abilities of children in a heterogeneous group.

Realistic fiction can help focus attention on behavior in school. The cruel taunting of a classmate in Judy Blume's *Blubber*, for example, or the racial prejudice (and later tolerance) demonstrated by the children in Vaunda Micheaux Nelson's *Mayfield Crossing* can provide object lessons and the basis of discussion.

Role-playing and creative dramatics are classroom activities that flow naturally from realistic fiction. Children can act out scenes that they find especially powerful or especially humorous. A writing extension can involve composing scripts for the characters.

Realistic fiction can be used to open the door for discussion of controversial topics. A book like Karen Hesse's *Phoenix Rising*, which dramatically describes the effects of an accident at a nuclear power plant, suggests debate on the advantages and disadvantages of nuclear power. Children may conduct research to inform these discussions and their own realistic stories on topics of concern.

At home, parents are sometimes concerned about the realistic fiction that their children read. They may be concerned with the language (a boy calling his kid brother "a real jerk") or occasional profanity, with what they consider inappropriate humor (some of which has been described as low-level "bathroom humor" that typically appeals to immature minds), and with some of the content that they may consider "racy" or too harsh for young readers. Parents are also sometimes uneasy about the way in which adults are portrayed in realistic fiction, which may involve exaggeration of faults and foibles that makes adults look silly.

Since it's likely that children will read the books that their friends are reading, parents have the opportunity to talk with their children in an honest and critical way about realistic fiction that their children are reading. Parents need to appreciate the appeal of the realistic fiction their children select, and children deserve to know what their parents think of these books. Judy Blume is reported to have said that she would not have to write about sensitive topics if parents talked to their children about them.

Parents can find another level of humor in some of the books their children read. Some of the scenes describing the interaction between parent and child in Jerry Spinelli's *Space Station Seventh Grade* are genuinely funny from a parent's point of view. Sharing the humor and content of realistic fiction is part of promoting a love of literature in the home.

CONCLUSION

Contemporary realistic fiction is a genre with which children feel comfortable. Books in this genre introduce children to characters they can recognize as part of their daily lives, describe situations that readers may have witnessed or experienced themselves, and provide insights into problem solving.

Realistic fiction provides variety in the reading diet of children. It gives them stories that make tears roll down their cheeks from laughing and from crying; stories in which they see portrayed their parents, aunts, and uncles, their brothers and sisters, their friends and enemies; stories in which characters their own age struggle to meet the ordinary and extraordinary challenges of growing up. Realistic fiction helps children come to grips with some of the everyday issues they confront in their immediate surroundings and with the dilemmas people unfamiliar to them must face.

Realistic fiction is a genre that children enjoy. The absurdities of characters' predicaments, the ingenious solutions that characters design often in the face of adult opposition, and the satisfaction that comes when characters conquer fears and grow as a result all contribute to making realistic fiction another reason for children to love literature.

Questions and Activities for Action and Discussion

1. Identify an author of contemporary realistic fiction who was one of your favorites when you were in elementary school. List the reasons why the work of this author appealed to you.

2. Compare a work of realistic fiction written during the 1950s or 1960s with one written within the past five years. Using a Venn diagram or other graphic organizer, compare and contrast the two books.

3. Characters in contemporary realistic fiction often don't behave like "little angels." They sometimes use profanity, get into trouble, show disrespect to parents, teachers, and each other, and behave in less-than-ideal ways. What would you say to parents who object to your using a fine piece of realistic fiction on the basis that it provides a "poor role model for my child"?

4. Examine some works of realistic fiction presented in picture story books for younger children. Add to the list of titles presented in Special Perspectives on Children's Literature.

5. Series books such as *Goosebumps* and *The Baby-Sitter's Club* are enormously popular with young readers. Describe how you might use series like these as part of the literacy program in your classroom.

CHILDREN'S & YOUNG ADULT BOOKS CITED IN THIS CHAPTER

Ada, Alma Flor. 1993. *My Name Is Maria Isabela*. New York: Atheneum.

Adler, David A. 1980–1988. *Cam Jensen Mysteries* (13 titles). New York: Penguin.

Blume, Judy. 1972. *Are You There, God? It's Me, Margaret*. New York: Dell.

_____ 1972. *Tales of a Fourth Grade Nothing*. New York: Dutton.

_____ 1978. *Freckle Juice*. New York: Dell.

_____ 1980. *Superfudge*. New York: Dutton.

_____ 1981. *The One in the Middle Is the Green Kangaroo*. Illustrated by Amy Atiken. New York: Bradbury.

Bosse, Malcolm. 1993. *Deep Dream of the Rainforest*. New York: Farrar, Straus and Giroux.

Buck, Pearl. 1968. *The Big Wave*. New York: Harper & Row.

Bunting, Eve. 1992. *Coffin on a Case*. New York: HarperCollins.

_____ 1994. *Smoky Night*. Illustrated by David Diaz. San Diego: Harcourt.

Burnford, Sheila. 1960. *Incredible Journey*. Illustrated by Carl Burger. New York: Bantam.

Byars, Betsy. 1970. *Summer of the Swans*. Illustrated by Ted Collins. New York: Viking.

_____ 1977. *The Pinballs*. New York: Harper & Row.

_____ 1987. *The Animal, the Vegetable, and John D. Jones*. Illustrated by Ruth Sanderson. New York: Delacorte.

_____ 1994–1996. *Hurculeah Jones Mysteries* (several titles). New York: Viking.

_____ 1996. *My Brother, Ant*. Illustrated by Marc Simont. New York: Viking.

Casey, Maude. 1994. *Over the Water*. New York: Henry Holt.

Christopher, Matt. 1995. *Fighting Tackle*. Boston: Little, Brown.

Cleary, Beverly. 1950. *Henry Huggins*. New York: Morrow.

_____ 1964. *Ribsy*. New York: Morrow.

_____ 1981. *Ramona Quimby, Age 8*. Illustrated by Alan Tiegreen. New York: Morrow.

_____ 1983. *Dear Mr. Henshaw*. Illustrated by Paul O. Zelinskyi. New York: Morrow.

Cleaver, Bill and Vera Cleaver. 1969. *Where the Lilies Bloom*. New York: New American Library.

Coerr, Eleanor. 1977. *Sadako and the Thousand Paper Cranes*. New York: Putnam.

Coleman, Michael. 1996. *Weirdo's War*. New York: Orchard.

Crew, Linda. 1989. *Children of the River*. New York: Dell.

Danzinger, Paula. 1990. *Make Like a Tree and Leave*. New York: Delacorte.

deClements, Barthe. 1981. *Nothing's Fair in Fifth Grade*. New York: Viking.

Fenner, Carol. 1995. *Yolanda's Genius*. New York: Simon and Schuster.

Ferris, Jean. 1998. Love Among the Walnuts. San Diego: Harcourt Brace.

Fitzhugh, Louise. 1964. *Harriet the Spy*. New York: Harper & Row.

Fletcher, Ralph. 1998. *Flying Solo*. Boston: Houghton Mifflin.

Fox, Paula. 1982. *The Slave Dancer*. New York: Doubleday.

George, Jean Craighead. 1959. *My Side of the Mountain*. New York: Dutton.

_____ 1972. *Julie of the Wolves*. Illustrated by John Schoenherr. New York: Harper & Row.

Gipson, Fred. 1956. *Old Yeller*. New York: Harper & Row.

Greenwald, Sheila. 1994. *Rosy Cole: She Walks in Beauty*. Boston: Little, Brown.

Grove, Vicki. 1998. *Reaching Dustin*. New York: Putnam.

Hamilton, Virginia. 1967. *Zeeley*. Illustrated by Simeon Shimin. New York: Macmillan.

_____ 1974. *M. C. Higgins, the Great*. New York: Simon and Schuster.

Heneghan, James. 1996. *Torn Away*. New York: Puffin.

Hesse, Karen. 1994. *Phoenix Rising*. New York: Penguin.

Hewett, Lorri. 1998. *Lives of Our Own*. New York: Dutton.

Holman, Felice. 1974. *Slake's Limbo*. New York: Macmillan.

Joosse, Barbara. 1991. *Mama, Do You Love Me?* Illustrated by Barbara Lavelle. San Francisco: Chronicle.

Konigsberg, E. L. 1967. *From the Mixed-up Files of Mrs. Basil E. Frankweiler*. New York: Atheneum.

Lowry, Lois. 1977. *A Summer to Die*. Boston: Houghton Mifflin.

_____ 1979. *Anastasia Krupnik*. Boston: Houghton Mifflin.

_____ 1986. *Anastasia on Her Own*. Boston: Houghton Mifflin.

MacLachlan, Patricia. 1985. *Sarah, Plain and Tall*. New York: Harper & Row.

Mathis, Sharon Bell. 1975. *The Hundred Penny Box*. New York: Viking.

McCulley, Emily Arnold. 1993. *Grandmas at Bat*. New York: HarperCollins.

Miles, Miska. 1971. *Annie and the Old One*. Boston: Houghton Mifflin.

Mohr, Nicholasa. 1979. *Felita*. Illustrated by Ray Cruz. New York: Dial.

Naidoo, Beverley. 1989. *Chain of Fire*. Illustrated by Eric Velasquez. New York: HarperCollins.

Naylor, Phyllis Reynolds. 1991. *Shiloh*. New York: Dell.

_____ 1996. *Shiloh Season*. New York: Atheneum.

_____ 1997. *Saving Shiloh*. New York: Atheneum.

Nelson, Vaunda Micheaux. 1993. *Mayfield Crossing*. New York: Putnam.

O'Dell, Scott. 1960. *Island of the Blue Dolphins*. Boston: Houghton Mifflin.

Park, Barbara. 1982. *Skinnybones*. New York: Knopf.

_____ 1987. *The Kid in the Red Jacket*. New York: Knopf.

Paterson, Katherine. 1980. *Jacob Have I Loved*. New York: Crowell.

Paulsen, Gary. 1987. *Hatchet* . New York: Bradbury.

_____ 1992. *The Haymeadow*. New York: Dell.

Pinkney, Brian. 1995. *Jo Jo's Flying Sidekick*. New York: Simon and Schuster.

Powell, Randy. 1988. *My Underrated Year*. New York: Farrar, Straus and Giroux.

Prior, Bonnie. 1997. *Toenails, Tonsils, and Tornadoes*. Illustrated by Helen Gogancherry. New York: Morrow.

Raskin, Ellen. 1978. *The Westing Game*. New York: Dutton.

Rawlings, Marjorie Kinnan. 1938. *The Yearling*. Illustrated by Edward Shenton. New York: Scribner's.

Rawls, Wilson. 1961. *Where the Red Fern Grows*. New York: Doubleday.

Robinson, Barbara. 1972. *The Best Christmas Pageant Ever*. New York: Harper & Row.

Rockwell, Thomas. 1973. *How to Eat Fried Worms*. Illustrated by Emily McCully. New York: Dial.

Rylant, Cynthia. 1993. *Missing May*. New York: Dell.

Savage, Deborah. 1997. *Under a Different Sky*. Boston: Houghton Mifflin.

Snyder, Zilpha Keatley. 1990. *Libby on Wednesday*. New York: Delacorte.

Sobol, Donald. 1967–1984. *Encyclopedia Brown Mysteries* (18 titles). New York: Bantam.

Soto, Gary. 1990. *Baseball in April*. San Diego: Harcourt Brace.

_____ 1991. *Taking Sides*. San Diego: Harcourt.

_____ 1992. *The Skirt*. Illustrated by Eric Velasquez. New York: Delacorte.

Sperry, Armstrong. 1940. *Call It Courage*. New York: Macmillan.

Spinelli, Jerry. 1990. *Maniac Magee*. Boston: Little, Brown.

_____ 1991. *Space Station Seventh Grade*. Boston: Little, Brown.

Surat, Michelle. 1989. *Angel Child, Dragon Child*. Illustrated by Vo-Dinh Mai. New York: Scholastic.

Taylor, Theodore. 1969. *The Cay*. New York: Doubleday.

Temple, Frances. 1995. *Tonight, by Sea*. New York: Orchard.

Thomas, Rob. 1997. *Slave Day*. New York: Simon and Schuster.

Tsuchiya, Yukio. 1988. *Faithful Elephants*. Boston: Houghton Mifflin.

Van Lann, Nancy. 1995. *Mama Rocks, Papa Sings*. Illustrated by Roberta Smith. New York: Knopf.

Voight, Cynthia. 1981. *The Homecoming*. New York: Atheneum.

_____ 1982. *Dicey's Song*. New York: Atheneum.

Waber, Bernard. 1972. *Ira Sleeps Over*. Boston: Houghton Mifflin.

Williams, Vera. 1982. *A Chair for My Mother*. New York: Greenwillow.

_____ 1993. *Scooter*. New York: Greenwillow.

Yep, Laurence. 1985. *Dragonwings*. New York: Harper & Row.

_____ 1995. *Thief of Hearts*. New York: HarperCollins.

Zolotow, Charlotte. 1972. *William's Doll*. Illustrated by Pane DuBois. New York: HarperCollins.

REFERENCES

Bennett. W. J. , ed. 1995. *The Children's Book of Virtues*. New York: Simon and Schuster.

Greenlee, A. A., D. L. Monson, and B. M. Taylor. 1996. The Lure of Series Books: Does It Affect Appreciation for Recommended Literature? *The Reading Teacher* 50:216–225.

Jenkins, C. A. 1997. The Baby-Sitters Club and Cultural Diversity: Or, Book # X: Jessi and Claudia Get Lost. In *Using Multiethnic Literature in the K–8 Classroom*, V. J. Harris, ed. Norwood, Mass.: Christopher-Gordon Publishers.

Kilpatrick, W., G. Wolfe, and S. Wolfe. 1994. *Books That Build Character: A Guide to Teaching Young Children Moral Values Through Stories*. New York: Simon and Schuster.

Motes, J. J. 1998. Teaching Girls to Be Girls: Young Adult Series Fiction. *The New Advocate* 11:39–53.

Russell, D. 1991. *Literature for Children: A Short Introduction*. New York: Longman.

Savage, J. F. 1998. *Teaching Reading and Writing: Combining Skills, Strategies, and Literature*. Boston: McGraw-Hill.

Temple, C., M. Martinez, J. Yokota, and A. Naylor. 1998. *Children's Books in Children's Hands*. Boston: Allyn and Bacon.

CHAPTER 8

HISTORICAL FICTION

T he recent past has witnessed a boom in historical fiction, the narrative accounts of past events and characters that are rooted in historical fact but built out of the imagination of an author. Historical fiction enables children to learn what life was like long ago. It injects a human element into the dates, places, events, and people that pupils study as part of history.

THIS CHAPTER

- examines how historical fiction enhances children's understanding of the past

- identifies important literary elements in this genre; and

- examines the historical fiction that is available for children's information and reading pleasure.

Historical fiction—narratives about the past that are rooted in historical facts but not restricted by those facts—is part of children's literary lives both inside and outside the classroom. Part history and part fiction, historical novels provide young readers with unique reading experiences that blend information and entertainment. Such stories are imaginary, yet they are based on known historical events. The genre is, in the words of historian Dale Porter, "an elusive child of mixed parentage. It claims the right of invention reserved for fiction, but claims, also, to be based on historical reality" (Porter 1993, 315).

Although fictional in nature, historical novels are carefully researched and their factual component is carefully described. Cynthia DeFelice (1998), an author of historical fiction, calls research the skeleton upon which the flesh of a historical novel is built. "For a book to come alive in the minds and hearts and imaginations of readers, the author must create a world that seems real" (30). Historical fiction meets the requirements of good history and good literature. It needs to be honest and authentic, the product of serious study, and must capture and captivate an audience.

What is the relationship between fact and fiction in historical novels? Traditionally, the expression *historical fiction* was considered an oxymoron, the conjoining of two irreconcilable elements. History was fact; fiction was fiction. This genre blends the two elements: historical events provide the foundation and framework for the story, but human personalities and conflicts provide the essence of the story. Historical novels are not merely stories set in the past. They are stories that reflect the spirit and culture of a former age, that show children what it was like to grow up in an earlier time. History documents events; historical fiction tells the story of those events.

Temple et al. (1998) describe three types of historical fiction: 1. *fictionalized memoirs*, in which authors draw upon their own experiences to recount incidents of the past, just as Laura Ingalls Wilder did in her *Little House* series; 2. *fictionalized family history*, in which stories are passed from generation to generation before being recorded in book form, such as Mildred D. Taylor's body of work and Patricia Polacco's *Pink and Say;* and 3. *fiction based on research*, which is the approach taken by most authors of historical fiction.

Sometimes, the categories of contemporary and historical fiction may overlap. Stories are generally considered historical when they are set at least a generation or more before the time when they are written. Mildred D. Taylor's Newbery Medal winner *Roll of Thunder, Hear My Cry* tells a story about life in the American South in the 1930s. However, it also deals realistically with a contemporary topic.

While it has classical and medieval roots, historical fiction is generally traced from the works of Sir Walter Raleigh, including *Waverley* (1814) and *Ivanhoe*, a book that made him a preeminent figure in this field. The genre reached a peak of excellence before the twentieth century and again came into its own in the 1920s. "Both in America and in Britain, the historical novel achieved its greatest flowering in the decades following World War II" (Rahn 1991, 13). The 1929 Newbery Medal was awarded to Eric Kelly for *Trumpeter of Krakow*, an adventure set in Medieval Poland. Laura Ingalls Wilder wrote her famous *Little House* series in the 1930s and 1940s. *Johnny Tremain* by Esther Forbes won the 1944 Newbery Medal, and many quality works of fiction based on history followed, as the genre became a well established and popular one for children. The genre continues to flourish today.

Works of historical fiction have garnered their share of top children's literature awards, most recently Newbery Medals in 1995 (for Karen Cushman's *The Midwife's Apprentice*), in 1989 (for Lois Lowry's *Number the Stars*), and in 1986 (for Patricia MacLachlan's *Sarah Plain and Tall*). The Scott O'Dell Award is given annually for excellence in historical fiction.

Novels, of course, are not the only literary forums for presenting history to children. Some picture books are based on historical events. The fantasy genre often overlaps with historical fiction. Biographies of figures from the past are available for children. The focus of this chapter, however, is on fiction—imaginative stories rooted in events of the past.

Why Historical Fiction?

Historical fiction animates the past in the minds of young readers. It enables children to develop an understanding of history beyond that which comes from memorizing dates, names, and locations of events—it presents history in the context terms of peoples' lives. By

LIST OF TEN

SCOTT O'DELL AWARD FOR HISTORICAL FICTION

The annual award given to the author of the most distinguished work of historical fiction is the Scott O'Dell Award, created by and named in honor of the author of so many quality historical novels for young adults. The book must be written by a U.S. citizen, set in the New World, and published in English by a U.S. publisher. Here are the winners for the past ten years:

1990 **Shades of Gray** by Carolyn Reeder
(Macmillan)

1991 **A Time of Troubles** by Peter van Raven
(Scribners)

1992 **Stepping on the Cracks** by Mary Downing Hahn
(Clarion)

1993 **Morning Girl** by Michael Dorris
(Hyperion)

1994 **Bull Run** by Paul Fleischman
(HarperCollins)

1995 **Under the Blood-Red Sun** by Graham Salisbury
(Delacorte)

1996 **The Bomb** by Theodore Taylor
(Harcourt Brace)

1997 **Jip: His Story** by Katherine Paterson
(Lodestar)

1998 **Out of the Dust** by Karen Hesse
(Scholastic)

1999 **Forty Acres and Maybe a Mule** by Harriet Gillem Robinet
(Simon and Schuster)

In addition to the Scott O'Dell Award, the Laura Ingalls Award, and the Carter Woodson Award, have been awarded to works of historical fiction. The National Council of Social Studies has included historical fiction in its annual selection of outstanding trade books.

transporting readers to different times and places, thus enabling them to assume new identities, historical novels give children opportunities to construct completely new perspectives and insights into the past.

In most high schools and junior high and middle schools, the textbook remains the backbone of the history curriculum. While elementary teachers usually rely less on textbooks than on other learning resources, text series are still important teaching tools, particularly in the upper elementary grades. Textbooks gather the material that children are expected to learn. They concentrate and organize information efficiently and provide easy access to what is deemed important. As such, they are integral to the instructional process in history and social studies classes.

Historical novels, however, can lead children into the past in ways that few textbooks can. In textbooks, material is necessarily selective and compressed, so many interesting details are omitted and important topics receive limited coverage. While history books "cover" the past, novels allow children to get under the covers, as they vicariously participate in the events they learn about. Historical fiction animates information found in textbooks. It "creates a sense of time and place that often eludes elementary children as they study the past" (Freeman and Levstik 1988, 329) and helps children reflect on the human consequences of historical events. Good historical novels propel children into the past, allowing them to learn what it was like to sail with the Vikings, enter battle with William the Conqueror, and travel across the open plains of the old American west, for example.

Historical fiction adds emotion to and elicits involvement in names, dates, and places. Fiction presents the human side of history, and children learn history better when they learn it as a good story. Novels can generate in children enthusiasm for learning about the past. They can also help children develop what has been called *historical empathy*, an awareness of past events as these events were experienced by people of past times (Tomlinson, Tunnell, and Richgels 1993).

By spending time through reading about individuals who lived long ago, today's young readers come to realize that history is made by real people, and this realization provides a link between the past and the present. Reading historical fiction "can breathe life into what students may have considered irrelevant and dull, thus allowing them to see that their *present* is part of a *living past*, that people as real as themselves struggled with problems similar to their own, and that today's way of life is a result of what these people did in finding solutions" (Jacobs and Tunnell 1996, 102).

While authors of historical fiction may approach their topics with clear instructional intent (Sipe 1997), few would suggest that history be taught with novels alone. What historical fiction does is add to children's learning a depth to understanding of events and conditions of the past. These novels also offer children insights into what writers must do to write about the past, what scholars call *doing history*. In addition to helping children learn about the past, these books can serve as resources for developing historical inquiry.

Historical fiction can also be used to help children develop a critical sense of historical accuracy and pay attention to writers' points of view. While authors of historical fiction must remain faithful to the facts, they filter the past through their own sociopolitical lenses. Jane Yolen's picture book *Encounter*, for example, is the story of the conquest by Columbus of the Americas, told through the eyes of a Tiano child whose tribe was brutalized and decimated by Columbus and his men. Historical fiction reflects reality, but that reality changes through differeng perspectives (MacLeod 1998).

Traditionally, historical novels tended to present history through rose-colored lenses, glorifying the past and the people who lived it. Today, writers don't sugarcoat history

Author Profile: SCOTT O'DELL

Scott O'Dell is one of the most prolific and best known authors of historical fiction for children. The annual award for the most distinguished work of historical fiction set in the New World was named in his honor.

O'Dell was born in Los Angeles, California, in 1898, a time when horses outnumbered automobiles on the American frontier. After attending Occidental College, he began a career as a writer.

A committed naturalist, O'Dell always had a deep respect for the environment. As part of a protest against hunting in the San Diego area, he wrote *Island of the Blue Dolphins*. This initial attempt at writing for children, the story of a Native American girl who survived for eighteen years on an island off the coast of California, won the 1961 Newbery Award and established O'Dell as a children's author. Three other Newbery Honor books followed: *The King's Fifth* (1966), *The Black Pearl* (1967), and *Sing Down the Moon* (1970).

O'Dell's work gives children unique insights into the past. His detailed work treats his subjects with sensitivity. Much of his work deals with the Spanish conquest and exploration of the New World and is based on his thorough study of the Incan, Mayan, and Aztec civilizations. His protagonists are typically people of native descent. His work presents a balanced view of history. For example, in his popular *Sing Down the Moon*, the story of a Navajo girl determined to return to the home of her ancestors after being forcibly removed, O'Dell does not whitewash the harsh treatment of the Navajo people by the U.S. Government. In addition to receiving the Newbery Medal, he has been honored with several national and international awards.

Scott O'Dell spent the last days of his writing career far from his native California in a remote setting in upstate New York, where he was able to enjoy the nature that was so central to his life and to his writing. When he died in 1989 at the age of ninety-one, he left us a literary legacy that includes the following books:

The Captive (1979)

The Feathered Serpent (1981)

The Amethyst Ring (1983)

The Serpent Never Sleeps (1987)

and include historical warts, blemishes, and all. For example, Yoshiko Uchida's three novels *Journey to Topaz*, *Journey Home*, and *The Bracelet* all document the unjust internment of Japanese-Americans following the attack on Pearl Harbor at the beginning of World War II. And Scott O'Dell vividly describes the forced resettlement of the Navajo people in *Sing Down the Moon* without softening the effects of this resettlement on the Navajo.

Children come to understand the American Revolution from different points of view as they read the following:

- Scott O'Dell's *Sarah Bishop,* a story told through the eyes of a girl whose family suffers the resentment of fellow citizens because they are loyal to the crown;
- Esther Forbes's *Johnny Tremain*, told through the eyes of a young patriot caught up in the excitement of the Revolution;
- James and Christopher Collier's *War Comes to Willy Freeman,* told through the eyes of a young black woman victimized by the Revolution;
- Avi's *The Fighting Ground,* told through the eyes of young Jonathan who comes to question the revolutionary values in which he once strongly believed;
- Richard Berleth's *Samuel's Choice,* about a slave in New York who must choose between helping the colonists fight for freedom and obeying his Loyalist master;
- Jean Fritz's *Early Thunder,* about a fourteen-year-old boy in Concord, Massachusetts, trying to decide whether to remain loyal to his king or to join the revolution; and
- James and Christopher Collier's *My Brother Sam Is Dead,* told in a way that enables young readers to experience the emotional conflict inherent in choosing a side in the Revolution.

Each of these books portrays the same event in very different ways and lets children form critical judgments about the past.

Johnson and Ebert (1992) summarize the advantages of "time travel" through historical fiction incorporated into the curriculum: it brings children closer to history by helping them experience the joy and despair of those who lived before them; it helps children develop a feeling for the continuity of life and their place in history; it promotes critical reading and thinking; and it helps children see the interdependence of humankind and develop a greater understanding of the relationship of the past to the future. Johnson and Ebert also describe how to set up a literature-based social studies unit using historical fiction.

Novels revitalize history and brings the past to life. "Reading historical fiction in conjunction with both textbooks and associated sources helps students to see history as the story of real people with feelings, values, and needs to which they themselves can relate, based on their own experiences and interests. This feeling of connection, of participation in the story, is crucial if students are to find history as exciting and stimulating as it actually is" (Coffey and Howard 1997, *xiii–xiv*).

HISTORICAL FICTION AS LITERATURE

Historical novels are primarily literary works, not merely veiled attempts to teach history. They contain all the qualities of good stories—well-developed characters, authentic settings, engaging plots, and relevant and appropriate themes. If the research baggage outweighs or overshadows the story line, the novel loses its appeal.

LIST OF TEN

BRIEF HISTORICAL FICTION BOOKS

Kathleen Sullivan (1997) has suggested a selection of picture books and short novels for young readers who are intimidated by, or don't have time for, longer works. Here are, from Sullivan's list, ten titles that cover different times and places:

Wagon Wheels by Barbara Brenner
an easy-reading chapter book about a black family who settled the American West as pioneers (HarperCollins, 1978)

Dandelions by Eve Bunting
about pioneer women as seen through the eyes of the daughter of a homesteading family (Harcourt, 1995)

Three Young Pilgrims by Cheryl Harness
based on the stories of three real people who came to America on the Mayflower (Simon and Schuster 1992)

Tears for Ashan by D. Marie
about a young African boy whose life is changed when his best friend is captured by slave traders (Creative Press, 1988)

Grandmother and the Runaway Shadow by Liz Rosenberg
a story about a young Eastern European girl who emigrates to America (Harcourt, 1996)

Love You, Soldier by Amy Hest
about a girl's experiences in New York during World War II (Simon and Schuster, 1991)

Skylark by Patricia MacLachlan
a sequel to Sarah Plain and Tall *in which Sarah takes her new family back to Maine for a visit (HarperCollins, 1994)*

Nettie's Trip South by Ann Turner
in which a Northern ten-year-old girl visits slave-owning relatives in the South (Simon and Schuster, 1987)

Meike and the Fifth Treasure by Eleanor Coerr
about the bombing of Nagasaki during World War II (Putnam, 1993)

This Is the Bird by George Shannon
chronicling the courage and perseverance of eight generations of strong women from pioneer to modern times (Houghton Mifflin, 1997)

Characters in historical fiction are unique and lifelike, not flat and stereotypical. Although they come out of the past, they are believable people to whom young readers can relate. Their activities, beliefs, and values are consistent with the historical period in which the story is set, yet they break through "expected" behavior of the time and show

Author Profile: KAREN CUSHMAN

Karen Cushman started her writing career relatively late in life, but it has since blossomed. Born in Chicago in 1941, Cushman moved to Los Angeles with her family when she was eleven. She recalls writing a play about Santa Claus going down the wrong chimney on Christmas Eve and ending up in the home of a Jewish family celebrating Hanukah and writing an epic poem about Elvis Presley. Although she enjoyed writing, her family didn't consider being an author a "real job."

The creative writing classes that she took at Stanford University helped change her mind. Her studies increased her interest in the past and honed her research skills. She graduated from Stanford with degrees in English and Greek and later earned a Master's degree in Museum Studies.

Over the years, Cushman had many book ideas. When she would share these ideas with her husband, he would reply, "Don't tell me. Write it down." After three years of research and writing, she published her first book *Catherine, Called Birdy* in 1994. It immediately won critical acclaim. The book was based on meticulous research about many aspects of life in the Middle Ages—beekeeping and sheep shearing, ointments and remedies, superstitions and fears, food and clothing, and much, much more.

Cushman's second book also focused on the life of a young girl during the Middle Ages. *The Midwife's Apprentice* won (among other awards) the 1996 Newbery Medal for the most distinguished contribution to children's literature published the previous year and quickly established the author's reputation in the field.

Cushman's third book, *The Ballad of Lucy Whipple* (1996), set in nineteenth-century America, tells the story of twelve-year-old Lucy and her family who head for California to search for gold only to find tattered tents, hungry miners, and other assorted problems.

Karen Cushman lives with her family in California. Her writing continues to bring the past alive for children.

---

individuality. The characters are generally fictional, although they may come in contact with real figures from history—for example, Johnny Tremain meets Paul Revere, John Hancock, and other historical figures from the Revolution. The main character is often young—like Kit Taylor in Elizabeth George Speare's *The Witch of Blackbird Pond* and Catherine in Karen Cushman's *Catherine, Called Birdy*. The universal aspects of character cut across time and space.

The settings for historical fiction are, obviously, in the past. It is not enough, however, for a historical novel to be set in the past; it must also accurately reflect the reality of its time period. Settings need to be detailed enough so that readers can get a sense of times and places that are probably unfamiliar to them yet not so detailed as to overwhelm the story. Writers must reflect the social conditions, customs, values, and everyday practices of their stories' settings. Some critics comment that contemporary historical fiction sometimes bends "historical narrative to modern models of social behavior" (MacLeod 1998, 32).

As in any good story, an interesting plot is essential. In historical fiction, the plot typically revolves around the ways characters respond to conflicts within the contexts of times and place.

The basic themes of historical fiction include loyalty, bravery, love and hate, the need to survive, and coming of age. Even though by its nature historical fiction deals with the past, its themes and ideas are related to issues that matter to children today. Children read historical fiction to meet their social and emotional needs, not primarily to acquire historical information. A single work may contain multiple universal themes, none of which is presented in a didactic fashion.

Language is of particular concern in historical fiction. Writing historical dialogue for young readers is a challenge, since speech that is different from today's speech needs to be understood by today's readers and yet be consistent with the time and place of the story, remain faithful to the historical context of the era, and accurately reflect the facts of history without compromising reality.

FACTORS FOR CONSIDERATION

EVALUATING HISTORICAL FICTION

When selecting historical fiction for use in your classroom, test each title by asking the following questions:

1. Does the content accurately reflect the history of the period in which the story takes place?
2. Is there a range of characters whose beliefs, words, and deeds are consistent with the historical time frame?
3. Is the theme appropriate for today's young readers?
4. Does the novel help children learn about people and cultures during a historical time period?
5. Are history and fiction fused in such a way as to hold the interest of the reader?

HISTORY THROUGH FICTION

Historical novels allow children to vicariously experience life in different eras of world history and in the history of their own country, from the time before recorded history until their parents' generation.

World History

Children can use the time machine of historical fiction to travel to the following eras:

- **Ancient times**: Rosemary Sutcliff's *Sun Horse, Moon Horse*, is a story set in ancient Britain before the Roman invasion, and Elizabeth George Speare's *The Bronze Bow*, is about a boy who lived in Palestine during the Roman occupation.

- **The Middle Ages**: Karen Cushman's *Catherine, Called Birdy* is a journal account of the daily activities of a headstrong girl who defied medieval standards of behavior, and *The Midwife's Apprentice* is about a homeless orphan who finds her identify as the servant of the village midwife, and Marguerite De Angeli's 1950 Newbery Medal winner *Door in the Wall* tells how a crippled lad saves the day during the siege of his lord's castle.

- **Explorations to the Americas**: Scott O'Dell's *The Amethyst Ring* is the story of the fall of the Mayan and Incan civilizations with the arrival of Cortez and Pizzaro, and Pam Conrad's *Pedro's Journal: A Voyage with Christopher Columbus* is a cabin boy's account of his experiences on the first voyage of Columbus in 1492.

- **The nineteenth and twentieth centuries**: Felice Holman's *The Wild Children* is set in Russia immediately following the Bolshevik Revolution, and Gary Disher's *The Bamboo Flute* is set in the Australian outback during the Great Depression.

Historical fiction helps children gain a view of the world beyond their borders by exploring the pasts of many nations and different peoples. Children can read about the histories of the following countries; for example:

- **Japan**: *Night of the Ninjas* by Mary Pope Osborne tells about two children who travel back in time to feudal Japan, and *Hiroshima No Pika* by Toshi Maruki is about the day Hiroshima was bombed.

- **Ireland**: In *Under the Hawthorn Tree*, Marita Conlon-McKenna tells the story of the struggle of three brave children during the Potato Famine of the mid-1800s and in *Beyond the Western Sea, Book One: The Escape from Home*, Avi describes the journey of a brother and a sister as they flee the Famine.

- **Sweden**: *The Long Way to a New Land* by Joan Sander tells how a family escaped a nineteenth-century famine by emigrating to America.

- **Korea**: *The Year of Impossible Good-Byes* by Sook Nyul Choi tells about the horrific experiences of the author's family during the Japanese occupation of Korea in World War II and their subsequent attempts to escape the Communist regime in North Korea.

- **Great Britain**: Ian Lawrence's *The Wreckers* is about nineteenth-century villagers who lured ships to the coast in order to wreck and plunder them, and Gary Blackwood's *The Shakespeare Stealer* is an intriguing story set in Elizabethan London in which a poor orphan is sent to steal Shakespeare's play "Hamlet."

Fiction that explains a nation's history helps children better understand the people whose lives and values have been shaped by that past. Among the most popular works of historical fiction for children are those based on American history. Historical novels at different levels cover the following historical events and periods:

- **Discovery and early settlement**: *Morning Girl* by Michael Dorris is the story of two Taino children living in the Bahamas prior to the arrival of Columbus, and Arnold Lobel's picture story book *On the Day Peter Stuyvesant Sailed into Town* recounts the early settlement of New York.

- **The arrival of the Pilgrims**: *Stranded at Plimoth Plantation 1626* by Gary Bowen and *Constance: A Story of Early Plymouth* by Patricia Clapp document life in early Plymouth.

- **Colonial America**: Elizabeth George Speare's popular *The Witch of Blackbird Pond* is about a girl who settles in a Puritan Connecticut colony, and *Tituba of Salem Village* by Ann Lane Petry recounts the horrors of the Salem witch trials.

- **The American Revolution**: *Katie's Trunk* by Ann Terner tells about a child who tries to hide when the Patriots arrive at her house; *The Fifth of March: A Story of the Boston Massacre* by Ann Renalder is an account of the famous historical event that helped fan the flames against the British; and *The Hatmaker's Sign: A Story Told by Benjamin Franklin* by Candice Fleming is based on an actual conversation between Franklin and Thomas Jefferson about a Boston hatmaker who tried hard to make a perfect sign, purportedly told by Franklin to Jefferson when the members of the Continental Congress were squabbling over the wording of the Declaration of Independence.

- **The opening of the West**: *Black-Eyed Susan* by Jennifer Armstrong is about life in the Dakota Territory and *Mr. Tuckett* is Gary Paulsen's story about a boy who celebrates his fourteenth birthday on a wagon train heading west on the Oregon Trail.

- **The Civil War**: *Bull Run* by Paul Fleischman tells the story of that famous first battle from many different perspectives; Carolyn Reeder's *Across the Lines* portrays the perspectives of two boys, one black and one white, living in the time of the Civil War; and Irene Hunt's *Across Five Aprils* is a powerful story about the effects of the war on a family whose sons are fighting for different sides.

- **Industrialization**: Emily Arnold McCully's *The Bobbin Girl* for younger children, Katherine Paterson's *Lyddie* for older readers, and Barry Denenberg's *So Far from Home: The Diary of Mary Driscoll, an Irish Mill Girl* all tell about the lives of young girls working in textile mills.

- **The Great Depression**: *Dotty's Suitcase* by Constance Greene is about Depression-era living, and *The Elderberry Thicket* by Joan T. Zeier is about the resilience of a Wisconsin Depression-era family.

- **World War II**: *Hang Out the Flag* by Katherine McGlade Marco describes the daily impact of the war on civilians as well as on the military, and *Summer of My German Soldier* is Bette Greene's touching novel about an escaped German prisoner of war befriended by a Jewish girl in Arkansas. Many books tell about the Holocaust and the internment of Japanese Americans.

- **The Civil Rights Movement**: Christopher Paul Curtis's *The Watsons Go to Birmingham—1963* chronicles the experiences of an African-American family from Detroit who visits the turbulent South at the beginning of the Civil Rights Movement, and Ozzie Davis's *Just Like Martin* is about violent and nonviolent clashes in the South.

- **America in the modern world**: Eve Bunting's picture book *The Wall* and, for older readers, Walter Dean Myers's *Fallen Angels* about a young soldier's life in the war, both focus on U.S. involvement in the Vietnam War.

Historical events that are often studied in the social studies curriculum are well supported by works of historical fiction. Teachers can find literature at different reading levels that teaches children about the following topics:

- **The Holocaust**: Jo Hoestlandt's *Star of Fear, Star of Hope*, Christopher Gallaz's and Roberto Innocenti's *Rose Blanche*, and Gudrun Pausewang's *The Final Journey* portray many aspects of the arrest, persecution, and extermination of European Jews during World War II. These books portray the prejudice and hatred of the persecutors of Jews and the courage and endurance of the victimized.

- **The Underground Railroad**: Books that range from picture books to more extensive historical novels including Deborah Hopkinson's *Sweet Clara and the Freedom Quilt*, Kathryn Lasky's *True North: A Novel of the Underground Railroad*, and F. N. Monjo's *The Drinking Gourd: A Story of the Underground Railroad* convey the courage and hope of those who tried to escape and those who helped them.

- **The Westward Movement**: Books from easy reading levels to more challenging materials include Betsy Byars's *The Golly Sisters Ride Again*, one of a series of books about two lively sisters who support themselves by dancing and singing for settlers as they travel through the Old West; G. Clifton Wisler's *Jerico's Journey*, an account of the hardships on a family making its way from Tennessee to Texas, and Elvira Woodruff's *Dear Levi: Letters from the Overland Trail*, a twelve-year-old boy's letters about traveling west on the Oregon Trail. These and other books relate the hardships and courage of early pioneers and give children insight into what the West was like in "the old days."

These titles identified for the Holocaust, the Underground Railroad, and the Westward Movement represent only a small fraction of the historical fiction available on the many topics included as part of the social studies curriculum.

Multicultural Dimensions of Historical Fiction

Historical fiction presents a picture of the diversity of the people who shaped the events of our nation and the world. Scores of fictional accounts tell about the role of African Americans in this nation's history, from the days of slavery in books like Paula Fox's *Slave Dancer*, the story of a boy who played the pipes to exercise the captured slaves being transported in the Middle Passage, to the opening of the West in books like *Wagon Wheels*, Barbara Brenner's easy-to-read story about African-American pioneers and their travel west in the 1800s, to relatively recent times in books like William Miller's *Richard Wright and the Library Card*, the story of how the great writer was denied because of his race the right to a library card in the 1920s.

Historical fiction about Latinos includes many stories about early Spanish explorers and pioneers in the Old West. Scott O'Dell's *Carlota* is about a Spanish-American girl in California during the Spanish-American War, and Albert Merrin's *The Empires Lost and Won: The Spanish Heritage in the Southwest* combines fact and fiction in tracing the history of Spanish people in poetry and prose for older readers.

Stories about Asian Americans focus heavily on the contributions of the Chinese immigrants to expansion in the American West and on the injustice suffered by Japanese Americans in the early days of World War II. Laurence Yep's *Dragon's Gate* tells about a boy who came from China to work on the transcontinental railroad. Three books by Yoshiko

Author Profile: PATRICIA AND FREDERICK MCKISSACK

Writers of historical fiction, biography, and other books related mainly to the African-American experience, Patricia and Frederick McKissack make a very talented team. Each has also written separately.

Patricia McKissack was born into a family of storytellers, so she was drawn easily into writing for children. After graduating from Tennessee State University, she began a teaching career. Having grown up in the segregated South, she set out to capture and convey to children the magic of African-American folk literature. The results of her effort were books like *Flossie and the Fox* (1986) and *Mirandy and Brother Wind* (1998).

Frederick McKissack had no intention of becoming a children's author. He studied civil engineering at Tennessee State University and began working as a contractor. After college, he and Patricia developed a romantic relationship and then the two teamed up both as a married couple and as an authorship team. Their first book together, *Look What You've Done Now, Moses*, was published in 1984.

The McKissacks share a love of books and a passion for black history. Their interests have produced a series of biographies of famous African-American figures: *Carter G. Woodson: The Father of Black History* (1991), *Frederick Douglas: Leader Against Slavery* (1991), *George Washington Carver: The Peanut Scientist* (1991), *Louis Armstrong: Jazz Musician* (1991), *Martin Luther King, Jr.: Man of Peace* (1991), *Langston Hughes: Great American Poet* (1992), and *Jesse Owens: Olympic Star* (1992). Two of their books—*A Long Hard Journey: The Story of Pullman Porter* (1990) and *Sojourner Truth: Ain't I a Woman* (1993)—have earned the Coretta Scott King Award for outstanding contributions to literature for children.

The historical fiction of the McKissacks covers a broad spectrum of topics. *Black Diamond* (1993), for example, is the story of the old Negro Baseball Leagues. *Christmas in the Big House, Christmas in the Quarters* (1994) is a brilliant piece of work that compares the holiday celebrations in the slave quarters with the celebrations in the home of the owner of a Virginia plantation in the pre–Civil War era.

The McKissacks live in St. Louis, Missouri, where they continue to use their special gifts for making history come alive for children. Here are some of the other books that the McKissacks have written:

> *The Story of Booker T. Washington* (1991)
>
> *Zora Neal Hurston* (1992)
>
> *African-American Scientists* (1994)

Uchida—*Journey to Topaz, Journey Home*, and *The Bracelet*—chronicle the experiences of Japanese Americans unjustly interned after the attack on Pearl Harbor at the beginning of World War II. Here are other books about this unfortunate time in American history:

- *Baseball Saved Us* by Ken Mochizuki, a young boy's account of playing baseball in the camps and his subsequent experiences;
- *So Far from the Sea* by Eve Bunting, the story of a Japanese family that visits the grandfather's grave and retells the old man's experiences in the camps; and
- *The Children of Topaz: The Story of a Japanese Internment Camp Based on a Classroom Diary* by M. O. Tunnell and G. W. Chilcoat, an historically accurate account from journal entries kept by third graders and their teacher.

In the past, historical fiction depicted Native Americans as wild and destructive people. Today, historical fiction about Indian Americans tells a very different story. Scott O'Dell's *Sing Down the Moon* tells about the injustices faced by the Navajo nation in their forced relocation to reservations, and his *Thunder Rolling in the Mountains,* co-authored with Elizabeth Hall, tells about the removal of the Nez Percé nation from their land in the Pacific Northwest. Joseph Bruchac's *The Arrow over the Door* is a well-researched account of an encounter between a group of Native Americans and a group of Quakers (Friends) who establish a place of mutual peace. Bruchac's *Children of the Long House* and Michael Dorris's *Guests* give insight into Native American tribal life and culture.

In sum, historical fiction written today is moving closer to more realistic portrayals of the pasts of diverse cultural groups.

HISTORICAL FICTION IN THE CLASSROOM AND AT HOME

In the classroom, historical fiction can be an integral part of instruction in social studies and language arts instruction. As children explore topics in world history (ancient civilizations, the Middle Ages, the Renaissance, immigration) and study topics in American history (Colonial America, the Westward Movement, the American Revolution, the Civil War), they can draw upon the knowledge and imagination of historical novelists to enhance their learning. Historical novels provide different perspectives on many aspects of the past.

Excellent picture books depict life and times of the past. Nelson (1996) has described how these books can be used effectively to enrich and enliven the reading and social studies programs, even in the upper elementary grades. "The human message of these picture books can be poignant and meaningful to the mature reader, be that person a fifth grader or their teacher" (6).

Teachers can use historical fiction in many ways as an integral part of the reading program, with readers workshops on such popular titles as Lois Lowry's *Number the Stars* or Katherine Paterson's *Lyddie.* For heterogeneous groups, teachers can select books at different reading levels but that focus on the same theme; for example, Alice Dalgliesh's *The Courage of Sarah Noble*, Elizabeth George Speare's *The Witch of Blackbird Pond*, and Scott O'Dell's *Island of the Blue Dolphins* all focus on the courage of strong female protagonists.

Writing is a natural outgrowth of the historical fiction that children read. Children can write reports based on their research of the historical periods reflected in historical novels. After reading a book such as Tony Johnson's *The Wagon*, the story of a boy born into slavery and freed by the Emancipation Proclamation, students can write before and after views of the boy's experience. Students can write in many modes—imaginary journals, letters, poems, next chapters, sequels, first person reactions, for example.

Norton (1993) suggests webbing to effectively engage children with historical fiction in the classroom. She suggests using semantic webs to teach vocabulary essential to any story, literacy webs to link important elements and characteristics of a specific novel, and unit webs for connecting different books related to a particular theme or topic. Students can develop webs for themes, characters, setting, and other literary elements as part of their guided book discussions. "Webbing allows students to identify areas of interest, brainstorm ideas, identify literature selections and other materials that are appropriate for each area, conduct research, authenticate fictional texts through nonfiction sources, and work together in groups to report information back to the class" (434).

Historical novels can be used for read alouds, booksharing, author studies, sustained silent reading, guided discussions, or any other activity that normally occurs as part of reading instruction in the literature-rich classroom.

Special Perspectives on Children's Literature

HISTORICAL FICTION BRINGS THE PAST ALIVE
by Ann Carmola

Reading aloud is a daily occurrence in my classroom, yet there is always an air of anticipation when we are about to begin a new book. My second and third graders sit on the floor, eagerly waiting for me to "open the box" and hand each of them his or her own copy of our next adventure.

Many of our read-aloud selections are historical fiction, books that take us back in time. Today, we are about to begin *Little House in the Big Woods* by Laura Ingalls Wilder. It's a perfect match for our social studies topic, the Westward Expansion.

As children explore the chapter titles and illustrations, they become more impatient and excited by the minute, and so I begin with chapter one. The children quickly learn that Laura lives with her Ma, Pa, and two sisters Mary and Carrie in a log cabin in Pepin, Wisconsin (around 1870). We stop for a minute to find Wisconsin on our large map of the United States and place a pin on its location. Later we will take time to find Pepin, but at the moment, we are off on our journey, and oh what fun we have!

Each chapter offers a new snapshot of pioneer life. The first book in the *Little House* series takes us through an entire year in the life of the Ingalls family. When we begin, it is fall, and the family is preparing for the long winter ahead. Pa is spending a great deal of time hunting, and when he brings home a deer, we are fascinated with the steps he takes to prepare the meat for winter. Most of my children have heard of smoked ham or turkey, but in the book they actually see a picture of a smokehouse and appreciate the work involved to prepare the meat of a single animal.

The slaughter of the pig really grabs their attention. They are surprised to learn that no part of the pig is wasted. They are all familiar with ham and pork chops and bacon, but they are amazed to find out about headcheese, cracklings, sausage, lard, and salt pork. They laugh and make faces when Pa blows up the pig's bladder and ties a string around the end of it for Mary and Laura to toss and kick around. For them, this is certainly a different form of entertainment!

Each day, I read one or two chapters, since most chapters are relatively short. We learn how the attic in the new house serves a dual purpose. As the weather turns colder, it becomes a place for Mary and Laura to play, but it is also a storage place for vegetables from the garden that the family will eat during the winter. We get to celebrate Christmas with Laura and her cousins, and later we learn how she and her family celebrate the Sabbath. We become involved as the family collects maple sap, and we can almost taste the maple syrup candy. A trip to the general store in the town of Pepin offers us a detailed look at what's available in comparison to today's malls. As spring becomes summer, we experience the family making cheese and gathering honey, and, before we know it, it's harvest time again.

We don't just read this book, we become part of the family. One of the first things we do is check out a copy of the *Little House Cookbook* from the school library. One day, we make Hasty Pudding, making sure we have "real" maple syrup to sweeten it. We try churning butter and using butter molds and making bread and pancakes. We even try to make our own cheese. My children are great list makers, so we make numerous lists. We make lists of activities that take place each season, a list of animals, a list of items available at the general store, a list of words we haven't seen before. We become fascinated with quilts and quilt patterns. Children plan and construct their own quilts with squares of construction paper.

When we finish the book, we have a day of celebration. We dress like pioneers, play games and sing songs that we have learned, and, with the help of parents, enjoy the foods that Laura and her family ate on numerous occasions. The walls and shelves of our classroom are filled with drawings, posters, lists, dioramas, puzzles, and other reminders of what we've learned about pioneer life. And this is just the beginning! All year long, we continue to use the Wilder books and other works of historical fiction to explore pioneer life.

Now the children have opportunities to choose another book from the *Little House* series to read independently. Multiple copies of the books are available in the classroom, so children can read alone or in pairs and talk about what they read. The series allows us to continue our journey, pinpoint where each story takes place, and learn why and how the family finally settles there. Each day, we meet to discuss similarities and differences among the books. We learn about the challenges that life in Minnesota, South Dakota, Oklahoma (Indian Territory), and Missouri present the Ingalls family. We enjoy the good times, but we suffer through the blizzards, prairie fires, floods, a grasshopper plague, and times of hunger.

Through it all, we learn that the home life of the Ingalls family is secure. My students feel the strength, cohesiveness, and love that the family members have for one another. The *Little House* books present us with a great deal of factual information about pioneer life in America, but they also clearly demonstrate that it took cooperation, hard work, and determination to survive. And those are important lessons to learn!

Ann Carmola is a teacher in the Newton, Massachusetts, public schools. Her classroom practices instill in her students a love of literature.

Historical fiction can be part of the reading diet of children outside the classroom as well. Simply written books like Kate Liea's *Potato: A Tale from the Great Depression*, based on the lives of the author's grandparents, can lead to stories about the history and background of one's own family.

Children who are introduced to the works of Scott O'Dell and Karen Cushman as part of their in-school reading regimen will more likely than not make these stories part of their home reading as well. Parents can be alerted to the availability of historical fiction and to the advantages of reading it, encouraging them to discuss and promote reading of this genre at home.

CONCLUSION

Historical fiction provides a nexus between the past and the present, between fact and fiction, between history and imagination. Historical novels present the human side of history and bring the past to life in appealing and memorable ways for children. While it is important that it be historically accurate, such fiction should also be judged by its story strength and the quality of its literary style. Within the classroom, historical novels can serve as a source of information about the past, provide material for recreational reading, or help to enrich a curriculum topic.

Questions and Activities for Action and Discussion

1. Select a period or event in American history and, using the Internet and other resources, make a "book cluster" of historical fiction titles that would be appropriate for studying that topic. Be sure to include books at different reading levels.

2. Read two or three historical novels for children about a historical event or period such as, the Renaissance, European exploration of the Americas, the American Revolution, or World War II. Compare and contrast the approaches taken in these

novels. Do these novels enhance your understanding of the event or period? If so, how? If not, why not?

3. Read a historical novel and a biography from the same time period. Using a graphic organizer, show what both books have in common and how they differ.

4. Compare a chapter in an elementary or middle school social studies textbook with a historical novel about a corresponding topic or period in history. Identify the advantages and the disadvantages that each offers as a learning resource.

5. Historical fiction is an effective way for helping children view the human side of history. Prepare a presentation that you might make to a skeptical group of school administrators, school board members, or parents who see historical fiction as a way of "watering down" the history curriculum.

CHILDREN'S & YOUNG ADULT BOOKS CITED IN THIS CHAPTER

Alder, Elizabeth. 1995. *The King's Shadow*. New York: Farrar, Straus and Giroux.

Armstrong, Jennifer. 1995. *Black-Eyed Susan*. New York: Crown.

Avi. 1987. *The Fighting Ground*. New York: Harper & Row.

_____ 1996. *Beyond the Western Sea, Book One: The Escape from Home*. New York: Orchard Books.

Berleth, Richard. 1990. *Samuel's Choice*. New York: Albert Whitman.

Blackwood, Gary. 1998. *The Shakespeare Stealer*. New York: Dutton.

Bowen, Gary. 1994. *Stranded at Plimouth Plantation 1626*. New York: HarperCollins.

Brenner, Barbara. 1978. *Wagon Wheels*. New York: Harper & Row.

Bruchac, Joseph. 1996. *Children of the Long House*. New York: Dial.

_____ 1998. *The Arrow over the Door*. Illustrated by James Watley. New York: Dial.

Bunting, Eve. 1990. *The Wall*. Illustrated by Ronald Himler. New York: Clarion.

_____ 1998. *So Far from the Sea*. Illustrated by David Diaz. New York: Harcourt Brace.

Byars, Betsy. 1994. *The Golly Sisters Ride Again*. New York: HarperCollins.

Choi, Sook Nyul. 1991. *The Year of Impossible Good-Byes*. New York: Dell.

Clapp, Patricia. 1991. *Constance: A Story of Early Plymouth*. Magnolia, Mass: Peter Smith.

Collier, James and Christopher Collier. 1974. *My Brother Sam Is Dead*. New York: Four Winds Press.

_____ 1987. *War Comes to Willy Freeman*. New York: Doubleday.

Conlon-McKenna, Marita. 1990. *Under the Hawthorn Tree*. Illustrated by Donald Teskey. Dublin, Ireland: O'Brien Press.

Conrad, Pam. 1991. *Pedro's Journal: A Voyage with Christopher Columbus*. Illustrated by Peter Koeppen. New York: Scholastic.

Curtis, Christopher Paul. 1995. *The Watsons Go to Birmingham—1963*. New York: Delacorte.

Cushman, Karen. 1994. *Catherine, Called Birdy*. New York: Clarion.

_____ 1995. *The Midwife's Apprentice*. New York: Clarion.

Dalgliesh, Alice. 1954. *The Courage of Sarah Noble*. New York: Scribner's.

Davis, Ossie. 1992. *Just Like Martin*. New York: Simon and Schuster.

De Angeli, Marguerite. 1949. *Door in the Wall*. New York: Dell.

Denenberg, Barry. 1997. *So Far from Home: The Diary of Mary Driscoll, an Irish Mill Girl*. New York: Scholastic.

Disher, Gary. 1993. *The Bamboo Flute*. New York: Ticknor and Fields.

Dorris, Michael. 1992. *Morning Girl*. New York: Hyperion.

_____ 1994. *Guests*. New York: Hyperion.

Fleischman, Paul. 1993. *Bull Run*. New York: HarperCollins.

Fleming, Candice. 1998. *The Hatmaker's Sign: A Story Told by Benjamin Franklin*. Illustrated by Robert A. Parker. New York: Orchard.

Forbes, Esther. 1994. *Johnny Tremain*. New York: Dell.

Fox, Paula. 1973. *Slave Dancer*. New York: Bradbury.

Fritz, Jean. 1987. *Early Thunder*. New York: Penguin.

Gallaz, Christopher and Roberto Innocenti. 1985. *Rose Blanche*. New York: Steward, Tabori and Chang.

Greene, Bette. 1973. *Summer of My German Soldier*. New York: Dial.

Greene, Constance. 1980. *Dotty's Suitcase*. New York: Viking.

Hoestlandt, Jo. 1993. *Star of Fear, Star of Hope*. Translated by Mark Polizzotti, Illustrated by Johanna Kang. New York: Walker and Co.

Holman, Felice. 1983. *The Wild Children*. New York: Scribners.

Hopkinson, Deborah. 1993. *Sweet Clara and the Freedom Quilt*. Illustrated by James Ransome. New York: Knopf.

Hunt, Irene. 1964. *Across Five Aprils*. Chicago: Follett.

Johnson, Tony. 1996. *The Wagon*. Illustrated by James Ransome. New York: Tambourine.

Kelly, Eric. 1928. *Trumpeter of Krakow*. New York: Macmillan.

Lasky, Kathryn. 1998. *True North: A Novel of the Underground Railroad*. New York: Scholastic.

Lawrence, Ian. 1998. *The Wreckers*. New York: Delacorte.

Liea, Kate. 1997. *Potato: A Tale from the Great Depression*. Illustrated by Lisa Campbell Ernst. Washington, D.C.: National Geographic Press.

Lobel, Arnold. 1971. *On the Day Peter Stuyvesant Sailed into Town*. New York: Harper & Row.

Lowry, Lois. 1989. *Number the Stars*. Boston: Houghton Mifflin.

MacLachlan, Patricia. 1985. *Sarah Plain and Tall*. New York: Harper & Row.

Marco, Katherine McGlade. 1992. *Hang Out the Flag*. New York: Macmillan.

Maruki, Toshi. 1980. *Hiroshima No Pika*. New York: Lothrup.

McCully, Emily Arnold. 1996. *The Bobbin Girl*. New York: Dial.

Miller, William. 1997. *Richard Wright and the Library Card*. Illustrated by Gregory Christe. New York: Lee and Low.

Mochizuki, Ken. 1993. *Baseball Saved Us*. Illustrated by Dom Lee. New York: Lee and Low.

Monjo, F. N. 1993. *The Drinking Gourd: A Story of the Underground Railroad*. Illustrated by Fred Brenner. New York: HarperCollins.

Myers, Walter Dean. 1988. *Fallen Angels*. New York: HarperCollins.

O'Dell, Scott. 1960. *Island of the Blue Dolphins*. Boston: Houghton Mifflin.

_____ 1970. *Sing Down the Moon*. Boston: Houghton Mifflin.

_____ 1980. *Sarah Bishop*. New York: Scholastic.

_____ 1981. *Carlota*. Boston: Houghton Mifflin.

O'Dell, Scott and Elizabeth Hall. 1992. *Thunder Rolling in the Mountains*. Boston: Houghton Mifflin.

Osborne, Mary Pope. 1995. *Night of the Ninjas*. New York: Random House.

Paterson, Katherine. 1991. *Lyddie*. New York: Lodestar.

Paulsen, Gary. 1994. *Mr. Tuckett*. New York: Delacorte.

Pausewang, Gudrun. 1996. *The Final Journey*. New York: Penguin.

Petry, Ann Lane. 1964. *Tituba of Salem Village*. New York: Crowell.

Polacco, Patricia. 1994. *Pink and Say*. New York: Philomel.

Reeder, Carolyn. 1997. *Across the Lines*. New York: Atheneum.

Renalder, Ann. 1993. *The Fifth of March: A Story of the Boston Massacre*. San Diego: Harcourt.

Sander, Joan. 1981. *The Long Way to a New Land*. New York: HarperCollins.

Speare, Elizabeth George. 1958. *The Witch of Blackbird Pond*. Boston: Houghton Mifflin.

_____ 1961. *The Bronze Bow*. Boston: Houghton Mifflin.

Sutcliff, Rosemary. 1978. *Sun Horse, Moon Horse*. New York: Dutton.

Taylor, Mildred D. 1976. *Roll of Thunder, Hear My Cry*. New York: Dial.

Terner, Ann. 1992. *Katie's Trunk*. New York: Macmillan.

Tunnell, Michael O. and George W. Chilcoat. 1996. *The Children of Topaz: The Story of a Japanese Internment Camp Based on a Classroom Diary*. New York: Holiday House.

Uchida, Yoshiko. 1971. *Journey to Topaz*. Illustrated by Donald Carrick. New York: Scribners.

_____ 1978. *Journey Home*. Illustrated by Charles Robins. New York: Atheneum.

_____ 1993. *The Bracelet*. Illustrated by Joanna Yardley. New York: Philomel.

Wisler, G. Clifton. 1993. *Jerico's Journey*. New York: Lodestar.

Woodruff, Elvira. 1994. *Dear Levi: Letters from the Overland Trail*. New York: Knopf.

Yep, Laurence. 1993. *Dragon's Gate*. New York: HarperCollins.

Yolen, Jane. 1992. *Encounter*. San Diego: Harcourt Brace.

Zeier, Joan T. 1990. *The Elderberry Thicket*. New York Atheneum.

REFERENCES

Coffey, R. K., and E. F. Howard. 1997. *America as Story* (2d ed.). Chicago: American Library Association.

DeFelice, C. 1998. Research: The Bones Beneath the Flesh of Historical Fiction. *Book Links* 8:30–34.

Freeman, E. B., and L. Levstik. 1988. Recreating the Past: Historical Fiction in the Social Studies Curriculum. *The Elementary School Journal* 88:329–337.

Jacobs, J. S., and M. O. Tunnell. 1996. *Children's Literature, Briefly*. Columbus, Ohio: Merrill.

Johnson, N. M., and M. J. Ebert. 1992. Time Travel Is Possible: Historical Fiction and Biography—Passport to the Past. *The Reading Teacher* 45:488-495.

MacLeod, A. S. 1998. Writing Backwards: Modern Models in Historical Fiction. *The Horn Book* 74:26–33.

Nelson, T. A. 1996. Pirates, Baseball and Explorers: A Fifth Grade Teacher and Her Students Discover Historical Fiction Picture Books. *The New England Reading Association Journal* 32:5–13.

Norton, D. E. 1993. Webbing and Historical Fiction. *The Reading Teacher* 46:432–436.

Porter, D. H. 1993. The Gold in Fort Knox: Historical Fiction in the Context of Historiography. *Soundings* 76:315–350.

Rahn, S. 1991. An Evolving Past: The Story of Historical Fiction and Nonfiction for Children. *The Lion and the Unicorn* 15:1–26.

Sipe, L. R. 1997. In Their Own Words: Authors' Views on Issues in Historical Fiction. *The New Advocate* 10:243–258.

Sullivan, K. 1997. Brief Books of Historical Fiction. *Book Links* 7:58–63.

Temple, C., M. Martinez, J. Yokota, and A. Nalyor. 1998. *Children's Books in Children's Hands*. Boston: Allyn and Bacon.

Tomlinson, C. M., M. O. Tunnell, and D. J. Richgels. 1993. The Content and Writing of History in Textbooks and Trade Books. In *The Story of Ourselves: Teaching History Through Children's Literature*, eds. M. O. Tunnell and R. Ammon. Portsmouth, N.H.: Heinemann.

CHAPTER 9

INFORMATIONAL BOOKS

 nformational trade books constitute the majority of books found in school libraries. Increasing attention is being devoted to the language and illustrations used in informational children's books, books that have become an important genre of children's literature.

THIS CHAPTER

- examines informational trade books as a genre of children's literature;
- describes characteristics of nonfiction writing for children; and

- identifies the popular areas in which informational children's trade books are most widely used.

When people are asked to identify their favorite piece of children's literature, they typically name books like *Madeline* or *The Velveteen Rabbit*. Yet much of what children read during their elementary school years is fact rather than fiction. Informational trade books are becoming increasingly popular with children and receiving more recognition as a genre in the field of children's literature.

Informational trade books have come a long way. In school libraries and classroom shelves of the past, these books were often utilitarian and usually dreary, with titles like *Rocks and Minerals* and *Let's Visit Afghanistan*. Traditionally, informational trade books were written by experts in their topics rather than by people with a sense of literary style or an understanding of young minds. Today, one finds "a bold profusion of titles, books written by authors who care about their subjects and produced by publishers who treat each book as a unique addition to the body of literature" (Greenlaw 1991, 41). Current authors of nonfiction for children are typically inspired to write about their topics instead of merely providing encyclopedic resources.

Nonfiction is the fastest-growing genre of juvenile literature. "Beginning in the 1960s and propelled by the information age, children's nonfiction books come into their own as a legitimate literary form led by acknowledged authors who employ rich writing styles and a variety of forms not just to convey knowledge or list facts but to infuse their subject with the same sense of wonder and awe that drew them to the topic in the first place" (Doiron 1995, 37). In the 1980s, informational trade books caught the attention of the Newbery Award committee. Three works of nonfiction were named Honor Books—Kathryn Lasky's and Christopher Knight's photo-essay *Sugaring Time* in 1983, Rhonda Blumberg's *Commodore Perry in the Land of Shogun* in 1986, and Patricia Lauber's *Volcano: The Eruption and Healing of Mount Saint Helens* in 1987. In 1988, Russell Freedman's *Lincoln: A Photobiography* was awarded the Newbery Medal. The unique illustrations and quality writing in these four books raised nonfiction to the level of other widely respected genres in children's literature and set the stage for new recognition and popularity of informational books.

Nonfiction children's trade books play an important part in both the learning-to-read and the reading-to-learn phase of children's school lives. Beyond the fact that these books satisfy children's natural curiosity and sense of wonder about the world around them, they provide the means through which some children find their "way into" the world of literacy (Caswell and Duke 1998).

Children use informational books to develop and practice the skills that will make them fluent and capable readers. At the same time, they use these books to acquire information and learn about their worlds. In using informational trade books as a basis for teaching, Farest, Miller, and Ferwin (1995) discovered that "children not only learned content, but that they did indeed move beyond information to develop newer and richer insights into, and deeper understandings of, both the content and the essence of literature" (273). Information books not only present facts; they encourage children to inquire, compare, analyze, imagine, and gain insight into new information. This genre of children's literature plays an important role in reading across the curriculum at all levels.

FACT AND FICTION

From their earliest years, children are introduced to literature in narrative form, stories that typically begin "Once upon a time" and end "happily ever after." Most of what children encounter in their early school years—estimates are as high as 90 percent—involves narrative text as well. Narrative text tells a story, is written primarily to entertain, contains the familiar elements of character, setting, plot, and theme that contribute to children's enjoyment and love of what they read, and consists of songs, poetry, and fiction in a variety of modes.

The purpose of expository text, on the other hand, is to inform, explain, instruct, or enlighten. It is structured and organized differently, and it doesn't always have the elements of the stories that children typically enjoy. Expository text may use description and narration to achieve its aims, but its purpose is not primarily to tell a story. Informational books are organized around particular topics or themes.

Reading informational material sometimes involves a different mind-set and a different set of skills than reading fiction. While both narrative and expository text require readers to recognize vocabulary, figure out the pronunciation and meaning of unknown words, and build meaning from the text on the printed page, authors of fact and authors of fiction often write from different perspectives. Children often read these different types of books for different purposes, and the different material often produces different responses.

Rosenblatt's (1991) well-known reader response theory draws a distinction between an aesthetic response to text and an efferent response to text. Readers typically approach stories and poems with an aesthetic stance to "get inside" or "live through" the stories and poems that they read. They approach factual material with an efferent stance to "gather information" or "take away" knowledge from the text.

Despite the differences between narrative and expository texts, the two types of text are not mutually exclusive. Doiron (1995) points out the aesthetic elements of children's nonfiction: the elements of language and style that skilled writers of nonfiction use can be appreciated for their aesthetics, and there is an aesthetic element to the pursuit of learning and to the discovery and construction of new knowledge.

In working with children, Spink (1996) found out "that stories can be highly informative without losing their appeal to our imaginative and aesthetic sensibilities and that informational texts can fuel our imaginations and fill us with delight, while at the same time provide us with empirical knowledge and concrete answers to specific questions" (136). Cognitive and emotional involvement in learning can be complementary processes. Even the most sophisticated adults are as fascinated with the information and illustrations presented in Aliki's *Mummies Are Made in Egypt* and David Macaulay's *The Way Things Work* as they are with the novels they read. Informational trade books can certainly be read for pleasure as well as for information.

WHAT MAKES GOOD NONFICTION LITERATURE FOR CHILDREN?

What are the characteristics of quality children's informational books? What should teachers and parents look for when selecting these books? In describing informational books as literature, Russell (1991) writes, "They can be books that excite young readers to further reading and books that young readers want to return to again and again— not only for information but for enjoyment. It is quite right to expect that nonfictional work be well written, beautifully illustrated, imaginatively laid out, as well as up-to-date, accurate, and thought-provoking" (Russell 1991, 138–139).

Dowd (1992) suggests the following criteria for judging the quality of children's informational books: accuracy/authenticity, content/perspective, style, organization, and illustrations/format. Sudol and King (1996), who have devised a checklist for evaluating nonfiction trade books, add the elements of vocabulary and reader interest.

Accuracy

Accuracy of information is obviously vital in nonfiction trade books. Children often take it for granted that whatever is printed is accurate, a dangerous assumption.

Accuracy begins with authorship. It's axiomatic that authors need to be qualified either through background or research to write on their topics. Some children's authors—like Franklin Branley who writes extensively about science in books like *Drip*

Author Profile: Gail Gibbons

Gail Gibbons is one of the most prolific author/illustrators of nonfiction books for young children. For twenty-five years she has fascinated children and adults with over fifty books on clocks and locks, on nature and diners.

Like many other authors and illustrators, Gibbons came to children's literature from other forms of media. Born and raised in Illinois, she received a BFA in graphic design from the University of Illinois. Her first job was as a graphic artist for a local CBS television affiliate in Champaign, and she later did freelance art and graphics for other television stations.

Although she enjoyed her work as a graphic artist, Gibbons never forgot a college instructor who had suggested she try her hand at illustrating children's books. This idea began to take hold in 1971 when she became the graphic artist for a children's program entitled "Take a Giant Step." She was working in a children's medium but not yet with children's literature. As she continued her work in graphic design for television shows, Gibbons began illustrating children's books that had been written by other authors. Her first original work was *Willie and His Wagon Wheel*, published in 1975. In the succeeding years, a wave of books on familiar topics of interest to children followed: *Clocks and How They Go*, (1979), *Trucks* (1981), *Dinosaurs* (1987), *How A House is Built* (1990), *Spiders* (1993), and *Cats* (1996).

As an author and illustrator, Gibbons takes meticulous care with her writing and her artwork. She researches topics with a fine-tooth comb, making sure she knows all she can before committing her subject to paper. In preparing to write *Clocks and How They Work* (1979), she explored the workings of clocks, took them apart, and studied different types of timepieces ranging from antique grandfather clocks to modern digital watches. The result was an instant success that won the 1980 American Institute of Graphic Arts Award.

Gibbons's research takes her around the country in search of just the right point of view. While researching *Martha's Diner* (1989), she visited old time New England diners. In preparing *The Moon Book* (1997), she didn't travel to the moon but meticulously researched the topic and consulted with scientists.

Gail Gibbons's books are informational and enjoyable. She combines clear and creative text with spectacular drawings to intrigue her audience and make learning a great experience. Her work has garnered many awards, including the American Library Association's Notable Books Award. She lives in rural Vermont, where she continues to produce books that continues to delight her audience. Among her recent books are the following:

Click (1997), a book about cameras

The Honey Makers (1997), a book about honeybees, how they live in colonies, how they produce honey, and how they are managed by beekeepers

Knights in Shining Armor (1995), a book about knights and knighthood

Sea Turtles (1995), an informative book about these fascinating sea creatures

Drop Raindrops and *Shooting Stars*—work exclusively in their areas of expertise. Authors who write informational books on a range of topics—like Gail Gibbons who has written on a range of topics from cows to clocks to cameras—are noted for the meticulous research they do on their subjects. Many nonfiction books contain authors' notes detailing the search for information and providing additional facts about a topic.

Timeliness contributes to accuracy. Information changes. Facts and concepts presented in nonfiction children's literature need to be up-to-date. The copyright date on a book on space, for example, is more important than the copyright date on a novel. As scientific discoveries add to our knowledge about such topics as dinosaurs, these discoveries need to be reflected in text. Comparing a current informational trade book about a timely topic with one written several years ago can be an interesting critical reading activity for children.

As in all children's literature, nonfiction books should avoid stereotypes. They should also realistically reflect the diversity of our society—women and girls in roles traditionally filled by men and boys, people of color in respected leadership positions.

In informational trade books, theories must be distinguished from confirmed facts. Informational books avoid anthropomorphism, or ascribing human characteristics to non-human creatures and inanimate objects.

Content

The content of nonfiction books needs to be appropriate for the interests and understanding of children. Content also must involve the cohesion of ideas. "Both unity and coherence are vital within individual paragraphs as well as throughout the text. . . . Unity of the whole text occurs when all ideas belong together and develop the thesis statement" (Sudol and King 1996, 422).

Content needs to both extend and support readers' background knowledge or schemata. Informational children's literature is used both to add to the child's existing knowledge and to build new areas of knowledge. Good informational books have an appropriate concept load, abstract concepts that are clarified with concrete examples, and content that does not take the readers' background knowledge for granted.

Style

As in any genre, style is an important element in informational trade books. "Quality nonfiction books for children satisfy the criterion of style when they (1) create a feeling of reader involvement, (2) use vivid and interesting language to present information in a clear and direct manner, and (3) convey a positive tone or attitude toward the subject" (Dowd 1992, 40).

Some information books create reader involvement by suggesting activities or experiments for children to do while they read. Some include children in text and illustrations. Style is enhanced by an upbeat tone that engages young readers.

Obviously, language contributes to style. Vivid words convey ideas, and vivid imagery makes concepts more clear.

Organization

Well-written informational material for children has a clear and logical structure. Content is organized according to structures familiar to young children—main ideas and details; sequence; comparison-contrast; cause-effect relationships. The presentation of text and illustrations supports the readers' ability to recognize these structures and comprehend the material presented.

Format

In nonfiction books, reference aids are important. These books frequently include a table of contents and an index, clear headings and subheadings that reflect the structure of the text, and bibliographies and glossaries to extend meaning.

Illustrations and graphic aids are very important. Photographs, maps, charts, diagrams, tables, and other visual devices are far more essential in nonfiction than in fiction because these visual devices reinforce authenticity and make meaning more clear. Timelines place information in a temporal context. Clear captions and labels clarify size and space relationships and add depth to and enhance the clarity of the information presented in the text. Nonfiction books use various forms of visual media both to present information and to make the work appeal to children. Appealing page layouts balance text and illustrations and vary the size and type of print for liveliness.

Vocabulary

Content-related reading material contains a technical and a specialized vocabulary. *Technical* words are those that are unique to a particular topic or subject area—words like *integer* in math, for example, or *longitude* in geography. *Specific* words are those that have a generally common meaning but that take on specialized meanings in relation to particular subjects—for example, the *bill* that Congress passes, the *bill* of the duck, the *bill* we pay at the end of the month. Skilled writers make sure that the meanings of these words are made clear to the young reader. Informational trade books define new words in context as they are introduced, use pictures and artwork to clarify meaning, and/or provide glossaries for reference.

Vocabulary is not watered down in informational books. Words are neither too advanced nor condescendingly simple. The ability to use language in this way is a mark of the skilled writer for children.

Interest

Interest is often generated by the reader. A child who is interested in gerbils or giraffes will seek out informational trade books about these animals. But there are qualities inherent in nonfiction books that will often grab and hold a young reader's attention. Colorful photos, attractive graphic design, appealing activities, engaging language all can entice readers to pick up and become engaged in a book.

Overall, the best indicator of a quality informational book is "clear prose that engages the reader, stirs the imagination, and awakens the mind" (Horning 1997, 36).

FACTORS FOR CONSIDERATION

EVALUATING INFORMATION BOOKS

In reviewing informational trade books to use with children, here are five factors to look for:

1. Is the information accurate and does it distinguish between fact and theory?
2. Is the content appropriate for the interest and understanding of young readers?
3. Is the tone of the writing clear and interesting?
4. Do photographs, drawings, diagrams, and other graphic devices support and extend information presented in the text?
5. Are author's notes or other information provided to help readers extend their knowledge of the subject?

CONCEPT BOOKS

A very basic type of informational trade book for children is the concept book. Concept books are books "in which examples and comparisons are used to present abstract ideas in concrete, understandable ways" (Harris and Hodges 1995, 40). These books convey a body of knowledge in an attractive and clear manner to a young audience. The purpose is to both teach and delight the young reader.

Language and mastery of concepts develop hand in hand in young children. The language in concept books is typically clear and simple. Some concept books are wordless, others have only label words, and others include simple narrative text. Illustrations—sometimes drawings but often photographs—show relationships among ideas and elements of the concept.

As in other categories of informational trade books, the range of topics addressed in concept books is incredibly wide. Simple books help children develop the concepts of shape, size, color, the senses, directions (as in *up* and *down*), time, and opposites among many others.

Technically, alphabet books and counting books are concept books as well, but consideration here is limited to books that convey information about a particular subject and help children answer questions about the world around them. There are concept books about objects and ideas that fascinate young children—trucks (Donald Crews's *Truck*), fire engines (Bruce McMillan's *Fire Engine Shapes*), trains (Donald Crews's *Freight Train*), parades (Donald Crews's *Parade*), guinea pigs (Dick King-Smith's *I Love Guinea Pigs*), and

LIST OF TEN

CONCEPT BOOKS FOR YOUNG CHILDREN

Much attention is given to helping young children learn the concepts of color, shape, size, and spatial relationships. Here are ten concept books, some of them classics, that children can enjoy as they learn:

My First Book of Colors by Eric Carle
one of a series of concept books that this brilliant writer/illustrator has created (Crowell, 1974)

Is It Red? Is It Yellow Is It Blue? by Tana Hoban
in which this popular author of concept books explores primary colors (Greenwillow, 1978).

Color Everywhere by Tana Hoban
a book filled with color photographs of familiar objects (Morrow, 1995)

Circles, Triangles, and Squares by Tana Hoban
a book that illustrates familiar geometric forms in everyday objects (Macmillan, 1974)

Shapes by John Reiss
goes beyond the familiar square, circle, and triangle to cubes, ovals, and rectangles (Bradbury, 1974)

Shapes by Anne Geddes
features the author's unique style of photographs and illustrations (Cedco, 1997)

Push-Pull, Empty-Full by Tana Hoban
a popular book comparing words and ideas that are different (Macmillan, 1972)

Fast-Slow, High-Low: A Book of Opposites by Peter Spier
another popular concept book illustrating opposites (Doubleday, 1972)

Dry or Wet? by Bruce MacMillan
with photographs of objects that are opposite to one another (Lothrup, 1998)

Opposites by Rosalinda Knightly
an engaging concept book illustrating the opposites (Little, Brown, 1986)

nursery school (Harlow Rockwell's *My Nursery School*). In short, teachers and parents of young children can find concept books on a huge array of topics.

Concept books convey knowledge. They enhance children's growing understanding of the world around them, help them develop ideas, sharpen their perceptions, stimulate their oral language, and provide early pleasurable experiences with books.

TYPES OF INFORMATIONAL BOOKS

Nonfiction trade books may assume any number of formats:

- **Straightforward presentations of facts and concepts**: Concept books for young children present information and ideas centered around a single topic, such as *Hiding* by Shirley Hughes, a charming book that illustrates the concept of hiding in all kinds of places—children hide behind the door, Daddy hides behind the newspaper, the moon hides behind the clouds.

- **Alphabet books**: Jerry Pallotta's *The Icky Bug Alphabet Book* and *The Yucky Reptile Alphabet Book* contain sophisticated science information tied to letters of the alphabet.
- **Wordless books**: These books present information without using text, such as Tom Feeling's *The Middle Passage* which tells the sad story of transportation of African slaves across the Atlantic.
- **Elaborately illustrated picture books**: Aliki's *A Medieval Feast* is a good example.
- **Photo-essays**: Russell Freedman's *Lincoln: A Photobiography* and Jill Krementz's *A Very Young Dancer* are good examples.

Biographies are also informational books in that they contain information on the lives of famous people, but they are considered here as a separate genre of children's literature.

Some nonfiction books combine more than one genre. For example, C. M. Millen's *A Symphony for the Sheep* contains information about wool production, from shearing the sheep to knitting woolen products, yet the information is presented in the form of a traditional Irish song.

Cultural diversity is reflected in informational books as it is in other genres of children's literature, and some of these books have a distinct multicultural and international focus. *Kofi and His Magic* by Maya Angelou, for example, is a lively, lyrical book about how a West African boy creates beautiful Kunte cloth, and it also gives a sense of life in his village. Another view of life in an African village is provided by Ifeoma Onyefulu in *Ogbo: Sharing Life in an African Village*, an informational photo-essay. Patricia and Frederick McKissack provide a history of the Civil Rights Movement in *The Civil Rights Movement in America from 1865 to the Present*. Deborah Chocolate's *My First Kwanzaa Book* describes the principles of this seven-day cultural holiday celebration.

Informational books about Latinos include the following:

- *The Mysteries of the Ancient Maya* by Carolyn Meyer and Charles Gallenkamp, which provides information about the rich history and achievements of the ancient Maya people;
- *Fiesta!* by June Behrens, an informational book describing the celebration of the Mexican holiday Cinco de Mayo;
- *In My Family/En mi familia* by Carmen Garza, an informational account that celebrates growing up in a Latino family in Texas;
- *Fernando's Gift—El regalo de Fernando* by Douglas Keister, which tells about life in a rural Costa Rican village; and
- *Day of the Dead: A Mexican-American Celebration* by Diane Hoyt-Goldsmith, a photo-essay about the feast that honors friends and relatives who have died.

These and other similar nonfiction books give all children insight into the values and traditions of Latino peoples.

Informational books relate to past and present aspects of Asian American and Native American cultures as well. Diane Hoyt-Goldsmith's *Hoang Anh: A Vietnamese-American Boy* is a photographic essay about the life of a young immigrant from Vietnam. Milton Meltzer provides an overview of Chinese immigration into the United States in *The Chinese Americans*. Arline Hirschfelder's *Happily May I Walk: American Indian and Alaska Natives Today* presents information about tribal governments, life on reservations, and other contemporary topics related to Native Americans. Virginia Driving Hawk Sneve's series *First Americans* (see p. 49) accurately portrays different groups of Native Americans.

In order to classify or categorize the topics found in informational children's literature, one would have to use a scheme as complex as the Dewey Decimal System. Children's informational trade books cover the gamut of human experience. There are hundreds and hundreds of trade books on popular topics of children's interests—dinosaurs, space travel, castles, wild animals, sports, and the like. For this book's purposes, information trade books will be divided into two broad categories: books of general interest and information, and those that cluster around content areas of the curriculum—science, social studies, math, and the arts. There are overlaps among categories, to be sure. An informational trade book about rain forests, for example, can provide geographic information about where in the world rain forests are located while also providing ideas about the social impact of the destruction of these resources.

General Interest and Information

Some books provide a cornucopia of merely trivial information, yet we keep returning to them again and again. Witness the adult fascination with the popular *Guinness Book of Records*, which also has a children's edition. Much of the information in these books is not especially important to our lives, yet it satisfies our basic need to know.

Children enjoy perusing books like Reginald Bragomer Jr. and David Fisher's *What's What: A Visual Glossary of the Physical World*, a book that contains illustrations and description of objects ranging from *aba* to *zipper*. Roland Morgan's *In the Next Three Seconds* is an ingenious and entertaining book that predicts what will happen in the world in successive periods of time—from the next three seconds to the next three million years—and helps children with the math involved in making these predictions. It predicts, for example, that Irish people will drink 200 potfuls of tea (in the next three seconds), Americans will eat four an a half head of cattle in take-out hamburgers (in the next three minutes), and 100 million European women will get married (in the next three decades).

Books like this, while they may not contain the most useful information and while children may not read them from cover to cover, provide many hours of entertainment.

Informational Trade Books About School Subjects

With the increased use of trade books in teaching, reading, and writing, informational literature has become an important vehicle for literacy across the curriculum. Nonfiction trade books are widely used in schools in the language arts and in other subject areas. Trade books are used to expand knowledge and to help students develop competencies in science, social studies, mathematics, the arts, and other areas of the curriculum.

Author Profile: SEYMOUR SIMON

From explaining what happens during a thunder and lightning storm to describing how the human brain functions to comparing wolves to human beings, Seymour Simon has a unique talent for making science understandable and interesting to young people and adults. With over 200 books to his credit, Simon knows how to communicate clearly with children.

Simon was born and raised in New York City. His interest in science began at a young age, when he spent all the time he could reading science fiction magazines. He attended the prestigious Bronx High School of Science and continued his education at City College of the City University of New York. After college, Simon became a teacher, a career he pursued for over twenty years.

Simon's first book, *Discovering What Earthworms Do*, was published in 1969. There followed several books on scientific topics related to the interests of children, books such as *The Paper Airplane Book* (1976) and *Pets in a Jar: Collecting and Caring for Small Animals* (1979). Simon's writing ventures into many different areas of science: the weather with books like *Storms* (1989) and *Lightning* (1997); animals with books like *Big Cats* (1991) and *Snakes* (1992); and outer space with books like *Galaxies* (1988) and *Our Solar System* (1992). More recently his series on the human body has featured books like *The Heart* (1996) explaining the circulatory system, *The Brain* (1997) explaining "the human control center" and *Bones: Our Skeletal System* (1998).

All of Simon's books are filled with accurate and interesting information and are characterized by striking photographs and illustrations. Over sixty of his books have been selected as Outstanding Science Trade Books by the National Association of Science Teachers and the Children's Book Council.

In addition to writing informational books, Simon has dabbled in fiction with his *Einstein Anderson Series of Mystery Stories*, which feature a young scientific genius with a fondness for bad puns. In these books, readers get not only the opportunity to solve mysteries but also the chance to learn about science. He has also edited *Star Walk* (1995), a collection of poetry and photographs about stars and space.

Seymour Simon continues to write books that inform and entertain children. Here are some of his other books:

Sharks (1995)

Wildfires (1996)

Spring Across America (1996)

Science

Most children are interested in the world around them, and science helps them account for much of what happens in that world. Informational trade books about science can transform interest into knowledge and satisfy children's curiosity about their world. In science-related information books, fascinating facts combine with interesting writing and informative illustrations to create in children a sense of wonder about science, while at the same time to provide enjoyable reading experiences.

In the world of science, information is exploding at an amazing rate. Informational trade books allow children to keep abreast of fast-moving developments in the fields of earth science, life science, and physical science and in related fields such as paleontology and ecology. Moreover, interacting with science books allows children to develop questioning, hypothesizing, analyzing, organizing, and other inquiry-based skills inherent in scientific literacy that will be so essential in the twenty-first century.

In examining informational trade books in science, it's important that children distinguish between fact and fiction. Ancient peoples created legends to account for events in their natural world, and authors of fiction have created engaging stories about scientific topics in which animals and objects think and act like people do. In science writing, however, accuracy demands the separation of fact and fiction and the recognition of the difference between the two.

LIST OF TEN

INFORMATIONAL TRADE BOOKS ABOUT SCIENCE

Extensive lists of science trade books are available to parents and teachers. Here is a sample of ten recently published books identified as outstanding by the National Science Teachers Association, in cooperation with the Children's Book Council:

A Drop of Water: A Book of Science and Wonder by Walter Wick
easy-to-read text and photographs explaining the concepts of evaporation, condensation, capillary attraction, and surface tension (Scholastic, 1997)

Earthquakes by Sally M. Walker
colorful diagrams and basic text explaining the scientific underpinnings of earthquakes (Carolrhoda, 1996)

The Big Rivers: The Missouri, the Mississippi, and the Ohio by Bruce Hiscock
with clear text and watercolors, describes how the three great rivers produced the floods of 1993 (Atheneum, 1997)

From Caterpillar to Butterfly by Deborah Heiligman, illustrated by Bari Weissman
detailed illustrations and interesting text presenting the growth stages of a butterfly as seen through the eyes of primary grade children (HarperCollins, 1996)

Weather Explained: A Beginner's Guide to the Elements by Derek Elsom
complex topics clearly presented with words, photographs, and diagrams (Henry Holt, 1997)

The Burrow Book: Tunnel into a World of Wildlife by Shaila Awan, illustrated by Richard Orr

a fascinating view of animals who live underground, from the Arctic tundra to the tropical forests of the world (DK Publishing, 1997)

Yikes! Your Body Up Close by Mike Janulewicz

an amazing close-up of various parts of the body shown through color photographs taken with an electron microscope (Simon and Schuster, 1997)

Fossil Feud: The Rivalry of the First American Dinosaur Hunters by Thom Holmes, illustrated by Cameron Clement

an account for upper elementary grade readers of two rival paleontologists seeking to organize fossil-hunting expeditions (Messner, 1997)

Turtle Bay by Saviour Pirotta, illustrated by Nilesh Mistry

a story that tells how a young boy in Japan waits for the turtles to return from the sea to lay their eggs (Farrar, Straus and Giroux, 1997)

Water Dance by Thomas Locker

poetic text and vivid oil paintings showing the natural movement of water (Harcourt Brace, 1997)

References such as *Science and Technology in Fact and Fiction: A Guide to Children's Books* by DayAnn M. Kennedy, Stella S. Spanger, and Mary Ann Vanderwerf (Bowker, 1990) contain lists of books related to specific branches of science. An annual list of outstanding science trade books for children is published in the March issue of *Science and Children*.

Trade books about science not only provide essential information about science, but they also give children a sense of what scientists do. Consider the following examples:

- Don Lessem's *Dinosaur Worlds: New Dinosaurs, New Discoveries* not only contains the latest information about dinosaurs but also details how scientists went about making their discoveries;

- Kathryn Lasky's *Surtsey, the Newest Place on Earth* describes a thirty-three-year-old volcanic island and what scientists are doing there;

- Lynn Curlee's *Into the Ice: The Story of Arctic Exploration* features wonderful illustrations and an informative narrative that take children on a journey to explore the North Pole; and

- Alfred B. Bortz's *To the Young Scientist: Reflections on Doing and Living Science* helps children understand the scientific process.

Mathematics

Math and language are closely related. The Standards of the National Council of Teachers of Mathematics (1989) place a heavy emphasis on reading and writing in learning math. Schiro (1997) has shown how children's literature can be used to help children understand and do math well.

Many fictional children's stories are built around mathematical concepts and can be used to teach mathematical operations. For example, Pat Hutchins's *The Doorbell Rang*, in which children sit around a kitchen table sharing cookies, is an effective way to teach division. Judith Viorst's *Alexander, Who Used to Be Rich Last Sunday* shows how money decreases through subtraction. Demi's *One Grain of Rice* is an exquisitely illustrated mathematical folktale from India about a clever young woman who outwits the greedy raja by requesting "only" one grain of rice doubled daily.

Some information books also present mathematical concepts. Counting books like Tana Hoban's *26 Letters and 99 Cents* and Peter Sis's brilliantly colorful *Going up* are effective ways of introducing children to numbers. David M. Schwartz's *How Much Is a Million?* illustrates large numbers in terms of children's experiences, and Hendrick Hertzberg's *One Million*, which contains a million dots interspersed with important and not-so-important facts, helps children begin to grasp the magnitude of large numbers. At the other end of the numerical spectrum, *Zero: Is It Something? Is it Nothing?* by Claudia Zaslavski helps children understand the mathematical concept of zero. Books about calculators and calculator games, such as Norvin Pallas's *Calculator Puzzles, Tricks and Games*, contain a great deal of information on the practice of mathematics.

Social Studies

Social studies—history, geography, economics, sociology, anthropology, and other social sciences—impacts heavily on children's (and adults') lives. Through informational trade books about social studies, children learn about people and places in other parts of their shrinking world, gain insights into events and people from the past, find out about the customs and traditions of other cultures, and read about events that shape their daily lives. These books cover topics that range from life in ancient civilizations to life in the modern world. Many of these books include diaries, letters, photographs, and other primary sources that provide firsthand accounts of places and times well beyond children's own immediate experience and environment.

Beyond providing interesting insights from times past and times present, informational trade books in social studies engage children in analyzing, interpreting, and evaluating what they read. These books provide valuable support for curriculum topics and may present views of historical events and perspectives on current issues different from those put forth in textbooks. Books about social studies are some of the best vehicles available to help children develop critical reading and thinking skills, encouraging children to make comparisons, test hypotheses, and engage in other activities involving higher mental processing.

As in the case of reading informational trade books about science, separating fact from fiction is an important part of reading social studies materials. Writers of fiction have some leeway in creating characters and describing events, but writers of nonfiction books are bound to present accurate information and be able to document their facts.

Social studies is basically about people's relationship with one another. As stories about people and cultures unfold and as children satisfy their curiosity with fascinating facts in informational trade books, social studies often takes on a new dimension in children's lives.

LIST OF TEN

INFORMATIONAL TRADE BOOKS ABOUT SOCIAL STUDIES

As in the case of science, hundreds of trade books on topics related to the social studies are published each year. Here is a sample of ten books published in 1997 and identified as outstanding by the National Council of the Social Studies, in cooperation with the Children's Book Council:

Dear Oklahoma City, Get Well Soon: America's Children Reach out to the People of Oklahoma edited by Jim Ross and Paul Myers
a touching collection of letters and drawings sent by children to the survivors of the Federal Building bombing in Oklahoma City and their rescuers (Walker, 1997)

Ogbo: Sharing Life in an African Village by Ifeoma Onyefulu
a photo-essay about a family in Nigeria (Gulliver, 1997)

My House Has Stars by Megan McDonald, illustrated by Peter Tatalanotto
a series of watercolors by children from many cultures of their homes, providing a geography lesson (Orchard, 1997)

The Flag We Love by Pam Munoz Ryan, illustrated by Ralph Masiello
patriotic verse and dazzling illustrations teaching the meaning of the stars and stripes (Charlesbridge, 1997)

Civil War by Martin W. Sandler
a vivid history of this tragic war presented with photographs, posters, songs, letters, and other primary source documents (HarperCollins, 1997)

Coming to America: The Story of Immigration by Betsy Maestro, illustrated by Susannah Ryan
an account of the past and present story of immigration (Scholastic, 1997)

Growing up in Coal Country by Susan Campbell Bartoletti
a historical account of life for children who worked in the coal mines during the early 1900s (Houghton Mifflin, 1997)

Pony Express! by Stephen Kroll, illustrated by Dan Andreasen
a lovely account in words and pictures of the history of the Pony Express (Scholastic, 1997)

Festivals by Myra Cohn Livingston, illustrated by Leonard Everett Fisher
poems and paintings about the traditions, customs, and stories of fourteen festivals celebrated around the globe (Holiday House, 1997)

Pyramids by Anne Millard
loaded with fascinating facts about the ancient pyramids of Egypt and the Americas (Kingfisher, 1997)

List of Ten continued

Additional references are listed in *Literature-Based Social Studies: Children's Books and Activities to Enrich the K–5 Curriculum* by M. Laughlin and P. Kardaleff, and the April/May issue of the journal *Social Education* contains an annotated bibliography of notable children's trade books in social studies—including fiction and biography—published the previous year.

The Arts

"Arts are basic" says the bumper sticker, and so they are. Music, painting, drama, dance, and literature are essential elements in the lives of children and adults alike. Informational trade books about the arts are an important part of children's literature. Well-designed and well-written picture story books, such as the following, make the arts accessible to young children:

- Wendy Kesselman's *Emma*, the touching story of an elderly woman living in a city apartment who overcomes her loneliness when she begins painting;
- Karen Ackerman's *Song and Dance Man*, the Caldecott Medal–winning story about an old vaudeville performer; and
- Karla Kuskin's *The Philharmonic Gets Dressed*, the amusing account of a symphony orchestra preparing for a performance.

A range of informational trade books on art, music, and other humanities are available for children. Books about art include Kathy Mallatt's *The Picture That Mom Drew*, which presents basic art elements in a clear and appealing way, and Joy Richardson's *Looking at Pictures: An Introduction to Art for Young People*, which pairs reproductions of famous paintings with commentary to appeal to children. Trade books about music cover a range of topics from Larry Kittelkamp's *Flutes, Whistles, and Reeds*, which explains how these instruments produce sound, to Craig Awmiller's *House on Fire: The Story of the Blues*, which tells about this musical background, to *i see the rhythm* by Toyomi Igus, a history of African-American music from the drum beats of Africa to contemporary rap and hip-hop, brilliantly illustrated by Michele Wood (King award in 1999 for illustration). Dance is portrayed in books like Jill Krementz's *A Very Young Dancer*, a photo-essay about a child who is studying ballet. Some children's trade books contain the lyrics (and the music) of songs, such as Woody Guthrie's *This Land Is Your Land* and Steve Graham's *Dear Old Donegal*.

Considerable information about the arts is contained in the biographies of painters, sculptors, singers, dancers, musicians, and writers. Collections of songs and artwork from other cultures also inform children about the arts. A plethora of how-to books related to the arts and leisure-time activities—drawing, painting, playing the guitar and other musical instruments, cooking, photography, model railroading, and filmmaking—fill the shelves of schools and libraries across the land.

Most children are interested in sports, and informational books on many different sports abound. In addition to scores of "How to Play . . ." or "How to Improve Your Game of . . ." books, there are many informational books that satisfy children's interest in athletics, books such as Dave Anderson's *The Story of Golf*, which recounts the history of the game, provides tips on playing, and profiles great men and women golfers, and *A Whole New Ball Game: The Story of the All-American Girls Professional Baseball League* by Sue Macy, an historical account of the women's professional baseball league that existed from 1943 to 1954.

What can be said of trade books in the arts can be said of all informational children's literature: "As never before, today's nonfictional literature for children is about to meet the needs and interests of young readers in quality, variety, and reader appeal. With these books, children's appetites for learning can be fed while their curiosity for more information is piqued" (Tomlinson and Lynch-Brown 1996, 190).

Books may overlap and apply to more than a single curriculum area. Books about the rain forest, for example, differ slightly in their content: *The Great Kapok Tree* is Lynne Cherry's fictional account of a man who is dissuaded from cutting down a tree by the animals whose lives depend on the tree; *The Most Beautiful Roof in the World*, is Kathryn Lasky's factual account of the scientific study of the canopy of the rain forests; and *Rain Forests* by Sara Oldfield is a comprehensive account of the history, present state, and future of these rich natural resources. All can be used to teach children geographical information about the locations of rain forests, to explaining the global ecological and social impact of the depletion of the rain forests, and to provide young people with hours of fascinating reading.

NONFICTION LITERATURE IN SCHOOL AND AT HOME

At home, most children are exposed to informational texts through concept books early in their lives. Children name the objects or animals in the illustrations for books like Denise Fleming's *In the Small, Small Pond* or for one of the many Richard Scarry books that have informed and entertained generations of young readers. These experiences are an important part of children's language and cognitive development.

As children's interest in their world expands, informational trade books can contribute to their learning. Nonfiction books that explain the background and significance of holidays like Christmas, Hanukah, and Kwanzaa, books that help children learn about their pet gerbils or guppies, books about cars, dolls, trucks, trains, or other objects that hold their interest, and books that connect with family activities such as Aliki's picture book *My Visit to the Aquarium* all can fill a child's mind with information and provide enjoyable reading experiences in a home setting.

In the classroom, the most obvious use of informational trade books is for thematic units in content areas of the curriculum. Nonfiction trade books are ideal research sources for oral and written reports. However, while these books are indeed useful for reading across the curriculum, they also belong as an integral part of regular classroom reading instruction. Publishers of basal readers have recognized this usefulness and included much more nonfiction in their programs.

Informational trade books can be full partners with other genres of literature in a balanced reading program. In addition to serving as sources of information for curriculum-related research projects, these books can be used in reading groups, as material for readers' workshops, and for sustained silent reading. The fascinating concepts in a simple book on skyscrapers, *Into the Sky* by Ryan Ann Hunter, and the rhyming text and spectacular illustrations in Diane Siebert's *Mojave* can help children learn as they enjoy themselves. Nonfiction literature can also be part of the daily read-aloud offerings.

AWARD-WINNING NONFICTION BOOKS

The Orbis Pictus Award for Outstanding Nonfiction for Children is given each year by the National Council of Teachers of English (NCTE) to promote and recognize excellence in the field of nonfiction. Established in 1990, the award has been given to the following books:

1990 **The Great Little Madison**
by Jean Fritz
(Putnam)

1991 **Franklin Delano Roosevelt**
by Russell Freedman
(Clarion)

1992 **The Journey of Charles Lindbergh**
by Robert Burleigh
(Philomel)

1993 **Children of the Dust Bowl: the True Story of the School at Weedpatch Camp**
by Jerry Stanley
(Crown)

1994 **Across America on an Emigrant Train**
by Jim Murphy
(Clarion)

1995 **Safari Beneath the Sea: The Wonder World of the North Pacific Coast**
by Diane Swanson
(Sierra)

1996 **The Great Fire**
by Jim Murphy
(Scholastic)

1997 **Leonardo da Vinci**
by Diane Stanley
(Morrow)

1998 **An Extraordinary Life: The Story of a Monarch Butterfly**
by Laurence Pringle
(Orchard)

Other awards are also given for nonfiction children's literature, including the *Boston Globe-Horn Book* Award (which also is given to fiction), the Carter G. Woodson Book Award for outstanding social science books related to ethnic minorities, the Eva L. Gordon Award for Children's Science Literature, and the Children's Book Guild Nonfiction Award given in recognition of an author's total body of nonfiction work. Lists of winners for many of these awards are presented in Appendix A.

Special Perspectives on Children's Literature

FICTION FORBIDDEN:
WHEN NONFICTION TAKES OVER THE SCHOOL
by Kathleen Tower

When you enter Lincoln School, a K–8 school in an economically and racially diverse area of Brookline, Massachusetts, you may encounter a sign in the lobby that reads, "FICTION FORBIDDEN." One month each year is designated as Nonfiction Month.

During this month, all teachers and children are concentrating on informational trade books and materials.

Over the years at Lincoln, the staff has worked tirelessly to help each child become someone who reads and enjoys reading. Despite all our efforts, we still had children who struggled with informational and nonfiction text. The faculty began to discuss how we could be more successful in helping pupils deal with this genre. Finally, we agreed that a month-long emphasis on reading and writing nonfiction material would be a good start.

As a Reading/Writing Specialist in the school, I have often found students who encounter difficulty dealing with informational or nonfiction material. Problems usually surface around grade four, when many of our middle grade students struggle with science and social studies texts. Yet it had always puzzled me that at-risk readers who had difficulty reading fiction could read the small print on the backs of sports cards or the information in video magazines. These children could recall minute details from their nonfiction reading but were unable to tell me about the characters, setting, or plot of a fictional story.

In the hallway one day I met Joey, one of my struggling fourth graders. I watched as he read the back of a baseball card. He could recognize words and comprehend information I did not realize he could understand. This was the same child who struggled with second and third grade text in my reading room! When I gave him other nonfiction material on baseball, he made amazing progress in reading.

I observed the same type of behavior in many of my other at-risk readers. They were so interested in information that they didn't find print an obstacle to obtaining it. With nonfiction material, they didn't have to read a whole book to feel that they were really reading. In addition, the information they discovered was based on their authentic interests and driven by their own curiosity. Pictures and text structure helped them to be successful. Students showed how much they enjoyed nonfiction! As a faculty, we decided to try nonfiction reading on a schoolwide basis for a month.

All teachers agreed to emphasize reading and writing information material. They encouraged all pupils to have nonfiction books or magazines in their desks. Teachers conducted book talks on informational trade books, and they shared these books during oral reading. Some classes did author studies on writers of nonfiction. The teachers themselves read informational books during Drop Everything and Read (DEAR) periods, and many students did the same.

Displays on informational books filled the hallways. For example, the display outside Ms. Lyons's room had pictures of students surrounded by books on topics of their personal interests: Tony with his books on birds, Allison with her books on baseball, Jamal with his books about space travel, Lena with her books on race cars. The students couldn't get their hands on enough books to satisfy their interests.

Our librarian was very supportive of the idea of Nonfiction Month. She arranged displays of informational trade books on different topics and at different reading levels, so that pupils of all abilities could find something of interest to read. We used the public library too. When one of my fifth grade problem readers went there to find references for a social studies report, she reported to me how amazed she was that "the library had so many books that were not story books."

In many classrooms, our nonfiction focus tied directly into reading and writing across the curriculum. Kindergartners developed books of important facts. Some second graders wrote books on sea life: each pupil chose a sea creature, researched it, and wrote about it. Other primary grade pupils read and wrote about curriculum topics of their choice. Fourth graders made Factual Playing Cards filled with questions and answers from research they had conducted. Fifth and sixth graders were studying ancient cultures, so different groups delved into reading about places where these ancient civilizations originated—Greece, Egypt, India, and Italy. Other classes, including seventh and eighth graders, investigated topics of interest and presented the results of their research in the form of books, reports, and news articles. Many students and teachers contributed reports of their reading to our schoolwide newsletter.

Lincoln students also explored biography. With the support of a local bookstore, our fifth graders enjoyed a visit from Natalie Bober, author of *Abigail Adams: Witness to a Revolution* and other works. Children were fascinated to meet a real author and to find out how she did her research. They were amazed to learn how she sometimes struggled with the writing process just as they often do. Students followed up the author visit by writing biographies of classmates, other students, or faculty whom they interviewed.

As a school community, we began to realize the importance of enabling everyone to experience nonfiction literature as a genre. Informational books need to be an important presence in the classroom. The Lincoln students are so much a part of the Information Age that it is essential for them to learn to read and understand informational material. Our students have an insatiable desire to learn about and explore their world. Nonfiction children's literature allows this to happen for them.

Kathleen Tower is the Reading/Writing Specialist at the Lincoln School.

Writers of nonfiction books can be the subject of author studies. Gail Gibbons, Kathryn Lasky, Russell Freedman, Seymour Simon, and others have created significant bodies of nonfiction work, and children can learn much about writing from studying their work.

Informational trade books provide terrific materials for teaching writing. Following a process writing model, children can, as part of prewriting, read different nonfiction books on a particular topic and compare the information they find as they collect it. As they draft written reports and other writing artifacts in the writing stage of the process, children can use nonfiction books as models of how information is presented effectively. As part of the postwriting stage, children can examine the structures of effective expository writing: main idea and detail, sequence, cause-effect, and comparison-contrast. They can also learn and practice appropriate word choice, improve the clarity of their sentence, study paragraph organization, and practice precise communication.

In school or at home, nonfiction material can be read at many levels. Yenka-Agbaw (1997) shows how the informational book *Christmas in the Big House, Christmas in the Quarters* by Patricia and Frederick McKissack, a book comparing different preparations for Christmas on a slave plantation in antebellum Virginia, can be read for information and pleasure, generating an aesthetic response that is reinforced by John Thompson's beautiful illustrations. At another level, this book allows the reader to focus on the injustice of slavery by comparing life in the big house to life in the slave quarters. Readers can construct other meanings by focusing on race, class, and gender. Beyond these levels of meaning, the book provides fascinating information about how Christmas was celebrated in a particular place and time.

Learning to read and reading to learn—informational children's literature plays a key role in both areas of children's literacy development.

CONCLUSION

When talking about children's literature, people are more apt to bring up Lois Lowry's novel *Number the Stars* than Franklyn Branley's information book *The Sky Is Full of Stars*. Yet nonfiction books constitute an important part of children's reading diet, and they have become a major genre in the field of literature for children.

Informational books are vital elements in children's school lives. As part of learning to read and write, children need to interact with many textual formats. Nonnarrative texts become catalysts in children's literacy development and provide a way for children to develop interest in, and acquire information about, a range of topics that they encounter while exploring their expanding worlds.

Reading is not either informative or pleasurable. It is both. Children can derive a great amount of personal satisfaction from seeking and finding information in print.

Questions and Activities for Action and Discussion

1. Select a topic in which you are especially interested. Using the public library or your school's curriculum resource center, gather five or six children's informational trade books on the topic. Compare and contrast the treatments of the topic in the books you select and be prepared to present the results of your research to a class of children or your peers.

2. Plan a reading lesson using a book by Seymour Simon or another writer of nonfiction for children. What prereading activities would you use to prepare children to read the text? List the comprehension questions and strategies that you might use. What follow-up writing, research, or discussion activities would you plan? In what ways would your lesson differ for a work of fiction?

3. As part of a group project explore the use of thematic teaching across the curriculum. Design a web to indicate which books you would use for specific themes in science or social studies.

4. Compare how subject matter is presented in a textbook and a trade book. Examine how a particular topic is presented in a content textbook designed for use in the upper elementary grades. Then look at two or three informational trade books on the same topic. Make a list of differences in the way the topic is treated by the print sources.

5. After reading the *Special Perspectives on Children's Literature* by Kathleen Tower describing the use of informational books at the Lincoln School, brainstorm and list additional ideas that might be used by classroom teachers to promote the use of informational trade books at various grade levels.

CHILDREN'S & YOUNG ADULT BOOKS CITED IN THIS CHAPTER

Ackerman, Karen. 1988. *Song and Dance Man*. Illustrated by Stephen Gammell. New York: Knopf.

Aliki. 1979. *Mummies Are Made in Egypt*. New York: HarperCollins.

_____ 1983. *A Medieval Feast*. New York: HarperCollins.

_____ 1993. *My Visit to the Aquarium*. New York: HarperCollins.

Anderson, Dave. 1998. *The Story of Golf*. New York: Morrow.

Angelou, Maya. 1996. *Kofi and His Magic*. Photos by Margaret Courtney Clarke. New York: Clarkson Potter.

Awmiller, Craig. 1996. *House on Fire: The Story of the Blues*. New York: Watts.

Behrens, June. 1978. *Fiesta!* Photos by Scott Taylor. San Francisco: Children's.

Blumberg, Rhoda. 1985. *Commodore Perry in the Land of Shogun*. New York: Lothrup, Lee and Shepherd.

Bortz, Alfred B. 1997. *To the Young Scientist: Reflections on Doing and Loving Science*. Danbury, Conn.: Watts.

Bragomer Jr., Reginald, and David Fisher. 1981. *What's What: A Visual Glossary of the Physical World*. Maplewood, N.J.: Hammond.

Branley, Franklin M. 1989. *The Sky Is Full of Stars*. Illustrated by Felicia Bond. New York: HarperCollins.

_____ 1989. *Shooting Stars*. Illustrated by Holly Keller. New York: HarperCollins.

_____ 1997. *Drip Drop Raindrops*. Illustrated by James Hale. New York: HarperCollins.

Cherry, Lynne. 1990. *The Great Kapok Tree: A Story of the Amazon Rain Forest*. San Diego: Harcourt Brace.

Chocolate, Deborah. 1992. *My First Kwanzaa Book*. New York: Scholastic.

Crews, Donald. 1978. *Freight Train*. New York: Greenwillow.

_____ 1983. *Parade*. New York: Greenwillow.

_____ 1980. *Truck*. New York: Greenwillow.

Curlee, Lynn. 1997. *Into the Ice: The Story of Arctic Exploration*. Boston: Houghton Mifflin.

Demi. 1997. *One Grain of Rice*. New York: Scholastic.

Downer, Marion. 1964. *The Story of Design*. New York: Lothrop, Lee and Shepherd.

Feelings, Tom. 1995. *The Middle Passage*: White Ships/Black Cargo. New York: Dial.

Fisher, Leonard E. 1987. *Look Around! A Book About Shapes.* New York: Viking.

Fleming, Denise. 1993. *In the Small, Small Pond*. New York: Henry Holt.

Freedman, Russell. 1987. *Lincoln: A Photobiography*. Boston: Houghton Mifflin.

Garza, Carmen. 1996. *In My Family/En mi familia*. San Francisco: Children's.

Graham, Steve. 1996. *Dear Old Donegal*. Illustrated by John O'Brien. New York: Clarion.

Guthrie, Woody. 1998. *This Land Is Your Land*. Boston: Little, Brown.

Hertzberg, Hendrick. 1970. *One Million*. New York: Simon and Schuster.

Hirschfelder, Arline. 1986. *Happily May I Walk: American Indians and Alaskan Natives Today*. New York: Simon and Schuster.

Hoban, Tana. 1987. *26 Letters and 99 Cents*. New York: Greenwillow.

Hoyt-Goldsmith, Diane. 1992. *Hoang Anh: A Vietnamese-American Boy*. Photographs by Lawrence Migdale. New York: Holiday House.

_____ 1995. *Day of the Dead: A Mexican-American Celebration*. Photographs by Lawrence Migdale. New York: Holiday House.

Hughes, Shirley. 1994. *Hiding*. Cambridge, Mass.: Candlewick Press.

Hunter, Ryan Ann. 1998. *Into the Sky*. Illustrated by Edward Miller. New York: Holiday House.

Hutchins, Pat. 1986. *The Doorbell Rang*. New York: Greenwillow.

Igus, Toyomi. 1998. *i see the rhythm*. Illustrated by Michele Wood. San Francisco: Children's.

Kesselman, Wendy. 1980. *Emma*. New York: Doubleday.

King-Smith, Dick. 1993. *I Love Guinea Pigs*. Cambridge, Mass.: Candlewick.

Kittlekamp, Larry. 1962. *Flutes, Whistles, and Reeds*. New York: Morrow.

Krementz, Jill. 1976. *A Very Young Dancer*. New York: Knopf.

Kuskin, Karla. 1982. *The Philharmonic Gets Dressed*. New York: Harper & Row.

Lasky, Kathryn. 1990. *Sugaring Time*. Photographs by Christopher Knight. New York: Macmillan.

_____ 1992. *Surtsey: The Newest Place on Earth*. Illustrated by Christopher Knight. New York: Hyperion.

_____ 1996. *The Most Beautiful Roof in the World*. Photographs by Christopher G. Knight. San Diego: Harcourt Brace.

Lauber, Patricia. 1986. *Volcano: The Eruption and Healing of Mount Saint Helens*. New York: Simon and Schuster.

Lessem, Don. 1996. *Dinosaur Worlds: New Dinosaurs, New Discoveries*. Honesdale, Penn.: Boyds Mills Press.

Lowry, Lois. 1989. *Number the Stars*. Boston: Houghton Mifflin.

Macaulay, David. 1988. *The Way Things Work*. Boston: Houghton Mifflin.

Macy, Sue. 1993. *A Whole New Ball Game: The Story of the All-American Girls Professional Baseball League*. New York: Holt.

Mallatt, Kathy. 1997. *The Picture That Mom Drew*. Illustrated by Bruce McMillan. New York: Walker.

McKissack, Patricia, and Frederick McKissack. 1991. *The Civil Rights Movement in America from 1865 to the Present*. San Francisco: Children's.

_____ 1994. *Christmas in the Big House, Christmas in the Quarters*. New York: Scholastic.

McMillan, Bruce. 1988. *Fire Engine Shapes*. New York: Lothrup, Lee and Shepard.

Meltzer, Milton. 1980. *The Chinese Americans*. New York: Harper & Row.

Meyer, Carolyn, and Charles Gallenkamp. 1995. *The Mystery of the Ancient Maya*. New York: Atheneum.

Millen, C. M. 1996. *A Symphony for the Sheep*. Illustrated by M. Azarian. Boston: Houghton Mifflin.

Morgan, Roland. 1997. *In the Next Three Seconds*. Illustrated by Rod Josey and Kira Josey. New York: Dutton.

Myers, Walter Dean. 1997. *Harlem*. Illustrated by Christopher Myers. New York: Scholastic.

Oldfield, Sara. 1997. *Rain Forests*. Minneapolis: Lerner.

Onyefulu, Ifeoma. 1996. *Ogbo: Sharing Life in an African Village*. San Diego: Harcourt Brace.

Pallas, Norvin. 1979. *Calculator Puzzles, Tricks and Games*. New York: Sterling.

Pallotta, Jerry. 1990. *The Icky Bug Alphabet Book*. Illustrated by Ralph Masiello. Watertown, Mass.: Charlesbridge.

_____ 1990. *The Yucky Reptile Alphabet Book*. Illustrated by Ralph Masiello. Watertown, Mass.: Charlesbridge.

Richardson, Joy. 1997. *Looking at Pictures: An Introduction to Art for Young People*. Illustrated by Charlotte Voake. New York: Abrams

Ride, Sally. 1992. *Voyager: An Adventure to the Edge of the Solar System*. New York: Crown.

Rockwell, Harlow. 1980. *My Nursery School*. New York: Greenwillow.

Schories, Pat. 1997. *Over Under in the Garden: An Alphabet Book*. New York: Farrar, Straus and Giroux.

Schwartz, David M. 1987. *How Much Is a Million?* New York: Lothrup.

_____ 1989. *If You Made a Million*. New York: Lothrup.

Siebert, Diane. 1997. *Mojave*. Illustrated by Wendell Minor. New York: HarperCollins.

Sis, Peter. 1989. *Going up*. New York: Greenwillow.

Viorst, Judith. 1978. *Alexander, Who Used to Be Rich Last Sunday*. New York: Macmillan.

Zaslavski, Claudia. 1989. *Zero: Is It Something? Is It Nothing?* New York: Watts.

REFERENCES

Caswell, L. J., and N. K. Duke. 1998. Non-Narrative as a Catalyst for Literacy Development. *Language Arts* 75:108–117.

Doiron, Ray. 1995. An Aesthetic View of Children's Nonfiction. *English Quarterly* 28:35–41.

Dowd, F. S. 1992. Trends and Evaluative Criteria for Informational Books for Children. In *Using Nonfiction Trade Books in the Elementary Classroom: From Ants to Zeppelins*, eds. E. B. Freeman and D. G. Person. Urbana, Ill.: National Council of Teachers of English.

Farest, C., C. J. Miller, and S. Ferwin. 1995. Lewis and Clark: An Incredible Journey into the World of Information Books. *The New Advocate* 8:271–288.

Greenlaw, M. J. 1991. Interacting with Informational Books. In *Invitation to Read: More Children's Literature in the Reading Program*, ed. B. Cullinan. Newark, Del.: International Reading Association.

Harris, T. L., and R. E. Hodges, eds. 1995. *The Literacy Dictionary*. Newark, Del.: International Reading Association.

Horning, K. 1997. *From Cover to Cover*. New York: HarperCollins.

National Council of Teachers of Mathematics. 1989. *Curriculum and Evaluation Standards for School Mathematics*. Reston, Va.: NCTM.

Rosenblatt, L. M. 1991. Literature—S.O.S.! *Language Arts* 68:444–448.

Russell, D. L. 1991. *Literature for Children: A Short Introduction*. New York: Longman.

Schiro, M. 1997. *Integrating Children's Literature and Mathematics in the Classroom: Children as Meaning-Makers, Problem Solvers, and Literary Critics*. New York: Teachers College Press.

Spink, J. K. 1996. The Aesthetics of Informational Reading. *The New Advocate* 9:135–149.

Sudol, P., and C. M. King. 1996. A Checklist for Choosing Nonfiction Trade Books. *The Reading Teacher* 49:422–424.

Tomlinson, C. M., and C. Lynch-Brown. 1996. *Essentials of Children's Literature* (2d ed.) Boston: Allyn and Bacon.

Yenka-Agbaw, V. 1997. Taking Children's Literature Seriously: Reading for Pleasure and Social Change. *Language Arts* 74:446–453.

GREAT WHITE SHARKS are famous for being the most dangerous and fiercest members of the shark family. They will eat large fish, other sharks and even whales.

Illustrations enhance the information presented in nonfiction books. Seymour Simon uses dramatic photographs to illustrate his many informational books, such as *Sharks* (top). By contrast, Gail Gibbons' highly informational books such as *Sharks* are illustrated with accurate drawings (bottom). © Doug Perrine/Innerspace Vissions (top).

A distant mountain

shimmers in the

dragonfly's eye.

A withered tree

blooms once again—

butterflies holding fast.

Art enhances the meaning and enjoyment of poetry. Kazuko G. Stone's delicate illustrations of the haiku of the Japanese poet Issa in Matthew Gollub's translation *Cool Melons—Turn to Frogs!* complements the beauty of the poems themselves. On the opposite page, the burst of color from Jan Spivey Gilchrest's illustration adds sight to the sounds of the poem "Fireworks" by Rebecca Kai Dotlich from *Lemonade Sun and Other Summer Poems*. The illustration of the green praying mantas painted in watercolor on a brown paper bag, adds a layer of symbolism to Douglas Florian's poem in *Insectlopedia*.

FIREWORKS

Emerald glitter
fills the sky;
a thousand dashing
dragon eyes
sparkle! flash!
spiral,
climb—
leaping,
leaving Earth
behind.
Roman candles
sizzle,
shatter,
diamonds dazzle,
rubies
scatter,
spilling silver
stars of fire—
blasting bits
of copper wire.
Sapphires crumble
in the sky,
tinsel
tumbles
down to die,
onto city streets
and roads;
CRACKLE—
POP!
The sky
explodes!

THE PRAYING MANTIS

Upon a twig
I sit and pray
For something big
To wend my way:
A caterpillar,
Moth,
Or bee—
I swallow them
Religiously.

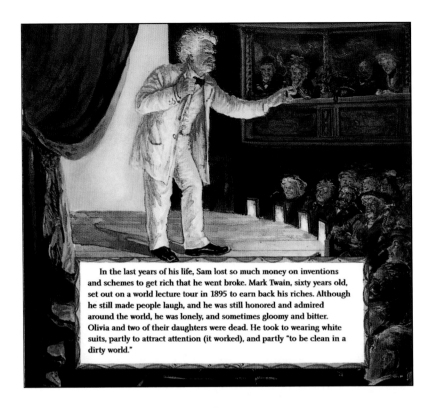

In the last years of his life, Sam lost so much money on inventions and schemes to get rich that he went broke. Mark Twain, sixty years old, set out on a world lecture tour in 1895 to earn back his riches. Although he still made people laugh, and he was still honored and admired around the world, he was lonely, and sometimes gloomy and bitter. Olivia and two of their daughters were dead. He took to wearing white suits, partly to attract attention (it worked), and partly "to be clean in a dirty world."

Illustrations is no less important in biographies. Illustrations by Cheryl Harness in her biography *Mark Twain and the Queens of the Mississippi* give children a sense of what this great author looked like in his later years (top). Not only do Yvonne Buchanan's illustration give a visual impression of what Bessie Coleman looked like in *Fly, Bessie, Fly* by Lynn Joseph — the biography of the first African American woman ever to earn a pilot's license; they also portray implements of the era — like the airplane, camera, and fountain pen (bottom).

CHAPTER 10

BIOGRAPHY AND AUTOBIOGRAPHY

ccounts of people's lives allow children to enhance their own lives. The genre of biography is often used to inspire, to inform, and to entertain. In this chapter, the qualities of good biographical writing and examples from popular trade books appropriate for use in the elementary school years are explored.

THIS CHAPTER

- examines biography as a genre of children's literature;
- identifies the range of biographical material available to young readers as part of their reading diets inside and outside of school; and

- focuses on autobiographies for children, especially those of well-known children's authors.

Bio-, a prefix from Greek meaning *life*, and *-graph*, a root from Greek meaning *written*, make *biography*, a written account of a person's life. Biography—and to a lesser extent autobiography—is an important genre in the world of children's literature. Biographies are books that describe and discuss the lives of real individuals, people whose words and deeds influenced the lives of others in some noteworthy way.

Why are biographies so popular with children? People—young and old alike—like to learn about people they admire. That's why so many magazines focus on the lives of celebrities in sports, entertainment, politics, and other fields that attract our interest. Biographies are popular with adults, and children's reading interests often parallel the interests of their elders.

Early biographies were shaped by religion and politics. Children were expected (or required) to read about inspirational and saintly people who did good deeds and eschewed evil, in the hope that their reading would lead them to emulate the virtues and qualities they read about. The subjects of early American biographies were presented as larger-than-life characters with exaggerated virtues and whose actions were driven by truth and goodness and followed the American way. Biographies of Christopher Columbus, for example, portrayed him as a brave explorer who was driven by the noblest of motives. History has shown otherwise.

Biographies for children have changed enormously in the past decade or so; never before have the lives of famous people been presented so authentically for a young audience. Writers for children have discovered that real lives can often be as interesting and as exciting as fiction. Biographies do more than inform and inspire; they also entertain.

Biographies have earned critical recognition as works of children's literature by winning both the Newbery Medal (*Invincible Louisa* by Cornelia Meigs in 1933, *Daniel Boone* by James Daugherty in 1940, and *Amos Fortune, Free Man* by Elizabeth Yates in 1951) and the Caldecott Medal (*Abraham Lincoln* by Edgar Parin D'Aulaire and Ingri D'Aulaire in 1940). More recently, Russell Freedman won the Newbery Award in 1988 for his *Lincoln: A Photobiography*, and many of the recent Carter Woodson awards for distinguished books related to social studies have been given to biographies (see Appendix A).

EXAMINING BIOGRAPHIES

What are the characteristics of quality biographies for children? "The three essential ingredients of good biography are history, the person, and literary artistry. Facts should be authentic and verifiable; the subject should be considered as an individual rather than as a paragon or type; and the writing should be a conscious work of art" (Sutherland 1997, 429).

As in the case of other informational books, accuracy and authenticity are essential. Instead of fictionalizing events in a person's life to convey a cohesive image, today's biographers carefully research historical accounts, review diaries and journals, and explore primary source documents and archives (if they exist) from the times when their subjects lived. Biographies are not fictionalized accounts of people's lives like historical fiction.

A distinction is made between *authentic biography* and *fictionalized biography*. The former sticks strictly to what is documented. Fictionalized biography is also rooted in thorough research, but the author may dramatize events and create conversations that may not actually have taken place even though they are based on some evidence. Some fictionalized biographies do stick closely to the facts of a person's life, however. Alan Schroeder's *Minty: A Story of Harriet Tubman* gives accurate information about Tubman's life and her role in the Underground Railroad, and Kathryn Lasky's *She's Wearing a Dead Bird on Her Head* is a delightfully illustrated picture book about Minna Hall and Harriet Hemenway who founded the Audubon Society to protect wildlife. Technically, however, these books more properly belong in the category of historical fiction since the authors do invent some scenarios. Children need to apply critical thinking in separating fact from fiction in the biographies they read.

A third category—*biographical fiction*—consists of fictionalized accounts of a person's life, liberally laced with anecdotes or events for which there is little historical documentation. For example, Robert Lawson told the story of Ben Franklin in *Ben and Me* through the eyes of a mouse that hid in Franklin's famous fur hat. Biographical fiction may be based on events in a person's life, but these events are reported in a thoroughly fictitious (and often facetious) fashion.

To help young readers construct meaning as they read about the lives of famous people, biographers often provide information that extends beyond the narrative such as side notes, footnotes, time lines, and additional references. For example, *Bill Pickett: Rodeo-Ridin' Cowboy* by Andrea Davis Pinkney, which depicts the life of the famous African-American cowboy and rodeo rider, contains additional information about the history of black cowboys in America. And on the back cover of *Louis Braille: The Boy Who Invented Books for the Blind* by Margaret Davidson, there is an embossed Braille alphabet that children can use to get a tactile sense of it.

Contemporary biographies typically present a more balanced picture than earlier biographies did, focusing on weaknesses and flaws along with strengths and accomplishments of their subjects. (Meltzer 1998). Books typically present their subjects as complex people with human natures, the type of people that children see around them all the time. Children enjoy learning about the quirky actions or amusing idiosyncrasies of famous people.

Biographies bring to life well-known (and sometimes not-so-well-known) people for young readers, adding flesh to the bones of old skeletons. Good biographies add depth to children's understanding. Many people think Crazy Horse is the enemy in the famous Battle of Little Big Horn, in which the Sioux defeated General George Custer and his troops. In *The Life and Death of Crazy Horse*, Russell Freedman presents a more in-depth picture of the great Sioux chief, describing him as a shy and sensitive man of principle with the courage and idealism to die for his beliefs.

Author Profile: JEAN FRITZ

Jean (Guttrey) Fritz has put her unique stamp on children's biographies (and historical fiction). Fritz combines an anecdotal writing style with a focus on interesting events in the lives of famous historical characters.

Fritz was born the daughter of American missionaries in Hankow, China, where she spent most of her childhood. She spent much of her free time writing. As a "stranger in a foreign land," she developed a deep interest in America and she returned to the United States as a teenager. After graduating from Wheaton College, she worked as a research assistant with a publishing company and as a librarian, while she combined her interest in history with writing.

Fritz's first book for children, *Bunny Hopwell's First Spring*, was published in 1954. Throughout the late 1950s and 1960s, a score of children's books followed, but Fritz really made her mark with the 1973 publication of *And Then What Happened, Paul Revere?* The book demonstrated the author's unique talent for presenting historical information in an interesting style.

Fritz wrote a series of biographies about famous people from American history, each with a title in the form of a question: *Why Don't You Get a Horse, Sam Adams?* (1974), *Where Was Patrick Henry on the 29th of May?* (1975), *Who's That Stopping on Plymouth Rock?* (1975), *Will You Sign Here, John Hancock?* (1976), *What's the Big Idea, Ben Franklin?* (1976), *Can't You Make Them Behave, King George?* (1977), *Where Do You Think You're Going, Christopher Columbus?* (1980), and others. In these books, Fritz created entertaining accounts of events in her subjects' lives, without invention or embellishment. Her books are thoroughly researched, and she does not compromise historical accuracy.

Fritz chronicled the lives of other famous figures from American history—Sam Houston, Stonewall Jackson, Benedict Arnold, Pocahontas, Teddy Roosevelt—as well as of those from other lands—Brendan the Navigator, St. Columba of Ireland, and great explorers from Henry the Navigator to Magellan.

The talents of Fritz are not limited to writing biographies and historical fiction for children. She has compiled a book of folktales, *The Good Giants and the Bad Bukwudgies* (1982), written an adult biography, *Cast for a Revolution: Some American Friends and Enemies, 1728–1814* (1972), and authored two very interesting autobiographies, *Homesick: My Own Story* (1982), and *China Homecoming* (1985).

Jean Fritz lives outside New York City, where she continues to make history fun to read. Here are some of her other books:

George Washington's Mother (1992)

Just a Few Words, Mr. Lincoln: The Story of the Gettysburg Address (1993)

Harriet Beecher Stowe and the Beecher Preachers (1994)

You Want Women to Vote, Lizzie Stanton? (1995)

In addition to being part of a balanced school-based reading program, biographies are essential components in reading across the curriculum. Biographies bring historical figures alive in social studies class. In science, children discover the process of scientific thinking as they see the world through the eyes of scientists who made important discoveries. By reading about the experiences of explorers, inventors, artists, singers, writers, and dancers, young readers gain insights into many areas of learning and life.

The essential question to ask in selecting biographies for children is, "Is it good literature?" Biography shares with other genres of children's literature the literary qualities of characterization, setting, plot, and theme.

Character is paramount, since biographers must present a person that children will want to read about. Often, biographers create characters the way novelists do—by showing what the character says and does and how others react to him or her. Because biographers don't have the freedom that fiction writers do, in that they need to remain historically accurate in relating events and conversations that create character, this task is especially challenging.

Since time and place heavily influence who a person is and what he or she does, and since biographies present individuals in the context of their times, setting is important as well. Settings for biographies range from ancient castles to contemporary space capsules. Setting provides the context in which the subject of a biography gains fame or notoriety. When available, photographs can help establish time and place. When photos are not available, illustrations may reflect the dress and artifacts of the period.

Since no story moves without a plot, biographers must present a story line that keeps the action moving. Biographers present events in a person's life in a dynamic fashion, not as a series of events strung together like beads on a string but in a way that reflects the interconnections and complex relationships of actual life.

Finally, themes like bravery, honesty, integrity, commitment, and hard work are illustrated through characters and their actions in biographies. Children may find biographies inspirational and motivating; for example, by reading accounts of the lives of famous contemporary women like Madeline Albright in Robert Maass's *UN Ambassador: A Behind-the-Scenes Look at Madeline Albright's World* or biographies like Henry Christopher's *Ruth Bader Ginsberg*, some children may be inspired to enter the world of government and politics. Or children may read biographies just for fun; for example, they may enjoy the humor of Robert M. Quackenbush's *Oh, What an Awful Mess!* the story of Goodyear's invention of rubber.

Biographies for children should reflect the qualities that mark literature in other genres. Artwork, illustrations, and photographs may contribute greatly to the portrayal of a person's life. Writing style should be appealing. They provide fine examples of language and content that children can read and enjoy.

FACTORS FOR CONSIDERATION

EVALUATING BIOGRAPHIES

Here are five factors to look for when reviewing biographies for children:

1. Is the book an authentic or fictionalized biography; does it fictionalize any part of the person's life?

2. Does the book present a balanced rather than a one-sided presentation of the person's life?

3. Does the book place the person's life within the contexts of the time and place?

4. Does the story meet the criteria of good children's literature?

5. Is a reader likely to talk about the person portrayed in the book and tell others about that person's life?

BIOGRAPHIES ABOUND

In the field of children's literature, biographies abound. They range in time from the life of Cleopatra—which children can explore in Diane Stanley's and Peter Vennema's picture book *Cleopatra* and Polly Schoyer Brooks's *Cleopatra* (for older readers)—to more contemporary times. Thousands of books written for young audiences recount the lives of the following categories of people:

- **Historical figures**: Diane Stanley's *Peter the Great* is an illustrated version of the life and times of the powerful Russian Emperor, and Aileen Fisher's *Jeanne d'Arc* explores the life of the French leader and saint.

- **Figures from American history**: Milton Meltzer's *Columbus and the World Around Him* tells the story of the explorer in the context of his time, and Anne Holler's

Pocahontas: Powhatan Peacemaker provides children with an authentic account as an alternative to the popular Disney image of this Native American princess.

- **Great leaders in our own history**: Rosemary Bray's picture book *Martin Luther King*, a brilliantly illustrated account of the life of the civil rights leader, portrays him as a man of courage and charisma, and Janet Klausner's *Sequoyah's Gift: Portrait of a Cherokee Leader*, tells the story of the chief who developed a writing system for the Cherokee language.

- **Political leaders from other nations**: David Adler's *Our Golda: The Story of Golda Meir*, tells about the Israeli prime minister, and Floyd Cooper's *Mandela: From the Life of the South African Statesman* is a picture book biography.

- **Inventors**: Examples are Russell Freedman's *The Wright Brothers: How They Invented the Airplane* and Andrea Davis Pinkney's *Dear Benjamin Banneker*, a picture book biography of the African-American inventor and scientist.

- **Visual artists**: Diane Stanley's *Leonardo da Vinci* is a picture book that portrays da Vinci as an artist, scientist, musician, and philosopher, and Bijou LeTord's *The Blue Butterfly: A Story About Claude Monet* introduces the French Impressionist to very young children.

- **Poets**: Audrey Osofsky's *Free to Dream: The Making of a Poet: Langston Hughes* includes accounts of the poet's life and samples of his poetry, and Catherine Reef's *Walt Whitman* is a candid account for older readers of the life of this American poet.

- **Athletes**: David Adler's *Jackie Robinson: He Was the First* describes this man not only as an athlete but also as someone who helped break the racial barrier in major league baseball, and Kathleen Krull's *Wilma Unlimited: How Wilma Rudolph Became the World's Fastest Woman* is a picture book biography of the Olympic athlete.

- **Scientists**: Peter Sis's *Starry Messenger: A Book Depicting the Life of a Famous Scientist, Mathematician, Astronomer, Philosopher, Physicist; Galileo Galilei* is a chronology of the life of this scientist, and Jacqueline Briggs Marten's *Snowflake Bently*, the story of Wilson Bentley whose photographic genius allowed him to capture on film the unique beauty of a snowflake.

- **Explorers**: Albert Marrin's *The Sea King: Sir Francis Drake and His Times* details the life of the English explorer, and Rhonda Blumberg's *The Remarkable Adventures of Captain Cook* tells about the man who explored Australia.

- **Musicians**: Mike Venezia's *Ludwig Van Beethoven* with an interesting combination of traditional and cartoon illustrations about this genius of classical music, and Andrea Davis Pinkney's *Duke Ellington: The Piano Prince and His Orchestra* about the life and world of this famous jazz artist.

- **Singers and dancers**: Tobi Tobias's biography *Maria Tallchief* chronicles the career of the ballerina, and Jeri Ferris's *What I Had Was Singing: The Story of Marian Anderson* chronicles the career of the American contralto.

- **Social leaders**: Betsy Harvey Kraft's *Mother Jones: One Woman's Fight for Labor* tells about the woman who fought for the interests of underrepresented labor groups, and Rosemary Wells's *Mary on Horseback: Three Mountain Stories* tells the story of Mary

Author Profile: DAVID A. ADLER

As a young man, David Adler had no idea that he wanted to be a writer. He dreamed about being a major league baseball player, an artist, an actor, and a lawyer. Unfortunately, he did much of this dreaming in school. When a teacher complained about his dreaming, an assistant principal said, "Maybe one day he will become a writer."

After earning a degree in economics from Queens College in New York City, Adler taught math in an intermediate school for nine years. While he was teaching, he earned a Master's degree in business and began work on a Ph.D. In response to being pestered by the questions of a nephew, Adler wrote *A Little at a Time* and sent it to a publisher. Published in 1976, this book launched Adler on a prolific career as a children's author.

Adler writes in many modes. He is the author of the Cam Jensen mystery books, an easy reading series about a young detective who solves mysteries and problems for her friends. He has written a number of books related to Judaism, including *A Picture Book of Jewish Holidays* (1981), *The Numbers on My Grandfather's Arm* (1987), and *Child of the Warsaw Ghetto* (1995).

But Adler is best known for his biographies. He has brought the lives of such diverse people as Christopher Columbus (1991), George Washington (1988), Paul Revere (1995), Benjamin Franklin (1992), Abraham Lincoln (1989), Sojourner Truth (1994), Robert E. Lee (1994), Golda Meir (1984), Jackie Robinson (1994), and John F. Kennedy (1990) to life for young children. In his picturebook biographies, David Adler paints his verbal portraits of people in the context of their times and in a way that helps children understand who they were.

Here are some of Adler's more recent books:

A Picture Book of Davy Crockett (1996)

A Picture Book of Louis Braille (1997)

One Yellow Daffodil: A Hanukkah Story (1995)

Chanukah in Chelm (1997)

Breckenridge who founded the Frontier Nursing Service to meet the needs of rural people in Kentucky.

Multicultural Dimensions

It's important that children read about all the people who have contributed significantly to our society, not just about men or about white people, for example, Patricia and Frederick McKissack (see pp. 198–199) have written about the lives of famous people of color in history, law, politics, athletics, the arts, and other fields. In addition to those identified earlier in the chapter, biographies of people who have made significant contributions to the Civil Rights Movement include Eloise Greenfield's *Rosa Parks* and Rosemary Bray's *Martin Luther King*, both written for younger readers. Walter Dean Myers's *Malcolm X: By Any Means Necessary* is a biography for older readers; Andrea Davis Pinkney's *Alvin Ailey* is a picture book biography of the famous dancer and choreographer; and James Haskins's *Thurgood Marshall: A Life for Justice* is about the first African-American justice appointed to the Supreme Court.

Biographies of Latinos, Asian Americans, American Indians, and other members of nonmainstream groups are not as readily available as those of African Americans. Nevertheless, biographies of notable Latino/a people include the life stories of interesting contemporary and historical figures. In *Cesar Chavez*, Bruce W. Conrad has chronicled the life of the famous labor leader who organized farm workers. Rae Bains's *Benito Juarez, Hero of Modern Mexico* tells about the former lawyer who was president of Mexico during the latter part of the nineteenth century. And Susan Maloney Clinton's *Everett Alvarez, Jr., a Hero for Our Times* tells about the navy pilot who was held captive for nine years during the Vietnam War.

Denis Fradin's *Sacageawea: Northwest Explorer* chronicles the contributions of the young Shoshoni woman who served as interpreter and guide for Lewis and Clark as they explored the Northwest Passage. It is based on letters, journals, and historical documents. Fradin has also written *Hiawatha: Messenger of Peace* about the Native American leader who brought together warring tribes to form the Iroquois Federation. Russell Freedman's *Indian Chiefs* contains photographs and biographical information about famous leaders of Native American nations.

Biographies of Asian Americans are even rarer than those of other nonmainstream cultures. A biography that children do enjoy is Allen Say's *El Chino*, the story of Billy Wong, a Chinese American who, because he was too small to play football, moved to Spain and became a famous bullfighter.

In sum, there is no shortage of fine books about interesting people of many different cultures and ethnic groups, books that meet children's need to know and that satisfy their curiosity, that broaden their horizons and enrich their lives, that inspire their hearts and enlighten their minds, and that provide enjoyment.

BIOGRAPHIES IN DIFFERENT FORMS

Biographies may be categorized by type:

- **Complete life stories**: These provide anecdotes and events from a person's childhood, adulthood, and old age; for example, Russell Freedman's *Franklin Delano Roosevelt* spans the president's lifetime, offering rich details about his personal life.
- **Partial biographies**: Instead of taking the cradle-to-the-grave approach, these biographies recount only noteworthy events from a person's experiences that children might find interesting. The time period covered may be as short as one day, as in Aliki's *The King's Day: Louis XIV of France*, featuring intriguing details about the Sun King. Most partial biographies, however, focus on a longer period of time. Jean Fritz's popular biographies *Will You Sign Here, John Hancock?* and *And Then What Happened,*

Paul Revere? recount single significant events in the lives of figures in American history.

- **Collective biographies**: These cover the lives of several people who are linked by some characteristic or theme. Examples are Paula Gunn Allen's and Patricia Clark Smith's *As Long as the Rivers Flow: The Stories of Nine Native Americans* and *The Smithsonian Book of the First Ladies: Their Lives, Times, and Issues* by Edith Mayo.

- **Photo biographies**: Russell Freedman's award-winning *Lincoln: A Photobiography* captures the life of the famous president in pictures.

Author Profile: RUSSELL FREEDMAN

Russell Freedman grew up in a household filled with books, sparked by lively conversations about literature, and interrupted by visits from published authors. At a young age, he knew he wanted to be a writer just like those who visited his family.

As a fifth grader, Freedman took a shot at writing by producing comic strips. In high school, he wrote mysteries. As an English major at the University of California at Berkeley, he wrote poetry and made his first money from writing—twenty-five dollars for one of his poems.

After serving with the U.S. Army in Korea, Freedman worked with the Associated Press in San Francisco. With a yen to travel, he went to New York where he became a publicity writer for network television shows. But he was still not satisfied with his work. He wanted to write about people and things that he cared about.

Freedman's first book was inspired by an article he read in *The New York Times* about Louis Braille and another article about a teenager who had invented a Braille typewriter. Russell's ensuing research resulted in a collection of biographies, *Teenagers Who Made History* (1961). He felt at home in the field of writing nonfiction for young adults and became a full-time author.

Freedman enjoys research, going to the library and looking through the pages of old books for new information, and living in areas where he can learn about his topics. For *Rattlesnakes* (1984), he spent three days on a rattlesnake farm in Maryland. Watching cowboys at work in Oklahoma helped inspire *Cowboys of the Wild West* (1985). For his Newbery Medal book *Lincoln: A Photobiography* (1987), he followed the footsteps of Abraham Lincoln from his log cabin birthplace to Ford's Theater, where Freedman sat in the back row and tried to imagine what it was like the night Lincoln was assassinated.

Russell Freedman's biographies—Abe Lincoln, Crazy Horse, the Wright Brothers, Franklin Roosevelt, Eleanor Roosevelt, and Louis Braille—are recognized as outstanding contributions to children's literature and have won the author awards and recognition as a giant in the field.

Here are some of Freedman's more recent works:

An Indian Winter (1992)
Kids at Work: Lewis Hind and the Crusade Against Child Labor (1994)
The Life and Death of Crazy Horse (1996)
Out of Darkness: The Story of Louis Braille (1997)

Biographies include picture books for young readers, such as Barbara Cooney's beautifully illustrated and poignantly written biography of the well-known first lady Eleanor Roosevelt, *Eleanor*, and Frances Ward Weller's *Madaket Millie,* a delightful biography of the less–well-known Millie Jewett, the tenacious and courageous first lady of Madaket Beach on Nantucket Island. Longer accounts for older children include Barry Denenberg's biography of Charles Lindbergh, *An American Hero: The True Story of Charles A. Lindbergh*, detailing the accomplishments and disappointments of this famous citizen. Some biographies come in series such as The Harper & Row I Can Read History Series and The Holiday House Picture Book Biography Series.

It has been said that we live in heroless times. Accounts of famous people give children heroes from the past and ideas about what makes a hero of the future. Whether long or short, simple or complex, individual or serialized, biographies give children a window through which to view the lives of other people in other places and at other times.

AUTOBIOGRAPHIES

In the field of children's literature, autobiographies—accounts of people's lives that are written by the people themselves—are far less popular than biographies. Also, for the most part, famous people don't write cradle-to-grave accounts about their own lives for young children, so such books are hard to come by.

Nevertheless, some people have written about their lives (or parts of their lives) for children. A powerful example is *Leon's Story* by Leon Walter Tillage, a riveting account of a man who grew up as a sharecropper's son and maintained his dignity in the face of cruelty and discrimination in North Carolina during the 1940s. Beth Bao Lord has written a delightful and humorous autobiographical account of her first year in the United States in *In the Year of the Boar and Jackie Robinson,* and astronaut Sally Ride tells about her experiences in space in *Voyager: An Adventure to the Edge of the Solar System.* In *Thank You, Mr. Falker*, Patricia Polacco tells about a young girl's trouble in learning how to read and about the patient fifth grade teacher who eventually helped her succeed. Readers learn at the end of the book that the story is an autobiographical account of the author's own struggle with reading in the early grades.

Children will find a few autobiographies of young people. The enormously popular *Ann Frank: The Diary of a Young Girl* tells of her years spent hiding from the Nazis in Amsterdam during the Second World War. Ann Frank did not know that some day her diary would be published; it was discovered by chance after the war and has since become a classic of young adult literature. A similar story has been told by Nelly S. Toll about hiding in Poland in *Behind the Secret Window: A Memoir of a Hidden Childhood During World War Two.*

People sometimes engage the help of professional writers to tell their own stories to young readers. *Rosa Parks: My Story*, the account of the woman whose refusal to sit at the back of the bus in Montgomery, Alabama, helped launch the 1960s Civil Rights Movement, was written with the assistance of Jim Haskins. Ryan White, the teenager who contracted AIDS from a blood transfusion, wrote his autobiography *Ryan White: My Own Story* with the help of Ann Marie Cunningham.

A notable exception to the dearth of autobiographies written for young children is the autobiographical work of famous children's authors. Why do children's authors write about themselves? It may be that they receive so much fan mail and so many letters of inquiry from their readers that they are inspired to write accounts of their own lives and work. Or maybe they're so tuned in to writing for children that their autobiographies are natural extensions of their work. Whatever the reason, autobiographical material exists for teachers to use in helping children develop a greater understanding and appreciation of the writing that children's authors produce.

LIST OF TEN

AUTOBIOGRAPHIES OF CHILDREN'S AUTHORS

Among children's author autobiographies for children are the following:

Girl from Yamhill: A Memoir and **My Own Two Feet: A Memoir** by Beverly Cleary
the author's life from childhood in Oregon through adolescence and into adulthood, with a focus on family life and her growing interest in writing

Bill Peet: An Autobiography by Bill Peet
illustrated in the same delightfully unique style that he uses to illustrate his other children's books

Homesick: My Own Story and **China Homecoming** by Jean Fritz
about her rather lonely life as the daughter of missionary parents living in China and about her later life

The Lost Garden by Laurence Yep
about growing up as a Chinese American in San Francisco and about how he came to use his writing as a means of celebrating his family and ethnic heritage

The Abracadabra Kid: A Writer's Life by Sid Fleischman
features the same humorous tone as his other books and advice for children about writing

The Invisible Thread by Yoshiko Uchida
about growing up as a second generation Japanese American in California

In Flight with David McPhail: A Creative Autobiography by David McPhail
about this illustrator's career and several of his books

Flora and the Tiger: 19 Very Short Stories from My Life by Eric Carle
personal and touching vignettes about his life and events that have influenced him

List of Ten continued

Lois Lowry: A Book of Memories by Lois Lowry
> *reflections (sometimes painful) and significant moments from her life, with photographs and brief passages from some of her children's books*

The World of William Joyce Scrapbook by William Joyce
> *an authentic account of his life and answers to children's questions about his life, his family, and his work, with delightful illustrations in the Joyce style*

Many of these and other children's authors and illustrators have created videotapes to describe their lives and work, which children and teachers find interesting. The World Wide Web makes it possible for contemporary authors to communicate spontaneously with their readers. Web pages exist for many authors of children's books. (See Appendix C.)

Reading about the lives of people as they tell their own stories can be interesting and informative for young readers. Insights that autobiographies provide may lead to insights into readers' own lives. Autobiographies written by children's authors typically contain information and advice that can serve children well in their own writing.

BIOGRAPHIES AND AUTOBIOGRAPHIES IN SCHOOL AND AT HOME

Within the home and within the classroom, biographies and autobiographies take their place alongside other genres of children's literature. Christine Duthie's *Special Perspectives on Children's Literature* (p. 247) suggests ideas for using biographies in the classroom. The lives of famous people often amaze and amuse children. These stories can be used to help children develop competency as independent readers. Biographies make fine subjects for literature groups, readers workshops, read-aloud selections, and free reading material. Comparing biographies of the same person written by different authors can be a valuable critical reading and thinking activity at any grade level.

Biographies also constitute an important part of the social studies curriculum. Accounts of historical figures provide insights into the past that enliven and inform children's view of historical events and periods. The lives of famous scientists can add depth to the study of science and help children become aware of what scientists do.

Most children find autobiographies, especially those of children's authors, extremely interesting. Many of these autobiographies contain information on how well-known children's authors get their ideas, the steps they follow to create stories, and advice for children about their own writing.

At home, biographies and autobiographies can become the stuff of shared family reading along with other genres of children's literature. Reading books about interesting characters—such as Don Brown's *Alice Ramsey's Great Adventure*, the story of the first woman to drive an auto across the United States, in 1909 (it took her fifty-nine days)—provide enjoyable experiences for children and adults alike.

Special Perspectives on Children's Literature

"IT'S JUST PLAIN REAL!": INTRODUCING YOUNG CHILDREN TO BIOGRAPHY AND AUTOBIOGRAPHY
by Christine Duthie

Since I believe that biography and autobiography compel young children and expand their possibilities as literate human beings, I include these genres as our read-aloud on a regular basis. They have enriched reading and writing workshops in my first grade classroom. My mini-lessons and discussions on biography/autobiography often focus on issues such as personal recall of a similar situation, why the subject chose to react in a particular way, or why the writer chose to include or exclude certain information.

Biography and autobiography have the unique ability to reach into the soil of human experience and till it for the reader; these genres embrace humanness and allow the reader to gaze at the world through the eyes and experiences of another. These genres provide instant role models with whom today's child can identify by offering the benefit of experience from those who have faced challenges or dilemmas. The journey of the reader through life, ever-toting personal experiences and influences, and the person whose journey is told through autobiography converge on the page. Often a young child asks, "Is that really true?" The affirmation which follows, when the text is biographic, is influential in the child's reflection. . . .

The presence of peers in the classroom presents the opportunity to mediate personal attitude with the opinions of others. In these genres, primary age children flourish with the opportunity to consider human possibilities within the context of the classroom; reflection with others blossoms to multiple perspectives. When authenticity boosts them to consider problems through and with others, I have often observed that quality biography and autobiography connect and carry readers to higher-level thinking. The combination of biography/autobiography and the dynamics of the group frequently launch children into interpretative discussion. . . .

The second reason for a biography/autobiography rebirth in my classroom has resulted from the availability of quality material for primary children. Writers and publishers of biography have come a long way since Ingri and Edgar d'Aulaire's 1939 Caldecott medal winner, *Abraham Lincoln*! Early biographies such as this one tended to be a life-to-death account of a historical figure and, more often than not, presented the person as someone with eminence and stature, yet whitewashed the reality of his or her lives. Young children were unable to relate to a stiff, unreal character. Many biographies and autobiographies currently written for primary age children present the main characters as ordinary people facing life's problems. . . .

The injection of social and personal focus and the abundance of quality material create a magnetism toward biography and autobiography not to be underestimated. Biography/autobiography are part of a genre awareness that I foster in my first grade classroom. I consider explicit exposure to all genres a goal in order to anchor a strong foundation for lifelong literacy.

Emerson said, "Language is a city, to the building of which every human being brings a stone." Young children are entitled to examine the "stones" of others in this part of the "Language City" for the pleasure and comfort found in biography and autobiography, for pure human experience, and for such books' high caliber and merit.

Seven-year-old Michael said it best when asked about biography and autobiography. With a smile and raised eyebrows, he answered, "It's just plain real." There is something pretty special about that; Michael knew it.

Christine Duthie teaches first grade in Trumansburg, New York, and is the author of True Stories: Nonfiction in the Primary Classroom *(Stenhouse, 1996). This essay is adapted from an article that appeared in the Summer 1998 issue of* The New Advocate *11(3): 219–227. Reprinted with permission of Christopher-Gordon Publishers, Inc*

CONCLUSION

It's no mean feat to develop accurate and realistic pictures of people in the contexts of their time and place, in language that is appropriate for young readers, in a scope that children will find manageable, and in a way that children will find interesting. Yet that's just what biographers who write for children do.

A far cry from the days when children were expected to read the lives of the saints and other prominent figures for inspiration and guidance, today young people are treated to realistic biographical accounts of historical and contemporary figures that interest, inform, and entertain. They enable young readers to extend beyond their own lives to the experiences of others.

Questions and Activities for Action and Discussion

1. Select a biography written for children about someone you admire. Critically review this work in terms of the information you already know about the person and the way in which the biographer portrays the person.

2. Collect three or four biographies written about the same person—Christopher Columbus, Dr. Martin Luther King Jr., or Pocahontas, for example. The biographies may be about the person's whole life or simply tell incidents from the person's life. Make a list of similarities and differences among these works.

3. As a genre of children's literature, biographies are often classified as information books. Make a list of the ways biographies can help children learn about the past.

4. While similar in some respects, autobiographies and biographies differ in some significant ways. Describe the ways a writer might approach writing about his or her own life as contrasted with how the writer would tackle the life of someone else. From biographical and autobiographical works written for children find examples to support your opinions.

5. Traditionally, biographers glorified their subjects by writing only glowing accounts of their lives. Contemporary biographers for children tend to be more accurate, writing about both positive and negative aspects of the lives of their subjects. Do you think biographies written for children ought to cloak some of the less positive aspects of the subjects' lives and personalities, or should authors paint "full pictures" of their subjects? Be prepared to support your position.

CHILDREN'S & YOUNG ADULT BOOKS CITED IN THIS CHAPTER

Adler, David. 1986. *Our Golda: The Story of Golda Meir.* New York: Puffin.

_____ 1989. *Jackie Robinson: He Was the First.* Illustrated by Robert Castill. New York: Holiday House.

Aliki. 1989. *The King's Day: Louis XIV of France.* New York: HarperCollins.

Allen, Paula Gunn, and Patricia Clark Smith. 1996. *As Long as the Rivers Flow: The Stories of Nine Native Americans.* New York: Scholastic.

Bains, Rae. 1993. *Benito Juarez, Hero of Modern Mexico.* Mahwa, N.J.: Troll.

Blumberg, Rhonda. 1991. *The Remarkable Adventures of Captain Cook.* New York: Simon and Schuster.

Bray, Rosemary. 1995. *Martin Luther King.* Illustrated by Malrah Zeldis. New York: Greenwillow.

Brooks, Polly Schoyer. 1995. *Cleopatra.* New York: HarperCollins.

Brown, Don. 1997. *Alice Ramsey's Great Adventure.* Boston: Houghton Mifflin.

Carle, Eric. 1998. *Flora and the Tiger: 19 Very Short Stories from My Life.* New York: Philomel.

Christopher, Henry. 1994. *Ruth Bader Ginsberg.* Danbury, Conn.: Watts.

Cleary, Beverly. 1988. *Girl from Yamhill: A Memoir.* New York: Morrow.

_____ 1995. *My Own Two Feet: A Memoir.* New York: Morrow.

Clinton, Susan Maloney. 1990. *Everett Alvarez, Jr., A Hero for Our Times.* San Francisco: Children's.

Conrad, Bruce W. 1992. *Cesar Chavez.* New York: Chelsea.

Cooney, Barbara. 1996. *Eleanor.* New York: Viking.

Cooper, Floyd. 1996. *Mandela: From the Life of the South African Statesman.* New York: Philomel.

D'Aulaire, Edgar Parin, and Ingri D'Aulaire. 1940. *Abraham Lincoln.* New York: Doubleday.

Daugherty, James. 1939. *Daniel Boone.* New York: Viking.

Davidson, Margaret. 1970. *Louis Braille: The Boy Who Invented Books for the Blind.* Illustrated by Janet Compere. New York: Scholastic.

Denenberg, Barry. 1996. *An American Hero: The True Story of Charles A. Lindbergh.* New York: Scholastic.

Ferris, Jeri. 1994. *What I Had Was Singing: The Story of Marian Anderson.* Minneapolis: Carolrhoda.

Fisher, Aileen. 1970. *Jeanne d'Arc.* Illustrated by Ati Forberg. New York: Crowell.

Fleischman, Sid. 1996. *The Abracadabra Kid: A Writer's Life.* New York: Greenwillow.

Fradin, Denis. 1992. *Haiawatha: Messenger of Peace.* New York: Macmillan.

_____ 1997. *Sacageawea: Northwest Explorer.* Illustrated by Nora Koeber. New York: Simon and Schuster.

Frank, Anne. 1967. *The Diary of a Young Girl.* New York: Doubleday.

Freedman, Russell. 1987. *Lincoln: A Photobiography.* New York: Clarion.

_____ 1987. *Indian Chiefs.* New York: Holiday House.

_____ 1990. *Franklin Delano Roosevelt.* New York: Clarion.

_____ 1991. *The Wright Brothers: How They Invented the Airplane.* New York: Holiday House.

_____ 1996. *The Life and Death of Crazy Horse.* Illustrated by A. B. H. Bull. New York: Holiday House.

Fritz, Jean. 1973. *And Then What Happened, Paul Revere?* Illustrated by Margot Tomes. New York: Putnam.

_____ 1976. *Will You Sign Here, John Hancock?* Illustrated by Trina Shart Hyman. New York: Putnam.

_____ 1984. *Homesick: My Own Story.* New York: Yearling.

_____ 1985. *China Homecoming.* New York: Putnam.

Greenfield, Eloise. 1995. *Rosa Parks.* Illustrated by Gil Ashby. New York: HarperCollins.

Haskins, James. 1992. *Thurgood Marshall: A Life for Justice.* New York: Henry Holt.

Holler, Anne. 1993. *Pocahontas: Powhantan Peacemaker.* New York: Chelsea House.

Joyce, William. 1997. *The World of William Joyce Scrapbook.* Photos by Philip Gould. New York: HarperCollins.

Klausner, Janet. 1993. *Sequoyah's Gift: Portrait of a Cherokee Leader.* New York: HarperCollins.

Kraft, Betsy Harvey. 1995. *Mother Jones: One Woman's Fight for Labor.* New York: Clarion.

Krull, Kathleen. 1996. *Wilma Unlimited: How Wilma Rudolph Became the World's Fastest Woman.* Illustrated by David Diaz. San Diego: Harcourt Brace.

Lasky, Kathryn. 1995. *She's Wearing a Dead Bird on Her Head.* Illustrated by D. Catrow. New York: Hyperion.

Lawson, Robert. 1939. *Ben and Me.* Boston: Little, Brown.

LeTord, Bijou. 1995. *The Blue Butterfly: A Story About Claude Monet.* New York: Doubleday.

Lord, Beth Bao. 1984. *In the Year of the Boar and Jackie Robinson.* New York: Harper & Row.

Lowry, Lois. 1998. *Looking Back: A Book of Memories.* Boston: Houghton Mifflin.

Maass, Robert. 1995. *UN Ambassador: A Behind-the-Scenes Look at Madeline Albright's World.* New York: Walker.

Marrin, Albert. 1995. *The Sea King: Sir Francis Drake and His Times.* New York: Atheneum.

Marten, Jacqueline Briggs. 1998. *Snowflake Bentley.* Illustrated by Mary Azarian. Boston: Houghton Mifflin.

Mayo, Edith. 1996. *The Smithsonian Book of the First Ladies: Their Lives, Times, and Issues.* New York: Henry Holt.

McKissack, Patricia C., and Frederick L. McKissack. 1998. *Young, Black, and Determined: A Biography of Lorraine Hansberry.* New York: Holiday House.

McPhail, David. 1996. *In Flight with David McPhail: A Creative Autobiography.* Portsmouth, N.H.: Heinemann.

Meigs, Cornelia. 1932. *Invincible Louisa.* Boston: Little, Brown.

Meltzer, Milton. 1990. *Columbus and the World Around Him.* New York: Watts.

Myers, Walter Dean. 1993. *Malcolm X: By Any Means Necessary.* New York: Scholastic.

Osofsky, Audrey. 1996. *Free to Dream: The Making of a Poet: Langston Hughes.* New York: Lothrop, Lee and Shepard.

Parks, Rosa, with Jim Haskins. 1992. *Rosa Parks: My Story.* New York: Dial.

Peet, Bill. 1989. *Bill Peet: An Autobiography.* Boston: Houghton Mifflin.

Pinkney, Andrea Davis. 1993. *Alvin Ailey.* New York: Hyperion.

_____ 1994. *Dear Benjamin Banneker.* Illustrated by Brian Pickney. San Diego: Harcourt Brace.

_____ 1996. *Bill Pickett: Rodeo-Ridin' Cowboy.* Illustrated by Brian Pickney. San Diego: Harcourt Brace.

_____ 1998. *Duke Ellington: The Piano Prince and His Orchestra.* Illustrated by Brian Pinkney. New York: Hyperion.

Polacco, Patricia. 1998. *Thank You, Mr. Falker.* New York: Putnam.

Quackenbush, Robert M. 1980. *Oh, What an Awful Mess!* Englewood Cliffs, N.J.: Prentice Hall.

Reef, Catherine. 1995. *Walt Whitman.* Boston: Houghton Mifflin

Ride, Sally. 1992. *Voyager: An Adventure to the Edge of the Solar System.* New York: Crown.

Say, Allan. 1990. *El Chino.* Boston: Houghton Mifflin.

Schroeder, Alan. 1996. *Minty: A Story of Harriet Tubman.* Illustrated by Jerry Pinkney. New York: Dial.

Sis, Peter. 1996. *Starry Messenger: A Book Depicting the Life of a Famous Scientist, Mathematician, Astronomer, Philosopher, Physicist; Galileo Galilei.* New York: Farrar, Straus and Giroux.

Stanley, Diane. 1996. *Leonardo da Vinci.* New York: Morrow.

_____ 1996. *Peter the Great.* New York: Morrow.

Stanley, Diane, and Peter Vennema. 1994. *Cleopatra.* Illustrated by Diane Stanley. New York: Morrow.

Tillage, Leon Walter. 1997. *Leon's Story.* Illustrated by Susan L. Roth. New York: Farrar, Straus and Giroux.

Tobias, Tobi. 1970. *Maria Tallchief.* New York: Crowell.

Toll, Nelly S. 1993. *Behind the Secret Window: A Memoir of a Hidden Childhood During World War Two.* New York: Dial.

Uchida, Yoshiko. 1991. *The Invisible Thread.* Englewood Cliffs, N.J.: Messner.

Venzia, Mike. 1996. *Ludwig Van Beethoven.* New York: Children's Press.

Weller, Frances Ward. 1997. *Madaket Millie.* Illustrated by Marcia Sewall. New York: Philomel.

Wells, Rosemary. 1998. *Mary on Horseback: Three Mountain Stories.* New York: Dial.

White, Ryan, with Ann Marie Cunningham. 1992. *Ryan White: My Own Story.* New York: Dial.

Yates, Elizabeth. 1950. *Amos Fortune, Free Man.* New York: Dutton.

Yep, Laurence. 1991. *The Lost Garden.* Englewood Cliffs, N.J.: Messner.

REFERENCES

Meltzer, M. 1998. If the Fish Stinks . . . *The New Advocate* 11:97–105.

Sutherland, Z. 1997. *Children and Books* (9th ed.). New York: Longman.

CHAPTER 11

POETRY

oetry is designed to delight. It appeals to the emotions and intellects of children and adults alike. From their earliest interaction with Mother Goose to their later encounters with poets like Robert Frost, children come to recognize and appreciate the elements that make poetry a special part of their reading experiences.

THIS CHAPTER

- examines different elements in children's poetry;

- describes the types of poems that children typically encounter as part of their literary experiences; and

- suggests ways to generate in children a love and appreciation of poetry.

Poetry has a major place in the world of children's literature. In its many forms, poetry broadens the minds, enriches the lives, and delights the ears of children.

What is poetry? *Webster's Dictionary* defines it as "the art of rhythmical composition . . . for exciting pleasure by beautiful, imaginative, or elevated thoughts" (1989, 1110). *The Literacy Dictionary* calls it "literature in metrical form—verse of 'high merit'" (Harris and Hodges 1995, 189).

Professional references variously define poetry as "a concise and memorable cast of language, with intense feeling, imagery, and qualities of sound that bounce pleasingly off the tongue, tickle the ear, and leave the mind something to ponder" (Temple et al. 1998, 227), and "the expression of ideas and feelings through a rhythmical composition of imaginative and beautiful words selected for their sonorous effects" (Tomlinson and Lynch-Brown 1996, 41).

Eleanor Farjeon, a noted children's poet, defines poetry in this way:

Poetry
What is poetry? Who knows?
Not the rose, but the scent of the rose;
Not the sky, but the light from the sky;
Not the fly, but the gleam of the fly;
Not the sea, but the sound of the sea;
Not myself, but something that makes me
See, hear, and feel something that prose
Cannot. What is it? Who knows?

Students have been known to describe poetry as "a bunch of metaphors buried under a pile of symbolism surrounded by a heap of imagery and obscured by analysis."

A precise definition of poetry is impossible because not all poems conform to a single form or achieve the same effect. A poem may be structured in fourteen lines as a sonnet or in five lines with a strict rhyme and rhythm scheme as a limerick. It may be written in the shape of a tree or the shape of a giraffe's neck. It may be a single line, written horizontally or vertically. It may rhyme or not. It may be passionate or cold, emotional or intellectual, clever or honest, painful or celebratory. No matter which definition one selects, one can always find an example of poetry that violates some element of that definition.

We might say that poetry is the expression of language in a deliberately chosen form to convey ideas and create images, but even this definition is inadequate. It blends ideas and images with language to generate impressions, moods, or emotions or to make commentary on something in a way that deliberately avoids generating emotion. All that can be said with any authority to define poetry is that it is writing in which language, form, and rhythm are all consciously chosen by the writer.

Young people seem to be intuitively drawn to the poetic elements—language, rhythm, rhyme, imagery, humor, and meaning—in children's verse. In the very early years, they respond to poetry by clapping, by spontaneously joining in as poems are read and recited, and by memorizing poems that have particular appeal to them. Schliesman (1998) summarizes the value of poetry in the lives of children: "In many ways, children, especially young children, take to poetry as naturally as breathing, and in some ways, poetry is as essential to their well-being as air that is clean. In addition to the captivating rhythms and sounds found in poetry, there is validation and counterpoint for thoughts and emotions. There is also delight and richness and liberation that can help sustain both heart and mind" (35).

Historically, as with other forms of children's literature, early poems for young people had a doom and gloom tone. In the late 1700s and early 1800s the tide began to turn as poets like William Blake, Edward Lear, Christina Rosetti, and Robert Louis Stevenson produced poems that appealed to children. Contemporary poets like John Ciardi, David McCord, Jack Prelutsky, and Shel Silverstein have produced a body of poetry that has enormous appeal to the young ears and minds of children.

Children's poetry and poetry for adults share some characteristics. Some poems have great appeal across age lines. The line of distinction between "adult" and "children's" poetry blurs, for example, in the children's trade book version of Robert Frost's *Stopping by the Woods on a Snowy Evening*, illustrated by Susan Jeffers.

Elements in Poetry

The elusiveness of a definition of poetry spills over into an elusiveness of a fixed description of form. There are obvious characteristics that distinguish poetry from prose genres, but not every poem has each of these qualities. In general, children's poetry uses language in unique forms, has particular patterns of rhythm and (sometimes) rhyme, creates images that allow us to see things in new ways, and deals in unique ways with content that appeals to children. The love of sound, word play, and the musical quality of verse are the stepping stones to get children interested in poetry.

Language

Language is one of the dimensions that distinguishes poetry from prose. Visually, the language is usually arranged differently. Words may be strung together in lines of prescribed syllable patterns, or they may be arranged in lines as short as one word, or the language may take on the shape of the subject of the poem. The words are rarely arranged on the page in the standard block paragraph form that characterizes prose.

Poetic language is fresh, imaginative, and economical. "Poets are word crafters. Each word matters—where it is placed on the page, its shades of meanings and how it works with the words adjacent to it" (Bownas, McClure, and Oxley 1997, 54).

The poet takes pains with language—choosing words and structure carefully. "The reason a successful poem works is not easy to sum up. There is a perfection in the selection of words and word order, an effective matching of the mood to the meter; a certain balance; a reaching out with language; a wholeness. To achieve this success, the poet-craftsman works hard with language" (Winch 1987, 126).

Rhythm

Rhythm is an essential element of poetry, another feature that often distinguishes poetry from prose. *Rhythm* refers to the beat or cadence of a poem. It involves the pronounced sound patterns that the poet uses to convey the thoughts and images contained in the work.

Sometimes, the beat of a poem suggests the action of the poem. One can hear the beat of the horse's hoofs in Alfred Noyes's "The Highwayman" ("*The highwayman came riding, riding, riding . . .*"), the cadenced marching step of the soldiers' boots in Rudyard Kipling's "Boots" ("*Boots, boots, boots, boots, moving up and down again . . .*"), the staccato beat of a stick being dragged by a child across a picket fence in David McCord's "The Pickety Fence" ("*The pickety fence/The pickety fence/ Give it a lick, it's/The Pickety fence*"). The rhythm of the language bespeaks the spirit of the poem.

Rhyme

Recurring sounds at the ends of lines are characteristic of much poetry, particularly for young children. Nevertheless, it's important for children (and many adults too) to realize that rhyme is not an essential element of poetry. Early experiences with Mother Goose, radio jingles, and popular songs create the impression that a poem is not a poem unless it has end-line rhyme. While rhyme is characteristic of some forms of poetry (limericks and sonnets, for example), the penchant for including rhyme in all forms of poetry often gets in the way of poetic expression. As children write their own poems, they often construct lines not to create mood or to convey image, but to get word pairs such as *hen* and *pen* and *nice* and *ice* to rhyme at the ends of the lines.

While it's important to disabuse children (and many adults) of the notion that all poetry has rhyme, it's also important to recognize that rhyme is part of what makes some poetry appealing. Rhymes such as

> Pat-a-cake-pat-a-cake, baker's man,
> Bake it and bake it as fast as you can,

and

> Hickory, dickory, dock,
> The mouse ran up the clock,

captivate children and draw them toward poetry from their earliest years. And rhyming elements in poems that older children find hilarious—Judith Viorst's "Mother Doesn't Want a Dog," in Jack Prelutsky's *The Random House Book of Poetry for Children*, for example, and Shel Silverstein's "Sarah Cynthia Sylvia Stout Who Would Not Take the Garbage Out" in his anthology *Where the Sidewalk Ends*—are part of what make these poems so enjoyable.

While end-line rhyme is characteristic of some types of poetry, skilled poets create images and moods in poetry with other sound elements such as:

- **assonance**, the internal repetition of similar vowel sounds followed by different consonant sounds—*the gloomy hoot of the cool shrew;*
- **alliteration**, the systematic repetition of initial consonant sounds in words—*sleek, slippery, slithery snakes;* and
- **onomatopoeia**, in which the sounds of a word imitate the sound the word names—*the buzz of the bee* or *the clickety-clack of the train as it speeds along the tracks.*

Imagery

"Imagery in literature is simply the quality that allows language to paint pictures with words" (Russell 1991, 78). The images of poetry make it a special form of writing. Poets write of "fog coming in on little cat's feet," describe a cat's "sandpaper kisses" on your cheek and refer to a towering apartment building as "a filing cabinet of human lives," to fish darting in the water as "little splinters of life," and to snowflakes as "pieces of quiet." Images such as these enable children to see the world in new ways.

Skilled poets create images that appeal to many senses. For example, in *Hailstones and Halibut Bones*, a collection of color poems, Mary O'Neill depicts the color red as a sunset, a firecracker, a rose, what "squiggles out when you cut your hand," and the feeling you get when you're embarrassed, suggesting the senses of sight, sound, smell, and touch and even emotion.

Content

The content of poetry for children can run the gamut from the sublime to the ridiculous, from "stopping by the woods on a snowy evening" to putting a bra on a camel.

For the most part, children's poets write about ordinary topics, the stuff of everyday life:

- **nature**: Kristine O'Connor Gerse's *Old Elm Speaks: Tree Poems* and Barbara Juster Esberson's *Echoes for the Eye: Poems to Celebrate Patterns in Nature;*
- **folk traditions**: Alvin Schwartz's *And the Green Grass Grew All Around*, a popular poem of some antiquity;
- **sports**: Lillian Morrison's collection of basketball poems *Slam Dunk* and Paul Janeczko's collection of baseball poems *That Sweet Diamond;*
- **holidays**: Eve Merriam's *Halloween ABC* and Jack Prelutsky's *It's Halloween;* and
- **seasons of the year**: Rebecca Kai Dotlich's *Lemonade Sun and Other Summer Poems.*

Individual poems and poetry collections for children can be found on virtually every imaginable topic—birthday parties and stray dogs, fantasies and fears, furry animals and feathery birds, worries and wishes, exotic secret thoughts and everyday school experiences. The meanings of the poems may be clear and literal or subtle and suggestive, but the subjects are all topics to which children can relate.

Humor

Children love to laugh. Humor is an essential element in poetry for children. Research (Kutiper and Wilson 1993) confirms what experience suggests: kids love humorous poems. Poets who write humorous poems make kids laugh and allow them to share this laughter with their teachers and parents. Two of the most popular poets with today's youngsters are Shel Silverstein and Jack Prelutsky. Perhaps the main reason for their widespread popularity is the spontaneous, irreverent, zany nature of much of the poetry they write (although some of their work is insightful and serious).

Children are introduced to humor and nonsense in their early encounters with nursery rhymes: a cow jumps over the moon, four and twenty blackbirds are baked in a pie, and an old woman lives in a shoe. The limericks and poems of Edward Lear and the explanation of Humpty Dumpty to Alice in Lewis Carroll's *Jabberwocky*, are classic examples of nonsense verse that children still enjoy. Most collections of children's poems contain humorous works (like John Ciardi's popular "Mummy Slept Late and Daddy Cooked Breakfast") that tickle children's funnybones. Anthologies of humorous poems such as David McCord's *Far and Few: Rhymes of the Never Was and Always Is* contain humor and nonsense verse that keep kids laughing throughout their childhood years.

Author Profile: Shel Silverstein

One of today's most popular children's poets is Shel Silverstein. His work is enjoyed by millions of children in classrooms every day.

Born in Chicago in 1932, Silverstein had no early inclination to be a writer for children. In the 1950s, as a member of the U.S. Armed Forces, he worked as a cartoonist for the military newspaper *Stars and Stripes*. Upon his discharge from the service, he worked for *Playboy* magazine, and he began to write country music. One of his songs was recorded by Johnny Cash and became a number-one hit. Convinced by his friends that his work would appeal to children, Silverstein wrote and illustrated *Lafcadio, the Lion Who Shot Back* (1963), launching his career as a children's writer.

Silverstein is best known for his poetry. His three collections of poems and drawings—*Where the Sidewalk Ends* (1974), *Light in the Attic* (1981), and *Falling Up* (1996) —are full of funny, zany, irreverent poems about topics to which children can relate, such as being sick (or faking it to miss school), child-friendly inventions like a homework machine or a remote control for manipulating the actions of one's father, and outlandish characters of all sorts. His poems range from short silly verses to longer narrative pieces. While his style includes free verse and concrete poems, most of Silverstein's work has strong rhythm and clear rhyme that appeal to children. His artistic style as an illustrator is uncomplicated, consisting of black and white line drawings, reflecting his background as a cartoonist.

While poetry is his stock in trade, Silverstein has also written some well-known children's prose. *The Giving Tree* (1964) is a story about a boy who wanted more and more from a tree that gave and gave and that he eventually cuts down. This book— which has been criticized by some arborists (because the tree is destroyed with impunity) and by some feminists (because Silverstein's narration does not criticize the boy for thoughtlessly taking and taking from a female tree that gives and gives)—has nevertheless become a favorite of many readers and purchased by many adults. (This is a perfect example of how different people construct different meanings from the same text.) *The Giving Tree* has been translated into several other languages.

Silverstein's other books—*The Missing Piece* (1976) and *The Missing Piece Meets the Big O* (1981)—are less well known but no less delightful.

In addition to writing for children and composing music, Shel Silverstein has written several plays for stage and screen. He is also a performing folksinger. But it is his poetry that provides a creative refuge for him and a refreshing read for children. His style draws readers to his poetry, and his approach, while light, entices children to share his love of literature.

Classroom encounters with poetry may involve analysis of poems. While awareness of the art and technique of poetry may at times be important, the emphasis in the early years needs to be on enjoyment.

TYPES OF POETRY

Poetry for children (and adults) can be classified by type. The genre includes nursery rhymes and verses, lyric poems, narrative poems, and structured poems that include limericks, haiku, concrete verse, and free verse.

The terms *poem, rhyme,* and *verse* are sometimes used interchangeably. Generally, rhymes and verses are poetic forms that have tight patterns of rhythm and sound. Some people make a distinction between poetry and verse on the basis of substance: Poetry deals

FACTORS FOR CONSIDERATION

FIVE FACTORS TO CONSIDER IN EVALUATING POETRY FOR CHILDREN

Here are five factors to look for when reviewing poetry for children:

1. Does the poem draw the child in; does it cause the child to clap, join in, or respond in some other way to the language and rhythm of the poem?

2. Does the poem use language that conveys ideas and images that children can understand and enjoy?

3. Do illustrations enhance the reader's understanding and/or appreciation of the verse?

4. Does the work have strong meter, rhyme, imagery, word play, and other elements that mark quality work?

5. Will the child be apt to remember (not necessarily memorize) the poem and want to hear it repeated again and again?

with lofty thoughts or impassioned feelings expressed in imaginative language, while verse merely conforms to metered rules and structure. Verse has been defined as "poetry without conceptual power" (Harris and Hodges 1995, 272). Rhymes and verses very often constitute young children's first experiences with poetry.

Rhymes and Chants

Rhymes and chants have long been popular with young children. Nursery rhymes constitute the first form of poetry that most children encounter and they remain enormously popular throughout the early years. Nursery rhymes are highly rhythmic and tightly rhymed verses produced by anonymous poets. Traditional nursery rhymes have a long history. "Rain, rain, go away," for example, predates the birth of Christ, and "Old King Cole" was a third-century British duke who is said to have built the city of Colchester in England.

Mother Goose Tales in its numerous incarnations is the oldest and best collection of nursery rhymes. Who "Mother Goose" really was is a matter of some speculation. The subtitle *Contes de ma mere l'oye (Tales of My Mother the Goose)* was used by Charles Perrault for his collection of French fairy tales in 1697. John Newbery's publishing house in London used *Mother Goose's Melody* when translating Perrault's work into English almost a century later. The American version of the origin of Mother Goose is that she was a woman named Elizabeth Foster Goose who wrote stories and songs for her sixteen children and stepchildren and is now buried in Boston's Old Granary Burial Ground. Newbery's collection of nursery rhymes was one of the first children's books ever published in England. And whatever the origin of the term, Mother Goose verses have been well loved by generations of children for centuries.

Many Mother Goose rhymes were originally created for adults, not for children. The rhymes originated as political commentaries on or social satire of events of the day. Jack Horner was a thief who, when delivering deeds of land which had been hidden in a pie for safekeeping, stuck in his thumb and stole one before reaching the court of King Henry VIII. "Ring Around the Rosie" is about the Great Plague that spread through Europe in the fourteenth century—people would notice a small rosy ring on their skin at the onset of the disease; carry herbs or posies in their pockets to ward off the sickness; sneeze "A-tishoo;" and fall down dead. Alan Trussell-Cullen presents the history of nursery rhymes in the very informative children's book *A Pocket Full of Posies*.

LIST OF TEN

A SAMPLER OF MOTHER GOOSE

Here is a sample of ten notable collections of Mother Goose rhymes from the hundreds of collections available:

My Very First Mother Goose, selected by Iona Opie, illustrated by Rosemary Wells
a collection that is whimsically illustrated to delight the eye as well as the ear (Candlewick, 1996)

Mother Goose's Words of Wit and Wisdom: A Book of Months by Tedd Arnold
an illustrated collection of rhymes that centers on months of the year (Dial, 1990)

Marguerite De Angeli's Book of Nursery and Mother Goose Rhymes by Marguerite De Angeli
a large book with traditional poems and illustrations (Doubleday, 1954)

The Random House Book of Mother Goose by Arnold Lobel
a richly illustrated collection of over 300 rhymes (Random House, 1986)

A Mother Goose Book, selected by Liz Van Doren, illustrated by Joan W. Anglund
a wonderful collection of Mother Goose rhymes (Harcourt Brace, 1991)

The Best Mother Goose Ever by Richard Scarry
a collection featuring Scarry's popular style and characters (Western, 1970)

Michael Foreman's Mother Goose by Michael Foreman
a large collection of popular rhymes (Harcourt Brace, 1991)

The Glorious Mother Goose by Cooper Edens
a collection illustrated by artists from the past (Atheneum, 1998)

Mother Goose: Or, the Old Nursery Rhymes by Kate Greenaway
a classic edition of the small version of Mother Goose illustrated by the famous British children's illustrator (Warne, 1881)

Tomie's Little Mother Goose by Tomie De Paola
rhymes illustrated with De Paola's unique popular style (Putnam, 1997).

Similar to nursery rhymes in their rhythm, rhyme, and appeal to young children are *playground chants*, verses that children chant on the playground as they are skipping rope or engaging in verbal play. Popular ditties like

> A my name is Alice and my sister's name is Ann . . .

are recited in time as children jump rope on the sidewalk or clap hands while sitting on the front steps.

Some of these playground verses are aimed to hurt or insult:

> I see London, I see France,
> I see (person's) underpants.

These rhymes are part of what Lurie (1990) calls "the tribal culture of childhood, and its sometimes subversive tales and rhymes."

Counting rhymes are very popular with young children too. Mother Goose poems such as

> "One, Two, Buckle my shoe"

and

> "One, two, three, four, five,
> I caught a hare alive"

help children with number concepts while engaging them in the joy of poetry at a very early age.

Narrative Poetry

Narrative poems tell stories that have beginnings, middles, and endings. The poetic quality of the rhythm and language contribute to the typically exciting action of the poem.

Among the classic American narrative poems that are presented as single children's books are the following:

- Henry Wadsworth Longfellow's *Paul Revere's Ride*, the story of the famous American revolutionary's ride to warn that the British were coming ("Listen, my children, and you shall hear/ Of the midnight ride of Paul Revere"), illustrated by Ted Rand;
- Robert Service's *The Cremation of Sam McGee*, the story of a gold prospector from Tennessee who freezes in the Arctic ("There are strange things done in the midnight sun/By the men who moil for gold"), illustrated by Ted Harrison; and
- Ernest Lawrence Thayer's *Casey at the Bat*, which recounts the mighty baseball player's disappointment of the hometown fans by striking out ("The outlook wasn't brilliant for the Mudville nine that day"), illustrated by Patricia Polacco.

A number of popular narrative poems have been illustrated many, many times:

- Clement Moore's well-known Christmas poem "A Visit from St. Nicholas" has been illustrated by scores of artists, including Tomie De Paola in his picture book *The Night Before Christmas* and Jan Brett with her wonderful style of brilliant colors and detailed borders; and
- Edward Lear's whimsical nonsense poem "The Owl and the Pussycat" has been presented for children a number of times, including in a richly illustrated version by Jan Brett.

Author Profile: JACK PRELUTSKY

When Jack Prelutsky was young, he thought that poetry was an unappealing subject that teachers forced upon children. So he decided to become a poet and create poetry that appealed to kids. Anyone who has enjoyed Prelutsky's entertaining and whimsical works knows that this children's poet has met his goals. Sometimes called "the poet laureate of the young generation," Prelutsky receives up to 100 letters a week from schoolchildren.

Prelutsky was born in 1940 in Brooklyn, New York. He attended Hunter College and studied music, with an eye to becoming an opera singer. As a young man, he tried his hand at a number of jobs: cab driver, waiter, actor, door-to-door salesman, and carpenter, among others. He was, in more ways than one, a Jack-of-all-trades.

As a child, Prelutsky was not allowed to have pets, so he created fabulous creatures in his imagination, creatures that found their way into his first book of poems, *A Gopher in the Garden and Other Animal Poems*, published in 1967. Prelutsky continued to produce original works that gained more and more popularity with children: *Rolling Henry Down the Hill* (1980, 1993), *The Sheriff of Rottenshot* (1982), *The Baby Uggs Are Hatching* (1982), *The New Kid on the Block* (1984), *Tyrannosaurus Was a Beast: Dinosaur Poems* (1988), and many others. Prelutsky writes about topics that children care about: the neighborhood bully, going to school, fear of the dark. His poems frequently feature animals and fantastic breasts that behave in surprising ways. His poetry is not only entertaining, but also frequently conveys a message.

While enormously popular with children, Prelutsky has not been without his critics. The irreverent approach he often takes, and his gruesome tales of macabre creatures in work like *The Headless Horseman Rides Tonight: Poems to Trouble Your Sleep* (1980) and *Nightmares: Poems to Trouble Your Sleep* (1993) have concerned some adults.

Prelutsky has also compiled and edited some wonderful collections of poems, including *Read-Aloud Rhymes for the Very Young* (1986), *Poems of A. Nonny Mouse* (1989), and *The Random House Book of Poetry for Children* (1983), which is perhaps the most highly acclaimed and widely used poetry anthology in schools. One of Prelutsky's latest works is *Hooray for Diffendoofer Day!* in which he collaborated with illustrator Lane Smith to turn some of the notes left by Dr. Seuss into a book after Seuss's death.

Jack Prelutsky lives in the Pacific Northwest, where he continues to write original poetry and compile anthologies that delight children. Here are some of his other works:

A. Nonny Mouse Writes Again!: Poems (1993)

For Laughing Out Louder: More Poems to Tickle Your Funnybone (1995)

Monday's Troll (1996)

Beauty of the Beast (1997)

Dinosaur Dinner with a Slice of Alligator Pie: Favorite Poems (1997)

Many poets have practiced their craft in narrative form. A. A. Milne, creator of *Winnie-the-Pooh*, also created *The World of Christopher Robin* which contains a number of narrative verses. Ogden Nash's older narrative poem *The Tale of the Custard Dragon* remains popular with children today. More contemporary poetry collections also contain narrative selections. Shel Silverstein's *Where the Sidewalk Ends* has clever story verses that tell about a boy being swallowed by a boa constrictor and a dentist being swallowed by a crocodile. Jack Prelutsky's *Rolling Harvey Down the Hill* contains a rhymed account of four friends who get sick of the neighborhood bully and roll him down the hill.

Ballads

The ballad, a form of narrative poetry, is part of folk literature. In the distant past, minstrels traveled the countryside entertaining people in courts and cottages with stories put to song. "Both the folk ballad and modern story poems have a common appeal: they tell a story in concentrated form, with a maximum of excitement and a minimum of words" (Sutherland 1997, 277). Children read ballads in illustrated books such as Alvin Schwartz's *And the Green Grass Grew All Around* and Jane Yolen's *The Ballad of the Pirate Queens*. Ballads are often included in anthologies of children's poetry as well.

Although we don't often think of them as narrative poems, many stories are told in verse. For example, Ludwig Bemelmans used rhythm and rhyme as he told about the antics of the popular *Madeline* and her friends in Miss Clavelle's school in Paris. And most of Dr. Seuss's stories were written in his unique rhyming style. Although these stories are told in language that contains the elements of poetry, the emphasis is on the story and not upon the quality of the language itself.

A powerful "story poem" is Karen Hesse's novel *Out of the Dust*, the 1998 Newbery Medal winner, a story told in free verse. Fourteen-year-old Billie Jo is orphaned when her mother and baby brother burn to death as a result of her father's carelessness. Billie Jo runs away but discovers that

> I didn't see anything better than what I already had.
> Home.

The language and the free verse that Hesse uses convey the starkness of the setting—the dust bowl of Oklahoma during the Great Depression—as well as propel a very moving story about an adolescent who must resolve serious conflicts.

Children love stories. Narrative poems tell stories in concentrated form with economy of language. A good way to get children interested in poetry is to introduce them to poetry in story form.

LIST OF TEN

A SAMPLER OF POETRY BOOKS

One or two comprehensive anthologies or collections of poetry with both traditional and contemporary selections on a range of topics ought to be at the fingertips of teachers or

List of Ten continued

on bookshelves at home. Although the terms are often used interchangeably, an *anthology* has poems by different poets and on different themes and topics, while a *collection* contains poems written by a single poet.

Here is a short list of some excellent compilations:

A Child's Garden of Verse by Robert Louis Stevenson
> *a classic collection of timeless poetry written by "the poet laureate of children" (Watts, 1966, one of many editions available)*

The Random House Book of Poetry selected by Jack Prelutsky, illustrated by Arnold Lobel
> *an outstanding comprehensive collection of poetry on a range of topics, with selections appropriate for virtually every occasion (Random House, 1983)*

Prelutsky has also edited and written other poetry collections including **The New Kid on the Block** (Greenwillow, 1984) and **A Pizza the Size of the Sun** (Greenwillow, 1996).

Where The Sidewalk Ends by Shel Silverstein
> *a collection of humorous poems that seem everlastingly popular with children and their teachers (Harper & Row, 1974)*

Silverstein has also written **Light in the Attic** (HarperCollins, 1981) and **Falling Up: Poems and Drawings** (HarperCollins, 1996).

Sing a Song of Popcorn: Every Child's Book of Poems edited by Beatrice Schenk De Regniers, Eva Moore, Mary Michaels White, and Jean Carr
> *a contemporary collection of poems arranged thematically (Scholastic, 1988)*

The New Oxford Book of Children's Verse edited by Neil Philip
> *an incredibly impressive collection that begins with poems written in the eighteenth century and ends with works produced in 1995, with over 350 poems by more than 200 poets (Oxford University Press, 1996)*

The New Oxford Treasury of Children's Poems edited by Michael Harrison and Christopher Stuart-Clark
> *a collection that brings together well-loved poems by well-known poets with some contemporary work (Oxford University Press, 1998)*

Pass the Poetry, Please edited by Lee Bennett Hopkins
> *the reissue of a collection of poems that have been very popular with teachers and children for a long time (HarperCollins, 1998)*

The Llama Who Had No Pajamas: 100 Favorite Poems by Mary Ann Hoberman
> *a compilation of old favorite poems for children to enjoy, enhanced by the illustrations of Betty Fraser (Harcourt Brace, 1998)*

The Beauty of the Beast: Poems from the Animal Kingdom selected by Jack Prelutsky
> *a collection of over 200 poems about animals, with watercolor illustrations by Meilo So that capture the beauty of the natural world (Knopf, 1997)*

I Am Writing a Poem About . . . : A Game of Poetry, edited by Myra Cohn Livingston
> *an interesting collection of work produced in a poetry class (Simon and Schuster, 1997)*

Also readily available are hundreds of specialized books of poetry with work by a particular author: books of poems on specific topics, such as cats or Halloween; and books with particular forms of poetry, such as like limericks. Of course, teachers and parents in love with poetry will have their own favorite collections available to share with children.

Lyric Poetry

Lyric poetry is a broadly inclusive term that is often used to refer to any short poem that is not a narrative poem. Lyric poems are melodic works that create an impression and evoke an emotion through their rhythmic use of language. Lyric poetry was originally intended to be sung; the term *lyric* is from the Greek expression "pertaining to the lyre." It has songlike qualities and usually explores personal feelings and emotions often in connection with human experiences.

Through language, lyric poems can create a mood that children can experience without being able to explain. In "The Swing," for example, Robert Louis Stevenson captures the exhilaration that children feel as they swing. The ability to capture a mood of childhood may explain the fact that much of the lyric poetry written in the nineteenth century for children still appeals to twenty-first-century children. The topics of these poems—wondering at nature, playing on the beach, learning to cope with growing up—endure.

Among the poets whose lyric work children continue to enjoy are the following:

- Robert Louis Stevenson, who has been called "the poet laureate of children," author of *A Child's Garden of Verse* (a number of editions of this famous poetry collection are available, including one illustrated by Brian Wildsmith);
- Eleanor Farjeon, a British poet whose poem defining poetry is in the opening part of this chapter, author of *The Children's Bells* and other wonderful works;
- Eloise Greenfield, whose collection *Honey, I Love* contains poetry that reflects the observations of a young African-American girl growing up (Greenfield has written other notable poetry collections that reflect the experience of young African Americans, including *Nathaniel Talking*, which uses the rap poetry of a young boy, and *Night on Neighborhood Street*, a book of poems that reflect the lives of urban youth); and
- David McCord, an American poet with the unique ability to see the world through the eyes of children and to capture that vision in wonderful lyric forms, author of several books of poetry including *One at a Time* and *Every Time I Climb a Tree*.

Lyric poems by other authors can be found in popular anthologies of children's poetry.

Free Verse

Free verse is a type of poetry without prescribed form; it is free of the traditional poetic elements of controlled stress, meter, and rhyme. Lines don't rhyme and rhythm is not as important as in other forms of poetry. This *vers libre* originated in France in the 1800s in

Author Profile: ELOISE GREENFIELD

Eloise Greenfield is a classic, popular, contemporary children's poet. Her work reflects for millions of children a love of life and a love of literature.

Born at the beginning of the Great Depression in North Carolina, Eloise Greenfield later moved with her family to Washington, D.C., where she went to college for two years and started working for the federal government. As a child, she loved to read, and, as a young adult, she tried her hand at writing but with little luck. In the 1970s, she joined the D.C. Black Writer's Workshop and, as a result of her work with this group, her writing career for children was launched with the publication of a biography about Rosa Parks.

While she has written picture books, biographies, and novels, Eloise Greenfield is best known for her poetry. Her first book of poems, *Honey, I Love and Other Love Poems* (1978) was an immediate hit, and it has become one of the most widely read books of children's poetry today. The work reflects the poet's experiences growing up in a warm and loving African-American family. The poems are marked by strong rhythm and expression of deep emotions to which children can relate. The title poem "Honey, I Love" was published as a picture book illustrated by Jan Spivy Gilchrest in 1995.

Greenfield has written other poetry collections—*Under the Sunday Tree* (1989), *Nathaniel Talking* (1989), and *Night on Neighborhood Street* (1991)—all of which reflect the African-American experience. She has also written single poems in picture book format, including *Africa Dream* (1977), *Daydreamers* (1981), and *For the Love of the Game: Michael Jordan and Me* (1997). Greenfield's work has been recognized by the National Council of Teachers of English, who presented her with their 1997 Award for Excellence in Poetry.

Music was an important part of Eloise Greenfield's childhood, and music is an integral part of her work as an author. The blues poem "My Daddy" and the poem "Nathaniel's Rap" from *Nathaniel Talking* are poems about music. She has said that when she writes, she hears "the music of speech" flow into her work, and if the words don't feel right musically, she doesn't use them. With musician Byron Morris, she has also made a musical version of the poems from *Honey, I Love*.

Despite a hectic schedule, which involves caring for two children and four grandchildren, Eloise Greenfield maintains ambitious goals for writing prose and poetry. Her continuing work will continue to delight generations of children to come.

Here are some of Eloise Greenfield's other books:

Bubbles (1972), a picture book

She Keep Bringing Me That Little Baby Girl (1974), a picture book

On My House (1975), a read-aloud book

Daddy and I (1991), a poetry board book

Kia Tanisha (1997), a poetry board book

Rosa Parks (1973), a biography

Paul Robeson (1975), a biography

Sister (1974), a novel

Koya Delaney and the Good Girl Blues (1992), a novel

an attempt to break away from the strict metrical rules that poets were expected to follow. Free verse has no discernible forms, no pattern of rhyme or rhythm; it does, however, "make its impressions with an intensity of insight or feeling, a clarity of vision, and sounds and rhythms that ebb and flow with the intensity of a poet's feelings about the subject matter (Temple et al., 1998, 232).

Free verse is not so free as to be formless or altogether unrhythmical, just as language is not formless or unrhythmical. Rather, the lines in free verse follow a varied pattern of spoken language. Each line contains various cadences of rhythm or beat and various numbers of syllables, just as speech does. The poet follows no predetermined pattern of rhythm or rhyme.

Children can encounter free verse in the work of such great poets as Carl Sandburg and Langston Hughes. Poems in free verse written for and by children can be found in the anthology *Miracles: Poems by Children of the English-Speaking World* edited by Richard Lewis.

Structured Poetry

Some poetry adheres to strict forms: limericks, haiku, cinquain, and concrete poems.

Limericks

Popularized in the mid-1800s by the poet Edward Lear, limericks adhere to a strict pattern of rhythm and rhyme: five lines, the first, second, and fifth having three feet and the third and fourth having two feet. The rhyming scheme is *aabba*:

> There was a young fellow named Jay
> Who liked to climb trees every day.
> Once he climbed up a tree,
> Waved and shouted, "See me!"
> But he fell when the branch gave away.

The content of limericks is usually humorous, and children enjoy reading and writing this type of poetry in the classroom. The classic book of limericks is Edward Lear's *There Was an Old Man . . . A Gallery of Nonsense Rhymes*. Other collections are John Ciardi's *The Hopeful Trout and Other Limericks* and Arnold Lobel's *A Book of Pigericks*.

Haiku

Haiku is a Japanese form of poetry that has seventeen syllables within three lines, one of five, one of seven, and one of five. The theme is a single thought or a phrase that reflects a human response to nature.

Flowers are blooming
Bringing beauty to our eyes,
A gift of springtime.

Haiku dates as far back as the Middle Ages. It has deep cultural and religious connections to Eastern thought. It expresses Zen beliefs about human kinship with the natural world. Its form suggests a momentary expression of humans' oneness with nature—"a breath-long expression of delight."

While structured according to a syllable count (the Japanese language has a syllabic rather than an alphabetic writing system like English), haiku is not servant to rhyme or meter. Teachers need to help children move beyond the line count and syllable count to recognize haiku as an elegant and sophisticated verse form that requires an austere, concise language.

Examples of haiku can be found in Richard Lewis's collection *In a Spring Garden*, illustrated by Ezra Jack Keats, and in Myra Cohn Livingston's *Cricket Never Dies: A Collection of Haiku and Tanka*, with pen and ink illustrations. The picture book *Grass Sandals: The Travels of Basho* by Dawnine Spivak chronicles the life of the Japanese poet Basho and is filled with examples of the famous poet's haiku.

Senryu is another type of Eastern poetry similar to haiku. Its scope is broader than nature.

Cinquain

Cinquain is a five-line verse form in which the first line has one word and gives the title; the second line has two words that usually describe the title; the third line has three words, usually expressing action related to the topic; the fourth line has four words that express a feeling; and the final one-word line is a synonym for the first line:

Happiness
Cheery Contentment
Sharing with others
How great it feels!
Joy.

Cinquain lacks the structured rhythm and rhyme elements found in other verse forms.

Concrete Poems

Children are often intrigued with concrete poems or "shape poems," poems in which words are arranged to represent the poem's subject. For example, Shel Silverstein's "Poem on the Neck of a Running Giraffe" (in *Where the Sidewalk Ends*) is written in the long, narrow shape of a giraffe's neck. Mary Ellen Solt and Willis Barnstone have put together a collection of this type of poetry in *Concrete Poems: A World View*.

Typically, concrete poems do not have a rhyme or rhythm scheme. They do, however, have eye-catching visual features that give them appeal.

With all the types of poetry available—narrative verse and lyric poems, free verse and structured forms—poetic variety can be the spice of life in a language arts classroom.

Children need to be given wide choice in poetry. They need to experience a mixed bag of poems—popular humorous light verse that makes them smile along with more serious work that leads them toward understanding their world; poems that stir their emotions as well as those that tickle their funny bones; narrative poems that tell good stories combined with free verse that relates to their personal experiences and emotions. The world of children's poetry is a rich world indeed.

Poetry: Multicultural Focus

Contemporary poetry often addresses issues important in the lives of children, reflecting the diversity that marks our society and promoting multiculturalism. The powerful words of Walter Dean Myers and the evocative art of Christopher Myers in *Harlem* portray a Harlem that people don't see on television. *Daddy Calls Me Man* by Angela Johnson features short verses that communicate a boy's feelings about his father, and *No Hickory, No Dickory, No Dock: Caribbean Nursery Rhymes* by John Agard and Grace Nichols, with original and traditional poetry from that part of the world, expresses the emotions and experiences of people of color. These are poems that all children can enjoy.

LIST OF TEN

BOOKS OF POETRY BY AND ABOUT AFRICAN AMERICANS

The following books are compilations of poems that reflect the experiences of poets of diverse cultures:

The Dream Keeper by Langston Hughes, illustrated by Brian Pinkney
a work by the great African American poet who wrote for adults as well as for children (Knopf, 1962)

Hughes also wrote **Carol of the Brown King: Poems**, a collection of Nativity poems that reflect the Black experience (Atheneum, 1998)

I Am the Darker Brother: An Anthology of Modern Poems by African Americans
an updated version of a compilation of poems first published in 1968, one of the most popular collection of poems by people of color (Simon and Schuster, 1997)

Soul Looks Back in Wonder illustrated by Tom Feelings
an outstanding anthology that celebrates African-American culture and history, blended beautifully with stunning illustrations (Dial, 1994)

In Daddy's Arms I Am Tall: African Americans Celebrating Fathers by Javaka Steptoe
a collection of poems from twelve African-American poets celebrating the strength of bonds between fathers and children (Lee and Low, 1997)

List of Ten continued

Not a Copper Penny in Me House by Monica Gunning
> *with language and images that reflect the culture of the Caribbean (Boyds Mills, 1993)*

Pass It On: African American Poetry for Children selected by Wade Hudson, illustrated by Floyd Cooper
> *a picture book that contains the work of well-known African-American poets (Scholastic, 1993)*

I, Too, Sing American: Three Centuries of African American Poetry selected by Catherine Clinton, illustrated by Stephen Alcorn
> *the works of African-American poets along with biographical sketches in a book the title of which comes from the first line of a Langston Hughes poem (Houghton Mifflin, 1998)*

The Sun Is So Quiet by Nikki Giovanni, illustrated by Ashley Bryan
> *poems about children of many ethnic backgrounds but especially of African descent*

The Palm of My Heart: Poetry by African American Children edited by Davida Adedjourma, illustrated by Gregory Christie
> *poems by children that reaffirm black culture and life (Lee and Low, 1996)*

Shimmy Shimmy Shimmy Like My Sister Kate: Looking at Harlem Renaissance Through Poems by Nikki Giovanni
> *a collection of African-American poetry more appropriate for the upper grades (Holt, 1996)*

The rich tradition of Latino cultures is reflected in Lori M. Carlson's collection *Cool Salsa: Bilingual Poems on Growing Up Latino in the United States* and Gary Soto's *Neighborhood Odes*, a collection of poems about the delights of growing up in a Hispanic neighborhood, and his *Canto Familiar*, interspersing the sounds and images of Mexican-American culture with Spanish words. *Sol a Sol* contains poems in English and Spanish collected by Lori Carlson and Emily Lisker celebrating activities of Latino family life, and Lulu Delacre's *Arroz con Leche: Popular Songs and Rhymes from Latin America* brings Latino traditions into the lives of children.

Poetry is a time-honored form of expression in Asian and Pacific cultures. For young children, *Chinese Mother Goose Rhymes*, edited by Robert Wyndham, a collection of nursery rhymes and ballads, illustrates the universal nature of language, culture, and themes by examining children's poetry from China. Charlotte B. De Forest's *The Prancing Pony: Nursery Rhymes from Japan* does the same thing with poetry from Japan. Janet Wong's books of poetry, *Good Luck Gold and Other Poems* and *The Seaweed Suitcase* address the Asian- and Pacific-American experiences with humor and skill.

Poetry, songs, and chants are important to Native American peoples. In *The Sacred Path: Spells, Prayers, and Power Songs of the American Indians*, John Bierhorst has gathered poetry from various Native American cultures. In *Touching the Distance: Native American Riddle Poems*, Brian Swann presents poetic images of different tribes in the form of riddles. Virginia Driving Hawk Sneve has given voices to the poetry of many Native American nations in *Dancing Teepees: Poems of American Indian Youth*, and Susan Jeffers's *Brother Eagle,*

Sister Sky: A Message from Chief Seattle is a poetic message about the Native American traditional respect for the earth.

A poetry anthology that is truly multicultural is *Chorus of Cultures Poetry Anthology: Developing Literacy Through Multicultural Poetry*, a collection of poems selected by noted authors and experts from different cultures: Alma Flor Ada, Violet Harris, and Lee Bennett Hopkins. Poems from different cultures contribute to children's appreciation of the rich diversity of our society. Books of poems that extend children's views across international borders include Nancy Van Laan's *Sleep, Sleep, Sleep: A Lullaby for Little Ones Around the World* and Floella Benjamin's *Skip Across the Ocean: Nursery Rhymes from Around the World*.

POETRY AT HOME AND IN SCHOOL

Many young children enjoy their first encounters with poetry at home. Parents and other caregivers involve them in the rhythm and rhyme of verses like "This little piggy went to market" and "One, two, buckle my shoe" as they engage in daily routines such as bathing and getting dressed. As a result of repeated exposure to *Mother Goose* during the preschool years, children will arrive at school already familiar with the farmer's wife who chases three blind mice and the cow who jumps over the moon. These rhymes and verses are often among children's first encounters with language.

Poetry becomes part of some families' experiences on Christmas Eve when parents share *The Night Before Christmas* with their children. John Foster's collection *First Verses* includes counting rhymes, finger rhymes, chanting rhymes, and action rhymes that elicit active responses from children. Alphabet books such as *Dr. Seuss's ABC* and picture books with rhyming text, such as Barbara Emberley's *Drummer Hoff*, provide children with early exposure to poetry as well. In some homes, parents provide a daily poetry break by reading from works like Sharon Taberski's energetic anthology *Morning, Noon, and Night: Poems to Fill Your Day*.

Poetry is an important part of the language arts curriculum. Many children receive their introduction to poetry as part of their classroom experiences, and the way it is presented to them can affect the way they view it for the rest of their lives.

Special Perspectives on Children's Literature

DIAMONDS IN THE ROUGH: HOW DO YOU TEACH SOMEONE TO LOVE POETRY?
by Elizabeth Gonsalves

I love baseball. As a kid, I played it in the backyard, my Mom or Dad pitching. Our family watched it on TV and went to Fenway Park to see the Red Sox play. My brothers played T-ball, minor league, then Little League and Babe Ruth; my sister played softball. As a family whose dad was in the Armed Forces, we moved a lot. My brothers and sister and I watched and played ball with kids in front yards on base and in the suburbs all over the Northeast. I understand baseball metaphors—"stepping up to the plate," "three strikes and you're out," "hit a home run." My favorite movies are baseball movies: *The Natural, A League of Their Own, Field of Dreams*. Nobody taught me about baseball from books or in front of a chalkboard; no one ever gave me a test. I learned the game from fans who followed teams, faithfully, in victory or defeat. I watched. I played.

I love poems. People taught me from books, in front of chalkboards. There were tests, and I didn't learn to love poems in schools. I loved nursery rhymes, jumprope chants, Sunday hymns. I found poems in anthologies and magazines; I cut out the ones I liked or copied them over. I memorized lyrics on record album covers and off sheet music. I knew the words by heart.

There *were* a few teachers who helped. One asked me to write a poem in seventh grade. And she didn't grade it! In the corner she wrote, "Very Good. Creative." I could write a poem; I was a poet. Another teacher, one I had in high school, rejoiced in poetry; she sang it, she danced it, she drew it, she wrote it. She invited us to join her—and we did. We memorized parts of poems she said we'd need for later. Emily Dickinson and T. S. Eliot were her close personal friends. I learned the thrill of recognizing the words that I placed in my memory and next to my heart. I love poetry because poets invite me into a world of words. I don't just stand on the sidelines and read—I play.

Some children *do* like *some* poetry: urban poetry, poetry by younger authors, war poetry, love poetry, depressing death poetry, angry-at-the-world poetry, I-can-change-the-world poetry, humorous kinds of purple cow poetry. Many of them write poetry and *are* poets, not just readers and memorizers.

Are They Good?

We show children pictures and then hand them crayons, finger paints,
masterpieces on refrigerator galleries—
they are artists.
We watch ball games with them and then teach them to throw and bat,
Little League, Babe Ruth, Triple A farm teams, big leagues—
they are athletes.
We show them cars and give them tricycles, bikes, mopeds, and their own
set of car keys, then a car—
they are drivers.
They watch the kitchen and we give them play sets, moving up to Easy
Bake and then into the real kitchen, cooking on their own—
they are chefs.
We show them babies and give them dolls, brothers and sisters, baby-
sitting, families of their own—
they are parents.
We read to them, show them poems, ask them to understand, and stay on
the outside . . . but they are not poets, writers—
they are only readers.

But *my* students won't be "writers"
or novelists, poets, playwrights.
Let them learn to appreciate, then to write expositorily—
arguments, narratives, descriptions, comparisons, contrasts—
an organized paragraph, sequence of organized paragraphs.

not stories, love letters, poems, protests, petitions, manifestoes, constitu-
tions, declaration, complaints, recommendations, predictions, fortunes
fairy tales,
autobiographies.

Ask them instead
When you write your poem, what form will you choose?
What rhythm, what rhyme?
What image will speak to your audience,
what metaphor will strike them?
Whose work will you model?
Here are some to browse through, to choose from.
Can you touch my mind, my heart, my imagination?

Talk to me.
Give me the poetry of now.

Here's the love poem I wrote yesterday
the poem I wrote on drugs
the poem I wrote after she broke up with me
the poem I wrote in my despair
the poem I slammed out in anger
the poem about my worlds, my tree, my river, my house, my rain,
my sun,
my happiness—
The words I wrote are from my heart.
Are they good?

(Gonsalves 1998)

How do you teach someone to love poetry? Learn to love something about poetry your-
self. Write a poem. Wander through an anthology of poems until something grabs
you—then step up to the plate and share it with your students. Maybe you'll strike out.
Maybe you'll hit a home run. You'll never know until you get in the game. And, by the
way, they're on your team. Let them play—and perhaps they'll learn to love the sport.

*Dr. Elizabeth Gonsalves is a poet and a teacher who chairs the English Department at
Abington High School in Abington, Massachusetts.*

When adults think of their experiences with poetry, many recall struggling to figure out if a poem was iambic pentameter or trying to decipher the meaning of poetic symbols. "The experience of poetry should come with so much pure pleasure that the taste for it will grow and become a permanent part of a child's emotional, intellectual, and aesthetic resources" (Sutherland 1997, 271). The emphasis ought to be on enjoyment rather than on analysis.

Poetry is written to be read aloud. The rhyme, rhythm, and language come alive through the voices of skilled readers and speakers. Poems need to be experienced. Children's poetry is made to be shared and enjoyed, savored and appreciated, but not to be forced upon the young.

Some simple rules apply to sharing poetry with children. Teachers need to read or recite poems that are their personal favorites, so that their own enthusiasm and love of poetry can be shared along with specific poems. Rehearsing a poem privately before reading it to the class will help the teacher capture the rhythm and mood a poem. Poems can also be recorded on tape. Children can follow the lines of print as they enjoy the poems at a listening center.

An effective way to engage children in reading poetry is choral reading, a technique that involves reading the poem aloud in a group. "Choral reading takes on new meaning for students because they begin to acquire a true appreciation of poetry and the poets who write it. . . . Engaging in choral reading of well-loved poems allows children the enjoyable experience of focusing on the images, rhyme, and rhythm created by the poet" (Farris 1997, 163). Choral reading helps develop effective speaking and reading skills, and it gives all children— including those who are shy and those who are less capable readers—an opportunity to have personal experiences with poetry.

Teachers can arrange poetry reading with students in several ways:

- In the line-a-child arrangement, each student or each pair of students reads one line in a poem of many similar lines, as in "My Name Is . . ." by Pauline Clarke from the *Random House Book of Poetry*:

    My name is Sluggery-wuggery
    My name is Worms-for-tea
    My name is . . .

- In a refrain arrangement, a soloist reads much of the poem, and the rest of the students join in on the refrain, as in Robert Louis Stevenson's "The Wind," featuring the following refrain after each stanza:

    Oh wind, a-blowing all day long!
    Oh wind, that sings so loud a song!

- In antiphonal or two-part choral reading, two groups are balanced against each other: girls and boys, for example, or high voices versus low ones. This is a popular arrangement in classrooms. Paul Fleischman's *Joyful Noise: Poems for Two Voices* contains poems that lend themselves to this arrangement.

- In unison arrangement, all children read together.

While the emphasis in choral reading is on enjoyment rather than on polished production, performances can be planned to share poetry with other classes.

What about memorizing poems, a popular practice in the past that many students have found odious? Typically, if a child finds a poem appealing enough, he or she will read it enough times to commit it to memory. Children who read Maurice Sendak's *Chicken Soup with Rice* as part of a class activity, for example, will soon find themselves repeating the verses from memory. Choral reading also helps children remember poems. Memorization for its own sake, however, is an educational practice not followed in many classrooms.

A practice that is followed in many classrooms is the writing of poetry. "Children grow rather naturally into poetry. . . . Children have a natural affinity to verse, songs, riddles, jokes, chants, and puns" (Tomkins and Hoskisson 1991, 395). Writing poetry is a very personal writing experience, and children need many experiences with poetry before they begin to write it. Writing should follow the reading, sharing, and enjoying of several poems.

Within the context of a process writing model followed in many classrooms, using poetry to express ideas becomes part of the prewriting stage. (Most professors don't allow college students the option of writing their papers as rhyming couplets, but those who do often get delightfully clever results!) Poetry gives children another way to respond in writing to what they read or feel.

Kenneth Koch, a professor of poetry at Columbia University, has worked to help children in the New York City schools learn to write poetry. He has operated on the premise that "children have a natural talent for writing poetry and anyone who teaches them should know that. Teaching is really not the right word for what takes place; it is more like permitting the children to discover something they already have (Koch 1970, 25). Koch uses "formula poems" with starters like "I wish . . ." and "I used to . . . but now I . . ." to get students started. In addition to describing techniques for getting children to write poetry, Koch's book *Wishes, Lies and Dreams* contains a wealth of poetry written by children. Another useful reference for teachers is *The Poetry Connection* by Kinereth Gensler and Nina Nyhart, another book based on the work of poets with children in classrooms.

Obviously, writing form poems such as limericks or haiku involves following a model and generating ideas and language to fit the model. Two or three class-generated examples often get students going in this direction.

Evaluating children's poetry can be tricky business. A letter grade can squash any further inclination to try one's hand at producing poems. The poetry incident described in the opening chapter of *Anastasia Krupnik* by Lois Lowry speaks to the danger of grading children's early attempts at poetry writing.

There are many ways to saturate children's classroom experiences with poems: selecting a Poem for the Day based on the season, the weather, or some other criterion (and inviting children to become involved in selection as well); having a Poet-Tree, a cardboard tree on which favorite poems for children are hung; planning a Poetry Show in which children are invited to read their own poems or their favorite poems and to which guest readers (the principal, the school secretary, other teachers) are invited to share their own favorites; and compiling a class book of children's best-loved poems. For teachers who love poetry and have good anthologies handy, the possibilities are virtually limitless.

CONCLUSION

Many people grow to dislike poetry even if, in their early years, they greatly enjoy it. From early delight, attitudes switch to dislike. Older children and many adults are often intimidated by poetry, unsure that they are making the "correct interpretation" of a poem or fearful of swimming in unfamiliar waters.

How to prevent this switch? To foster a love of literature, teachers and parents must help children happily enter the world of poetry with what has been called "unfettered exposure." Throughout children's preschool and elementary school years, the emphasis in poetry needs to be on pleasure.

To be sure, there will be times when oral or written responses to poems will be appropriate in readers' workshop discussions or in personal literature journals. And by the time students get to high school they can expect test items that require them to read and interpret a passage of poetic text. But as children are gaining early experiences with poetry, the primary emphasis needs to remain on enjoyment. Children's poetry was not written to be dissected or to be butchered and brutalized in the name of generating understanding and "appreciation."

Poetry is more than a subject to be studied. It's a universal art form that enriches our lives, an adventure to be enjoyed in language and literature and living. The gift of poetry is one of the greatest gifts we can give to the young.

Questions and Activities for Action and Discussion

1. Part of your education has undoubtedly involved the study of poetry. What are your recollections of these experiences with poetry? As a parent or classroom teacher, how would you approach poetry with children?

2. Gather a collection of children's poems on a particular theme or topic—Thanksgiving, birds, monsters, pets, or humor, for example. Make a list of the similarities you find among the poems and the reasons these poems would appeal to children.

3. Explore the work of a person who has written poetry for children, such as John Ciardi, Eloise Greenfield, or David McCord. Practice reading some of the poet's work and prepare to share some of the poems with a group of children.

4. How does poetry reflect the multicultural values of our diverse society? Read selections from Latino, African-American, Asian-American, or Native American poets. List elements that you think make these works "multicultural."

5. Choose a particular type of poetry (lyric or narrative poems, for example) and find several poems in this category. Share one or two of these poems with classmates or with children in an elementary classroom and gather information from your listeners about their responses to the poems.

CHILDREN'S & YOUNG ADULT BOOKS CITED IN THIS CHAPTER

Ada, Alma Flor, Violet Harris, and Lee Bennett Hopkins. 1993. *Chorus of Cultures Poetry Anthology: Developing Literacy Through Multicultural Poetry.* Carmel, Calif.: Hampton Brown.

Agard, John, and Grace Nichols. 1994. *No Hickory, No Dickory, No Dock: Caribbean Nursery Rhymes.* New York: Candlewick.

Bemelmans, Ludwig. 1962. *Madeline.* New York: Viking.

Benjamin, Floella. 1995. *Skip Across the Ocean: Nursery Rhymes from Around the World.* Illustrated by Sheila Moxley. New York: Orchard.

Bierhorst, John. 1983. *The Sacred Path: Spells, Prayers, and Power Songs of the American Indians.* New York: Morrow.

Carlson, Lori, ed. 1994. *Cool Salsa: Bilingual Poems on Growing up Latino in the United States.* New York: Holt.

Carlson, Lori, and Emily Lisker, eds. 1998. *Sol a Sol.* New York: Holt.

Carroll, Lewis. 1977. *Jabberwocky.* Illustrated by Jane Breskin Zalben. New York: Warne.

Ciardi, John. 1992. *The Hopeful Trout and Other Limericks.* Illustrated by Susan Meddaugh. Boston: Houghton Mifflin.

De Forest, Charlotte B. 1968. *The Prancing Pony: Nursery Rhymes from Japan.* Illustrated by Keiko Hida. New York: Walter Wetherhill.

Delacre, Lulu. 1988. *Arroz con Leche: Popular Songs and Rhymes from Latin America.* New York: Scholastic.

Dotlich, Rebecca Kai. 1998. *Lemonade Sun and Other Summer Poems.* Illustrated by Jan Sapaivey Gilchrest. Honesdale, Penn.: Boyds Mill Press.

Emberley, Barbara. 1967. *Drummer Hoff.* Illustrated by Ed Emberley. New York: Simon and Schuster.

Esberson, Barbara Juster. 1996. *Echoes for the Eye: Poems to Celebrate Patterns in Nature.* Illustrated by Helen Davie. New York: HarperCollins.

Farjeon, Eleanor. 1960. *The Children's Bells.* Illustrated by Peggy Fornum. London: Welch.

Fleischman, Paul. 1989. *Joyful Noise: Poems for Two Voices.* New York: HarperCollins.

Foster, John. 1996. *First Verses.* Illustrated by Carol Thompson. New York: Oxford University Press.

Frost, Robert. 1978. *Stopping by the Woods on a Snowy Evening.* Illustrated by Susan Jeffers. New York: Dutton.

Geisel, Theodore (Dr. Seuss). 1963. *Dr. Seuss's ABC.* New York: Random House.

Gerse, Kristine O'Connor. 1998. *Old Elm Speaks: Tree Poems.* Illustrated by Kate Kiesler. Boston: Houghton Mifflin.

Greenfield, Eloise. 1978. *Honey, I Love.* New York: HarperCollins.

_____ 1988. *Nathaniel Talking.* New York: Writers and Readers.

_____ 1991. *Night on Neighborhood Street.* New York: Puffin.

Hesse, Karen. 1997. *Out of the Dust.* New York: Scholastic.

Janeczko, Paul. 1998. *That Sweet Diamond: Baseball Poems.* Illustrated by Carole Katchen: New York: Atheneum.

Jeffers, Susan. 1991. *Brother Eagle, Sister Sky: A Message from Chief Seattle.* New York: Dial.

Johnson, Angela. 1978. *Daddy Calls Me Man.* Illustrated by Rhonda Mitchell. New York: Orchard.

Lear, Edward. 1991. *The Owl and the Pussycat.* Illustrated by Jan Brett. New York: Putnam.

_____ 1994. *There Was an Old Man . . . A Gallery of Nonsense Rhymes.* Illustrated by Michele Lemieux. New York: Morrow.

Lewis, Richard, ed. 1966. *Miracles: Poems by Children of the English-Speaking World.* New York: Simon and Schuster.

_____ ed. 1989. *In a Spring Garden.* Illustrated by Ezra Jack Keats. New York: Dial.

Livingston, Myra Cohn. 1997. *Cricket Never Dies: A Collection of Haiku and Tanka.* Illustrated by Kees de Kiefte. New York: Simon and Schuster.

Lobel, Arnold. 1983. A Book of Pigericks. New York: Harper & Row.

Longfellow, Henry Wadsworth. 1990. *Paul Revere's Ride.* Illustrated by Ted Rand. New York: Dutton.

Lowry, Lois. 1984. *Anastasia Krupnik.* New York: Dell.

McCord, David. 1952. *Far and Few: Rhymes of the Never Was and Always Is.* Illustrated by Henry B. Kane. Boston: Little, Brown.

_____ 1967. *Every Time I Climb a Tree.* Illustrated by Marc Simont. Boston: Little, Brown.

_____ 1971. *One at a Time.* Illustrated by Henry B. Kane. Boston: Little, Brown.

Merriam, Eve. 1995. *Halloween ABC.* New York: Simon and Schuster.

Milne, A. A. 1988. *The World of Christopher Robin.* New York: Dutton.

Moore, Clement. 1980. *The Night Before Christmas.* Illustrated by Tomie De Paola. New York: Holiday House.

_____ 1998. *The Night Before Christmas.* Illustrated by Jan Brett. New York: Putnam.

Morrison, Lillian, ed. 1995. *Slam Dunk: Basketball Poems.* Illustrated by Bill James. New York: Hyperion.

Myers, Walter Dean. 1997. *Harlem.* Illustrated by Christopher Myers. New York: Scholastic.

Nash, Ogden. 1995. *The Tale of the Custard Dragon.* Illustrated by Lynn Munsinger. Boston: Little Brown.

O'Neill, Mary. 1990. *Hailstones and Halibut Bones.* New York: Doubleday.

Prelutsky, Jack. 1980. *Rolling Harvey Down the Hill.* New York: Greenwillow.

_____ 1983. *The Random House Book of Poetry for Children.* Illustrated by Arnold Lobel. New York: Random House.

_____ 1997. *It's Halloween.* New York: Greenwillow.

Schwartz, Alvin. 1992. *And the Green Grass Grew All Around.* Illustrated by Sue Trusdell. New York: HarperCollins.

Sendak, Maurice. 1986. *Chicken Soup with Rice.* New York: Scholastic.

Service, Robert W. 1987. *The Cremation of Sam McGee.* Illustrated by Ted Harrison. New York: Greenwillow.

Silverstein, Shel. 1974. *Where the Sidewalk Ends.* New York: Harper & Row.

Sneve, Virginia Driving Hawk. 1989. *Dancing Teepees: Poems of American Indian Youth.* New York: Holiday House.

Solt, Mary Ellen, and Willis Barnstone, eds. 1980. *Concrete Poetry: A World View.* Bloomington, Ind.: University of Indiana Press.

Soto, Gary. 1992. *Neighborhood Odes.* Illustrated by David Diaz. San Diego: Harcourt Brace.

_____ 1995. *Canto Familiar.* Illustrated by Annika Nelson. San Diego: Harcourt Brace.

Spivak, Dawnine. 1997. *Grass Sandals: The Travels of Basho.* Illustrated by Demi. New York: Atheneum.

Stevenson, Robert Louis. 1966. *A Child's Garden of Verse.* Illustrated by Brian Wildsmith. New York: Watts.

Swann, Brian. 1998. *Touching the Distance: Native American Riddle Poems.* Illustrated by Maria Rendon. San Diego: Harcourt Brace.

Taberski, Sharon, ed. 1996. *Morning, Noon, and Night: Poems to Fill Your Day.* Illustrated by Nancy Doniger. Greenvale, N.Y.: Mondo.

Thayer, Ernest Lawrence. 1992. *Casey at the Bat.* Illustrated by Patricia Polacco. New York: Putnam.

Trussell-Cullen, Alan. 1989. *A Pocket Full of Posies.* Auckland, New Zealand: Shortland Publications.

Van Laan, Nancy. 1995. *Sleep, Sleep, Sleep: A Lullaby for Little Ones Around the World.* Illustrated by Holly Meade. Boston: Little, Brown.

Wong, Janet. 1994. *Good Luck Gold and Other Poems.* New York: Simon and Schuster.

_____ 1995. *The Seaweed Suitcase.* New York: Simon and Schuster.

Wyndham, Robert. 1968. *Chinese Mother Goose Rhymes.* New York: Philomel.

Yolen, Jane. 1995. *The Ballad of the Pirate Queens.* Illustrated by David Shannon. San Diego: Harcourt.

REFERENCES

Bownas, J., A. A. McClure, and P. Oxley. 1997. Bring the Rhythm of Poetry into the Classroom. *Language Arts* 75:48–55.

Farris, P. J. 1997. *Language Arts: Process, Product and Assessment* (2d ed.). Boston: McGraw-Hill.

Gensler, K., and N. Nyhart. 1992. *The Poetry Connection.* New York: Teachers and Writers Collaborative.

Harris, T. L., and R. E. Hodges, eds. 1995. *The Literacy Dictionary: The Vocabulary of Reading and Writing.* Newark, Del.: International Reading Association.

Jacobs, J. S., and M. O. Tunnell. 1996. *Children's Literature Briefly*. Columbus, Ohio: Merrill.

Koch, K. 1970. *Wishes, Lies and Dreams*. New York: Random House.

Kutiper, K., and P. Wilson. 1993. Updating Poetry Preferences: A Look at the Poetry Children Really Like. *The Reading Teacher* 47:28–35.

Lurie, A. 1990. *Don't Tell the Grown-ups: Subversive Children's Literature*. Boston: Little, Brown.

Russell, D. L. 1991. *Literature for Children: A Short Introduction*. New York: Longman.

Schliesman, M. 1998. Poetry for Every Child. *Book Links* 7:35–39.

Sutherland, Z. 1997. *Children and Books* (9th ed.). New York: Longman.

Temple, C., M. Martinez, J. Yokota, and A. Naylor. 1998. *Children's Books in Children's Hands: An Introduction to their Literature*. Boston: Allyn and Bacon.

Tomkins, G., and K. Hoskisson. 1991. *Language Arts: Content and Teaching Strategies* (2d ed.). Columbus, Ohio: Merrill.

Tomlinson, C. M., and C. Lynch-Brown. 1996. *Essentials of Children's Literature* (2d ed.). Boston: Allyn and Bacon.

Webster. 1989. *Webster's Encyclopedic Unabridged Dictionary of the English Language*. New York: Gramercy Books.

Winch, G. 1987. The Supreme Fiction: On Poetry and Children. In *Give Them Wings: The Experience of Children's Literature*, eds. M. Saxby and G. Winch. Melbourne, Australia, Macmillan of Australia.

CHAPTER 12

Media, Technology, and Children's Literature

 his chapter identifies technological devices related to children's literature and examines how these resources can best be used to create lifelong readers by promoting the love of literature.

This Chapter

- examines traditional audiovisual devices such as tape and video recordings as a means of sharing literature with children;

- describes technological devices, such as CD-ROMs, that present children's books in alternative formats; and

- considers other forms of information technology, such as personal computers and the Internet, that support the study, teaching, and enjoyment of literature for children.

Media and technology are pervasive forces in today's world. People rely on radio and television for much of their information and entertainment. From the automotive technology that helps keep our cars running to the medical technology that helps keep our bodies running, computers are an important part of our day-to-day lives. Virtually every family has a television set. Almost half our homes have personal computers, and the number increases every year. We use computers for all kinds of reasons—for shopping, managing personal finances, entertainment, information, and maintaining contact with others. Children use computers to do their homework and to play educational (and other) games. Personal computers promise to be as essential in the future as telephones are today.

Technology is dramatically changing the contour of the educational landscape as well. Three-quarters of all classrooms have computers, and about half of all teachers use computers as instructional tools (Jerald 1998a). A plethora of programs flow from software development houses for many different uses in the classroom. Although a significant portion of school computer time is spent learning about computers and how to use them, children continue to utilize computers as learning tools in all areas of the curriculum. Given the twenty-first-century need for citizens to be skilled in computer use, the very definition of *literacy* has been expanded to include computer literacy or electronic literacy.

Classrooms of the future will be far more technologically driven than classrooms of today. It's not surprising, then, to see technology impacting children's literature in so many ways. Children can interact with their favorite stories on CD-ROMs. Internet sites provide all kinds of information about children's literature, from references for term papers to citations that address the issue of gender bias and stereotyping in children's books. We can find sales figures and book reviews on-line. Children can link up with other children to exchange information about books and connect with the home pages of many well-known authors. Parents can tap into Web pages that advise them on which books to buy, advise them on how to use books at home, offer topical book lists (such as of children's books to read around Mother's Day), and provide a wealth of other information about buying books for children. Teachers can find lessons built around books that they use in their classrooms and connect with other teachers for cybertalk about books. We can order books conveniently and reasonably over the Internet by connecting with book vendors, some of which will even provide personal profiles of our preferences in children's literature. In short, technology and telecommunications in their many forms have enormously expanded possibilities for encounters with children's literature. The computer has been called "the ubiquitous icon of the digital age" (Walter 1998, 37).

Author Profile: JAN BRETT

Jan Brett is a children's author and illustrator who uses technology to connect with children in classrooms. Born in the seaside town of Hingham, Massachusetts, Brett loved to read and draw as a child, foreshadowing the career that she enjoys in her adult life. She attended the Boston Museum School and began her career by illustrating books written by other children's authors, such as Eve Bunting's *St. Patrick's Day in the Morning* (1980).

Two qualities that characterize Jan Brett's work are meticulous detail and authenticity. Not only are the illustrations on each page rich in vivid detail, but the margins are filled with detailed depictions of people (and animals), places, and things directly and indirectly related to the story. These borders enhance the reader's enjoyment.

In preparation for a book, Brett carefully researches setting before she draws the pictures. She traveled to Denmark and sketched the Danish countryside as the basis for her artwork in *The Hat* (1997). She spent time in the Caribbean before producing her rich rendition of Edward Lear's poem *The Owl and the Pussycat* (1992). Her intimate familiarity with Nantucket Island and its people are evident in *Comet's Nine Lives* (1996), the story of a cat who survives a series of mishaps.

Brett connects story characters to people and animals in her real life, and she tells her readers all about the connections. Berliotz, the main character in *Berliotz the Bear* (1991), for example, is modeled after her musician husband Joe. Other animal characters in the story (which is about a group of musicians who get stuck on their way to a concert) are based on her husband's colleagues in the Boston Symphony Orchestra. Her book *The Hat* (1997) was suggested by the misadventures of her own pet hedgehog when he got his head caught in a stocking slipper.

Brett connects with kids by providing newsletters about her books and by answering questions on the Internet. Her newsletters tell about the children who inspired her stories, describe the people who helped her research her topics, provide information about her work on a book, make suggestions about how to use her books in the classroom, encourage children in their own work, and even contain simple drawing lessons related to the topic of a book. Through the personal insights that she provides, readers are able to develop a greater appreciation of who Jan Brett is and the perspective from which she works as an author/illustrator of children's literature. Her Web page address is: http://www.janbrett.com.

Here are some of Brett's other well-known works:

Armadillo Rodeo (1995)

Town Mouse, Country Mouse (1994)

The Mitten: A Ukrainian Folktale (1989)

Goldilocks and the Three Bears (1987)

The Twelve Days of Christmas (1986)

Technology also holds promise for improving the reading achievement of young children. Based on its research summary, the National Research Council's Committee on the Prevention of Reading Difficulties in Young Children concludes, "Preliminary evaluations indicate that well designed software programs for supporting early literacy development can produce gains in student performance. Such software can reinforce, motivate, and extend early literacy instruction" (Snow, Burns, and Griffin 1998, 342).

As technology has yet-unanticipated potential to change our lives both inside and outside the classroom, it will surely impact the way that young children interact with literature. Media and technology already provide important alternatives to print as a means of presenting literature to children, and the use of these tools is bound to increase in the future.

Literature and Media

While computers provide new means of presenting literature to children, older audio- and videotape technology remains effective for giving children access to literature. "Audio and visual technologies and their respective media can make a significant contribution to a literature-based reading curriculum . . . " (Rickelman and Henk 1990, 682). Besides enhancing the already provocative appeal of children's literature, audiovisual activity with literature "solidifies children's concept of story, encourages the use of prediction strategies, expands receptive vocabularies, captures the imagination, and most importantly, promotes further literacy involvement" (Ibid.).

Audiotapes

Tape recorders have been around for so long that many people consider them an "ancient" form of technology. Nevertheless, taped books can play an important part in children's encounters with literature at home and in school.

Hearing a tape before reading a book can enhance the reading experience enormously. A personal experience brought this home in connection with Frank McCort's bestselling, Pulitzer Prize–winning *Angela's Ashes*. When that book was first published, a friend enthusiastically recommended it to me. I requested it from my local public library and was told that I was number 292 on the list. Shortly thereafter, I borrowed a friend's taped copy of the book read by the author himself. When my number finally came up at the library, I read the book with the author's voice inside my head. Song lyrics and dialogue came alive in the rich Irish accent of the author. Descriptions and events from the story were not just words on the page but were brought alive through McCort's personal account of his own experiences. My reading experience with the book was enhanced tremendously by the tape.

Taped books can enhance the reading experience of children in the same way. When they hear books on tape before (or while) reading them, children share reactions like, "It's sure fun because they do the voices," "I like to listen and follow along," and "Books on tape help me when I get tongue-tied. I read a lot more with tapes" (Mooney and O'Day, 1999).

Audiotapes enable children to experience and interact with literature. Children who hear taped books are in a better position to understand and appreciate what they read. The tapes expose them to the language of the texts and students can then anticipate the events of the plot. They know who the characters are and can understand their motivations. When they see the words on the page, they can hear the conversations among the Tuck family in Natalie Babbitt's *Tuck Everlasting*, and they can "hear" what is happening in Lois Lowry's *Number the Stars*. These tapes give children access to literature that is beyond their reading ability and provide a form of scaffolding for later reading. They provide an oral fluency model and can be the means to increase motivation and confidence.

For children who are reading well below grade level—remedial readers, learning disabled pupils, second language learners, bilingual speakers, and others who are typically at risk of reading failure—taped books provide an entree into the literacy community. When classmates are engaged in classroom book talks about John Reynolds Gardiner's *Stone Fox* or when friends are discussing Katherine Paterson's *The Great Gilly Hopkins* in the cafeteria, children whose reading ability does not allow them to read these books are empowered to join in the conversation if they have heard the books on tape. Being able to talk about a book that everyone else is talking about enhances confidence and sense of self.

But what if a child decides never to read a book after hearing the tape? In the worst case scenario, the child has become familiar with a piece of literature that he or she otherwise would not have known. In the best case scenario, the child will be motivated to pick up the book and attempt to read it on his or her own or will be in a better position to read the book if it is introduced as reading material in the classroom. As teachers build literacy lessons around core trade books and other pieces of literature, children will be necessarily engaged in reading by the taped versions that provide background and help with comprehending the story.

Taped books are effective instructional devices and tools that often lead to independent reading. Besides, most children love to hear stories read to them, and taped books thus contribute to developing a love of literature.

Movies and Videotapes

Television is a powerful medium in today's society. From the preschool years through old age, people spend a significant amount of time watching TV, more time than they typically spend reading. Movies and videos constitute a major staple in our entertainment diet.

Children's initial encounters with literature often come through the visual media of television and movies. As part of their preschool experiences, children watch television programs such as "Reading Rainbow," the well-known PBS series that opens the door to literature by reading quality books aloud. "Reading Rainbow" provides a unique exposure to books, additional information, and discussions that allow children to expand their knowledge and develop their understanding of related topics and contents. It also offers unique opportunities to inject another dimension of multicultural literature into the lives of young children. (Videocassettes of "Reading Rainbow" with supporting instructional materials are available for classroom use; information about these materials can be found at *http://gpn.unl.edu/index.htm*.) Other television shows bring children's literature into the lives of preschoolers. Some programs feature Marc Brown's character Arthur who was born in books but is now a television character enormously popular among young children. Local cable outlets sometimes air programs related to children's literature.

Videotapes provide another medium for presenting literature to young children. Beyond Disney's renditions of traditional folk classics like *Cinderella* and *Snow White*, motion pictures and television shows have featured fine works of literature—Ludwig Bemelmans's *Madeline*, Phyllis Naylor's *Shiloh*, Patricia MacLachlan's *Sarah, Plain and Tall*, to name a few. On video, children can enjoy the animated version of Maurice Sendak's delightful *Pierre* (the boy who didn't care) and listen to the classic *Mike Mulligan and His Steam Shovel* while viewing Virginia Lee Burton's original illustrations on the screen.

By actually presenting stories in dramatized, animated, or read-aloud formats, videotapes open other doors to children's literature for young readers. Videos allow children to enter the studios of author/illustrators like Eric Carle and Robert McCloskey and watch these incredibly talented individuals create their books as they talk about their work. Through videos children and their teachers make connections with award-winning Russell Freedman and Jean Craighead George, interact with Mildred D. Taylor's *Roll of Thunder, Hear My Cry* as they hear the story read and see scenes from the book depicted on the screen, and watch talented actress Glenn Close create the title role in *Sarah, Plain and Tall*. In short, videos offer children opportunities to engage in many dimensions of children's literature in a number of ways.

Videotaped versions of children's literature offer the same advantages that audiotapes do, and they also offer a visual impact. Viewing a video based on a well-known story can build a schema for later reading and may motivate children to read the original version. Watching the video *after* reading the book is an interesting and valuable critical reading/writing/thinking activity. Children can compare and contrast the video version with the original version and make critical judgments about which version is better and why. Writing critical reviews comparing print and media presentations is an authentic and valuable writing experience for children.

While audiovisual devices are useful means for promoting knowledge and enjoyment of children's literature, the computer will constitute the most powerfully promising technological force of the twenty-first century.

COMPUTER TECHNOLOGY

Computers have long been used as instructional tools in language arts. Programs are available to provide drill and practice exercises, the electronic equivalents of ditto worksheets. Programs with carefully designed instructional sequences and intriguing visual images present phonics, vocabulary, sentence-building, grammar, and other exercises that enable children to develop and practice language and literacy competencies. Child-oriented word-processing programs are widely used in composing, editing, revising, illustrating, and publishing stories and poems as part of classroom writing programs. More and more teachers are using computers for more and more reasons as part of language arts instruction.

Computer programs are also used as instructional devices to present literature to children in classroom and home settings. In a school setting, the computer can be the vehicle for presenting books to children on CD-ROM or for teaching about and testing children on stories that they have read. With access to the Internet, computers can be the means of learning more about children's literature and the people who write it, and a vehicle for sharing ideas with others.

The computer has brought momentous changes to our lives. Many aspects of our world are changing before our eyes, and we can expect schools in the twenty-first century to change apace. With computers, children will continue to interact with and respond to literature in new ways.

Books on CD-ROM

When most people think of children's literature, they think of books, of quietly turning pages bound between a front and back cover, of static words and stable pictures arranged on paper. Many members of the younger generation have already encountered literature in a very different form—on a computer screen, with digitally enhanced pictures that move in response to the click of a mouse, with text that is highlighted as it is read, with the option of hearing the story read in more than one language, and with built-in technology that invites the reader to become actively involved in the story. Many children enjoy very early encounters with books presented on CD-ROMs.

A CD-ROM (Compact Disk Read-Only Memory) is an optical disk designed to store digitally coded information that is permanently recorded for use with a computer. A CD-ROM can store up to the equivalent of half a million pages of text; sets of encyclopedias that formerly occupied many library shelves are now contained on a couple of disks, supplemented by audio, video, and other features not found in conventional sources of print. With this storage capacity, a single CD-ROM can accommodate a whole collection of children's literature.

FACTORS FOR CONSIDERATION

FIVE FACTORS TO CONSIDER IN EVALUATING CD-ROM PRESENTATIONS OF CHILDREN'S BOOKS

Here are five factors to look for when reviewing CD-ROM presentations of children's books:

1. Is the book worthwhile; is it a book that a child would enjoy in its conventional print form?

2. Are there worthwhile opportunities for the child to interact with the story and respond appropriately in various ways?

3. Are there ways for children to read the text without being overly distracted from the story itself?

4. Does the program provide multiple learning options to develop the child's language, reading, writing, thinking, and other literacy-related abilities?

5. Does the program provide or suggest ways to help a child move toward independence in reading?

Some skills-oriented CD-ROMs use characters from children's literature to facilitate skill-development activities; for example, *Curious George Learns to Spell* has more to do with spelling than with literature, and *Dr. Seuss Kindergarten* offers reading and math games that feature familiar Seuss characters. However, within a literature program, the CD-ROMs uses should present books to children without focusing primarily on skills.

CD-ROMs present books in a way that can extend and enrich a child's interaction with and involvement in stories and poems that comprise literature for children. Electronic texts typically incorporate more features than conventional texts can—animation, speech (in different languages), sound effects, live action, instructional support, dialogue, and the like.

A CD-ROM presentation can extend and enrich a child's interaction with a trade book. The CD-ROM presentation of Beatrix Potter's classic story *The Tale of Peter Rabbit*, for example, provides the original text and illustrations on screen and reads the story aloud with a musical background. Text is highlighted as the story is read and children can point to words they don't understand.

In the CD-ROM presentation of *Chickka Chicka Boom Boom*, the popular alphabet book written in an animated narrative style by Bill Martin Jr. and John Archambault, five lively youngsters on the screen offer the young reader six options for interacting with the text and illustrations of the book:

1. **Read-Along**: Ray Charles reads the story aloud, and each word is highlighted in color as it is read so the child can more easily follow the words.

2. **Sing-Along**: The words of the book are sung to several different tunes; again, each word is highlighted in color as it is sung. The original illustrations from the book are animated as the words are being sung.

3. **Bang and Clang**: The child listens to the story being read to a lively beat.

4. **Jump and Jingle**: As the child clicks on a letter, kids on the screen recite a playground chant or jump-rope rhymes using words beginning with that letter.

5. **Explore S'more**: When the child clicks on a letter, he or she hears sentences featuring words that begin with that letter ("*R* is for *rainbow*") and sees the upper- and lowercase forms of the letter transformed into the objects named by the words.

6. **Letter Line-up**: The child clicks on letters randomly arranged on the screen to place each letter in the proper alphabetical order.

The *Chicka Chicka Boom Boom* CD-ROM not only presents the actual book in an animated format, but also gives children help in learning letter names, sounds, upper- and lowercase forms, and alphabet sequence, while providing a delightful multimedia performance. Suggestions for parents are included as well.

LIST OF TEN

CHILDREN'S BOOKS AVAILABLE ON CD-ROM

The children's literature titles available in electronic format are increasing. Some are animated versions of printed books, while others incorporate games, music, and interactive activities. Here is a sample of books available:

If You Give a Mouse a Cookie by Laura Numeroff
The animated version of this very popular delightful picture book allows children to control the pace of the reading and to interact with various parts of the book (HarperCollins Interactive, 1995).

Dr. Seuss's ABC by Dr. Seuss
In addition to letting children point to and click on objects, this version offers an alphabet song to go along with text (Living Books, 1995).

Scary Poems for Rotten Kids by Sean O'Huigin
Text is highlighted as it is read and children can point to and click on words to hear them read aloud (Discis Books, 1990).

Sheila Ray, the Brave by Kevin Henkes
Characters act out the story and add dialogue; there's also an interactive map game (Living Books, 1996).

Cinderella: The Original Fairy Tale by Greg Guderian
The point-and-click feature makes words appear when the reader points to objects on the screen (Discis Books, 1990).

Arthur's Teacher Trouble by Marc Brown
Clever animation allows children to participate in the story in different ways; other Arthur titles are also available (Living Books, 1992).

How the Leopard Got His Spots by Rudyard Kipling
This electronic version of the famous "Just So Story" is read by Danny Glover, with music by Ladysmith Black Mambazo, and allows users to solve puzzles and play games with figures embedded in the illustrations (Rabbit Ears Productions, 1995).

The Paper Bag Princess by Robert Munsch
Point-and-click features allow children to interact with illustrations and text in this delightful story (Discis Books, 1990).

The New Kid on the Block by Jack Prelutsky
A cartoon version of the poet guides children through playful interactions with the poems (Living Books, 1993).

Just Grandma and Me by Mercer Mayer
Children can enter the story and play interactively by manipulating figures in the illustrations on each page (Living Books, 1993).

Many other children's titles and quality trade books are available on CD-ROM, and more are appearing in the educational and commercial marketplace all the time.

Some children's literature comes with CD-ROMs as part of a "package," the disk included inside the cover of the book itself. Bernadine Connelly's retelling of the famous African-American folk ballad about the Underground Railroad, *Follow the Drinking Gourd*, for example, comes with a CD-ROM that allows the reader to follow the lines of the text while listening to Morgan Freeman read the story of the flight of a young girl and her family from slavery.

CD-ROM storybooks have some distinct advantages over conventional print. Electronic text incorporates speech, animation, sound effects, music, and other features that encourage readers to interact with stories in a number of different ways. It engages the child more actively in the book, and it recognizes multiple modes of learning. Electronic storybooks can help young children explore basic concepts of print; the highlighting of text, for example, helps emergent readers trace print from left to right and top to bottom. Most presentations provide instant feedback, giving the definitions of words to which children point. Such programs help children learn to recognize words and construct meaning from text. Research suggests that comprehension can improve with the use of electronic text; studies of the impact of electronic text on the reading comprehension of third graders found that comprehension measured by retelling was significantly better for children who read CD-ROM versions of the story than for those who read the conventional print versions of the books (Matthew 1997).

While stories presented on CD-ROMs offer distinct advantages, they come with downsides as well. By their nature, computers eliminate physical interaction with a book. The screen is, in a sense, removed from the personal control that the child feels while holding a book. Electronic text does not provide the portability of a book. Readers can't make page selections on the screen the way they can with a book. Also, the computer is an unequal substitute for a human in sharing a story. Some critics fear that electronic books will contribute to what Kraft (1997–1998) calls "vidiocy," by drawing children's attention away from text. Children may become so engrossed with the bells and whistles that they fail to attend to the text and the story itself.

Databases of Children's Literature

Children's literature databases are resources that today's teachers find enormously valuable. These databases list thousands of children's book titles and their authors, illustrators, publishers, publication dates, genres, reading levels, interest levels, topics, and they provide summary annotations, and sometimes other information as well. Databases give teachers, parents, librarians, students, and other users of children's literature instant access to all of this information. Need a list of stories to prepare for Halloween? Check the database. How about some poems about springtime? Check the database. Soccer stories for a child with an intense interest in that sport? Books for children of different reading abilities for a curriculum unit on rocks and minerals? A list of children's trade books written by Virginia Hamilton? Check the database!

Self-contained databases are available on floppy disk and are typically provided with children's literature texts like this one. Lists of annotated childrens' books can also be found at various Web sites on the Internet.

Children's Literature on the Internet

The Internet—the vast global system for connecting computers linked by the World Wide Web—is the leading edge of technology and an important teaching/learning tool in today's classroom. About 85 percent of schools are wired to the Internet, and virtually every school will soon be connected (Jerald 1998b). Teachers regularly use the Internet as part of their instructional regimen. The Internet makes a world of information instantaneously available.

The Internet has created a global classroom, as it allows teachers and children to communicate instantly with others across the country and across the world. Classroom walls dissolve as children conduct on-line conversations about favorite books and share the information they have gathered. Reading and writing communities grow beyond children's immediate environments. Classes share their responses to books and participate in other authentic literacy experiences that support their development as readers and writers. The Internet provides a vehicle for communication heretofore unimagined.

The Internet can be used to enhance and expand access to children's literature and information about that literature. The vast connections that the Internet provides enable students to explore many dimensions of a literary genre; for example, children might use the Internet to explore folktales from different parts of the world and to share folktales that they have written with children in other parts of the world. In their classroom-based on-line research, children can find fiction and nonfiction children's books related to curriculum topics such as the rain forest, earthquakes, the Holocaust, or developing democracies in Eastern Europe. By making accessible resources and references, the computer enhances and enriches the study of children's literature.

Using the Internet, children can find a wealth of information about children's authors. In seeking information about a poet like Jack Prelutsky, for example, a student might access the Web site *galenet.com*, open the Contemporary Authors database, and type in the author's name. The Web site will list personal information, awards that the author has won, a list of the author's publications, media adaptations of the author's work, interesting insights into the author and his work, and sources of information for further reading. The whole process takes only a few minutes.

Children can also use search engines like Yahoo and Alta Vista for information about authors and other children's literature topics. Plenty of information can often be found through these sources, and sometimes the amount of information provided can be overwhelming, consisting of thousands of Web sites linked to the author's name, for example. Many of these links contain only incidental information (a book may be included on a reading list of a school or library); many are commercial (telling where and how to order the book); and children may encounter some Web site links that are entirely inappropriate for young readers. A list of helpful Internet sites for many authors is presented in Appendix C.

As a research tool, the Internet offers enormous advantages. However, it does not entirely replace books. Children often prefer to sift through informational children's books at their own pace than to search for information on-line. Nonfiction trade books usually present information in more organized formats and in styles that are useful and appealing to children. While the Internet provides flexibility and open-endedness, information trade books present manageable pieces of specific information in an organized context and framework. In this way, informational children's literature is an important support for the Internet, and vice versa.

LIST OF TEN

INTERNET SITES RELATED TO CHILDREN'S LITERATURE

Children's literature is all over the Internet, consisting of literally millions of references. A child, parent, or teacher who goes looking for information on a particular children's author, for example, will be struck by the vast array of information available.

Here is a list of ten Internet sites related to children's literature. Some valuable and useful sites have been necessarily omitted. By the time you read this chapter, it's likely that scores of additional Web sites pertaining to children's literature will have appeared on the World Wide Web. However, there's enough information to mine in these sites to keep one engaged and interested for a long time!

The Children's Literature Homepage
> (http://www.parentsplace.com/readroom/childnew/index.html)
> *designed to help adults find children's books, also profiles prominent authors and illustrators*

Children's Literature—Guide to Research and Resources
> (http://indiana.edu/~eric_rec/ieo/bibs/childlit.html)
> *a general guide to research and resources available through the ERIC system (related ERIC Web sites contain information on gender issues and other topics related to children's books)*

List of Ten continued

Literacy Prizes and Awards (http://www.ccc.govt.nz/Library/Lit_Prizes/)
links to numerous award sites for children's literature

Children's Literature and Resources Home Page
(http://www.conroe.isd.tenet.deu/cisd/instruc_resources/language_arts/child_lit.html)
includes reviews of hardback books, electronic books, and multimedia materials

The Children's Literature Web Guide
(http://www.ucalgary.ca/%7Edkbrown/index.html)
a very informative compilation and categorization of the growing number of Internet resources related to literature for children and young adults

Carol Hurst's Children's Literature Site (http://www.carolhurst.com/)
written by Carol Otis Hurst and Rebecca Otis, contains a collection of reviews of children's books, ideas on how to use the books in the classroom, and heaps of additional information about children's literature

Vandergift's Children's Literature Page
(http://www.scils.rutgers.edu/special/kay/childlit.html) and
(http://www.scils.rutgers.edu/special/kay/yalit/html)
commentaries and bibliographies of children's books and young adult books

Children's Literature Center (Library of Congress)
(gopher://marvel.loc.gov/11/research/reading.rooms/children)
an information center serving various constituencies with an interest in children's literature

Children's Literature Gopher
(gopher://lib.nmsu.edu:70/11/.subjects/Education/.childlit)
a potpourri of resources and information about children's literature and those who use it

Children's and YA Authors Internet Links
(http://falcon.jmu.edu/~ramseyil/bioyahome.htm)
links to many author sites on the Web

Those interested in children's literature can find additional information from the Web pages of the following organizations:

Association for Library Service to Children (http://www.ala.org/alsc/)

Children's Book Council (http://www.cbcbooks.org/)

Cooperative Children's Book Center (http://www.soemadison.wisc.edu/ccbc/)

International Reading Association (http://reading.org/)

Young Adult Library Services Association (http://www.ala,org/yalsa/)

Additional Web addresses are presented in Appendices C and D.

At Web sites related to children's literature, teachers can find literature units, information about children's authors (often provided at authors' own Web sites), lessons and teaching ideas for books, suggestions for writing activities, suggestions for oral language activities related to stories and poems at different grade levels, minilessons that link literature and skills, questions to stimulate critical thinking, and activities to extend understanding and enrich learning related to children's literature. A cornucopia of resources and information is available to expand teachers' knowledge of and appreciation for children's literature and to help foster a corresponding knowledge and appreciation in their students. But, like any teaching tool, teachers need to use the Internet judiciously and view what they find with a critical eye. Just because information and ideas are in cyberspace does not mean they are accurate or useful.

TECHNOLOGY AND CHILDREN'S LITERATURE IN SCHOOL AND AT HOME

At home and in the classroom, many opportunities exist for using media and technology to promote in children a love of literature. Both public libraries and school libraries offer stories on tape, video, and CD-ROM and in conventional printed form.

Cassette tape-and-book packages are readily available for use at home, some of them featuring well-known entertainment personalities such as Meryl Streep reading *The Tale of Peter Rabbit* and Robin Williams reading *Pecos Bill*. These performers add a whole new dimension to stories for children and they can provide hours of home entertainment for children to enjoy on their own. Taped books can also provide on long car trips entertainment for adults and children alike, making the journey seem shorter and forestalling the repeated question, "When will we get there?"

Video versions of children's literature also provide home entertainment for children. They engage children in animated or dramatized versions of a story they have read or will read in book form. Talking about the classic children's stories that children view on video provides a context for parent-child interaction about literature from a very young age.

Some parents use CD-ROM presentations of children's books as a means of making their preschool children comfortable with the computer before kindergarten. The accessibility of electronic books is far less than the accessibility of printed versions, and books on CD-ROM are certainly no substitute for lap reading; however, at their best, such digitized electronic companions never tire of the repeated request, "Read it again!"

In the classroom, taped books can become important learning tools in a literature program. A listening center where children can go to hear the story read while they follow the print is part of an enriched learning environment. Using taped books as part of the instructional program increases children's vocabularies and encourages speech-print interaction, while helping children become aware of their literary legacy. Upper-grade children can make tapes for younger pupils as a functional and authentic exercise in oral reading.

Videos of children's stories belong in a classroom literature program as well. Many teachers develop students' critical thinking skills by having children read a book and then view the video based on the story. More often than not, children discover that they enjoy the book better than the movie. Some teachers occasionally reverse the process, having children view a video version of a book before introducing the book as part of readers workshop, directed lessons, or other instructional activity. With a selection that reflects diversity, videos also have the potential to increase the amount of multicultural literature in the classroom.

The powerful medium of books presented on CD-ROM can be valuable supplements to the classroom literature program. Sharp (1996) suggests partnering electronic books with conventional print versions of children's books by starting with the printed versions and sharing and discussing the story in its conventional form with children before introducing the electronic version. Having pairs or small groups of children read together a story on the computer provides a social context for reading and opportunities for human interaction not inherent in electronic forms of text. Follow-up activities that encourage children to compare electronic versions with print versions are also useful. Follow-up reading for fluency and enjoyment is essential. "CD-ROM technology has enabled the producers of electronic books to pack more sights, sounds, and information together than can be found on any traditional printed page. The potential for exploration is enormous—but random clicking on the screen without any accompanying reflection is not likely to lead to much learning" (Sharp 1996, 24).

In selecting and using media and technology for presenting children's literature in the classroom, the school librarian/media specialist can be an incredibly valuable resource. In most schools, the library is the epicenter of literature and a very special place for those who love books. Although they have different jobs, teachers and librarians have similar goals—to help children develop the ability and the inclination to read. Good librarians work on the cutting edge of technology and serve as resident experts on books, so they are in a perfect position to support the work of the classroom teacher in print and electronic contexts.

Special Perspectives on Children's Literature

INTEGRATING LITERATURE AND TECHNOLOGY IN THE CLASSROOM
by Robin Fitzgerald and Mary Carr

Technology is becoming an integral part of the lives of children the world over. By integrating literature and technology units, we have developed a means of using computers to improve literacy skills, while at the same time offering children opportunities to respond to novels in different ways. Developing both literacy and technological skills in students is essential for their future success. Our units enable children to do both in a natural and appealing way.

Our units start with literature. Novels are presented in the classroom in conventional ways—by reading aloud; by building meaning and connecting with the story through discussion; by multiple writing opportunities. For virtually every literacy activity, there's a corresponding technological connection.

As they read, children write their responses and record their journal entries with word processors. For the study of literary elements, they create graphic organizers like character clusters and story maps with *Inspiration*, a program that allows them to create webs in a variety of formats and with attractive graphics. They use *Crossword Puzzle*

Companion to create puzzles that range from simple to complicated, using the new vocabulary from the story. For descriptive writing and other writing assignments related to the book, they use *The Ultimate Writing and Creativity Center*, which lets them add graphics, sounds, and animation to their writing.

For each book, students do an author study using *Netscape Communicator* to locate the author's Web page on the Internet. Children develop twenty-first-century research skills as they formulate questions and mine the Web for answers. When they finish, they use *Print Shop Press Writer* to write newspaper reports about what they have learned. Children's final products are book reports and advertisements for the novel that they create with *Microsoft Power Point*. Their presentations include sound and animation that reflect their responses to books.

The following chart summarizes the integrated literature/technology unit that we developed for Judy Blume's *Tales of a Fourth Grade Nothing*. We chose this book because it has been a longtime favorite with children, full of humor and experiences that children from different cultures relate to in their own lives.

Unit Plan: *Tales of a Fourth Grade Nothing*

Concept/skill	Literacy activity	Technology application
Summary and reflection	Daily logs and journals	Animation, music, LOGO programming with *MicroWorlds*
Story structure	Designing of graphic organizers and writing short narratives in class	Creation of Webs and other graphic organizers with *Inspiration*
Exploring adjectives; descriptive writing	Introduction of sense words; use of adjectives to write descriptive paragraphs	Addition of color, art, animation, and sound to charts with *The Ultimate Writing and Creativity Center*
Vocabulary development	Brainstorming of new vocabulary words encountered in class	Creation of crossword puzzles with *Crossword Companion* for class and homework
Author study	K-W-L activity on Judy Blume; generating of questions based on activity	Use of *Netscape Communicator* to do research on the Internet at *www.judyblume.com* and other Web sites
Research writing	Writing of a factual newspaper about Judy Blume	Use of *Printshop Press Writer* to format and publish newspaper
Persuasive writing	Discussion; examples of ads and commercials, persuasive language and words	Creation of animated presentations with voice-overs in *Power Point*

Other activities	Summaries, signs; writing practice	*Microsoft Word*
	Making illustrations to go with chapters	*Microsoft Paint*
	Adding images captured from Internet and other sources	*PowerPoint*
	Using the digital camera	*Word* and *PowerPoint*

Children used the Internet to learn about Judy Blume and to get tips about writing. They sent the author copies of *Judy News*, the newspaper that they had created. They received a personal e-mail from the author in return. Overall, the unit produced a genuine engagement with literature for the children.

Other books that we have used in integrated literature and technology units are C. S. Lewis's *The Lion, the Witch, and the Wardrobe*, Roald Dahl's *James and the Giant Peach*, and books in the *Goosebumps* series. We have found that, after doing each unit, the students are motivated to read more books by the same author or in the same series. We try to choose books that will hook our pupils; these are displayed in the classroom Book Corner.

We've discovered the enormous advantages of integrating technology in the study of literature. Motivation is never a problem. Children become so excited and interested in their work that reading and writing take on new dimensions. The many applications of technology address the multiple intelligences of children in the class. Throughout the unit, children continually engage in the four types of language: reading, writing, speaking, and listening. The quality of their work improves, since children have multiple opportunities to construct meaning, write, and edit their work in different modes. For children whose first language is not English, new dimensions are added by technology to their language learning. Since children of different abilities work both alone and in pairs or small groups, every member of the class is able to experience success.

After teaching with literature for many years, integrating literature with technology has enhanced our students' learning experiences beyond our expectations. We've found that children are able to work at their level of competence and then, motivated by the technology, challenge themselves with more complex tasks. The sense of enthusiasm is catching! Not only do we lead the students in their exploration of literature, but the students also lead us to places we never anticipated. We truly believe that the technological integration of these units has made experiences with literature more meaningful, interesting, and enjoyable, not only for the children but for the two of us as well. More importantly, we are able to achieve our overall unit goal: to create a positive learning environment in which our students experience the pleasures of children's literature while preparing themselves for the future.

Robin Fitzgerald and Mary Carr both teach at the American School of Barcelona, Spain, where Dr. Fitzgerald is the computer coordinator and Ms. Carr is a fifth grade teacher.

The keys to using media and technology as part of a classroom literature program are integration and balance. Videos, audio-tapes, and CD-ROMs need to be balanced with conventional print to enrich and enliven children's enjoyment of literature. Teachers need to select software in which the educational value is at least as great as the entertainment value, software that will address children's needs and satisfy the demands of the curriculum. They need to use nonprint material that will support children's learning to read and write as well as present literature in its original form. In the classroom, technology related to children's literature should meet children's individual needs and promote independence. Otherwise, technology can become a mere extension of Saturday morning cartoon shows, where the entertainment value outweighs the instructional value by far.

CONCLUSION

Audiotapes of stories and poems that are well read, videos that faithfully reflect children's literature, and electronic books that don't let the bells and whistles overpower the text are the tools of the future in children's literature. While there are potential dangers to using computers with young children (Healy 1998), technology has become so much a part of the fabric of our lives that it is bound to influence children's interaction with literature.

We have a deep attraction to books. "Cuddling up with a good book" is more appealing to us than "cuddling up with a good CD-ROM." In the best of circumstances, media and technology are integrated into a comprehensive literacy program that has children's literature as its centerpiece. Technology is used as a means of heightening children's knowledge and appreciation of literature.

With the availability of children's literature in alternative forms, is there a danger that literature presented technologically will replace print? In the words of librarian David K. Brown on his Internet site The Children's Literature Web Guide, "The Internet is a tremendous resource, but it will never compete with a children's librarian with a gleam in his eye." To those who say computers will sometime replace children's interaction with literature in books, I say the same thing that Madeline said to the tigers in the zoo.

Questions and Activities for Action and Discussion

1. Research the topic of technology and children's literature. Write a brief report based on your research, citing some of the advantages and disadvantages of using technological devices for presenting literature to children.

2. Concern is often expressed about using taped books or videotapes of popular stories with children. Some people argue that children who listen to or view a story on tape will not experience the true joy of reading it. Others argue that seeing or hearing the story will better prepare the child for the reading experience. What do you think? Choose a side in this debate and be prepared to defend your position.

3. Review a popular children's book presented on CD-ROM. Describe the features of the program and list the pros and cons of engaging with the story electronically. Compare your reaction to this type of presentation with your response to reading the story in book form.

4. Observe a classroom and/or interview a teacher about his or her use of technology in the children's literature program. Identify ways in which children are using technological devices to interact with books and to develop skills and strategies that will help make them better readers and writers.

5. Explore the topic of children's literature on the Internet. Using some of the Web sites listed on page p.p. 291–2, mine the Web for interesting or useful information about your favorite children's author or book.

CHILDREN'S & YOUNG ADULT BOOKS CITED IN THIS CHAPTER

Babbitt, Natalie. 1976. *Tuck Everlasting.* New York: Farrar, Straus and Giroux.

Bemelmans, Ludwig. 1962. *Madeline.* New York: Viking.

Burton, Virginia Lee. 1939. *Mike Mulligan and His Steam Shovel.* Boston: Houghton Mifflin.

Connelly, Bernadine. 1997. *Follow the Drinking Gourd.* Illustrated by Yvonne Buchanan. New York: Simon and Schuster.

Gardiner, John Reynolds. 1980. *Stone Fox.* New York: Harper & Row.

Kellogg, Stephen. 1986. *Pecos Bill.* New York: Morrow. (Other editions available.)

Lowry, Lois. 1990. *Number the Stars.* Boston: Houghton Mifflin.

MacLachlan, Patricia. 1985. *Sarah Plain and Tall.* New York: Harper & Row.

Naylor, Phyllis. 1991. *Shiloh.* New York: Simon and Schuster.

Paterson, Katherine. 1978. *The Great Gilly Hopkins.* New York: Harper & Row.

Potter, Beatrix. 1903. *The Tale of Peter Rabbit.* New York: Dover. (Other editions available.)

Seeger, Pete. 1994. *Abiyoyo.* Illustrated by Michael Hays. New York: Macmillan.

Sendak, Maurice. 1962. *Pierre: A Cautionary Tale.* New York: HarperCollins.

Taylor, Mildred D. 1976. *Roll of Thunder, Hear My Cry.* New York: Dial.

Van Allsburg, Chris. 1981. *Jumanji.* Boston: Houghton Mifflin.

CD-ROMS CITED IN THIS CHAPTER

Martin Jr., Bill, and John Archambault. 1996. *Chicka Chicka Boom Boom.* Illustrated by Lois Ehlert. New York: Davidson and Associates, Inc. and Simon and Schuster.

Potter, Beatrix. 1991. *The Tale of Peter Rabbit.* Toronto, Ontario: Discis Books.

The Learning Company. 1998. *Dr. Seuss Kindergarten.* Cambridge, MA.

The Learning Company. 1998. *Curious George Learns to Spell.* Cambridge, MA.

REFERENCES

Healy, J. M. 1998. *Failure to Connect: How Computers Affect Our Children's Minds, for Better and Worse.* New York: Simon and Schuster.

Jerald, C. D. 1998a. How Technology Is Used. *Education Week* 18(5):110–113.

_____ 1998b. By the Numbers. *Education Week* 18(5):102–105.

Kraft, E. 1997–1998. Killing the Text, Digitally. *The Reading Teacher* 51:337.

Matthew, K. 1997. A Comparison of the Influence of Interactive CD-ROM Storybooks and Traditional Print Storybooks on Reading Comprehension. *Journal of Computing in Education* 29:263–275.

Mooney, J. and P. O'Day. 1999. Children's Thoughts About Books on Tape. Unpublished Manuscript. Chestnut Hill, MA: Boston College.

Rickelman, R. J., and W. A. Henk. 1990. Children's Literature and Audio/Visual Technologies. *The Reading Teacher* 43:182–184.

Sharp, D. 1996. Partnering with Electronic Books and Literature. *Media & Methods* 32:24–25.

Snow, C. E., M. S. Burns, and P. Griffin. eds. 1998. *Preventing Reading Difficulties in Young Children.* Washington, D.C.: National Academy Press.

Walter, V. A. 1998. Girl Power: Multimedia and More. *Book Links* 7:37–41.

CHAPTER 13

CHILDREN'S LITERATURE IN THE CURRICULUM

 iterature-based language arts instruction has swept the nation. Trade books are being used widely as vehicles for teaching reading and writing, and basal readers are saturated with unexpurgated literature selections produced by widely respected and well-recognized authors. Instead of being an "enrichment" part of the curriculum, children's literature has moved to center stage and has become an integral part of language arts instruction.

THIS CHAPTER

- traces the path of literature into the heart of the reading-writing curriculum;

- describes the qualities of a literature-based language arts program; and

- examines ways in which trade books are used to teach reading and writing in the classroom.

Reading and writing are at the heart of the elementary school curriculum. From the time children enter school, their success is defined by how well they learn to read. More time is devoted to teaching reading and writing than to any other school subject. Virtually the entire curriculum in the early grades centers around literacy, and school effectiveness is often judged by reading test scores. Reading provides a cornerstone for much of children's later learning. In short, two of the three R's, readin' and writin', continue to occupy a central space in education.

For a very long time, reading was viewed and taught in schools as a skill-development process. Teachers prepared lessons in vocabulary, phonics, structural analysis, and a myriad of comprehension skills. Children did worksheets on synonyms and antonyms, long vowels and short vowels, prefixes and suffixes, sequencing and cause-effect relationships. Reading was equated with skills mastery.

Basal reading programs dominated instruction. These programs were designed around a scope and sequence of skills, and stories were written so that children could master these skills. Words were repeated over and over so that children could recognize the words by sight. ("Oh, oh. Look, look. See, see. See Dick run. Run, Dick, run.") Stories were constructed around particular phonetic elements (a story about thunder and lightning contained information about "the loud pounding sound of thunder in the clouds" to help children learn the relationship between the letter combination *ou* and the vowel element in the word *sound*). After reading each story, children completed worksheets designed to reinforce and practice the skill that the story was designed to teach.

The effect of this practice was that many children came to see reading as a school subject, not something to be enjoyed and savored beyond the classroom walls. Developing the ability to read overshadowed the emphasis on the inclination to read. Children spent up to 70 percent of their reading instructional time completing workbooks and skills sheets (which most viewed as a chore) rather than interacting with stories they could enjoy (Anderson et al. 1985).

Enter children's literature. In the latter decades of the 1900s, psycholinguists promoted the view of reading as an authentic language activity. Instead of dealing with "the stuff and guff of Dick and Jane," educators began to place real books written by real people into the hands of children as a means of helping them learn to read and write. Literature became a more integral part of the language arts curriculum. Workshops on how to teach reading with trade books dominated teachers' conferences; professional journals bulged with articles on the topic; and a whole new generation of professional texts on teaching reading through a literature-based approach were used in teacher preparation programs (Routman 1988; Reutzel and Cooter 1992; Wiseman 1992; Cox and Zarrillo 1993; Savage 1994). Even the "good old" basals changed. While much emphasis remained on skills, programs were infused with quality literature written by recognized children's authors.

Within the more recent past, there has been a call for a more balanced approach to teaching reading. Based on a fear that basic skills are being neglected, schools are being urged to provide more instruction in phonics and related skills. But even those who promote an increased emphasis on explicit skills instruction continue to recognize the importance of literature in learning to read. For example, the California Department of Education (1995), while calling for organized skills instruction in schools, identifies a strong literature program as the first element in a balanced and comprehensive approach to reading. Its report says that "every elementary classroom should have at least 1,500 books" (10). In the practical reality of most classrooms, skilled teachers synthesize skills and literature-based instruction in a way that makes sense for students while helping them develop the ability and the inclination to read.

The "literature-based revolution" that has occurred in the elementary school curriculum has dramatically changed the face of language arts instruction. Even as the pendulum swings back toward a greater emphasis on direct instruction in basic skills, children's literature remains a powerful force in classroom reading instruction.

ENCOUNTERING LITERATURE IN THE CLASSROOM

Children encounter literature in the classroom in a number of ways. Their initial classroom encounters, like their initial home encounters, consist of hearing stories and poems read aloud. Then, throughout the grades, literature finds its way into the classroom through basal readers, core literature books, anchor books, and classroom libraries.

Reading Aloud

Sharing literature through oral reading has long been recognized as the mark of good teaching. Children first experience literature listening to stories read to them at home or in school, and reading aloud remains an essential part of reading instruction throughout the grades. In the lower grades, reading aloud is used as a means of sharing literature with young children who are not yet able to read the stories independently. In the upper grades, reading to students introduces them to authors and genres that may yet be unfamiliar. At all levels, reading aloud provides pleasure that helps children fall in love with literature.

Teachers read aloud to children every day, often several times a day. Peterson and Eeds (1990) identify the values of reading aloud: it exposes children to literature that they may never have discovered on their own; it provides enjoyment; it connects the language of literature to the mind of the child; and it builds community and gives children different ways of thinking about stories. Reading aloud is not only a way of injecting literature directly into the school experiences of children on a daily basis; research suggests that it is also an essential activity for building knowledge required for eventual success in reading (Lesiak 1997).

LIST OF TEN

FAVORITE BOOKS TO READ ALOUD IN SCHOOL

Obviously, any good piece of literature about which a teacher is enthusiastic is good material for reading aloud. Many classroom occasions will suggest a particular read-aloud title—a book for a holiday, a collection of poems to fit the mood of a class, an information book related to a topic of interest or theme, a seasonal selection, and the like. Here are ten "hardy perennials" that have remained popular with children over the years:

Charlotte's Web by E. B. White
from preschool until the time that children can read it on their own, a favorite of children (Harper & Row, 1952)

James and the Giant Peach by Roald Dahl
outrageous characters that continue to fascinate and engage children whenever they hear the story (Knopf, 1961)

How to Eat Fried Worms by Thomas Rockwell
outrageous and improbable story that seems to appeal to children's sense of humor and the absurd (Dell, 1973)

The Lion, the Witch, and the Wardrobe by C. S. Lewis
masterpiece of high fantasy that often introduces children to the genre and induces them to read other books in the Chronicles of Narnia (Macmillan, 1961)

A Wrinkle in Time by Madeline L'Engle
for space-age children, a work of science fiction that still holds pleasure and fascination (Farrar, Straus and Giroux, 1962)

List of Ten continued

The Secret Garden by Frances Hodgson Burnett
> *written in 1911, a beloved British story about friendship and hope that still captures the imagination and attention of elementary school pupils when it is read well to them (Knopf, 1993)*

The House of Dies Drear by Virginia Hamilton
> *a mystery story about runaway slaves who hid in the walls of a mysterious house that keeps children on the edge of their seats (Simon and Schuster, 1968)*

Stone Fox by John Reynolds Gardiner
> *a story dominated by love, loyalty, and action to which children of different grade levels respond (Crowell, 1980)*

Ramona the Pest by Beverly Cleary
> *about an outspoken young person who experiences the trials and travails of school, well loved by children in the primary grades (Morrow, 1968)*

Where the Red Fern Grows by Wilson Rawls
> *a favorite story to read to children, difficult to read without crying (Doubleday, 1961)*

Other titles—thousands of them—also make excellent read-aloud selections across the grades.

Basal Readers

Ironically, basal reading programs have become a source of literature for children. For decades, basals dictated the way reading was taught, since these series constituted the primary (if not exclusive) source of children's reading material in school. Basals were the primary tools for teaching reading in well over 90 percent of elementary classrooms, and educators considered them to embody scientific truth when it came to teaching reading (Shannon 1983).

In the 1980s, basals came under fire for both content and methodology (Goodman et al. 1988; Shannon, 1989). Concern was expressed about the unexciting content, stilted language, emphasis on isolated skills mastery over reading, tedious workbook exercises that bored children to tears, and scripted lessons that cramped teachers' imagination, initiative, and style.

As more and more teachers became aware of the value of using children's literature as a vehicle for teaching reading, basal publishers began to include more and more literature in their programs. Today, virtually every basal series on the market is literature-based. The table of contents of a typical basal today lists stories by authors like Chris Van Allsburg and Julius Lester, poems by Nikki Giovanni and Myra Cohn Livingston, informational pieces by Seymour Simon and Ray Brockel, folk literature from different cultures, and complete stories from award-winning books. Additional independent trade books are often included as part of basal packages. While publishers sometimes make minor adjustments to stories, the literature is largely unexpurgated (Reutzel and Larsen 1995).

The use of basals has become an important means of connecting children and literature. Given the role that basals continue to play in classroom reading instruction, this shift to literature-based programs is a significant shift indeed (Langer and Allington 1992).

Core Books

Core books form the nucleus of a reading program in the classroom. Quality books judged to be appropriate for a particular grade level—Arnold Lobel's *Frog and Toad Together* in grade one, for example, or Natalie Babbitt's *Tuck Everlasting* in the upper grades—are used for instructional purposes with all students, either apart from or in conjunction with basal programs. Multiple copies of the same title provide common reading material for large groups, sometimes a whole class.

With core books, teachers provide direct instruction in vocabulary activities, strategies for comprehension, oral reading to develop fluency, writing activities, and other lessons designed to help children develop competency in reading. Some educators worry about having all children read the same core book because it eliminates children's choices. However, these books are deemed important in providing a common reading experience for all children, and they often provide springboards for students to other literature, such as books by the same author or books about the same topic.

Anchor Books

Anchor books are trade books that teachers use in language arts but that extend to other curriculum areas as well (Routman 1996). A book like *The Great Fire* by Jim Murphy is not only used for instructional purposes in reading; it is also used to extend children's learning in social studies, as it tells about the 1871 fire that destroyed the city of Chicago. These books are the primary vehicles for reading and writing instruction, and they are used to support concepts and reinforce content in all areas of the curriculum.

Classroom Libraries

If children are going to interact with literature, they need access to books—lots and lots of books. A well-stocked classroom library contains books on a variety of reading levels. In the early grades, wordless books, picture story books, simple books of poetry, familiar folk literature, and easy informational trade books dominate the collection. Plenty of books for children who develop early independence are available as well, including books with easily decodable text. Teachers are certain to include an ample selection of books that reflect the cultural diversity of our society. In the upper grades, the collection accommodates the expanding interests and increasing reading abilities of students. While there is normally an emphasis on realistic fiction, a full range of genres is included. A classroom environment where literature is treasured will include all kinds of books.

Author Profile: JANE YOLEN

Jane Yolen is a talented and prolific writer of literature for children. Her work is enjoyed by readers from the preschool years to adulthood and she has contributed to virtually every genre of children's literature.

Born in New York City, Yolen graduated from Smith College in 1960 and began working for several publishing companies in New York. These positions, she acknowledges, prepared her well for her career as a writer. Yolen launched her illustrious career by writing juvenile nonfiction such as *Pirates in Petticoats* (1963) and fiction such as *The Witch Who Wasn't* (1964). She continued to produce prolifically, writing or editing as many as eight or nine books a year.

Yolen has written books for children of all ages, from the charming *Baby Bear's Bedtime Book* (1990) to the powerful young adult novel *Armageddon Summer* (1998), which she coauthored with Bruce Coville. She has also written science fiction (*Cards of Grief*, 1984) and short stories (*Dragonfield and Other Stories*, 1985) for adults. But she has made her mark on literature by writing for children such books as the evocative *Owl Moon* (1987), a moving story of the Holocaust called *The Devil's Arithmetic* (1987), and the fantastic *Here There Be Unicorns* (1994).

The tradition of storytelling runs strongly in Yolen's family, and her writing style reflects this. Her great-grandfather was a teller of tales in his European village, and both of her parents wrote short stories. Yolen's use of language owes much to this oral tradition. When she writes, she reads each sentence aloud before moving on.

Yolen has contributed to many genres of children's literature. She has written a trilogy of fantasy novels for young adults: *Dragon's Blood: A Fantasy* (1981), *Heart's Blood* (1984), and *A Sending of Dragons* (1987). Her book *Encounter* (1992) is a historical fiction picture book about the landing of Christopher Columbus, told through the eyes of a native Taino child. She has written informational books such as *Simple Gifts: The Story of the Shakers* (1976) and books of poetry such as *The Originals: Animals That Time Forgot* (1998). She has gathered folktales from around the world. She moves from one genre to another with fluency and flexibility.

Yolen does not illustrate her own work. Her books have been illustrated by talented artists well known to children: Anne Hunter, Diane Stanley, David Shannon, and Ted Lewin, among others.

Jane Yolen currently splits her time between homes in New York and the Berkshire Mountains in western Massachusetts, where ideas for new stories come out (in her own words) as from a spigot. Children—and their parents and teachers—continue to enjoy Jane Yolen creations. Here are some other of her books:

Nocturne (1997)

Merlin (1997), the final book of a young Merlin trilogy

The Sea Man (1997)

Miz Berlin Walks (1997)

Twelve Impossible Things Before Breakfast (1997)

Teachers use many strategies to build as large a classroom library as possible. As administrators make a strong commitment to literature in the curriculum, more school funds become available for the purchase of trade books. Minigrants are sometimes available, and parent-teacher organizations are often willing to provide funds for classroom book collections. Teachers use bonus points from commercial book clubs to purchase books for common use. In some schools, parents donate books to the classroom library instead of sending cupcakes for their child's birthday or other special occasions. Teachers scour yard sales and white elephant tables and visit discount book stores, using their own resources to buy trade books for the classroom. Often, school and public libraries are happy to arrange for short-term loans for specific classroom collections. Over the years, a creative and energetic teacher will build an enviable classroom collection.

The classroom schedule allows children to interact with the literature that is available to them. Sustained Silent Reading (SSR) occurs every day, when everybody in the classroom (including the teacher) drops everything and reads. All engage in uninterrupted reading of self-selected books for the purpose of pure enjoyment. The teacher's role in this activity is crucial. While there is a strong temptation to use SSR time to correct students' work or put the finishing touches on report cards, teachers who read their own books model that reading is an important and enjoyable activity.

In sum, teachers who use literature as a central focus of their language arts curriculum find varied ways of making literature an integral component of their students' everyday lives in the classroom. From browsing in a well-stocked classroom library when they arrive in the morning, to engaging in directed reading activities with trade books during the day, to enjoying opportunities to read favorite books as part of sustained silent reading, to hearing stories or poems read aloud as they get ready to leave at the end of the day, children experience literature as an ongoing part of their school lives.

How Children's Literature Is Used in the Classroom

How are children's trade books used for instructional purposes in the classroom? Previous chapters of this book have addressed the use of children's literature at home and in school. Professional resource books offer specific suggestions for using particular titles for specific purposes (Bromley 1996; Yopp and Yopp 1996; Zarrillo 1994), and programs with materials related to children's books are accessible to teachers (*Literature Enrichment Activities Packets* by Sundance Publishers; *Novel Ties* by Learning Links; *Novel Units* by Novel Units; *Literature And Multiple Intelligences* by Pathways Publishing). In instructional settings at different grade levels, trade books are used as part of shared reading, guided reading, literature circles and readers' workshops, skills and strategy development, thematic teaching, writing, and other instructional activities.

Shared Reading

In the early years, children typically have formal classroom encounters with trade books through shared reading, an instructional strategy that introduces young readers to the essentials of beginning literacy. In shared reading, children see the text and are invited to participate as the teacher reads the book with fluency and expression. Children start to act as readers and see themselves as readers as they share the reading experience in a classroom, in the same way they have shared bedtime stories in their homes. Under the direction of an expert reader, children become familiar with text and how it works.

McGee and Richgels (1996) identify the three steps in shared reading: "The teacher reads aloud a selection printed in large text on a chart or in a big book; the teacher and students read the selection together; students do individual activities with the selection" (271). Shared reading helps children learn basic concepts about print, introduces them to word recognition and decoding techniques, and engages them in techniques for making meaning from text.

The first reading allows children to hear the story and to absorb its mood and content. The teacher introduces the book, sets the purpose, and invites the children's participation. The teacher points to the words to establish speech-print relationships and sweeps her hand under the lines to establish the left-to-right orientation of our writing system. She also models meaning-making strategies, points out familiar words, and uses comments and questions that invite children to think and act like skilled readers. In subsequent shared readings, the teacher typically asks children to join in the reading at predictable parts, focuses on familiar words and phrases, or otherwise draws children's attention to features of print. In the third phase of shared reading, children respond to the book by talking about the story, reading their small book versions alone or with a partner, and engaging in follow-up art, drama, or writing activities.

In a shared reading lesson, a teacher might use a book like Pat Hutchins's *Rosie's Walk*, the story of a hen who is followed around the barnyard by a hapless fox. The teacher introduces the book by calling attention to the title and the author's name, and the group discusses the colorful cover illustration and predicts what the story might be about. As the teacher reads the story aloud, he points to the words on the page and responds to students' comments. After reading, the children respond by talking about the story. Questions are designed to get children involved through discussion rather than to elicit a "right answer." In subsequent readings, as teacher and children share the book again, the teacher may use *Rosie's Walk* as a focus for

- **word recognition** ("Who can point to the word *hen*?");
- **decoding skills** ("Look, Rosie's name begins with the letter *R*, just like the names of *Rob* and *Rachel*—who can think of other *r-r-r-r* words?");
- **comprehension components** ("Where did Rosie walk after she walked around the pond?");
- **prediction strategies** ("What do you think will happen next?");
- **critical thinking** ("Do you think Rosie knew that the fox was following her? Why do you think so?"); and
- **shared writing** ("Let's write our own story about Rosie's walk.").

Repeated readings and follow-up activities make the text of the story very familiar to children, familiar enough so that they can read it on their own.

In the very earliest stages of their school careers, children who experience daily sessions of shared readings with predictable books like Bill Martin Jr.'s popular *Brown Bear, Brown Bear, What Do You See?* and Wanda Gag's classic *Millions of Cats*, acquire essentials of beginning literacy and, at the same time, become familiar with stories, poems, and informational books that are part of their literary heritage. They learn to recognize repeated words, apply skills needed to make meaning from print, and create their own predictable stories ("First grade, first grade, what do we see?" or "Millions of dogs").

Guided Reading

As children's early reading ability increases, teachers use trade books for guided reading activities. "Guided reading is a context in which a teacher supports each reader's development of effective strategies for processing novel texts at increasingly challenging levels of difficulty" (Fountas and Pinnell 1996, 2). The purpose of guided reading is to help children, with teacher support, develop and apply effective reading strategies early in their school lives so that they can use these strategies to become successful readers.

Guided reading is typically carried on in small groups of children with similar reading ability. The teacher briefly introduces a book by using the pictures and some of the language of the story. As children read the book aloud in a very soft voice, the teacher attends to the reading of each child so that she can provide help with words that the child may not recognize, interacts with individual children to help them with problems, and focuses the attention of the group on the meaning of the text. Children move toward independence based on the support and guidance they receive.

Afterwards, the teacher discusses the story, inviting children's personal responses and returning to the text to locate evidence to support responses. Perhaps the group engages in a follow-up activity involving art or writing related to the book. Later, children can return to the book to read it independently or to a partner.

Through guided reading, children learn critical concepts about print and how to use it independently. They engage with texts rather than with a list of isolated skills. Teachers guide and support their efforts as they move toward independence and a love of literature.

LIST OF TEN

CHARACTERISTICS OF LITERATURE-BASED CLASSROOM PROGRAMS

A universal definition or boilerplate description of a literature-based reading/writing program does not exist. There are, however, ten qualities that characterize such programs in action:

Trade books with stories, poems, and informational materials are an integral part of all aspects of classroom life.
Literature is woven into classroom activities throughout the day, not just studied from 9:00 to 9:45 each morning. Children encounter good literature every day, all day long.

The learning environment bespeaks the love of literature.
Books are everywhere. Before school and during reading time, children use a classroom library well-stocked with books purchased by the school or borrowed from the local public

List of Ten continued

library. A reading corner with a rug remnant, a comfortable chair or two, some posters, and a brightly painted bookcase provides an attractive space that invites children to come in and read.

Literature is shared by reading aloud all the time.

The teacher reads a "poem for the day," a chapter from a chapter book, a piece of informational literature. Guests are invited to share their favorite story or poem. Tapes and CD-ROMs are available for children to listen to and enjoy.

Literature is used for instructional purposes.

Trade books are shared as part of language experience activities. Planned and incidental literacy lessons are related to books that are part of the reading curriculum. New words are featured as children encounter them in the context of stories and poems. Questions and discussions about books expand children's interpretive and critical thinking skills. Teachers "tease" minilessons on skills and strategies from books that children are reading.

Sustained Silent Reading (or Drop Everything and Read) is a daily feature of the classroom program.

Time is set aside for everyone—including the teacher—to read self-selected material for the pure purpose of enjoyment.

Writing about literature is part of the program.

Children keep logs and response journals about what they read. Literature is the stimulus for all kinds of writing activities—stories, poems, letters, sequels, next chapters, new endings, parodies, and other forms of writing. Children study authors with a view to improving their own writing technique and style. Based on their encounters with literature, they write their own books, which then become part of the classroom library for classmates to share.

Author studies help children become familiar with those who write what they read.

A bulletin board on Our Author/Illustrator of the Week (or Month) is prominently displayed. Children write letters to authors, use the Internet to learn more about their favorite authors, and use the Web to contact authors and illustrators as appropriate.

Literature is used across the curriculum.

Displays of books on rocks and minerals, baseball and race cars, immigration and exploration, and other topics that children are interested in or studying in math, science, social studies, and the arts are in evidence throughout the classroom.

Displays of children's involvement with literature are all around.

Newly designed book jackets made in art class, limericks written after reading Edward Lear, charts comparing crosscultural versions of fairy tales, "index card responses" to books that they have read, stories involving their favorite characters, and other materials provide evidence of children's encounters with books.

Children are excited about books.

They take pride in talking to visitors about what they have read. They enthusiastically engage in book talks among themselves. Their attitudes and behaviors make it plain that they see themselves as a community of readers.

Literature Circles and Readers' Workshops

"Integral to the success of learning from and through literature is the need to discuss and share the literary experience" (Pike, Compain, and Mumper 1997, 259). In literature-based programs, children carry on this discussion in literature circles or readers' workshops. While literature circles can range from informal book talks to more formal discussion, readers' workshops tend to involve a more structured approach to talking about literature that is part of the curriculum.

In readers' workshop, children exchange ideas about the books they are reading. Groups typically are small (five to seven students), heterogeneous, and flexible and feature teacher-guided but student-directed discussion of literature (Daniels 1994).

Sometimes, all children read the same book; at other times, the text set involves single copies of different books that are related to each other in some way (Klassen and Short 1993). Depending on grade level, groups meet at least two or three times a week for periods of up to an hour. Books are sometimes selected by the teacher, sometimes by the children, and sometimes as part of the core curriculum. A planning sheet may be used to outline the format, to suggest guide questions or concepts to focus on, and to stipulate rules for good discussion. As students become more experienced and more at ease in discussing trade books, formal planning materials become less and less important.

Prereading activities might include discussion designed to activate students' prior knowledge, introduce key vocabulary words, set purposes, and make predictions based on an initial examination of the book or based on the author's prior work. In class, time is set aside for actual reading, and once students become engaged in the book, they typically read on their own time as well. As they read, students may respond by writing in their journals or sharing their thinking and questions with classmates or with the teacher.

As children respond to books in workshop groups, they talk about stories they read, not in a "this is what happened and this is my favorite part" mode, but in a much more personal way. Through discussion, children connect what they read to their own lives, compare their books to what others in the group are reading, compare what they are reading to other stories they have read, identify aspects of authors' styles, and move into deeper levels of meaning.

Minilessons—short structured periods of five to fifteen minutes of direct instruction on a specific area of common need—can be part of readers' workshop. The focus of minilessons typically runs the gamut from introducing a particular genre of literature, to demonstrating strategies for using context clues to figure out the meaning of an unknown word, to teaching the punctuation conventions of dialogue. Skilled teachers teach minilessons at the beginning, middle, or end of a workshop period, but they never usurp the entire reading/discussion time, and they teach lessons that are aimed at common needs.

After the readers' workshop experience, students can engage in a variety of follow-up activities:

- **further research on a topic**: researching the topic of homelessness after reading Jerry Spinelli's *Maniac McGee;*
- **writing a new chapter or sequel to a story**: writing about what happened to Gabe and Jonas when they entered the "real world" in *The Giver* by Lois Lowry;
- **creating a play or dramatizing a scene from a book**: acting out a scene from Sid Fleischman's *The Whipping Boy;* and

- **engaging in an art activity**: drawing a map of the museum in which the children spend the weekend in *From the Mixed-up Files of Mrs. Basil E. Frankweiler* by E. L. Konigsburg or a sketch of the rats' abode in *Mrs. Frisby and the Rats of NIMH* by Robert C. O'Brien.

These follow-up activities are a long way from the conventional book reports.

In a readers' workshop, the teacher plays many roles—facilitator, model, coach, collaborator, supporter, and audience for what students have to say. Teachers also have a direct instructional role in planning minilessons and diagnosing student needs. The idea of these literature circles is to create a community of learners in which the teacher is a member.

Small groups meet daily or several times a week. Group membership remains flexible, not carved in stone. Children decide how much they want to read, share their reactions, discuss their responses, plan extension projects, and engage in follow-up collaborative writing projects. For assessment, teachers monitor the quality of discussion or use a checklist that focuses on elements of effective participation in literature response groups.

Hill, Johnson, and Noe (1995) put literature circles in a broader context. They focus on inquiry-centered instruction using literature discussion groups. While literature is used, it is the inquiry process rather than the literature itself that drives instruction.

Transactional Literature Discussions

Duggan (1997) suggests another model for having children talk about trade books in literature circles or readers' workshops, transactional literature discussions (TLD). Based upon reader response theory, TLD is an instructional approach for helping children read and react to trade books in a structured fashion. Groups of between five and seven children select a trade book for reading and discussion and they follow a six-step process:

1. **Getting ready**: a prereading activity consisting of previewing the book selected and making predictions about the story;

2. **Reading and thinking aloud**: pausing at intervals to share thoughts about the story;

3. **Wondering on paper**: writing short written responses during or immediately following reading;

4. **Talking**: sharing of thoughts about the book for fifteen to thirty minutes, following a structured respond-question-listen-link strategy that helps children respond to and link the story to their own experiences and the ideas of others;

5. **Thinking on paper**: journal writing that helps children explore and extend ideas; and

6. **Looking back**: enriching learning by reflecting on what has been learned and how it was learned.

Teachers participate in TLD groups by modeling questions and responses, reinforcing student comments, providing scaffolding for children's meaning-making activities, guiding discussions with open-ended questions, and actively participating in the literacy activity.

Grand Conversations

Grand conversations is a term that Peterson and Eeds (1990) use to describe literature discussion in the classroom. Designed for "teachers who teach with story," grand conversations provide a means of helping children explore and expand meaning in what they read. The expression refers to a dialogue among groups of students about books. "Grand books," Petersen and Eeds maintain, "will produce grand conversations."

In grand conversations, groups of mixed ability students participate in a readers' workshop about the same book. Ground rules are set: children take turns and don't interrupt; everyone gets a chance to talk; children can disagree with one another but they must do so politely; everyone respects the ideas of others. Dialogue is built on the trust that each contribution will be valued.

When a book is selected, the teacher sets expectations as to how many pages or chapters are to be read each day. During the initial reading, the teacher meets with the group to check progress and to determine students' initial reactions to what they are reading.

After they have finished the story, discussion moves to critical interpretation. Participants enter the dialogue with an open mind. Discussion extends beyond comprehension (relating what happened in the story) to interpretation (identifying the meanings of what happened). Children share their personal interpretations. Literary elements—setting, characters, plot, theme, mood, language—are essential components of the conversation. Students examine how writers develop and use these elements, and make comparisons between different works by the same author and among the works of different writers. Conversations connect the story to the children's own lives and allow them to enter the world that the writer has created. Grand conversations move beyond the level of literal comprehension to multiple levels of meaning and point of view. They move readers beyond the lines of the text to interpretive and critical levels of meaning.

The teacher plays a diminishing role over time in grand conversations; that is, the teacher models, guides, and monitors discussions heavily at the beginning but says less and less as the dialogues progress. Children come to understand that their ideas, interpretations, and responses make the dialogue successful. Grand conversations can start early in a child's school life, as teachers engage very young children in dialogue about the books that they have read aloud.

Each of these approaches—literature circles, readers' workshops, transactional literature discussions, grand conversations—and other approaches not examined help children interact with literature in a more meaningful fashion. Activities lead children beyond literal comprehension to a deeper understanding of what they read. The aim is to have children think actively and critically. Through discussions, children respond to reading with an efferent and/or aesthetic stance and maintain active engagement through reader response (Rosenblatt 1978, 1982). Each technique is a means of helping children become more thoughtful readers and thinkers, while helping them appreciate the literature they will encounter throughout their lifetimes.

Skills and Strategy Development

Children learn to read by reading, so meaningful encounters with literature are a direct way for children to improve their reading ability. Shared reading and guided reading directly address children's strategies for deriving meaning from text. Lessons to help children improve their ability are also part of reading instruction in the classroom. Teachers use trade books for direct opportunities to teach reading skills and strategies throughout the grades.

In a conventional skills-emphasis program, reading skills come first. Children learn lists of isolated words; sound-symbol relationships are learned outside the context of connected discourse; passages are constructed around main ideas and details, cause-effect relationships, sequence, or some other component of comprehension. By contrast, in a literature-based approach, the story comes first and teachers "tease" lessons out of the books. Consider the following examples:

- After reading *Alexander and the Terrible, Horrible, No Good, Very Bad Day* by Judith Viorst, the teacher plans a vocabulary lesson on synonyms and antonyms for which children brainstorm a list of words with the same and different meanings as those words in the title and then dictate or write sentences with those words.

- Using Nancy Shaw's *Sheep on a Ship* (or her other books such as *Sheep in a Jeep*), the teacher makes a chart of the *sh* words (*sheep, ship, shake*), the short *a* words (*lap, flap, raft,*), or the rhyming words (*hail, sail, rail*) found in this story, and then, in a strategy of direct phonics instruction, asks children to create their own stories using the words that they generated.

- As the class is reading *My Side of the Mountain* by Jean Craighead George, the teacher keeps a list of compound words found in the book (*snowstorm, knothole, deerskin*, and so on) to use to discuss this construction as part of a vocabulary lesson.

In teaching skills and strategies through literature, meaning and a love of literature are paramount. Conventional instruction on cause-effect relationships typically consists of a worksheet with ten decontextualized sentences and directions such as "In the first five sentences, circle the cause and underline the effect; in the second five sentences, underline the cause and circle the effect." In a literature-based approach, instruction starts with a book, such as Maurice Sendak's *Where the Wild Things Are,* and children discuss the causes and effects of a character's actions in the story. Both approaches have the same focus, but they differ in their respect for literature.

Thematic Teaching

Thematic teaching involves the linking of subject areas through a theme. "In the world outside of school we don't compartmentalize our thinking as math, science, and social studies. Instead, we apply the content, skills, and processes we have learned to think about, discuss, and solve real-life problems and situations. In thinking about topics of high interest to students, . . . natural links occur across all curricular areas incorporating language arts and children's literature" (Freeman and Person 1998, 19).

Within the context of literature-based instruction, thematic teaching involves content units and literature units using children's trade books.

Special Perspectives on Children's Literature

THE IMPACT OF LITERATURE IN THE CLASSROOM
by Pamela G. Amster

Today our first grade classroom was filled with new books; twenty-one new books and authors. The books were makeshift combinations of red and green lined paper. Some pages were stapled on the right fold; just as many were stapled on the left fold. Some books were straight; most were crooked. Some of the books read front to back; just as many read back to front. One story even included every word and sentence written right to left!

The authors, six and just-turned-seven year olds vied for the Author's Chair. Their audience of peers sat with rapt attention, hanging onto every word (featuring some of the most creatively inventive spelling you could ever see) and every sentence (with or without punctuation). They exclaimed at the illustrations. I sat speechless, humbled and awed by the scene. This is our twenty-third day of school. Almost half of these authors came to me as at-risk readers. Today they are on fire!

While all of my pupils find their way to the author's chair eventually, this is the first time such a wave of writing occurred so early in the school year and was so all-inclusive. Today everyone wrote a book.

When I reflect on and consider the circumstances that might have contributed to this tidal wave of shared literacy this year, I'm impressed with the power of literature. Like last year, I began the year with a unit on color. This year, with a grant from our town's educational foundation, I supplemented the color unit with multiple copies of witty, charming, and gorgeous books such as

- Bill Martin Jr.'s *Brown Bear, Brown Bear, What Do You See?;*
- Kathleen Sullivan Carrol's *One Red Rooster;*
- Mary Serfozo's *Who Said Red?;*
- Dr. Seuss's *Green Eggs and Ham* and *My Many Colored Days*, (published posthumously);
- Ellen Stoll Walsh's *Mouse Paint;*
- Lois Ehlert's *Red Leaf, Yellow Leaf;*
- Ed Young's *Seven Blind Mice;*
- Leo Lionni's *A Color of His Own;*
- Daniel Manus Pinkwater's *The Big Orange Splot;*
- Sam Swope's *The Araboolies of Liberty Street;*
- Bruce McMillan's *Growing Colors;*

and many other children's fiction and nonfiction trade books, along with basal stories featuring colors.

I read several of these books aloud to my children every day. They shared the books in pairs and in small groups. We talked about them in instructional settings and used them in our science unit on the rainbow. As children became familiar with the text, they read the books on their own.

I saw the impact of these delicious titles today. In these and other books, the children continue to enjoy language at the hands of talented and inspirational storytellers like Leo Lionni, Sam Swope, and Dr. Seuss. And the children have been inspired and delighted by the charming and intoxicating illustrations of Eric Carle, Lois Ehlert, and Ed Young.

Today, each one of my children felt the magic and power of their ideas in words and pictures on paper. They beamed and giggled under the accolades of their peers and teacher. Literature at best takes us someplace. Today, it took my children into that most indescribably wondrous place—their own imaginations.

Pamela Amster is a primary grade teacher at the Plymouth River School in Hingham, Massachusetts.

Content Themes

Teachers use trade books to help children learn about topics in science, mathematics, social studies, and other content areas of the curriculum (see Chapter 9). For a science unit on space, for example, teachers might select the following trade books:

- Heather Couper and Nigel Henbest's *The Space Atlas: A Pictorial Atlas of Our Universe*, with detailed information about space presented in large book format;
- Seymour Simon's many books about space, such as *Our Solar System*, and his many books about the planets, such as *Jupiter* and *Mars;*
- Franklin Branley's *Neptune: Voyager's Final Target* and other books in this Voyager into Space series;
- Jacqueline Milton's *Zoo in the Sky*, which presents an astronomer's fascinating view of the constellations of our galaxy;
- Sally Ride's and Tam O'Shaughnessy's *The Third Planet: Exploring Earth from Space*, a book coauthored by an astronaut, using satellite photography to explain physical forces on the earth;
- Gloria Skurzynski's *Discover Mars*, which offers children an opportunity to explore Mars through three-dimensional illustrations; and
- Elaine Scott's *Close Encounters: Exploring the Universe with the Hubble Space Telescope*, which combines information about the universe with some spectacular photographs.

These books and literally hundreds of others like them provide effective means of helping children acquire information in all areas of the curriculum.

Sometimes, a single piece of literature can be used in several different subject areas. For example, a book such as the Caldecott Award–winning *The Glorious Flight: Across the Channel with Louis Bleriot* by Alice and Martin Provensen not only provides a wonderful reading experience for children, but also leads to topics of study in history (development of aviation), geography (of Europe), science (principles of flight), drawings that depict France in the early 1900s, math (computing distance, speed, and time), and other topics.

Literature Themes

In literature units, teachers use a literature circle or readers' workshop format to focus on topics, authors, and genres of children's books.

Topic groups focus on topics commonly found in children's stories. The teacher gathers several titles related to a certain theme. For example, the teacher might gather books about survival (see pp. 173–174), books of animal stories, or mysteries. Children read these books and share the stories, comparing and contrasting the characters, settings, and plots. They relate the stories to their own lives, create their own stories related to the topic or theme, and (more often than not) continue to read on their own books that classmates in the group have read.

Author groups provide another focus for literature themes. Some children's authors, such as Lois Lowry, Judy Blume, and Beverly Cleary, have written so many children's books that they can easily provide a range of reading material for a group. Group members read books by the same writer—perhaps after doing research on the life of the author—and discuss their responses to the author's work. With some authors students may be able to focus on a single subject as they read different books by the same person; for example, the work of Laura Ingalls Wilder.

Genre units involve children in reading and discussing books of the same genre. As children read stories about the legendary folk heroes Robin Hood, Paul Bunyan, and Fin McCool, for example, they can discuss how they represent the cultures of England, America, or Ireland, the lands from which each hero comes. Students can read biographies of great world leaders, such as those found in Chapter 10; they can compare and contrast the qualities that made these people great and place these qualities within the context of the times in which they lived. They can relate the qualities of these leaders to those found in contemporary leaders. These make good topics for literature discussion and grand conversations. In genre groups, children can read historical fiction (see Chapter 8) and compare different presentations of the same historical event or time period.

In studying genres, children develop critical thinking as they compare different versions of a favorite story. For example, as part of a genre unit on traditional folk literature, students might read several versions of a familiar story such as the following:

- *The Three Little Pigs* by Paul Galdone or one of the many other *traditional* versions of the story of the three pigs and the big bad wolf;
- *The True Story of the Three Little Pigs* by Jon Scieszka, which tells the story from the point of view of Alexander T. Wolf who portrays himself as an innocent victim who has been framed;
- *The Three Little Javelinas* by Susan Lowell, about three wild pigs in the desert Southwest who build their houses out of tumbleweed, saguaros, and adobe and who are chased by a coyote;

- *The Three Hawaiian Pigs and the Magic Shark* by Donivee Martin Laird, about three pigs who build their houses of pili grass, driftwood, and lava rock and who are hunted by a magic shark who sees them when they are surfing;
- *The Three Little Wolves and the Big Bad Pig* by Eugene Trivizas, in which three cuddly little wolves build houses of brick, concrete, and reinforced armored plates, all of which are destroyed by a big bad pig who is eventually tamed by a house of flowers;
- *The Fourth Little Pig* by Teresa Celsi, the story of the three pigs' older sister who tells her brothers, to, in effect, "Get a life!"; and
- *The Three Little Pigs* by Steven Kellogg, an offbeat, upbeat version in which the three pigs (Percy, Pete, and Prudence) run a successful waffle business until the wolf Tempesto comes along.

The teacher helps children create a wall chart comparing the various versions of the story. As groups construct the wall chart, they acquire vocabulary, develop decoding and encoding skills, construct meaning, and engage in critical thinking activities that will serve them well as readers.

Literature units related to topics, authors, and genres have the advantage of meeting a range of reading levels in heterogeneous reading groups. Selecting books by theme or genre allows the teacher to use books at different levels of difficulty for children of different abilities working together in the same group. In a mystery topic group, for example, Valerie reads Ellen Raskin's challenging mystery story *The Westing Game*, while Atilla reads David Adler's more basic *Cam Jensen and the Fourth Floor Twins*. In a Judy Blume author group, Valerie reads the more sophisticated *Are You There, God? It's Me, Margaret,* while Atilla reads *Freckle Juice*. Of course, teachers always need to be ready for damage control when Valerie blurts out, "That's a baby book!" or "I read that when I was in second grade!"

Literature units help take literature to another level in the school experience of children. Using the techniques of literature circles, children construct meaning and make connections between literature and their own lives. The activities provide useful alternatives to the fill-in-the-blank activities that dominate so much traditional reading instruction. Teachers cannot evaluate these new activities in the old conventional ways that rely on literal levels of understanding. Checklists, observation, daily notes, anecdotal records, portfolios, and other forms of alternative assessment are called for. Also necessary is a focus on procedural matters: whether all members of the group had a chance to contribute, whether disagreements were handled appropriately, and so on.

In addition to monitoring the quality of discussion, teachers can often assess children's interpretation of literature through the entries in their reading response journals. Responding in writing is part of the reading-writing connection that is integral to literature-based literacy programs.

Literature Logs or Reader Response Journals

Response journals or literature logs are records of children's thinking, their questions, and the observations they make during reading. Journals and logs are a means of helping children reflect on the books they read and generate personal written responses. Children record their thoughts, raise questions, and make personal connections between literature and their own lives.

Author Profile: CYNTHIA RYLANT

When Cynthia Rylant was growing up in a rural mountain town in West Virginia, she had no access to libraries or bookstores, so she relied on comic books for her reading material. As a children's author, however, she gives young readers a legacy far richer than that of Archie and Jughead.

Rylant was born in Hopewell, Virginia. She was raised and educated in West Virginia and earned degrees from Morris Harvey College, Marshall University, and Kent State University.

Rylant draws heavily upon her childhood experiences, and her writing is often intensely personal. Her first book, *When I Was Young in the Mountains* (1982), was based on her life with her grandparents, with whom she lived after the tumultuous divorce of her parents. The book was recognized as a Caldecott Honor Book in 1983. Much of her other work is related to her life as well. *A Blue-Eyed Daisy* (1985) and the poetry in *Waiting to Waltz: A Childhood* (1984) are about her experiences growing up.

In her novels, Rylant writes with sensitivity and perception. Books like *The Relatives Came* (1985) and *A Fine White Dust* (1986), draw young readers in by making the concerns of her young protagonists as important as those of the adults. In 1993, Cynthia Rylant won the Newbery Medal for *Missing May*, a touching story about the death of a loved one and the effect on a family. Not all of her stories are sad, however. She has written *A Couple of Kooks and Other Stories About Love* (1989), several stories about Mr. Putter and Tabby (1994–1995), and fifteen stories about the adventures of *Henry and Mudge*.

Here are some of Rylant's other books:

The Blue Hill Meadows (1997)

Silver Packages: An Appalachian Christmas Story (1997)

Poppleton (1997)

Scarecrow (1997)

The Bird House (1998)

Response journals serve many purposes. They give students opportunities to express their thinking about a piece of literature. They provide an ongoing record of stories and poems that children have encountered in the classroom, along with their responses to it. Journals allow students to reflect on their own experiences in relation to the literature that they read. They provide the glue that cements the reading-writing connection. Besides, research suggests that journals promote improvement in children's understanding and appreciation of what they read (Wollman-Bonilla and Werchadlo 1995, Smith 1995).

As children begin to keep journals, they have a tendency to summarize what they read. As they get used to interpreting literature, responses typically increase in length, fluency, and depth of understanding. At the beginning stages, teachers often provide prompts:

- "How did the story make you feel?"
- "What made you happy/sad/upset/scared?"
- "What did the story make you think of in your own life?"
- "What do you think will happen if . . . ?
- "My favorite character was . . . because . . . ."

Teachers often begin the journal writing process by modeling responses, sometimes with a chapter book that they read aloud, until students gain fluency and independence.

Literature logs can take various forms—personal or critical responses recorded in notebooks; a buddy journal, in which pairs of children share and react to what they have written; electronic dialogue journals in which students share their responses to literature with someone in another classroom, school, town, state, or country via the Internet.

Literature journals not only connect reading and writing. They also provide occasions for greater involvement in literature through reader response in the classroom.

PARENTS AS PART OF A LITERATURE-BASED PROGRAM

The home is where the love of literature usually begins. Given the importance of early learning and the important role of the home in a child's school success, parent education and family training have become a national priority. Local schools reach out to families in an effort to use books to forge a closer link between home and school.

Education is experiencing more family involvement in children's learning than ever before, and schools are typically using whatever family involvement is available in children's education (Allington and Cunningham 1996). Schools are beginning to make parents more aware of the importance of literature in the home and to emphasize the vital role of parents during the children's preschool years.

In a home setting, parents and other caregivers can share the following:

- books such as *Jamberry* by Bruce Degen and *Each Peach Pear Plum* by Janet and Allan Ahlberg in which lively language explodes off the page;
- board book reproductions of old favorites such as Eric Carle's *The Very Hungry Caterpillar* and *The Very Busy Spider* and other board books for the very young;
- books with repetitive language such as one of the many versions of *The Gingerbread Man* or *There Was an Old Lady Who Swallowed a Fly* by Simms Taback;
- Mother Goose rhymes and other poems that engage children;
- alphabet books with rhymes such as Jane Yolen's *Alphabestiary* and counting books such as Eileen Christelow's *Five Little Monkeys Jumping on the Bed*, featuring familiar chants, creating in young children an enjoyable awareness of letters and numbers;
- concept books such as Tana Hoban's *All About Where* and Ellen Stoll Walsh's *Mouse Paint*, in which children come to discover various parts of their young worlds;
- familiar fairy tales that have stood the test of time for centuries such as Robert Holden's rhymed retelling of *The Pied Piper of Hamlin* (intricately illustrated by Drahos Zak);

- picture story books such as *Caps for Sale* by Esphyr Slobodkina and simple chapter books such as *Mr. Popper's Penguins* by Richard and Florence Atwater, which generations of children have loved;

- trickster tales such as those told in different cultures retold by Virginia Hamilton in *A Ring of Tricksters*, which delight young minds;

- informational books such as Gail Gibbon's *Planet Earth/Inside Out* and Wendell Minor's *Grand Canyon: Exploring the Natural Wonder*, through which children learn more about topics of interest; and

- simple picture books such as Uri Shulevitz's *Snow* and more complex picture books like Peter Sis's *Tibet Through the Red Box*.

More than enough literature exists for parents to fill children's lives throughout the entire emergent literacy stage.

The importance of reading to children at home does not diminish when the child starts school. In the early school years, sharing books at home continues to convey the message that reading is important and continues to reinforce and extend children's classroom experiences with books. As children begin to learn to read on their own, they can take turns reading with their parents. Even as they progress beyond the primary grades and into independence in reading, regular reading time can remain a precious part of family rituals.

In short, the home plays a vital role in fostering children's love of literature. Parents who read to their children provide a gift—or a series of gifts—of incalulable value. They give children expanded language opportunities and intellectual stimulation. They give children a pleasant introduction to print and hours of imaginative engagement. They give children a sense of story that will continue to serve them well in reading and writing in school. Finally, they give children a love of literature that often lasts a lifetime.

CONCLUSION

Children's literature has moved to center stage in the curriculum of the elementary school. Rather than serving as "something extra" that enriches classroom experiences, literature for children has become an integral part of teaching and learning language arts and other school subjects. Teachers use trade books for many purposes—for shared reading and guided reading, for direct instruction and recreational reading, to stimulate writing and help learning across the curriculum. Children are the beneficiaries of this "literature-based revolution" that has occurred in schools. Parents, too, have become more aware of the importance of literature in the lives of their children. The increase in the number of juvenile books published each year is testimony to parents' interest and awareness of children's books.

The way in which children's literature is used as part of the school curriculum is limited only by the creativity and ingenuity of the classroom teacher. But, even as teachers use trade books for instructional purposes, the bottom line remains the love of literature. Teachers who use literature to develop literacy run the risk of facing a point of diminishing returns, a point at which using the book becomes a chore rather than a pleasure. There are no strict rules, but good teachers have a sense of when the line is close.

Every classroom encounter with trade books need not be the occasion for a directed literacy lesson. There are many occasions when a book can be read, shared, enjoyed, and left alone as far as instruction goes. When programs generate a love of literature, students are more likely to make these "just for fun" stories part of their classroom experiences.

Children's literature doesn't teach reading; teachers do. Of all the forces in education—parental and administrative pressures, wealth or dearth of resources, school organization and facilities, school policies and procedures, and everything else that impacts the school lives of teachers and students—the teacher is the most powerful force of all. Teachers are at the heart of the instructional process. When in the hands of competent teachers, quality literature can make fantastic things happen in the classroom.

Questions and Activities for Action and Discussion

1. Research the development of reading instruction in schools. If possible, examine some older basal reading books that were published twenty or thirty years ago. Compare these basals with materials currently used in schools. Make a list of the differences, maintaining a specific focus on the literature contained in the programs.

2. Observe (or if possible, engage in) a shared or guided reading lesson using an early level trade book. Prepare a brief report on your experiences, noting what the teacher (or you) did and how the children responded to the lesson.

3. The educational marketplace is full of commercial packages and workbook programs related to using children's literature to help children develop literacy competency. Critique one of these programs. Focus on how it approaches literature and indicate why you would (or would not) use it in your own classroom.

4. Make a list of informational trade books that you might use as part of a science or social studies unit, such as on dinosaurs or aviation. Describe how these books are related to one another, and how they approach the content you want children to learn and how you might use them as part of a thematic unit in the classroom.

5. Interview a teacher on the use of children's trade books to teach reading and writing. List the advantages and potential problems of a literature-based program and indicate some of the strategies you would implement in your own classroom.

CHILDREN'S & YOUNG ADULT BOOKS CITED IN THIS CHAPTER

Adler, David A. 1985. *Cam Jensen and the Fourth Floor Twins.* New York: Penguin.

Ahlberg, Janet, and Allan Ahlberg. 1979. *Each Peach Pear Plum.* New York: Viking.

Atwater, Richard, and Florence Atwater. 1938. *Mr. Popper's Penguins.* Boston: Little, Brown.

Babbitt, Natalie. 1976. *Tuck Everlasting.* New York: Farrar, Straus and Giroux.

Blume, Judy. 1971. *Freckle Juice.* New York: Dell.

_____ 1972. *Are You There, God? It's Me, Margaret.* New York: Dell.

Branley, Franklin M. 1992. *Neptune: Voyager's Final Target.* New York: HarperCollins.

Carle, Eric. 1969. *The Very Hungry Caterpillar.* New York: Philomel.

_____ 1995. *The Very Busy Spider.* New York: Putnam.

Celsi, Teresa. 1990. *The Fourth Little Pig.* Austin, Texas: Steck Vaughn.

Christelow, Eileen. 1989. *Five Little Monkeys Jumping on the Bed.* New York: Clarion.

Couper, Heather, and Nigel Henbest. 1992. *The Space Atlas: A Pictorial Atlas of Our Universe.* San Diego: Harcourt Brace.

Degen, Bruce. 1983. *Jamberry.* New York: Harper & Row.

Fleischman, Sid. 1986. *The Whipping Boy.* New York: Greenwillow.

Gag, Wanda. 1928. *Millions of Cats.* New York: Putnam.

Galdone, Paul. 1979. *The Three Little Pigs.* Boston: Houghton Mifflin.

George, Jean Craighead. 1959. *My Side of the Mountain.* New York: Dutton.

Gibbons, Gail. 1995. *Planet Earth/Inside Out.* New York: Morrow.

Hamilton, Virginia. 1997. *A Ring of Tricksters: Animal Tales from America, the West Indies, and Africa.* Illustrated by Barry Moser. New York: Scholastic.

Hoban, Tana. 1991. *All About Where.* New York: Greenwillow.

Holden, Robert. 1998. *The Pied Piper of Hamlin.* Illustrated by Drahos Zak. Boston: Houghton Mifflin.

Hutchins, Pat. 1968. *Rosie's Walk.* New York: Scholastic.

Kellogg, Steven. 1997. *The Three Little Pigs.* New York: Morrow.

Konigsburg, E. L. 1967. *From the Mixed-up Files of Mrs. Basil E. Frankweiler.* New York: Atheneum.

Laird, Donivee Martin. 1981. *The Three Hawaiian Pigs and the Magic Shark.* Waipahu, Hawaii: Barnaby Books.

Lobel, Arnold. 1972. *Frog and Toad Together.* New York: HarperCollins

Lowell, Susan. 1992. *The Three Little Javelinas.* Flagstaff, Ariz.: Northland Arizona.

Lowry, Lois. 1993. *The Giver.* Boston: Houghton Mifflin

Martin, Bill Jr. 1983. *Brown Bear, Brown Bear, What Do You See?* New York: Henry Holt.

Milton, Jacqueline. 1989. *Zoo in the Sky.* Illustrated by Christina Balit. Washington, D.C.: National Geographic Press.

Minor, Wendell. 1998. *Grand Canyon: Exploring the Natural Wonder.* New York: Scholastic.

Murphy, Jim. 1995. *The Great Fire.* New York: Scholastic.

O'Brien, Robert C. 1971. *Mrs. Frisby and the Rats of NIMH.* New York: Macmillan.

Provensen, Alice, and Martin Provensen. 1983. *The Glorious Flight: Across the Channel with Louis Bleriot.* New York: Viking.

Raskin, Ellen. 1978. *The Westing Game.* New York: Dutton.

Ride, Sally, and Tam O'Shaughnessy. 1994. *The Third Planet: Exploring Earth from Space.* New York: Crown.

Scieszka, Jon. 1989. *The True Story of the Three Little Pigs.* Illustrated by Lane Smith. New York: Viking.

Scott, Elaine. 1998. *Close Encounters: Exploring the Universe with the Hubble Space Telescope.* New York: Hyperion.

Sendak, Maurice. 1963. *Where the Wild Things Are.* New York: Harper & Row.

Shaw, Nancy. 1988. *Sheep in a Jeep.* Boston: Houghton Mifflin.

_____ 1989. *Sheep on a Ship.* Boston: Houghton Mifflin.

Shulevitz, Uri. 1998. *Snow.* New York: Farrar, Straus and Giroux.

Simon, Seymour. 1985. *Jupiter.* New York: Morrow.

_____ 1987. *Mars.* New York: Morrow.

_____ 1992. *Our Solar System.* New York: Morrow.

Sis, Peter. 1998. *Tibet Through the Red Box.* New York: Farrar, Straus and Giroux.

Skurzynski, Gloria. 1998. *Discover Mars.* Washington, D.C.: National Geographic Press.

Slobodkina, Esphyr. 1940. *Caps for Sale.* New York: Harper & Row.

Spinelli, Jerry. 1990. *Maniac McGee.* Boston: Little, Brown.

Taback, Simms. 1997. *There Was an Old Lady Who Swallowed a Fly.* New York: Penguin.

Trivizas, Eugene. 1993. *The Three Little Wolves and the Big Bad Pig.* New York: Simon and Schuster.

Viorst, Judith. 1972. *Alexander and the Terrible, Horrible, No Good, Very Bad Day.* New York: Atheneum.

Walsh, Ellen Stoll. 1989. *Mouse Paint.* San Diego: Harcourt Brace.

Yolen, Jane, ed. 1995. *Alphabestiary.* Illustrated by Allan Eitzen. Honesdale, Penn.: Boyds Mills Press.

REFERENCES

Allington, R. L., and P. M. Cunningham. 1996. *Schools That Work.* New York: HarperCollins.

Anderson, R. C., et al. 1985. *Becoming a Nation of Readers: The Report of the Commission on Reading.* Washington, D.C.: The National Institute of Education, U.S. Department of Education.

Bromley, K. D. 1996. *Webbing with Literature* (2d ed.). Boston: Allyn and Bacon.

California Department of Education. 1995. *Every Child a Reader: Report of the California Reading Task Force.* Sacramento: California Department of Education.

Cox, C., and J. Zarrillo. 1993. *Teaching Reading with Children's Literature.* New York: Macmillan.

Daniels, H. 1994. *Literature Circles: Voice and Choice in the Student Centered Classroom.* York, ME: Stenhouse Publishers.

Duggan, J. 1997. Transactional Literature Discussions: Engaging Students in the Appreciation and Understanding of Literature. *The Reading Teacher* 51:86–96.

Fountas, I. C., and G. S. Pinnell. 1996. *Guided Reading: Good First Reading Teaching for All Children*. Portsmouth, N.H.: Heinemann.

Freeman, E. B., and D. G. Person. 1998. Connecting Informational Children's Books with Content Area Learning. Boston: Allyn and Bacon.

Goodman, K. S., P. Shannon, Y. S. Freeman , and S. Murphy. 1988. *Report Card on Basal Readers*. Katonah, N.Y.: Richard C. Owens, Publishers.

Hill, B. C., N. J. Johnson, and K. L. S. Noe. 1995. *Literature Circles and Responses*. Norwood, Mass.: Christopher Gordon Publishers.

Kismaric, C., and M. Heiferman. 1996. *Growing up with Dick and Jane*. San Francisco: Collins Publishers.

Klassen, C., and K. G. Short. 1993. Literature Circles: Hearing Children's Voices. In *Children's Voices: Talk in the Classroom*, ed. B. E. Cullinan, Newark, Del.: International Reading Association.

Langer, J. A., and R. L. Allington. 1992. Curriculum Research in Writing and Reading. *Handbook on Research in Curriculum*, ed. Philip W. Jackson. New York: Macmillan.

Lesiak, J. L. 1997. Research Based Answers to Questions About Emergent Literacy in Kindergarten. *Psychology in Schools* 34:143–159.

McGee, L. M., and D. J. Richgels. 1996. *Literacy's Beginnings: Supporting Young Readers and Writers* (2d ed.). Boston: Allyn and Bacon.

Peterson, R., and M. Eeds. 1990. *Grand Conversations: Literature Groups in Action*. New York: Scholastic.

Pike, K., R. Compain, and J. Mumper. 1997. *New Connections: An Integrated Approach to Literacy*. New York: Longman.

Reutzel, D. R., and R. B. Cooter. 1992. *Teaching Children to Read: From Basals to Books*. Columbus, Ohio: Merrill.

Reutzel, D. R., and N. S. Larsen. 1995. Look What They've Done to Real Children's Books in the New Basal Readers. *Language Arts* 72:495–507.

Rosenblatt, L. M. 1978. *The Reader, the Text and the Poem*. Carbondale, Ill.: University of Southern Illinois Press.

_____ 1982. The Literacy Transaction: Evocation and Response. *Theory Into Practice* 21:268–277.

Routman, R. 1988. *Transitions: From Literature to Literacy*. Portsmouth, NH: Heinemann.

_____ 1996. *Literacy at the Crossroads*. Portsmouth, N.H.: Heinemann.

Savage, J. F. 1994. *Teaching Reading Using Literature*. Madison, WI: Brown and Benchmark.

Shannon, P. 1983. The Use of Commercial Reading Materials in American Elementary Schools. *Reading Research Quarterly* 19:68–85.

_____ 1989. *Broken Promises: Reading Instruction in Twentieth Century America*. Granby, Mass.: Bergin and Garrey, Publishers.

Smith, E. B. 1995. Anchored in Our Literature: Students Responding to African American Literature. *Language Arts* 72:571–574.

Wiseman, D. L. 1992. *Learning to Read with Literature*. Boston: Allyn and Bacon.

Wollman-Bonilla, J. E., and B. Werchadlo. 1995. Literature Response Journals in a First-Grade Classroom. *Language Arts* 72:562–570.

Yopp, H. K., and R. H. Yopp. 1996. *Literature-Based Reading Activities* (2d ed.). Boston: Allyn and Bacon.

Zarrillo, J. 1994. *Multicultural Literature, Multicultural Teaching: Units for the Elementary Grades*. Fort Worth, Texas: Harcourt Brace.

APPENDIX A

AWARD-WINNING CHILDREN'S LITERATURE

Each year, numerous awards are given to children's books that are distinguished in some way and/or that have made significant contributions to the field.

THE CALDECOTT MEDAL AND HONOR AWARDS

The Caldecott Medal, first awarded in 1938, is presented annually to the illustrator of the most distinguished picture book published in the United States. The award is named after Randolph Caldecott, a British illustrator, and is given by the Children's Services Division of the American Library Association.

1938   **Animals of the Bible**   by Helen Dean Fish, illustrated by Dorothy P. Lathrop (Frederick A. Stokes)
Honor Books:
Seven Simeons: A Russian Tale   by Boris Artzybasheff (Viking)
Four and Twenty Blackbirds: Nursery Rhymes of Yesterday Recalled for Children of Today   by Helen Dean Fish, illustrated by Robert Lawson (Frederick A. Stokes)

1939   **Mel Li**   by Thomas Handforth (Doubleday Doran)
Honor Books:
The Forest Pool   by Laura Adams Armer (Longmans Green)
Wee Gillis   by Munro Leaf, illustrated by Robert Lawson (Viking)
Snow White and the Seven Dwarfs   by Wanda Gag (Coward-McCann)
Barkis   by Clare Newberry (Harper and Brothers)
Andy and the Lion: A Tale of Kindness Remembered or the Power of Gratitude   by James Daugherty (Viking)

1940   **Abraham Lincoln**   by Ingrid and Edgar Parin D' Aulaire (Doubleday Doran)
Honor Books:
Cock-a-Doodle Doo: The Story of a Little Red Rooster   by Berta and Elmer Hader (Macmillan)
Madeline   by Ludwig Bemelmans (Simon & Schuster)
The Ageless Story   by Lauren Ford (Dodd Mead)

1941   **They Were Strong and Good**   by Robert Lawson (Viking)
Honor Book:
April's Kittens   by Clare Newberry (Harper and Brothers)

1942   **Make Way for Ducklings**   by Robert McCloskey (Viking)
Honor Books:
An American ABC   by Maud and Miska Petersham (Macmillan)
In My Mother's House   by Ann Nolan Clark, illustrated by Velino Herrera (Viking)
Paddle-to-the-Sea   by Holling C. Holling (Houghton Mifflin)
Nothing at All   by Wanda Gag (Coward-McCann)

1943   **The Little House**   by Virginia Lee Burton (Houghton Mifflin)
Honor Books:
Dash and Dart   by Mary Buff and Conrad Buff (Viking)
Marshmallow   by Clare Newberry (Harper and Brothers)

1944   **Many Moons**   by James Thurber, illustrated by Louis Slobodkin (Harcourt Brace)
Honor Books:
Small Rain: Verses from the Bible   selected by Jessie Orton Jones, illustrated by Elizabeth Orton Jones (Viking)
Pierre Pigeon   by Lee Kingman, illustrated by Arnold E. Bare (Houghton Mifflin)
The Mighty Hunter   by Berta Hader and Elmer Hader (Macmillan)
A Child's Good Night Book   by Margaret Wise Brown, illustrated by Jean Charlot (W. R. Scott)
Good-Luck Horse   by Chih-Yi Chan, illustrated by Plato Chan (Whittlesey)

1945   **Prayer for a Child**   by Rachel Field, illustrated by Elizabeth Orton Jones (Macmillan)
Honor Books:
Mother Goose: Seventy-Seven Verses with Pictures   illustrated by Tasha Tudor (Henry Z. Walck)
In the Forest   by Marie Hall Ets (Viking)
Yonie Wondernose   by Marguerite de Angeli (Doubleday)
The Christmas Anna Angel   by Ruth Sawyer, illustrated by Kate Seredy (Viking)

1946   **The Rooster Crows**   (traditional Mother Goose), illustrated by Maud Petersham and Miska Petersham (Macmillan)
Honor Books:
Little Lost Lamb   by Golden MacDonald, illustrated by Leonard Weisgard (Doubleday)
Sing Mother Goose   by Opal Wheeler, illustrated by Margorie Torrey (E. P. Dutton)
My Mother Is the Most Beautiful Woman in the World   by Becky Reyher, illustrated by Ruth Gannett (Howell, Soskin)
You Can Write Chinese   by Kurt Wiese (Viking)

1947 **The Little Island** by Golden MacDonald, illustrated by Leonard Weisgard (Doubleday)
Honor Books:
Rain Drop Splash by Alvin Tresselt, illustrated by Leonard Weisgard (Lothrop, Lee & Shepard)
Boats on the River by Marjorie Flack, illustrated by Jay Hyde Barnum (Viking)
Timothy Turtle by Al Graham, illustrated by Tony Palazzo (Robert Welch)
Pedro, the Angel of Olvera Street by Leo Politi (Charles Scribner's Sons)
Sing in Praise: A Collection of the Best-Loved Hymns by Opal Wheeler, illustrated by Marjorie Torrey (E. P. Dutton)

1948 **White Snow, Bright Snow** by Alvin Tresselt, illustrated by Roger Duvoisin (Lothrop, Lee & Shepard)
Honor Books:
Stone Soup: An Old Tale by Marcia Brown (Charles Scribner's Sons)
McElligot's Pool by Dr. Seuss (Random House)
Bambino the Clown by George Schreiber (Viking)
Roger and the Fox by Lavinia Davis, illustrated by Hildegard Woodward (Doubleday)
Song of Robin Hood edited by Anne Malcolmson, illustrated by Virginia Lee Burton (Houghton Mifflin)

1949 **The Big Snow** by Betta Hader and Elmer Hader (Macmillan)
Honor Books:
Blueberries for Sal by Robert McCloskey (Viking)
All Around the Town by Phyllis McGinley, illustrated by Helen Stone (J. B. Lippincott)
Juanita by Leo Politi (Charles Scribner's Sons)
Fish in the Air by Kurt Wiese (Viking)

1950 **Song of the Swallows** by Leo Politi (Charles Scribner's Sons)
Honor Books:
America's Ethan Allen by Stewart Holbrook, illustrated by Lynd Ward (Houghton Mifflin)
The Wild Birthday Cake by Lavinia Davis, illustrated by Hildegard Woodward (Doubleday)
The Happy Day by Ruth Krauss, illustrated by Marc Simont (Harper and Brothers)
Bartholomew and the Oobleck by Dr. Seuss (Random House)
Henry Fisherman by Marcia Brown (Charles Scribner's Sons)

1951 **The Egg Tree** by Katherine Milhous (Charles Scribner's Sons)
Honor Books:
Dick Whittington and His Cat by Marcia Brown (Charles Scribner's Sons)
The Two Reds by William Lipkind, illustrated by Nicholas Mordvinoff (Harcourt)
If I Ran the Zoo by Dr. Seuss (Random House)

The Most Wonderful Doll in the World   by Phyllis McGinley, illustrated by Helen Stone (J. B. Lippincott)
T-Bone, The Baby Sitter   by Clare Newberry (Harper and Brothers)

1952   **Finders Keepers**   by William Lipkind, illustrated by Nicholas Mordvinoff (Harcourt)
Honor Books:
Mr. T. W. Anthony Wood: The Story of a Cat and a Dog and a Mouse   by Marie Hall Ets (Viking)
Skipper John's Cook   by Marcia Brown (Charles Scribner's Sons)
All Falling Down   by Gene Zion, illustrated by Margaret Bloy Graham (Harper and Brothers)
Bear Party   by William Pene du Bois (Viking)
Feather Mountain   by Elizabeth Olds (Houghton Mifflin)

1953   **The Biggest Bear**   by Lynd Ward (Houghton Mifflin)
Honor Books:
Puss in Boots   by Charles Perrault, illustrated and translated by Marcia Brown (Charles Scribner's Sons)
One Morning in Maine   by Robert McCloskey (Viking)
Ape in a Cape: An Alphabet of Odd Animals   by Fritz Eichenbert (Harcourt)
The Storm Book   by Charlotte Zolotow, illustrated by Margaret Bloy Graham (Harper and Brothers)
Five Little Monkeys   by Juliet Kepes (Houghton Mifflin)

1954   **Madeline's Rescue**   by Ludwig Bemelmans (Viking)
Honor Books:
Journey Cake, Ho!   by Ruth Sawyer, illustrated by Robert McCloskey (Viking)
When Will the World be Mine?   by Miriam Schlein, illustrated by Jean Charlot (W. R. Scott)
The Steadfast Tin Soldier   by Hans Christian Andersen, translated by M. R. James, illustrated by Marcia Brown (Charles Scribner's Sons)
A Very Special House   by Ruth Krauss, illustrated by Maurice Sendak (Harper and Brothers)
Green Eyes   by Abe Birnbaum (Capitol)

1955   **Cinderella, or the Little Glass Slipper**   by Charles Perrault, translated and illustrated by Marcia Brown (Charles Scribner's Sons)
Honor Books:
Book of Nursery and Mother Goose Rhymes   illustrated by Marguerite de Angeli (Doubleday)
Wheel on the Chimney   by Margaret Wise Brown, illustrated by Tibor Gergely (J. B. Lippincott)
The Thanksgiving Story   by Alice Dalgliesh, illustrated by Helen Sewell (Charles Scribner's Sons)

1956   **Frog Went a-Courtin** edited by John Langstaff, illustrated by Feodor Rojankovsky (Harcourt)
Honor Books:
Play with Me by Marie Hall Ets (Viking)
Crow Boy by Taro Yashima (Viking)

1957   **A Tree Is Nice** by Janice May Udry, illustrated by Marc Simont (Harper and Brothers)
Honor Books:
Mr. Penny's Race Horse by Marie Hall Ets (Viking)
1 Is One by Tasha Tudor (Henry A. Walck)
Anatole by Eve Titus, illustrated by Paul Galdone (Whittlesey)
Gillespie and the Guards by Benjamin Elkin, illustrated by James Daugherty (Viking)
Lion by William Pene du Bois (Viking)

1958   **Time of Wonder** by Robert McCloskey (Viking)
Honor Books:
Fly High, Fly Low by Don Freeman (Viking)
Anatole and the Cat by Eve Titus, illustrated by Paul Galdone (Whittlesey)

1959   **Chanticleer and the Fox** adapted from Chaucer by Barbara Cooney (Thomas Y. Crowell)
Honor Books:
The House That Jack Built: A Picture Book in Two Languages by Antonio Frasconi (Harcourt Brace)
What Do You Say, Dear? by Sesyle Joslin, illustrated by Maurice Sendak (W. R. Scott)
Umbrella by Taro Yashima (Viking)

1960   **Nine Days to Christmas** by Marie Hall Ets and Aurora Labastida, illustrated by Marie Hall Ets (Viking)
Honor Books:
Houses from the Sea by Alice E. Goudey, illustrated by Adrienne Adams (Charles Scribner's Sons)
The Moon Jumpers by Janice May Udry, illustrated by Maurice Sendak (Harper and Brothers)

1961   **Baboushka and the Three Kings** by Ruth Robbins, illustrated by Nicolas Sidjak (Parnassus Imprints)
Honor Book:
Inch by Inch by Leo Lionni (Obolensky)

1962   **Once a Mouse . . .** by Marcia Brown (Charles Scribner's Sons)
Honor Books:
The Fox Went Out on a Chilly Night: An Old Song by Peter Spier (Doubleday)
Little Bear's Visit by Else Holmelund Minarik, illustrated by Maurice Sendak (Harper and Brothers)

The Day We Saw the Sun Come Up   by Alice E. Goudey, illustrated by Adrienne Adams (Charles Scribner's Sons)

1963   **The Snowy Day**   by Ezra Jack Keats (Viking)
Honor Books:
The Sun Is a Golden Earring   by Natalia M. Belting, illustrated by Bernarda Bryson (Holt, Rinehart & Winston)
Mr. Rabbit and the Lovely Present   by Charlotte Zolotow, illustrated by Maurice Sendak (Harper & Row)

1964   **Where the Wild Things Are**   by Maurice Sendak (Harper & Row)
Honor Books:
Swimmy   by Leo Lionni (Pantheon)
All in the Morning Early   by Sorche Nic Leodhas, illustrated by Evaline Ness (Holt, Rinehart & Winston)
Mother Goose and Nursery Rhymes   illustrated by Philip Reed (Atheneum)

1965   **May I Bring a Friend?**   by Beatrice Schenk de Regniers, illustrated by Beni Montresor (Atheneum)
Honor Books:
Rain Makes Applesauce   by Julian Scheer, illustrated by Marvin Bileck (Holiday House)
The Wave   by Margaret Hodges, illustrated by Blair Lent (Houghton Mifflin)
A Pocketful of Crickets   by Rebecca Caudill, illustrated by Evaline Ness (Holt, Rinehart & Winston)

1966   **Always Room for One More**   by Sorche Nic Leodhas, illustrated by Nonny Hogrogian (Holt, Rinehart & Winston)
Honor Books:
Hide and Seek Fog   by Alvin Tresselt, illustrated by Roger Duvoisin (Viking)
Tom Tit Tot   by Evaline Ness (Charles Scribner's Sons)

1967   **Sam, Bangs and Moonshine**   by Evaline Ness (Holt, Rinehart & Winston)
Honor Book:
One Wide River to Cross   by Barbara Emberley, illustrated by Ed Emberley (Prentice-Hall)

1968   **Drummer Hoff**   by Barbara Emberley, illustrated by Ed Emberley (Prentice-Hall)
Honor Books:
Frederick   by Leo Lionni (Pantheon)
Seashore Story   by Taro Yashima (Viking)
The Emperor and the Kite   by Jane Yolen, illustrated by Ed Young (World)

1969   **The Fool of the World and the Flying Ship**   by Arthur Ransom, illustrated by Uri Shulevitz (Farrar, Straus & Giroux)
Honor Book:
Why the Sun and the Moon Live in the Sky: An African Folktale   by Elphinstone Dayrell, illustrated by Blair Lent (Houghton Mifflin)

1970   **Sylvester and the Magic Pebble**   by William Steig (Windmill/Simon & Schuster)
Honor Books:
Goggles!   by Ezra Jack Keats (Macmillan)
Alexander and the Wind-Up Mouse   by Leo Lionni (Pantheon)
Pop Corn and Ma Goodness   by Edna Mitchell Preston, illustrated by Robert Andrew Parker (Viking)
Thy Friend, Obadiah   by Brinton Turkle (Viking)
The Judge: An Untrue Tale   by Harve Zemach, illustrated by Margot Zemach (Farrar, Straus & Giroux)

1971   **A Story, a Story**   by Gail E. Haley (Atheneum)
Honor Books:
The Angry Moon   by William Sleator, illustrated by Blair Lent (Little, Brown)
Frog and Toad Are Friends   by Arnold Lobel (Harper & Row)
In the Night Kitchen   by Maurice Sendak (Harper & Row)

1972   **One Fine Day**   by Nonny Hogrogian (Macmillan)
Honor Books:
If All the Seas Were One Sea   by Janina Domanska (Macmillan)
Moja Means One: A Swahili Counting Book   by Muriel Feelings, illustrated by Tom Feelings (Dial)
Hildilid's Night   by Cheli Duran Ryan, illustrated by Arnold Lobel (Macmillan)

1973   **The Funny Little Woman**   by Arlene Mosel, illustrated by Blair Lent (E. P. Dutton)
Honor Books:
Anansi the Spider: A Tale from the Ashanti   adapted and illustrated by Gerald McDermott (Holt, Rinehart & Winston)
Hosie's Alphabet   by Hosea, Tobias, and Lisa Baskin, illustrated by Leonard Baskin (Viking)
Snow White and the Seven Dwarfs   translated by Randall Jarrell, illustrated by Nancy Ekholm Burkert (Farrar, Straus & Giroux)
When Clay Sings   by Byrd Baylor, illustrated by Tom Bahti (Charles Scribner's Sons)

1974   **Duffy and the Devil**   by Harve Zemach, illustrated by Margot Zemach (Farrar, Straus & Giroux)
Honor Books:
Three Jovial Huntsmen   by Susan Jeffers (Bradbury)
Cathedral: The Story of Its Construction   by David Macaulay (Houghton Mifflin)

1975   **Arrow to the Sun**   adapted and illustrated by Gerald McDermott (Viking)
Honor Book:
Jambo Means Hello: A Swahili Alphabet Book   by Muriel Feelings, illustrated by Tom Feelings (Dial)

1976   **Why Mosquitoes Buzz in People's Ears**   by Verna Aardema, illustrated by Leo and Diane Dillon (Dial)
Honor Books:
The Desert Is Theirs   by Byrd Baylor, illustrated by Peter Parnall (Charles Scribner's Sons)
Strega Nona   retold and illustrated by Tomie De Paola (Prentice-Hall)

1977   **Ashanti to Zulu: African Traditions**   by Margaret Musgrove, illustrated by Leo and Diane Dillon (Dial)
Honor Books:
The Amazing Bone   by William Steig (Farrar, Straus & Giroux)
The Contest   retold and illustrated by Nonny Hogrogrian (Greenwillow)
Fish for Supper   by M. B. Goffstein (Dial)
The Golem: A Jewish Legend   by Beverly Brodsky (McDermott)
Hawk, I'm Your Brother   by Byrd Baylor, illustrated by Peter Parnall (Charles Scribner's Sons)

1978   **Noah's Ark**   by Peter Spier (Doubleday)
Honor Books:
Castle   by David Macaulay (Houghton Mifflin)
It Could Always Be Worse   retold and illustrated by Margot Zemach (Farrar, Straus & Giroux)

1979   **The Girl Who Loved Wild Horses**   by Paul Goble (Bradbury)
Honor Books:
Freight Train   by Donald Crews (Greenwillow)
The Way to Start a Day   by Byrd Baylor, illustrated by Peter Parnall (Charles Scribner's Sons)

1980   **Ox-Cart Man**   by Donald Hall, illustrated by Barbara Cooney (Viking)
Honor Books:
Ben's Trumpet   by Rachel Isadora (Greenwillow)
The Treasure   by Uri Shulevitz (Farrar, Straus & Giroux)
The Garden of Abdul Gasazi   by Chris Van Allsburg (Houghton Mifflin)

1981   **Fables**   by Arnold Lobel (Harper & Row)
Honor Books:
The Bremen-Town Musicians   by Ilse Plume (Doubleday)
The Grey Lady and the Strawberry Snatcher   by Molly Bang (Four Winds)
Mice Twice   by Joseph Low (Atheneum)
Truck   by Donald Crews (Greenwillow)

1982   **Jumanji**   by Chris Van Allsburg (Houghton Mifflin)
Honor Books:
A Visit to William Blake's Inn: Poems for Innocent and Experienced Travelers   by Nancy Willard, illustrated by Alice and Martin Provensen (Harcourt Brace Jovanovich)

Where the Buffaloes Begin by Olaf Baker, illustrated by Stephen Gammell (F. Warne)

On Market Street by Arnold Lobel, illustrated by Anita Lobel (Greenwillow)

Outside Over There by Maurice Sendak (Harper & Row)

1983 **Shadow** by Blaise Cendrars, illustrated by Marcia Brown (Charles Scribner's Sons)

Honor Books:

When I Was Young in the Mountains by Cynthia Rylant, illustrated by Diane Goode (E. P. Dutton)

A Chair for My Mother by Vera B. Williams (Morrow)

1984 **The Glorious Flight: Across the Channel with Louis Bleriot, July 25, 1909** by Alice and Martin Provensen (Viking)

Honor Books:

Ten, Nine, Eight by Molly Bang (Greenwillow)

Little Red Riding Hood retold and illustrated by Trina Schart Hyman (Holiday House)

1985 **St. George and the Dragon** by Margaret Hodges, illustrated by Trina Schart Hyman (Little, Brown)

Honor Books:

Hansel and Gretel retold by Rika Lesser, illustrated by Paul O. Zelinsky (Dodd)

Have You Seen My Duckling? by Nancy Tafuri (Greenwillow)

The Story of Jumping Mouse by John Steptoe (Lothrop, Lee & Shepard)

1986 **The Polar Express** by Chris Van Allsburg (Houghton Mifflin)

Honor Books:

King Bidgood's in the Bathtub by Audrey Wood, illustrated by Don Wood (Harcourt Brace Jovanovich)

The Relatives Came by Cynthia Rylant, illustrated by Stephen Gammell (Bradbury)

1987 **Hey, All** by Arthur Yorinks, illustrated by Richard Egielski (Farrar, Straus & Giroux)

Honor Books:

Alphabatics by Suse MacDonald (Bradbury)

Rumpelstiltskin retold and illustrated by Paul O. Zelinsky (E. P. Dutton)

The Village of Round and Square Houses by Ann Grifalconi (Little, Brown)

1988 **Owl Moon** by Jane Yolen, illustrated by John Schoenherr (Philomel)

Honor Book:

Mufaro's Beautiful Daughters: An African Tale by John Steptoe (Lothrop, Lee & Shepard)

1989   **Song and Dance Man**   by Karen Ackerman, illustrated by Stephen Gammell (Alfred A. Knopf)
Honor Books:
The Boy of the Three-Year Nap   by Dianne Snyder, illustrated by Allen Say (Houghton Mifflin)
Free Fall   by David Wiesner (Lothrop, Lee & Shepard)
Goldilocks   retold and illustrated by James Marshall (Dial)
Mirandy and Brother Wind   by Patricia C. McKissack, illustrated by Jerry Pinkney (Alfred A. Knopf)

1990   **Lon Po Po: A Red-Riding Hood Story from China**   by Ed Young (Philomel)
Honor Books:
Bill Peet: An Autobiography   by Bill Peet (Houghton Mifflin)
Color Zoo   by Lois Ehlert (J. B. Lippincott)
Hershel and the Hanukkah Goblins   by Eric Kimmel, illustrated by Trina Schart Hyman (Holiday House)
The Talking Eggs   by Robert D. San Souci, illustrated by Jerry Pinkey (Dial)

1991   **Black and White**   by David Macaulay (Houghton Mifflin)
Honor Books:
"More More More," Said the Baby: Three Love Stories   by Vera B. Williams (Greenwillow)
Puss in Boots   by Charles Perrault, translated by Malcolm Arthur, illustrated by Fred Marcellino (Farrar, Straus & Giroux)

1992   **Tuesday**   by David Weisner (Clarion)
Honor Book:
Tar Beach   by Faith Ringgold (Crown)

1993   **Mirette on the High Wire**   by Emily Arnold McCully (G. P. Putnam's Sons)
Honor Books:
Stinky Cheese Man and Other Fairly Stupid Tales   by Jon Scieszka, illustrated by Lane Smith (Viking)
Working Cotton   by Sherley Anne Williams, illustrated by Carol Byard (Harcourt Brace)
Seven Blind Mice   by Ed Young (Philomel)

1994   **Grandfather's Journey**   by Allen Say (Houghton Mifflin)
Honor Books:
Peppe the Lamplighter   by Elisa Bartone, illustrated by Ted Lewin (Lothrop, Lee & Shepard)
In the Small, Small Pond   by Denise Fleming (Henry Holt)
Owen   by Kevin Henkes (Greenwillow)

1995   **Smoky Night**   by Eve Bunting, illustrated by David Diaz (Harcourt Brace)
Honor Books:
John Henry   by Julius Lester, illustrated by Jerry Pickney (Dial)
Swamp Angel   by Paul Zelinsky, illustrated by Anne Isaacs (E. P. Dutton)
Time Flies   by Eric Rohmann (Crown)

1996 **Officer Buckle and Gloria** by Peggy Ratham (Putnam)
Honor Books:
Alphabet City by Stephen T. Johnson (Viking)
Zin! Zin! Zin! A Violin by Lloyd Moss, illustrated by Marjorie Priceman (Simon and Schuster)
The Faithful Friend by Robert San Souci, illustrated by Brian Pinkney (Simon and Schuster)
Tops and Bottoms by Janet Stevens (Harcourt Brace)

1997 **Golem** by David Wisniewski (Clarion)
Honor Books:
The Graphic Alphabet edited by Neal Porter, illustrated by David Pelletier (Orchard)
Hush! A Thai Lullaby by Minfong Ho, illustrated by Holly Meade (Orchard)
The Paperboy illustrated by Dav Pilkey (Orchard)
Starry Messenger by Peter Sis (Farrar, Straus & Giroux)

1998 **Rapunzel** by Paul Zelinsky (Dutton)
Honor Books:
The Gardener by Sarah Stewart, illustrated by David Small (Live Oak Media)
Harlem by Walter Dean Myers, illustrated by Christopher Myers (Scholastic)
There Was an Old Lady Who Swallowed a Fly by Simms Taback (Viking)

1999 **Snowflake Bentley** by Jaqueline Briggs Martin, illustrated by Mary Azarian (Houghton Mifflin)
Honor Books:
Duke Ellington: The Piano Prince and His Orchestra by Andrea Davis Pinkney, illustrated by Brian Pinkney (Hyperion)
No, David by David Shannon (Scholastic)
Snow by Uri Shulevitz (Farrar, Straus and Giroux)
Tibet: Through the Red Box by Peter Sis (Farrar, Straus and Giroux)

THE NEWBERY MEDAL AND HONOR AWARDS

First presented in 1922, the Newbery Medal is awarded for the most distinguished contribution to children's literature published in the United States. The award is named after John Newbery, the first English publisher of books for children. It is given by the Children's Services Division of the American Library Association.

1922 **The Story of Mankind** by Hendrik Willem van Loon (Boni & Liveright)
Honor Books:
The Great Quest by Charles Hawes (Little, Brown)
Cedric the Forester by Bernard Marshall (Appleton)

The Old Tobacco Shop: A True Account of What Befell a Little Boy in Search of Adventure   by William Bowen (Macmillan)
The Golden Fleece and the Heroes Who Lived Before Achilles   by Padraic Colum (Macmillan)
Windy Hill   by Cornelia Meigs (Macmillan)

1923   **The Voyages of Doctor Dolittle**   by Hugh Lofting (Frederick A. Stokes)

1924   **The Dark Frigate**   by Charles Hawes (Atlantic Monthly Press)

1925   **Tales from Silver Lands**   by Charles Finger (Doubleday, Page)
Honor Books:
Nicholas: A Manhattan Christmas Story   by Anne Carroll Moore (G. P. Putnams' Sons)
Dream Coach   by Anne Parrish (Macmillan)

1926   **Shen of the Sea**   by Arthur Bowie Chrisman (E. P. Dutton)
Honor Book:
Voyagers   by Padraic Colum (Macmillan)

1927   **Smoky, the Cowhorse**   by Will James (Charles Scribner's Sons)

1928   **Gayneck, the Story of a Pigeon**   by Dhan Gopal Mukerji (E. P. Dutton)
Honor Books:
The Wonder Smith and His Son: A Tale from the Golden Childhood of the World   by Ella Young (Longmans, Green)
Downright Dencey   by Caroline Snedeker (Doubleday)

1929   **The Trumpeter of Krakow**   by Eric P. Kelly (Macmillan)
Honor Books:
Pigtail of Ah Lee Ben Loo   by John Bennett (Longmans, Green)
Millions of Cats   by Wanda Gag (Coward-McCann)
The Boy Who Was   by Grace Hallock (E. P. Dutton)
Clearing Weather   by Cornelia Meigs (Little, Brown)
Runaway Papoose   by Grace Moon (Doubleday, Doran)
Tod of the Fens   by Elinor Whitney (Macmillan)

1930   **Hitty, Her First Hundred Years**   by Rachel Field (Macmillan)
Honor Books:
Daughter of the Seine: The Life of Madame Roland   by Jeanette Eaton (Harper and Brothers)
Pran of Albania   by Elizabeth Miller (Doubleday, Doran)
Jumping-Off Place   by Marian Hurd McNeely (Longmans, Green)
Tangle-Coated Horse and Other Tales: Episodes from the Fionn Saga   by Ella Young (Longmans, Green)
Vaino: A Boy of New England   by Julia Davis Adams (E. P. Dutton)
Little Blacknose   by Hildegarde Swift (Harcourt)

1931   **The Cat Who Went to Heaven**   by Elizabeth Coatsworth (Macmillan)

Honor Books:
Floating Island   by Anne Parrish (Harper and Brothers)
The Dark Star of Itza: The Story of a Pagan Princess   by Alida Malkus (Harcourt)
Queer Person   by Ralph Hubbard (Doubleday, Doran)
Mountains Are Free   by Julia Davis Adams (E. P. Dutton)
Spice and the Devil's Cave   by Agnes Hewes (Alfred A. Knopf)
Meggy Macintosh   by Elizabeth Janet Gray (Doubleday)
Garram the Hunter: The Boy of the Hill Tribes   by Herbert Best (Doubleday, Doran)
Ood-Le-Uk the Wanderer   by Alice Lide and Margaret Johansen (Little, Brown)

1932   **Waterless Mountain**   by Laura Adams Armer (Longmans, Green)
Honor Books:
The Fairy Circus   by Dorothy P. Lathrop (Macmillan)
Calico Bush   by Rachel Field (Macmillan)
Boy of the South Seas   by Eunice Tietjens (Coward-McCann)
Out of the Flame   by Eloise Lownsbery (Longmans, Green)
Jane's Island   by Marjorie Allee (Houghton Mifflin)
Truce of the Wolf and Other Tales of Old Italy   by Mary Gould Davis (Harcourt)

1933   **Young Fu of the Upper Yangtze**   by Elizabeth Foreman Lewis (John C. Winston)
Honor Books:
Swift Rivers   by Cornelia Meigs (Little, Brown)
The Railroad to Freedom: A Story of the Civil War   by Hildegarde Swift (Harcourt Brace)
Children of the Soil: A Story of Scandinavia   by Nora Burglon (Doubleday, Doran)

1934   **Invincible Louisa: The Story of the Author of 'Little Women'**   by Cornelia Meigs (Little, Brown)
Honor Books:
The Forgotten Daughter   by Caroline Snedeker (Doubleday, Doran)
Swords of Steel   by Elsie Singmaster (Houghton Mifflin)
ABC Bunny   by Wanda Gag (Coward-McCann)
Winged Girl of Knossos   by Erik Berry (Appleton-Century)
New Land   by Sarah Schmidt (R. M. McBride)
Big Tree of Bunlahy: Stories of My Own Countryside   by Padraic Colum (Macmillan)
Glory of the Seas   by Agnes Hewes (Alfred A. Knopf)
Apprentice of Florence   by Ann Kyle (Houghton Mifflin)

1935   **Dobry**   by Monica Shannon (Viking)
Honor Books:
Pageant of Chinese History   by Elizabeth Seeger (Longmans, Green)

Davy Crockett   by Constance Rourke (Harcourt Brace)
Day on Skates: The Story of a Dutch Picnic   by Hilda Van Stockum (Harper)

1936   **Caddie Woodlawn**   by Carol Ryrie Brink (Macmillan)
Honor Books:
Honk, the Moose   by Phil Stong (Dodd, Mead)
The Good Master   by Kate Seredy (Viking)
Young Walter Scott   by Elizabeth Janet Gray (Viking)
All Sail Set: A Romance of the Flying Cloud   by Armstrong Sperry (John C. Winston)

1937   **Roller Skates**   by Ruth Sawyer (Viking)
Honor Books:
Phoebe Fairchild: Her Book   by Lois Lenski (Frederick A. Stokes)
Whistler's Van   by Idwal Jones (Viking)
Golden Basket   by Ludwig Bemelmans (Viking)
Winterbound   by Margery Bianco (Viking)
Audubon   by Constance Rourke (Harcourt Brace)
The Codfish Musket   by Agnes Hewes (Doubleday, Doran)

1938   **The White Stag**   by Kate Seredy (Viking)
Honor Books:
Pecos Bill   by James Cloyd Bowman (Little, Brown)
Bright Island   by Mabel Robinson (Random House)
On the Banks of Plum Creek   by Laura Ingalls Wilder (Harper and Brothers)

1939   **Thimble Summer**   by Elizabeth Enright (Holt, Rinehart & Winston)
Honor Books:
Nino   by Valenti Angelo (Viking)
Mr. Popper's Penguins   by Richard and Florence Atwater (Little, Brown)
"Hello the Boat!"   by Phyllis Crawford (Henry Holt)
Leader by Destiny: George Washington, Man and Patriot   by Jeanette Eaton (Harcourt Brace)
Penn   by Elizabeth Janet Gray (Viking)

1940   **Daniel Boone**   by James Daugherty (Viking)
Honor Books:
The Singing Tree   by Kate Seredy (Viking)
Runner of the Mountain Tops: The Life of Louis Agassiz   by Mabel Robinson (Random House)
By the Shores of Silver Lake   by Laura Ingalls Wilder (Harper and Brothers)
Boy with a Pack   by Stephen W. Meader (Harcourt Brace)

1941   **Call It Courage**   by Armstrong Sperry (Macmillan)
Honor Books:
Blue Willow   by Doris Gates (Viking)
Young Mac of Fort Vancouver   by Mary Jane Carr (Thomas Y. Crowell)

The Long Winter   by Laura Ingalls Wilder (Harper and Brothers)
Nansen   by Anna Gertrude Hall (Viking)

1942   **The Matchlock Gun**   by Walter D. Edmonds (Dodd, Mead)
Honor Books:
Little Town on the Prairie   by Laura Ingalls Wilder (Harper and Brothers)
George Washington's World   by Genevieve Foster (Charles Scribner's Sons)
Indian Captive: The Story of Mary Jemison   by Lois Lenski (Frederick A. Stokes)
Down Ryton Water   by Eva Roe Gaggin (Viking)

1943   **Adam of the Road**   by Elizabeth Janet Gray (Viking)
Honor Books:
The Middle Moffat   by Eleanor Estes (Harcourt Brace)
Have You Seen Tom Thumb?   by Mabel Leigh Hunt (Frederick A. Stokes)

1944   **Johnny Tremain**   by Esther Forbes (Houghton Mifflin)
Honor Books:
The Happy Golden Years   by Laura Ingalls Wilder (Harper and Brothers)
Fog Magic   by Julia Sauer (Viking)
Rufus M.   by Eleanor Estes (Harcourt Brace)
Mountain Born   by Elizabeth Yates (Coward-McCann)

1945   **Rabbit Hill**   by Robert Lawson (Viking)
Honor Books:
The Hundred Dresses   by Eleanor Estes (Harcourt Brace)
The Silver Pencil   by Alice Dalgliesh (Charles Scribner's Sons)
Abraham Lincoln's World   by Genevieve Foster (Charles Scribner's Sons)
Lone Journey: The Life of Roger Williams   by Jeanette Eaton (Harcourt Brace)

1946   **Strawberry Girl**   by Lois Lenski (J. B. Lippincott)
Honor Books:
Justin Morgan Had a Horse   by Marguerite Henry (Wilcox & Follett)
The Moved-Outers   by Florence Crannell Means (Houghton Mifflin)
Bhimsa, the Dancing Bear   by Christine Weston (Charles Scribner's Sons)
New Found World   by Katherine Shippen (Viking)

1947   **Miss Hickory**   by Carolyn Sherwin Bailey (Viking)
Honor Books:
Wonderful Year   by Nancy Barnes (J. Messner)
Big Tree   by Mary and Conrad Buff (Viking)
The Heavenly Tenants   by William Maxwell (Harper and Brothers)
The Avion My Uncle Flew   by Cyrus Fisher (Appleton-Century)
The Hidden Treasure of Glaston   by Eleanore Jewett (Viking)

1948   **The Twenty-One Balloons**   by William Pene du Bois (Viking)
Honor Books:
Pancakes-Paris   by Claire Huchet Bishop (Viking)

Le Lun, Lad of Courage   by Carolyn Treffinger (Abingdon-Cokesbury)
The Quaint and Curious Quest of Johnny Longfoot   by Catherine Bester-man (Bobbs Merrill)
The Cowtail Switch and Other West African Stories   by Harold Courlan-der (Henry Holt)
Misty of Chincoteague   by Marguerite Henry (Rand McNally)

1949   **King of the Wind**   by Marguerite Henry (Rand McNally)
Honor Books:
Seabird   by Holling C. Holling (Houghton Mifflin)
Daughter of the Mountains   by Louis Rankin (Viking)
My Father's Dragon   by Ruth S. Gannett (Random House)
Story of the Negro   by Arna Bontemps. Alfred A. Knopf)

1950   **The Door in the Wall**   by Marguerite de Angeli (Doubleday)
Honor Books:
Tree of Freedom   by Rebecca Caudill (Viking)
The Blue Cat of Castle Town   by Catherine Cobletz (Longmans, Green)
Kildee House   by Rutherford Montgomery (Doubleday)
George Washington   by Genevieve Foster (Charles Scribner's Sons)
Sons of the Pines: A Story of Norwegian Lumbering in Wisconsin   by Walter and Marion Havighurst (John C. Winston)

1951   **Amos Fortune, Free Man**   by Elizabeth Yates (E. P. Dutton)
Honor Books:
Better Known as Johnny Appleseed   by Mabel Leigh Hunt (J. B. Lippincott)
Gandhi, Fighter Without a Sword   by Jeanette Eaton (Morrow)
Abraham Lincoln, Friend of the People   by Clara Ingram Judson (Wilcox & Follett)
The Story of Appleby Capple   by Anne Parrish (Harper)

1952   **Ginger Pye**   by Eleanor Estes (Harcourt Brace)
Honor Books:
Americans Before Columbus   by Elizabeth Baity (Viking)
Minn of the Mississippi   by Holling C. Holling.
The Defender   by Nicholas Kalashnikoff (Charles Scribner's Sons)
The Light at Tern Rock   by Julia Sauer (Viking)
The Apple and the Arrow   by Mary and Conrad Buff (Houghton Mifflin)

1953   **Secret of the Andes**   by Ann Nolan Clark (Viking)
Honor Books:
Charlotte's Web   by E. B. White (Harper)
Moccasin Trail   by Eloise McGraw (Coward-McCann)
Red Sails to Capri   by Ann Weil (Viking)
The Bears on Hemlock Mountain   by Alice Dalgliesh (Charles Scribner's Sons)
Birthdays of Freedom, Vol. 1   by Genevieve Foster (Charles Scribner's Sons)

1954   **And Now Miguel**   by Joseph Krumgold (Thomas Y. Crowell)
Honor Books:
All Alone   by Claire Huchet Bishop (Viking)
Shadrach   by Meindert DeJong (Harper)
Hurry Home, Candy   by Meindert DeJong (Harper)
Theodore Roosevelt, Fighting Patriot   by Clara Ingram Judson (Follet)
Magic Maize   by Mary and Conrad Buff (Houghton Mifflin)

1955   **The Wheel on the School**   by Meindert DeJong (Harper)
Honor Books:
The Courage of Sarah Noble   by Alice Dalgliesh (Charles Scribner's Sons)
Banner in the Sky   by James Ullman (J. B. Lippincott)

1956   **Carry on, Mr. Bowditch**   by Jean Lee Latham (Houghton Mifflin)
Honor Books:
The Secret River   by Marjorie Kinnan Rawlings (Charles Scribner's Sons)
The Golden Name Day   by Jennie Lindquist (Harper)
Men, Microscopes, and Living Things   by Katherine Shippen (Viking)

1957   **Miracles on Maple Hill**   by Virginia Sorensen (Harcourt Brace)
Honor Books:
Old Yeller   by Fred Gipson (Harper)
The House of Sixty Fathers   by Meindert DeJong (Harper)
Mr. Justice Holmes   by Clara Ingram Judson (Follett)
The Corn Grows Ripe   by Dorothy Rhoads (Viking)
Black Fox of Lorne   by Marguerite de Angeli (Doubleday)

1958   **Rifles for Watie**   by Harold Keith (Thomas Y. Crowell)
Honor Books:
The Horsecatcher   by Mari Sandoz (Westminister)
Gone-Away Lake   by Elizabeth Enright (Harcourt Brace)
The Great Wheel   by Robert Lawson (Viking)
Tom Paine, Freedom's Apostle   by Leo Gurko (Thomas Y. Crowell)

1959   **The Witch of Blackbird Pond**   by Elizabeth George Speare (Houghton Mifflin)
Honor Books:
The Family Under the Bridge   by Natalie Savage Carlson (Harper)
Along Came a Dog   by Meindert DeJong (Harper)
Chucaro: Wild Pony of the Pampa   by Francis Kalnay (Harcourt Brace)
The Perilous Road   by William O. Steele (Harcourt Brace)

1960   **Onion John**   by Joseph Krumgold (Thomas Y. Crowell)
Honor Books:
My Side of the Mountain   by Jean Craighead George (E. P. Dutton)
America Is Born   by Gerald W. Johnson (Morrow)
The Gammage Cup   by Carol Kendall (Harcourt Brace)

1961   **Island of the Blue Dolphins**   by Scott O'Dell (Houghton Mifflin)
Honor Books:
America Moves Forward   by Gerald W. Johnson (Morrow)
Old Ramon   by Jack Schaefer (Houghton Mifflin)
The Cricket in Times Square   by George Selden (Farrar, Straus & Giroux)

1962   **The Bronze Bow**   by Elizabeth George Speare (Houghton Mifflin)
Honor Books:
Frontier Living   by Edwin Tunis (World)
The Golden Goblet   by Eloise McCraw (Coward-McCann)
Belling the Tiger   by Mary Stolz (Harper)

1963   **A Wrinkle in Time**   by Madeleine L'Engle (Farrar, Straus & Giroux)
Honor Books:
Thistle and Thyme: Tales and Legends from Scotland   by Sorche Nic Leodhas (Holt, Rinehart & Winston)
Men of Athens   by Olivia Coolidge (Houghton Mifflin)

1964   **It's Like This, Cat**   by Emily Cheney Neville (Harper & Row)
Honor Books:
Rascal   by Sterling North (E. P. Dutton)
The Loner   by Ester Wier (D. McKay)

1965   **Shadow of a Bull**   by Maia Wojciechowska (Atheneum)
Honor Book:
Across Five Aprils   by Irene Hunt (Follett)

1966   **I, Juan de Pareja**   by Elizabeth Borton de Trevino (Farrar, Straus & Giroux)
Honor Books:
The Black Cauldron   by Lloyd Alexander (Holt, Rinehart & Winston)
The Animal Family   by Randall Jarrell (Pantheon)
The Noonday Friends   by Mary Stolz (Harper & Row)

1967   **Up a Road Slowly**   by Irene Hunt (Follett)
Honor Books:
The King's Fifth   by Scott O'Dell (Houghton Mifflin)
Zlateh The Goat and Other Stories   by Isaac Bashevis Singer (Harper & Row)
The Jazz Man   by Mary H. Weik (Atheneum)

1968   **From the Mixed-Up Files of Mrs. Basil E. Frankweiler**   by E. L. Konigsburg (Atheneum)
Honor Books:
Jennifer, Hecate, Macbeth, William McKinley, and Me, Elizabeth   by E. L. Konigsburg (Atheneum)
The Black Pearl   by Scott O'Dell (Houghton Mifflin)
The Fearsome Inn   by Isaac Bashevis Singer (Charles Scribner's Sons)
The Egypt Game   by Zilpha Keatley Snyder (Atheneum)

1969   **The High King** by Lloyd Alexander (Holt, Rinehart & Winston)
Honor Books:
To Be a Slave by Julius Lester (Dial)
When Shlemiel Went to Warsaw and Other Stories by Isaac Bashevis Singer (Farrar, Straus & Giroux)

1970   **Sounder** by William H. Armstrong (Harper & Row)
Honor Books:
Our Eddie by Sulamith Ish-Kishor (Pantheon)
The Many Ways of Seeing: An Introduction to the Pleasures of Art by Janet Gaylord Moore (World)
Journey Outside by Mary Q. Steele (Viking)

1971   **Summer of the Swans** by Betsy Byars (Atheneum)
Honor Books:
Kneeknock Rise by Natalie Babbitt (Farrar, Straus & Giroux)
Enchantress from the Stars by Sylvia Louise Engdahl (Atheneum)
Sing Down the Moon by Scott O'Dell (Houghton Mifflin)

1972   **Mrs. Frisby and the Rats of NIMH** by Robert C. O'Brien (Atheneum)
Honor Books:
Incident at Hawk's Hill by Allan W. Eckert (Little, Brown)
The Planet of Junior Brown by Virginia Hamilton (Macmillan)
The Tombs of Atuan by Ursula K. LeGuin (Atheneum)
Annie and the Old One by Miska Miles (Little, Brown)
The Headless Cupid by Zilpha Keatley Snyder (Atheneum)

1973   **Julie of the Wolves** by Jean Craighead George (Harper & Row)
Honor Books:
Frog and Toad Together by Arnold Lobel (Harper & Row)
The Upstairs Room by Johanna Reiss (Thomas Y. Crowell)
The Witches of Worm by Zilpha Keatley Snyder (Atheneum)

1974   **The Slave Dancer** by Paula Fox (Bradbury)
Honor Book:
The Dark Is Rising by Susan Cooper (Atheneum)

1975   **M. C. Higgins, the Great** by Virginia Hamilton (Simon & Schuster)
Honor Books:
Figgs & Phantoms by Ellen Raskin (E. P. Dutton)
My Brother Sam Is Dead by James Lincoln Collier and Christopher Collier (Four Winds)
The Perilous Gard by Elizabeth Marie Pope (Houghton Mifflin)
Philip Hall Likes Me, I Reckon Maybe by Bette Greene (Dial)

1976   **The Grey King** by Susan Cooper (Atheneum)
Honor Books:
The Hundred Penny Box by Sharon Bell Mathis (Viking)
Dragonwings by Laurence Yep (Harper & Row)

1977   **Roll of Thunder, Hear My Cry**   by Mildred D. Taylor (Dial)
Honor Books:
Abel's Island   by William Steig (Farrar, Straus & Giroux)
A String in the Harp   by Nancy Bond (Atheneum)

1978   **Bridge to Terabithia**   by Katherine Paterson (Thomas Y. Crowell)
Honor Books:
Ramona and Her Father   by Beverly Cleary (Morrow)
Anpao: An American Indian Odyssey   by Jamake Highwater (J. B. Lippincott)

1979   **The Westing Game**   by Ellen Raskin (E. P. Dutton)
Honor Book:
The Great Gilly Hopkins   by Katherine Paterson (Thomas Y. Crowell)

1980   **A Gathering of Days: A New England Girl's Journal 1830–32**   by Joan Blos (Charles Scribner's Sons)
Honor Book:
The Road from Home: The Story of an Armenian Girl   by David Kherdian (Morrow)

1981   **Jacob Have I Loved**   by Katherine Paterson (Thomas Y. Crowell)
Honor Books:
The Fledgling   by Jane Langton (Harper & Row)
A Ring of Endless Light   by Madeleine L'Engle (Farrar, Straus & Giroux)

1982   **A Visit to William Blake's Inn: Poems for Innocent and Experienced Travelers**   by Nancy Willard (Harcourt Brace Jovanovich)
Honor Books:
Ramona Quimby, Age 8   by Beverly Cleary (Morrow)
Upon the Head of the Goat: A Childhood in Hungary, 1939–1944   by Aranka Siegal (Farrar, Straus & Giroux)

1983   **Dicey's Song**   by Cynthia Voigt (Atheneum)
Honor Books:
Blue Sword   by Robin McKinley (Greenwillow)
Doctor DeSoto   by William Steig (Farrar, Straus & Giroux)
Graven Images   by Paul Fleischman (Harper & Row)
Homesick: My Own Story   by Jean Fritz (Putnam)
Sweet Whisper, Brother Rush   by Virginia Hamilton (Philomel)

1984   **Dear Mr. Henshaw**   by Beverly Cleary (Morrow)
Honor Books:
The Sign of the Beaver   by Elizabeth George Speare (Houghton Mifflin)
A Solitary Blue   by Cynthia Voigt (Atheneum)
The Wish Giver   by Bill Brittain (Harper & Row)
Sugaring Time   by Kathryn Lasky (Macmillan)

1985   **The Hero and The Crown**   by Robin McKinley (Greenwillow)

Honor Books:
Like Jake and Me   by Mavis Jukes (Alfred A. Knopf)
The Moves Make the Man   by Bruce Brooks (Harper & Row)
One-Eyed Cat   by Paula Fox (Bradbury)

1986   **Sarah, Plain and Tall**   by Patricia MacLachlan (Harper & Row)
Honor Books:
Commodore Perry in the Land of the Shogun   by Rhoda Blumber (Lothrop, Lee & Shepard)
Dogsong   by Gary Paulsen (Bradbury)

1987   **The Whipping Boy**   by Sid Fleischman (Greenwillow)
Honor Books:
A Fine White Dust   by Cynthia Rylant (Bradbury)
On My Honor   by Marion Dane Bauer (Clarion)
Volcano: The Eruption and Healing of Mount St. Helens   by Patricia Lauber (Bradbury)

1988   **Lincoln: A Photobiography**   by Russell Freedman (Clarion)
Honor Books:
After the Rain   by Norma Fox Mazer (Morrow)
Hatchet   by Gary Paulsen (Bradbury)

1989   **Joyful Noise: Poems for Two Voices**   by Paul Fleischman (Harper & Row)
Honor Books:
In the Beginning: Creation Stories from Around the World   by Virginia Hamilton (Harcourt Brace Jovanovich)
Scorpions   by Walter Dean Myers (Harper & Row)

1990   **Number the Stars**   by Lois Lowry (Houghton Mifflin)
Honor Books:
Afternoon of the Elves   by Janet Taylor Lisle (Orchard)
Shabanu, Daughter of the Wind   by Susan Fisher Staples (Alfred A. Knopf)
The Winter Room   by Gary Paulsen (Orchard)

1991   **Maniac Magee**   by Jerry Spinelli (Little, Brown)
Honor Book:
The True Confessions of Charlotte Doyle   by Avi (Orchard)

1992   **Shiloh**   by Phyllis Reynolds Naylor (Atheneum)
Honor Books:
Nothing but the Truth   by Avi (Orchard)
Wright Brothers   by Russell Freedman (Holiday House)

1993   **Missing May**   by Cynthia Rylant (Orchard)
Honor Books:
What Hearts   by Bruce Brooks (HarperCollins)
Dark Thirty: Southern Tales of the Supernatural   by Patricia C. McKissack (Alfred A. Knopf)
Somewhere in the Darkness   by Walter Dean Myers (Scholastic)

1994   **The Giver**   by Lois Lowry (Houghton Mifflin)
Honor Books:
Crazy Lady!   by Jane Leslie Conly (HarperCollins)
Dragon's Gate   by Laurence Yep (HarperCollins)
Eleanor Roosevelt: A Life of Discovery   by Russell Freedman (Clarion)

1995   **Walk Two Moons**   by Sharon Creech (HarperCollins)
Honor Books:
Catherine, Called Birdy   by Karen Cushman (Clarion)
The Ear, the Eye, and the Arm   by Nancy Farmer (Orchard)

1996   **The Midwife's Apprentice**   by Karen Cushman (Clarion)
Honor Books:
What Jamie Saw   by Carolyn Coman (Front Street)
The Watsons Go to Birmingham—1963   by Christopher Paul Curtis (Dellacourt)
Yolanda's Genius   by Carol Fenner (Margaret K. McElderry Books)
The Great Fire   by Jim Murphy (Scholastic)

1997   **The View from Saturday**   by E. L. Konigsburg (Atheneum)
Honor Books:
A Girl Named Disaster   by Nancy Farmer (Orchard)
Belle Prater's Boy   by Ruth White (Farrar, Straus & Giroux)
Moorchild   by Eloise McGraw (Simon & Schuster)
The Thief   by Megan Whalen Turner (Greenwillow)

1998   **Out of the Dust**   by Karen Hesse (Scholastic)
Honor Books:
Ella Enchanted   by Gail Carson Levine (HarperCollins)
Lily's Crossing   by Patricia Reilly Giff (Dell)
Wringer   by Jerry Spinelli (HarperCollins)

1999   **Holes**   by Louis Sachar (Farrar, Straus and Giroux)
Honor Book:
A Long Way from Chicago   by Richard Peck (Dial)

CORETTA SCOTT KING AWARD

The Coretta Scott King Awards honor African-American writers and illustrators of outstanding educational and inspirational books for children and young adults, books that demonstrate sensitivity to the worth of all people. Awards are given for both writing (fiction and nonfiction) and for illustration. Winners of the Coretta Scott King Awards are listed in Chapter 2 on page 43.

BOSTON GLOBE/HORN BOOK AWARDS

These awards, sponsored by *The Boston Globe* newspaper and *The Horn Book Magazine* are given to an author of outstanding fiction or poetry for children and to an illustrator for outstanding illustration in a picture book. In 1976, an award was added for the author of an outstanding work of nonfiction for children.

1967   Text: **The Little Fishes**   by Erik Christian Haugaard (Houghton
Illustration: **London Bridge Is Falling Down**   by Peter Spier (Doubleday)

1968   Text: **The Spring Rider**   by John Lawson (Crowell)
Illustration: **Tikki Tikki Tembo**   by Arlene Mosel, illustrated by Blair Lent (Holt)

1969   Text: **A Wizard of Earthsea**   by Ursula K. Le Guin (Houghton)
Illustration: **The Adventures of Paddy Pork**   by John S. Goodall (Harcourt)

1970   Text: **The Intruder**   by John Rowe Townsend (Lippincott)
Illustration: **Hi, Cat!**   by Ezra Jack Keats (Macmillan)

1971   Text: **A Room Made of Windows**   by Eleanor Cameron (Atlantic/Little)
Illustration: **If I Built a Village**   by Kazue Mizumura (Crowell)

1972   Text: **Tristan and Iseult**   by Rosemary Sutcliff (Dutton)
Illustration: **Mr. Gumpy's Outing**   by John Burningham (Holt)

1973   Text: **The Dark Is Rising**   by Susan Cooper (Atheneum/McElderry)
Illustration: **King Stork**   by Trina Schart Hyman (Little, Brown)

1974   Text: **M. C. Higgins, the Great**   by Virginia Hamilton (Macmillan)
Illustration: **Jambo Means Hello**   by Muriel Feelings, illustrated by Tom Feelings (Dial)

1975   Text: **Transport 7—41–R**   by T. Degens (Viking)
Illustration: **Anno's Alphabet**   by Mitsumasa Anno (Crowell)

1976   Fiction: **Unleaving**   by Jill Paton Walsh (Farrar, Straus and Giroux)
Nonfiction: **Voyaging to Cathay: Americans in the China Trade**   by Alfred Tamarin and Shirley Glubok (Viking)
Illustration: **Thirteen**   by Remy Charlip and Jerry Joyner (Parents)

1977   Fiction: **Child of the Owl**   by Laurence Yep (Harper)
Nonfiction: **Chance, Luck and Density**   by Peter Dickinson (Atlantic/ Little, Brown)
Illustration: **Granfa' Grif Had a Pig and Other Rhymes**   by Wallace Tripp (Little, Brown)

1978   Fiction: **The Westing Game**   by Ellen Raskin (Dutton)
Nonfiction: **Mischling, Second Degree: My Childhood in Nazi Germany** by Ilse Koehn (Greenwillow)
Illustration: **Anno's Journey**   by Mitsumasa Anno (Philome)

1979   Fiction: **Humbug Mountain**   by Sid Fleischman (Atlantic/Little, Brown)
Nonfiction: **The Road from Home: The Story of an Armenian Girl**   by David Kherdian (Greenwillow)
Illustration: **The Snowman**   by Raymond Briggs (Random)

1980   Fiction: **Conrad's War**   by Andrew Davies (Crown)
Nonfiction: **Building: The Fight Against Gravity**   by Mario Salvadori (Atheneum/McElderry)
Illustration: **The Garden of Abdul Gasazi**   by Chris Van Allsburg (Houghton)

1981   Fiction: **The Leaving**   by Lynn Hall (Scribner's)
Nonfiction: **The Weaver's Gift**   by Kathryn Lasky (Warne)
Illustration: **Outside Over There**   by Maurice Sendak (Harper)

1982   Fiction: **Playing Beatie Bow**   by Ruth Park (Atheneum)
Nonfiction: **Upon the Head of the Goat: A Childhood in Hungary, 1939–1944**   by Aranka Siegal (Farrar, Straus and Giroux)
Illustration: **A Visit to William Blake's Inn: Poems for Innocent and Experienced Travelers**   by Nancy Willard, illustrated by Alice and Martin Provensen (Harcourt)

1983   Fiction: **Sweet Whispers, Brother Rush**   by Virginia Hamilton (Philomel)
Nonfiction: **Behind Barbed Wire: The Imprisonment of Japanese Americans During World War II**   by Daniel S. Davis (Dutton)
Illustration: **A Chair for My Mother**   by Vera B. Williams (Greenwillow)

1984   Fiction: **A Little Fear**   by Patricia Wrightson (McElderry/Atheneum)
Nonfiction: **The Double Life of Pocahontas**   by Jean Fritz (Putnam)
Illustration: **Jonah and the Great Fish**   retold and illustrated by Warwick Hutton (McElderry/Atheneum)

1985   Fiction: **The Moves Make the Man**   by Bruce Brooks (Harper)
Nonfiction: **Commodore Perry in the Land of the Shogun**   by Rhoda Blumber (Lothrop)
Illustration: **Mama Don't Allow**   by Thatcher Hurd (Harper)

1986   Fiction: **In Summer Light**   by Zibby Oneal (Viking Kestrel)
Nonfiction: **Auks, Rocks, and the Odd Dinosaur**   by Peggy Thomson (Crowell)
Illustration: **The Paper Crane**   by Molly Bang (Greenwillow)

1987   Fiction: **Rabble Starkey**   by Lois Lowry (Houghton)
Nonfiction: **Pilgrims of Plimouth**   by Marcia Sewall (Atheneum)
Illustration: **Mufaro's Beautiful Daughters**   by John Steptoe (Lothrop)

1988   Fiction: **The Friendship**   by Mildred Taylor (Dial)
Nonfiction: **Anthony Burns: The Defeat and Triumph of a Fugitive Slave** by Virginia Hamilton (Knopf)
Illustration: **The Boy of the Three-Year Nap**   by Diane Snyder, illustrated by Allen Say (Houghton)

1989   Fiction: **The Village by the Sea**   by Paula Fox (Orchard)
Nonfiction: **The Way Things Work**   by David Macaulay (Houghton)
Illustration: **Shy Charles**   by Rosemary Wells (Dial)

1990   Fiction: **Maniac Magee**   by Jerry Spinelli (Little, Brown)
Nonfiction: **The Great Little Madison**   by Jean Fritz (Putnam)
Illustration: **Lon Po Po: A Red-Riding Hood Story from China**   retold and illustrated by Ed Young (Philomel)

1991   Fiction: **The True Confessions of Charlotte Doyle**   by Avi (Orchard)
Nonfiction: **Appalachia: The Voices of Sleeping Birds**   by Cynthia Rylant, illustrated by Barry Moser (Harcourt)
Illustration: **The Tale of the Mandarin Ducks**   retold by Katherine Paterson, illustrated by Leo and Diane Dillon (Lodestar)

1992   Fiction: **Missing May**   by Cynthia Rylant (Orchard)
Nonfiction: **Talking with Artists**   by Pat Cummings (Bradbury)
Illustration: **Seven Blind Mice**   by Ed Young (Philomel)

1993   Fiction: **Ajeemah and His Son**   by James Berry (Harper)
Nonficton: **Sojourner Truth: Ain't I a Woman?**   by Patricia and Fredrick McKissack (Scholastic)
Illustration: **The Fortune-Tellers**   by Lloyd Alexander, illustrated by Trina Schart Hyman (Dutton)

1994   Fiction: **Scooter**   by Vera B. Williams (Greenwillow)
Nonfiction: **Eleanor Roosevelt: A Life of Discovery**   by Russell Freedman (Clarion)
Illustration: **Grandfather's Journey**   by Allen Say (Houghton)

1995   Fiction: **Some of the Kinder Planets**   by Tim Wynne-Jones (Orchard)
Nonfiction: **Abigail Adams: Witness to a Revolution**   by Natalie S. Bober (Simon and Schuster)
Illustration: **John Henry,** retold by Julius Lester, illustrated by Jerry Pinkney (Dial)

1996   Fiction: **Poppi**   by Avi, illustrated by Brian Floca (Orchard)
Nonfiction: **Orphan Train Rider: One Boy's True Story**   by Andrea Warren (Houghton Mifflin)
Illustration: **In the Rain with Baby Duck**   by May Hest, illustrated by Jill Barton (Candlewick)

1997   Fiction: **The Friends**   by Kazumi Yumoto (Dell)
Nonfiction: **A Drop of Water: A Book of Science and Wonder**   by Walter Wick (Scholastic)
Illustration: **The Adventures of Sparrow Boy**   by Brian Pinkney (Simon and Schuster)

1998   Fiction: **The Circuit: Stories from the Life of a Migrant Child**   by Francisco Jimenez (University of New Mexico Press)
Nonfiction: **Leon's Story**   by Leon Tillage (Farrar, Straus and Giroux)
Illustration: **And If the Moon Could Talk**   by Kate Banks, illustrated by Georg Hallensleben (Farrar, Straus and Giroux)

Laura Ingalls Wilder Award

Named in honor of the *Little House* author, this award was given every five years until 1980 and every three years thereafter to authors and illustrators who have made a lasting contribution to literature for children. It is given by the Association of Library Service to Children of the American Library Association.

1954	**Laura Ingalls Wilder**
1960	**Clara Ingram Judson**
1965	**Ruth Sawyer**
1970	**E. B. White**
1975	**Beverly Cleary**
1980	**Theodor Geisel (Dr. Seuss)**
1983	**Maurice Sendak**
1986	**Jean Fritz**
1989	**Elizabeth George Speare**
1992	**Marcia Brown**
1995	**Virginia Hamilton**
1998	**Russell Freedman**

NCTE Award for Excellence in Poetry for Children

Given annually from 1977 to 1982 and every three years thereafter, this award recognizes a living American poet for his or her entire body of work for children.

1977	**David McCord**
1978	**Aileen Fisher**
1979	**Karla Kuskin**
1980	**Myra Cohn Livingston**
1981	**Eve Merriam**
1982	**John Ciardi**
1985	**Lillian Moore**
1988	**Arnold Adoff**
1991	**Valerie Worth**
1994	**Barbara Esbensen**
1997	**Eloise Greenfield**

MILDRED L. BATCHELDER AWARD

Established in 1966, the Mildred Batchelder Award honors outstanding books originally published in another country in a language other than English, then translated, and finally published in the United States. The award is sponsored by the American Library Association's Committee for Library Service to Children.

1968 **The Little Man** by Erich Kästner, translated from German by James Kirkup, illustrated by Rick Schreiter (Knopf)

1969 **Don't Take Teddy** by Babbis Friis-Baastad, translated from Norwegian by Lise Sömme McKinnon (Scribner's)

1970 **Wildcat Under Glass** by Alki Zei, translated from Greek by Edward Fenton (Holt)

1971 **In the Land of Ur: The Discovery of Ancient Mesopotamia** by Hans Baumann, translated from German by Stella Humphries, illustrated by Hans Peter Renner (Pantheon)

1972 **Friedrich** by Hans Peter Richter, translated from German by Edite Kroll (Holt)

1973 **Pulga** by Siny Rose Van Iterson, translated from Dutch by Alexander and Alison Gode (Morrow)

1974 **Petros' War** by Alki Zei, translated from Greek by Edward Fenton (Dutton)

1975 **An Old Tale Carved Out of Stone** by Aleksandr M. Linevski, translated from Russian by Maria Polushkin (Crown)

1976 **The Cat and Mouse Who Shared a House** written and illustrated by Ruth Hürlimann, translated from German by Anthea Bell (Walck)

1977 **The Leopard** by Cecil Bödker, translated from Danish by Gunnar Poulsen (Atheneum)

1978 No award.

1979 **Konrad** by Christine Nöstlinger, translated from German (Austrian) by Anthea Bell, illustrated by Carol Nicklaus (Watts)
Rabbit Island by Jörg Steiner, translated from German (Swiss) by Ann Conrad Lammers, illustrated by Jörg Müllen (Harcourt)

1980 **The Sound of Dragon's Feet** by Alki Zei, translated from Greek by Edward Fenton (Dutton)

1981 **The Winter When Time Was Frozen** by Els Pelgrom, translated from Dutch by Raphael and Maryka Rudnik (Morrow)

1982 **The Battle Horse** by Harry Kullman, translated from Swedish by George Blecher and Lone Thygesen-Blecher (Bradbury)

1983   **Hiroshima No Pika**   written and illustrated by Toshio Maruki, translated from Japanese through Kurita-Bando Literary Agency (Lothrop)

1984   **Ronia, the Robber's Daughter**   by Astrid Lindgren, translated from Swedish by Patricia Crampton (Viking)

1985   **The Island on Bird Street**   by Uri Orlev, translated from Hebrew by Hillel Halkin (Houghton)

1986   **Rose Blanche**   by Christophe Gallaz and Roberto Innocenti, translated from French by Martha Coventry and Richard Graglia, illustrated by Roberto Innocenti (Creative Education)

1987   **No Hero for the Kaiser**   by Rudolf Frank, translated from German by Patricia Crampton, illustrated by Klaus Steffans (Lothrop)

1988   **If You Didn't Have Me**   by Ulf Nilsson, translated from Swedish by Lone Thygesen-Blecher and George Blecher, illustrated by Eva Eriksson (McElderry)

1989   **Crutches**   by Peter Härtling, translated from German by Elizabeth D. Crawford (Lothrop)

1990   **Buster's World**   by Bjarne Reuter, translated from Danish by Anthea Bell (Dutton)

1991   **A Hand Full of Stars**   by Rafik Schami, translated from German by Rika Lesser (Dutton)
Honor Book:
Two Short and One Long   by Nina Ring Aamundsen, translated from Norwegian by the author (Houghton)

1992   **The Man from the Other Side**   by Uri Orlev, translated from Hebrew by Hillel Halkin (Houghton)

1993   No Award.

1994   **The Apprentice**   by Pilar Molina Llorente, illustrated by Juan Ramón Alonso, translated from Spanish by Robin Longshaw (Farrar, Straus and Giroux)
Honor Books:
Anne Frank, Beyond the Diary: A Photographic Remembrance   by Ruud van der Rol and Rian Verhoeven, translated from Dutch by Tony Langham and Plym Peters (Viking)
The Princess in the Kitchen Garden   by Annemie and Margriet Heymans, translated from Dutch by Johanna H. Prins and Johanna W. Prins (Farrar, Straus and Giroux)

1995   **The Boys from St. Petri**   by Bjarne Reuter, translated from Danish by Anthea Bell (Dutton)

1996   **The Lady with the Hat**   by Uri Orlev, translated from Hebrew by Hillel Halkin (Houghton Mifflin)

1997 **The Friends** by Kazumi Yumoto, translated from Japanese by Cathy Hirano (Farrar, Straus and Giroux)

1998 **The Robber and Me** by Joseph Holob, translated from German by Elizabeth D. Crawford (Holt)

1999 **Thanks to My Mother** by Schoschana Rabinovici, translated from Hebrew by James Skofield (Dial)

The Scott O'Dell Award

Funded by the noted author Scott O'Dell and administered by Zena Sutherland of the University of Chicago, this award is given to a distinguished work of historical fiction for children or young adults set in the New World. Winners of the Scott O'Dell Award for the past ten years are listed in Chapter 8 on page 188.

Ezra Jack Keats Award

This is a biennial award given to a promising young artist and a promising young writer of children's literature who have had six or fewer books published. Named after the Caldecott Medal–winning author, the award is administered by the Ezra Jack Keats Foundation.

1987 **Valerie Flournoy** for *The Patchwork Quilt*, illustrated by Jerry Pinkney (Dial)

1989 **Juanita Havill** for *Jamaica's Friend*, illustrated by Anne Siubley O'Brien (Houghton Mifflin)

1991 **Angela Johnson** for *Tell Me a Story, Mama* (Orchard)

1993 **Faith Ringgold** for *Tar Beach* (Crown)

1995 **Carrie Best** for *Taxi, Taxi*, illustrated by Dale Gottlieb (Little, Brown)

1997 **Juan Felipe Herrera** for *Calling the Doves/El canto de las palomas* (Children's Book Press)

Orbis Pictus Award

This annual award is given by the National Council of Teachers in English in recognition of outstanding nonfiction writing for young readers. The award-winning titles for the 1990s are presented in Chapter 9 on page 226.

Americas Award

This award is given in recognition of U.S. works of children's fiction, poetry, folklore, or selected nonfiction that authentically and engagingly relate to Latin America, to the Caribbean, or to Latinos in the United States. The award is sponsored by the National

Consortium of Latin American Studies Programs. A list of award-winning books is presented in Chapter 2 on page 45.

Pura Belpe Award

Given every two years by the Association for Library Service for Children and the National Association to Promote Library Services to the Spanish, this award honors Latino writers and illustrators whose literary work for children portrays, affirms, and celebrates the Latino cultural experience. The first awards, given in 1996, were selected from books published between 1990 and 1995 and are listed in Chapter 2 on page 45.

And So On . . .

A host of other awards, too numerous to list here, are given to books of distinction and outstanding contributions to the field of children's literature. Some of these awards of special interest to teachers follow:

Children's Choices: a unique award in that the winners are chosen by children rather than by adults; sponsored by the International Reading Association and the Children's Book Council. Winners in different categories—beginning readers, young readers, intermediate readers, and advanced readers—are announced every year in the October issue of *The Reading Teacher.*

The International Reading Association's Children's Book Award: This award is given each year to an author of a first or second book whose work shows unusual promise.

Carter G. Woodson Award: Named after the eminent African-American historian and educator, this award is sponsored by the National Council for the Social Studies to "encourage the writing, publishing, and dissemination of outstanding social studies books for young readers which treat topics related to ethnic minorities and race relations sensitively and accurately." The award is given to nonfiction books with a U.S. setting and focus on ethnicity.

The Phoenix Award: This award is for the author of a book first published twenty years earlier for work that did not receive a major book award.

The Edgar Allan Poe Award: This award is given by the Mystery Writers of America for the best juvenile mystery of the year.

***The New York Times* Best Illustrated Children's Books of the Year:** This award is given to ten books annually.

Most state or regional children's literature and/or professional reading organizations designate children's books for awards in various categories.

INTERNATIONAL BOOK AWARDS

In addition to the Mildred L. Batchelder Award, a number of international awards are given to books and authors of literature for children and young adults. Some of these follow:

The Hans Christian Andersen Prize: the first international children's book award, established in 1956 to honor an illustrator and an author from different countries

The Amelia Frances Howard-Gibbon Medal: awarded only to Canadian citizens, for the most distinguished illustrations in a children's book published in Canada

The Canadian Children's Book of the Year Award: given to the author of a children's book of outstanding literary merit published in Canada and, since 1954, also to the author of a children's book published in French

The Kate Greenaway Medal: given to the illustrator of the most distinguished work in illustration published in the United Kingdom, named in honor of the nineteenth-century British illustrator

The Carnegie Medal: awarded to the most outstanding children's book published in the United Kingdom, sponsored by the British Library Association

The Australian Children's Book of the Year Awards: sponsored by the Australian Children's Book Council, three awards given to the best illustrated book, the best book for younger readers (i.e., a book that bridges the gap between picture books and longer novels), and the best book for older readers

The Russell Clark Award for Illustrations and The Esther Glen Award: the former given for distinguished illustrations and the latter given for distinguished contributions to children's literature published in New Zealand

The Mother Goose Award: given each year to the most exciting newcomer to the field of illustration of children's books in Great Britain

The number of international, national, regional, state, and local awards grows every year as works of quality in children's literature come to be more highly valued. An extensive list of these awards, with descriptions of the awards, and a list of award-winning titles and people is published each year in *Children's Books in Print* (Bowker).

APPENDIX B

SOURCES OF INFORMATION ABOUT GOOD BOOKS

Choosing just the right book for the appropriate purpose is a challenge for parents, teachers, librarians, and others concerned with children's literature. Where does one find out about the thousands of children's books that are published annually? Here are some useful reference sources that provide information:

A to Zoo: Subject Access to Children's Picture Books   by Carolyn W. Lima and John A. Lima
an incredibly comprehensive guide, which lists picture books by topics from aardvarks to Zuni Indians, updated regularly (Bowker, 1998).

Best Books for Children Preschool Through Grade 6 (6th ed.)   by John T. Gillespie
over 17,600 titles of children's books listed, all briefly annotated and classified by topics (Bowker, 1998).

Adventuring with Books: A Booklist for Pre-K–Grade 6   edited by Wendy Sutton
a very useful and comprehensive guide updated regularly and annotated by genre (NCTE).

More Books Kids Will Sit Still for: A Read-Aloud Guide   by Judy Freeman
a reference guide to great books for reading aloud, classified by genre with useful annotations (Bowker, 1995).

Multicultural Resources for Young Readers   edited by Daphne Muse
highly informative annotations of children's literature related to many different cultural groups and issues (The New Press, 1997).

Kaleidoscope: A Multicultural Booklist for Grades K–8   edited by Rosalinda Barrera, Verlkinda D. Thompson, and Mark Dressman
an annotated bibliography of over 500 works of fiction and nonfiction by or about African Americans, Asian Americans, Hispanic Americans, and Native Americans (NCTE, 1998).

Connecting Cultures: A Guide to Multicultural Literature for Children by Rebecca L. Thomas
includes books from preschool to high school with classification by subject, title, index, and illustrator (Bowker, 1996).

Our Family, Our Friends, Our World: An Annotated Guide to Significant Multicultural Books for Children and Teenagers   by Lynn Miller-Lachman
a comprehensive guide for learning about cultures and countries around the world (Bowker, 1992).

Portraying Persons with Disabilities   by Joan B. Friedberg, June B. Mullins, and Adelaide Weir Sukiennik
a bibliography of nonfiction books for children and teenagers that gives a fairly detailed annotation for books appropriate from the early grades through high school (a similar volume is available for fiction) (Bowker, 1992).

***The New York Times* Parent's Guide to the Best Books for Children**   by Eden Ross Lipson
an extensive guide with paragraph-length annotations on different types of literature (Times Books, 1991).

***The Horn Book* Guide to Children's and Young Adult Books**
published twice a year, with annotations by the highly respected editorial staff of The Horn Book Magazine *(The Horn Book, 1998).*

Great Books for Girls: More Than 600 Books to Inspire Today's Girls and Tomorrow's Women and **Great Books for Boys: More Than 600 Books for Boys 2 to 14**
two resource books that do just about what their titles suggest (Ballantine Books, 1997).

Science and Technology in Fact and Fiction   by DayAnn M. Kennedy, Stella S. Spangler, and Mary Ann Vanderweif
contains annotated references of fiction and nonfiction books (Bowker, 1990).

From Biography to History   edited by Catherine Barry
contains an annotated list of biographies about people ranging from Abigail Adams to Mildred (Babe Didrickson) Zaharias, with recommendations for related titles (Bowker, 1998).

The Reading Rainbow Guide to Children's Books: The 101 Best Titles   by Twila C. Liggett and Cynthia Mayer
lists of books from the popular PBS television series (Citadel, 1994).

Notable Children's Books and Best Books for Young Adults
pamphlets published annually, listing outstanding books for children and young adults (American Library Association, 1998).

These titles are only a sample of references and guides available to assist parents, teachers, and others in choosing and using books for children. One can find annotated guides to books that help children cope with separation and loss, annotated bibliographies for children's books on the environment, guides to fantasy children's literature, lists of books for children about mathematics, books on humorous topics, children's literature related to music, children's books about war and peace, guides to wordless books and guides on many, many more topics.

Magazines and journals such as the following, regularly feature reviews of children's books:

School Library Journal
publishes in the December issue the annual list of best books reviewed in the journal during the year

The Horn Book Magazine
contains articles about children's authors and reviews of books, published six times a year

Book Links
contains highly informative concise articles and thematic bibliographies, published six times a year

The Lion and the Unicorn
a more scholarly treatment of topics, with lengthy analysis of books, published twice a year by Johns Hopkins University

The New Advocate
a quarterly devoted entirely to children's literature, with fine articles and excellent book reviews

The Reading Teacher (International Reading Association) **and Language Arts** (National Council of Teachers of English)
professional journals that contain reviews of children's books in each issue

The WEB (Wonderfully Exciting Books)
published by the Center for Language, Literature, and Reading at Ohio State University, features articles about children's books and how to use them

With the growing popularity of children's literature, many newspapers make reviews of trade books for children a regular feature of their book review or education sections.

Recommended lists can be found all over the World Wide Web. See Chapter 12 and Appendix C for a list of Web sites.

APPENDIX C

SOURCES OF INFORMATION ABOUT CHILDREN'S AUTHORS

For those interested in planning author studies in the classroom and in finding out more information about children's authors, the following reference sources are available:

Children's Books and Their Creators   edited by Anita Silvey (Houghton Mifflin, 1995)
encyclopedic compendium of information about authors and other topics in the field of children's literature

Pauses: Autobiographical Reflections of 101 Creators of Children's Books by Lee Bennett Hopkins (Harper Collins, 1995)
a book of sketches of well-known authors, illustrators, and poets, compiled by one of the first authors who profiled authors for children in Books Are by People *(Citation, 1969) and* More Books by More People *(Citation, 1974)*

Once Upon a Time: An Encyclopedia for Successfully Using Children's Literature with Young Children (DLM, 1990) and **Long Ago and Far Away: An Encyclopedia for Successfully Using Children's Literature with Young Children** (DLM, 1991)   by Carol Otis Hurst
one-page biographical sketches of authors, along with practical teaching suggestions for using their books

Meet the Authors and Illustrators: 60 Creators of Favorite Children's Books Talk About Their Work, Vol. I (1991) **and Vol. II** (1993)   by Deborah Kovacs and James Preller (Scholastic)
sixty informative biographical sketches of creators of picture books and novels for young readers

The Seventh Book of Junior Authors and Illustrators   edited by Sally Holmes Holtz (H. W. Wilson Co., 1996)
a series with very valuable information on contemporary children's authors

Something About the Author   by Ann Commaire (Gale Research)
over eighty volumes in print, informational essays on contemporary authors and illustrators (additional volumes appear regularly)

Many writers have provided detailed information about their own lives in autobiographies written for children, samples of which are presented in Chapter 10. These books offer insights that no other source of information could possibly contain.

Professional journals and magazines such as *Language Arts*, *The Horn Book Magazine*, and *The New Advocate* regularly feature profiles of authors of children's books.

The Internet abounds with Web sites containing up-to-the-minute information about writers and illustrators of children's books:

Index to Internet Sites: Children's and Young Adult Authors and Illustrators
http://falcon.jmu.edu/~ramseyil/biochildhome.htm

Yahoo's Directory of Children's Authors
http://dir.yahoo.com/arts/humanities/literature/genres/children_s/authors

Authors and Illustrators on the Web (includes links to individual author Web sites)
http://www.acs.ucalgary.ca/~dkborwn/authors.html

The Author Corner
http://ccpl.carr.lib.md.us/authco/

A Celebration of Women Writers
http://www.cs.cmu.edu/people/mmbt./women/writers.html

Children's Author Directory
http://www.inkspot.com/author/directory.html

Children's Authors Websites
http://www.park-ridge.il.us/library/cdauthors.html

GaleNet
http://www.galenet.gale.com/

Links to collections of author and illustrator pages on the Web often change rapidly, so it is a good idea to visit these sites occasionally to check for the addition of new information.

Via the Internet, some authors can be contacted directly through their own Web pages. Some occasionally respond! These Web pages may be set up by the author him- or herself or by fans and others interested in the author's work. Here is a small sample of the Web pages of some popular authors and illustrators of children's literature:

Judy Blume
http://www.judyblume.com/home.html

Jan Brett
http://www.janbrett.com

Eric Carle (official Web site)
http://www.eric-carle.com/

Virginia Hamilton
http://www.virginiahamilton.com/

Roald Dahl
http://www.nd.edu/~khoward1/Roald.html

Jean Craighead George
http://www.jeancraigheadgeorge.com/

Maurice Sendak
http://falcom.jmu.edu/~ramseyil/sendak.htm

Chris Van Allsburg
http://www.eduplace.com/rdg/author/cva/index.html

Publishers of children's books also provide direct and easy access to biographical and other information about their authors and illustrators. While these sites may contain interesting and valuable information for children, they are typically designed to promote the sale of books.

Finally, videos can be fruitful sources of information about authors. Here are some interesting videos that can be used as part of author studies:

Sendak
although a little dated, an interview with Sendak that gives the viewer insight into the author's genius (Weston Woods, 1986)

A Visit with Jerry Pinkney
featuring the illustrator talking about the research that goes into his illustrations (Penguin, 1995)

A Visit with Lloyd Alexander
in which the author turns reality into fantasy (Penguin, 1994)

Eric Carle: Picture Writer
in which Carle demonstrates the special technique he uses to produce the delightful books that he writes and illustrates (Philomel/Scholastic, 1993)

Other videos enable children to "visit" with and learn about their favorite authors.

APPENDIX D

PUBLISHERS AND THEIR ADDRESSES

Following is a list of the addresses of the publishers of the children's and young adult books cited in this text. Publishing companies merge and addresses change all the time, so for more up-to-date information, consult the most current edition of *Children's Books in Print*.

Alyson Publishing, Inc.
see Liberation Publications, Inc.
Web site: *www.alyson.com*

Atheneum Publishers
see Simon and Schuster

Avon Books
1350 Avenue of the Americas, New York, NY 10019
Tel: 800-223-6834
Web site: *http://avonbooks.com*

Bantam Doubleday Dell
1540 Broadway, New York, NY 10019
Tel.: 800-223-6834
Web site: *www.bdd.com*

Boyds Mills Press
815 Church St., Honesdale, PA 18431
Tel.: 800-949-7777

Bradbury Press
See Simon and Schuster

Candlewick Press
2067 Massachusetts Ave., Cambridge MA 02140
Tel.: 617-661-3330

Carolrhoda Books, Inc.
241 First Avenue North, Minneapolis, MN 55401

Charlesbridge Publishing, Inc.
85 Main St., Watertown, MA 02172
Tel.: 800-225-3214
Web site: *www.charlesbridge.com*

Chatto & Windus
see Trafalgar Square

Children's Book Press
246 First St. Suite 101, San Francisco, CA 94105
Tel.: 800-788-3123
E-mail: *cbookpress@lgc.apc.org*

Clarion Books
215 Park Ave., New York, NY 10003
Tel.: 212-420-5800

Coward-McCann
see Putnam Publishing Group, The

Crocodile Books
see Interlink Publishing Group, Inc.

Thomas Y. Crowell
see HarperCollins

Crown Publishers
see Knopf

Delacorte Press
see Bantam Doubleday Dell

Dell Publishing
see Bantam Doubleday Dell

Dial
see Penguin USA

DK Publishing, Inc. (formerly Dorling Kindersley Publishing, Inc.)
95 Madison Ave., 10th floor, New York, NY 10016
Tel.: 212-213-4800
Web site: *http://www.dk.com*

Doubleday
see Bantam Doubleday Dell

Dover Publications, Inc.
31 E. Second St., Mineola, NY 11501
Tel.: 800-223-3130

Dutton Children's Books
see Penguin USA

Farrar, Straus and Giroux, Inc.
see VHPS

Firefly Books, Ltd.
P.O. Box 1338, Ellicott Station, Buffalo, NY 14205
Tel.: 800-387-5085

Follett Educational Services
5563 Archer Ave., Chicago, IL 60638-3098
Tel.: 800-621-4272
Web site: *www.fes.follett.com*

Four Winds Press
see Simon and Schuster

Front Street Books, Inc.
20 Battery Park Ave., Asheville, NC 28801-2734
Tel.: 828-236-3097
Web site: *www.frontstreetbooks.com*

Fulcrum Publishing
350 Indiana St., Suite 350, Golden, CO 80401
Tel.: 800-992-2908
Web site: *www.fulcrum-books.com*

Golden Books
10101 Science Dr., Sturtevent, Wisconsin 53177
Tel.: 800-558-3291
Web site: *www.goldenbooks.com*

Greenwillow Books
1350 Avenue of the Americas, New York, NY 10019
Tel.: 800-631-1199
Web site: *www.williammorrow.com*

Hamilton, Hamish
see Penguin

Hammond Inc.
515 Valley St., Maplewood, NJ 07040
Tel.: 800-526-4953
Web site: *www.Hammondmap.com*

Hampton Brown Co., Inc.
26385 Carmel Rancho Blvd., Carmel, CA 93923
Tel.: 800-933-3510
Web site: *www.hampton-brown.com*

Harcourt Brace Children's Books
525 B St., Suite 1900, San Diego, CA 92101-4495
Tel.: 800-831-7799
Web site: *www.ideallibrary.com*

HarperCollins Children's Books
10 East 53rd St., New York, NY 10022
Tel.: 800-242-7737
Web site: *http://www.harpercollins.com*

Harper Trophy Paperbacks
see HarperCollins

Heinemann
88 Post Rd. N., P.O. Box 5007, Westport, CT 06881-5007
Tel.: 800-541-2086
Web site: *www.heinemann.com*

Henry Holt and Company, Inc.
115 W. 18th St., New York, NY 10011
Tel.: 800-488-5233
Web site: *www.henryholt.com*

Holiday House
425 Madison Ave., New York, NY 10017
Tel.: 212-688-0085

Houghton Mifflin
222 Berkley St., Boston, MA 02116-3764
Tel.: 617-351-5000
Web site: *www.hmco.com*

Hyperion Books
114 Fifth Ave., New York, NY 10011
Tel.: 212-633-4400
Web site: *www.disney.com*

Interlink Publishing Group, Inc.
99 7th Ave., Brooklyn, NY 11215
Tel.: 800-238-5465
Web site: *www.interlinkbooks.com*

Kane Miller Book Publishers
P.O. Box 310529, Brooklyn, NY 11231-0529
Tel.: 718-624-5120
Web site: *www.kanemiller.com*

Kids Can Press
distributed by General Distribution Services, Inc., 85 River Rock Dr., Suite
202, Buffalo, NY 14207-2170
Tel.: 800-805-1083
Web site: *www.genpub.com*

Alfred A. Knopf
see Random House

Lee & Low Books, Inc.
95 Madison Ave., Room 606, New York, NY 10016
Tel.: 212-779-4400
Web site: *www.leeandlow.com*

Lerner Publications Co.
241 First Ave. N., Minneapolis, MN 55401
Tel.: 800-328-4929
Web site: *www.lernerbooks.com*

Liberation Publications, Inc.
6922 Hollywood Blvd., 10th floor, Los Angeles, CA 90028
Tel.: 323-871-1225

Linnet Professional Publications
see Shoe String Press, Inc.

Little, Brown & Co.
3 Center Plaza, Boston, MA 02108-2084
Tel.: 800-759-0190
Web site: *www.littlebrown.com*

Lodestar Publishing
375 Hudson St., New York, NY 10014

Lothrop, Lee, Shepard Books
see William Morrow

Macmillan Publishing Co.
see Simon and Schuster

Messner, Julian
see Silver Burdett Publishers

Mondo Publishing
One Plaza Rd., Greenvale, NY 11548
Tel.: 800-242-3650
Web site: *www.mondopub.com*

Morrow Junior Books
see William Morrow

William Morrow & Co., Inc.
1350 Avenue of the Americas, New York, NY 10019
Tel.: 800-843-9389
Web site: *www.williammorrow.com*

National Geographic Society
1145 17th St. NW, Washington, DC 20036
Tel.: 800-638-4077
Web site: *www.nationalgeographicsociety.com*

O'Brien Press, Ltd., The
20 Victoria Road, Rathgar, Dublin, Ireland

Orchard Books
see Franklin Watts

Oxford University Press
198 Madison Ave., New York, NY 10016-4314
Tel.: 212-726-6000
Web site: *http://www.oup-usa.org*

Penguin Putnam, Inc.
375 Hudson St., New York, NY 10014
Tel.: 212-366-2000
Web site: *http://www.penguinputnam.com*

Philomel Books
see Putnam

Pocket Books
see Simon and Schuster

Prentice Hall
division of Simon and Schuster, Customer Service, P.O. Box 11075, Des
Moines, IA 50336-1075
Tel.: 800-282-0693
Web site: *www.prenhall.com*

Puffin Books
see Penguin USA

G. P. Putnam's Sons
see Putnam Publishing Group, The

Putnam Publishing Group, The
see Penguin Putnam, Inc.

Raintree Steck-Vaughn Publishing
see Steck-Vaughn Co.

Random House
201 E. 50th St., New York, NY 10022
Tel.: 800-726-0600
Web site: *http://www.randomhouse.com*

Scholastic, Inc.
555 Broadway, New York, NY 10012
Tel.: 212-343-6100
Web site: *http://www.scholastic.com*

Charles Scribner's Sons
see Simon and Schuster

Shoe String Press, Inc.
P.O. Box 657, 2 Linsley St., North Haven, CT 06473-2517
Tel.: 203-239-2702
E-mail: *sspbooks@aol.com*

Shortland Publications
360 Dominion Road, Mt. Eden, Auckland, New Zealand

Simon & Schuster Books for Young Readers
see Simon & Schuster Children's

Simon & Schuster Children's
see Simon & Schuster

Simon & Schuster
1230 Avenue of the Americas, New York, NY 10020
Tel.: 800-223-2348
Web site: *www.simonsays.com*

Steck-Vaughn Co.
Box 26015, Austin, TX 78755
Tel.: 800-531-5015
Web site: *http://www.steck-vaughn.com*

Sterling Publishing Co., Inc.
387 Park Ave. S., 5th floor, New York, NY 10016-8810
Tel.: 800-367-9692
Web site: *www.sterlingpub.com*

Steward, Tabori & Chang
115 W. 18th St., 5th floor, New York, NY 10011
Tel.: 212-519-1200

Tambourine Books
see William Morrow & Co., Inc.

Trafalgar Square
P.O. Box 257, Howe Hill Rd., North Pomfret, VT 05053
Tel.: 800-457-1911
E-mail: *tsquare@sover.net*

VHPS
4419 West 1980, Salt Lake City, UT 84104
Tel.: 888-330-8477

Vanguard Foundation
6900 Newman Rd., Clifton, VA 20124-1613
Tel.: 703-803-3728
E-mail: *wmcommsfdn@aol.com*

Viking
see Penguin Putnam, Inc.

Walker & Co.
435 Hudson St., New York, NY 10014
Tel.: 800-AT-WALKER

Walter Wetherhill
568 Broadway, Suite 705, New York, NY 10012
Tel.: 212-966-3080
Web site: *www.wetherhill.com*

Frederick Warner & Co., Inc.
see Penguin Putnam, Inc.

Franklin Watts, Inc.
A Grolier Company, 90 Sherman Turnpike, Danbury, CT 06816
Tel.: 203-797-3500
Web site: *http://publishing.grolier.com*

Albert Whitman & Co.
6340 Oakton St., Morton Grove, IL 60053-2723
Tel.:800-255-7675
Web site: *www.awhitmanco.com*

Yearling Books
see Bantam Doubleday Dell Books for Young Readers

CREDITS

Chapter 1

Reprinted by permission of Paul Fleischman. p. 12. *Publishers Weekly*, February 5, 1996. Reprinted by permission of Publishers Weekly. pp. 8-10. Reprinted by permission of Julia Lowd. p. 12. Reprinted by permission of Monique Lowd. p. 23. Reprinted by permission of Kim Keller. p. 15.

Chapter 2

Reprinted by permission of Marilyn Cochran-Smith. p. 52.

Chapter 3

Reprinted by permission of Maureen E. Kenny. p. 75.

Chapter 4

Reprinted by permission of Amy Seldin. p. 103.

Chapter 5

Reprinted by permission of Audrey Friedman. p. 127.

Chapter 6

Reprinted by permission of Bonnie Rudner. p. 136.

Chapter 7

Reprinted by permission of Pamela O'Day. p. 166.

Chapter 8

Reprinted by permission of Ann Caramola. p. 201.

Chapter 9

Reprinted by permission of Kathleen Tower. p. 226.

Chapter 10

Reprinted by permission of *The New Advocate*. p. 247.

Chapter 11

Reprinted by permission of Harold Ober Associates Incorporated. Copyright 1957 by Eleanor Farjeon. p. 254. Reprinted by permission of Elizabeth Gonsalves. p. 271.

Chapter 12

Reprinted by permission of Robin Fitzgerald and Mary Carr. p. 294.

Chapter 13

Reprinted by permission of Pamela G. Amster. p. 315.

CREDITS

Color Inserts

Insert A   From *Millions Of Cats* by Wanda Gag. Copyright 1928 by Wanda Gag, renewed © 1956 by Robert Janssen. Used by permission of Coward-McCann, Inc., a division of Penguin Putnam Inc. p. 1; From *Little Black Sambo* by Helen Bannerman. Reproduced by permission. From *Sam And The Tigers* by Julius Lester, illustrated by Jerry Pinkney. Copyright © 1996 by Jerry Pinkney, art. Used by permission of Dial Books for Young Readers, a division of Penguin Putnam Inc. p. 2, top; From *The Snowy Day* by Ezra Jack Keats. Copyright © 1962 by Ezra Jack Keats, renewed © 1990 by Martin Pope, Executor. Used by permission of Viking Penguin, a division of Penguin Putnam Inc. p. 3, top; Reprinted with the permission of Atheneum Books for Young Readers, an imprint of Simon & Schuster Children's Publishing Division from *Ma Dear's Aprons* by Patricia C. McKissack, illustrated by Floyd Cooper. Illustrations copyright © 1997 Floyd Cooper. p. 3, bottom; From *Snapshots From The Wedding* by Gary Soto, illustrated by Stephanie Garcia. Copyright © 1997 by Stephanie Garcia. Used by permission of G.P. Putnam's Sons, a division of Penguin Putnam Inc. p. 4, top; Illustration from *Grandfather's Journey* by Allen Say. Copyright (c) 1993 by Allen Say. Reprinted by permission of Houghton Mifflin Company. All rights reserved.

Insert B: From *Rapunzel* by Paul O. Zelinsky. Copyright © 1967 by Paul O. Zelinsky. Used by permission of Dutton Children's Books, a division of Penguin Putnam Inc. p. 1, top; From *The Mitten* by Jan Brett. Copyright © 1989 by Jan Brett. Used by permission of G.P. Putnam's Sons, a division of Penguin Putnam Inc. p. 1, middle; From *Tar Beach* by Faith Ringgold. Copyright © 1991 by Faith Ringgold. Reprinted by permission of Crown Publishers, Inc. p. 1, bottom; From *Make Way For Ducklings* by Robert McCloskey. Copyright 1941, renewed © 1969 by Robert McCloskey. Used by permission of Viking Penguin, a division of Penguin Putnam Inc. p.2, top; From *And To Think That I Saw It On Mulberry Street* by Dr. Seuss. Trademark and copyright © 1937 and renewed 1964 by Dr. Seuss Enterprises, L.P. Reprinted by permission of Random House, Inc. p. 2, bottom; From *Miss Spider's Tea Party* by David Kirk. Copyright © 1994 by Callaway Editions, Inc. Reprinted by permission of Scholastic Inc. p. 3, top; From *Very Hungry Caterpillar* by Eric Carle. Copyright © 1969 by Eric Carle. Used by permission of Philomel Books, a division of Penguin Putnam Inc. p. 3, middle; From *The Leaf Men* by William Joyce. Copyright © 1996 by William Joyce. Used by permission of HarperCollins Publishers. p. 3, bottom; Illustration from *The Polar Express*. Copyright (c) 1985 by Chris Van Allsburg. Reprinted by permission of Houghton Mifflin Co. All rights reserved. p. 4, top; Illustration from *The Napping House*, text copyright © 1984 by Audrey Wood, illustrations © 1984

by Don Wood, reproduced by permission of Harcourt, Inc. p. 4 bottom; From *Frog Goes To Dinner* by Mercer Mayer. Copyright © 1974 by Mercer Mayer. Used by permission of Dial Books for Young Readers, a division of Penguin Putnam Inc. p. 5, top; Illustration from *Tuesday*. Copyright © 1991 by David Wiesner. Reprinted by permission of Clarion Books/Houghton Mifflin Co. All rights reserved. p. 5, bottom; Illustration from *Black and White*. Copyright (c) 1990 by David Macaulay. Reprinted by permission of Houghton Mifflin Co. All rights reserved. p. 6, top; From *The Stinky Cheeseman and Other Fairly Stupid Tales* by Jon Scieszka, illustrated by Lane Smith. Copyright © 1992 by John Scieszka, text. Copyright © 1992 by Lane Smith, illustrations. Used by permission of Viking Penguin, a division of Penguin Putnam Inc. p. 6, bottom; Illustration from *Castle*. Copyright (c) 1977 by David Macaulay. Reprinted by permission of Houghton Mifflin Co. All rights reserved. p. 7, top; From *The Giving Tree* by Shel Silverstein. Copyright © 1964 by Evil Eye Music, Inc. Used by permission of HarperCollins Publishers. p. 7, bottom; From *Anansi the Spider* adapted and illustrated by Gerald McDermott, © 1972 by Landmark Production, Incorporated. Reprinted by permission of Henry Holt and Company, Inc. p. 8, top; From *Why Mosquitoes Buzz In People's Ears* by Verna Aardema, pictures by Leo and Diane Dillon. Copyright © 1975 by Leo and Diane Dillon, pictures. Used by permission of Dial Books for Young Readers, a division of Penguin Putnam Inc. p. 8, middle; Reprinted with the permission of Atheneum Books for Young Readers, a imprint of Simon & Schuster Children's Publishing Division from *Shadow* translated and illustrated by Marcia Brown. Copyright © 1982 Marcia Brown. p. 8 bottom.

Insert C   Copyright (c) 1992 by Gail Gibbons. Reprinted from *Sharks* by permission of Holiday House, Inc. p. 1, bottom; Illustrations copyright © 1998 Kazuko G. Stone from the book *Cool Melons - Turn to Frogs*. Permission granted by Lee & Low Books Inc., 95 Madison Avenue, New York, NY 10016. p. 2; Illustration copyright © 1998 by Jan Spivey Gilchrist from *Lemonade Sun and Other Summer Poems* by Rebecca Kai Dotlich. Published by Boyds Mills Press, Inc. Reprinted by permission. p. 3, top; Illustration from *Insectlopedia*, copyright © 1998 by Douglas Florian, reproduced by permission of Harcourt Inc. p. 3, bottom; Reprinted with the permission of Simon & Schuster Books for Young Readers, an imprint of Simon & Schuster Children's Publishing Division from *Mark Twain And The Queens Of The Mississippi* by Cheryl Harness. Copyright © 1998 Cheryl Harness. p. 4, top; Reprinted with the permission of Simon & Schuster Books for Young Readers, an imprint of Simon & Schuster Children's Publishing Division from *Fly, Bessie, Fly* by Lynn Joseph, illustrated by Yvonne Buchanan. Illustrations copyright © 1998 Yvonne Buchanan. p. 4, bottom.

NAME INDEX

Note: Page numbers in **bold** type indicate author profiles; Page numbers in *italics* indicate color plates. Names of authors, illustrators and translators are found in this index; all other names may be found in the subject index.

Aamundsen, Nina Ring, 354
Aardema, Verna, 15, 28, 100, 107, 144, 146, **153–154**, 156, 157, 334, *B.8*
Aarza, Carman Lomas, 45
ABC Bunny, 339
Abel's Island, 346
Abigail Adams: Witness to a Revolution, 228, 351
Abiyoyo, 155, 161, 298
The Abracadabra Kid: A Writer's Life, 245, 250
Abraham Lincoln, 236, 247, 249, 327
Abraham Lincoln, Friend of the People, 342
Abraham Lincoln's World, 341
Abuela, 46, 59
The Accidental Zucchini, 95
Ackerman, Karen, 224, 230, 336
A Collection of Haiku and Tanka, 278
Across America on an Emigrant Train, 226
Across Five Aprils, 197, 205, 344
Across the Lines, 197, 206
Ada, Alma Flor, 38, 46, 59, 146, 157, 165, 183, 271, 277
Adam of the Road, 341
Adams, Adrienne, 331, 332
Adams, Harriet Stratemeyer (Carolyn Keene), 180
Adams, Julia Davis, 338, 339
Adedjourma, Davida, 270
Adler, David A., 175, 183, 240, **241,** 249, 318, 322
Adoff, Arnold, 50, 59, 352
The Adopted One, 69, 81
The Adventures of Huckleberry Finn, 26, 31, 164
The Adventures of Paddy Pork, 349
The Adventures of Sparrow Boy, 351
The Adventures of Tom Sawyer, 164
Aesop, 151, 157
Aesop's Fables, 84, 152, 157
Africa Dream, 43, 266
African-American Scientists, 199
Afternoon of the Elves, 347
After the Rain, 347
Agard, John, 38, 269, 277
The Ageless Story, 327
Ahlberg, Allan, 15, 28, 88, 107, 320, 322
Ahlberg, Janet, 15, 28, 88, 107, 320, 322
Aïda, 44
A Is for Aloha, 38
A Is for Asia, 38
Aitken, Amy, 183
Ajeemah and His Son, 351
Alcorn, Stephen, 270
Alcott, Louisa May, 5, 28, 164
Alder, Elizabeth, 204
Alexander, Lloyd, 115, 124, 131, 344, 345, 351, 365
Alexander, Martha, 92, 107
Alexander, Who Used to Be Rich Last Sunday, 222, 232
Alexander and the Terrible, Horrible, No Good, Very Bad Day, 11, 19–20, 31, 90, 111, 314, 323
Alexander and the Wind-Up Mouse, 333

The Alfred Summer, 73, 81
Alice Ramsey's Great Adventure, 246, 249
Alice's Adventures in Wonderland, 5, 14, 29, 115, 119, 130, 131
Alien Secrets, 126, 132
Aliki, 138, 157, 211, 217, 225, 230, 242, 249
All About Where, 320, 323
All Alone, 343
Allard, Harry, 126, 131
All Around the Town, 329
Allee, Marjorie, 339
Allen, Laura Jen, 121
Allen, Paula Gunn, 249
Allen, Thomas B., 88, 107
All Falling Down, 330
Alligators All Around: An Alphabet Book, 97
All in the Morning Early, 332
Allison, 69, 74, 81, 91
All Sail Set: A Romance of the Flying Cloud, 340
All the Colors of the Earth, 50, 60
Along Came a Dog, 343
Alonso, Juan Ramón, 354
Alphabatics, 335
Alphabestiary, 320, 323
Alphabet City, 337
Alphabet Soup: A Feast of Letters, 95
Alvin Ailey, 242, 251
Always Room for One More, 332
Amazing and Incredible Counting Stories, 96
The Amazing Bone, 334
Amazing Grace, 19, 30
Amelia Bedelia, 119
America is Born, 343
America Moves Forward, 344
An American Hero: The True Story of Charles A. Lindbergh, 244
Americans Before Columbus, 342
America's Ethan Allen, 329
The Amethyst Ring, 191, 196
Amigo, 36, 59
Amos Fortune, Free Man, 236, 252, 342
An American ABC, 328
An American Hero: The True Story of Charles A. Lindbergh, 250
Anansi and the Talking Melon, 144, 159
Anansi Does the Impossible: An Ashanti Tale, 146, 157
Anansi Finds a Fool, 154
Anansi the Spider: A Tale from the Ashanti, 88, 109, 145, 333, *B.8*
Anastasia Krupnik, 170, 185, 275, 278
Anastasia on Her Own, 171, 185
Anatole, 331
Anatole and the Cat, 331
Ancona, George, 67, 79
Andersen, Hans Christian, 5, 114, 122, 131, 137, 147, 157, 158, 330

Anderson, David A., 44, 224, 230
And If the Moon Could Talk, 86, 109, 351
And Now Miguel, 343
Andreasen, Dan, 223
Andrews, Benny, 89, 108
Androcles and the Lion, 152, 160
And the Green Grass Grew All Around, 257, 263, 278
And Then What Happened, Paul Revere?, 237, 242–243, 250
And To Think That I Saw It on Mulberry Street, 3, B.1
*Andy and the Lion: A Tale of Kindness Remembered or the Power of
      Gratitude*, 327
Angela's Ashes, 284
Angel Child, Dragon Child, 48, 56–57, 61, 178, 186
Angelo, Valenti, 340
Angelou, Maya, 217, 230
Anglund, Joan W., 260
The Angry Moon, 333
The Animal, the Vegetable, and John D. Jones, 69, 71, 80, 171, 184
The Animal Family, 344
Animalia, 95
Animals of the Bible, 327
An Mei's Strange and Wondrous Journey, 69, 81
Anna in Charge, 52, 61
Anne Frank, Beyond the Diary: A Photographic Remembrance, 354
Anne Frank: The Diary of a Young Girl, 244
Anne of Green Gables, 24, 30
Annie and the Old One, 66, 77, 81, 179, 185, 345
Anno, Mitsumasa, 93, 94, 96, 349
Anno's Alphabet, 94, 349
Anno's Counting Book, 96
Anno's Journey, 93, 349
A. Nonny Mouse Writes Again!: Poems, 262
Anpao: An American Indian Odyssey, 346
Anthony Burns: The Defeat and Triumph of a Fugitive Slave, 350
Antics! An Alphabet Anthology, 94, 108
Ant Plays Bear, 71
The Apaches, 49
Ape in a Cape: An Alphabet of Odd Animals, 330
Appalachia: The Voices of Sleeping Birds, 351
Apple, Margot, 31, 131
The Apple and the Arrow, 342
Appleton, Victor, 115
The Apprentice, 354
Apprentice of Florence, 339
April's Kittens, 328
The Arabookies of Liberty Street, 315
Archambault, John, 73, 81, 94, 109, 287, 299
Are You There, God? It's Me, Margaret, 7, 9, 27, 29, 164, 168, 183,
      318, 323
Armadillo Rodeo, 283
Armageddon Summer, 22, 31, 306
Armer, Laura Adams, 327, 339
Armstrong, Jennifer, 197, 204
Armstrong, William H., 10, 21, 28, 345
Arnold, Tedd, 260
The Arrow over the Door, 200, 204
Arrow to the Sun: A Pueblo Indian Tale, 88, 109, 145, 156, 160, 333
Arroyo, Imna, 60
Arroz con Leche: Popular Songs and Rhymes from Latin America, 270, 277
Arthur, High King of Britain, 152, 160
Arthur, Malcolm, 336
Arthur's Teacher Trouble, 288
Artzybasheff, Boris, 327
Asafe, Meshack, 159
Ashanti to Zulu: African Traditions, 39, 94, 109, 334

Ashby, Gil, 250
As Long as the Rivers Flow: The Stories of Nine Native Americans,
      243, 249
As the Crow Flies, 68, 77, 81
Atomics for the Millions, 97
The A to Z Beastly Jamboree, 94
A to Zen, 39
Atwater, Florence, 321, 323, 340
Atwater, Richard, 321, 323, 340
Auch, Herm, 59
Auch, Mary Jane, 51, 59
Audubon, 340
August, Louise, 150
Auks, Rocks, and the Odd Dinosaur, 350
Aunt Flossie's Hats (and Crab Cakes Later), 38, 60
Aunt Harriet's Underground Railroad in the Sky, 85
The Aunt in Our House, 165
Avalanche, 95, 110
Avi, 192, 196, 204, 347, 351
The Avion My Uncle Flew, 341
Awan, Sheila, 221
The Awful Aardvarks Go To School, 95, 109
Awmiller, Craig, 224, 230
Aylesworth, Jim, 149, 158
Azarian, Mary, 232, 250, 337

BAAA, 105
Babbitt, Natalie, 15, 28, 121, 131, 284, 298, 305, 323, 345
Baboushka and the Three Kings, 331
Babuska Baba Yaga, 100, 110
Baby Bear's Bedtime Book, 306
The Baby-Sitter's Club, 24, 179
The Baby Uggs Are Hatching, 262
A Bag of Moonshine, 148
Bahti, Tom, 333
Bailey, Carolyn Sherwin, 341
Bailey, Pearl, 43
Baines, Rae, 242, 249
Baity, Elizabeth, 342
Baker, Leslie, 161
Baker, Olaf, 335
Bald Eagle, 102, 109
Balit, Christina, 323
The Ballad of Lucy Whipple, 194
The Ballad of the Pirate Queens, 263, 279
Bambino the Clown, 329
The Bamboo Flute, 196, 205
Bang, Molly, 96, 334, 335, 350
Banks, Kate, 86, 107, 351
Banks, Lynne Reid, 53, 118, 131
Banner in the Sky, 343
Bannerman, Helen, 39, 40, 59, A.2
Barbour, Karen, 72, 79
Bare, Arnold E., 328
Barkis, 327
Barnes, Nancy, 341
Barnstone, Willis, 268, 279
Barnum, Jay Hyde, 329
Baron, Elisa, 336
Barrett, Judi, 122, 131
Barron, T. A., 123, 131, 152, 158
Bartholomew and the Oobleck, 329
Bartoletti, Susan Campbell, 89, 107, 223

Barton, Jill, 351
Base, Graeme, 95
Baseball in April and Other Stories, 46, 177, 185
Baseball Saved Us, 200, 206
Basho, 268
Baskin, Hosea, 333
Baskin, Leonard, 333
Baskin, Lisa, 333
Baskin, Tobias, 333
Bateman, Teresa, 145, 158
The Battle Horse, 353
Battle-Lavert, Gwendolyn, 41
Bauer, Marion Dane, 347
Baum, Frank, 6, 29, 115, 131
Baumann, Hans, 353
Baumgartner, Barbara, 158
Bayard, Carole, 43
Baylor, Byrd, 20, 29, 36, 59, 333, 334
A Bear Called Paddington, 117, 131
Bear Party, 330
The Bears on Hemlock Mountain, 342
Beat the Story Drum, Pum-Pum, 43
The Beauty of the Beast: Poems from the Animal Kingdom, 262, 264
The Beggar's Ride, 73, 81
Behind Barbed Wire: The Imprisonment of Japanese Americans During World War II, 350
Behind the Secret Window: A Memoir of a Hidden Childhood During World War Two, 244, 252
Behrens, June, 217, 230
Bell, Anthea, 353, 354
Belle Prater's Boy, 348
Belling the Tiger, 344
Belting, Natalia M., 332
Bemelmans, Ludwig, 1, 29, 89, 107, 263, 277, 285, 298, 327, 330, 340
Ben and Me, 236, 250
Bench, Carolyn, 30
Bender, Robert, 94
Benito Juarez, Hero of Modern Mexico, 242, 249
Benjamin, Floella, 271, 277
Bennett, John, 338
Benson, Patrick, 132
Ben's Trumpet, 334
Bent, Jennifer, 38
Beowulf, 154
Berenstain Bears series, 10
Berleth, Richard, 192, 204
Berliotz the Bear, 282
Bernsten, Ruth, 81
Berry, Erik, 339
Berry, James, 351
Best, Carrie, 355
Best, Herbert, 339
The Best Christmas Pageant Ever, 176, 185
Besterman, Catherine, 342
The Best Mother Goose Ever, 260
The Best Word Book Ever, 13, 23, 31
Betrayed, 49
Betsy Tacy series, 24
Better Known as Johnny Appleseed, 342
Between Earth and Sky: Legends of Native American Sacred Places, 49, 59
Beyond the Western Sea, Book One: The Escape from Home, 196, 204
The BFG, 119, 132
Bhimsa, the Dancing Bear, 341
Bianco, Margery, 340
The Bicycle Man, 91

Bidken, Odds, 146, 158
Bierhorst, John, 146, 158, 270, 277
Big Blue Whale, 4, 29
Big Cats, 219
The Biggest Bear, 330
The Big Orange Splot, 315
The Big Rivers: The Missouri, the Mississippi, and the Ohio, 220
The Big Snow, 329
Big Tree, 341
Big Tree of Bunlahy: Stories of My Own Countryside, 339
The Big Wave, 178, 183
Bileck, Marvin, 332
Bill Peet: An Autobiography, 245, 251, 336
Bill Pickett: Rodeo-Ridin' Cowboy, 237, 251
Bingo Brown series, 71
The Bird House, 319
Birnbaum, Abe, 330
Birthdays of Freedom, Vol. 1, 342
Bishop, Claire Hutchet, 341, 343
Black and White, 98, 104, 109, 336, *B.6*
Black Beauty, 176
The Black Cauldron, 344
Black Child, 43
Black Diamond, 199
Black-Eyed Susan, 197, 204
Black Fox of Lorne, 343
Black is Brown Is TAN, 50, 59
The Black Pearl, 191, 344
Black Ships Before Troy: The Story of the Iliad, 154, 161
Black Troubador: Langston Hughes, 43
Blackwood, Gary, 196, 204
Blake, Quentin, 132
Blake, William, 254
Blecher, George, 353, 354
The Bloody Chamber and Other Stories, 138
Blos, Joan, 346
Blubber, 7, 21, 27, 29, 181
The Blue and the Gray, 65
Blueberries for Sal, 329
The Blue Butterfly: A Story About Claude Monet, 240, 250
The Blue Cat of Castle Town, 342
A Blue-Eyed Daisy, 319
The Blue Hill Meadows, 319
Blue Sword, 346
Blue Willow, 340
Blumberg, Rhoda, 230, 240, 249, 347, 350
Blume, Judy, 2, **6–7,** 9, 10, 21, 27, 29, 164, 166, 168, 170, 171, 177, 181, 182, 183, 295–296, 317, 318, 323, 364
Boats on the River, 329
The Bobbin Girl, 197, 205
Bober, Natalie S., 228, 351
Bobo's Dream, 92, 107
Bödker, Cecil, 353
The Boggart, 121
The Bomb, 189
Bond, Felicia, 230
Bond, Michael, 117, 131
Bond, Nancy, 346
Bone Button Borscht, 143, 158
Bones: Our Skeletal System, 219
Bonsall, Crosby, 11, 29
Bontemps, Arna, 342
Book of Nursery and Mother Goose Rhymes, 330
A Book of Pigericks, 267, 278
The Book of Three, 115, 124, 131

"Boots," 255
BoRabbit Smart for True: Folktales from the Gullah, 148
Borden, Louise, 88, 107
Bored–Nothing to Do!, 122, 133
Borreguita and the Coyote, 153
The Borrowers, 120, 132
Bortz, Alfred B., 221, 230
Bosse, Malcolm, 174, 183
"Bound for Discovery," 12
Bowen, Gary, 196, 204
Bowen, William, 338
Bowman, James Cloyd, 340
Boy: Tales of Childhood, 120
Boy of the South Seas, 339
The Boy of the Three-Year Nap, 61, 91, 146, 161, 336, 350
Boys at Work, 47
The Boys from St. Petri, 354
The Boy Who Cried Wolf, 152, 160
The Boy Who Was, 338
Boy with a Pack, 340
The Bracelet, 57, 61, 191, 199, 206
Bragomer, Reginald, Jr., 218, 230
The Brain, 219
Branley, Franklin M., 211, 229, 230, 316, 323
Bray, Rosemary, 240, 242, 249
Breck, Judith, 73, 79
The Bremen-Town Musicians, 155, 161, 334
Brenner, Barbara, 36, 59, 193, 198, 204
Brenner, Fred, 206
Brett, Jan, 65, 89, 99, 108, 143, 152, 158, 261, 278, **282–283**, 364, *B.2*
Brian's Winter, 173
Bridge to Terabithia, 4, 10, 15, 26, 30, 67, 77, 78, 81, 174, 181, 346
Briggs, Raymond, 349
Bright Island, 340
Bringing the Rain to the Kapiti Plain: A Nandi Tale, 146, 153, 156, 157
Brink, Carol Ryrie, 340
Brittain, Bill, 123, 131, 346
Brockel, Ray, 304
Brodsky, Beverly, 334
The Bronze Bow, 195, 206, 344
The Bronze Cauldron, 153, 160
Brooks, Bruce, 69, 79, 347, 350
Brooks, Polly Schoyer, 239, 249
Brother Eagle, Sister Sky: A Message from Chief Seattle, 270–271, 278
Brown, Don, 246, 249
Brown, Marc, 285, 288
Brown, Marcia, 99, 143, 158, 329, 330, 331, 335, 352, *B.8*
Brown, Margaret Wise, 2, 4, 6, 9, 29, 83, 107, 108, 328, 330
Brown Bear, Brown Bear, What Do You See? 99, 103, 109, 308, 315, 323
Bruchac, Joseph, 39, 49, 59, 147, 200, 204
Brunhoff, Jean de, 23
Bryan, Ashley, 43, 270
Bryson, Bernarda, 332
Bubbles, 266
Buchanan, Yvonne, 158, 298, *C.4*
Buck, Pearl, 178, 183
Buff, Conrad, 328, 341, 342, 343
Buff, Mary, 328, 341, 342, 343
Buffalo Woman, 146, 159
Building: The Fight Against Gravity, 350
Bull, A. B. H., 250
Bull Run, 189, 197, 205
Bummer Summer, 69, 81
Bunnicula, 127, 132
Bunny Hopwell's First Spring, 237

Bunting, Eve, 25, 29, 50, 59, **64–65**, 67, 72, 74, 77, 79, 89, 91, 108, 167, 170, 175, 183, 193, 197, 200, 204, 282, 336
Burger, Carl, 183
Burglon, Nora, 339
Burkert, Nancy Ekholm, 131, 333
Burleigh, Robert, 226
Burnett, Frances Hodgson, 6, 29, 164, 304
Burnford, Sheila, 176, 183
Burningham, John, 349
The Burrow Book: Tunnel into a World of Wildlife, 221
Burton, Virginia Lee, 118, 131, 147, 158, 285, 298, 328, 329
Bury My Bones but Keep My Words: African Tales for Retelling, 146, 159
Buster's World, 354
Butler, David, 110
The Butter Battle Book, 3
Buzz Said the Bee, 14, 30
Byard, Carol, 336
Byars, Betsy, 6, 69, **70–71**, 72, 73, 74, 80, 171, 175, 181, 184, 198, 204, 345
By the Shores of Silver Lake, 340

Caddie Woodlawn, 340
Caduto, Michael J., 147, 158
Caines, Jeannette, 41, 72, 80
Calculator Puzzles, Tricks and Games, 222, 232
Caldecott, Alfred, 151
Caldecott, Randolph, 5, 18, 84, 151, 158, 327, *A.1*
The Caldecott Aesop: Twenty Fables Illustrated by Randolph Caldecott, 151, 158
Calico Bush, 339
Calling on Dragons, 123, 133
Calling the Doves/El canto de las palomas, 355
Call It Courage, 174, 185
The Calypso Alphabet, 38
Cameron, Eleanor, 349
Cam Jensen and the Fourth Floor Twins, 318, 322
Cam Jensen Mysteries, 175, 183
Campbell, Tracey, 109
El canto de las palomas/Calling the Doves, 355
Canto Familiar, 270, 279
Can't You Make Them Behave, King George?, 237
Caps for Sale, 155, 161, 321, 323
The Captive, 191
Cards of Grief, 306
Caribbean Alphabet, 38
Carle, Eric, 6, 9, 14, 29, 87, 89, 95, 97, 108, 109, 152, 158, 216, 245, 249, 285, 316, 320, 323, 364, *B.3*
Carlota, 57, 60, 199, 206
Carl's Christmas, 93
Carlson, Lori M., 270, 277
Carlson, Natalie Savage, 72, 80, 343
Carlstrom, Nancy White, 102, 108
Carol of the Brown King: Poems, 269
Carpenter, Nancy, 41
Carr, Jean, 264
Carr, Mary Jane, 340
Carrick, Donald, 61, 206
Carrol, Kathleen Sullivan, 315
Carroll, Lewis. *See* Dodgson, Charles
The Carrot Seed, 16
Carry on, Mr. Bowditch, 343
Carter, Angela, 137, 138
Carter G. Woodson: The Father of Black History, 199

Caseley, Judith, 67, 80
Casey, Maude, 171, 184
Casey at the Bat, 261, 279
*Cast for a Revolution: Some American Friends and Enemies,
        1728–1814*, 238
Castle, 334
Castles, B.7
The Cat and Mouse Who Shared a House, 353
Cathedral: The Story of Its Construction, 333
Catherine, Called Birdy, 194, 196, 204, 348
The Cat in the Hat, 3, 9, 99, 108
The Cat in the Hat Comes Back, 4
Catling, Patrick S., 123, 131
Catrow, David, 158, 250
Cats, 212
The Cat's Meow, 47
The Cat Who Went to Heaven, 338
Caudill, Rebecca, 332, 342
Cauley, Lorinda B., 159
The Cay, 164, 174, 186
Cedric the Forester, 337
Celsi, Teresa, 318, 323
Cendrars, Blaise, 335
Cepeda, Joe, 47, 61
Cesar Chavez, 242, 249
Chain of Fire, 51, 60, 168, 185
A Chair for My Mother, 68, 74, 77, 81, 89, 91, 111, 167, 170, 186,
        335, 350
Chan, Chih-Yi, 328
Chan, Plato, 328
Chance, Luck and Density, 349
Changes, Changes, 93
Chanticleer and the Fox, 331
Chanukah in Chelm, 241
Charlie and the Chocolate Factory, 119, 132
Charlie and the Great Glass Elevator, 119
Charlip, Remy, 349
Charlot, Jean, 328, 330
Charlotte's Web, 9, 116, 117, 119, 127, 133, 303, 342
Chato's Kitchen, 45, 47, 117, 133
Chaucer, Geoffrey, 331
The Cherokees, 49
Cherries and Cherry Pits, 41
Cherry, Lynne, 225, 230
Chess, Victoria, 161
Chicka Chicka Boom Boom, 94, 109, 287, 288
Chicka Chicka Boom Boom (CD-ROM), 299
Chicken Soup with Rice, 97, 275, 279
Chilcoat, George W., 200, 206
Child of the Owl, 178, 179, 349
Child of the Warsaw Ghetto, 241
The Children of Lir, 143, 160
*Children of the Dust Bowl: the True Story of the School at Weedpatch
        Camp*, 226
Children of the Long House, 200, 204
Children of the River, 48, 59, 178, 184
Children of the Soil: A Story of Scandinavia, 339
*The Children of Topaz: The Story of a Japanese Internment Camp Based on a
        Classroom Diary*, 200, 206
The Children's Bells, 265, 277
Children's Books from Other Countries, 51
A Child's Garden of Verse, 5, 31, 264, 265, 279
A Child's Good Night Book, 328
Chills in the Night: Tales That Will Haunt You, 121
Chilly Stomach, 72, 80

China Homecoming, 245, 250
Chinatown, 48, 60
The Chinese Americans, 218, 232
Chinese Mother Goose Rhymes, 270, 279
Chin-La, Cynthia, 38
El Chino, 91, 242, 251
Chitty Chitty Bang Bang, 120
Chocolate, Deborah, 217, 230
The Chocolate Touch, 123, 131
Choi, Sook Nyul, 48, 59, 196, 204
Choi, Yansook, 60
*Chorus of Cultures Poetry Anthology: Developing Literacy Through
        Multicultural Poetry*, 271, 277
Chrisman, Arthur Bowie, 338
Christelow, Eileen, 11, 29, 320, 323
Christiansen, C. B., 68, 80
Christie, Gregory, 270
The Christmas Anna Angel, 328
Christmas in the Big House, Christmas in the Quarters, 44, 199, 229, 232
Christopher, Henry, 239, 249
Christopher, Matt, 176, 184
The Chronicles of Narnia, 24, 124, 139
Chucaro: Wild Pony of the Pampa, 343
Ciardi, John, 6, 254, 257, 267, 277, 352
El Cid, 154
Cinder Edna, 142, 159
Cinderella, 86, 114, 120, 285
"Cinderella," 14, 26, 99, 136, 149
Cinderella, or the Little Glass Slipper, 330
Cinderella: The Original Fairy Tale, 288
Circles, Triangles, and Squares, 216
The Circuit: Stories from the Life of a Migrant Child, 45, 351
The Civil Rights Movement in America from 1865 to the Present, 217, 232
Civil War, 223
Clancy's Coat, 65
Clapp, Patricia, 196, 204
Clark, Ann Nolan, 328, 342
Clarke, Margaret Courtney, 230
Clarke, Pauline, 274
Clearing Weather, 338
Cleary, Beverly, 6, 64, 68, 74, 80, 94, 118, 127, 131, 168, 170, 171, 175,
        184, 245, 249, 304, 317, 346, 352
Cleaver, Bill, 172, 184
Cleaver, Vera, 172, 184
Clemens, Samuel (Mark Twain), 5, 26, 31, 164
Clement, Cameron, 221
Clementine, 71
Cleopatra, 239, 249, 252
Clever Tom and the Leprechaun, 145, 161
Click, 213
Clifford, Judy, 79
Clifton, Lucille, 43, 66, 80
Climo, Shirley, 48, 59, 141, 150, 158
Clinton, Catherine, 270
Clinton, Susan Maloney, 242, 249
Clocks and How They Work, 212
Close Encounters: Exploring the Universe with the Hubble Space Telescope,
        316, 323
Cloudy with a Chance of Meatballs, 122, 129, 131
Coast to Coast, 71
Coatsworth, Elizabeth, 338
Cobletz, Catherine, 342
Cock-a-Doodle Doo: The Story of a Little Red Rooster, 327
The Codfish Musket, 340
Coerr, Eleanor, 178, 184, 193

Coffer, Judith Ortiz, 45
Coffin on a Case, 175, 183
Coffin on a Crime, 65
Cohen, Barbara, 37, 59
Cole, Babette, 142, 158
Cole, Joanna, 69, 80
Coleman, Evelyn, 89, 108
Coleman, Michael, 174, 184
Colliding with Chris, 88, 108
Collier, Christopher, 11, 29, 36, 50, 192, 204, 345
Collier, James, 11, 29, 36, 50, 192, 204, 345
Collins, Ted, 184
A Color of His Own, 315
Colors Everywhere, 11, 30, 216
Color Zoo, 336
Colum, Padraic, 338, 339
Columbus and the World Around Him, 239, 251
Coman, Carolyn, 72, 80, 348
Comenius, John, 5
Comet's Nine Lives, 89, 108, 282
Coming to America: The story of Immigration, 223
Commodore Perry in the Land of the Shogun, 210, 230, 347, 350
"The Company of Wolves," 137, 138
Compere, Janet, 250
The Complete Grimm's Fairy Tales, 138
Concrete Poems: A World View, 268, 279
Conlon-McKenna, Marita, 196, 204
Conly, Jane Leslie, 73, 74, 80, 130, 131, 348
Connelly, Bernadine, 155, 158, 289, 298
Connelly, Jan Bourdeau, 49, 59
Conrad, Bruce W., 242, 249
Conrad, Pam, 196, 204
Conrad's War, 350
Constance: A Story of Early Plymouth, 196, 204
Contes de ma mere l'oye (Tales of My Mother the Goose), 259
The Contest, 334
Coolidge, Olivia, 344
Cool Melons — Turn to Frogs! C.2
Cool Salsa: Bilingual Poems on Growing Up Latino in the United States, 270, 277
Cooney, Barbara, 6, 24, 59, 89, 101, 108, 244, 249, 331, 334
Cooper, Floyd, 60, 240, 249, 270, *A.3*
Cooper, Susan, 121, 345, 349
Corduroy, 10, 116, 118, 126, 132
The Corn Grows Ripe, 343
Cornrows, 38, 43, 57, 61
Couper, Heather, 316, 323
A Couple of Kooks and Other Stories About Love, 319
The Courage of Sarah Noble, 200, 205, 343
Courlander, Harold, 342
Coutant, Helen, 67, 80
Coventry, Martha, 354
Coville, Bruce, 22, 31, 306
Cowboys of the Wild West, 243
The Cowtail Switch and Other West African Stories, 342
Coyote: A Trickster Tale from the American Southwest, 144, 145, 160
Cracker Jackson, 71, 72, 80
Crampton, Gertrude, 8
Crampton, Patricia, 354
The Crane Wife, 146, 158
Crawford, Elizabeth D., 354, 355
Crawford, Phyllis, 340
The Crayon Counting Book, 96
Crazy Lady! 73, 74, 80, 348
The Creation, 44

Creech, Sharon, 175, 348
The Cremation of Sam McGee, 261, 279
Crespo, George, 151, 158
Crew, Donald, 215, 230, 231, 334
Crew, Garry, 51, 59
Crew, Linda, 48, 59, 178, 184
The Cricket in Times Square, 10, 344
Cricket Never Dies: A Collection of Haiku and Tanka, 268, 278
The Crocodile and the Ostrich: A Tale from the Akambba of Kenya, 154
Crow Boy, 52, 61, 331
Crown, Jerry Stanley, 226
Crutches, 354
Cruz, Ray, 31, 185
The Crystal Heart: A Vietnamese Legend, 146, 161
Cummings, Pat, 41, 43, 351
Cunningham, Ann Marie, 245, 252
Curious George, 23, 46, 117, 133
Curious George Learns to Spell, 287
Curious George Learns to Spell (CD-ROM), 299
Curlee, Lynn, 221, 231
Curtis, Christopher Paul, 42, 59, 197, 204, 348
Cushman, Karen, 8, 72, 80, 188, **194**, 196, 203, 204, 205, 348
Cut from the Same Cloth: African American Women of Myth, Legend, and Tall Tale, 148

Daddy and I, 266
Daddy Calls Me Man, 165, 269, 278
Daddy's Roommate, 26, 31, 69, 81
Dahl, Roald, 10, 13, 21, 24, 26, 29, 114, **119–120**, 123, 127, 128, 129, 131, 132, 296, 303, 365
Dalgliesh, Alice, 200, 205, 330, 341, 342, 343
Dancing Teepees: Poems of American Indian Youth, 49, 61, 270, 279
Dancing with Dziadziu, 89, 107
Dandelions, 193
Daniel Boone, 236, 250, 340
Daniel O'Rorke, 145
Danny, Champion of the World, 119
Danzinger, Paula, 177, 184
The Dark Frigate, 338
The Dark is Rising, 345, 349
Darkness and the Butterfly, 41
The Dark Star of Itza: The Story of a Pagan Princess, 339
The Dark Thirty: Southern Tales of the Supernatural, 44, 121, 347
Darling, Louis, 131
Dash and Dart, 328
Daugherty, James, 236, 250, 327, 331, 340
Daughter of the Mountains, 342
Daughter of the Seine: The Life of Madame Roland, 338
D'Aulaire, Edgar Parin, 236, 247, 249, 327
D'Aulaire, Ingri, 236, 247, 249, 327
Davenier, Christine, 117, 132
David, Joseph, 161
Davidson, Margaret, 237, 250
Davie, Helen, 277
Davies, Andrew, 350
Davies, Nichola, 4, 29
Davis, Aubrey, 143, 158
Davis, Daniel S., 350
Davis, Jenny, 68, 80
Davis, Lavinia, 329
Davis, Mary Gould, 339
Davis, Ossie, 43, 197, 205
Davy Crockett, 340

Day, Alexandra, 93
Daydreamers, 266
Day of the Dead: A Mexican-American Celebration, 217, 231
Day on Skates: The Story of a Dutch Picnic, 340
Dayrell, Elphinstone, 332
Days of the Dead, 67, 80
A Day's Work, 65
The Day We Met You, 69, 80
The Day We Saw the Sun Come Up, 332
de Angeli, Marguerite, 196, 205, 260, 328, 330, 342, 343
Dear Benjamin Banneker, 240, 251
Dearden, Carmen Diana, 159
Dear Levi: Letters from the Overland Trail, 198, 206
Dear Mr. Henshaw, 68, 74, 171, 175, 184, 346
Dear Oklahoma City, Get Well Soon: America's Children Reach out to the People of Oklahoma, 223
Dear Old Donegal, 224, 231
Death's Door, 71
Deathwatch, 19, 31
December, 65, 72, 79
deClements, Barthe, 172, 184
Deenie, 7
Deep Dream of the Rainforest, 174, 183
The Defender, 342
Defoe, Daniel, 2, 164
De Forest, Charlotte B., 270, 277
Degen, Bruce, 98, 108, 320, 323
Degens, T., 349
de Jenkins, Lyll Becerra, 189
DeJong, Meindert, 343
Delacre, Lulu, 45, 270, 277
Demi, 146, 158, 222, 231, 279
Denenberg, Barry, 197, 205, 244, 250
de Paola, Tomie, 93, 100, 108, 143, 146, 158, 159, 260, 261, 278, 334
de Regniers, Beatrice Schenk, 97, 264, 332
Derraux, Isabelle, 109
de Saint Exupéry, Antoine, 122, 132
The Desert Is Theirs, 334
Desimini, Lisa, 157, 160
de Trevino, Elizabeth Borton, 344
The Devil's Arithmetic, 306
The Devil's Donkey, 123, 131
Diamond, Donna, 80
The Diary of a Young Girl, 250
Diaz, David, 59, 65, 79, 89, 95, 108, 109, 167, 183, 204, 250, 279, 336
Dicey's Song, 169, 171, 175, 186, 346
Dickens, Charles, 25
Dickinson, Peter, 349
Dick Whittington and His Cat, 329
Digging, 15, 31
Dillon, Diane, 28, 44, 59, 60, 107, 109, 132, 148, 153, 157, 334, 351, *B.8*
Dillon, Leo, 28, 44, 59, 60, 107, 109, 132, 148, 153, 157, 334, 351, *B.8*
Dinner at Aunt Connie's House, 85
Dinosaur Dinner with a Slice of Alligator Pie: Favorite Poems, 262
Dinosaurs, 212
Dinosaur Stomp! A Monster Pop-Up Book, 87, 110
Dinosaur Worlds: New Dinosaurs, New Discoveries, 221, 231
The Disappearing Alphabet, 95, 111
Discovering What Earthworms Do, 219
Discover Mars, 316, 323
Disher, Gary, 196, 205
The Diverting History of John Gilpin, *A.1*
Dobry, 339
Dr. De Soto, 117, 133, 346
Dr. Seuss Kindergarten, 287

Dr. Seuss Kindergarten (CD-ROM), 299
Dr. Seuss's A B C, 3, 271, 277, 288
Dodgson, Charles (Lewis Carroll), 5, 29, 115, 131, 257, 277
Dogsong, 50, 60, 173, 347
Do Like Kyla, 165
The Doll in the Garden: A Ghost Story, 121
Domanska, Janina, 333
Donde Viven los Monstruos (Where the Wild Things Are), 46
Doniger, Nancy, 279
Don't Bet on the Prince, 136, 138
Don't Forget to Write, 167
Don't Take Teddy, 353
The Doorbell Rang, 222, 231
The Door in the Wall, 196, 205, 342
Dorris, Michael, 189, 196, 200, 205
Dorros, Arthur, 46, 59, 102, 108
Dotlich, Rebecca Kai, 257, 277, *C.3*
Dotty's Suitcase, 197, 205
The Double Life of Pocahontas, 350
Doucet, Sharon Arms, 145, 158
Downer, Marion, 231
Down in the Garden: An Alphabet Book, 95
Downright Dencey, 338
Down Ryton Water, 341
Dragonfield and Other Stories, 306
Dragonfly's Tail, 151, 160
Dragon Kyn, 132
Dragon Lost at Sea, 179
Dragon's Blood: A Fantasy, 306
The Dragon's Boy, 152, 161
Dragon's Gate, 57, 61, 179, 199, 206, 348
Dragon Slayer, 154, 161
Dragonwings, 38, 48, 61, 178, 186, 345
Dragonwings, Crescent, 43
Draper, Sharon M., 44
Dream Coach, 338
The Dream Keeper, 269
The Drinking Gourd: A Story of the Underground Railroad, 198, 206
Drip Drop Raindrops, 211, 230
A Drop of Water: A Book of Science and Wonder, 220, 351
Drummer Hoff, 101, 271, 277, 332
Dry or Wet?, 216
DuBois, Pane, 186
du Bois, William Pene, 330, 331, 341
Duckett, Alfred, 43
Duey's Tale, 43
Duffy and the Devil, 333
Duke Ellington: The Piano Prince and His Orchestra, 240, 251, 337
Dumpling Soup, 50, 60
Duvoisin, Roger, 329, 332

Each Peach Pear Plum, 88, 103, 107, 320, 322
The Ear, the Eye, and the Arm, 126, 132, 348
Early Thunder, 192, 205
Earthquakes, 220
East of the Sun and West of the Moon, 144, 159
Eaton, Jeanette, 338, 340, 341, 342
Echoes for the Eye: Poems to Celebrate Patterns in Nature, 257, 277
Eckert, Allan W., 345
Edens, Cooper, 100, 108, 260
Edmonds, Walter D., 341
Edward and the Pirates, 25, 30
The Egg Tree, 329

Egielski, Richard, 149, 158, 335
The Egypt Game, 344
The Egyptian Cinderella, 150
Ehlert, Lois, 87, 108, 299, 315, 316, 336
Eichenbert, Fritz, 330
Eight Hands Round: A Patchwork Alphabet, 94, 110
Einstein Anderson Series of Mystery Stories, 219
Eitzen, Allan, 324
The Elderberry Thicket, 197, 206
Eleanor, 244, 249
Eleanor Roosevelt: A Life of Discovery, 348, 351
The Elephant Child, 147, 159
Elkin, Benjamin, 331
Ella Enchanted, 348
Elsom, Derek, 220
Emberley, Barbara, 101, 271, 277, 332
Emberley, Ed, 101, 277, 332
Emberley, Michael, 149, 158
Emma, 224, 231
Emma's Magic Winter, 99, 109
Emma's Rug, 91
The Emperor and the Kite, 122, 133, 332
"The Emperor's New Clothes," 147
The Emperor's New Clothes, 122, 131, 147, 158
The Empires Lost and Won: The Spanish Heritage in the Southwest, 199
Empty Window, 67, 79
Enchantress from the Stars, 345
Encounter, 191, 206, 306
Encyclopedia Brown Mysteries, 175, 185
Engdahl, Sylvia Louise, 345
England, Linda, 41, 59
Enright, Elizabeth, 340, 343
Eriksson, Eva, 354
Ernst, Lisa Campbell, 205
The Eruption and Healing of Mount Saint Helens, 231
Esberson, Barbara Juster, 257, 277, 352
Escape to Freedom, 43
Estes, Eleanor, 341, 342
Ets, Marie Hall, 328, 330, 331
Evans, Leslie, 99, 108
Even More Short and Shivery, 121
Everett Alvarez, Jr., A Hero for Our Times, 242, 249
Everett Anderson's Good-Bye, 43, 66, 80
Everyday Children, 87, 110
Every Time I Climb a Tree, 265, 278
The Extinct Alphabet Book, 95
An Extraordinary Life: The Story of A Monarch Butterfly, 226

Fables, 152, 160, 334
The Face at the Window, 42, 45, 60
Fairman, Tony, 146, 159
The Fairy Circus, 339
"A Fairy Tale for Our Time," 136, 138
Fairytales, 147, 157
Faithful Elephants, 178, 186
The Faithful Friend, 141, 337
Fallen Angels, 44, 197, 206
Falling Up: Poems and Drawings, 258, 264
The Family Under the Bridge, 72, 80, 343
Fantastic Mr. Fox, 119
Far and Few: Rhymes of the Never Was and Always Is, 257, 278

Farjeon, Eleanor, 253, 265, 277
Farmer, Nancy, 126, 132, 348
Fast-Slow, High-Low: A Book of Opposites, 11, 31, 216
Father Water, Mother Woods: Essays about Fishing and Hunting in the North Woods, 173
Faulkner, Keith, 87, 108
Fax, Elton C., 43
The Fearsome Inn, 344
The Feathered Serpent, 191
Feather Mountain, 330
Feelings, Muriel, 39, 96, 108, 333, 349
Feelings, Tom, 39, 43, 44, 96, 108, 217, 231, 269, 333, 349
Feiffer, Jules, 88, 89, 108, 116, 132
Felecia, 185
Felitia, 165
Fenner, Carol, 172, 184, 348
Fenton, Edward, 353
Fernando's Gift—El regalo de Fernando, 217
Ferris, Jean, 175, 184
Ferris, Jeri, 240, 250
Festivals, 223
Field, Rachel, 328, 338, 339
Fiesta! 96, 217, 230
The Fifth of March: A Story of the Boston Massacre, 197, 206
Figgs & Phantoms, 345
The Fighting Ground, 192, 204
Fighting Tackle, 176, 184
The Final Journey, 198, 206
Finders Keepers, 330
A Fine White Dust, 319, 347
Finger, Charles, 338
Fin M'Coul: The Giant of Knockmany Hill, 100, 108
Fire Engine Shapes, 215, 232
Fire Truck, 98, 110
The First Americans, 49, 61, 218
First Snow, 67, 80
First Verses, 4, 29, 271, 277
Fish, Helen Dean, 327
Fisher, Aileen, 239, 250, 352
Fisher, Cyrus, 341
Fisher, David, 218, 230
Fisher, Leonard Everett, 223, 231
Fish for Supper, 334
Fish in the Air, 329
Fitzhugh, Louise, 6, 29, 164, 184
The 500 Hats of Bartholomew Cubbins, 3, 122, 132
Five Little Monkeys Jumping on the Bed, 11, 29, 320, 323, 330
Flack, Marjorie, 329
The Flag We Love, 223
Flavin, Theresa, 59
The Fledgling, 346
Fleischman, Paul, 12, 189, 197, 205, 274, 277, 346, 347
Fleischman, Sid, 245, 250, 311, 323, 347, 349
Fleming, Candice, 197, 205
Fleming, Denise, 225, 231, 336
Flesher, V., 81
Fletcher, Ralph, 172, 184
Fletcher, Susan, 132
Floating Island, 339
Floca, Brian, 351
Flora and the Tiger: 19 Very Short Stories from My Life, 245, 249
Florian, Douglas, *C.3*

Flossie and the Fox, 146, 160, 199
Flournoy, Valerie, 42, 43, 59, 355
Flutes, Whistles, and Reeds, 224, 231
Fly, Bessie, Fly, C.4
Fly Away Home, 65, 72, 77, 79
Fly High, Fly Low, 331
Flying Solo, 172, 184
Fog Magic, 341
Folktales from India: A Selection of Oral Tales from Twenty-Two Languages, 148
Follow the Drinking Gourd, 155, 158, 289, 298
The Fool of the World and the Flying Ship, 332
Forbert, Ati, 250
Forbes, Esther, 11, 29, 188, 192, 205, 341
Ford, George, 43
Ford, Lauren, 327
Foreman, Michael, 148, 260
The Forest Pool, 327
The Forestwife, 123, 133
Forged by Fire, 44
The Forgotten Daughter, 339
For Laughing Out Louder: More Poems to Tickle Your Funnybone, 262
For the Love of the Game: Michael Jordan and Me, 266
Fortnum, Peggy, 131, 277
The Fortune-Tellers, 351
Fossil Feud: The Rivalry of the First American Dinosaur Hunters, 221
Foster, Genevieve, 341, 342
Foster, John, 4, 29, 271, 277
Four and Twenty Blackbirds: Nursery Rhymes of Yesterday Recalled for Children of Today, 327
The Fourth Little Pig, 318, 323
Fox, Paula, 19, 29, 73, 80, 177, 184, 198, 205, 345, 347, 350
The Fox Went Out on a Chilly Night: An Old Song, 331
Fradin, Denis, 242, 250
Frank, Anne, 244, 250
Frank, Rudolf, 354
Frankenstein, 125
Franklin Delano Roosevelt, 226, 242, 250
Frasconi, Antonio, 331
Freckle Juice, 7, 27, 29, 177, 183, 318, 323
Frederick, 332
Frederick Douglass: Leader Against Slavery, 199
Freedman, Ina, 50, 59
Freedman, Russell, 59, 210, 217, 226, 228, 231, 236, 237, 240, 242, **243–244,** 250, 285, 347, 348, 351, 352
Free Fall, 336
Freeman, Don, 10, 116, 118, 132, 331
Free to Dream: The Making of a Poet: Langston Hughes, 240, 251
Freight Train, 215, 230, 334
Friedman, Ina, 91
Friedman, Judith, 80
Friedrich, 353
The Friends, 351, 355
The Friendship, 40, 44, 350
Friis-Baastad, Babbis, 353
Fritz, Jean, 59, 192, 205, 226, **237–238,** 242, 245, 250, 346, 350, 351, 352
Frog and Toad Are Friends, 15, 30, 99, 109, 333
Frog and Toad series, 99
Frog and Toad Together, 305, 323, 345
Frog Goes to Dinner, B.5
Frog Went a-Courtin', 331
From Caterpillar to Butterfly, 220

From the Mixed-up Files of Mrs. Basil E. Frankweiler, 164, 175, 184, 312, 323, 344
Frontier Living, 344
Frost, Robert, 254, 277
Fudge-A-Mania, 7
The Funny Little Woman, 333

Gackenbach, Dick, 11, 29
Gag, Wanda, 6, 29, 84, 88, 308, 323, 327, 328, 338, 339, *A.1*
Gaggin, Eva Roe, 341
Galaxies, 219
Galdone, Paul, 99, 131, 149, 159, 317, 323, 331
Gallaz, Christopher, 198, 205, 354
Gallenkamp, Charles, 217, 232
The Gammage Cup, 343
Gammell, Stephen, 230, 335, 336
Gandhi, Fighter Without a Sword, 342
Gannett, Ruth S., 328, 342
Garcia, Stephanie, 45, 47, 61, 85, 89, 110, *A.4*
The Gardener, 337
The Garden of Abdul Gasazi, 334, 350
Gardiner, John Reynolds, 10, 29, 181, 284, 298, 304
Gardner, James Finn, 142, 159
Garner, Alan, 148
Garner, James Finn, 52, 56
Garram the Hunter: The Boy of the Hill Tribes, 339
Garza, Carmen, 217, 231
Gates, Doris, 340
A Gathering of Days: A New England Girl's Journal 1830-32, 346
Gathering the Sun: An Alphabet in Spanish and English, 38
Gauthier, Gail, 172
Gayneck, the Story of a Pigeon, 338
Geddes, Anne, 95, 216
Geisel, Theodor Seuss (Dr. Seuss), 2, **3–4,** 6, 9, 14, 24, 29, 83, 89, 92, 98, 99, 101, 108, 122, 132, 262, 263, 277, 287, 288, 315, 316, 329, 352, *B.1*
Geisert, Arthur, 96
Gensler, Kinereth, 275
George, Jean Craighead, 19, 29, 50, 59, 77, 80, 173, 174, 184, 285, 314, 323, 343, 345, 365
George's Marvelous Medicine, 120
George Washington, 342
George Washington Carver: The Peanut Scientist, 199
George Washington's Mother, 238
George Washington's World, 341
Gergely, Tibor, 330
Gerse, Kristine O'Connor, 257, 277
Geter, Tyrone, 61
Ghost Abbey, 122
The Ghost Comes Calling, 121
The Ghost of Grania O'Malley, 152, 160
Gibbons, Gail, 8, **212–213,** 228, 321, 323, *C.1*
Gilchrist, Jan Spivey, 44, 277, *C.3*
Gillespie and the Guards, 331
The Gingerbread Boy, 149, 158, 159
"The Gingerbread Boy," 149
The Gingerbread Man, 99, 149, 158, 320
"The Gingerbread Man," 144, 155
The Gingerbread Rabbit, 149, 159
Ginger Pye, 342
Giovanni, Nikki, 270, 304
Gipson, Fred, 176, 184, 343

A Girl Called Boy, 123, 132
Girl from Yamhill: A Memoir, 245, 249
A Girl Named Disaster, 348
The Girl Who Dreamed Only Geese and Other Tales of the Far North, 148
The Girl Who Loved Wild Horses, 334
The Giver, 11, 30, 77, 80, 115, 126, 127, 129, 130, 132, 311, 323, 348
The Giving Tree, 2, 31, 88, 110, 258, *B.7*
Glanzma, Lois S., 132
Glass, Andrew, 131
The Glorious Flight: Across the Channel with Louis Bleriot, July 25, 1909, 100, 110, 317, 323, 335
The Glorious Mother Goose, 100, 108, 260
Glory of the Seas, 339
Glubok, Shirley, 349
Goble, Paul, 144, 146, 159, 334
Godden, Rumer, 24
Gode, Alexander, 353
Gode, Alison, 353
The Gods and Goddesses of Olympus, 138, 157
Goetzel, Robert F., 39
Goffstein, M. B., 334
Gogancherry, Helen, 185
Goggles!, 333
Going Home, 65, 108
Going Solo, 120
Going Up!, 95, 110, 222, 232
The Gold Cadillac, 40
Golden Basket, 340
The Golden Carp and Other Tales from Vietnam, 148
The Golden Compass, 126, 133
The Golden Fleece and the Heroes Who Lived Before Achilles, 338
The Golden Goblet, 344
The Golden Name Day, 343
The Golden Sandal: A Middle Eastern Cinderella Story, 150
Goldilocks, 336
Goldilocks and the Three Bears, 283
"Goldilocks and the Three Bears," 26, 147
Golem, 337
The Golem: A Jewish Legend, 334
Gollub, Matthew, *C.2*
The Golly Sisters Ride Again, 198, 204
The Golly Sisters series, 71
Gone-Away Lake, 343
Gone-a-Whaling: The Lure of the Sea and the Hunt for the Great Whale, 11, 30
Good, Diane, 29
Goodall, John S., 93, 108, 349
Good-Bye and Keep Cold, 68, 80
Good-Bye Charles Lindbergh: Based on a True Story, 88, 107
Good Dog, Carl, 93
Goode, Diane, 335
The Good Giants and the Bad Bukwudgies, 238
Good Luck Gold and Other Poems, 270, 279
Good-Luck Horse, 328
The Good Master, 340
Goodnight, Moon, 2, 4, 9, 23, 29, 83, 107, 108
Goodnight, Owl!, 99, 109
Good Work, Amelia Bedelia, 119, 133
Goosebumps, 179
Goosebumps series, 296
A Gopher in the Garden and Other Animal Poems, 262
Gottlieb, Dale, 355
Goudey, Alice E., 331, 332
Gould, Philip, 250
Graeber, Charlotte, 66, 74, 80

Graglia, Richard, 354
Graham, Al, 329
Graham, Kenneth, 6, 29
Graham, Margaret Bloy, 330
Graham, Steve, 224, 231
Grahame, Kenneth, 118, 132
Gramatky, Hardie, 118, 132
Grand Canyon: Exploring the Natural Wonder, 321, 323
Grandfather's Journey, 48, 60, 91, 336, 351, *A.4*
Grandmas at Bat, 176, 185
Grandmother and the Runaway Shadow, 193
Granfa' Grif Had a Pig and Other Rhymes, 349
The Graphic Alphabet, 337
Grass Sandals: The Travels of Basho, 268, 279
Graven Images, 346
Gray, Elizabeth Janet, 339, 340, 341
The Great Fire, 226, 305, 323, 348
The Great Gilly Hopkins, 26, 30, 70, 81, 284, 298, 346
The Great Kapok Tree: A Story of the Amazon Rain Forest, 225, 230
The Great Little Madison, 226, 351
The Great Quest, 337
The Great Wheel, 343
Greenaway, Kate, 5, 84, 260
Greene, Bette, 197, 205, 345
Greene, Constance, 197, 205
Green Eggs and Ham, 3, 9, 99, 108, 315
Green Eyes, 330
Greenfield, Eloise, 15, 43, 44, 57, 59, 242, 250, 265, **266–267**, 352
Greenwald, Sheila, 177, 184
The Gremlins, 119
Grenfield, Eloise, 277
The Grey King, 345
The Grey Lady and the Strawberry Snatcher, 334
Griego, Margot, 46, 59
Grifalconi, Ann, 41, 335
Griff, Patricia Reilly, 348
Griffith, Gershom, 41
Grimes, Nikki, 43
Grimes, Vicki, 38, 60
Grimm, Jacob, 5, 63, 136, 138, 155
Grimm, Wilhelm, 5, 63, 136, 138, 155
Grove, Vicki, 172, 184
Grover, Max, 95, 96
Growing Colors, 315
Growing up in Coal Country, 223
Guderian, Greg, 288
Guests, 200, 205
Guevara, Susan, 45, 47, 133
Guinness Book of Records, 218
Gulliver's Travels, 2, 115
Gundersheimer, Karen, 24
Gunning, Monica, 270
Gurko, Leo, 343
Gustafson, Scott, 95
Guthrie, Woody, 155, 159, 224, 231
Gutierrez, Douglas, 146, 159
Guy, Ginger Furglesong, 96
Guy, Rosa, 43

Hader, Berta, 327, 328, 329
Hader, Elmer, 327, 328, 329
Hague, Kathleen, 144, 159
Hague, Michael, 144, 159

Hahn, Mary Downing, 121, 189
Hailstones and Halibut Bones, 256, 278
Hale, James, 230
Haley, Gail E., 100, 108, 159, 333
Half-Chicken/Medio Pollito, 46, 59
Half Moon and One Whole Star, 43
Halkin, Hillel, 354
Hall, Anna Gertrude, 341
Hall, Donald, 89, 108, 334
Hall, Elizabeth, 200, 206
Hall, Lynn, 350
Hallensleben, Georg, 351
Hallock, Grace, 338
Halloween ABC, 26, 30, 257, 278
Hamanaka, Sheila, 41, 50, 60
Hamilton, Virginia, 7, 43, 44, 73, 80, 148, 151, 159, 165, 171, 174, 184, 290, 304, 321, 323, 345, 346, 347, 349, 350, 352, 365
Hamm, Diane, 96
Handforth, Thomas, 327
A Hand Full of Stars, 354
The Handmade Alphabet, 94
Hands, 87, 108
Hang Out the Flag, 197, 205
Hans Brinker and the Silver Skates, 24
Hansel and Gretel, 114, 335
"Hansel and Gretel," 99, 135, 136
Hanson, Regina, 42, 45, 60
Happily May I Walk: American Indians and Alaska Natives Today, 218, 231
The Happy Day, 329
The Happy Golden Years, 341
Happy Winter, 24
Harder, Dan, 88, 108
Hardy Boys series, 9
The Hare and the Tortoise, 152, 159
Harlem, 232, 269, 278, 337
The Harmony Arms, 68, 80
Harness, Cheryl, 193, *C.4*
Harper, Dan, 4, 29
The Harper & Row I Can Read History Series, 244
Harriet Beecher Stowe and the Beecher Preachers, 238
Harriet the Spy, 6, 29, 164, 184
Harris, Violet, 271, 277
Harrison, Michael, 264
Harrison, Ted, 261, 279
Harry and the Terrible Whatzit, 11, 29
Harry Potter and the Sorcerer's Stone, 115–116, 133
Härtling, Peter, 354
Hartmann, Wendy, 96
Haskins, James, 43, 242, 245, 250, 251
The Hat, 282, 283
Hatchet, 164, 173, 174, 185, 347
Hathorn, Libby, 89, 108
The Hatmaker's Sign: A Story Told by Benjamin Franklin, 197, 205
Haugaard, Erik Christian, 349
Have You Seen My Duckling?, 335
Have You Seen Tom Thumb?, 341
Havighurst, Marion, 342
Havighurst, Walter, 342
Havill, Juanita, 50, 60, 355
Hawes, Charles, 337, 338
Hawk, I'm Your Brother, 334
Hayashi, Akiki, 61
The Haymeadow, 172, 173, 185
Hays, Michael, 161, 298

The Headless Cupid, 345
The Headless Horseman Rides Tonight: Poems to Trouble Your Sleep, 262
The Heart, 219
Heart's Blood, 306
Heather Has Two Mommies, 70, 81
Heaven, 44, 69, 80, 165
The Heavenly Tenants, 341
Hector Protector, 98
Heiligman, Deborah, 220
Heller, Holly, 230
Heller, Ruth, 150
"Hello the Boat!", 340
Henbest, Nigel, 316, 323
Henegan, James, 168, 184
Henkes, Kevin, 16, 288, 336
"Henny Penny," 136, 144
Henry, Marguerite, 341, 342
Henry and Mudge: The First Book of Their Adventures, 99, 110
Henry and Mudge series, 99, 319
Henry Fisherman, 329
Henry Huggins, 64, 80, 170, 184
Heo, Yumi, 38
Hepworth, Cathy, 94, 108
Herculeah Jones Mysteries, 71, 175, 184
Here's to You, Rachel Robinson, 7
Here There Be Unicorns, 306
Hermes, Patricia, 70, 80
The Hero and The Crown, 346
Herrera, Jan Felipe, 355
Herrera, Velino, 328
Hershel and the Hanukkah Goblins, 336
Her Stories, 44
Hertzberg, Hendrick, 222, 231
Hesse, Karen, 22, 30, 66, 74, 80, 182, 184, 263, 277, 348
Hest, Amy, 193, 351
Hewes, Agnes, 339, 340
Hewett, Lorri, 172, 184
Hey, All, 335
Heymans, Annemarie, 354
Heymans, Margriet, 354
Hi, Cat!, 349
Hiawatha: Messenger of Peace, 242, 250
Hickox, Rebecca, 150
Hida, Keiko, 277
The Hidden Treasure of Glaston, 341
Hide and Seek Fog, 332
Hiding, 217, 231
High Elk's Treasure, 49
The High King, 345
Highwater, Jamake, 346
"The Highwayman," 255
Hilderbrand, Will, 150
Hildilid's Night, 333
Himalayan Trails, 12
Himler, Ronald, 79, 204
Hindu Ways, 12
Hinton, S. E., 9, 10, 15, 30
Hirano, Cathy, 355
The Hired Hand: An African American Folktale, 141, 146, 160
Hiroshima, 179
Hiroshima No Pika, 51, 60, 196, 205, 354
Hirschfelder, Arline, 218, 231
Hiscock, Bruce, 220
Hitty, Her First Hundred Years, 338
Ho, Minfong, 337

Hoang Anh: A Vietnamese-American Boy, 218, 231
Hoban, Tana, 11, 30, 87, 92, 109, 216, 222, 231, 320, 323
The Hobbitt, 124, 133
Hoberman, Mary Ann, 264
Hodges, Margaret, 332, 335
Hoestlandt, Jo, 198, 205
Hoffman, Mary, 19, 30
Hogrogian, Nonny, 144, 155, 159, 332, 333, 334
Holbrook, Stewart, 329
Holden, Robert, 320, 323
A Hole Is to Dig, 97
Holes, 348
The Holiday House Picture Book Biography Series, 244
Hollennleben, Georg, 107
Holler, Anne, 239, 250
Holling, Holling C., 328, 342
Holman, Felice, 174, 184, 196, 205
Holmes, Thom, 221
Holob, Joseph, 355
Homecoming, 70, 81
The Homecoming, 24, 168, 186
Homesick: My Own Story, 59, 238, 245, 250, 346
"Honey, I Love," 266
Honey, I Love and Other Poems, 57, 59, 265, 266, 277
The Honey Makers, 213
Honk, the Moose, 340
The Honorable Prison, 189
Hooray for Diffendoofer Day!, 3, 101, 262
The Hopeful Trout and Other Limericks, 267, 277
The Hopi, 49
Hopkins, Lee Bennett, 264, 271, 277
Hopkinson, Deborah, 198, 205
The Horse and His Boy, 125
The Horsecatcher, 343
Horton Hatches the Egg, 3
Horton Hears a Who! 3
Hosie's Alphabet, 333
The Hound of Ulster, 154
The House in the Sky, 141
The House of Dies Drear, 304
The House of Sixty Fathers, 343
House on Fire: The Story of the Blues, 224, 230
Houses from the Sea, 331
The House that Jack Built: A Picture Book in Two Languages, 331
Houston, Gloria, 24
How A House is Built, 212
Howard, Elizabeth Fitzgerald, 38, 60
Howard, Kim, 59
Howe, Deborah, 127, 132
Howe, James, 72, 80, 127, 132
Howell, Frank, 61
How I Was Adopted, 69, 80
How Many Days to America? A Thanksgiving Story, 65
How Many Feet in the Bed? 96
How Much Is a Million? 222, 232
How My Parents Learned to Eat, 50, 59, 91
How the Camel Got Its Hump, 147, 159
How the Grinch Stole Christmas, 83, 108
How the Leopard Got His Spots, 289
How the Rhinoceros Got Its Skin, 147, 159
How the Sea Began: A Tiano Myth, 151, 158
How the Stars Fell Into the Sky, 144, 160
How to Eat Fried Worms, 176, 185, 303
Hoyt-Goldsmith, Diane, 217, 218, 231
Hubbard, Ralph, 339

Huck, Charlotte, 150
Hudson, Wade, 270
Hughes, Langston, 267, 269
Hughes, Shirley, 217, 231
Hullaboo ABC, 94
Humbug Mountain, 349
Humming Whispers, 165
Humphries, Stella, 353
The Hundred Dresses, 341
The Hundred Penny Box, 41, 60, 177, 185, 345
Hundreds of Cats, A.1
Hunt, Irene, 197, 205, 344
Hunt, Jonathan, 94, 109
Hunt, Mabel Leigh, 341, 342
Hunter, Anne, 107, 306
Hunter, Ryan Ann, 225, 231
Hunterly, Jamichael, 160
Hurd, Clement, 29, 108
Hurd, Thacher, 24, 350
Hürlimann, Ruth, 353
Hurmence, Brenda, 123, 132
Hurry Home, Candy, 343
Hush! A Thai Lullaby, 337
Hutchins, Pat, 93, 97, 99, 109, 222, 231, 308, 323
Hutton, Warwick, 350
Hyman, Trina Schart, 26, 30, 99, 250, 335, 336, 349, 351
Hyun, Peter, 148

I, Juan de Paraja, 344
I, Too, Sing American: Three Centuries of African American Poetry, 270
I Am Angela, 15, 30
I Am Not Going to Get up Today, 4
I Am the Darker Brother: An Anthology of Modern Poems, 269
I Am Writing a Poem About...: A Game of Poetry, 264
Ian's Walk: A Story about Autism, 73, 80
Ibbotson, Eva, 124, 132
The Icky Bug Alphabet Book, 94, 110, 217, 232
If a Bus Could Talk: The Story of Rosa Parks, 85
If All the Seas Were One Sea, 333
If I Built a Village, 349
If I Ran the Circus, 4
If I Ran the Zoo, 3, 329
If People Could Fly: American Black Folktales, 43
If You Are a Hunter of Fossils, 20, 29
If You Didn't Have Me, 354
If You Give A Moose A Muffin, 98, 110
If You Give A Mouse A Cookie, 9, 98, 110, 288
If You Give A Pig A Pancake, 98, 110
If You Made a Million, 232
Iggy's House, 7
Igus, Toyomi, 224, 231
I Hadn't Meant to Tell You This, 72, 81
Iktomi and the Berries, 144, 159
I'll Always Love You, 66, 81
Illuminations, 94
I Lost My Bear, 88, 89, 108
I Love Guinea Pigs, 215, 231
In a Spring Garden, 268, 278
Inch by Inch, 331
Incident at Hawk's Hill, 345
Incredible Journey, 176, 183
In Daddy's Arms I Am Tall: African Americans Celebrating Fathers, 44, 269

Indian Captive: The Story of Mary Jemison, 341
Indian Chiefs, 59, 242, 250
The Indian in the Cupboard, 53–55, 118, 131
An Indian Winter, 244
I Never Had It Made, 43
In Flight with David McPhail: A Creative Autobiography, 245, 251
In My Family/En mi familia, 45, 217, 231
In My Mother's House, 328
The Inn-Keeper's Apprentice, 91
Innocenti, Roberto, 198, 205, 354
Insectlopedia, C.3
In Summer Light, 350
In the Beginning: Creation Stories from Around the World, 151, 159, 347
In the Forest, 328
In the Land of Ur: The Discovery of Ancient Mesopotamia, 353
In the Next Three Seconds, 218, 232
In the Night Kitchen, 26, 31, 98, 333
In the Rain with Baby Duck, 351
In the Small, Small Pond, 225, 231, 336
In the Year of the Boar and Jackie Robinson, 48, 60, 244, 251
Into the Ice: The Story of Arctic Exploration, 221, 231
Into the Sky, 225, 231
The Intruder, 349
Invincible Louisa: The Story of the Author of 'Little Women,' 236, 251, 339
The Invisible Princess, 85
The Invisible Thread, 245, 252
Ira Sleeps Over, 98, 108, 167, 170, 186
Irene and the Big Fine Nickel, 38, 61
The Irish Cinderlad, 141, 150, 158
Irving, Washington, 5, 30
Isadora, Rachel, 160, 334
i see the rhythm, 44, 224, 231
Ish-Kishor, Sulamith, 345
Is It Red? Is It Yellow? Is It Blue?, 216
The Island, 173
An Island Like You: Stories from the Barrio, 45
Island of the Blue Dolphins, 10, 174, 185, 191, 200, 206, 344
The Island on Bird Street, 354
Issa, C.2
Issacs, Anne, 153, 159, 336
It Could Always Be Worse, 334
It's Halloween, 257, 278
It's Like This, Cat, 344
It's Mine—A Greedy Book, 11, 29
Ivanhoe, 188
I Want to Be, 41
I Was a Third Grade Science Project, 51, 59

Jabar, Cynthia, 108
Jabberwocky, 257, 277
Jackal's Flying Lesson: A Khoskhoi Tale, 154
Jack and the Beanstalk, 114
"Jack and the Beanstalk," 99, 135, 139
Jackie Robinson: He Was the First, 240, 249
Jackson, Bryon, 8
Jackson, Ellen, 142, 159
Jackson, Kathryn, 8
Jacob Have I Loved, 168, 171, 185, 346
Jacobson, Cathy, 159
Jacques, Brian, 24, 118, 132
Jaffe, Nina, 150
Jamaica and Brianna, 50, 60
Jamaica's Friend, 355

Jamberry, 98, 108, 320, 323
Jambo Means Hello: A Swahili Alphabet Book, 39, 333, 349
James, Bill, 278
James, M. R., 330
James, Will, 338
James and the Giant Peach, 119, 127–128, 131, 296, 303
Janeczko, Paul, 257, 278
Jane's Island, 339
Janulewicz, Mike, 221
Jaquith, Patricia, 148
Jarrell, Randall, 149, 159, 333, 344
Jasmin's Notebook, 38, 60
The Jazz Man, 344
Jeanne d'Arc, 239, 250
Jed's Junior Space Patrol, 126, 132
Jeffers, Susan, 254, 270, 277, 278, 333
Jennifer, Hecate, Macbeth, William McKinley, and Me, Elizabeth, 344
Jenny Reen and the Jack Muh Lantern, 41
Jerico's Journey, 198, 206
Jerome, Anita, 231
Jesse Owens: Olympic Star, 199
Jewett, Eleanore, 341
Jimenez, Francisco, 45, 351
Jimmy Yellow Hawk, 49
Jip: His Story, 189
Johansen, Margaret, 339
John Henry, 153, 160, 336, 351
John Midas in the Dreamtime, 123, 131
Johnny Appleseed, 159
Johnny Tremain, 11, 29, 188, 192, 205, 341
Johnson, Angela, 41, 44, 60, 69, 80, 88, 109, **165**, 278, 355
Johnson, Crockett, 16
Johnson, Gerald W., 343, 344
Johnson, James Weldon, 44
Johnson, Stephen T., 337
Johnson, Tony, 155, 159, 200, 205
JoJo's Flying Side Kick, 41, 176, 185
The Jolly Postman, 15, 28
Jonah and the Great Fish, 350
Jones, Carol, 152, 159
Jones, Elizabeth Orton, 328
Jones, Idwal, 340
Jones, Jessie Orton, 328
Jordan, Mary Kate, 66, 80
Jorge el Curioso (Curious George), 46
Joseph, Lynn, 45, C.4
Josey, Kira, 232
Josey, Rod, 232
Joslin, Sesyle, 331
Jossee, Barbara, 179, 184
Journey, 70, 74, 81
Journey Cake, Ho!, 330
Journey Home, 191, 199, 206
The Journey of Charles Lindbergh, 226
Journey Outside, 345
Journey to the Center of the Earth, 125
Journey to Topaz, 36, 61, 191, 199, 206
The Joy Boys, 71
Joyce, William, 22, 30, 246, 250, B.3
Joyful Noise: Poems for Two Voices, 274, 277, 347
Joyner, Jerry, 349
Juanita, 329
The Judge: An Untrue Tale, 333
Judson, Clara Ingram, 342, 343, 352
Jukes, Mavis, 347

Julie of the Wolves, 19, 29, 77, 80, 174, 184, 345
Julius, 88, 109, 165
Jumanji, 89, 111, 299, 334
Jumping-Off Place, 338
Jupiter, 316, 323
Just a Few Words, Mr. Lincoln: The Story of the Gettysburg Address, 238
Juster, Norman, 122, 132
Just Grandma and Me, 289
Justin and the Best Bisquits in the World, 43
Justin Morgan Had a Horse, 341
Just Like Martin, 197, 205
"Just So" stories, 147
Just Us Women, 41

Kalashnikoff, Nicholas, 342
Kalnay, Francis, 343
Kane, Henry B., 278
Kang, Johanna, 205
Kardaleff, P., 224
Kästner, Erich, 353
Katchen, Carole, 278
Katie's Trunk, 197, 206
Katy and the Big Snow, 118, 131
Katz, Karen, 69, 80
Katz, Susan, 66, 80
Keats, Ezra Jack, 7, 11, 24, 30, 38, 60, 85, 90, 109, 268, 278, 332, 333, 349, 355, *A.3*
Keene, Carolyn. *See* Adams, Harriet Stratemeyer
Keepers of the Earth: Native American Stories and Environmental Activities for Children, 147, 158
Keister, Douglas, 217
Keith, Harold, 343
Keller, Holly, 15, 30
Kellogg, Steven, 24, 100, 109, 153, 159, 298, 318, 323
Kelly, Eric P., 188, 205, 338
Kendall, Carol, 343
Kennedy, DayAnn M., 221
Kepes, Juliet, 330
Kesselman, Wendy, 224, 231
The Khan's Daughter, 179
Kherdian, David, 346, 349
Kia Tanisha, 266
The Kid in the Red Jacket, 172, 185
Kidnapped, 5, 31, 164
Kids at Work: Lewis Hind and the Crusade Against Child Labor, 244
Kiefte, Kees de, 60, 278
Kiesler, Kate, 277
Kildee House, 342
Kimmel, Eric A., 144, 149, 159, 336
Kind Hearts and Gentle Monsters, 179
King Bidgood's in the Bathtub, 335
King Long Shanks, 147, 161
Kingman, Lee, 328
King of the Wind, 342
The King's Day: Louis XIV of France, 242, 249
The King's Fifth, 191, 344
King-Smith, Dick, 215, 231
The King's Shadow, 204
King Stork, 349
Kipling, Rudyard, 5, 12, 114, 147, 159, 255, 289
Kirk, David, 97, 102, 109, 117, 132, *B.3*
Kirkup, James, 353
Kittelkamp, Larry, 224, 231

Klause, Annette Curtis, 126.132
Klausner, Janet, 240, 250
Klevin, Elisa, 59
Kliros, Thea, 31
Kneeknock Rise, 345
Kneen, Maggie, 161
Knight, Christopher G., 80, 210, 231
Knightly, Rosalinda, 216
Knights in Shining Armor, 213
Knots on a Counting Rope, 73, 81
Koch, Kenneth, 275
Koeber, Nora, 250
Koehn, Ilse, 349
Koeler, Phoebe, 69, 80
Koeppen, Peter, 204
Koertge, Ron, 68, 80
Kofi and His Magic, 217, 230
Konisberg, E. L., 164, 175, 184, 312, 323, 344, 348
Konrad, 353
The Korean Cinderella, 48, 59, 150
Korea's Favorite Tales and Lyrics, 148
Koya Delaney and the Good Girl Blues, 267
Kraft, Betsy Harvey, 240, 250
Krahn, Fernando, 93
Kraus, Ruth, 16
Krauss, Ruth, 97, 329, 330
Krementz, Jill, 217, 224, 231
Kroll, Edite, 353
Kroll, Stephen, 223
Kroll, Virginia, 41
Krull, Kathleen, 102, 109, 240, 250
Krumgold, Joseph, 343
Krupinski, Loretta, 150, 158
Kuchera, Kathleen, 157
Kullman, Harry, 353
Kunhardt, Dorothy, 9, 88, 109
Kuroi, Ken, 108
Kuskin, Karla, 87, 102, 106, 109, 224, 231, 352
Kyle, Ann, 339

Labastida, Aurora, 331
The Lady of Guadeloupe, 146, 158
The Lady with the Hat, 354
Lafcadio, the Lion Who Shot Back, 258
Laird, Donivee Martin, 318, 323
The Land I Lost: Adventures of a Boy in Vietnam, 48, 60
Langham, Tony, 354
Langstaff, John, 155, 331
Langston Hughes: Great American Poet, 199
Langton, Jane, 346
Lasky, Kathryn, 67, 80, 205, 210, 221, 225, 228, 231, 236, 250, 346, 350
The Last Battle, 125
Later, Gator, 179
Latham, Jean Lee, 343
Lathrop, Dorothy P., 327, 339
Laubner, Patricia, 210, 231, 347
Laughlin, M., 224
Lavelle, Barbara, 184
Lawrence, Ian, 196, 205
Lawson, John, 349
Lawson, Robert, 6, 21, 30, 84, 88, 109, 115, 132, 236, 250, 327, 328, 341, 343

Leader by Destiny: George Washington, Man and Patriot, 340
Leaf, Munro, 88, 109, 127, 132, 327
The Leaf Man, 22, 30, *B.3*
Lear, Edward, 5, 254, 257, 261, 267, 278, 282, 310
The Learning Company, 299
Lears, Laurie, 73, 80
The Leaving, 350
The Leaving Morning, 165
Lee, Alan, 161
Lee, Dom, 206
Lee, Milly, 38, 60
Lee, Tanith, 138
The Legend of Africana, 43
The Legend of Bluebonnet, 146, 155, 158
The Legend of Fa Mulen, 141
The Legend of Scarface, 140
The Legend of Sleepy Hollow, 5, 30
LeGuin, Ursula K., 345, 349
Le Lun, Lad of Courage, 342
Lemieux, Michele, 278
Lemonade Sun and Other Summer Poems, 257, 277, *C.3*
L'Engle, Madeleine, 9, 26, 30, 126, 127, 128, 129.132, 303, 344, 346
Lenski, Lois, 340, 341
Lent, Blair, 331, 332, 333, 349
Lentil, 64, 81
Leodhas, Sorche Nic, 332, 344
Leon and Albertine, 117, 132
Leonardo da Vinci, 226, 240, 251
Leon's Story, 244, 252, 351
The Leopard, 353
Leprechaun's Gold, 145, 158
Lessac, Frane, 38
Lessem, Don, 221, 231
Lesser, Rika, 335, 354
Lester, Julius, 39, 60, 144, 153, 159, 160, 304, 336, 345, 351, *A.2*
LeTord, Bijou, 240, 250
Letters from Atlantis, 126, 133
Letters to Judy: What Kids Wish They Could Tell You, 7, 27
Letters to Rifka, 24, 29
Let the Circle Be Unbroken, 40, 43
Levine, Gail Carson, 348
Lewin, Ted, 306, 336
Lewis, Clive Staples, 6, 13, **124–125,** 129, 132, 139, 296, 303
Lewis, Elizabeth Foreman, 339
Lewis, Richard, 267, 268, 278
Lewison, Wendy Cheyette, 14, 30
Liang and the Magic Paintbrush, 146, 158
Libby on Wednesday, 172, 185
The Library Card, 25, 31
Lide, Alice, 339
Liea, Kate, 203, 205
The Life and Death of Crazy Horse, 237, 244, 250
The Light at Tern Rock, 342
A Light in the Attic, 26, 31, 258, 264
Lightning, 219
Like Jake and Me, 347
Lily's Crossing, 348
Li Ming, 133
Lincoln: A Photobiography, 210, 217, 231, 236, 243, 250, 347
Lindbergh, Reeve, 95, 109
Lindgren, Astrid, 119, 132, 354
Lindquist, Jennie, 343
Linevski, Aleksandr M., 353
Lion, 331

The Lion, the Witch, and the Wardrobe, 116, 124, 132, 296, 303
Lionni, Leo, 315, 316, 331, 332, 333
Lipkind, William, 329, 330
Lisker, Emily, 270, 277
Lisle, Janet Taylor, 347
Literature-Based Social Studies: Children's Books and Activities to Enrich the K–5 Curriculum, 224
Little, Jean, 99, 109
A Little at a Time, 241
Little Bear's Visit, 331
Little Blacknose, 338
The Little Engine That Could, 9, 86, 118, 126, 133
A Little Fear, 350
The Little Fishes, 349
The Little House, 328
Little House Cookbook, 202
Little House in the Big Woods, 10, 201–203
Little House on the Prairie, 10
Little House stories, 6, 18, 49, 53, 188, 201, 202, 203
The Little Island, 329
Little Lost Lamb, 328
The Little Man, 353
The Little Mermaid, 147
"The Little Mermaid," 5, 147
The Little Mermaid, the Original Story, 158
The Little Prince, 122, 132
The Little Red Hen, 99, 149, 159
Little Red Riding Hood, 335
"Little Red Riding Hood," 26, 30, 99, 137, 138, 149, 155
The Littles, 133
The Little Seven-Colored Horse, 140
"Little Snow-White," 138
The Littlest Angel, 9
Little Toot, 118, 132
Little Town on the Prairie, 341
Little Women, 5, 28, 164, 166
Litzinger, Rosanne, 158
Lives of Our Own, 172, 184
Livingston, Myra Cohn, 223, 264, 268, 278, 304, 352
Living up the Street, 46
The Llama Who Had No Pajamas: 100 Favorite Poems, 264
Llorente, Pilar Molina, 354
Lloyd, Megan, 159
Lobel, Anita, 24, 150, 335
Lobel, Arnold, 15, 30, 99, 109, 111, 152, 160, 196, 205, 260, 264, 267, 278, 305, 323, 333, 334, 335, 345
Local News, 45, 46, 60
Locker, Thomas, 59, 221
Loener, Jean, 131
Lofting, Hugh, 338
Lois Lowry: A Book of Memories, 246
London Bridge Is Falling Down, 349
Lone Journey: The Life of Roger Williams, 341
The Lonely Lioness and the Ostrich Chicks, 154
The Loner, 344
Longfellow, Henry Wadsworth, 261, 278
A Long Hard Journey: The Story of a Pullman Porter, 44, 199
Longshaw, Robin, 354
A Long Way from Home, 348
The Long Way to a New Land, 110, 196, 206
The Long Winter, 341
Lon Po Po: A Red-Riding Hood Story from China, 48, 61, 155, 161, 336, 351
Look Around! A Book About Shapes, 231

Looking at Pictures: An Introduction to Art for Young People, 224, 232
Looking Back: A Book of Memories, 251
Look! Look! Look!, 11, 30, 87, 109
Look What You've Done Now, Moses, 199
The Lorax, 3
Lord, Beth Bao, 48, 60, 244, 251
The Lord of the Rings, 116
Losing Uncle Tim, 66, 80
The Lost Garden, 245, 252
The Lost Years of Merlin, 123, 131, 152, 158
Louie, Ai-Ling, 48, 60, 141, 150, 160
Louis Armstrong: Jazz Musician, 199
Louis Braille: The Boy Who Invented Books for the Blind, 237, 250
Love Among the Walnuts, 175, 184
Lovelace, Maud Hart, 24
Love You, Soldier, 193
Love You Forever, 2, 30
Low, Joseph, 334
Low, William, 48, 60
Lowell, Susan, 317, 323
Lownsbery, Eloise, 339
Lowrey, Jeanette Sebring, 8
Lowry, Lois, 6, 11, 15, 30, 77, 80, 115, 126, 132, 170, 171, 184, 188,
    200, 205, 229, 231, 246, 251, 275, 278, 284, 298, 311, 317,
    323, 347, 348, 350
Lubin, Leonard, 131
Ludwig Van Beethoven, 240, 252
Lunn, Janet, 123, 132
Lyddie, 197, 200, 206
Lynch, Patrick James, 148

M. C. Higgins, the Great, 171, 174, 184, 345, 349
Maass, Robert, 239, 251
Macaulay, David, 98, 104, 109, 211, 231, 333, 334, 336, 350, *B.6, B.7*
McCaughrean, Geraldine, 153, 160
McClintock, Barbara, 158
McCloskey, Robert, 6, 9, 20, 23, 30, 64, 81, 84, 100, 109, 285, 328,
    329, 330, 331, *B.1*
McCord, David, 6, 254, 255, 257, 265, 278, 352
McCort, Frank, 284
McCully, Emily Arnold, 59, 100, 109, 153, 160, 176, 185, 197,
    205, 336
McDermott, Gerald, 88, 109, 144, **145**, 156, 160, 333, *B.8*
MacDonald, Golden, 328, 329
McDonald, Megan, 223
MacDonald, Sue, 41, 335
McElligot's Pool, 3, 329
McElrath-Eslick, Lori, 30
MacGill-Callahan, Sheila, 143, 160
McGinley, Phyllis, 329, 330
McGovern, Ann, 152, 160
McGrath, Barbara Barbieri, 96
McGraw, Eloise, 342, 344, 348
McGreft, J. K., 12
McGuffey Eclectic Readers, 64
McKinley, Robin, 346
McKinnon, Lise Sömme, 353
McKissack, Frederick L., 44, 52, **198–199**, 217, 229, 232, 241,
    251, 351
McKissack, Patricia C., 41, 44, 50, 52, 60, 121, 146, 160, **198–199,**
    217, 229, 232, 241, 251, 336, 347, 351, *A.3*
MacLachlan, Patricia, 6, 10, 11, 20, 30, 70, 74, 81, 177, 185, 188, 193,
    205, 285, 298, 347

McMillan, Bruce, 96, 215, 216, 232, 315
McMummy, 71
McNeely, Marian Hurd, 338
McPhail, David, 25, 30, 245, 251
Macy, Sue, 225, 232
Madaket Millie, 244, 252
Ma Dear's Aprons, 41, 60, *A.3*
Madeline, 1, 23, 30, 89, 107, 209, 263, 277, 285, 298, 327
Madeline's Rescue, 330
Maestro, Betsy, 223
Magic and the Night River, 91
The Magician's Nephew, 125
Magic Maize, 343
Mahy, Margaret, 47, 60, 144, 160
Mai, Vo-Dinh, 61, 186
Make Like a Tree and Leave, 177, 184
Make Way for Ducklings, 9, 100, 103, 109, 328, *B.1*
Maland, Nick, 29
Malcolmson, Anne, 329
Malcolm X: By Any Means Necessary, 242, 251
Malkus, Alida, 339
Mallatt, Kathy, 224, 232
Mama, Do You Love Me?, 179, 184
Mama, Let's Dance, 70, 80
Mama, Raouf, 51, 60
Mama Don't Allow, 350
Mama One, Mama Two, 70, 81
Mama Rocks, Papa Sings, 177, 186
Mandela: From the Life of the South African Statesman, 240, 249
The Man from the Other Side, 354
Maniac Magee, 73, 74, 81, 164, 175, 185, 311, 323, 347, 351
The Man Who Tricked a Ghost, 121
Many Moons, 328
Many Nations: An Alphabet Book of Native Americans, 39
The Many Ways of Seeing: An Introduction to the Pleasures of Art, 345
Marcello, Fred, 40, 59, 336
Marco, Katherine McGlade, 197, 205
Marguerite De Angeli's Book of Nursery and Mother Goose Rhymes, 260
Maria Tallchief, 240, 252
Marie, D., 193
Market Day, 65
Mark Twain and the Queens of the Mississippi, C.4
Marrin, Albert, 240, 251
Mars, 316, 323
Marshall, Bernard, 337
Marshall, James, 336
Marshmallow, 328
Marten, Jacqueline Briggs, 240, 251
Martha's Diner, 212
Martin, Ann, 24
Martin, Ann M., 69, 81, 179
Martin, Bill, Jr., 73, 81, 89, 94, 99, 109, 287, 299, 308, 315, 323
Martin, Jaqueline Briggs, 337
Martin, Rafe, 141, 150, 155, 160
Martinez, Ed, 47
Martinez, Victor, 45
Martin Luther King, 240, 242, 249
Martin Luther King, Jr.: Man of Peace, 43, 199
Maruki, Toshi, 51, 60, 196, 205, 354
Mary on Horseback: Three Mountain Stories, 240, 252
Mary Poppins, 31, 115
Marzollo, Claudio, 126, 132
Marzollo, Jean, 126, 132
Masai and I, 41
Masiello, Ralph, 110, 223, 232

Massola, Frank, 96
The Matchlock Gun, 341
Mathis, Sharon Bell, 41, 43, 60, 177, 185, 345
Matilda, 119
Max's Bath, 87, 111
Maxwell, William, 341
Mayer, Mercer, 93, 289, *B.5*
Mayfield Crossing, 172, 181, 185
May I Bring a Friend?, 332
Mayo, Edith, 251
Mazer, Norma Fox, 72, 81, 347
Meade, Holly, 279, 337
Meader, Stephen W., 340
Means, Florence Crannell, 341
Meanwhile . . . , 116, 132
Meddaugh, Susan, 11, 30, 65, 99, 109, 277
A Medieval Feast, 217, 230
Medio Pollito/Half-Chicken, 46, 59
Meggy Macintosh, 339
Meigs, Cornelia, 236, 251, 338, 339
Meike and the Fifth Treasure, 193
Mei Li, 327
Meltzer, Milton, 218, 232, 239, 251
Men, Microscopes, and Living Things, 343
The Mennyms, 120, 133
Men of Athens, 344
Merlin, 306
Merlin and the Dragons, 124, 133
The Mermaid's Twin Sister, 45
Merriam, Eve, 26, 30, 257, 278, 352
Merrin, Albert, 199
"Merseyside Snow White," 137
Mertorel, Antonio, 160
Messenger, Norman, 158
Meyer, Carolyn, 217, 232
Mice Twice, 334
Michael Foreman's Mother Goose, 260
The Middle Moffat, 341
The Middle Passage: White Ships, Black Cargo, 44, 93, 108, 217, 231
Midnight Dance of the Snowshoe Hare: Poems About Alaska, 102, 108
The Midwife's Apprentice, 72, 80, 188, 194, 196, 205, 348
Migdale, Lawrence, 231
The Mighty Hunter, 328
Mike Mulligan and His Steam Shovel, 285, 298
Miles, Miska, 66, 77, 81, 179, 185, 345
Milhous, Katherine, 329
Millard, Anne, 223
Millen, C. M., 217, 232
Miller, Edward, 231
Miller, Elizabeth, 338
Miller, William, 198, 205
Millions of Cats, 29, 88, 308, 323, 338
Milly and Tilly: The Story of a Town Mouse and a Country Mouse, 152, 161
Milne, A. A., 6, 9, 115, 118, 132, 263, 278
Milton, Jacqueline, 316, 323
Mine's the Best, 11, 29
Minn of the Mississippi, 342
Minor, Wendell, 321, 323
The Minpins, 120, 132
Minty: A Story of Young Harriet Tubman, 44, 236, 251
Miracles: Poems by Children of the English-Speaking World, 267, 278
Miracles on Maple Hill, 343
Mirandy and Brother Wind, 44, 199, 336
Mirette on the High Wire, 100, 109, 336

Mischling, Second Degree: My Childhood in Nazi Germany, 349
Miss Hickory, 341
Missing May, 66, 74, 81, 164, 175, 185, 319, 347, 351
The Missing Piece, 258
The Missing Piece Meets the Big O, 258
Mississippi Bridge, 36, 40, 61
Miss Nelson is Missing, 126, 131
Miss Rumphius, 101
Miss Spider's New Car, 102, 109
Miss Spider's Tea Party, 97, 109, 117, 132, *B.3*
Miss Spider's Wedding, 102, 109
Mr. Bow Tie, 72, 79
Mr. Gumpy's Outing, 349
Mr. Justice Holmes, 343
Mr. Penny's Race Horse, 331
Mr. Popper's Penguins, 321, 323, 340
Mr. Rabbit and the Lovely Present, 332
Mr. T. W. Anthony Wood: The Story of a Cat and a Dog and a Mouse, 330
Mr. Tuckett, 197, 206
Mrs. Frisby and the Rats of NIMH, 118, 130, 133, 312, 323, 345
Mistry, Nilesh, 221
Misty of Chincoteague, 342
Mitchell, Margaree King, 52, 60
Mitchell, Rhonda, 278
The Mitten: A Ukrainian Folktale, 143, 158, 283, *B.2*
Mitzi's Honeymoon with Nana Potts, 68, 81
Miz Berlin walks, 306
Mizumura, Kazue, 349
The M&M's Brand Chocolates Counting Book, 96
Moccasin Trail, 342
Mochizuki, Ken, 200, 206
Mohr, Nicholasa, 146, 160, 165, 185
Moinarik, Else Holmelund, 331
Moja Means One: A Swahili Counting Book, 96, 108, 333
Mojave, 225, 232
Mollel, Tololwa, 151, 160
Molly's Pilgrim, 37, 59
Molly the Brave and Me, 41
Molnar-Fenton, Stephan, 69, 81
Monday's Troll, 262
Monjo, F. N., 198, 206
Monkey Island, 73, 80
The Monkey's Haircut and Other Stories Told by the Maya, 146, 158
Montgomery, L. M., 6, 24, 30
Montgomery, Rutherford, 342
Montresor, Beni, 332
Moon, Grace, 338
The Moon Book, 212
The Moon Jumpers, 331
Moonlight, 92, 110
Moonstick, 65
Moorchild, 348
Moore, Anne Carroll, 338
Moore, Clement C., 24, 261, 278
Moore, Eva, 264
Moore, Janet Gaylord, 345
Moore, Lillian, 147, 158, 352
Mordvinoff, Nicholas, 329, 330
"More More More," Said the Baby: Three Love Stories, 336
Morgan, Roland, 218, 232
Morin, Paul, 160
Morning, Noon, and Night: Poems to Fill Your Day, 271, 279
Morning Girl, 189, 196, 205
Morning on the Lake, 49
Morpurgo, Michael, 152, 160

Morrill, Leslie, 132
Morrison, Gordon, 102, 109
Morrison, Lillian, 257, 278
Mosel, Arlene, 47, 60, 333, 349
Moser, Barry, 29, 159, 323, 351
Moser, Cara, 29
Moss, Lloyd, 96, 109, 337
Moss, Thylias, 41
The Most Beautiful Roof in the World, 225, 231
The Most Wonderful Doll in the World, 330
Mother Crocodile: An Uncle Amadou Tale from Senegal, 43
"Mother Doesn't Want a Dog," 256
Mother Goose, 86, 271
Mother Goose: Or, the Old Nursery Rhymes, 260
Mother Goose: Seventy-Seven Verses with Pictures, 328
Mother Goose and Nursery Rhymes, 332
A Mother Goose Book, 260
Mother Goose rhymes, 255, 320
Mother Goose's Melody, 259
Mother Goose's Words of Wit and Wisdom: A Book of Months, 260
Mother Goose Tales, 2, 5, 14, 15, 100, 259
Mother Jones: One Woman's Fight for Labor, 240, 250
Motown and Didi, 43
Mountain Born, 341
Mountains are Free, 339
The Mouse and the Motorcycle, 118, 127, 131
Mouse Mess, 99, 110
Mouse Paint, 315, 320, 323
The Moved-Outers, 341
The Moves Make the Man, 347, 350
Much Bigger Than Martin, 24
Mufaro's Beautiful Daughters: An African Tale, 44, 100, 110, 146, 150, 155, 161, 335, 350
Mugabane, Peter, 43
Mukerji, Dhan Gopal, 338
Müllen, Jörg, 353
Mummies Are Made in Egypt, 211, 230
"Mummy Slept Late and Daddy Cooked Breakfast," 257
Munsch, Robert, 2, 30, 289
Munsinger, Lynn, 278
Murphy, Jim, 11, 30, 226, 305, 323, 348
Musgrove, Margaret, 39, 94, 109, 334
Musicians of the Sun, 144, 145, 160
Mustard, 66, 74, 80
My Brother, Ant, 71, 171, 184
My Brother Sam is Dead, 11, 29, 192, 204, 345
"My Daddy," 266
Myers, Christopher, 232, 269, 278, 337
Myers, Paul, 223
Myers, Walter Dean, 43, 44, 197, 206, 232, 242, 251, 269, 278, 337, 347
My Father's Dragon, 342
My First Book of Colors, 216
My First Kwanzaa Book, 217, 230
My First Word Book, 13, 31
My House Has Stars, 223
My Mama Needs Me, 43
My Many Colored Days, 315
My Mom Can't Read, 25, 31
My Mother is the Most Beautiful Woman in the World, 328
My Mother's House, My Father's House, 68, 80
"My Name Is . . .", 274
My Name Is Maria Isabela, 165, 183
My Nursery School, 216, 232
My Own Two Feet: A Memoir, 245, 249

My Side of the Mountain, 173, 184, 314, 323, 343
The Mysteries of the Ancient Maya, 217, 232
My Two Uncles, 70, 81
My Underrated Year, 176, 185
My Very First Mother Goose, 101, 260
My Visit to the Aquarium, 225, 230

Naidoo, Beverley, 51, 60, 168, 185
Namioka, Lensey, 48, 60
Nancy Drew series, 9, 180
Nansen, 341
Nanta's Lion: A Search-and-Find Adventure, 41
The Napping House, B.4
Nash, Ogden, 263, 278
Nate the Great, 167
"Nathaniel's Rap," 266
Nathaniel Talking, 44, 265, 266, 277
Navajo ABC: A Dine Alphabet Book, 39
Naylor, Phyllis Reynolds, 4, 30, 175, 176, 185, 285, 298, 347
Neighborhood Odes, 47, 270, 279
Neitzel, Shirley, 4, 30
Nelson, Annika, 89, 107, 279
Nelson, Theresa, 73, 81
Nelson, Vaunda Micheaux, 172, 181, 185
Neptune: Voyager's Final Target, 316, 323
Ness, Evaline, 21, 30, 88, 92, 109, 331, 332
Nettie's Trip South, 193
Neville, Emily Cheney, 344
Newberry, Clare, 327, 328, 330
New Found World, 341
The New Kid on the Block, 262, 264, 289
New Land, 339
Newman, Lesléa, 70, 81
Newman, Shirlee P., 24
The New Oxford Book of Children's Verse, 264
The New Oxford Treasury of Children's Poems, 264
Nhuong, Huynh Quang, 48, 60
Nicholas: A Manhattan Christmas Story, 338
Nicholas Pike, 141
Nichols, Grace, 269, 277
Nicholson, William, 133
The Night Before Christmas, 261, 271, 278
"The Night Before Christmas," 24
Nightjohn, 173
Nightmares: Poems to Trouble Your Sleep, 262
Night of the Ninjas, 196, 206
Night of the Stars, 146, 159
Night on Neighborhood Street, 265, 266, 277
Night Swimmers, 71
Nilsson, Ulf, 354
Nim and the War Effort, 38, 60
Nine Candles, 74, 81
Nine Days to Christmas, 331
Nine-In-One, Grr! Grr!, 146, 161
Nino, 340
Nix, Garth, 124, 132
No, David!, 83, 110, 337
Noah's Ark, 334
Nocturne, 107, 111, 306
No Hero for the Kaiser, 354
No Hickory, No Dickory, No Dock: Caribbean Nursery Rhymes, 269, 277
Nolan, Dennis, 152, 160
The Noonday Friends, 344

No Place to Be: The Voices of Homeless Children, 73, 79
Norman, Howard, 148
North, Sterling, 344
Northern Indian Cooking, 12
Norton, Mary, 120, 132
Nöstlinger, Christine, 353
Not a Copper Penny in Me House, 270
Nothing at All, 328
Nothing but the Truth, 347
Nothing Ever Happens on My Block, 22, 31
Nothing's Fair in Fifth Grade, 172, 184
The Not-Just-Anybody Family, 71
No Turning Back, 51, 60
Now It's Your Time! The African-American Struggle for Freedom, 44
Noyes, Alfred, 255
The Numbers on My Grandfather's Arm, 241
Number the Stars, 15, 30, 200, 205, 229, 231, 284, 298, 347
Numeroff, Laura Jaffe, 9, 98, 110, 288
Nursery and Household Tales, 136
Nyhart, Nina, 275

O'Brien, Edna, 148
O'Brien, Robert C., 118, 130, 133, 312, 323, 345
O'Connor, Jane, 41
O'Dell, Scott, 10, 57, 60, 174, 185, **190–191,** 192, 196, 199, 200, 203, 206, 344, 345, 355
Odysseus, 139
Odyssey, 154
Off and Running, 47
Officer Buckle and Gloria, 101, 110, 337
Off to School, 41
Ogbo: Sharing Life in an African Village, 217, 223, 232
Oh, the Places You'll Go, 2, 3, 29
Oh, What an Awful Mess!, 239, 251
O'Huigin, Sean, 288
Old Cotton Blues, 41, 59
Old Elm Speaks: Tree Poems, 257, 277
Oldfield, Sara, 225, 232
"Old King Cole," 259
The Old Man and His Door, 46, 47, 61
Old Ramon, 344
Olds, Elizabeth, 330
An Old Tale Carved Out of Stone, 353
The Old Tobacco Shop: A True Account of What Befell a Little Boy in Search of Adventure, 338
Old Yeller, 176, 184, 343
Oliver, Maria Fernandez, 146, 159
O'Malley, Kevin, 88, 108, 159
Omerod, Jan, 92, 93, 110
Once a Mouse . . . , 331
"One, two, buckle my shoe," 271
One, Two, One Pair, 96
Oneal, Zibby, 350
One at a Time, 265, 278
One-Eyed Cat, 19, 29, 347
One Fine Day, 144, 155, 159, 333
One Fish, Two Fish, Red Fish, Blue Fish, 3, 9, 99, 108
One Grain of Rice, 222, 231
O'Neill, Mary, 256, 278
The One in the Middle Is the Green Kangaroo, 7, 27, 29, 171, 183
1 is One, 331
One Million, 222, 231
One Morning in Maine, 330

One of Three, 165
One Red Rooster, 315
One Sun Rises: An African Wildlife Counting Book, 96
1, 2, 3 to the Zoo, 95, 108
One Wide River to Cross, 332
One Yellow Daffodil: A Hanukkah Story, 241
Onion John, 343
On Market Street, 335
On My Honor, 347
On My House, 266
On the Banks of Plum Creek, 340
On the Day Peter Stuyvesant Sailed into Town, 196, 205
Onyefulu, Ifeoma, 217, 223, 232
Ood-Le-Uk the Wanderer, 339
Opie, Iona, 101, 260
Opposites, 216
Orbis Sensualum Pictus, 5
The Originals: Animals That Time Forgot, 306
Origins of Life on Earth: An African Creation Myth, 44
Orlev, Uri, 354
The Orphan Boy, 151, 160
Orphan Train Rider: One Boy's True Story, 351
Orr, Richard, 221
Osborne, Mary Pope, 196, 206
O'Shaughnessy, Tam, 316, 323
Osofsky, Audrey, 240, 251
Otherwise Known as Sheila the Great, 7
Oughton, Jerrie, 144, 160
Our Eddie, 345
Our Golda: The Story of Golda Meir, 240, 249
Our Solar System, 219, 316, 323
Out of Darkness: The Story of Louis Braille, 244
Out of the Dust, 22, 30, 66, 74, 80, 263, 277, 348
Out of the Flame, 339
Outside Over There, 98, 335, 350
The Outsiders, 9, 15, 30
Over the Moon: An Adoption Tale, 69, 80
Over the Water, 171, 184
Over Under in the Garden: An Alphabet Book, 232
Owen, 16, 336
The Owl and the Pussycat, 278, 282
"The Owl and the Pussycat," 261
Owl Moon, 101, 306, 335
Ox-Cart Man, 89, 108, 334

Pablo Remembers: The Fiesta of the Day of the Dead, 67, 79
Paddle-to-the-Sea, 328
Pageant of Chinese History, 339
Palazzo, Tony, 329
Pallas, Norvin, 222, 232
The Palm of My Heart: Poetry by African American Children, 270
Palotta, Jerry, 94, 95, 110, 217, 232
Pancakes for Breakfast, 93, 108
Pancakes-Paris, 341
The Paper Airplane Book, 219
The Paper Bag Princess, 289
The Paperboy, 337
The Paper Crane, 350
Parade, 215, 230
Parish, Peggy, 119, 133
Park, Barbara, 172, 176, 185
Park, Dong-il, 148
Park, Ruth, 350

Parker, Nancy Winslow, 30
Parker, Robert Andrew, 158, 205, 333
Parks, Rosa, 245, 251
Parnall, Peter, 29, 81, 334
Parrish, Anne, 338, 339, 342
Parrot in the Oven: Mi Vida, 45
Paschal, Francine, 179
Pass It On: African American Poetry for Children, 270
Pass the Poetry, Please, 264
The Patchwork Quilt, 42, 43, 59, 355
Paterson, Katherine, 4, 6, 10, 15, 26, 30, 67, 70, 78, 81, 168, 171, 174, 181, 185, 189, 197, 200, 206, 284, 298, 346, 351
Patricic, Dusan, 158
Patterson, Lillie, 43
Pat the Bunny, 9, 88, 109
Paul, Ann Whitford, 94, 110
Paul Bunyan, 100, 109, 159
Paul Revere's Ride, 261, 278
Paul Robeson, 267
Paulsen, Gary, 50, 60, 164, 166, 172, **173**, 174, 181, 185, 197, 206, 347
Pausewang, Gudrun, 198, 206
The Pea Patch Jig, 24
Pearson, Tracey Campbell, 95
Peck, Richard, 67, 81, 348
Pecos Bill, 159, 293, 298, 340
Pedro, the Angel of Olvera Street, 329
Pedro's Journal: A Voyage with Christopher Columbus, 196, 204
Peet, Bill, 245, 251, 336
Pelgrom, Els, 353
Pelletier, David, 337
Penn, 340
The People Could Fly: American Black Folktales, 148
Peppe the Lamplighter, 336
The Perilous Gard, 345
The Perilous Road, 343
Perrault, Charles, 5, 63, 136, 137, 138, 259, 330, 336
Perrault's Fairy Tales, 138
Peter Rabbit, 86
Peters, Plym, 354
Peter's Chair, 11, 30, 38, 60, 85, 109
Petersham, Maud, 328
Petersham, Miska, 328
Peterson, John, 133
Peter Spier's Christmas! The Story of Holly and Ivy, 24
Peter the Great, 102, 110, 239, 251
Petros' War, 353
Petry, Ann Lane, 197, 206
Pets in a Jar: Collecting and Caring for Small Animals, 219
The Phantom Tollbooth, 122, 132
The Philharmonic Gets Dressed, 224, 231
Philip, Neil, 264
Philip Hall Likes Me, I Reckon Maybe, 345
Phoebe Fairchild: Her Book, 340
Phoenix Rising, 182, 184
"The Pickety Fence," 255
A Picture Book of Davy Crockett, 241
A Picture Book of Jewish Holidays, 241
A Picture Book of Louis Braille, 241
The Picture That Mom Drew, 224, 232
The Pied Piper of Hamelin, 320, 323
Pierre: A Cautionary Tale, 98, 285, 298
Pierre Pigeon, 328
Pigs from 1 to 10, 96
Pigtail of Ah Lee Ben Loo, 338
Pilgrims of Plimouth, 350

Pilkey, Dav, 88, 109, 337
A Pillow for My Mom, 66, 81
The Pinballs, 70, 71, 74, 80, 171, 184
Pink and Say, 25, 30, 50, 60, 106, 110, 188, 206
Pinkney, Andrea Davis, 36, 60, 74, 81, 237, 240, 242, 251, 337
Pinkney, Brian, 41, 60, 141, 148, 176, 185, 250, 269, 337, 351
Pinkney, Jerry, 8, 39, 41, 43, 44, 59, 60, 85, 89, 101, 153, 159, 160, 250, 336, 351, 355, 365, *A.2*
Pinkwater, Daniel Manus, 315
Piper, Watty, 9, 118, 133
Pippi in the South Seas, 119, 132
Pippi Longstocking, 119
The Pirate Queen, 153, 160
Pirates in Petticoats, 306
Pirotta, Saviour, 221
A Pizza the Size of the Sun, 264
Planet Earth/Inside Out, 321, 323
The Planet of Junior Brown, 73, 80, 345
Playing Beatie Bow, 350
Play with Me, 331
Plecas, Jennifer, 109
Plume, Ilse, 334
Pocahontas: Powhatan Peacemaker, 240, 250
A Pocket Full of Posies, 260, 279
A Pocketful of Crickets, 332
"Poem on the Neck of A Running Giraffe," 268
Poems of A. Nonny Mouse, 262
The Poetry Connection, 275
Poitier, Sidney, 43
The Poky Little Puppy, 8
Polacco, Patricia, 25, 30, 50, 60, 100, 106, 110, 188, 206, 244, 251, 261, 279
The Polar Express, 13, 22, 24, 31, 98, 101, 335, *B.4*
Politi, Leo, 329
Politically Correct Bedtime Stories: Modern Tales for Our Life and Times, 52, 56, 142, 159
Polizzotti, Mark, 205
Polushkin, Maria, 353
Pony Express!, 223
Pop Corn and Ma Goodness, 333
Pope, Elizabeth Marie, 345
Poppi, 351
Poppleton, 319
Poppleton Everyday, 117, 133
Porter, Neal, 337
Postman Pig and His Busy Neighbors, 53
Potato: A Tale from the Great Depression, 203, 205
Potter, Beatrix, 6, 8, 9, 30, 83, 84, 89, 115, 117, 133, 287, 298, 299, *A.1*
Poulsen, Gunnar, 353
Powell, Randy, 176, 185
The Prancing Pony: Nursery Rhymes from Japan, 270, 277
Pran of Albania, 338
Prayer for a Child, 328
Prelutsky, Jack, 3, 8, 15, 101, 254, 256, 257, **262**, 263, 264, 278, 289, 290
Preston, Edna Mitchell, 333
A Pretty Little Pocketbook, 5
Price, Leontyne, 44
Priceman, Marjorie, 337
Prince Caspian, the Return to Narnia, 125
The Princess and the Pea, 122, 131
Princess Furball, 150
The Princess in the Kitchen Garden, 354
Princess Smartypants, 142, 158
Pringle, Laurence, 226

Prins, Johanna H., 354
Prins, Johanna W., 354
Prior, Bonnie, 177, 185
Priscilla Twice, 67, 80
Proust, Marcel, 25
Provensen, Alice, 100, 110, 317, 323, 334, 335, 350
Provensen, Martin, 100, 110, 317, 323, 334, 335, 350
Prueman, Marjorie, 109
Prydan Chronicles, 124
Pulga, 353
Pullman, Philip, 126, 133
Push-Pull, Empty-Full, 216
Puss in Boots, 149, 159, 330, 336
"Puss in Boots," 136, 144
Pyramids, 223

Quackenbush, Robert M., 239, 251
The Quaint and Curious Quest of Johnny Longfoot, 342
Queer Person, 339

Rabbit and the Moon, 147, 161
Rabbit Hill, 21, 30, 115, 132, 341
Rabbit Island, 353
Rabbit Makes a Monkey out of Lion, 154
Rabble Starkey, 350
Rabinovici, Schoschana, 355
Rackham, Arthur, 147, 157
Raglan, Tim, 159
Rahasman, Vashanti, 25, 30
The Railroad to Freedom: A Story of the Civil War, 339
"Rain, rain, go away," 259
The Rainbow People, 148, 179
Rain Drop Splash, 329
Rain Forests, 225, 232
Rain Makes Applesauce, 332
Ramanujan, A. K., 148
Ramona and Her Father, 346
Ramona Quimby, Age 8, 170, 184, 346
Ramona the Pest, 64, 80, 304
Rand, Ted, 94, 261, 278
The Random House Book of Mother Goose, 260
The Random House Book of Poetry for Children, 256, 262, 264, 274, 278
Rankin, Laura, 94
Rankin, Louis, 342
Ransom, Arthur, 332
Ransome, James E., 44, 60, 79, 205
Rapunzel, 99, 111, 149, 161, 337, *B.2*
Rascal, 344
Rasco and the Rats of NIMH, 130.131
Raskin, Ellen, 22, 31, 175, 185, 318, 323, 345, 346, 349
Rathman, Peggy, 101, 110, 337
Rattigan, Jama Kim, 50, 60
Rattlesnakes, 243
Raven: A Trickster Tale from the Pacific Northwest, 144, 145, 160
Raven in a Dove House, 74, 81
Rawlings, J. K., 116, 133
Rawlings, Marjorie Kinnan, 176, 185, 343
Rawls, Wilson, 9, 78, 81, 176, 185, 304
Ray Charles, 43
Reaching Dustin, 172, 184
Read-Aloud Rhymes for the Very Young, 262
Read for Me, Mama, 25, 30
Really Rosie, 98

The Real Mother Goose, 23
Rebecca of Sunnybrook Farm, 5, 31, 164, 166
Red as Blood or Tales from the Sisters Grimmer, 138
Red Leaf, Yellow Leaf, 315
Red Sails to Capri, 342
Redwall, 118, 132
Redwall series, 24
Reed, Philip, 332
Reeder, Carolyn, 189, 197, 206
Reef, Catherine, 240, 251
Reiss, Johannna, 345
Reiss, John, 216
The Relatives Came, 319, 335
The Remarkable Adventures of Captain Cook, 240, 249
Remember the Good Times, 67, 81
Renalder, Ann, 197, 206
Rendon, Maria, 279
Renner, Hans Peter, 353
Reuter, Bjarne, 354
Revolting Rhymes, 120
Rey, H. A., 117, 133
Rey, Margaret, 117, 133
Reyher, Becky, 328
Reynolds, John Gardner, 15
Rhoads, Dorothy, 343
Ribbons, 48, 61, 179
Ribsy, 168, 184
Richardson, Joy, 224, 232
Richard Wright and the Library Card, 198, 205
Richter, Hans Peter, 353
Ride, Sally, 232, 244, 251, 316, 323
Rifles for Watie, 343
Riley, Linnea, 99, 110
"Ring Around the Rosie," 260
Ringgold, Faith, 8, 44, **85,** 122, 133, 336, 355, *B.2*
A Ring of Endless Light, 346
A Ring of Tricksters: Animal Tales from America, the West Indies, and Africa, 321, 323
Ritz, Karen, 80
A River Dream, 91
The Road from Home: The Story of an Armenian Girl, 346, 349
The Road to Memphis, 40, 44
The Robber and Me, 355
Robbins, Ruth, 331
Robin Hood of Sherwood Forest, 152, 160
Robins, Charles, 206
Robinson, Aminah Brenda Lynn, 89, 108
Robinson, Barbara, 176, 185
Robinson, Dorothy, 43
Robinson, Jackie, 43
Robinson, Mabel, 340
Robinson Crusoe, 2, 164
Rockwell, Harlow, 216, 232
Rockwell, Thomas, 176, 185, 303
Rodanas, Kristina, 151, 160
Roger and the Fox, 329
Rogers, Jacqueline, 31
Rohmann, Eric, 336
Rojankovsky, Feodor, 331
Roller Skates, 340
Rolling Harvey Down the Hill, 263, 278
Rolling Henry Down the Hill, 262
The Rolling Stone, 165
Rollins, Charlemae, 43
Rollo and Tweedy and the Ghost at Dougal Castle, 121

Roll of Thunder, Hear My Cry, 4, 7, 10, 31, 36, 40, 61, 174, 188, 206, 285, 299, 346
Ronia, the Robber's Daughter, 354
A Room Made of Windows, 349
The Rooster Crows, 328
The Rooster Who Went to His Uncle's Wedding, 146, 157
The Root Cellar, 123, 132
Rosa Parks: My Story, 242, 245, 250, 251, 266
Rose, David, 132
Rose Blanche, 198, 205, 354
Rosen, Michael J., 95, 110
Rosenberg, Liz, 193
Rosetti, Christina, 254
Rosie's Walk, 97, 109, 308, 323
Ross, Christine, 81
Ross, Jim, 223
Rosy Cole: She Walks in Beauty, 177, 184
Roth, Susan L., 251
Rothman, Eric, 93, 110
The Rough-Faced Girl, 141, 150, 155, 160
Rounds, Glen, 149, 160
Rourke, Constance, 340
Ruby, 149, 158
Rudnik, Maryka, 353
Rudnik, Raphael, 353
Rufus M., 341
Rumpelstiltskin, 149, 159, 161, 335
"Rumpelstiltskin," 5, 155
Rumpelstiltskin's Daughter, 149, 155, 161
Run Away Home, 50, 60
Runaway Papoose, 338
Runaway Ralph, 118, 131
Runner of the Mountain Tops: The Life of Louis Agassiz, 340
Ruth Bader Ginsberg, 239, 249
Ryan, Cheli Duran, 333
Ryan, Pam Munoz, 96, 223
Ryan White: My Own Story, 245, 252
Rylant, Cynthia, 66, 74, 81, 87, 99, 110, 117, 164, 175, 185, **319**, 335, 347, 351

Sacagawea: Northwest Explorer, 242, 250
Sachar, Louis, 15, 31, 348
Sacred Fire, 49, 61
The Sacred Path: Spells, Prayers, and Power Songs of the American Indians, 270, 277
Sadako and the Thousand Paper Cranes, 178, 184
Safari Beneath the Sea: The Wonder World of the North Pacific Coast, 226
Saggy Baggy Elephant, 8
Sailing: From Jibs to Jibing, 173
St. George and the Dragon, 335
St. Patrick's Day in the Morning, 65, 282
Saito, Manabu, 148
Salisbury, Graham, 189
Salter, Safaya, 152, 157
Salvadori, Mario, 350
Sam, Bangs and Moonshine, 21, 30, 88, 92, 109, 332
Sam and the Tigers, 39, 60, *A.2*
Sam and the Zamboni Man, 101, 110
Samuel's Choice, 192, 204
The Samurai's Daughter, 141
Sandburg, Carl, 267
Sander, Joan, 196, 206
Sanderson, Ruth, 184

Sandin, Joan, 81, 110
Sandler, Martin W., 223
Sandoz, Mari, 343
San Souci, Daniel, 141, 147, 158
San Souci, Robert D., 101, 121, **140–141,** 146, 148, 152, 160, 336, 337
Santore, Charles, 147, 158
Saport, Linda, 60
Sarah, Plain and Tall, 10, 11, 20, 30, 177, 185, 188, 205, 285, 298, 347
Sarah Bishop, 192, 206
"Sarah Cynthia Sylvia Stout Who Would Not Take the Garbage Out," 256
Sarny, a Life Remembered, 173
Sauer, Julia, 341, 342
Savage, Deborah, 172, 185
Saving Shiloh, 4, 30, 176, 185
Sawyer, Ruth, 328, 330, 340, 352
Say, Allen, 7, 48, 60, 61, 69, 74, 81, 85, **91,** 161, 242, 251, 336, 350, 351, *A.4*
Saying Good-Bye to Grandma, 66, 81
Scarecrow, 319
Scarry, Richard, 9, 13, 23, 31, 53, 225, 260
Scary Poems for Rotten Kids, 288
Schaefer, Jack, 9, 344
Schaffer, Manda, 81
Schami, Rafik, 354
Schechter, Ellen, 152, 160
Scheer, Julian, 332
The Schernoff Discoveries, 173
Schick, Eleanor, 39
Schindelman, Joseph, 132
Schindler, S. D., 108
Schlein, Miriam, 330
Schmidt, Sara, 339
Schoenherr, John, 101, 184, 335
Schories, Pat, 232
Schreiber, George, 329
Schreiter, Rick, 353
Schroeder, Alan, 44, 236, 251
Schroeder, Ann, 150
Schwartz, Alvin, 257, 263, 278
Schwartz, David M., 222, 232
Science and Technology in Fact and Fiction: A Guide to Children's Books, 221
Scieszka, Jon, 22, 31, 99, 104, 110, 147, 149, 152, 160, 161, 317, 323, 336, *B.6*
Scooter, 172, 186, 351
Scorpions, 347
Scott, Elaine, 316, 323
Scott, Sir Walter, 188
The Screwtape Letters, 125
Scuffy the Tugboat, 8
Seabird, 342
Sea Glass, 178
The Sea King: Sir Francis Drake and His Times, 240, 251
The Sea Man, 306
Seashore Story, 332
Sea Turtles, 213
The Seaweed Suitcase, 270, 279
The Secret Garden, 6, 29, 164, 304
The Secret of Platform 13, 124, 132
Secret of the Andes, 342
The Secret of the Indian, 118, 131
The Secret River, 343
Seeger, Elizabeth, 339
Seeger, Pete, 155, 161, 298

Selden, George, 10, 344
Selway, Martina, 167
The Seminoles, 49
Sendak, Maurice, 6, 9, 26, 31, 84–85, **97–98**, 100, 110, 122, 133, 275, 279, 285, 298, 314, 323, 330, 331, 332, 333, 335, 350, 352, 365
A Sending of Dragons, 306
Sequoyah's Gift: Portrait of a Cherokee Leader, 240, 250
Seredy, Kate, 328, 340
Serfozo, Mary, 315
The Serpent Never Sleeps, 191
Service, Robert W., 261, 279
Seuss, Dr. *See* Geisel, Theodor Seuss
Seven Blind Mice, 315, 336, 351
Seven Candles for Kwanzaa, 36, 60
The Seven Chinese Brothers, 47, 60, 144, 160
Seven Simeons: A Russian Tale, 327
The Seven Songs of Merlin, 152, 158
17 Black Artists, 43
Sewall, Marcia, 251, 350
Sewell, Anna, 176
Sewell, Helen, 330
Sgouros, Charissa, 66, 81
Shabanu, Daughter of the Wind, 347
Shades of Gray, 189
Shadow, 335, B.8
Shadow of a Bull, 344
Shadrach, 343
The Shakespeare Stealer, 196, 204
Shane, 9
Shannon, David, 83, 110, 141, 150, 160, 279, 306, 337
Shannon, George, 193
Shannon, Monica, 339
Shapes (Geddes), 216
Shapes (Reiss), 216
Sharks, 220
Sharks (Gibbons), C.1
Sharks (Simon), C.1
Sharmat, Marjorie Weinman, 167
Shaw, Nancy, 14, 31, 314, 323
Sheep in a Jeep, 14, 31, 314, 323
Sheep on a Ship, 14, 31, 314, 323
Sheep out to Eat, 14, 31
Sheila Ray, the Brave, 288
She Keep Bringing Me That Little Baby Girl, 266
Shelley, Mary, 125
Shen of the Sea, 338
Shenton, Edward, 185
Shepard, Aaron, 146, 161
Shepard, E. H., 132
The Sheriff of Rottenshot, 262
She's Wearing a Dead Bird on Her Head, 236, 250
Shiloh, 4, 30, 175, 176, 185, 285, 298, 347
Shiloh Season, 4, 30, 176, 185
Shimin, Simeon, 184
Shimmy Shimmy Shimmy Like My Sister Kate: Looking at Harlem Renaissance Through Poems, 270
Shimpei, Noro, 91
Shippen, Katherine, 341, 343
Shoes Like Ms. Alice's, 165
Shooting Stars, 211, 230
Short and Shivery series, 141
Shortcut, 105
Shulevitz, Uri, 321, 323, 332, 334, 337
Shurzynski, Gloria, 323

Shute, Linda, 145, 161
Shy Charles, 350
Sibley, Anne, 355
Sidjak, Nicolas, 331
Siebert, Diane, 225, 232
Siegal, Aranka, 346, 350
The Sign of the Beaver, 346
Silva, Simon, 38
Silverberg, Robert, 126, 133
The Silver Chair, 125
Silver Packages: An Appalachian Christmas Story, 319
The Silver Pencil, 341
Silverstein, Shel, 2, 8, 9, 26, 31, 88, 110, 254, 256, **257–258**, 263, 264, 268, 279, B.7
The Silver Treasure: Myths and Legends of the World, 153, 160
Simon, Seymour, 8, **219–220**, 228, 304, 316, 323, C.1
Simont, Marc, 184, 278, 329, 331
Simple Gifts: The Story of the Shakers, 306
Sing a Song of Popcorn: Every Child's Book of Poems, 264
Sing Down the Moon, 191, 192, 200, 206, 345
Singer, Isaac Bashevis, 344, 345
The Singing Tree, 340
Sing in Praise: A Collection of the Best-Loved Hymns, 329
Singmaster, Elsie, 339
Sing Mother Goose, 328
Sis, Peter, 95, 98, 110, 222, 232, 240, 251, 321, 323, 337
Sister, 267
Sked, Greg, 89, 109
Skinnybones, 176, 185
Skip Across the Ocean: Nursery Rhymes from Around the World, 271, 277
Skipper John's Cook, 330
Skip to My Lou, 155, 161
The Skirt, 177, 185
Skofield, James, 355
Skurzynski, Gloria, 316
The Sky Is Always the Sky, 102, 109
The Sky is Full of Stars, 229, 230
Skylark, 193
Sky Sash So Blue, 89, 108
Slade's Children, 124, 132
Slake's Limbo, 174, 184
Slam!, 44
Slam Dunk: Basketball Poems, 257, 278
The Slave Dancer, 177, 184, 198, 205, 345
Slave Day, 177, 186
Sleator, William, 333
Sleep, Sleep, Sleep: A Lullaby for Little Ones Around the World, 271, 279
Slepian, Jan, 73, 81
Slobodkin, Louis, 328
Slobodkina, Esphyr, 155, 161, 321, 323
Small, David, 337
Small, Irene, 38, 41, 61
Small Rain: Verses from the Bible, 328
Smith, Doris, 67, 74, 81
Smith, Kathleen Atkins, 44
Smith, Lane, 3, 8, 30, 31, 85, 89, 99, 101, 104, 110, 152, 160, 161, 262, 324, 336, B.6
Smith, Patricia Clark, 249
Smith, Roberta, 186
The Smithsonian Book of the First Ladies: Their Lives, Times, and Issues, 243, 251
Smoky, the Cowhorse, 338
Smoky Mountain Rose: An Appalachian Cinderella, 150
Smoky Night, 50, 59, 65, 74, 79, 89, 108, 167, 170, 183, 336
Snakes, 219

Snapshots from the Wedding, 45, 46, 47, 61, 89, 110, *A.4*
Snedeker, Caroline, 338, 339
Sneed, Brad, 150
Sneve, Virginia Driving Hawk, 7, **49**, 61, 218, 270, 279
Snow, 321, 323, 337
Snow Dance, 99, 108
Snowdrops for Cousin Ruth, 66, 81
Snowflake Bentley, 240, 251, 337
The Snowman, 349
Snow White, 120, 285
"Snow White," 5, 14, 136
Snow White and the Seven Dwarfs, 327, 333
The Snowy Day, 7, 30, 85, 90, 109, 332, *A.3*
Snyder, Diane, 61, 91, 146, 161, 336, 350
Snyder, Zilpha Keatley, 172, 185, 344, 345
Sobol, Donald, 175, 185
So Far from Home: The Diary of Mary Driscoll, an Irish Mill Girl, 197, 205
So Far from the Sea, 65, 200, 204
Sojourner Truth: Ain't I a Woman?, 199, 351
Sol a Sol, 270, 277
A Solitary Blue, 346
Solt, Mary Ellen, 268, 279
Some of the Kinder Planets, 351
Something on My Mind, 43
Somewhere in the Darkness, 347
Song and Dance Man, 224, 230, 336
The Song of el Coqui and Other Tales of Puerto Rico, 146, 160
Song of Robin Hood, 329
Song of Roland, 154
Song of Senda, 140
Song of the Swallows, 329
Song of the Trees, 36, 40, 57, 61
Sons of the Pines: A Story of Norwegian Lumbering in Wisconsin, 342
Sootface: An Ojibwa Cinderella Story, 141
Sorensen, Virginia, 343
SOS Titanic, 65
Soto, Gary, 7, 45, **46–47**, 61, 89, 110, 117, 133, 177, 185, 270, 279, *A.4*
Soul Looks Back in Wonder, 44, 269
Sounder, 10, 21, 28, 345
The Sound of Dragon's Feet, 353
Souza, Diana, 81
The Space Atlas: A Pictorial Atlas of Our Universe, 316, 323
Space Station Seventh Grade, 182, 185
Spagnoli, Cathy, 161
Spanger, Stella S., 221
Speare, Elizabeth George, 194, 195, 197, 200, 206, 343, 344, 346, 352
Special War, 173
Sperry, Armstrong, 174, 185, 340
Spice and the Devil's Cave, 339
Spiders, 212
Spier, Peter, 11, 31, 93, 122, 133, 216, 331, 334, 349
Spinelli, Jerry, 6, 15, 25, 31, 73, 74, 81, 164, 175, 181, 182, 185, 311, 323, 347, 348, 351
Spirin, Gennady, 158, 160
Spivak, Dawnene, 268, 279
Spring Across America, 220
The Spring Rider, 349
Spying on Miss Muller, 65
Squids Will Be Squids: Fresh Morals, Beastly Fables, 152, 161
Stanek, Muriel, 25, 31
Stanley, Diane, 102, 110, 149, 155, 161, 226, 239, 240, 251, 252, 306
Staples, Susan Fisher, 347
The Star Fisher, 178
Star of Fear, Star of Hope, 198, 205

Starry Messenger: A Book Depicting the Life of a Famous Scientist, Mathematician, Astronomer, Philosopher, Physicist: Galileo Galilei, 240, 251, 337
Star Walk, 219
The Steadfast Tin Soldier, 330
Steele, Mary Q., 345
Steele, William O., 343
Steffans, Klaus, 354
Steig, William, 14, 20, 31, 117, 133, 333, 334, 346
Stein, Sara Burnett, 69, 81
Stepping on the Cracks, 189
Steptoe, Javaka, 44, 269
Steptoe, John, 7, 43, 44, 85, 100, 110, 146, 150, 161, 335, 350
Stevens, Janet, 155, 159, 161, 337
Stevenson, Harvey, 110
Stevenson, James, 101, 110
Stevenson, Robert Louis, 5, 31, 164, 254, 264, 265, 274, 279
Stevie, 85, 110
Stewart, Sarah, 337
Stine, R. L., 179
The Stinky Cheese Man and Other Fairly Stupid Tales, 3, 99–100, 104, 110, 147, 161, 336, *B.6*
Stoltz, Mary, 344
Stone, Erika, 81
Stone, Helen, 329, 330
Stone, Kazuko G., *C.2*
The Stonecutter, 145
Stone Fox, 10, 15, 29, 181, 284, 298, 304
Stone Soup: An Old Tale, 143, 158, 329
Stopping by Woods on a Snowy Evening, 254, 277
The Storm Book, 330
Storms, 219
A Story, a Story: An African Tale, 100, 108, 159, 333
The Story of an English Castle, 93
The Story of an English Village, 93, 108
The Story of Appleby Capple, 342
The Story of Babar, 23
The Story of Booker T. Washington, 199
The Story of Design, 231
The Story of Ferdinand, 88, 109, 127, 132
The Story of Golf, 224, 230
The Story of Jumping Mouse, 335
The Story of Little Babaji, 40, 59
The Story of Little Black Sambo, 38, 59, *A.2*
The Story of Mankind, 337
The Story of Stevie Wonder, 43
Story of the Negro, 342
Stranded at Plimoth Plantation 1626, 196, 204
Stratmeyer, Edward, 6
Strawberry Girl, 341
Strega Nona, 100, 108, 143, 158, 334
Strickland, Paul, 87, 110
Strider, 68, 80
A String in the Harp, 346
Strong, Phil, 340
Stuart-Clark, Christopher, 264
Stuart Little, 10
Suen, Anastasia, 101, 110
Sugaring Time, 210, 231, 346
Sugarman, Tracy, 160
Sukey and the Mermaid, 141
A Summer Life, 46
The Summer of My German Soldier, 197, 205
Summer of the Monkeys, 78, 81
Summer of the Swans, 71, 73, 74, 80, 171, 184, 345

Summers, Kate, 152, 161
Summer Sisters, 7
A Summer to Die, 171, 184
Sundiata: Lion King of Mali, 154
Sun Horse, Moon Horse, 195, 206
The Sun Is a Golden Earring, 332
The Sun Is So Quiet, 270
Sunshine, 92, 110
Sunshine Home, 65
Superfudge, 7, 170, 183
Surat, Michele, 48, 56–57, 61, 178, 186
Surtsey: The Newest Place on Earth, 221, 231
Sutcliff, Rosemary, 154, 161, 195, 206, 349
Swamp Angel, 153, 159, 336
Swann, Brian, 270, 279
Swanson, Diane, 226
Sweat, Lynn, 133
Sweet Clara and the Freedom Quilt, 198, 205
Sweet Valley High, 179
Sweetwater, 178
Sweet Whispers, Brother Rush, 43, 346, 350
Swift, Hildegarde, 338, 339
Swift, Jonathan, 2, 115
Swift Rivers, 339
Swimmy, 332
"The Swing," 265
Swope, Sam, 315, 316
Swords of Steel, 339
Sylvester, 117
Sylvester and the Magic Pebble, 14, 20, 31, 333
A Symphony for the Sheep, 217, 232

Taback, Simms, 87, 110, 320, 323, 337
Taberski, Sharon, 271, 279
Tafuri, Nancy, 335
Taking Sides, 47, 177, 185
The Tale of Peter Rabbit, 6, 8, 14, 30, 115, 117, 118, 119, 133, 287, 293, 298, *A.1*
The Tale of Peter Rabbit (CD-ROM), 299
The Tale of Rabbit and Coyote, 155, 159
The Tale of Squirrel Nutkin, 117, 133
The Tale of the Custard Dragon, 263, 278
The Tale of the Flopsy Bunnies, 117, 133
The Tale of the Mandarin Ducks, 351
Tales, Flora and Fauna of Southern Asia, 12
Tales for the Telling, 148
Tales from Silver Lands, 338
Tales of a Fourth Grade Nothing, 7, 9, 164, 170, 183, 295–296
Tales of My Mother the Goose (Contes de ma mere l'oye), 259
Tales of Oliver Pig, 99, 111
The Tales of Uncle Remus: The Adventures of Brer Rabbit, 144, 159
The Talking Earth, 50, 59
The Talking Eggs: A Folktale from the American South, 101, 140, 146, 160, 336
Talking to Dragons, 123, 133
Talking with Artists, 351
Tamarin, Alfred, 349
Tangle-Coated Horse and Other Tales: Episodes from the Fionn Saga, 338
Tapahonso, Luci, 38
Tar Beach, 44, 85, 122, 133, 336, 355, *B.2*
A Taste of Blackberries, 67, 74, 81
Tatalanotto, Peter, 223
Taxi, Taxi, 355

Taylor, Mildred D., 4, 7, 10, 31, 36, **40**, 43, 44, 57, 61, 165, 174, 188, 206, 285, 299, 346, 350
Taylor, Scott, 230
Taylor, Theodore, 164, 174, 186, 189
Tazewell, Charles, 9
T-Bone, the Baby Sitter, 330
Teague, Mark, 133
Tears for Ashan, 193
Teenagers Who Made History, 243
Telling Time with Big Mama Cat, 4, 29
Tell Me, Grandma, Tell Me, Grandpa, 24
Tell Me a Story, Mama, 165, 355
Temple, Frances, 45, 168, 186
Temple, Herbert, 43
Ten, Nine, Eight, 96, 335
Teng, Jean, 160
The Tenth Good Thing About Barney, 66, 81
Terner, Ann, 197, 206
Teskey, Donald, 204
Testa, Maria, 74, 81
The Thanksgiving Story, 330
Thanks to My Mother, 355
Thank You, Mr. Falker, 25, 30, 244, 251
That Sweet Diamond: Baseball Poems, 257, 278
Thayer, Ernest Lawrence, 261, 279
Then Again, Maybe I Won't, 7, 27, 29
Theodore Roosevelt, Fighting Patriot, 343
There Was an Old Lady Who Swallowed a Fly, 87, 110, 320, 323, 337
There Was an Old Man. . .A Gallery of Nonsense Rhymes, 267, 278
They Were Strong and Good, 328
The Thief, 348
Thief of Hearts, 178, 179, 186
Thimble Summer, 340
The Third Planet: Exploring Earth from Space, 316, 323
Thirteen, 349
This Is the Bird, 193
This Land is Your Land, 155, 159, 224, 231
This Life, 43
"This little piggy went to market," 271
Thistle and Thyme: Tales and Legends from Scotland, 344
Thomas, Jane Rush, 66, 81
Thomas, Rob, 177, 186
Thompson, Carol, 29, 277
Thompson, John, 229
Thomson, Peggy, 350
"The Three Bears," 136
The Three Billygoats Gruff, 149, 160
"The Three Billygoats Gruff," 136
The Three Hawaiian Pigs and the Magic Shark, 318, 323
Three Jovial Huntsmen, 333
The Three Little Javelinas, 317, 323
The Three Little Pigs, 317, 318, 323
"The Three Little Pigs," 136, 149
The Three Little Pigs and the Big Bad Wolf, 149, 160
The Three Little Wolves and the Big Bad Pig, 318, 323
Three Young Pilgrims, 193
Thunder Rolling in the Mountains, 200, 206
Thurber, James, 328
Thurgood Marshall: A Life for Justice, 242, 250
Thy Friend, Obadiah, 333
Thygesen-Blecher, Lone, 353, 354
Tibet: Through the Red Box, 321, 323, 337
Tiegreen, Alan, 184
Tietjens, Eunice, 339
Tiger Eyes, 7

Tikki Tikki Tembo, 47, 60, 349
Tillage, Leon Walter, 244, 252, 351
'Til We Have Faces: A Myth Retold, 125
Time Flies, 93, 110, 336
A Time for Andrew: A Ghost Story, 121
A Time of Troubles, 189
A Time of Wonder, 20, 23, 30, 331
Timothy Turtle, 329
Tim O'Toole and the Wee Folks, 145
Tituba of Salem Village, 197, 206
Titus, Eve, 331
To Be a Drum, 89, 108
To Be a Slave, 345
Tobias, Tobi, 240, 252
Tod of the Fens, 338
Toenails, Tonsils, and Tornadoes, 177, 185
Tolkien, J. R. R., 116, 124, 129, 133
Toll, Nelly S., 244, 252
Tolstoy, Leo, 25
The Tombs of Atuan, 345
Tomes, Margot, 59, 250
Tomie's Little Mother Goose, 260
Tomlinson, Carl M., 51
Tomlinson, Theresa, 123, 133
Tom Paine, Freedom's Apostle, 343
Tom Swift stories, 115
Tom Tit Tot, 332
Tonight, by Sea, 45, 168, 186
Toning the Sweep, 41, 44, 60, 165
Too Many Tamales, 45, 47, 61
Too Short Fred, 11, 30, 99, 109
Tootle, 8
Tops and Bottoms, 337
Torn Away, 168, 184
Torrey, Marjorie, 328, 329
Tortillas para Mamá and Other Spanish Nursery Rhymes, 46, 59
To the Young Scientist: Reflections on Doing and Loving Science, 221, 230
Touching the Distance: Native American Riddle Poems, 270, 279
Town Mouse, Country Mouse, 152, 158, 283
"The Town Mouse and the Country Mouse," 155
Townsend, John Rowe, 349
Train to Somewhere, 65
Transport 7—41-R, 349
Traveling to Tondo: A Tale of the Knundo of Zaire, 154
Travels in India, 12
Travers, Pamela, 6, 31, 115
The Treasure, 334
Treasure Island, 5, 31, 164
A Tree is Growing, 102, 108
A Tree is Nice, 331
Tree of Cranes, 91
Tree of Freedom, 342
Treffinger, Carolyn, 342
Tresselt, Alvin, 329, 332
Tripp, Wallace, 349
Tristan and Iseult, 349
Trivas, Irene, 80
Trivizas, Eugene, 318, 323
Truce of the Wolf and Other Tales of Old Italy, 339
Truck, 212, 215, 231, 334
The True Confessions of Charlotte Doyle, 347, 351
True North: A Novel of the Underground Railroad, 198, 205
The True Story of the Three Little Pigs, 22, 31, 104, 106, 110, 149, 160, 317, 323
Trumpeter of Krakow, 188, 205, 338

Trusdell, Sue, 278
Trussell-Cullen, Alan, 260, 279
Tsan, Jean, 60
Tsan, Moo-Sien, 60
Tseng, Mouslen, 160
Tsuchiya, Yukio, 178, 186
Tsutsui, Yoriko, 52, 61
Tucket's Ride, 173
Tuck Everlasting, 15, 28, 121, 127, 131, 284, 298, 305, 323
Tudor, Tasha, 328, 331
Tuesday, 65, 93, 101, 111, 128, 336, *B.5*
Tunis, Edwin, 344
Tunnell, Michael O., 200, 206
A Turkey for Thanksgiving, 65
Turkle, Brinton, 333
Turner, Ann, 193
Turner, Megan Whalen, 348
The Turning Year, 89, 109
Turtle Bay, 221
Twain, Mark. *See* Clemens, Samuel
The Twelve Days of Christmas, 283
Twelve Impossible Things Before Breakfast, 306
The Twelve Moons, 49
Twelve Tales from Aesop, 152, 158
The Twenty-One Balloons, 341
26 Letters and 99 Cents, 92, 109, 222, 231
20,000 Leagues Under the Sea, 125
Twinnies, 65
The Twits, 120
The Two Giants, 64
The Two Reds, 329
Two Short and One Long, 354
The Two Thousand Pound Goldfish, 71
Tyrannosaurus Was a Beast: Dinosaur Poems, 262

Uchida, Yoshiko, 36, 57, 61, 191, 199, 206, 245, 252
Udry, Janice May, 331
The Ugly Duckling, 147, 158
"The Ugly Duckling," 5, 147
Ullman, James, 343
Umbrella, 331
UN Ambassador: A Behind-the-Scenes Look at Madeline Albright's World, 239, 251
Uncle Jed's Barbershop, 52, 60
Under a Different Sky, 172, 185
Under the Blood-Red Sun, 189
Under the Hawthorn Tree, 196, 204
Under the Sunday Tree, 266
Unleaving, 349
Up a Road Slowly, 344
Upon the Head of the Goat: A Childhood in Hungary, 1939-1944, 346, 350
The Upstairs Room, 345

Vaino: A Boy of New England, 338
The Valentine Bears, 65
Van Allsburg, Chris, 8, 13, 22, 24, 31, 85, 89, 94, 98, 101, 111, 299, 304, 334, 335, 350, 365, *B.4*
van der Rol, Ruud, 354
Vanderwerf, Mary Ann, 221
Van Doren, Liz, 260
Van Iterson, Siny Rose, 353

Van Laan, Nancy, 177, 186, 271, 279
Van Leeuwen, Jean, 99, 111
van Loon, Hendrik Willem, 337
van Raben, Peter, 189
Van Stockum, Hilda, 340
Vejigante Masquerader, 45
Velasquez, Eric, 60, 185
The Velveteen Rabbit, 10, 118, 127, 128, 133, 209
Venezia, Mike, 240, 252
Vennema, Peter, 239, 252
Verne, Jules, 5, 125
The Very Busy Spider, 320, 323
The Very Hungry Caterpillar, 9, 14, 23, 29, 87, 97, 103, 108, 320, 323, *B.3*
The Very Quiet Cricket, 87, 108
A Very Special House, 330
A Very Young Dancer, 217, 224, 231
The Vicar of Wibbleswicke, 120
Vidal, Beatriz, 157
The View from Saturday, 348
Vigna, Judith, 70, 81
The Village by the Sea, 350
The Village of Round and Square Houses, 335
Viorst, Judith, 11, 19–20, 31, 66, 81, 90, 111, 222, 232, 256, 314, 323
"A Visit from St. Nicholas," 261
A Visit to William Blake's Inn: Poems for Innocent and Experienced Travelers, 334, 346, 350
Vivels, Jackie, 121
Voight, Cynthia, 24, 70, 81, 168, 169, 171, 175, 186, 346
Volcano: The Eruption and Healing of Mount St. Helens, 210, 347
The Voyage of Osiris, 145
The Voyage of the Dawn Trader, 125
Voyage of the Frog, 173
Voyager: An Adventure to the Edge of the Solar System, 232, 244, 251
Voyagers, 338
The Voyages of Doctor Dolittle, 338
Voyaging to Cathay: Americans in the China Trade, 349
Vuong, Lynette Dyer, 148

Waber, Bernard, 98, 111, 167, 170, 186
The Wagon, 200, 205
Wagon Wheels, 36, 59, 193, 198, 204
Waiting to Waltz: A Childhood, 319
Walker, Sally M., 220
Walk Two Moons, 24, 175, 348
The Wall, 65, 197, 204
Walsh, Ellen Stoll, 315, 320, 323
Walsh, Jill Paton, 349
Walter, Mildred Pitts, 43
Walt Whitman, 240, 251
War Comes to Willy Freeman, 36, 59, 192, 204
Ward, Lynd, 329, 330
Warren, Andrea, 351
The Watcher, 72, 80
Water Dance, 221
Waterless Mountain, 339
The Watertower, 51, 59
Watley, James, 204
The Watsons Go to Birmingham—1963, 42, 59, 197, 204, 348
Waugh, Sylvia, 120, 133
The Wave, 332
Waverly, 188
The Way Meat Loves Salt: A Cinderella Tale from the Jewish Tradition, 150
The Way Things Work, 211, 231, 350
The Way to Start a Day, 334

We Are All in the Digs with Jack and Guy, 98
Weather Explained: A Beginner's Guide to the Elements, 220
A Weave of Words, 141
The Weaver's Gift, 350
Wednesday's Surprise, 65
The Wednesday Surprise, 25, 29
Wee Gillis, 327
Weeping Willow, 72, 81
Weik, Mary H., 344
Weil, Ann, 342
Weirdo's War, 174, 184
Weisgard, Leonard, 328, 329
Weisner, David, 336
The Well, 40
Weller, Frances Ward, 244, 252
Wells, Rosemary, 87, 101, 111, 240, 252, 260, 350
Wells, Ruth, 38
We're Making Breakfast for Mother, 4, 30
Wescott, Nadine, 155, 161
Westall, Robert, 122
The Westing Game, 175, 185, 318, 323, 346, 349
Weston, Christine, 341
What Can You Do with a Shoe?, 97
What do You Say, Dear?, 331
What Hearts, 69, 79, 347
What I Had Was Singing: The Story of Marian Anderson, 240, 250
What Jamie Saw, 72, 80, 348
What's So Funny, Ketu?: A Nuer Tale, 153–154
What's the Big Idea, Ben Franklin? 237
What's What: A Visual Glossary of the Physical World, 218, 230
Wheeler, Opal, 328, 329
Wheel on the Chimney, 330
The Wheel on the School, 343
The Wheels on the Bus, 87, 111
When Clay Sings, 333
When I Am Old Like You, 165
When I Was Young in the Mountains, 319, 335
When She Was Good, 72, 81
When Shlemiel Went to Warsaw and Other Stories, 345
"When the Clock Strikes," 138
When Will the World be Mine?, 330
Where Do You Think You're Going, Christopher Columbus?, 237
Where's Waldo, 9
Where the Buffaloes Begin, 335
Where the Lilies Bloom, 172, 184
Where the Red Fern Grows, 9, 81, 176, 185, 304
Where the Sidewalk Ends, 256, 258, 263, 264, 268, 279
Where the Wild Things Are, 9, 46, 97, 98, 100, 110, 122, 126, 133, 314, 323, 332
Where Was Patrick Henry on the 29th of May?, 237
The Whipping Boy, 311, 323, 347
Whistle for Willie, 85, 109
Whistler's Van, 340
White, E. B., 6, 9, 10, 114, 117, 127, 128, 303, 342, 352
White, Keinyo, 41
White, Mary Michaels, 264
White, Robb, 19, 31
White, Ruth, 72, 81, 348
White, Ryan, 245, 252
White Snow, Bright Snow, 329
The White Stag, 340
Whitney, Elinor, 338
A Whole New Ball Game: The Story of the All-American Girls Professional Baseball League, 225, 232
Who Said Red, 315

Who's That Stopping on Plymouth Rock? 237
Why Don't You Get a Horse, Sam Adams? 237
Why Goats Smell So Bad and Other Stories from Benin, 51, 60
Why Lapin's Ears Are So Long and Other Tales from the Louisiana Bayou, 145, 158
Why Mosquitoes Buzz in People's Ears, 15, 28, 100, 107, 144, 153, 157, 334, *B.8*
Why the Sun and the Moon Live in the Sky: An African Folktale, 332
Wick, Walter, 220, 351
The Wide-Mouthed Frog: A Pop Up Book, 87, 108
Wier, Ester, 344
Wiese, Kurt, 328, 329
Wiesner, David, 8, 65, 93, 101, 111, 127, 128, 148, 336, *B.5*
Wifey, 7
Wiggins, Kate Douglas, 5, 31, 164
Wilbur, Richard, 95, 111
The Wild Birthday Cake, 329
Wildcat Under Glass, 353
The Wild Children, 196, 205
Wilder, Laura Ingalls, 6, 10, 48–49, 53, 188, 201–203, 340, 341, 352
Wildfires, 220
Wildsmith, Brian, 265, 279
Wilhelm, Hans, 30, 66, 81
Willard, Nancy, 334, 346, 350
Willey, Bee, 160
Willhoite, Michael, 26, 31, 69, 81
Williams, Barbara, 68, 81
Williams, Garth, 59, 80, 159
Williams, Margery, 118, 127, 128, 133
Williams, Marjorie, 10
Williams, Sherley Anne, 336
Williams, Vera B., 41, 68, 74, 77, 81, 89, 91, 111, 167, 170, 172, 186, 335, 336, 350, 351
William's Doll, 170, 186
Willie and His Wagon Wheel, 212
Will You Sign Here, John Hancock? 237, 242, 250
Wilma Unlimited: How Wilma Rudolph Became the World's Fastest Woman, 102, 109, 240, 250
"The Wind," 274
The Wind in the Willows, 6, 29, 118, 130, 132
Window Music, 101, 110
Windy Hill, 338
Winged Girl of Knossos, 339
Winnie-the-Pooh, 115, 118, 126, 132, 263
Winterbound, 340
Winterdance, 173
Winterkill, 173
The Winter Room, 347
The Winter When Time Was Frozen, 353
Winthrop, Elizabeth, 68, 77, 81
Wishes, Lies and Dreams, 275
The Wish Giver, 346
Wisler, G. Clifton, 198, 206
Wisniewski, David, 154, 161, 337
The Witches, 26, 29, 119, 123, 132
The Witches of Worm, 345
The Witch of Blackbird Pond, 194, 197, 200, 206, 343
The Witch Who Wasn't, 306
A Wizard of Earthsea, 349
Wojciechowska, Maia, 344
Wolf, A. *See* Scieszka, Jon
Wollman, Steven, 59
The Wonderful Wizard of Oz, 6, 20, 115, 127, 130, 131
Wonderful Year, 341
The Wonder Smith and His Son: A Tale from the Golden Childhood of the World, 338

Wong, Janet, 270, 279
Wood, Audrey, 335, *B.4*
Wood, Don, 335, *B.4*
Wood, Douglas, 147, 161
Wood, Michele, 44, 61, 224, 231
Wood, Nancy, 49
Woodruff, Elvira, 198, 206
Woodson, Jacqueline, 72, 81
Woodsong, 173
Woodward, Hildegard, 329
Working Cotton, 336
The World of Christopher Robin, 263, 278
The World of William Joyce Scrapbook, 246, 250
Worth, Valerie, 352
The Wreckers, 196, 205
Wrede, Patricia, 123, 133
Wright, Betty Ren, 121
Wright Brothers, 347
The Wright Brothers: How They Invented the Airplane, 240, 250
Wrightson, Patricia, 350
Wringer, 15, 31, 348
A Wrinkle in Time, 9, 26, 30, 126, 127, 129, 132, 303, 344
Wyndham, Robert, 270, 279
Wynne-Jones, Tim, 351

Xiong, Blia, 146, 161

Yang the Youngest and His Terrible Ear, 48, 60
Yarborough, Camile, 38, 43, 57, 61
Yardley, Joanna, 61, 206
Yashimo, Taro, 52, 61, 331, 332
Yates, Elizabeth, 236, 252, 342
The Yearling, 176, 185
The Year of Impossible Good-Byes, 48, 59, 196, 204
The Year of the Perfect Christmas Tree: An Appalachian Story, 24
A Year with Butch and Spike, 172
Yeh-Shen: A Cinderella Story from China, 48, 60, 141, 150, 160
Yep, Laurence, 7, 38, 48, 52, 57, 61, 121, 148, **178–179**, 186, 199, 206, 245, 252, 345, 348, 349
Yertle the Turtle, 3, 92, 108
Yikes! Your Body Up Close, 221
Yolanda's Genius, 172, 184, 348
Yolen, Jane, 22, 31, 101, 107, 111, 122, 124, 133, 147, 152, 161, 191, 206, 263, 279, **306**, 320, 323, 332, 335
Yonie Wondernose, 328
Yorinks, Arthur, 335
You Can Write Chinese, 328
Young, Black, and Determined: A Biography of Lorraine Hansberry, 251
Young, Ed, 48, 61, 133, 148, 150, 155, 160, 315, 316, 332, 336, 351
Young, Ella, 338
Young Arthur, 141, 152, 160
Young Fu of the Upper Yangtze, 339
Young Guinevere, 141, 152, 160
Young Lancelot, 141
The Young Landlords, 43
Young Mac of Fort Vancouver, 340
Young Walter Scott, 340
You're Only Old Once!, 2, 29, 98, 108
Your Move, 65, 74, 79
You Want Women to Vote, Lizzie Stanton? 238
The Yucky Reptile Alphabet Book, 217, 232
Yumoto, Kazumi, 351, 355

Zahares, Wade, 110
Zak, Drahos, 320, 323
Zalben, Jane Breskin, 277
Zaslavski, Claudia, 222, 232
Zeeley, 165, 184
Zei, Alki, 353
Zeier, Joan T., 197, 206
Zeldis, Malrah, 249
Zelinsky, Paul O., 80, 87, 99, 111, 149, 161, 184, 335, 336, 337, *B.2*
Zemach, Harve, 333
Zemach, Margot, 333, 334

Zero: Is It Something? Is It Nothing?, 222, 232
Zin! Zin! Zin! a Violin, 96, 109, 337
Zion, Gene, 330
Zipes, Jack, 136, 138
Zlateh the Goat and Other Stories, 344
Zolotow, Charlotte, 170, 186, 330, 332
Zoo in the Sky, 316, 323
Zora Neal Hurston, 199
Zumo the Rabbit, 145
The Z Was Zapped,

SUBJECT INDEX

Note: Page numbers followed by *n* indicate notes.

AAVE (African-American Vernacular English), 42

Abandonment, 70
Accuracy, in informational books, 211–213
Additive approach, to multicultural literature, 36
Adolescence, in realistic fiction, 172
Adoption, 69
Adults
    fables and folktales for, 63
    picture books for, 98
    young adult titles, 72, 180
Aesop fables, 151–152
African American(s), 39–42, 39*n*
African-American literature, 39–42
    biography, 241–242
    black heroines of, 41
    folk literature, 142, 144, 146
    picture books, 85
    poetry, 269–270
African-American Vernacular English (AAVE), 42
African folktales, 153–154
Age groups, 2
Allegorical narratives, 151
Alliteration, 256
Alphabet books, 84, 320
    informational, 217
    multicultural, 38–39
    picture books, 94–95, 103
Alternative family structures, 68–70, 171
Amelia Frances Howard-Gibbon Medal, 357
American history, in fiction, 191, 196–197, 200
American Institute of Graphic Arts Award, 212
American Library Association, 18, 27, 43, 45, 174–175, 212,
        327, 337, 352, 353
Americas Award, 45, 355–356
Amster, Pamela G., 315–316
Anchor books, 305
Animal stories
    fantasy, 117
    realistic, 176
    talking beast tales, 144
Annual sales, 2
Anthologies (poetry), 263–265, 271
Anthropomorphism, 117, 118
Antiphonal choral reading, 274
Art(s)
    biography of artists, 240
    informational books on, 224–225
    in picture books, 86, 88–90
Asian-American literature, 47–48
    folk literature, 145, 146
    poetry, 270
Asian Americans, 47–48, 47*n*
    biographies of, 242
    in historical fiction, 199–200
    in informational books, 218
    in realistic fiction, 178
Asian poetry, 270
Association for Library Service to Children (ALA), 292,
        352, 353, 356

Assonance, 256
At-risk readers
    audiotaped books and, 284
    nonfiction and, 227
Attention span, plot and, 90
Audiotaped books, 284, 293
Australian Children's Book Council, 357
Australian Children's Book of the Year Awards, 357
Authentic biography, 236
Authenticity in multicultural literature, 37–38
Author groups, 317
Authors
    author studies, 228, 310
    autobiographies of, 245–246
    interaction with, on Internet, 283, 292, 295, 364–365
    sources of information about, 363–365
Autobiography, 244–246. *See also* Biography
    autobiographical stories, 48
    of children's authors, 245–246
    collaborative writing in, 245
    introducing young children to, 247–248
    in school and home setting, 246
Award-winning books. *See also specific awards*
    biography, 236, 247
    historical fiction, 188–189
    informational, 226
    multicultural, 43–44, 45
    on sensitive subjects, 68, 71, 73, 74

Ballads, 154–155, 263
Basal readers, 14, 301–302, 304–305
"Bed-to-bed" plot, 19–20, 90
Best-selling books, 8–10
Bibliotherapy, 10–11, 168
Big books, 88
Bilingual literature, 46
Biographical fiction, 236
Biography, 217, 224, 228. *See also* Autobiography
    of artists, 240
    aspects of, 236–239
    award-winning, 236, 247
    introducing young children to, 247–248
    kinds of subjects, 239–241
    multicultural, 241–242
    picture books, 102
    in school and home setting, 246
    of scientists, 219–221
    series books, 244
    in social studies curriculum, 240–241, 246
    types of, 242–244
Board books, 13, 87, 103, 320
Book awards, 17–19
Book selection
    self-selection, 26
    written policies on, 27
Boston Globe–Horn Book Award, 18, 226, 348–351

Boston Globe newspaper, 348
British Library Association, 357

Caldecott Honor Books, 319
  list of winners, 327–337
  picture books, 85, 104
Caldecott Medal, 7, 17, 18, 48
  biography, 236, 247
  folk literature, 144, 145, 149, 152, 153
  informational books, 224
  list of winners, 327–337
  picture books, 85, 88, 91, 98, 99,
    104–105
Canadian Children's Book of the Year
    Award, 357
Carmola, Ann, 201–203
Carnegie Medal, 357
Carol Hurst's Children's Literature Site, 292
Carr, Mary, 294–297
Carter G. Woodson Award, 189, 236, 356
Cartoon style, in picture books, 89
Castle tales, 135
Catharsis, fantasy as, 114
Caxton, William, 4, 5, 84
CD-ROM books, 282, 286–290, 293, 294
  available titles, 288–289
  evaluating, 287
  interactive, 287–288
Censorship, 25–27
  fantasy, 120, 126
  homosexuality and, 69–70
  targets of, 7, 27
Chants, 260–261
Chapbooks, 4, 84
Character, 20–21
  in biography, 238
  in fantasy, 115–116, 119, 124, 129
  folk literature, 140
  hero tales, 154, 244
  in historical fiction, 193–194
  in picture books, 90
  realistic fiction, 169
  sensitive subjects and, 74
  supernatural characters, 123
Child abuse, 71–72
Child development
  cognitive, 11–13
  language, 13–14
  personal/social, 10–11
Childhood, concept of, 63–64
Children's and YA Authors Internet
    Links, 292
Children's Book Council, 18, 219, 223,
    292, 356
Children's Book Guild Non-fiction
    Award, 226
Children's Choice award, 18, 356
Children's literature, 1–28
  awards for (*See* Award-winning books;
    specific awards)
  best-sellers, 8–10
  censorship of, 25–27
  child's perspective of, 12–13

Children's literature—*Cont.*
  features of, 14–15, 17
  history of, 4–8, 84–85
  impact on language arts curriculum,
    315–316
  importance of story in, 15–16
  learning to read and, 22–23, 25
  literary elements in, 19–22
  parent's perspective of, 23–25
  sources of information about, 359–361
  therapeutic use of, 75–76
  traditional, 68
Children's Literature and Resources Home
    Page, 292
Children's Literature Center (Library of
    Congress), 292
Children's Literature Gopher, 292
Children's Literature-Guide to Research and
    Resources, 291
Children's Literature Homepage, The, 291
Children's Literature Web Guide, The, 292
Children's Services Division (ALA), 327, 337
Choral reading, of poetry, 274
Cinderella stories, multicultural, 149–150
Cinquain, 268
Civil Rights Movement, 33
Classic works, censorship and, 26
Classroom libraries, 305, 307
Classroom setting. *See* School setting
Cochran-Smith, Marilyn, 52–56
Cognitive development, 11–13
Cognitive disabilities, stories about, 73
Collections (poetry), 264–265
Collective biographies, 243
Color, importance of, 88
Community-based learning, 76
Compact Disk Read-Only Memory. *See* CD-
    ROM books
Comparing and contrasting, 11
Computer technology. *See also* Media
  CD-ROM books, 286–290
  computers, 286–293
  in home and school settings,
    293–294, 297
  integrating with literature, 294–297
  Internet resources, 290–293
  literature databases, 290
  media and, 281–298
Concept books, 11, 16, 320
  informational, 215–216, 217
  picture books, 97, 103
Concrete poems, 268
Conflict
  in plotting, 19
  stories about, 48
Consortium of Latin American Studies
    Programs, 45
Contemporary Authors database, 290–291
Content
  of informational books, 213
  in poetry, 256–257
Content themes, 316–317
Contributions approach to multicultural
    literature, 36
Controversial topics, 6–7, 165–166, 182

Conventions, postmodernism and, 104
Cooperative Children's Book Center, 292
Coping skills, 75
Core books, 305
Coretta Scott King Award, 18, 43–44, 348
  historical fiction, 199
  informational books, 224
Cottage tales, 135
Council for Children's Books, 17
Counting books, 84, 95–97, 103, 222
Creative thinking, fantasy and, 114
Critical interpretation, 313
Critical reading, 191
Critical thinking, 11, 105
Cross-curricular studies
  folk literature in, 156
  in language arts curriculum, 310
  nonfiction in, 228
Cultural capital, 35
Culturally generic books, 38
Culturally neutral books, 38
Culturally specific books, 38
Culture. *See also specific cultural groups*
  folk literature and, 141, 152
Cumulative tales, 144
Curriculum(a). *See also* Cross-curricular
    studies
  application of books to, 226
  biography in social studies, 240–241, 246
  fantasy in, 129
  language arts (*See* Language arts
    curriculum)
  transformation to multiethnic focus,
    36–37

Databases, on literature, 290
DEAR (Drop Everything and Read)
    program, 227, 310
Death, 65–67
Design of picture books, 89
Didactic works, 4–5, 63–64
Die-cut books, 87
Disabled persons, 73
Displays, 310
Diversity, valuing, 35
Divorce, 67–68
Doing history, 190
Drop Everything and Read (DEAR)
    program, 227, 310
Duthie, Christine, 246, 247–248

Easy-to-read stories, 99
Ebonics, 42
Edgar Allan Poe Award, 356
Emotional development, 75–77
Enthusiasm, 310
Epics, 154
Esther Glen Award, 357
Eurocentric perspective, 36, 57
Eva L. Gordon Award for Children's
    Science Literature, 226
Expository text, 210–211
Expressionistic style in picture books, 89

Eye dialect, 42
Ezra Jack Keats Award, 18, 355
Ezra Jack Keats Foundation, 355

Fables, 63, 151–152
Fairy tales, 7, 136–138, 147, 320
    Cinderella stories, 149–150
    feminist, 136–137
    Marxist, 137
    in picture books, 99–100
Families (family life)
    alternative structures, 68–70, 171
    death of family member, 66
    in fantasy, 120–121
    foster families, 70
    in realistic fiction, 170–171
    in traditional literature, 68
Famous people, biographies of, 237
Fantasy, 113–130
    about animals, 117
    about royalty, 122
    about toys, 118
    evaluating, 116
    family stories, 120–121
    fantastic characters in, 119
    ghost stories, 121–122
    heroic fantasy, 123–124
    historical, 123
    at home, 126–127, 129
    literary qualities, 115–116, 129
    in picture books, 101–102
    preposterous, 122–123
    reading aloud, 127
    role of, 114–115
    in school setting, 127, 129–130
    science fiction, 125–126
    visualizing, 127–129
Feminist fairy tales, 136–137
Fictionalized biography, 236
Fictionalized family history, 188
Fictionalized memoirs, 188
Fiction based on research, 188
Fitzgerald, Robin, 294–297
Flat characters, 140
Folk literature, 135–157
    African American, 142, 144, 146
    African American literature, 142,
        144, 146
    Asian-American, 145, 146
    award-winning, 144, 145, 149, 152, 153
    ballads and folk songs, 154–155
    Cinderella stories, 149–150
    epics, 154
    evaluating, 143
    fables, 151–152
    fairy tales (See Fairy tales)
    folktales (See Folktales)
    at home and in school, 155–156
    in language arts curriculum, 317–318
    legends, 152–153
    literary elements, 138–142
    myths, 150–151
    Native American, 142, 144, 145,
        146–147

Folk Literature—Cont.
    types of, 142–155
Folk songs, 154–155
Folk style, in picture books, 89
Folktales, 143–147
    for adults, 63
    African, 153–154
    Latino, 146
    "literary," 147
    multicultural, 143–144, 148
    in picture books, 99–100, 143
    traditional, 7, 57
Follow-up activities, 311–312
Formats, 87–88, 214
"Formula poems," 275
Foster families, 70
Free verse, 265, 267
Friedman, Audrey A., 127–129
Friends, death of, 67

Gangs, stories about, 74
General interest books, 218
Genres, 17, 99
Genre units, 317
Ghost stories, 121–122
Golden Books, 9, 84–85
Gonsalves, Elizabeth, 271–273
Good verses evil in folk literature, 139
Grand conversations, 313
Graphic aids, 214
Grimm's Law, 136
Growing up, in realistic fiction, 172–174
Guided reading, 309, 313–314

Haiku, 267–268
Hans Christian Andersen Prize, 18, 357
Hero cycle, 116, 139
Heroic fantasy, 123–124
Hero tales, 154, 244
Heterogeneous reading groups, 318
High fantasy, 123–124
Historical empathy, 190
Historical fantasy, 123
Historical fiction, 187–203
    American history, 191, 196–197, 200
    classroom activities based on, 201–203
    evaluating, 195
    historical fantasy, 123
    in home and school settings,
        200–201, 203
    literary elements in, 192–195
    multicultural dimensions of, 198–200
    picture books, 100
    realistic fiction and, 164
    Scott O'Dell Award, 188–189
    uses of, 189–192
    world history, 195–198
    for young readers, 193
History
    American history, 191, 196–197, 200
    biography of historical figures,
        239–240
    of children's literature, 4–8, 84–85

History—Cont.
    realistic fiction, 177
    world history, 195–198
Homelessness, 72–73
Home setting
    biography in, 246
    computer technology in, 293
    fantasy in, 126–127
    folk literature in, 155
    historical fiction in, 203
    informational books in, 225
    multicultural literature in, 51–52
    picture books in, 102–103
    poetry in, 271
    realistic fiction in, 182
    sensitive subjects in, 74, 75, 77–78
Homosexuality, censorship and, 69–70
Horn Book Magazine, The, 348, 364
Hornbooks, 4
Humor
    in picture books, 95
    in poetry, 256, 257
    in realistic fiction, 170–171,
        176–177, 182
    sensitive subjects and, 68
    tall tales, 153

Illiteracy, 25
Illustrations, 5, 6. See also Art(s);
        Picture books
    in informational books, 214
    of narrative poetry, 261
    in picture books, 83–84, 90–91, 94
Imagery, in poetry, 256
Imagination
    fantasy and, 114
    picture books and, 86
    realistic fiction and, 168
Immigrants, stories about, 48
Informational books, 84, 209–229, 321
    about mathematics, 221–222
    about social studies, 222, 223–224
    accuracy of, 211–213
    arts books, 224–225
    award-winning, 226
    concept books, 97, 215–216, 217
    content of, 213
    emphasizing, 226–228
    evaluating, 211, 215
    fact and fiction, 210–211
    formats of, 214, 216–217
    general interest, 218
    interest in, 214–215
    in language arts curriculum, 310
    multicultural, 217–218
    organization of, 214
    picture books, 90, 94, 102
    in school and home settings, 225,
        228–229
    scientific, 219–221
    style of, 213–214
    vocabulary of, 214
    wordless books, 93
Inspiration (computer program), 294, 295

Instructional activities with multicultural literature, 56
Integrated literature/technology unit, 295–296
Interaction with literature, 284
Interactive books, 87–88
International adoption, 69
International book awards, 357
International literature, 51, 56
International Reading Association, 18, 292, 356
The International Reading Association's Children's Book Award, 356
Internet
    author interaction on, 283, 292, 295, 364–365
    literature on, 290–293
    literature Web pages, 282, 291–292
Irony, 22

Kate Greenaway Medal, 357
Keller, Kim, 15–16
Kenny, Maureen E., 75–77

Language
    in concept books, 215
    development of, 13–14, 86, 94
    in historical fiction, 195
    in poetry, 255
Language arts curriculum, 301–322. See also Cross-curricular studies; Curriculum(a)
    anchor books, 305
    basal readers, 301–302, 304–305
    classroom libraries, 305, 307
    content themes, 316–317
    core books, 305
    grand conversations, 313
    guided reading, 309, 313–314
    impact of literature on, 315–316
    literature-based programs, 302, 309–310
    literature circles in, 311, 312
    literature themes, 317–318
    poetry in, 271, 274–275
    reader response journals, 318–320
    readers' workshops, 311–312
    reading aloud, 303–304
    role of parents in, 320–321
    shared reading, 307–309, 310, 313–314
    skills and strategy development, 313–314
    thematic teaching, 314
    transactional discussions, 312
Language Arts journal, 364
Language development, 13–14, 86, 94
"Lap reading," 102
Latino literature, 42, 44–47, 67
    biography, 242
    folktales, 146
    historical fiction, 199
    informational books, 217
    poetry, 270
    realistic fiction, 177
Latinos/Latinas, 42, 42n, 44–47

Laura Ingalls Wilder Award, 18, 189, 352
Learning environment, 309–310
Legends, 152–153
Life stories, complete, 242
Limericks, 267
Literacy Dictionary, The, 34
Literacy Prizes and Awards (Web page), 292
Literary elements, 19–22
    character (See Character)
    in fantasy, 115
    in folk literature, 138–142
    in historical fiction, 192–195
    minor devices, 21–22
    in picture books, 90–92
    plot (See Plot)
    in poetry, 255–258
    setting (See Setting)
    theme (See Theme)
Literary fantasies, 114
Literary folktales, 147
Literature and Multiple Intelligences (resource material), 307
Literature-based programs, 302, 309–310
Literature circles, 311, 312
Literature Enrichment Activities Packets (resource material), 307
Literature groups, 181
Literature logs, 318–320
Literature themes, 317–318
Locke, John, 63
Lowd, Julia, 12–13
Lowd, Monique, 23–25
Lyric poetry, 265

Magic, in fairy tales, 149
Marxist fairy tales, 137
Mathematics, 221–222
Meaning, in postmodern picture books, 104
Media
    literature and, 283–286
    movies and videotapes, 285–286, 293
    in picture books, 89
Memorizing poetry, 275
Merged families, 69
Microsoft Paint (computer program), 296
Microsoft Power Point (computer program), 295
Microsoft Word (computer program), 296
MicroWorlds (computer program), 295
Mildred L. Batchelder Award, 18, 51, 353–355, 357
Minilessons, 311
Minorities, 34
Modern fantasies, 114
Mood, 21
Moralistic tales, 164
Moral values, in realistic fiction, 169
Mother Goose Award, 357
Mother Goose rhymes, 259–260
Movies, 285
Multicultural curriculum, 156
Multicultural literature, 33–58
    African-American (See African-American literature)

Multicultural literature—Cont.
    African folktales, 153–154
    alphabet books, 38–39
    Asian-American (See Asian-American literature)
    Asian poetry, 270
    authenticity in, 37–38
    award-winning books, 40, 43–44, 45
    biography, 241–242
    Cinderella stories, 149–150
    on death, 66–67
    definitions of, 34
    folk literature (See Folk literature)
    folktales, 143–144, 148
    historical fiction, 196, 198–200
    at home and in school, 51–52, 56–57
    informational, 217–218
    international, 51, 56
    Latino (See Latino literature)
    Native American (See Native American literature)
    picture books, 94, 100, 143–144
    poetry, 269–271
    political correctness and, 52–56
    realistic fiction, 165, 177–179
    reasons for, 35–38
    on television, 285
    trickster tales, 144–145
Multiethnic literature, 7, 34, 50, 85
Music, 224
Mysteries, 175
Mystery Writers of America, 356
Myths, 150–151

Narrative form, 210–211
Narrative poetry, 261, 263
National Association of Science Teachers, 219
National Association to Promote Library Services to the Spanish, 356
National Consortium of Latin American Studies Programs, 355–356
National Council for the Social Studies, 356
National Council of Teachers of English (NCTE), 18, 27, 226, 352, 355
National Council of Teachers of Mathematics, 221
National Council of the Social Studies, 189, 223
National Research Council, 283
Native American literature, 48–50
    folk literature, 142, 144, 145, 146–147
    poetry, 270–271
Native Americans, 48–50, 48n
    biographies of, 242
    in historical fiction, 200
    informational books, 218
    in realistic fiction, 179
NCTE (National Council of Teachers of English), 18, 27, 226, 355
NCTE Award for Excellence in Poetry for Children, 352
Netscape Communicator (computer program), 295

The New Advocate journal, 364
Newbery, John, 5, 18, 63, 258, 337
Newbery Honor Books
    list of winners, 337–348
    nonfiction, 210
Newbery Medal, 17, 18, 21
    biography, 236, 243
    books on sensitive subjects, 66, 68, 71,
        73, 74
    for fantasy, 126
    for historical fiction, 188, 196
    list of winners, 337–348
    multicultural books, 40
    nonfiction books, 210
    realistic fiction, 164, 174–175, 176
The New York Times Best Illustrated
        Children's Books of the
        Year, 356
New York Times Book Review, The, 42
    Nonfiction reading programs, 226–228
Notable Books Award (ALA), 212
Novel Ties (resource material), 307
Novel Units (resource material), 307

Occult topics, 120
O'Day, Pamela, 166–167
Older children
    books on homelessness, 72–73
    fantasy for, 117–118
    personal connections to literature, 167
    picture books for, 98
Onomatopoeia, 256
Oral tradition, 135, 136
Orbis Pictus Award, 18, 226, 355
Organization of informational books, 214
Outstanding Science Trade Books, 219

Parents. *See also* Families (family life); Home
        setting
    discussions on sensitive subjects, 74
    perspective of children's literature, 23–25
    role in language arts curriculum,
        320–321
    single parent families, 68
Parodies
    of fables, 152
    of fairy tales, 149
Partial biographies, 242–243
Peer relationships, 172
Personal connections to literature, 166–167
Personal/social development, 10–11
Pets, death of, 66
The Phoenix Award, 356
Phonemic awareness, 14
Photographs
    photo biographies, 243
    photo-essays, 217
    in picture books, 89
Physical disabilities, stories about, 73
Picture books, 6, 83–107, 321
    art in, 86, 88–90

Picture books—*Cont.*
    biographies, 244
    evaluating, 92
    fables, 152
    folktales, 99–100, 143
    formats for, 87–88
    historical fiction, 193, 200
    history of, 84–85
    in home setting, 102–103
    imagination and, 86
    informational, 217
    language development and, 86, 94
    learning to read and, 86–87
    literary elements in, 90–92
    multicultural, 94, 100, 143–144
    picture story books (*See* Picture story
        books)
    postmodern, 103–105
    in school setting, 106
    types of, 92–97
Picture story books, 84, 97–102, 321
    biography, 102
    essential collection of, 100–101
    fantasy, 101–102
    folk and fairy tales, 99–100
    historical stories, 100
    informational, 102
    poetry, 102
    realistic stories, 101
Playground chants, 260–261
Plot, 19–20
    in biography, 238–239
    in fantasy, 116, 129
    folk literature, 139
    in historical fiction, 195
    of picture books, 90
    realistic fiction, 169, 181
Poetry, 253–276
    ballads, 263
    cinquain, 268
    compilations of, 263–265
    evaluating, 259
    free verse, 265, 267
    haiku, 267–268
    in home and school settings, 271,
        274–275
    in language arts curriculum, 271,
        274–275
    limericks, 267
    literary elements in, 255–258
    lyric, 265
    Mother Goose, 260
    multicultural, 269–271
    narrative, 261, 263
    picture books, 102
    reading aloud, 274
    rhymes and chants, 259–261
    shape poems, 268
    structure of, 254
    teaching love of, 271–273
Point of view, 22
Political correctness, 52–56
Political satire, 115, 259–260

Popularity of series books, 180
Pop-up books, 87
Postmodern picture books, 103–105
Pourquoi tales, 144, 151
Poverty, stories about, 74
Predictable story books, 99
Prediction, 11
Prejudice, in realistic fiction, 172
Preposterous events, 122–123
Prereading activities, 311
Pressure groups, censorship and, 26
Print Shop Press Writer (computer
        program), 295
Problem solving, 75
Psychological needs, folk literature and,
        141–142
Publishers, list of, 367–374
Publishers Weekly, 8–10
Pulitzer Prize, 284
Pura Belpre Award, 45, 356

Quilt stories, 85

Race
    in picture books, 85
    stereotypical portrayals, 7
Racism, 36, 53–56, 120
Read-aloud books, on sensitive subjects,
        77–78
Reader response journals, 78, 318–320
Reader response theory, 211
Readers' workshops, 311–312
Reading
    learning to read, 22–23, 25
    metalinguistic aspects of, 86
    picture books and, 86–87
Reading aloud, 24
    fantasy, 127
    historical fiction, 201–203
    in language arts curriculum, 303–304
    picture books, 87, 99
    poetry, 274
Reading programs
    biography in, 238
    fantasy in, 127
    folk literature in, 155–156
    historical fiction in, 200
    informational books in, 225
    nonfiction, 226–228
    technology in, 283
"Reading Rainbow" program, 285
Reading Teacher, The, 18, 356
Realistic fiction, 163–183
    animal stories, 176
    appeal of, 166, 168–169
    connecting with, 166–167
    evaluating, 169–170
    family life in, 170–171
    growing up in, 172–174
    history, 177

Realistic fiction—*Cont.*
  in home and school settings,
      181–182
  humor in, 176–177
  literary qualities in, 169
  multicultural stories, 165, 177–179
  mysteries, 175
  Newbery Medal winners, 164, 174–175
  picture books, 101
  school life in, 171–172
  series books, 179–181
  sports in, 175–176
Recall (memory skills), 11
Reference aids, 214
Refrain arrangements, of poetry, 274
"Relationship novels," 53
Repetition, in folk literature, 139
Representational style, in picture books, 89
Research tools, Internet, 291
Response to multiethnic literature, 37
Rhyme
  in folk literature, 139
  Mother Goose rhymes, 259–260
  in poetry, 255–256, 258–259
Rhythm, in poetry, 255
Royalty, 122
Rudner, Bonnie, 136–138
Russell Clark Award for Illustrations, 357

School life, in realistic fiction, 171–172
School setting. *See also* Language arts
      curriculum; *specific subjects*
  biography in, 238, 246
  computer technology in, 293–294, 297
  fantasy in, 127, 129–130
  folk literature in, 155–156
  historical fiction in, 200–201
  informational books in, 225, 228–229
  integrating technology with literature,
      294–297
  literature in, 2
  multicultural literature in, 52, 56–57
  picture books in, 106
  poetry in, 271, 274–275
  realistic fiction in, 181–182
  sensitive subjects in, 74, 75, 77–78
Science
  book awards for, 226
  informational books on, 219–221
  in language arts curriculum, 316
Science fantasy, 125–126
Science fiction, 125–126
Scott O'Dell Award, 188–189, 355
Search engines, 291
Seldin, Amy, 100–105
Self-selection, 26
Semantic webs, 201
Senryu, 269
Sensitive subjects, 63–78
  abuse, 71–72
  death, 65–67
  divorce, 67–68
  family structures, 68–70, 171

Sensitive subjects—*Cont.*
  foster families, 70
  in home and school settings, 74, 77–78
  homelessness, 72–73
  persons with special needs, 73
  social and emotional development and,
      75–77
Series books
  biographies, 244
  realistic fiction, 179–181
Service learning, 76
Setting, 20
  in biography, 238
  in fantasy, 115, 129
  folk literature, 140
  in historical fiction, 194–195
  of picture books, 90
  realistic fiction, 169
Sexism, in folk literature, 142
Shape poems, 268
Shared reading, 307–309, 310, 313–314
Sibling(s), 70
Sibling rivalry, in realistic fiction, 171
Single parent families, 68
Skill-development activities
  with CD-ROMs, 287
  reading as, 301
  skills and strategy development, 313–314
Skills-emphasis programs, 314
Social action approach, 36
Social change, 64
Social development, 10–11, 75–77
Social studies
  biography in, 240–241, 246
  historical fiction and, 197–198, 200
  informational books on, 222, 223–224
Sports
  informational books on, 224–225
  in realistic fiction, 175–176
SSR (Sustained Silent Reading), 307, 310
Stereotypes, avoiding, 213
Story, 16
Stress, response to literature and, 76
Structured poetry, 267–269
Style, 21–22, 213–214
Supernatural characters, 123
Surrealistic style, in picture books, 89
Survival stories, 173–174
Sustained Silent Reading (SSR), 307, 310
Sutherland, Zena, 355
Symbolism, 22

Talking beast tales, 144
Tall tales, 153
Technical vocabulary, 214
Technology. *See* Computer technology;
      Media
Television, 285
Thematic teaching, 314
Theme, 20–21
  in biography, 239
  content themes, 316–317
  in fantasy, 116, 126, 129

Theme—*Cont.*
  in folk literature, 141–142
  in historical fiction, 195
  literature themes, 317–318
  in picture books, 91–92
  in realistic fiction, 169
Three-dimensional books, 87
"Time slip" novels, 123
"Time travel," through historical fiction, 192
TLD (transactional literature
      discussions), 312
Tone, 21
Topic groups, 317
Topics
  controversial, 6–7, 165–166, 182
  occult, 120
  sensitive (*See* Sensitive subjects)
Tower, Kathleen, 226–228
Toy fantasies, 118
Trade books
  informational (*See* Informational books)
  in language arts curriculum, 309
  in school setting, 52
Traditional children's literature, 68
Transactional literature discussions (TLD),
      312
Transformation approach, 36
Trickster tales, 144–145, 321

The Ultimate Writing and Creativity Center
      (computer program), 295
Unison arrangements, of poetry, 274
University of Chicago, 355
Urban violence, stories about, 74

Vandergrift's Children's Literature Page, 292
Videotaped author information, 365
Videotaped books, 285–286, 293
Violence, 120, 142
Visualizing fantasy, 127–129
Vocabulary, 13, 214

Webbing, 201
Web pages, on literature, 282, 291–292
Women/girls
  black heroines, 41
  feminist fairy tales, 136–137
  in folk literature, 142
Wonder tales, 147, 149
Wordless books, 84, 92–93, 217
Word-processing programs, 286
World history, 195–198
World knowledge, 168
World Wide Web. *See* Internet
Writing
  effect of literature on, 23
  informational books and, 228
  in language arts curriculum, 310
  poetry, 275
Writing programs
  fantasy, 129–130
  folk literature in, 156

Writing programs—*Cont.*
    historical fiction, 200–201

Young adult(s), 72, 180
Young adult fiction series, 180

Young Adult Library Services
    Association, 292
Younger children
    books on homelessness, 72
    historical fiction for, 193
    introducing biography to, 247–248

Younger children—*Cont.*
    personal connections to literature, 167
    picture books for, 87, 88, 98, 106